DIRECTING IN INDIAN CINEMA

A COMPREHENSIVE GUIDE TO FILMMAKING IN THE LAND OF DIVERSITY

SOUMEN SARKAR

Dedicated to my parents and wife, who have been my unwavering pillars of love, support, and inspiration throughout this incredible journey.

Contents

Foreword

"Directing in Indian Cinema" stands as an all-encompassing tome, an invaluable guide that plunges into the intricate artistry and technical finesse required in one of the globes most prolific and culturally diverse film landscapes. Amidst the extravagant splendour of Bollywood and the understated profundity of regional cinema, this book embarks on a profound journey into the pivotal role of the director. It unfurls the director's profound influence in crafting narratives that resonate with audiences, meticulously curating the visual aesthetics that adorn the silver screen, and channelling the profound cultural impact that Indian films wield. With insights that traverse genres, languages, and traditions, this book offers a comprehensive roadmap for aspiring and seasoned directors, illuminating the dynamic and ever-evolving world of Indian cinema.

Preface

What you're holding in your hands is a part of my personal notebook. This unassuming collection of pages bears witness to my daily ritual, post-dinner, where I diligently dedicate hours to the pursuit of knowledge, meticulously recording notes and insights. This section marks the beginning of my ongoing work, an unfinished tapestry of thoughts and ideas. I have converted this portion of my notebook into the form of a book. For any suggestions and for the improvement of the book, please reach out to me via email at:

thefacetheeyes@gmail.com

About The Author

Soumen Sarkar's existence has been a mesmerizing odyssey replete with unforeseen twists and multifaceted obsessions. Born in the modest surroundings of Jamshedpur, India, he ventured forth to Berhampore, West Bengal to pursue his education and commenced his professional journey as a junior audit officer. However, his ardour for computer programming and hardware engineering spurred him to establish his own company, all while indulging in his passion for playing guitar at a professional level. Soumen's imaginative endeavours knew no bounds, as he co-founded Varanasi Film and Television Institute which now belongs to the annals of history. With his acumen in sound engineering, he collaborated with both national and international artists, leading him to conduct enlightening workshops and eventually, become a revered instructor at a college, honing his pupils' skills in sound recording and music theory. In the wide span of his existence, Soumen embarked on a daring quest to wield the power of the written word, distilling invaluable knowledge about sound for aspiring novices in the domain of cinema, television, games, podcasts and audio storytelling. He loves to relate sound experimentally with other fields like visual design, yoga, indoor and outdoor games, acoustics for industry, ancient artwork, temple art, medical therapy, travel and tourism etc.

Feel free to share your valuable feedback with us at

thefacetheeyes@gmail.com

Introduction

"Directing in Indian Cinema" serves as an invaluable resource for filmmakers, students, scholars, and enthusiasts interested in understanding the intricacies of filmmaking in one of the world's most culturally rich and diverse cinematic landscapes. The book offers a detailed examination of various aspects related to directing Indian cinema. It celebrates India's rich cultural diversity, explores the dynamic landscape of regional cinema, and emphasizes the role of the director in shaping narratives, visuals, and cultural impact within Indian cinema. With meticulous insight, the book unravels the multifaceted responsibilities that rest upon the director's shoulders, encompassing the realms of conceptualization, script evolution, casting, visual aesthetics, and storytelling. The director is portrayed as the visionary architect who channels creativity and precision to give shape to the intricate interplay of characters, narrative arcs, and visual elements, ultimately creating a cohesive tapestry on the screen.

The guide also delves into the rich terrain of culturally infused narrative techniques within Indian cinema, where myths, legends, and indigenous traditions intertwine to engender emotional and intellectual engagement with audiences. It highlights the significance of visual aesthetics in storytelling, showcasing the collaborative partnership between directors and cinematographers and unveiling the techniques used to craft visually stunning and emotionally resonant scenes. Furthermore, the book provides a comprehensive analysis of India's cinematic landscape, encompassing both Bollywood and the diverse regional film industries, celebrating their shared heritage while acknowledging their individual contributions. The guide explores how Indian cinema acts as a cultural mirror, adeptly capturing the intricacies of society, ever-evolving values, and dynamic shifts. It scrutinizes the relationship between cinema and society, revealing how directors utilize their creative agency to present compelling commentary on the sociocultural fabric and challenge established norms. Additionally, the book examines the global impact of Indian cinema, showcasing the director's role as a cultural ambassador in crafting narratives that bridge the gap between Indian origins and international appeal. It offers practical insights through case studies of iconic films and profiles of renowned Indian directors, highlighting their approaches, techniques, and styles in achieving their artistic and storytelling goals.

1. Nature of Indian Cinema

The nature of Indian cinema is a complex and multi-dimensional concept that encompasses various aspects of storytelling, cultural representation, industry dynamics, and societal impact. Its cultural diversity, narrative versatility, and emotional engagement set it apart, while its global impact and ability to reflect societal issues make it a significant player in the global film industry. What makes Indian cinema truly unique is its remarkable ability to blend tradition with innovation, offering a dynamic and evolving force in the world of filmmaking. It consistently contributes unique stories and perspectives to global cinema, bridging gaps and fostering cross-cultural understanding.

Indian Cinema: A Kaleidoscope of Cultural Diversity and Regional Pride

Indian cinema is a remarkable reflection of the profound cultural diversity and regionalism that characterizes the subcontinent. It thrives as a rich mosaic of regional film industries, each with its own unique linguistic, cultural, and storytelling identity. From the grandeur of Bollywood in Hindi to the poignant narratives of Tollywood in Telugu, the energetic spirit of Kollywood in Tamil, and many others, these regional film hubs collectively form the intricate tapestry of Indian cinema. This diversity mirrors India's kaleidoscopic cultural heritage, where traditions, languages, and customs flourish abundantly. It showcases the country's cultural plurality and the coexistence of numerous identities, each contributing to the cinematic canvas, ultimately enriching the discourse on Indian cinema as an embodiment of cultural diversity and regional pride.

Versatile Narratives: Indian Cinema's Unique Blend of Genres and Styles

Indian cinema's standout feature is its narrative versatility, effortlessly navigating various genres and storytelling styles. These films blend drama, romance, action, comedy, and music into a cohesive narrative, setting them apart globally. This versatility mirrors life's complexities, making Indian cinema appealing to diverse audiences. It creates immersive and multifaceted cinematic experiences that cater to viewers of all ages and backgrounds. This fusion of genres within a single film represents Indian storytelling's holistic nature, combining emotions and entertainment for a diverse cinematic journey. Indian cinema's versatility has propelled it onto the global stage, resonating with audiences worldwide and enriching the medium with its distinctive storytelling prowess.

The Art of Melodrama: Indian Cinema's Emotional Connection with Audiences

At the heart of Indian cinema's enduring appeal lies its remarkable capacity for emotional engagement and the art of melodrama. This distinctive characteristic, often marked by heightened emotions and fervent performances, serves as a cornerstone of the cinematic experience. Within the world of Indian films, characters passionately articulate their emotions, their tears and laughter echoing with an intensity that transcends the screen, forging a powerful connection with audiences. This melodramatic prowess, far from being a mere theatrical affectation, becomes a conduit for empathetic resonance, as viewers are drawn into the characters' emotional landscapes, feeling their joys and sorrows as if they were their own. This potent emotional engagement serves as the lifeblood of Indian cinema's popularity, fueling the fervor of its ardent fan base. It is through this shared emotional journey that Indian films not only entertain but also leave an indelible mark on the hearts of viewers, creating lasting memories and fostering a deep connection that endures long after the credits roll. In essence, Indian cinema's embrace of melodrama and emotional intensity is a testament to its ability to tap into the core of human experience, rendering it a universal language that transcends cultural boundaries and unites audiences in a shared tapestry of feelings and sentiment.

Harmonious Melodies and Enchanting Dance: The Soulful Essence of Indian Cinema

In Indian cinema, music and dance are integral components that elevate storytelling and emotional expression. Songs, with their poetic lyrics and soulful melodies, allow characters to convey their deepest emotions and desires, connecting profoundly with audiences. Choreographed dance sequences, whether grand or intimate, advance the plot, enhance aesthetics, and offer moments of spectacle, transporting viewers into a world of rhythmic expression. This fusion of music and dance isn't just cinematic embellishment but an intrinsic aspect of Indian cinema's identity. It distinguishes it as a unique medium where emotions are sung, steps narrate, and every beat resonates with the narrative's heartbeat. Through this fusion, Indian films create a lasting impact, offering a sensory experience that transcends language and culture, forging a strong connection with audiences worldwide.

Indian Cinema: Reflecting Culture, Inspiring Change - A Chronicle of Society's Narratives and Transformation

Indian cinema, in its profound role as a cultural mirror, serves as an eloquent and evocative chronicle of societal landscapes, offering poignant reflections of the nation's cultural norms, rich traditions, and pressing contemporary concerns. Beyond its role as a source of entertainment, it emerges as a potent platform for dialogue and catalyst for social change, tackling pertinent issues with remarkable sensitivity and depth. Whether unraveling the intricacies of gender equality, illuminating the shadows of social injustice, or shedding light on the complex contours of political landscapes, Indian cinema navigates these multifaceted narratives with an artistry that transcends its artistic boundaries. It not only exposes the underbelly of societal challenges but also becomes a conduit for empathy and advocacy, galvanizing audiences to engage with these issues and fostering a collective consciousness that extends beyond the confines of the silver screen. This profound ability to meld art and activism, to reflect the culture while challenging its norms, endows Indian cinema with a transformative power that resonates far beyond the world of entertainment, making it a vibrant instrument for cultural discourse and societal impact.

Indian Cinema's Global Impact: Bridging Cultures and Connecting Hearts Across Borders

Indian cinema, especially Bollywood, has crossed borders to create a strong global presence, captivating audiences worldwide. It has a diverse following, drawing cinephiles, enthusiasts, and curious viewers into its spellbinding world. Bollywood serves as a radiant beacon, sharing its cinematic brilliance with the world and has a passionate fan base, especially among the South Asian diaspora. For many expatriates and immigrants, Indian films are a cherished link to their cultural roots, offering nostalgia and familiarity that transcends time and distance. These movies are more than entertainment; they connect diaspora communities to their heritage, language, and traditions, maintaining a deep link with their Indian identity. Indian cinema's global reach transcends linguistic and cultural barriers, forging a global community of cinema lovers and deeply impacting the South Asian diaspora's cultural identity and sense of belonging. In essence, Indian cinema serves as a cultural ambassador and unifying force, connecting people across continents and fostering a shared heritage and a love for cinematic magic.

Innovative Indian Cinema: Pushing Boundaries and Redefining Creativity in Film

Indian cinema consistently demonstrates a spirit of cinematic innovation, with filmmakers fearlessly venturing into diverse narrative forms, visual effects, and storytelling techniques, resulting in groundbreaking works that challenge conventions and push the boundaries of creative expression. This adventurous approach to filmmaking has led to the emergence of revolutionary works that captivate audiences far and wide. As the industry enthusiastically embraces technological advancements, it remains in a state of perpetual evolution, adapting to changing audience preferences and expanding the possibilities of storytelling. Directors venture into a myriad of genres, from experimental narratives and edgy storytelling to imaginative visual effects and innovative soundscapes, thus weaving an ever-evolving tapestry of creativity. This relentless pursuit of cinematic excellence has not only enriched the artistic discourse within Indian cinema but has also enabled it to remain relevant and captivating to audiences both within the country and on the global stage, demonstrating its enduring vitality and capacity for creative exploration. In essence, Indian cinema's commitment to innovation is a testament to its resilience, adaptability, and unwavering commitment to delivering fresh and inspiring narratives that continue to captivate and inspire.

Indian Cinema's Economic Diversity: From Modest Masterpieces to Blockbuster Spectacles

The landscape of Indian cinema is marked by a striking economic diversity that encapsulates a broad spectrum of filmmaking endeavors. On one end of the spectrum, there are films crafted with modest budgets, driven by compelling narratives, strong performances, and a commitment to storytelling that resonates with audiences across the socio-economic spectrum. These films often rely on creative storytelling and resourcefulness to make their mark. On the other end of the spectrum, there's a discernible trend of high-budget productions that stand shoulder to shoulder with international standards in terms of visual effects, production values, and sheer grandeur. These big-budget extravaganzas leverage state-of-the-art technology, opulent sets, and international collaborations to create cinematic spectacles that captivate audiences not just in India but across the globe. This economic diversity within Indian cinema underscores its ability to cater to a wide range of tastes and preferences, making it a thriving and multifaceted industry that accommodates both passion-driven independent filmmaking and blockbuster spectacles that rival the best of global cinema.

Challenges and Triumphs: Navigating the Complex Terrain of Indian Cinema

The Indian cinema industry faces significant challenges like widespread piracy, which harms revenues and intellectual property, and complex distribution issues in a vast and diverse country. Balancing traditional storytelling with modern audience tastes is an ongoing challenge. Nevertheless, the industry has shown resilience and adaptability. It is combating piracy through technology and digital rights management while developing innovative distribution models to reach audiences across India. Filmmakers are creatively blending traditional and modern narrative techniques. These efforts have expanded the industry's global reach, and its ability to navigate these challenges exemplifies its adaptability and resilience. Moreover, filmmakers have exhibited a keen awareness of evolving storytelling styles, leveraging both traditional and modern narrative techniques to craft engaging and resonant narratives. The industry's efforts have borne fruit, resulting in an expanded global reach and an increasing presence at international film festivals and markets. This ongoing journey of progress exemplifies Indian cinema's ability to navigate the turbulent seas of challenges, transforming them into opportunities for growth, innovation, and a continued role as a global cinematic force.

Indian Cinema: Bridging Cultural Identity and Global Expression

Indian cinema thrives at the crossroads of cultural identity and globalization, reflecting India's heritage while absorbing global cinematic influences. It acts as a bridge, connecting traditional Indian customs, languages, and traditions with global cinema trends. Indian filmmakers delicately balance cultural authenticity with international appeal, blending traditional narratives and rituals with modern storytelling techniques. This fusion of the familiar and the novel allows Indian cinema to captivate a diverse international audience while retaining its unique essence. It showcases India's ability to maintain its cultural integrity in a connected world and serves as a global ambassador for its rich cultural tapestry. In this dance between roots and global appeal, Indian cinema continues to evolve, enriching its identity and global presence.

CHAPTER - 02

2. Filmmaking Styles of Indian Film

Indian cinema is celebrated for its diverse approach to filmmaking, encompassing various styles that cater to a wide range of audience preferences. Melodrama, marked by heightened emotional expressions and dramatic conflicts, often forms the core of narratives. Iconic song and dance sequences are integral for conveying emotions, character development, and entertainment. Indian films adeptly blend different genres, from romance and drama to action and comedy, within a single cinematic canvas. Social realism is a powerful style addressing societal issues and challenging norms. Mythology taps into India's cultural heritage, infusing narratives with timeless tales and archetypal motifs. Character-driven narratives explore protagonists' motivations, flaws, and growth. Symbolism adds layers of meaning, while grand-scale productions create cinematic spectacles. Regional authenticity is preserved, celebrating unique cultural identities. Artistic experimentation pushes the boundaries of conventional storytelling, fostering thought and intellectual discourse. These diverse styles enrich the cinematic tapestry of Indian cinema, offering a plethora of experiences for audiences in India and around the world.

Melodrama, the Heartbeat of Indian Cinema: Exploring the Art of Emotional Intensity in Narratives

Indian cinema's distinctive penchant for melodrama is characterized by its ability to heighten emotional intensity in narratives. In this tradition, characters are depicted as passionate and their emotions are vividly portrayed with a dramatic flair that goes beyond the subtleties of realism. This often involves exaggerated facial expressions, intense and emotive dialogues, and theatrical performances that amplify the emotional connection between the characters and the audience. Whether it's the euphoria of a long-awaited reunion, the heart-wrenching agony of separation, or the sheer ecstasy of love's consummation, these emotions are magnified to a level that transcends the boundaries of realism. This melodramatic approach serves multiple purposes: it provides viewers with a cathartic release of emotions, allowing them to vicariously experience the characters' highs and lows. Furthermore, it creates a strong empathetic bond between the audience and the characters, making the storytelling deeply relatable and emotionally resonant. It is this unique ability of Indian cinema to evoke intense emotions and immerse viewers in a world of heightened feelings that distinguishes it as a captivating and emotionally charged storytelling medium.

Dance and Music: The Heartbeat of Indian Cinema

In Indian cinema, song and dance sequences play a multifaceted role in storytelling. They are integral to the narrative structure, serving several essential functions. Firstly, they convey characters' emotions and feelings, allowing them to express love, joy, sorrow, or conflict in ways that words alone cannot. Secondly, these sequences advance the plot, marking turning points or revelations in the storyline. Thirdly, they showcase cultural traditions, reflecting the richness of Indian culture and providing insight into characters' lives. Moreover, these sequences are an essential part of the entertainment value, with meticulous choreography, stunning costumes, mesmerizing music, and intricate dance moves that captivate and delight the audience. In essence, song and dance in Indian cinema are vital components that add vibrancy, energy, and emotional depth to storytelling, creating an immersive and multi-sensory cinematic experience for viewers.

Genre Fusion: The Multifaceted World of Indian Cinema

Indian cinema's narrative versatility is a hallmark of its storytelling approach, characterized by its seamless blending of multiple genres within a single film. This unique cinematic tradition offers audiences a diverse and multifaceted experience, catering to a broad spectrum of tastes and preferences. In an Indian film, one can encounter a harmonious coexistence of romance, comedy, action, drama, and even elements of mythology or folklore, all artfully interwoven. This genre-mixing is a deliberate strategy that allows filmmakers to craft narratives with wide-ranging appeal, ensuring that there's something to captivate every segment of the audience. Moreover, it contributes to the dynamic nature of Indian cinema, liberating storytelling from the confines of genre boundaries and enabling the exploration of a vast spectrum of emotions, themes, and narrative styles within a single, coherent narrative tapestry. This approach not only enriches the cinematic experience but also reflects the diverse and inclusive nature of Indian storytelling, where storytelling conventions are subverted, and creative boundaries are constantly pushed to offer viewers an engaging and multifaceted cinematic journey.

Social Impact Cinema: Indian Films as Agents of Change

Indian cinema often engages with social realism and message-driven content, serving as a powerful medium for addressing pressing societal issues and cultural norms. These films act as platforms for storytelling, using cinema to raise awareness and initiate discussions on contemporary topics. They go beyond entertainment to highlight and challenge social problems, encouraging viewers to critically examine the status quo and question prevailing norms. By addressing issues like gender inequality, caste discrimination, poverty, and corruption, Indian cinema plays a vital role in shaping public opinion, fostering social awareness, and sparking conversations that can drive meaningful change in society. This genre of filmmaking emphasizes the industry's commitment to not only entertain but also educate and inspire, reflecting its broader social responsibility and its role as an advocate for positive societal transformation.

Mythology Meets Modernity: Indian Cinema's Timeless Tales

The integration of mythology, epics, and folklore in Indian cinema represents a captivating fusion of tradition and modernity. Filmmakers draw upon the rich tapestry of Indian mythology, skillfully reimagining legendary characters and ancient tales within contemporary contexts. In doing so, they offer audiences a vital cultural bridge connecting the past and the present. This narrative approach goes beyond mere entertainment; it strengthens cultural connections and traditions, rendering these timeless stories accessible and relevant to new generations. By revisiting age-old narratives, Indian cinema underscores the enduring relevance of ancient wisdom and the timeless appeal of stories cherished for centuries. In this manner, it ensures that India's cultural heritage thrives and evolves in the dynamic cinematic realm, fostering a deeper appreciation of the nation's rich traditions while breathing new life into ageless tales for contemporary audiences.

Character-Centric Narratives: Indian Cinema's Exploration of the Human Journey

Character-driven narratives hold a prominent place in Indian cinema, where the personal journeys and growth of characters take precedence. These films delve deep into the intricate facets of the human experience, intricately exploring the emotional landscapes of their protagonists. Character arcs are meticulously crafted to strike a chord with audiences, often mirroring the real-life trials and tribulations people face. Whether it's a compelling rags-to-riches story, a journey of profound self-discovery, or the intricate evolution of complex relationships, Indian cinema places a strong emphasis on fostering emotional engagement among viewers. Audiences are invited to emotionally invest in the characters' growth, empathizing with their struggles and joyously celebrating their triumphs. This intense focus on character-driven storytelling enables Indian cinema to leave a profound and enduring impact, as it taps into universal themes of humanity, resilience, and personal transformation that resonate deeply across cultures and borders, fostering a genuine connection between viewers and the stories portrayed on screen.

Symbolism and Allegory in Indian Cinema: Layers of Meaning in Visual Storytelling

Indian cinema excels in employing symbolism and allegory to add depth and meaning to its storytelling. Filmmakers use visual motifs, metaphors, and allegorical elements to convey profound messages and explore intricate themes. These symbols can represent cultural values, address societal issues, or delve into philosophical concepts, offering viewers a thought-provoking and introspective journey. Whether through nature symbolizing human emotions, recurring visual motifs signifying character growth, or complex allegorical storytelling addressing political or social commentary, Indian cinema embraces symbolism as a powerful tool that elevates narratives and encourages audiences to explore hidden meanings, fostering a richer and more contemplative cinematic experience.

Epic-Scale Productions in Indian Cinema: Creating Cinematic Spectacles of History and Mythology

Indian cinema's exploration of epic-scale productions, particularly in historical or mythological narratives, is characterized by a dedication to grandeur and spectacle. These films spare no expense in creating lavish sets, opulent costumes, and embracing larger-than-life production values. Directors and production designers meticulously recreate historical periods or mythological realms to transport the audience to entirely different worlds. Whether depicting majestic ancient palaces, sprawling epic battlefields, or ethereal divine realms, these films use every visual and technical element to create breathtaking and immersive experiences. The attention to detail and state-of-the-art technology result in awe-inspiring cinematic spectacles, contributing to the rich legacy of Indian cinema and showcasing the industry's ability to craft grand visual narratives, offering audiences a taste of historical and mythological worlds on an epic scale.

Regional Authenticity in Indian Cinema: Celebrating the Diverse Cultural Tapestry

Indian cinema's regional authenticity is a captivating facet, wherein diverse film industries within India proudly showcase their distinct styles, vividly reflecting the rich cultural, linguistic, and artistic tapestry of their respective regions. For example, Bengali films are renowned for their emphasis on intellectual depth, artistic storytelling, and a profound connection to the literary and artistic traditions of Bengal. In contrast, Tamil cinema often leans towards action-packed narratives, passionately delving into pertinent social issues, perfectly mirroring the vibrant ethos of Tamil Nadu. Each regional film industry brings its unique flavor and sensibilities to the cinematic tableau, celebrating and preserving the kaleidoscope of India's cultural diversity while offering audiences a plethora of cinematic experiences tailored to their specific regional identities. This regional authenticity not only enriches the larger spectrum of Indian cinema but also lends depth and dimension to the narratives, creating a more resonant and immersive experience for local audiences who find stories that intimately relate to their own cultural milieu and experiences.

Indian Cinema: Pioneering Innovation in Storytelling and Visual Artistry

Indian filmmakers have a long-standing tradition of experimentation and innovation in their craft, constantly pushing the boundaries of storytelling techniques, visual effects, and narrative structures. This penchant for innovation has resulted in the creation of unconventional narratives and distinct visual experiences that challenge traditional cinematic norms. Directors in India are unafraid to explore diverse genres, from thought-provoking social dramas to mind-bending science fiction, and they often incorporate cutting-edge visual effects and technology to enhance storytelling. This spirit of experimentation infuses Indian cinema with vitality and ensures that it continues to evolve, adapting to changing audience preferences and global cinematic trends while staying true to its artistic roots.

CHAPTER - 03

3. Analyzing the Handling of Visual Elements

Visual elements take a commanding role in Indian cinema, contributing significantly to the art of storytelling, the aesthetics of the film, and the holistic cinematic experience. Indian filmmakers employ a diverse and expansive palette of visual techniques to create captivating and immersive films. With meticulous attention to detail and a flair for creativity, these visual elements serve as potent tools, enriching the narrative, eliciting a broad spectrum of emotions, and transporting the audience into the captivating world of the film. The diversity in these visual elements is evident as Indian cinema traverses different genres and time periods, capturing the grandeur of historical epics with intricate set designs, period-specific costumes, and elaborate detailing that transports viewers to bygone eras. Simultaneously, vibrant song sequences are brought to life with mesmerizing choreography, colorful cinematography, and the inherent energy of Indian musical traditions, creating moments of pure cinematic delight.

In stark contrast, Indian cinema excels at portraying the gritty realism of contemporary dramas through innovative camera work, unique lighting setups, and a keen eye for capturing the nuances of everyday life. These visual elements are more than just complements to the narrative; they assume a life of their own within the film, becoming iconic and unforgettable aspects of the cinematic experience. In Indian cinema, the celebration of visual spectacle is deeply woven into the fabric of storytelling, where filmmakers elevate visuals to a central position, making it an integral and revered tradition that continues to captivate audiences and contribute to the rich tapestry of the global cinematic landscape.

A. Cinematography

Camera Work

Indian cinema, renowned for its diverse and innovative storytelling, employs a rich tapestry of camera techniques to capture scenes with precision and creativity. Within this cinematic landscape, filmmakers utilize an array of methods, each carefully chosen to match the mood and narrative requirements of a given scene. Static shots, characterized by their stable and unchanging composition, are often employed to convey stability and contemplation. Dynamic tracking shots, on the other hand, add a sense of movement and energy, smoothly following characters or objects to draw the audience into the action. Sweeping crane shots elevate the grandeur of epic sequences, offering breathtaking aerial perspectives that showcase the scale of the production. Meanwhile, handheld camera work injects an immediate and visceral quality into intense or chaotic scenes, immersing viewers in the midst of the drama. These diverse camera techniques are not only technical tools but storytelling devices that contribute significantly to the emotional impact and visual aesthetics of Indian cinema, making it a dynamic and captivating cinematic experience. In filmmaking and cinematography, various camera techniques are used to capture shots and convey emotions, storytelling elements, and artistic expressions. Here are some different types of camera techniques commonly employed by filmmakers:

Static Shots in Filmmaking: Capturing Stability and Composure

In cinematography, static shots entail keeping the camera entirely motionless, resulting in a stable and meticulously composed image. This technique is frequently employed in filmmaking for scenes involving dialogues, interviews, or moments that require a heightened sense of stability and visual clarity. By keeping the camera still, filmmakers can emphasize the characters and their interactions, allowing viewers to focus on the nuances of the performance and the narrative. Static shots are instrumental in establishing a sense of visual equilibrium and control within a film, contributing to the overall cinematic experience by providing a foundation for more dynamic shots and enhancing the storytelling in moments of stillness and contemplation.

Handheld Camera Techniques: Creating Immersive Realism and Dynamic Chaos

The handheld camera technique involves a camera operator physically holding the camera and deliberately introducing shake and movement to the shot, emulating a raw and documentary-style effect. This approach is instrumental in infusing a scene with a palpable sense of immediacy, unpredictability, and authenticity. The natural handheld movement can evoke a feeling of chaos or urgency, making it particularly effective for capturing intense, emotionally charged moments or simulating a fly-on-the-wall perspective. This technique's inherent instability and kinetic energy create a heightened sense of realism, immersing the audience in the scene and allowing them to experience it as if they were present in the moment, contributing significantly to the overall storytelling and visual impact of the film.

Steadicam and Smooth Tracking Shots: Achieving Dynamic Fluidity and Precision

In cinematography, a Steadicam or similar stabilizing device is employed by a camera operator to execute smooth and fluid tracking shots, offering a unique cinematic experience that seamlessly blends dynamic movement with the steadiness of a static shot. This technique revolutionizes the way the camera follows subjects or explores scenes by eliminating the inherent shakiness associated with handheld shots. The Steadicam's precision and agility enable the camera to glide effortlessly through environments, capturing intricate and immersive sequences that maintain a polished and professional visual quality. This approach is instrumental in enhancing the storytelling by providing filmmakers with the creative freedom to choreograph intricate movements, track characters in action, or navigate through complex environments while delivering a visual experience that feels both dynamic and refined, ultimately enriching the narrative and engaging the audience.

Dolly Shots in Cinematography: Smooth Tracking and Revealing Camera Movement

Dolly shots in cinematography involve mounting the camera on a wheeled platform known as a dolly, which travels along a track, allowing for controlled and precise camera movements. This versatile technique serves multiple purposes in filmmaking, including smooth tracking shots that follow characters or objects in motion, as well as revealing shots that emphasize a specific element within the scene. Dolly shots are prized for their ability to add a layer of cinematic finesse by providing a graceful and elegant camera movement. They can contribute to the narrative by dynamically capturing the unfolding action, establishing spatial relationships, heightening tension, or drawing attention to crucial details. The combination of the dolly's mobility and the track's guidance results in visually striking sequences that enhance the storytelling, making dolly shots a fundamental tool in the cinematographer's arsenal.

Crane and Jib Shots in Cinematography: Elevating Cinematic Perspective and Drama

In cinematography, a camera is affixed to a crane or jib, enabling the capture of high or low-angle shots and facilitating sweeping camera movements. Crane shots are celebrated for their ability to introduce a dramatic and cinematic flair to a scene. By raising or lowering the camera and executing expansive horizontal movements, crane shots provide filmmakers with the means to create visually striking compositions that transcend traditional camera perspectives. These shots are frequently employed to convey a sense of grandeur, emphasize key moments, or evoke awe and wonder in the audience. The crane's dynamic capabilities, including soaring overhead views and graceful swoops, enrich the visual storytelling, contributing to the film's overall impact and immersing viewers in a captivating cinematic experience.

Aerial Cinematography: Capturing Bird's-Eye Perspectives and Dynamic Landscapes

Aerial shots, captured from aircraft, drones, or helicopters, offer a breathtaking and expansive bird's-eye perspective of a location or scene. These shots are a potent storytelling tool in cinematography, frequently utilized for various purposes. Firstly, they excel at serving as establishing shots, setting the scene by revealing the broader context and geography of a location, instantly immersing viewers in the film's world. Secondly, aerial shots are instrumental in showcasing landscapes, from sweeping natural vistas to urban cityscapes, allowing the audience to appreciate the scale, beauty, and diversity of the environment. Finally, the dynamic perspectives achieved through aerial cinematography can infuse a scene with energy, drama, or a unique visual impact, enriching the storytelling by offering a fresh and captivating viewpoint that elevates the film's overall aesthetic and narrative depth.

Zooming in Cinematography: Altering Perspective and Focusing Attention

Zooming in cinematography refers to the technique of adjusting the camera's focal length to alter the framing of a shot, allowing the subject to appear closer or farther away within the frame. This versatile tool serves various storytelling purposes. Zooming in can be employed for dramatic effect, drawing the audience's attention to a specific detail, emotion, or revelation within the scene. Conversely, zooming out can create a sense of context or isolation by encompassing more of the environment or characters within the frame. Zooms are also utilized to dynamically shift the viewer's focus, guiding their perception and interpretation of the narrative. This technique's inherent ability to manipulate the visual perspective, combined with its seamless, fluid motion, makes it an invaluable resource in the cinematographer's toolkit, capable of enhancing the storytelling, emphasizing emotional beats, and engaging the audience on both an intellectual and emotional level.

Racking Focus in Cinematography: Shifting Attention and Creating Depth

Racking focus in cinematography is the technique of shifting the focus from one subject or object in the frame to another, typically within the same shot. This dynamic technique is frequently employed to direct the viewer's attention precisely where the filmmaker intends, guiding the audience's perception and engagement with the narrative. By transitioning the focus smoothly from one element to another, racking focus can unveil new information, emphasize crucial details, or facilitate visual storytelling in a seamless and visually engaging manner. Furthermore, this technique has the added benefit of creating a sense of depth within the shot, enhancing the cinematic experience by allowing the audience to explore the frame's spatial dimensions and perceive the relationships between various elements within the scene.

Whip Pan Camera Technique: Rapid Transitions and Dynamic Visual Effects

Whip pans in cinematography involve the rapid panning of the camera from one subject or object to another within a single shot, resulting in a blur or transitional effect that imparts a dynamic and disorienting quality to the scene. This technique is employed to achieve specific storytelling goals, primarily serving as a visually impactful means for transitioning between scenes or highlighting abrupt shifts in narrative tone or focus. The swift and abrupt nature of whip pans can create a sense of urgency, disorientation, or surprise, effectively engaging the audience's attention and prompting them to reorient themselves within the story. This technique's kinetic energy and suddenness make it a valuable tool for filmmakers to infuse a sequence with a burst of energy, underscore dramatic developments, or evoke a heightened emotional response from the viewers.

Tilt Shots in Cinematography: Revealing Scale and Emphasizing Verticality

Tilt shots in cinematography involve the deliberate vertical movement of the camera, either upward (tilt up) or downward (tilt down), to reveal, emphasize, or draw attention to a subject or object within the frame. This versatile technique serves multiple narrative purposes, with the primary goal of showcasing the scale and perspective of a location, emphasizing vertical elements, or highlighting specific details within a scene. Tilt shots can provide the audience with a visual sense of height, depth, or grandeur by capturing the full vertical extent of a subject, whether it's a towering skyscraper, a majestic waterfall, or a character descending into a subterranean world. This technique's ability to shift the viewer's perspective within a shot makes it an effective storytelling tool for directors and cinematographers, enhancing the visual impact and thematic depth of a film.

Pan Shots in Cinematography: Capturing Motion and Expansive Views

Pan shots in cinematography entail the horizontal swiveling or rotation of the camera from one side to another within a single shot, capturing a panoramic view of the surroundings or expertly tracking a subject's movement. This dynamic technique serves a crucial role in visual storytelling, offering filmmakers the flexibility to seamlessly follow characters or objects in motion or unveil the breadth of a scenic vista. Pans are particularly adept at creating a sense of continuity and engagement by smoothly connecting various elements within the frame, whether it's tracing a character's path through a bustling city or highlighting the vastness of a natural landscape. The camera's lateral movement, whether it's a slow, deliberate pan or a rapid whip pan, adds depth, context, and momentum to a scene, effectively conveying spatial relationships, capturing action sequences, and enhancing the overall narrative flow.

Tracking Shots in Cinematography: Creating Dynamic Immersion and Action Sequences

Tracking shots in cinematography involve the camera moving in synchronization with or following a subject, typically facilitated by a dolly or handheld rig, imparting a sense of dynamic immersion and energy to a scene. This technique is a powerful storytelling tool, allowing filmmakers to engage the audience on an intimate level by literally tracking characters or objects in motion. Tracking shots are instrumental in creating a heightened sense of presence and continuity, enabling viewers to feel as if they are actively participating in the unfolding narrative. They excel in capturing dynamic action sequences, chase scenes, or moments of heightened tension, as the camera elegantly glides alongside the action, seamlessly connecting the audience to the characters and events. Whether executed with precision on a dolly or with the kinetic rawness of a handheld rig, tracking shots enrich the cinematic experience by providing a dynamic visual perspective that heightens the emotional impact and narrative engagement.

Point of View (POV) Shots in Cinematography: Immersive Character Perspectives and Subjective Storytelling

The first-person perspective shot, also known as the subjective camera or point-of-view (POV) shot, involves the camera capturing a scene from the viewpoint of a character or object within the story, allowing viewers to perceive the world as if they were that character. This technique creates an extraordinarily immersive and subjective experience, drawing the audience into the character's shoes and fostering a profound connection with their experiences, emotions, and perspectives. It serves to make the audience an active participant in the narrative, allowing them to witness events through the character's eyes, fostering empathy, suspense, or intrigue, depending on the character's state of mind or the story's context. The first-person perspective shot is a potent tool in cinema, as it intensifies the audience's emotional engagement and helps convey the character's inner world and the unfolding events from a deeply personal and subjective vantage point.

Over-the-Shoulder (OTS) Shots in Filmmaking: Establishing Character Relationships and Dialogue Dynamics

The over-the-shoulder (OTS) shot, a commonly employed cinematic technique, offers a perspective from behind one character's shoulder, showcasing another character typically engaged in dialogue. This shot serves a crucial purpose in dialogue-driven scenes by establishing the spatial relationship between characters. By providing viewers with a visual context that includes both characters and their interactions, the OTS shot enhances the understanding of the dynamics, emotions, and nonverbal cues at play during the conversation. It allows the audience to observe the character in the foreground while simultaneously gauging the reactions, expressions, and positioning of the character facing away. This shot's effectiveness lies in its ability to facilitate a nuanced and immersive comprehension of the characters' interactions, making it a fundamental element in cinematic storytelling, particularly during pivotal dialogue exchanges.

Split-Screen Technique in Filmmaking: Simultaneous Storylines and Perspectives

A split-screen technique in filmmaking involves dividing the frame into multiple sections, each depicting distinct scenes, characters, or perspectives concurrently. This technique serves as a powerful visual tool for conveying parallel storylines, actions, or events within the same frame, allowing the audience to observe multiple facets of the narrative simultaneously. By juxtaposing different scenes or characters side by side, the split-screen technique offers a dynamic and visually engaging means of illustrating interconnected storylines, emphasizing the synchronicity of events, and highlighting contrasts or comparisons between characters or situations. It enhances the storytelling by enabling viewers to comprehend the complexity of the narrative, appreciate thematic nuances, and experience a heightened sense of immersion as they navigate between multiple simultaneous story elements within a single frame.

These camera techniques are just a few examples of the many tools filmmakers use to convey their stories and artistic vision. Each technique has its own unique impact on the audience and can be combined and customized to create visually compelling and emotionally resonant films.

Use of Lenses

In Indian cinema, the choice of lenses plays a pivotal role in shaping the visual narrative. Wide-angle lenses, with their expansive field of view, are employed to capture breathtaking landscapes, immersing the audience in the grandeur of the surroundings, whether it's the rugged terrains of a historical epic or the picturesque landscapes of a romantic saga. On the other hand, telephoto lenses come into play to bring distant objects or characters into sharp focus, forging an intimate connection with the viewer and accentuating emotions and expressions amidst vast cinematic canvases. Versatile prime lenses, renowned for their fixed focal lengths, are prized for their ability to create a shallow depth of field, enabling filmmakers to precisely isolate subjects and blur backgrounds for a dreamlike ambiance or enhanced character presence. These carefully chosen lenses, serving as visual instruments in the hands of cinematographers, allow Indian cinema to weave a visual tapestry that enriches storytelling, evokes emotions, and immerses the audience in the on-screen world. Each type of lens brings its unique characteristics and creative possibilities to cinematography, enabling filmmakers to select the one that best complements their artistic vision for a particular project. Here are some of the most common types of lenses used in filmmaking:

Prime Lenses in Cinematography: Sharpness, Cinematic Aesthetics, and Shallow Depth of Field

Prime lenses, a staple in the toolkit of cinematographers, are distinguished by their fixed focal lengths, meaning they cannot zoom in or out. These lenses are highly regarded for their exceptional sharpness and optical quality, consistently delivering images with outstanding clarity and detail. What sets prime lenses apart and contributes to their cinematic appeal is their wider maximum aperture settings, often ranging from f/1.2 to f/2.8 or even wider. This wider aperture allows for a substantial amount of light to enter the lens, making prime lenses ideal for low-light conditions and achieving a shallow depth of field. The shallow depth of field, in turn, results in a beautifully blurred background, known as bokeh, which not only isolates the subject but also adds a dreamy, cinematic quality to the imagery. Cinematographers frequently turn to prime lenses when they seek to create visually stunning shots with striking visual separation between the subject and its surroundings, ultimately contributing to the film's artistic and storytelling elements.

Zoom Lenses in Cinematography: Versatility, Focal Length Control, and Image Quality Considerations

Zoom lenses, a versatile tool in cinematography, feature variable focal lengths that grant cinematographers the ability to adjust the framing of a shot by zooming in or out without the need to switch lenses. This adaptability simplifies the shooting process by offering flexibility on set and is particularly valuable in scenarios where quick changes in framing are required, such as documentary filmmaking or live event coverage. However, it's essential to note that while zoom lenses excel in convenience and adaptability, they may not always match the image quality and depth of field control achieved by prime lenses. Prime lenses, with their fixed focal lengths and wider apertures, often deliver superior optical quality and the ability to create a more pronounced shallow depth of field, resulting in creamy bokeh and subject isolation. Cinematographers frequently choose between zoom and prime lenses based on the specific requirements of their projects, balancing the need for versatility against the desire for maximum image quality and creative control.

Wide-Angle Lenses in Cinematography: Expansive Views and Creative Distortion Effects

Wide-angle lenses, characterized by their short focal length and broad field of view, are invaluable tools in cinematography for capturing expansive landscapes, confined spaces, and creative distortion effects. Their ability to encompass a vast expanse within the frame makes them ideal for shooting sweeping outdoor vistas, architectural interiors, or any scenario where capturing a wide perspective is essential. Moreover, wide-angle lenses come into their own when shooting close to a subject, allowing cinematographers to exaggerate the proximity of elements in the foreground while maintaining a significant background, creating dynamic and visually striking compositions. Additionally, the inherent distortion introduced by wide-angle lenses, such as the stretching of objects near the edges of the frame, can be harnessed creatively to add a sense of surrealism, exaggeration, or visual impact to a scene, making them a versatile choice in a cinematographer's toolkit for both their practicality and artistic potential.

Normal Lenses in Cinematography: Natural Perspective and Human Eye Equivalence

Normal lenses, often referred to as standard or prime lenses, boast a focal length roughly equivalent to the diagonal size of the camera's sensor or film frame, resulting in a perspective that closely mimics what the human eye naturally perceives. This close resemblance to human vision makes normal lenses an incredibly popular choice among cinematographers for capturing scenes with a natural and lifelike appearance. They excel in reproducing the way the world is seen by the human eye, making them ideal for a wide range of applications, from everyday life scenarios to intimate character-driven storytelling. Normal lenses facilitate a genuine and relatable visual experience, maintaining minimal distortion and avoiding the exaggerated perspectives associated with wide-angle or telephoto lenses. As a result, they are cherished for their ability to produce images that feel inherently familiar, enhancing the audience's connection with the narrative and contributing to a film's overall realism and authenticity.

Telephoto Lenses in Cinematography: Capturing Distant Subjects and Compressed Perspectives

Telephoto lenses, characterized by their extended focal lengths, play a vital role in cinematography, primarily serving two distinct purposes. First, they excel at capturing distant subjects with exceptional clarity and detail, making them indispensable for long-range shots where physically getting closer to the subject isn't possible or practical. This capability is particularly advantageous in wildlife filmmaking, sports coverage, or any scenario where the cinematographer needs to bridge significant distances without sacrificing image quality. Second, telephoto lenses are highly effective in compressing the perspective within a shot, giving the impression that objects in the foreground and background are closer together than they actually are. This compression effect is often used artistically to isolate subjects from the background, making them stand out with a striking visual separation. Telephoto lenses are a versatile tool in the cinematographer's arsenal, providing both the means to capture distant details and the creative potential to sculpt visually compelling compositions by controlling perspective and depth of field.

Anamorphic Lenses in Cinematography: Distinctive Widescreen Cinematic Aesthetics

Anamorphic lenses, revered for their ability to infuse a cinematic production with a distinctive and iconic visual style, employ a unique optical principle. These lenses squeeze a wide aspect ratio onto a standard film frame during shooting, a process that enhances the cinematic experience by expanding the horizontal field of view while maintaining the vertical dimensions. The squeezed image, characterized by its oval bokeh and horizontal lens flares, offers a unique widescreen aesthetic that is instantly recognizable and synonymous with the cinematic grandeur of classic Hollywood films. In post-production, the squeezed image is digitally unsqueezed, restoring the intended widescreen format. This process not only creates a visual signature but also imparts a sense of cinematic nostalgia, making anamorphic lenses a preferred choice for filmmakers aiming to capture a timeless and visually captivating look that adds depth, character, and a touch of nostalgia to their productions.

Macro Lenses in Cinematography: Extreme Close-Up Detail and Texture Capture

Macro lenses, purpose-built for extreme close-up photography, serve as indispensable tools for capturing intricate details, textures, and the minuscule wonders of the world. Their unique optical design enables cinematographers and photographers to delve into the microscopic realm, revealing hidden beauty and complexity that often goes unnoticed by the naked eye. These lenses are widely employed in various creative disciplines, from nature documentaries where they unveil the intricate patterns on insects' wings or the delicate veins of a leaf, to product photography where they showcase the fine textures and craftsmanship of objects. The ability to capture such close-up, high-resolution imagery makes macro lenses invaluable for both scientific exploration and artistic expression, allowing viewers to explore the fascinating intricacies of the microcosmos in all its splendor and detail.

Fisheye Lenses in Cinematography: Extreme Wide-Angle and Distorted Visual Effects

Fisheye lenses, renowned for their distinctive optical characteristics, deliver an extreme wide-angle perspective marked by pronounced distortion, resulting in a unique circular or hemispherical field of view. These lenses, celebrated for their ability to warp reality, are a popular choice among filmmakers and photographers seeking to inject surrealism, stylization, or a bold visual impact into their work. By distorting straight lines and stretching objects near the edges of the frame, fisheye lenses create a visually arresting and otherworldly effect, bending reality in creative and imaginative ways. This makes them a preferred tool for capturing avant-garde compositions, immersive action sequences, and experimental shots that push the boundaries of conventional cinematography, adding a touch of the extraordinary to storytelling and allowing filmmakers to craft visuals that are both captivating and unconventional.

Tilt-Shift Lenses in Cinematography: Selective Focus Control and Creative Perspective Manipulation

Tilt-shift lenses, renowned for their unique and creative capabilities, offer cinematographers precise control over focus and perspective, enabling them to craft captivating visual effects. These lenses are particularly cherished for their ability to create a "miniature" or "toy-like" effect, where the area of sharp focus is selectively narrowed to mimic the shallow depth of field one might associate with macro photography. This effect is often used to make real-world scenes appear as if they are miniaturized models, adding a whimsical and surreal quality to the imagery. Additionally, tilt-shift lenses allow for the adjustment of the lens elements to control perspective distortion, effectively correcting converging lines and maintaining verticality, which is especially valuable when photographing architecture or landscapes. By offering such nuanced creative control over focus and perspective, tilt-shift lenses empower cinematographers to explore new realms of visual storytelling, resulting in compositions that are both artistically intriguing and technically precise.

Vintage Lenses in Cinematography: Unique Character and Optical Qualities

Many cinematographers deliberately choose older or vintage lenses as a means to imbue their footage with a distinct visual character and atmosphere. Vintage lenses, often revered for their unique optical qualities and imperfections, can contribute an air of nostalgia, warmth, and charm to a production. These lenses may exhibit characteristics like softness, flaring, chromatic aberration, or vignetting that, while considered flaws in modern optics, are celebrated for their ability to evoke a sense of authenticity and timelessness. The use of vintage lenses can transport viewers to a different era, create a dreamlike quality, or imbue a narrative with a sense of history and tradition. By selecting vintage lenses, cinematographers exercise creative control over the visual storytelling, deliberately embracing the idiosyncrasies of these optics to craft a distinctive and evocative look that complements the narrative's thematic intent and enhances its emotional resonance.

Cinema Lenses: Precision, Durability, and Image Quality for Filmmaking

Cinema lenses, purpose-built for the demanding requirements of filmmaking, stand as a testament to precision and craftsmanship in the world of optics. These lenses are meticulously engineered with features tailored to the cinematic process, including geared focus rings and calibrated markings that facilitate precise and repeatable focus pulling, a crucial skill in filmmaking for maintaining sharpness on moving subjects. Available in both prime and zoom options, cinema lenses offer filmmakers the flexibility to choose the best tool for their storytelling needs while ensuring consistency in image quality and colour rendition throughout a production. Furthermore, cinema lenses are renowned for their robust construction and durability, designed to withstand the rigors of on-set use and the demands of various shooting conditions. Their optical quality is exceptional, delivering pristine imagery with minimal distortion and aberration, making them a trusted choice for professionals seeking to achieve the highest standards of visual excellence in their cinematic works.

Lighting

In Indian cinema, the art of lighting stands as a cornerstone of visual storytelling. Meticulously planned and expertly executed, lighting serves as the painter's brushstroke, shaping the mood and ambiance of every scene. Collaborating closely with directors, cinematographers craft specific lighting effects to evoke emotions and enhance narrative depth. High-key lighting, characterized by even, bright illumination, is often employed to infuse romantic sequences with a soft, dreamy glow, accentuating the beauty of characters and surroundings. Conversely, low-key lighting, which emphasizes strong contrasts between light and shadow, lends an air of mystery and suspense to pivotal moments, intensifying the audience's engagement. The interplay of light and shadow in Indian cinema isn't merely technical but a profound artistic choice, influencing the emotional resonance of every frame and enveloping the viewer in the intended atmosphere, making lighting an indispensable tool in the storytelling arsenal of Indian cinema. These are just a few of the many lighting techniques used in cinema. The choice of lighting technique depends on the director's vision, the genre of the film, and the emotional impact the scene needs to convey. Effective lighting can transform a simple scene into a visually captivating and emotionally resonant moment in a film. Here are some different types of lighting techniques used in cinema:

Three-Point Lighting Setup in Filmmaking: Key, Fill, and Backlight Techniques

The Three-Point Lighting Setup is an essential and versatile technique in filmmaking, photography, and cinematography, offering a structured approach to illuminate subjects and create visually compelling scenes. It consists of three core lights, each with a specific role that collectively contributes to the overall aesthetic and mood of a shot.

Firstly, the Key Light takes center stage as the primary and brightest source of illumination. This light is strategically positioned to cast light on the subject, illuminating their features and setting the visual tone for the scene. The Key Light's intensity and angle can be adjusted to create various effects, from soft, flattering illumination for a warm and inviting atmosphere to harsh, dramatic lighting for tension and suspense. It establishes the fundamental lighting direction and defines the subject's primary contours.

Complementing the Key Light is the Fill Light, a softer source placed on the opposite side of the subject. Its role is to mitigate harsh shadows produced by the Key Light, reducing the overall contrast in the scene. By doing so, it provides a more balanced and natural appearance to the subject, ensuring that important details are not lost in deep shadows. The Fill Light helps create a sense of depth and dimensionality while maintaining a comfortable level of brightness, making it an invaluable component for achieving a well-exposed and aesthetically pleasing shot.

Lastly, the Backlight or Rim Light occupies a distinct position behind the subject. Its purpose is to separate the subject from the background by casting a subtle but defining rim of light along the edges of the subject. This effect not only adds dimensionality but also visually isolates the subject, making them stand out against their surroundings. The Backlight is particularly effective in creating a sense of depth and preventing the subject from blending into the background, enhancing their presence in the frame.

The Three-Point Lighting Setup serves as a foundational tool for cinematographers and photographers, offering them the flexibility to adapt and tailor the lighting to suit the specific requirements of a scene or narrative. By mastering this technique, visual storytellers can manipulate light and shadow to convey emotions, emphasize important elements, and craft captivating and evocative imagery that resonates with audiences.

High-Key Lighting: Creating Bright, Cheerful Atmospheres in Film

High-key lighting is a lighting technique characterized by its use of bright, even illumination that effectively minimizes shadows, resulting in a scene or shot that exudes a cheerful and upbeat atmosphere. This lighting style is a staple in genres like comedies and musicals, where a sense of lightheartedness, optimism, and joy is paramount. By evenly illuminating the entire frame and reducing the contrast between light and shadow, high-key lighting creates a soft and flattering look on the subjects, making them appear youthful and vibrant. Shadows are nearly eliminated, allowing the audience to focus on the characters' expressions and actions without distraction. The absence of harsh shadows contributes to an overall sense of positivity and mirth, making high-key lighting an indispensable tool for filmmakers seeking to convey a sense of joy and exuberance in their storytelling.

Low-Key Lighting: Crafting Dramatic and Tense Cinematic Experiences

Low-key lighting is a lighting technique renowned for its ability to craft dramatic and high-contrast scenes, characterized by deep shadows and limited fill light. This approach deliberately accentuates the interplay of light and shadow, creating an atmosphere that is laden with mystery and tension. Commonly employed in genres like film noir and horror, low-key lighting casts intricate patterns of light and shadow across the frame, often obscuring parts of the scene in darkness, leaving viewers on edge and intensifying the emotional engagement. The stark contrast between illuminated and shadowed areas heightens the visual drama, concealing details and emphasizing select elements, making it a favored choice for filmmakers aiming to evoke a sense of foreboding, suspense, or psychological unease. In the world of cinematic storytelling, low-key lighting stands as a powerful tool to immerse the audience in a narrative where darkness and secrets lurk just beyond the reach of light.

Soft Lighting Techniques: Crafting Gentle and Flattering Cinematic Illumination

Soft lighting is a lighting technique employed in filmmaking and photography to produce a gentle and diffused illumination that bathes the subject in a flattering and delicate glow, effectively minimizing the appearance of harsh shadows and creating a visually appealing aesthetic. Achieved through the use of diffusers, bounce surfaces, or by filtering light through materials like silk or frosted glass, soft lighting serves as a cinematic touch to capture beauty, intimacy, and romance. This technique is often a top choice for beauty shots, where it enhances the appearance of actors, models, or subjects by rendering smooth skin tones and concealing imperfections. Similarly, in romantic scenes, soft lighting adds a dreamy and ethereal quality to the frame, evoking emotions and emphasizing the connection between characters. By reducing the contrast between light and shadow, soft lighting creates a serene and inviting ambiance, making it a valuable tool for filmmakers seeking to craft visually captivating and emotionally resonant imagery.

Hard Lighting: Emphasizing Texture and Detail in Cinematic Scenes

Hard lighting is a lighting technique that deliberately generates sharp and well-defined shadows while accentuating high-contrast scenes. This approach is often utilized to place a spotlight on texture, detail, and depth, making it a favored choice for filmmakers and photographers looking to create dramatic and stylized visuals. By employing intense, directional light sources, hard lighting casts distinct and prominent shadows that can carve out intricate patterns on surfaces, enhancing the three-dimensionality of objects and subjects. This technique excels in bringing out the fine details in scenes, be it the rugged textures of a character's face, the rough surfaces of props and settings, or the sculptural qualities of the environment. Frequently embraced in genres like film noir, where stark visuals heighten tension and intrigue, hard lighting serves as a potent tool to create visually striking and emotionally evocative imagery that captures the essence of storytelling with boldness and precision.

Natural Light Filmmaking: Achieving Authenticity and Realism on Screen

The use of natural sunlight or ambient light sources in filmmaking is a technique cherished for its ability to infuse a scene with a genuine and authentic atmosphere, lending a sense of realism that is often sought after in documentaries and films aiming for a naturalistic and uncontrived feel. This approach leverages the existing light available in the shooting environment, whether it be sunlight streaming through windows, the soft glow of practical lamps, or the dappled light filtering through foliage. By relying on natural lighting, filmmakers capture the organic nuances of a location or setting, allowing the scene to unfold in a way that mirrors real-life experiences. This technique fosters a sense of immersion and immediacy, connecting the audience to the authenticity of the narrative and the genuine emotions of the characters. In essence, the use of natural light sources serves as a means to transport viewers into a world that feels remarkably genuine, making it a valuable choice for filmmakers committed to capturing the unfiltered essence of their stories.

Practical Lighting in Filmmaking: Crafting Warm and Intimate Cinematic Candlelight or Firelight Atmospheres

The use of practical light sources, such as candles or fires, to illuminate a scene is a cinematic technique cherished for its capacity to craft a warm and intimate ambiance. This approach evokes a sense of nostalgia and authenticity, frequently finding its place in period pieces and romantic scenes where it can transport viewers to a bygone era or envelop them in the passionate connection between characters. Practical light sources infuse the frame with a soft, flickering glow that casts gentle and dancing shadows, evoking feelings of intimacy and serenity. This technique not only captures the visual allure of the scene but also elicits emotional depth, enhancing the romanticism or historical charm of the narrative. In essence, the use of practical light sources stands as a testament to the art of storytelling, adding a layer of authenticity and emotional resonance that resonates profoundly with the audience.

Silhouette Lighting: Crafting Dramatic Cinematic Silhouettes and Concealing Emotions

Silhouette lighting is a captivating lighting technique that strategically employs backlighting to create a striking visual effect where the subject appears as a dark, featureless silhouette against a brilliantly lit background. This approach is often harnessed for its dramatic impact, as it lends an air of mystery and intrigue to a scene, obscuring the subject's identity or emotions, and allowing the audience to focus on the outline and posture of the character. Silhouette lighting is particularly powerful in situations where concealing a character's face or identity is essential, such as in suspenseful moments or when emphasizing the universality of a character's emotions or experiences. By utilizing strong backlighting, filmmakers can craft visually arresting and emotionally charged imagery that resonates with viewers on a subconscious level, drawing them deeper into the narrative and heightening the cinematic experience.

Motivated Lighting in Filmmaking: Enhancing Realism and Depth through Natural Light Sources

Motivated lighting, a fundamental technique in filmmaking, centers on the strategic use of light sources that naturally exist within the scene itself, such as lamps, streetlights, or windows. By incorporating these ambient sources into the lighting design, filmmakers infuse their scenes with a heightened sense of realism and depth. Motivated lighting not only serves to illuminate the environment in a manner that mirrors everyday life but also plays a crucial role in character development and narrative storytelling. For instance, the warm glow of a table lamp in a cozy living room can evoke feelings of comfort and intimacy, while the harsh beams of streetlights cutting through a dark alley can heighten tension and suspense. This technique underscores the artistry of filmmaking by seamlessly integrating lighting into the narrative, allowing it to become an intrinsic part of the story's emotional and visual landscape.

Chiaroscuro Lighting: Evoking Artistry and Drama through Contrast and Dimensionality

Chiaroscuro lighting is a mesmerizing lighting technique deeply rooted in the aesthetics of Renaissance painting. It masterfully employs stark contrasts between light and shadow to craft a cinematic experience that accentuates the three-dimensionality of objects and subjects, rendering them with an almost sculptural quality. This technique is celebrated for its artistic and dramatic effects, which unfold on the screen like a living masterpiece. By carving out bold and distinct areas of illumination and shadow, chiaroscuro lighting not only adds depth and texture to the visuals but also instills a sense of mystery, intrigue, and emotional resonance in a scene. The interplay of light and dark, reminiscent of the works of Caravaggio and Rembrandt, is frequently employed in filmmaking to imbue scenes with a timeless and timeless quality, transforming them into visually striking and emotionally charged canvases.

Colour Gels and Lighting: Transforming Mood and Evoking Emotions in Cinematic Scenes

The utilization of coloured gels or lights stands as a transformative technique in filmmaking, capable of profoundly altering the mood and atmosphere of a scene. Each colour carries its own emotional resonance, and when strategically employed, it can evoke specific feelings and add layers of depth to the narrative. For example, the warm and inviting hues of red and orange can convey passion, romance, or urgency, while cool blues and greens might evoke tranquility, sadness, or a sense of unease. Filmmakers deftly wield coloured lighting to accentuate the emotional undercurrents of a story, guide the viewer's perception, and underscore the thematic elements of a scene. Whether it's the eerie green glow of a laboratory in a sci-fi thriller or the romantic red hues of a candlelit dinner in a love story, coloured lighting serves as a potent visual language, enriching the storytelling palette and imbuing the visuals with depth and emotional resonance.

Top Lighting: Crafting Drama and Mystery through Overhead Illumination

Top lighting, a striking cinematographic technique, involves illuminating the subject from an overhead angle, casting intriguing shadows over the eyes and accentuating the contours of the forehead and cheekbones. This approach infuses a scene with a sense of drama and mystery, as the interplay of light and shadow lends depth and texture to the subject's facial features. The shadows that envelop the eyes can evoke a sense of secrecy or concealment, adding complexity to the character's emotions or intentions. Top lighting is frequently employed in film noir to heighten the suspense and ambiguity of characters, but it can also be harnessed in various genres to craft visually captivating and emotionally resonant imagery. It exemplifies the artistry of lighting in filmmaking, where the mere positioning of a light source can dramatically shape the narrative's tone and character dynamics.

Underlighting: Evoking Eerie and Unsettling Atmospheres with Bottom Illumination

Underlighting is a powerful cinematic technique that involves positioning light sources below the subject, resulting in a striking and often eerie or unsettling visual effect. This lighting strategy is a hallmark of horror and thriller genres, as it has the capacity to cast haunting shadows across the subject's facial features, emphasizing their sinister or mysterious qualities. By illuminating the subject from below, underlighting creates a sense of unease and ambiguity, heightening tension and suspense within the narrative. It obscures details, distorts facial expressions, and conjures an otherworldly aura that is conducive to crafting chilling and enigmatic scenes. Underlighting stands as a testament to the versatile and evocative nature of lighting in film, where even the placement of a light source can evoke profound emotional and psychological responses from the audience.

Cross Lighting: Enhancing Dimension and Depth through Angled Illumination

Cross lighting, a sophisticated lighting technique in filmmaking, hinges on the strategic placement of light sources at right angles to each other. This meticulous arrangement engenders a dynamic interplay of light and shadow that imparts a tangible three-dimensionality to subjects and scenes. By casting contrasting illumination from opposing directions, cross lighting creates striking highlights and deep shadows, bringing out the texture and contours of characters or objects. It enhances the sense of depth within the frame, lending an element of visual drama and complexity to the narrative. This technique is frequently employed in both film and photography to imbue visuals with a captivating and immersive quality, underscoring the significance of meticulous lighting design in storytelling and cinematography.

Colour Grading

Colour grading is an essential post-production process in cinema that involves adjusting the colours and tones of a film to achieve a desired look, mood, or style. Different colour grading techniques are used to enhance storytelling and create specific visual aesthetics. In Indian cinema, colour grading is a fundamental aspect of the cinematic art, serving as a powerful tool to elevate the visual appeal of scenes. This meticulous craft encompasses a wide spectrum of techniques, each meticulously chosen to augment the storytelling and aesthetic impact of a given sequence. Desaturation, for instance, is often utilized to infuse a sense of nostalgia, lending scenes a vintage, timeless quality that transports viewers to a different era. In contrast, vibrant and saturated colours burst forth during exuberant song sequences, painting the screen with a kaleidoscope of emotions and energy. Moreover, specific colour schemes are deftly employed to invoke particular emotions, with warm hues like reds and oranges evoking passion and intensity, while cooler blues and greens might be employed to convey calmness or melancholy. This nuanced manipulation of colour in Indian cinema serves as a visual language that resonates with the audience, deepening their emotional connection to the narrative and enhancing the overall cinematic experience. Here are some common types of colour grading techniques used in cinema:

Colour Correction: Balancing Hue, Saturation, and Brightness for True-to-Life Footage

Colour correction is a fundamental post-production technique employed to rectify colour imbalances and inconsistencies present in video footage, ensuring that the colours depicted on screen are faithful to reality. This process encompasses the adjustment of three key elements: hue, saturation, and brightness. By finely tuning these parameters, colour correction aims to achieve a harmonious and accurate representation of the original scene's colours. It serves as the initial phase in the broader colour grading process, setting the foundation for subsequent creative adjustments. Through meticulous manipulation of hue, saturation, and brightness, colour correction seeks to eliminate unwanted colour casts, restore natural skin tones, and create an authentic visual experience for the audience, making it an indispensable tool in professional video production.

The Art of Contrast: Shaping Mood and Style Through Shadow and Highlight Adjustments

The art of contrast manipulation involves the deliberate adjustment of an image's contrast by controlling the interplay between shadows and highlights, thereby exerting a profound influence on the mood and visual style of a scene. When contrast is heightened by accentuating the brightness of highlights and deepening the darkness of shadows, it yields a striking and intense visual aesthetic, fostering a sense of drama and excitement within the frame. Conversely, reducing contrast by softening the divide between shadows and highlights results in a gentler, more ethereal atmosphere, often evoking a dreamy or nostalgic quality. This nuanced play with contrast is a pivotal aspect of cinematography and photography, enabling creators to sculpt the emotional impact and artistic expression of their visuals, making it an indispensable tool in visual storytelling.

Perfecting Colour Balance: Crafting Mood and Temperature with RGB Levels

Perfecting colour balance is a pivotal process in colour grading that revolves around the precise manipulation of the red, green, and blue (RGB) colour channels within an image. By meticulously adjusting these channels, colourists can achieve a desired colour temperature, thereby exerting significant influence over the overall mood and ambiance of the scene. Shifting the balance towards warmer tones, characterized by heightened reds and yellows, can evoke a cozy, inviting atmosphere or even convey a sense of nostalgia. Conversely, leaning towards cooler hues with pronounced blues and greens can create a crisp, refreshing, or somber ambiance. Striking a neutral balance, on the other hand, aims for faithful colour representation, maintaining the scene's authenticity. This versatile technique enables filmmakers and photographers to use colour temperature as a powerful storytelling tool, enhancing the emotional resonance and visual cohesion of their work.

Saturation Control: Amplifying or Subduing Colour Vibrancy for Expressive Visual Impact

Saturation control, a pivotal element of colour grading, empowers creators to dynamically shape the visual impact of their work by deliberately adjusting the vibrancy of colours within a scene. By amplifying saturation, colours become vivid, intense, and eye-catching, often instilling a sense of energy and dynamism into the frame. This heightened saturation can be used to convey excitement, intensity, or to create a visually striking composition. Conversely, when saturation is subdued, colours lose their vibrancy, adopting a muted or desaturated appearance, thus imparting a more subdued, understated mood. This technique proves invaluable in conveying a wide spectrum of emotions and visual styles, enabling storytellers to evoke nostalgia, serenity, or even stark realism. As a versatile tool in the creative arsenal of filmmakers and photographers, saturation control serves to enhance the overall visual impact and narrative depth of their work.

Desaturation (Selective Colour): Directing Focus and Creating Visual Emphasis

Desaturation, particularly in the context of selective colour, is a powerful tool in visual storytelling that allows creators to strategically manipulate colours within an image. This technique involves the intentional desaturation of specific colours in a scene while preserving others in their full vibrancy, resulting in a striking visual effect. By isolating certain elements or subjects in colour against a desaturated backdrop, attention is sharply directed toward those coloured elements, creating a focal point and emphasizing their significance within the composition. Selective colour desaturation can be employed to underscore emotions, highlight key narrative elements, or guide the viewer's gaze in a deliberate and impactful manner, making it an invaluable technique for enhancing visual storytelling and creating compelling, memorable images or scenes.

Cross Processing: Crafting Surreal and Unconventional Colour Palettes

Cross processing is a creative colour grading technique that seeks to replicate the unique and visually captivating aesthetics associated with the cross-processing of film stocks. This method involves deliberately altering the colour balance in an image by developing it using chemicals intended for a different type of film stock, resulting in a surreal and unconventional colour palette. Typically, cross-processing produces striking contrasts, heightened saturation, and unexpected shifts in hues, giving the image an otherworldly or dreamlike quality. By applying cross-processing in digital post-production, filmmakers and photographers can craft visually distinctive and emotionally evocative scenes, often lending a sense of nostalgia, fantasy, or a futuristic edge to their work, making it an artistic tool for pushing creative boundaries and achieving extraordinary visual impact.

Grayscale or Sepia Toning: Evoking Timeless Nostalgia in Visual Storytelling

Grayscale and sepia toning are classic techniques in visual storytelling that can evoke a sense of timeless nostalgia. When an image is converted to grayscale, it removes all colour information, leaving only shades of gray, which can imbue a scene with a stark and dramatic quality. On the other hand, adding a sepia tone imparts a warm, brownish tint, reminiscent of antique photographs, and it often carries a sentimental or historical connotation. These techniques are frequently employed in filmmaking and photography to transport audiences to different eras or to create a sense of history and reminiscence, making them powerful tools for evoking emotions and enriching the narrative depth of period pieces, flashbacks, or any visual story seeking to tap into the allure of the past.

Teal and Orange Colour Grading: Balancing Warmth and Coolness for Aesthetic Harmony

Teal and Orange colour grading is a widely employed technique in visual storytelling that aims to strike an aesthetic balance between warmth and coolness. By accentuating the contrast between warm orange and cool teal tones in an image, this technique creates a visually pleasing and harmonious colour scheme that is known to be particularly eye-catching and emotionally engaging. The warm, inviting tones of orange often evoke feelings of intimacy and vitality, while the cool, serene teal hues convey a sense of tranquility and depth. This interplay not only adds vibrancy and richness to the visuals but also provides a psychological and emotional resonance for the audience. Teal and Orange colour grading is a go-to choice for many filmmakers and photographers looking to enhance the visual impact of their work and create an aesthetically pleasing and complementary colour palette.

Day-for-Night: Transforming Daytime into Moonlit Magic through Colour Grading

Day-for-night is a sophisticated colour grading technique that allows filmmakers to transform daytime footage into a convincing nighttime scene. Through meticulous colour grading, this process manipulates the original colours and brightness levels to simulate the atmosphere of a moonlit night or night vision effect, giving the impression that the scene was shot after dark. It typically involves reducing the overall brightness and warmth of the image while emphasizing cool, bluish tones to replicate the subdued lighting conditions of nighttime. By adding contrast and adjusting the colour balance, shadows are deepened, and highlights are subdued, creating the illusion of a nocturnal setting. Day-for-night is a valuable tool in filmmaking, enabling filmmakers to overcome logistical challenges and create visually engaging night scenes while maintaining control over lighting and shooting conditions. It adds depth and atmosphere to the narrative, enhancing the overall cinematic experience for the audience.

Bleach Bypass: Embracing High Contrast and Reduced Saturation for Cinematic Impact

Bleach bypass is a cinematic technique inspired by traditional film processing methods, particularly during the development stage, where the bleach step is partially skipped. This unique approach results in a visually striking and distinctive aesthetic characterized by several key features. Firstly, it introduces high contrast by allowing silver halide to remain in the emulsion, resulting in darker shadows and brighter highlights. Secondly, it reduces colour saturation, producing a desaturated appearance where colours appear muted and less vibrant. Additionally, the process often accentuates film grain, contributing to a gritty and textured visual quality. This combination of elements provides a distinct cinematic impact, adding an edgy, dramatic quality to the imagery that is particularly well-suited for enhancing the mood and tone of various film genres, creating a visually compelling and emotionally resonant viewing experience.

Vintage or Retro Grading: Time-Traveling through Colour to Capture Nostalgia

Vintage or retro grading is a creative colour grading technique that aims to transport viewers back in time by replicating the distinct colour characteristics associated with older film stocks and formats, such as 8mm or 16mm film. This process involves careful adjustment of colour balance, contrast, and saturation to emulate the visual aesthetics of a bygone era. It typically introduces warm, slightly faded tones, reminiscent of aged photographs or vintage film reels. By mimicking the colour signatures of the past, vintage or retro grading invokes a sense of nostalgia and historical authenticity, making it a powerful tool for filmmakers and photographers seeking to evoke specific time periods, create a timeless ambiance, or capture the sentimentality of days gone by, enriching the visual storytelling experience with a delightful touch of the past.

High Dynamic Range (HDR) Grading: Elevating Visual Splendor with Enhanced Highlight and Shadow Detail

High Dynamic Range (HDR) grading is an advanced color grading technique that transforms the visual impact of an image by precisely adjusting its dynamic range, enhancing both highlight and shadow details. This process involves merging multiple exposures or finely tuning a single exposure to capture a broader range of luminance values. It allows scenes to showcase an extraordinary level of visual detail, particularly in challenging lighting conditions. HDR grading accentuates highlights, revealing intricate textures, subtle nuances, and vibrant colors, creating a stunning and immersive visual spectacle. It also enhances shadow detail, making previously hidden elements visible and adding depth to the composition. Filmmakers and photographers rely on HDR grading to deliver captivating and lifelike visuals, setting a new standard for visual excellence and immersive storytelling.

Muted or Washed-Out Colours: Crafting Subdued Atmospheres for Dramatic Storytelling

Muted or washed-out colors in color grading are a powerful tool used to create a subdued atmosphere that complements certain dramatic or dystopian narratives. This technique involves intentionally reducing the vibrancy and saturation of colors, resulting in a visual palette with subdued and desaturated hues. It conveys emotions like bleakness, melancholy, or despair, enhancing the emotional depth and tone of the story. Muted colors can evoke realism and intensify depictions of harsh environments, adding gritty authenticity to the narrative. Filmmakers and photographers use this approach to control mood and ambiance, crafting a unique visual language that resonates with audiences and enhances the storytelling experience, making it a crucial tool for shaping the aesthetics of dramatic and dystopian narratives.

Daylight vs. Artificial Light: Enhancing Visual Contrast to Convey Location and Mood Shifts

Emphasizing the contrast between natural daylight and artificial indoor lighting is a cinematographic technique that plays a pivotal role in visual storytelling. It accentuates differences in location and mood within a scene, creating a visual dichotomy that communicates various narrative elements. This contrast signifies shifts in physical locations and conveys emotional and psychological shifts. Daylight symbolizes openness and purity, while artificial light carries connotations of confinement and tension. This technique enhances the audience's understanding of the narrative by visually reinforcing transitions between different aspects of the story, contributing to the impact and cohesiveness of the visual storytelling experience.

Split Toning: Unleashing Creative Colour Harmony in Shadows and Highlights

Split toning is a dynamic colour grading technique that enables creators to exercise precise control over the colour harmony within shadows and highlights independently. This process entails the deliberate assignment of distinct colours to these two key areas of an image. By doing so, it unleashes a world of creative possibilities, as it allows for the crafting of unique colour combinations that can evoke specific moods and atmospheres. For example, warm tones in highlights can create a sense of cosiness or nostalgia, while cooler shadows might instill a calm, serene ambiance. Split toning can be employed to intensify visual storytelling by reinforcing the emotional resonance of a scene, enhancing contrast and dimensionality, and even helping to guide the viewer's eye to essential elements within the composition. It is a versatile technique that lends depth and artistic flair to photography and filmmaking, offering a powerful tool for creators to express their creative vision and elevate the impact of their visuals.

These are just a few examples of the many colour grading techniques used in cinema. The choice of technique depends on the filmmaker's vision and the storytelling goals of the project. Effective colour grading can significantly impact the visual storytelling and emotional impact of a film.

B. Set design and production design

Set design and production design are integral aspects of Indian cinema, profoundly shaping the visual and narrative landscapes of films. These creative disciplines are vital for immersing audiences in the worlds filmmakers intend to create. Production designers and set decorators meticulously craft authentic sets, replicating real-world locations or conjuring fantastical realms with attention to detail. Whether recreating historical eras, constructing modern urban environments, or crafting intricate dreamscapes, these designers enrich Indian cinema with visual spectacles. Sets often become integral characters in the story, seamlessly integrating with the narrative. Production design extends to props, lighting, and aesthetics, influencing the film's mood, tone, and atmosphere. In essence, set and production design are the silent architects behind the magic of Indian cinema, fostering emotional connections between viewers and the cinematic world, elevating storytelling to new heights of grandeur and artistry.

Crafting Cinematic Splendor: The Artistry of Indian Cinema's Production Designers and Art Directors

Indian cinema consistently showcases grandeur and artistry through its meticulously crafted sets that transport audiences to real-world locales or fantastical realms. Production designers and art directors collaborate to bring these visual spectacles to life with intricate attention to detail, ensuring an authentic and immersive experience that seamlessly integrates with the narrative. They unleash boundless creativity when constructing awe-inspiring landscapes, palaces, and dreamscapes for fantasy worlds. These sets, often on an epic scale, become integral characters in the story, significantly contributing to the visual language of Indian cinema and elevating it to a realm where imagination knows no bounds.

Period and Cultural Accuracy in Indian Cinema: Bringing History to Life with Meticulous Detail

In historical or period films within Indian cinema, an unwavering commitment to authenticity and precision is paramount. Meticulous attention is dedicated to every aspect of set design and costume creation, showcasing filmmakers' dedication to transporting viewers back in time. Set designers painstakingly research and recreate architectural marvels with historical accuracy, bringing ancient palaces, forts, and cities to life in exquisite detail. Simultaneously, costume designers delve into historical archives to source fabrics, designs, and embellishments that faithfully reflect the fashion of the era, ensuring that actors are dressed authentically. This dedication enhances the visual splendor of the film and fosters a profound connection between the audience and the historical narrative, immersing viewers in a bygone era and making these films a visual feast for history and cinema enthusiasts alike.

The Artistry of Costume Design in Indian Cinema: Crafting Character and Narrative Through Wardrobe

Within the intricate tapestry of Indian cinema, costume designers wield their artistry to fashion outfits that serve as a mirror to characters' personalities, social standings, and the temporal backdrop of the narrative. Every stitch, fabric choice, and accessory is a carefully calculated expression of character identity, aligning seamlessly with the film's era and socio-cultural context. Costume changes, more than mere sartorial transitions, metamorphose into potent visual cues that signify character evolution and narrative progression. A character's journey is mirrored in their wardrobe choices, from initial appearances that reveal their societal roles and personal quirks to subsequent transformations that reflect emotional growth or shifts in fortune. These meticulously crafted costumes, far from being mere attire, become vital elements of character development, facilitating a deeper connection between the audience and the personas unfolding on screen, and enriching the storytelling canvas of Indian cinema.

C. Visual Effects (VFX)

Realism and Fantasy

The importance of VFX in Indian cinema lies in its ability to seamlessly blend realism and fantasy, offering audiences a cinematic experience where creativity knows no bounds. VFX has become a vital tool for filmmakers, allowing them to craft awe-inspiring action sequences that defy the laws of physics, bring mythical creatures to life with astonishing detail, and transport viewers to breathtaking, otherworldly landscapes. Whether it's the gravity-defying stunts in action blockbusters, the mesmerizing portrayal of mythical beings in epic sagas, or the integration of actors into digitally crafted environments, VFX enhances the visual splendor of Indian cinema, pushing the boundaries of what's visually possible and opening doors to unexplored genres and narratives. As Indian cinema continues to evolve, VFX remains an indispensable part of its storytelling arsenal, creating a fusion of reality and imagination that leaves a lasting impact on the cinematic landscape. Here are different types of VFX used in cinema to create both realistic and fantastical elements:

Realism and Fantasy: Realistic VFX

Enhancing Practical Sets: The Role of Digital Set Extensions in Immersive Filmmaking

Digital set extensions serve as a pivotal tool in modern filmmaking, allowing filmmakers to breathe life into practical sets by augmenting or extending them digitally. This versatile technique enables the incorporation of intricate details, breath-taking backgrounds, or entire environments that were either logistically impossible or cost-prohibitive to construct physically during filming. Whether it's transforming a nondescript city street into a bustling, otherworldly metropolis, transporting characters to exotic landscapes, or embellishing historical settings with architectural grandeur, digital set extensions provide filmmakers with the creative freedom to craft immersive worlds that captivate audiences and enrich the storytelling experience. These enhancements seamlessly integrate with the live-action elements, blurring the line between reality and imagination to bring forth cinematic narratives that transcend the limitations of physical production.

Bringing CGI Characters to Life: Interactions with Live-Action Actors in Film

In modern filmmaking, computer-generated characters and creatures have become integral, seamlessly blending into live-action settings and convincingly interacting with human actors. The range of CGI characters is vast, encompassing lifelike animals, mythical beings, and more. This technology has transformed storytelling, enabling filmmakers to breathe life into creatures, characters, and settings that were once confined to the realm of imagination. Whether it's the majestic dragons in fantasy adventures, realistic animals in wildlife documentaries, or animated anthropomorphic heroes, CGI characters expand creative horizons and deepen the audience's sense of wonder and engagement with cinematic tales. The remarkable versatility of CGI characters continues to redefine filmmaking, pushing the boundaries of what's achievable on screen, and enabling the creation of captivating worlds and characters that enthrall audiences like never before.

Crafting Immersive Worlds: The Art of Matte Paintings in Film

Matte paintings are a fundamental yet often underappreciated aspect of filmmaking, serving as the unsung heroes in the creation of immersive cinematic experiences. These intricate works of art involve the meticulous crafting of static backgrounds or environments, which are seamlessly integrated into live-action footage. Matte paintings find their niche in scenarios where practical or physical construction of expansive landscapes or historically accurate settings is either impractical or cost-prohibitive. Through the skillful application of digital or traditional painting techniques, artists breathe life into these canvases, infusing them with depth, texture, and intricate details. The result is a visual marvel that transports audiences to worlds both real and fantastical, where the line between reality and artistry blurs. Whether it's recreating ancient cities, envisioning alien landscapes, or conjuring the grandeur of a bygone era, matte paintings are the invisible architects behind the film's visual storytelling, enriching the narrative tapestry with their evocative beauty and contributing to the overall cinematic magic.

Age Manipulation through Visual Effects (VFX): Redefining Performances on Screen

Visual effects (VFX) represent a transformative force in the world of filmmaking, introducing a dimension of creative freedom that was previously unparalleled. One of the most striking applications of VFX is the ability to digitally manipulate actors' appearances, revolutionizing how age is portrayed on screen. Filmmakers can now leverage this technology to make actors appear younger or older with incredible precision. De-aging, in particular, has garnered significant attention for its ability to seamlessly rejuvenate actors, allowing them to revisit iconic roles or participate in flash-forward sequences. The intricacy of these digital processes means that facial expressions, movements, and emotional nuances are faithfully retained, preserving the integrity of the actors' performances.

Seamless Integration of Special Effects Makeup with VFX: Redefining Imagination on Screen

Furthermore, VFX enhances the traditional art of special effects makeup by digitally integrating it into live-action sequences. This integration permits fantastical transformations that would be impractical, hazardous, or even impossible to achieve solely with physical prosthetics. From the creation of otherworldly beings with intricate, computer-generated features to subtle enhancements that emphasize a character's personality traits, VFX offers filmmakers a versatile toolset to unlock unprecedented storytelling possibilities. In doing so, they infuse their narratives with greater depth, visual impact, and creative flexibility, ensuring that the audience is transported to realms where the imagination knows no bounds, all while preserving the authenticity of the performances that lie at the heart of their cinematic tales.

Defying Gravity: The Magic of Removing Wires and Harnesses Through Digital Editing in Film

The art of filmmaking has evolved significantly with the advent of digital technology, and one remarkable application of this progress is the removal of wires and harnesses from stunts or scenes involving suspended actors. During the filming of daring stunts or gravity-defying sequences, safety often requires the use of wires and harnesses to protect actors, but these elements can be visually obtrusive when not intended to be part of the narrative. Here, the magic of post-production comes into play. Skilled visual effects artists can meticulously erase these visible supports from the final footage, seamlessly restoring the illusion of unrestricted movement and weightlessness. This digital wizardry not only enhances the believability of the action but also ensures the safety of the performers, allowing them to push the boundaries of physicality while achieving spectacular, gravity-defying feats that captivate and immerse audiences in a world of cinematic wonder.

Creating Crowded Spectacles: VFX Duplication for Large Gatherings in Film

In filmmaking, the illusion of large crowds or formidable armies has been significantly advanced through the use of visual effects (VFX). Rather than assembling hordes of extras, which can be logistically challenging and expensive, a small group of actors can be cleverly duplicated multiple times in post-production, effectively creating the illusion of a massive gathering. Skilled VFX artists employ techniques such as rotoscoping, motion tracking, and compositing to seamlessly integrate these duplicate characters into the scenes, ensuring that they move realistically within the context of the narrative. This not only streamlines the production process but also allows filmmakers to maintain precise control over every aspect of the scene, from the positioning of the individuals to their actions and interactions. The result is a cinematic spectacle that convinces audiences of the presence of vast crowds or armies, enhancing the scale and impact of the storytelling while preserving the filmmaker's creative vision and budgetary constraints.

Green and Blue Screen Magic: Transforming Settings with Chroma Key Techniques in Film

The filmmaking techniques involving green or blue screen technology have revolutionized the way filmmakers craft their narratives, offering unprecedented flexibility in terms of locations and environments. By filming actors against a uniform, solid-coloured backdrop, typically green or blue, filmmakers can easily extract and replace that background in post-production with digital elements. This process, known as chroma keying, opens up a world of creative possibilities. Filmmakers can transport their characters to exotic landscapes, historical settings, or fantastical realms without the need for extensive physical sets or locations. It not only streamlines the production process but also allows for the creation of visually stunning and diverse worlds, all while maintaining complete control over lighting, camera angles, and other aspects of the scene. The end result is a seamless integration of live-action performances with digitally generated settings, enhancing the storytelling by immersing audiences in environments that might otherwise be impossible to achieve or visit, all while preserving the creative vision and budgetary considerations of the filmmakers.

Fantasy and Sci-Fi VFX

Unleashing the Magic of VFX: Transforming Characters into Werewolves, Vampires, and Aliens

Visual effects (VFX) wield a remarkable creative power in the world of filmmaking, allowing characters to undergo astonishing metamorphoses and emerge as fantastical beings, be they menacing werewolves, seductive vampires, or enigmatic extraterrestrial entities. Achieving these transformations is a complex process that typically entails meticulous digital character modeling and animation. Through these techniques, VFX artists meticulously craft every detail of these otherworldly personas, from their eerie skin textures and supernatural appendages to their fluid and graceful movements. This fusion of artistic imagination and cutting-edge technology ensures that these mythical creatures seamlessly integrate into the cinematic narrative, captivating audiences and bringing the realms of fantasy and science fiction vividly to life on the silver screen.

Enhancing Safety and Spectacle: VFX Simulations for Explosions, Collapsing Buildings, and Destruction Sequences

Explosions, collapsing buildings, and high-octane destruction sequences in films often rely heavily on the intricate artistry of visual effects (VFX) simulations, primarily for the paramount concern of safety during the filming process. These dramatic and visually stunning spectacles necessitate meticulous planning and execution. VFX professionals use computer-generated imagery (CGI) to craft these scenes, allowing for a controlled environment where the safety of cast and crew is paramount. By using VFX, filmmakers can meticulously choreograph the chaos of explosions, building collapses, and other destructive events while ensuring that every element is precisely timed and controlled, thereby mitigating the inherent risks involved in such sequences. These VFX simulations not only guarantee the physical well-being of everyone on set but also enable filmmakers to achieve a level of realism and spectacle that would be impractical or dangerous to attain through practical effects alone, resulting in awe-inspiring cinematic moments that leave audiences on the edge of their seats.

Elevating Characters with Extraordinary Abilities: VFX's Magic in Adding Superhuman Powers and Energy Effects

When it comes to portraying characters with superhuman abilities or magical powers on screen, visual effects (VFX) serve as the ultimate conduit for bringing these extraordinary feats to life. VFX artists harness their creative prowess to infuse characters with a dazzling array of supernatural elements, from crackling energy effects and elemental manipulation to the manifestation of mystical powers. These effects often involve a meticulous fusion of digital artistry and technical expertise, where VFX teams work tirelessly to ensure that every manifestation of superhuman capability is not only visually compelling but also seamlessly integrated into the cinematic narrative. Whether it's a superhero harnessing the forces of nature or a sorcerer conjuring spells beyond imagination, VFX magic is the driving force that transcends the boundaries of reality, allowing audiences to suspend disbelief and immerse themselves in the awe-inspiring world of the extraordinary.

Breathing Life into Fantasy: VFX's Artistry in Crafting Fictional Creatures, Dragons, Monsters, and Alien Species

Visual effects (VFX) stand as the gateway to summoning the most fantastical and mythical creatures to the screen, breathing life into the wildest of imaginations. VFX artists employ their immense talent and cutting-edge technology to craft these extraordinary beings, be they majestic dragons soaring through the skies, hulking and terrifying monsters lurking in the shadows, or enigmatic and otherworldly alien species. Every detail, from the creature's anatomy to its movements and behaviors, is meticulously designed and rendered with the utmost precision, blurring the lines between reality and fantasy. The synthesis of artistic creativity and technological prowess ensures that these entirely fictional entities not only captivate the audience's imagination but also become integral characters in the narrative, their presence and actions profoundly shaping the storyline and invoking a sense of wonder and awe that is the hallmark of cinematic magic.

Mastering Time: VFX's Cinematic Wizardry in Time Manipulation Effects, Slow Motion, Loops, and Time Trave

Time manipulation effects, including the mesmerizing realms of slow motion, time loops, or the mind-bending concept of time travel, are made possible through the wizardry of visual effects (VFX). VFX artists wield their creative mastery to bend the laws of time, capturing moments with exquisite detail by slowing them down to a fraction of reality's pace or distorting the temporal continuum to create mesmerizing loops that defy causality. In time travel, VFX professionals transport characters and audiences alike to different epochs, seamlessly integrating them into historical events or propelling them into a speculative future. These intricate effects demand an intricate blend of technological prowess and artistic finesse, ensuring that every frame resonates with temporal intrigue, sparking wonder, and leaving an indelible mark on the cinematic experience. Whether it's a bullet-riddled action sequence frozen in time or a character navigating the complexities of temporal paradoxes, VFX time manipulation weaves a tapestry of visual wonders that tantalize the senses and ignite the imagination.

Exploring the Cosmos: VFX's Stellar Role in Depicting Space Travel, Alien Worlds, and Cosmic Marvels

Visual effects (VFX) serve as the cosmic artists of the cinematic universe, enabling filmmakers to traverse the vast expanse of space, explore alien planets, and unveil the majestic mysteries of the cosmos. Through VFX, space travel becomes an awe-inspiring voyage, with spacecraft soaring through star-studded voids, and alien planets taking shape as intricate, otherworldly landscapes that stretch the limits of imagination. Cosmic phenomena, such as the ethereal dance of nebulae, the dark and ominous presence of black holes, or the enigmatic portals of wormholes, are crafted with meticulous attention to scientific accuracy and artistic grandeur. VFX professionals employ a fusion of cutting-edge technology and creative ingenuity to manifest these celestial wonders on screen, enveloping audiences in a breathtaking tapestry of the universe's majesty. With each frame, VFX redefine the boundaries of exploration, sparking wonder and curiosity while transporting viewers to the far reaches of the cosmos, where the laws of physics blend seamlessly with the magic of storytelling.

Metamorphosis Unleashed: Astonishing Shape-Shifting and Transformations Through VFX Mastery

Visual effects (VFX) wield an astonishing transformative power, capable of reshaping characters and objects into forms that defy imagination. Through the intricate artistry of VFX, characters can undergo jaw-dropping metamorphoses, shifting from one state to another with seamless fluidity. Be it the transformation of an ordinary human into a fearsome beast, a mundane object into a wondrous artifact, or a subtle change in appearance to convey hidden powers, VFX techniques provide the canvas upon which filmmakers paint these incredible changes. The process often involves a meticulous combination of digital modeling, animation, and compositing, with each frame meticulously crafted to ensure that the transformation feels not only visually spectacular but also emotionally resonant, serving as a pivotal moment in the narrative. In VFX, the possibilities for shape-shifting and morphing are limitless, allowing storytellers to unleash their creativity and leave audiences in awe of the boundless potential of cinematic magic.

Crafting Dreamscapes: VFX's Power to Shape Entire Virtual Worlds and Surreal Landscapes

Visual effects (VFX) possess the extraordinary capacity to craft entire universes, each a unique tapestry of creativity and imagination that beckons viewers into uncharted territories of wonder and enchantment. With the precision of digital artistry, VFX professionals design and construct these virtual worlds from scratch, fashioning breathtaking landscapes that defy the constraints of reality. Whether it's traversing the ethereal realms of a dream, embarking on epic adventures through fantastical kingdoms, or delving into surreal landscapes where the laws of physics bow to artistic expression, VFX transports audiences into the heart of these fictional domains. Every pixel, every nuance of light and shadow, is meticulously rendered to evoke a sense of immersion and wonder, captivating viewers and igniting their imagination. In the field of VFX, storytellers become architects of entire cosmos, inviting audiences to lose themselves in these digital dreams where the boundaries of the tangible world blur and the magic of cinematic storytelling unfolds in its full splendor.

Capturing the Elements: VFX's Mastery in Simulating Realistic and Fantastical Particle Effects

Visual effects (VFX) harness the artistry of particle simulations to breathe life into cinematic environments, conjuring everything from the ethereal wisps of smoke to the roaring infernos of fire, the fluid serenity of water, and the gritty textures of dust. With meticulous precision, VFX artists orchestrate the movement and behavior of these particles, ensuring that they react to the virtual world's dynamics in a way that is both scientifically accurate and artistically compelling. These simulations are the backbone of creating immersive and immersive environments, whether it's conjuring the realistic ambience of a bustling city street or the fantastical spectacle of a mystical ritual. VFX particle simulations, with their capacity for versatility and creativity, blur the line between reality and fantasy, enabling filmmakers to craft stunning and captivating worlds that captivate the senses and draw audiences into the heart of the cinematic experience.

Unlocking Realism: Exploring the World of Motion Capture Technology (Mo-Cap) for Lifelike Digital Character Animation

Motion capture technology, often referred to as mocap, stands as the bridge between the physical performances of actors and the digital realm, revolutionizing the way characters come to life on the screen. This sophisticated technology meticulously records the subtlest nuances of an actor's movements, translating every gesture, expression, and step into data that can be applied to digital character models. The result is a level of realism and nuance in animation that was once unimaginable. Through mocap, characters take on a lifelike quality, from the way they walk and talk to the emotions that play across their faces. This fusion of the human touch with cutting-edge technology breathes authenticity into characters, creating a seamless connection between the actors and their digital counterparts. Whether it's a dynamic action sequence or a heartfelt conversation, motion capture technology is the key to elevating the art of animation, ensuring that characters resonate with audiences on a profound and emotional level, all while pushing the boundaries of what is achievable in cinematic storytelling.

Doubling Down on Safety and Spectacle: The Role of Digital Doubles in Complex Stunts and Hazardous Scenes

Digital doubles, the pinnacle of visual effects (VFX) artistry, are meticulously crafted digital replicas of actors, designed to seamlessly step in for them during complex stunts, hazardous scenes, or any situation where the safety of the actor is paramount. These highly detailed virtual doppelgängers embody every facet of the actor's physical appearance, from their facial features and body proportions to their distinctive mannerisms and expressions. Through the magic of VFX, these digital avatars are brought to life with astonishing fidelity, enabling them to undertake perilous feats or navigate treacherous environments that would be impractical or dangerous for the real actor. This ingenious fusion of technology and artistry ensures that the character's presence remains consistent and convincing, regardless of the situation, while safeguarding the physical well-being of the actor. Digital doubles exemplify the transformative potential of VFX, where the boundaries between reality and digital artistry blur, allowing filmmakers to push the limits of cinematic storytelling while preserving the safety of their cast.

Vanishing Acts and Particle Puzzles: Unveiling VFX's Mastery in Invisibility and Disintegration Effects

Visual effects (VFX) wield an extraordinary ability to manipulate the visibility and physical integrity of characters and objects, orchestrating the dramatic illusion of invisibility or disintegration into particles. When a character becomes invisible, VFX artists employ intricate techniques to mask their presence, such as compositing the background behind them or digitally erasing their form while ensuring that the scene's lighting and shadows remain consistent. Conversely, when objects disintegrate into particles, VFX specialists choreograph a meticulously choreographed dance of pixels, fragmenting the subject into minuscule elements that cascade, float, or scatter, evoking a vivid sense of dissolution. These effects demand a delicate balance of technical precision and artistic finesse, captivating audiences by imbuing characters and objects with an ethereal quality that challenges the boundaries of reality. In the hands of skilled VFX professionals, the concept of invisibility and disintegration is transformed into a mesmerizing and unforgettable visual spectacle that serves as a pivotal narrative element in the world of cinema.

Seamless Integration

In the world of Indian cinema, the seamless integration of Visual Effects (VFX) with practical elements has become a defining feature, reflecting the meticulous craftsmanship of filmmakers. What sets Indian cinema apart is the extraordinary attention to detail in ensuring that digital effects harmoniously coexist with live-action sequences. Every frame is a delicate balance between the real and the digital, with utmost care taken to maintain the authenticity and continuity of the narrative. Whether it's epic battles, gravity-defying stunts, or the creation of awe-inspiring worlds, VFX is harnessed to enhance the storytelling without overshadowing the live performances. The success lies in the ability of Indian filmmakers to make the unbelievable appear tangible, creating a cinematic experience that immerses the audience in a world where the lines between reality and fantasy blur effortlessly. This commitment to integrating VFX seamlessly into the fabric of the film not only upholds the visual standards but also preserves the authenticity of storytelling, solidifying its place in the rich tapestry of Indian cinema. Here are different types of techniques used to seamlessly blend practical elements with VFX in cinema:

Chroma Key Magic: Transforming Scenes with Green and Blue Screen Technology in Post-Production

Shooting actors or objects against a green or blue screen, a technique known as chroma keying, offers filmmakers a powerful tool for achieving complex visual effects. During the filming process, the green or blue background serves as a placeholder, making it easier to isolate the subject from its surroundings in post-production. This isolation facilitates the removal of the background and replacement with digital elements, such as other locations, fantastical landscapes, or computer-generated characters. This technique is particularly versatile and finds application in a broad spectrum of cinematic scenarios. For instance, it enables the portrayal of space travel, where actors can perform in front of a green screen, and the vast cosmos is added later digitally. Similarly, period dramas often employ chroma keying to recreate historical settings, allowing actors to interact with environments that may not exist anymore. Overall, this technique empowers filmmakers to bridge the gap between imagination and reality, opening up endless creative possibilities in modern cinema.

Seamless Integration: The Art of Match-Moving in VFX for Synchronized Realism

Match-moving, a crucial process in modern filmmaking, entails meticulously tracking and recording the movement of the camera during a live-action shot. This tracking data serves as the foundation for seamlessly integrating visual effects (VFX) into the scene. By precisely capturing the camera's movements, match-moving enables VFX artists to position and animate digital elements within the shot with remarkable accuracy. This synchronization ensures that the digital components, be it fantastical creatures, explosive effects, or otherworldly backgrounds, seamlessly blend with the live-action elements. It's the magic that makes a dragon appear to soar through the sky alongside actors, or a superhero to effortlessly navigate a digitally enhanced cityscape. Essentially, match-moving is the technical backbone that allows filmmakers to weave the realms of reality and imagination into a cohesive and visually stunning cinematic experience.

Elevating Practical Magic: Enhancing Real-World Effects with VFX for Dynamic Realism

Practical effects, encompassing tangible elements like explosions, pyrotechnics, or animatronics, can be elevated to greater levels of dynamism and realism through the strategic integration of Visual Effects (VFX). This synergy involves enhancing practical effects with digital elements to achieve results that are not only more visually stunning but also safer and more controllable on set. For instance, by augmenting a practical explosion with digital fire or smoke, filmmakers can create a spectacle that surpasses the limitations of purely physical effects. This approach not only enhances the impact of the explosion but also allows for fine-tuning and precision in post-production, ensuring the safety of the cast and crew during filming. The seamless blending of practical and digital effects in this manner showcases the evolving artistry of filmmaking, providing filmmakers with a versatile toolkit to craft increasingly immersive and breathtaking cinematic experiences.

Illuminating Realism: The Art of Seamlessly Integrating VFX Shadows and Lighting with Practical Scenes

Achieving a high level of realism in visual effects (VFX) hinges on the meticulous integration of shadows and lighting. It's imperative to ensure that the VFX elements seamlessly coexist with the practical scene, and this involves a careful orchestration of various factors. First and foremost, the angle, intensity, and colour of light sources in the live-action scene must align with those in the digital elements to maintain consistency and authenticity. Shadows, whether cast by real objects or digitally created ones, should interact naturally with the environment, responding to the direction and quality of light. This meticulous attention to lighting details ensures that VFX elements appear as if they genuinely exist within the practical scene, eliminating any visual discrepancies and reinforcing the viewer's immersion in the cinematic world. Essentially, it's the harmony of light and shadow that bridges the gap between reality and fantasy, contributing significantly to the overall believability and impact of the final visual composition.

Harmonizing Realities: Crafting Convincing VFX Interactions with the Practical World Through Lighting and Shading

When a VFX element, like a spaceship, needs to interact seamlessly with the practical environment in a scene, meticulous attention to lighting and shading is paramount to create a convincing interaction. This process involves not only matching the angle, intensity, and colour of the light sources in both the live-action and digital elements but also accounting for the way light behaves when it interacts with surfaces. The VFX team must ensure that the spaceship's glow, for instance, realistically illuminates the ground and objects around it, casting shadows and highlights that align with the lighting conditions of the scene. By meticulously harmonizing these elements, the VFX seamlessly integrates with the practical environment, allowing the audience to suspend disbelief and fully immerse themselves in the narrative. Such attention to detail ensures that the visual effects element appears as an organic and integral part of the scene, enhancing the overall realism and impact of the cinematic experience.

Seamless Set Expansion: The Fusion of Practical and Digital Elements for Cinematic Enhancement

Expanding or enhancing practical sets with digital elements is a prevalent and versatile technique in modern filmmaking. This approach involves seamlessly integrating digital components to augment or transform the practical set, opening up creative possibilities that might be impractical or cost-prohibitive to achieve physically. For example, it allows filmmakers to add a sprawling city skyline to a rooftop scene, extending the visual scope of the environment and enhancing the atmosphere. Similarly, it enables the extension of the size or scale of a practical building, making it appear larger or more grandiose than it actually is. This technique not only enhances the visual aesthetics but also provides filmmakers with greater control over the cinematic world they wish to create, allowing them to craft immersive and visually captivating scenes that align with the storytelling vision.

Precision in Isolation: The Art of Rotoscoping for Targeted VFX Enhancements in Film

Expanding or enhancing practical sets with digital elements is a prevalent technique in contemporary filmmaking, and within this realm, rotoscoping plays a crucial role. Rotoscoping involves the meticulous process of isolating specific objects, actors, or elements within a scene, essentially creating a digital "mask" around them. Once isolated, visual effects (VFX) can be applied exclusively to these selected areas while leaving the remainder of the scene untouched. This technique finds diverse applications, such as adding digital makeup or costumes to actors. For example, it allows filmmakers to alter an actor's appearance by applying intricate makeup or elaborate costumes digitally, offering a level of precision and creative freedom that traditional makeup and wardrobe might not afford. Rotoscoping essentially acts as a digital canvas, enabling filmmakers to selectively enhance or modify elements within a practical set, resulting in seamless and captivating visual effects that blend effortlessly with the live-action components of the scene.

Capturing Character Essence: The Fusion of Motion Capture and Digital Models for Lifelike Animations

Motion capture, a widely-used technique in filmmaking and video game development, involves recording the movements of actors or performers and integrating them with digital character models to create realistic animations. Actors wear specialized suits or markers to track their every move, which is translated into data points and mapped onto digital character models. Success lies in synchronizing the live-action performance with the digital representation for fluid and convincing animations. Motion capture is instrumental in bringing various characters and creatures to life, achieving a level of realism and expressiveness challenging to attain through traditional animation. It acts as a bridge between the physical and digital worlds, enhancing the immersive experience for audiences in cinema and video games.

Blurring Realms: Crafting Characters with a Blend of Practical and Digital Elements for Authenticity and Artistry

In certain cinematic scenarios, characters or creatures are ingeniously brought to life through a combination of practical effects, such as animatronics or prosthetics, and judiciously applied digital enhancements. This hybrid approach capitalizes on the strengths of each technique, offering the benefits of physical realism and tactile interaction with the practical elements while incorporating the finesse and flexibility of digital effects for added details or complex movements. Practical elements provide a tangible presence for actors to interact with and react to, ensuring that physical interactions appear genuine and convincing. Simultaneously, digital enhancements can be employed to refine the character's appearance or to achieve movements or expressions that may be challenging to execute practically. This synergy between practical and digital techniques permits filmmakers to strike a harmonious balance, crafting characters or creatures that seamlessly blend the tactile authenticity of the physical world with the creative potential of the digital realm, resulting in captivating and believable on-screen personas.

Bringing Realism to the Screen: The Revolution of Physics Simulations in Modern Filmmaking

Leveraging physics simulations in modern filmmaking represents a remarkable technological advancement that has revolutionized the way filmmakers integrate digital and practical elements. These simulations provide a means to emulate the laws of physics within a digital environment, allowing digital objects or phenomena to interact with real-world elements in a realistic manner. One of the most striking applications of this technique is the recreation of the physical behavior of digital objects when they come into contact with physical surfaces. For instance, in an action sequence, a digital object can be made to realistically crumble, shatter, or bounce upon impacting the ground, mirroring how it would behave in the physical world. This level of detail not only enhances the visual authenticity of a scene but also elevates the narrative by introducing intricate and captivating interactions between digital and real-world elements. As a result, audiences are immersed in a cinematic world where the boundaries between the physical and digital realms seamlessly blend, enhancing the overall viewing experience.

Fluid Dynamics Unleashed: Physics Simulations in Crafting Realistic Water Scenes in Film

Moreover, physics simulations are employed to replicate the complex interaction of digital fluids, such as water, with practical props. This dynamic process allows for the creation of lifelike splashes, ripples, and reflections, contributing to the overall realism of scenes involving water. Whether it's a character wading through a river, a ship navigating stormy seas, or a glass of water shattering during an intense moment, physics simulations enable these interactions to appear convincing and visually compelling. As such, the use of physics simulations not only adds a layer of visual sophistication to filmmaking but also extends the creative possibilities for storytellers, who can now seamlessly integrate digital and practical elements to craft captivating narratives that push the boundaries of what is visually achievable on screen.

Invisible Enhancements: The Subtle Art of Unobtrusive VFX for Seamless Scene Polishing

At times, the artistry of visual effects (VFX) is so discreet that it becomes nearly imperceptible to the viewer's eye. This subtlety often comes into play during post-production to refine a scene, involving tasks like meticulous cleanup, wire removal, or subtle background enhancements. Such interventions are designed to make the final shot appear flawless and seamless, without drawing attention to the fact that digital manipulation has taken place. For instance, wire removal can eliminate the presence of safety harnesses or cables used during stunts, ensuring that the actors' movements appear entirely unencumbered. Background enhancements might involve adjusting lighting, colours, or details to create a more polished and visually cohesive environment. In essence, these subtle VFX interventions serve to enhance the overall quality of a scene, allowing the audience to remain fully immersed in the story without being distracted by the telltale signs of digital manipulation, underscoring the remarkable versatility and subtlety of modern visual effects techniques.

Protecting Performers: VFX as Safety Net in Stunt Filmmaking

Safety is an absolute priority in filmmaking, and visual effects (VFX) play a pivotal role in safeguarding the well-being of actors and crew members. This involves the strategic deployment of digital elements or the enhancement of practical ones to minimize the inherent risks associated with complex stunts and action sequences. For example, digital stunt doubles or characters can be used to perform dangerous actions, allowing actors to stay out of harm's way. Additionally, VFX can be employed to augment practical effects, making them more controllable and less perilous. This approach not only protects the physical safety of those involved but also provides filmmakers with greater flexibility and precision in achieving their creative vision. Ultimately, the seamless integration of safety-focused VFX ensures that the exhilaration of action-packed scenes is accompanied by the peace of mind that the well-being of the cast and crew is upheld, underscoring the crucial role that visual effects play in responsible filmmaking.

Expanding Crowds Through VFX: The Art of Compositing Multiple Passes for Larger Practical Scenes

In order to depict larger and more densely populated crowds in practical scenes, filmmakers often employ a clever technique involving a relatively small number of extras. This process entails filming the same group of extras in multiple passes, with each pass featuring a different arrangement or positioning of the individuals. Subsequently, visual effects (VFX) techniques are utilized to composite these various passes together, seamlessly merging them into a single cohesive crowd scene. The beauty of this approach lies in its ability to create the illusion of a much larger and more dynamic crowd while working within the practical limitations of available extras and physical space. The result is a convincing and visually rich crowd scene that enhances the authenticity and scale of the narrative, all achieved through the creative application of VFX technology.

The key to successful integration is meticulous planning, close collaboration between VFX teams and on-set crews, and a deep understanding of how practical and digital elements will interact within the scene. When done effectively, the audience is immersed in the story, and the VFX enhance the storytelling without drawing undue attention to themselves.

D. Makeup and Prosthetics

Character Transformations

Makeup artists and prosthetic experts wield significant influence in the film industry by facilitating the transformation of actors into compelling characters. Their vital role encompasses a wide range of tasks, from aging characters convincingly, crafting historical appearances with precision, to concealing or enhancing specific facial features as needed by the narrative. Through the deft application of makeup and prosthetic materials, these professionals enable actors to undergo profound physical metamorphoses, seamlessly blurring the line between the performer and their on-screen persona. Utilizing a diverse array of techniques, from subtle enhancements to elaborate prosthetic creations, they contribute significantly to the authenticity and immersive quality of the cinematic experience, ensuring that characters come to life in a visually compelling and emotionally resonant manner. Here are different types of techniques used to develop character transformations through makeup and prosthetics in cinema:

Transforming Appearances: The Art of Prosthetic Appliances in Filmmaking

Prosthetic appliances are meticulously crafted, custom-designed pieces often composed of materials such as foam latex, silicone, or gelatin, and they serve as transformative tools in makeup artistry. These appliances are skillfully applied to an actor's skin to achieve a wide array of visual effects, ranging from scars and wounds to intricate aging effects, and can even extend to full-face masks for characters undergoing radical transformations. The process begins with the careful creation of the prosthetic piece to match the character's specific requirements, followed by its precise application on the actor's face or body. Once affixed, these appliances seamlessly blend with the actor's skin, achieving a remarkably realistic appearance that enhances the character's depth and authenticity. Whether used to age a character over decades or create fantastical beings, prosthetic appliances exemplify the marriage of artistry and technology in the world of film and theater, facilitating the captivating transformation of actors into their on-screen personas.

Sculpting Faces: The Magic of Shading and Highlighting in Makeup Artistry

Makeup artists possess a remarkable arsenal of techniques, among them, the art of shading and highlighting, which allows them to sculpt and reshape an actor's facial features with precision and subtlety. By deftly applying makeup shades darker than the actor's natural skin tone, certain areas of the face can be shadowed to create the illusion of depth, while lighter shades can be used to emphasize and lift other features. This transformative method allows makeup artists to enhance or diminish specific aspects of an actor's appearance, such as accentuating cheekbones, refining noses, or chiseling jawlines. This technique is frequently employed to align the actor's facial characteristics with those of a specific character or historical figure, ultimately achieving a stunning metamorphosis that extends beyond superficial makeup, underlining the artistry and expertise of makeup professionals in character creation and portrayal.

Timeless Transformations: Aging and De-Aging Makeup in Film and Television

Aging makeup is a transformative art within the world of special effects makeup, meticulously employed to age actors and characters convincingly by simulating the natural effects of time on the skin. This technique involves the strategic application of makeup elements like wrinkles, age spots, and other nuanced details to evoke the appearance of advancing years. It's an art of subtlety and precision, aimed at creating a realistic portrayal of aging. Conversely, de-aging makeup is its counterpart, where makeup artists employ their expertise to reverse the hands of time, erasing or softening the signs of aging to make actors appear younger. This process can involve techniques like smoothing out wrinkles and rejuvenating skin texture, often used in flashback sequences or to maintain consistency in long-running franchises. In both cases, aging and de-aging makeup showcase the remarkable skill of makeup artists in transforming actors' appearances, enabling them to embody characters of various ages with astonishing authenticity on the screen.

Masters of Illusion: Exploring Special Effects Makeup (SFX Makeup) in Film and Beyond

Special effects makeup, often referred to as SFX makeup, stands as a dynamic and multifaceted discipline within the world of makeup artistry. It encompasses a wide spectrum of techniques, merging the talents of makeup artists and effects specialists to craft astonishingly realistic and sometimes otherworldly transformations. SFX makeup involves the skillful application of prosthetics, makeup, and on occasion, animatronics, to bring characters to life with authenticity. This versatile craft can span from the creation of subtle injuries like bruising, wounds, or scars for gritty realism in crime dramas, to intricate and elaborate designs that give birth to fantastical creatures and supernatural entities in the realms of horror and fantasy. Whether it's the meticulous recreation of historical battle wounds, the crafting of iconic cinematic monsters, or the subtle manipulation of facial features, special effects makeup represents an intricate fusion of artistry and technology, a craft that blurs the line between the real and the surreal on the silver screen.

Dental Prosthetics: Transforming Smiles and Character Appearances in Film and Theater

Dental prosthetics, encompassing various elements like fake teeth, dental plates, or veneers, play a pivotal role in the art of character transformation within the area of film and theater. These specialized pieces, meticulously designed and customized to suit the character's needs, serve as potent tools in the hands of makeup artists and costume designers. By precisely altering an actor's dental features, these prosthetics can create dramatic shifts in their smile and overall facial appearance, achieving a level of authenticity that is paramount in character portrayal. Such dental transformations are particularly invaluable for characters with distinctive dental attributes, as they can be instrumental in not only evoking the physical traits but also the personality and backstory of the character. Whether it's the creation of misaligned teeth for a quirky supporting character or the perfect set of dentures for a historical figure, dental prosthetics underscore the profound impact that even the smallest details can have on an actor's performance and the overall visual narrative of a production.

Head-Turning Transformations: The Art of Bald Caps and Wigs in Costume Design

Bald caps and wigs are transformative tools in the world of costume and character design, facilitating the alteration of an actor's hair and scalp appearance. Bald caps, skillfully applied to an actor's head, serve as a blank canvas, creating the illusion of a completely bald scalp and allowing for the portrayal of characters with no hair or a dramatically different hairline. Conversely, wigs, available in a wide range of styles, colours, and lengths, offer the versatility to change an actor's hair dramatically to suit the character's requirements. They can be used to transform a brunette into a blonde, add vibrant colours, or recreate period-specific hairstyles with remarkable authenticity. These hair-related techniques enable costume designers and makeup artists to achieve significant character transformations by manipulating an actor's hair and scalp appearance, making them integral to the art of creating visually striking and emotionally resonant characters in film and theater.

Shaping Characters: The Role of Padding and Body Suits in Physical Transformation

The utilization of padding and body suits represents a sophisticated and invaluable facet of character transformation within the realms of film and theater. These versatile tools serve as a means to physically manipulate an actor's physique, effectively enhancing, diminishing, or entirely redefining their body proportions to suit the specific demands of a role. Whether it's making an actor appear larger, smaller, or possessing entirely unique body characteristics, such as exaggerated muscles or distinctive body shapes, padding and body suits enable the creation of characters with diverse and distinct physical attributes. This artistry is often employed for characters with unique body types, ensuring that the actor embodies the character's physicality convincingly. The seamless integration of these elements into costume and character design underscores their significance in achieving the visual authenticity and storytelling nuances essential to captivating audiences on the stage or screen.

Hair and Facial Transformation: Crafting Character Appearances Through Wigs and Makeup

The art of altering an actor's hairstyle and adding facial hair through makeup and wigs is crucial for character transformation in film and theater. This technique allows makeup artists and costume designers to create unique character appearances by adjusting hair color, length, and style. Using wigs, they can drastically change an actor's hair to match the character's personality or historical context. Meticulously applying facial hair with makeup techniques like crepe hair or spirit gum enables the creation of various styles, from moustaches to beards. This not only enhances the actor's appearance but also establishes the character's identity, reflecting their era, background, and personality. Makeup and wigs are potent tools for character development, allowing actors to authentically embody their roles on both stage and screen.

Ink and Artistry: Transforming Actors with Temporary Tattoos and Body Art

The application of temporary tattoos and body art represents a versatile and impactful technique within the arena of character design in film and theater. These artful adornments are meticulously applied to an actor's skin to create the illusion of character-specific tattoos, scars, or distinctive markings. Temporary tattoos, which come in a wide variety of designs and styles, are ideal for characters with intricate or culturally significant body art. On the other hand, body art techniques, which include hand-painted designs or makeup applications, allow for customized and highly detailed markings that can convey specific narratives or character histories. This artistry serves as an essential tool in character development, enabling actors to embody their roles authentically and visually communicate essential aspects of their characters, such as personal history, affiliations, or cultural backgrounds, enhancing the overall depth and impact of the narrative on both stage and screen.

Eyes of Transformation: The Power of Coloured Contact Lenses in Character Portrayal

The use of coloured contact lenses in makeup and character design holds transformative power, enabling makeup artists and costume designers to alter an actor's eye colour with remarkable effect. By precisely selecting and applying coloured contact lenses, the actor's natural eye colour can be dramatically changed to achieve a specific aesthetic or character look. This simple yet highly effective technique can have a profound impact on an actor's appearance, enhancing their ability to embody a character and convey distinct personality traits, emotions, or even supernatural qualities. The shift in eye colour can be a subtle tool for character development or a bold statement, serving as a visual cue that informs the audience about the character's identity and backstory. Whether it's for a period piece, a fantasy realm, or a character with unique attributes, coloured contact lenses represent a pivotal element in the artistry of character portrayal, allowing actors to step into the shoes (or eyes) of their roles with captivating authenticity.

Mastering the Macabre: Crafting Realistic Blood and Gore Effects in Film and Theater

The art of creating realistic blood and gore effects in makeup is a specialized and impactful facet of film and theater. Makeup artists employ an array of materials and techniques to achieve gruesome and authentic effects. Fake blood, typically made from a combination of syrup and food colouring, serves as the foundation, allowing for the depiction of wounds, injuries, and bloody scenes. Prosthetic wounds, which are custom-crafted to match the character's injuries, are then meticulously applied to the actor's skin, creating the illusion of gashes, lacerations, and deformities. Squibs, small explosive devices, are strategically placed beneath the prosthetic wounds and rigged to simulate gunshot wounds, creating explosive and dramatic effects. The combination of these materials and techniques enables makeup artists to craft visceral and chilling scenes, from graphic injuries to intense action sequences, lending authenticity and impact to the storytelling process while highlighting the artistry and technical prowess of makeup professionals in creating visual effects that truly captivate audiences.

Artistry with Purpose: The Intricate Research and Design of Character Transformations in Makeup Artistry

The process of crafting character transformations through makeup and prosthetics involves a meticulous and research-driven approach. Makeup artists embark on a comprehensive journey of character exploration, delving into the character's background, personality traits, and the historical or fictional context of the narrative. This research serves as the foundation for informed design decisions, enabling makeup artists to create looks that align seamlessly with the character's identity and the story's setting. They consider various factors, such as the character's age, social status, cultural background, and personal experiences, all of which influence the character's appearance. Additionally, attention to historical accuracy or adherence to the visual style of a particular time period is crucial in achieving authenticity. This holistic approach ensures that the makeup and prosthetics not only enhance the actor's physical transformation but also contribute significantly to the depth and consistency of the character within the narrative, highlighting the meticulous craftsmanship and storytelling synergy at the heart of character design in film and theater.

Seamless Synergy: The Collaboration Between Makeup, Prosthetics, and Costume Design for Character Transformations

The synergy between makeup, prosthetics, and costume design is a pivotal aspect of character transformation in film and theater. These creative disciplines work in harmony to craft a cohesive and visually convincing character portrayal. Makeup artists and costume designers collaborate closely to ensure that the makeup and prosthetics align seamlessly with the character's overall appearance and storytelling context. This entails considering factors such as the character's personality, background, and the era or culture they belong to, which collectively influence their visual identity. The character's makeup, prosthetic elements, and costumes are carefully coordinated to create a unified and authentic look that resonates with the audience and enhances the storytelling experience. This collaborative approach underscores the importance of visual consistency in character design, showcasing the artistry and attention to detail that contribute to the compelling and immersive world of film and theater.

On-Set Artistry: The Vital Role of Makeup Artists in Maintaining Consistency During Filming

Throughout the filming process, makeup artists play a vital role in maintaining the visual continuity of characters by continuously monitoring, maintaining, and touching up makeup and prosthetics. This meticulous and ongoing effort is essential to ensure that the characters' appearance remains consistent not only throughout different scenes but also over the course of multiple shooting days, which may be non-sequential. Makeup artists pay close attention to factors like sweat, lighting changes, and the natural wear and tear that occurs during filming to make necessary adjustments and touch-ups. Their expertise ensures that scars, wounds, aging effects, or any other character transformations remain realistic and unblemished, preserving the seamless illusion created by makeup and prosthetics and contributing to the overall cohesiveness of the film or television production. This dedication to detail underscores the crucial role of makeup artists in maintaining the integrity of the characters' appearances and the storytelling process throughout the shooting schedule.

Character transformations through makeup and prosthetics are a collaborative effort between makeup artists, prosthetic designers, costume designers, and the actors themselves. These techniques allow actors to fully immerse themselves in their roles and bring characters to life on the screen.

Special Effects Makeup

In Indian cinema, the application of special effects makeup stands as a remarkable craft, serving as the transformative gateway for characters with extraordinary and fantastical attributes, be they supernatural beings or mythical creatures. This specialized form of makeup artistry requires a unique skill set and imaginative vision to bring these extraordinary characters to life on screen. It enables actors to undergo astounding physical alterations, transcending the boundaries of reality to fully embody their roles in film, television, theater, and other forms of entertainment. Through a myriad of techniques, ranging from intricate prosthetics to innovative paintwork and creative use of materials, special effects makeup artists elevate the art of character transformation, ensuring that the most imaginative and fantastical characters seamlessly integrate into the cinematic narrative, captivating audiences with their visually striking and otherworldly appearances. Here are different types of techniques commonly employed in this process:

The Artistry of Prosthetic Appliances: Crafting Custom Transformations for the Screen

Prosthetic appliances constitute meticulously crafted, custom-designed pieces that are individually sculpted and molded to precisely conform to an actor's facial contours or body, achieving a seamless and natural fit. These versatile creations serve as transformative tools in the world of makeup and character design, offering a wide array of possibilities.

Prosthetic appliances can encompass diverse effects, from simulating wounds, scars, and injuries to creating otherworldly creature features and dramatic character alterations. Typically composed of specialized materials such as foam latex, silicone, or gelatin, these appliances offer both the pliability to adapt to an actor's movements and the ability to replicate realistic skin textures, ensuring a convincing and authentic appearance on screen or stage. In essence, prosthetic appliances epitomize the fusion of artistry and technology, enabling actors to undergo profound physical transformations and breathe life into their characters within the realms of film and theater.

Capturing Character Essence: The Role of Life Casting in Custom Prosthetics

A life cast is a crucial step in the creation of custom prosthetic pieces, serving as the foundational mold from which these transformative elements are crafted. This intricate process begins by applying a specialized material, often alginate or silicone, directly onto the actor's face or body, meticulously capturing their unique features and contours. The material is carefully applied to ensure a precise and accurate replication of the actor's anatomy. Once the material sets and solidifies, it forms a detailed negative impression, essentially a replica of the actor's face or body. This life cast then serves as the basis for the creation of custom prosthetic appliances, ensuring that they fit flawlessly and harmoniously with the actor's natural features. The accuracy and attention to detail inherent in the life casting process are paramount, as they lay the groundwork for achieving convincing and authentic character transformations in the realms of film and theater.

Sculpting Transformation: From Clay to Custom Prosthetic Masterpieces

The art of crafting prosthetic appliances begins with skilled sculptors who employ a diverse array of tools and materials to meticulously bring the original design to life. Sculptors may utilize traditional materials such as clay, which offers tactile and hands-on sculpting capabilities, or opt for digital sculpting software for precision and efficiency. These talented artists sculpt intricate and detailed designs that encapsulate the desired character transformation, ensuring that every contour and feature is expertly replicated. Once the sculpting process is complete, the resulting sculpture serves as the master mold—a blueprint of the prosthetic piece's final form. This master mold becomes the key to reproducing prosthetic pieces with unwavering fidelity, and it serves as the starting point for the casting process, where materials like foam latex, silicone, or gelatin are used to create the final prosthetic appliances, each one crafted to match the sculpted design with exquisite accuracy.

Molding the Magic: Transforming Sculpted Designs into Prosthetic Reality

Following the intricate sculpting process, the next critical step is the creation of molds that serve as the means to reproduce the finely crafted design in a flexible material, typically foam latex. These molds can be crafted from various materials, with common choices including plaster, silicone, or fiberglass, each offering distinct advantages. Plaster molds are cost-effective and widely used for smaller-scale projects, while silicone molds provide exceptional detail and are favored for intricate and delicate designs. Fiberglass molds are known for their durability and resilience to frequent use. Regardless of the material chosen, the mold-making process involves meticulously layering the selected material over the sculpted piece and allowing it to cure and harden. Once the mold is completed and carefully separated from the original sculpture, it becomes the essential tool for casting multiple prosthetic pieces, ensuring that each subsequent piece faithfully replicates the sculpted design with precision and consistency.

Crafting Character: The Art of Casting Prosthetic Pieces from Molds

The casting of prosthetic pieces represents the transformative culmination of the creative process, where molds, carefully crafted from materials like plaster, silicone, or fiberglass, are utilized to reproduce the sculpted design. These molds are meticulously prepared, and the chosen material for the prosthetic piece, typically foam latex, silicone, or gelatin, is carefully poured or injected into the mold cavity. The casting material takes the form of the sculpted design as it sets and solidifies. This process is performed with meticulous attention to detail, ensuring that each prosthetic piece is an exact replica of the original sculpt, capturing every nuance and intricacy. Once cured, the prosthetic pieces are delicately removed from the molds, revealing finely crafted, flexible, and detailed creations that are ready for the subsequent stages of application and transformation on the actor's face or body, ultimately bringing characters to life in the world of film and theater.

Seamless Transformation: The Precision of Applying Prosthetic Pieces in Makeup Artistry

The application of prosthetic pieces by skilled makeup artists is a precise and intricate process that forms the cornerstone of character transformation in film and theater. Using specialized adhesives and blending techniques, these artists carefully affix the custom-crafted prosthetic pieces onto the actor's skin, ensuring a seamless fusion between the prosthetic and the actor's natural features. This step demands a keen eye for detail and a mastery of makeup techniques, as the artists must delicately manipulate the edges of the prosthetic to seamlessly integrate it with the actor's skin texture, colour, and contours. Achieving this seamless merger is essential to creating a convincing and authentic transformation, allowing actors to step into their characters with a sense of realism that captivates audiences. The artistry lies in the ability to make the boundaries of the prosthetic virtually disappear, thus enabling actors to embody their roles with captivating authenticity and bringing the characters to life on screen or stage.

Vanishing Boundaries: The Art of Blending Prosthetic Edges for a Seamless Look

The process of concealing the edges of prosthetic appliances represents a meticulous and artful endeavor undertaken by makeup artists to achieve seamless integration with the actor's skin. To make these edges virtually disappear, artists employ an array of specialized techniques. Feathering involves gently thinning and tapering the edges of the prosthetic, ensuring a gradual transition from the prosthetic to the actor's skin, eliminating any abrupt lines. Blending entails skillfully layering makeup products, such as foundation or concealer, over the edges to soften their appearance and match the colour and texture of the actor's skin precisely. Additionally, artists may use painting techniques to further camouflage the edges by meticulously recreating the surrounding skin's natural tone and texture. This intricate process demands both technical precision and an artistic eye, resulting in a flawless integration of the prosthetic appliance into the actor's skin, achieving a convincing and authentic transformation that captivates audiences.

Harmonizing Hues: The Artistry of Matching Prosthetic Appliance Colours to Skin Tone

Makeup artists employ a combination of specialized techniques and materials to achieve a natural and cohesive look when matching the colour and texture of prosthetic appliances to the actor's skin. This process begins with the careful selection of paints and pigments that closely resemble the actor's natural skin tones, considering factors like undertones and shading. Artists then meticulously layer and blend these materials, ensuring a seamless transition from the prosthetic to the actor's skin. Airbrushing, a precise and controlled application method, is often employed to achieve even coverage and realistic texture, replicating the subtleties of the surrounding skin. The result is a harmonious integration of the prosthetic piece with the actor's features, erasing any visible distinctions and creating a convincingly natural appearance. This attention to detail not only enhances the character's authenticity but also showcases the remarkable artistry and technical expertise of makeup professionals in achieving seamless character transformations in the world of film and theater.

Hair and Character: Crafting Facial Hair and Eyebrows for Prosthetic Transformations

Makeup artists adeptly handle the intricacies of character design for roles requiring facial hair, eyebrows, or other hair-related features, utilizing various techniques to achieve authenticity. In some instances, they meticulously apply real human or synthetic hair directly onto the prosthetic pieces, matching the colour and texture to the character's requirements. This process involves painstakingly positioning individual hair strands or small hair patches on the prosthetic, allowing for a customized and natural appearance. Alternatively, artists may opt for pre-made hair appliances designed for specific character needs, such as moustaches or beards, which can be easily adhered to the prosthetic. The choice of technique depends on factors like the character's style, the level of detail required, and the actor's comfort. This artistry in handling facial hair not only contributes to the character's visual authenticity but also exemplifies the skill and precision of makeup professionals in achieving seamless character transformations on screen or stage.

Eyes of Enchantment: Transforming Gaze with Coloured and Specialty Contact Lenses

The use of coloured or specialty contact lenses in makeup and character design is a transformative artistry that allows makeup artists to manipulate the actor's eye colour and create captivating visual effects. Coloured lenses, available in an extensive array of hues, enable artists to change the actor's eye colour to suit the character's persona or enhance a specific look. These lenses are carefully selected to match the character's desired eye colour, creating a striking and realistic effect. Additionally, specialty lenses are employed to craft otherworldly or supernatural eyes, including designs featuring patterns, textures, or unique visual elements like cat-like pupils or eerie sclera. These lenses play a pivotal role in defining character traits and enhancing the storytelling experience, capturing the essence of characters with a distinct and captivating gaze that mesmerizes audiences while showcasing the skill and precision of makeup artists in achieving these remarkable visual transformations.

Canvas of Expression: The Artistry of Body Painting in Character Design

Body painting techniques are a versatile and creative form of artistic expression employed in character design to craft intricate designs, tattoos, or various markings directly onto the actor's skin. These techniques encompass a wide range of possibilities, from tribal patterns and cultural tattoos to fantastical designs and abstract artistry. Body painters utilize specialized body paints, brushes, and sponges to meticulously apply and blend colours and textures onto the actor's skin, achieving stunning visual effects. The process demands precision and attention to detail, as artists work to bring the character's personality and backstory to life through the artful application of paint. Whether enhancing a character's cultural heritage or conveying a mystical quality, body painting techniques serve as a powerful tool in storytelling, captivating audiences and demonstrating the incredible artistry of makeup professionals in creating immersive and visually captivating character transformations.

Texturing Reality: Elevating Prosthetic Realism with Intricate Details

In film and theater, adding texture to prosthetic pieces is a crucial step in enhancing their realism and character transformations. Makeup artists use various techniques and materials to create intricate details. For instance, crafting reptilian scales involves precise sculpting and layering of textures on the prosthetic, followed by detailed painting and shading to replicate the look and feel of scales. Similarly, creating wrinkles for aging or character-specific features involves sculpting to mimic natural skin contours. Intricate painting of veins on prosthetic appliances simulates the subtle vascular patterns beneath the skin's surface. This meticulous focus on texture provides depth and dimension, making character appearances more authentic and highlighting the artistic and technical expertise of makeup professionals in achieving lifelike transformations.

Safety and Comfort: Prioritizing Actor Well-Being During Prosthetic Application

Ensuring the safety and comfort of actors throughout the prosthetic application process is paramount in the world of makeup and character design. This multifaceted approach to actor well-being begins with managing ventilation, as prosthetic adhesives and materials can emit fumes that may be uncomfortable or harmful if inhaled. Adequate ventilation systems are employed to maintain a safe and breathable environment. Additionally, makeup artists use specialized, skin-friendly adhesives to minimize any potential discomfort or allergic reactions during the application. Prosthetic removal techniques are also carefully considered, using products and methods that are gentle on the skin to avoid any unnecessary irritation. Actors are given regular breaks during lengthy makeup sessions to ensure their comfort and alleviate physical strain, fostering a collaborative and respectful atmosphere on set. Overall, this holistic approach to actor safety and comfort underscores the professionalism and consideration of makeup professionals in the pursuit of exceptional character transformations.

Character-Centric Makeup: The Collaborative Process Between Artists, Directors, and Actors

The collaboration between makeup artists, directors, and actors is a fundamental aspect of character design in film and theater, and it begins with a deep understanding of the character's background, personality, and context. Makeup artists work closely with directors to gain insights into the character's narrative arc and visual representation within the story. This collaboration involves extensive research into the character's historical or cultural context, motivations, and emotional journey, as well as discussions with actors to understand their interpretation and vision for the role. Armed with this knowledge, makeup artists meticulously design and execute makeup that aligns with the character's depth, effectively conveying their inner world and external appearance. The makeup becomes a visual language that enhances storytelling, capturing the essence of the character and ensuring a harmonious fusion of aesthetics and narrative in the final performance, showcasing the integral role of makeup artists in the art of character portrayal.

Harmonizing Artistry: The Collaborative Synergy of Makeup, Costumes, and Lighting Design

The collaboration between makeup artists, costume designers, and lighting directors is an essential aspect of creating a cohesive and visually striking character portrayal in film and theater. Makeup artists work closely with costume designers to ensure that the makeup complements the overall look of the character, considering factors like clothing, accessories, and hairstyles. This collaboration ensures that the character's appearance is harmonious and coherent, contributing to a unified and memorable visual aesthetic. Additionally, makeup artists coordinate with lighting directors to account for how different lighting setups will affect the makeup's appearance on camera or stage. This includes considerations such as the colour temperature of lighting, intensity, and direction, which can significantly impact the makeup's colours sand textures. The synergy between these creative disciplines ensures that the makeup enhances the character's mood, appearance, and narrative presence, highlighting the collaborative nature of production in achieving a compelling and immersive on-screen or on-stage experience.

Perfecting the Look: The Importance of Makeup Tests and Rehearsals Before Filming

Before the cameras roll, makeup artists engage in a crucial pre-production process by conducting makeup tests and rehearsals with the actors. This essential step is undertaken to refine and perfect the makeup application, aligning it precisely with the desired character vision. During these sessions, artists work closely with the actors, experimenting with various makeup techniques, colours, and styles to ensure that the character's appearance is both visually striking and emotionally resonant. Makeup tests allow for adjustments to be made, addressing any issues related to colour accuracy, blending, or overall aesthetics. Furthermore, these rehearsals provide actors with the opportunity to become familiar with the makeup application process and ensure they are comfortable with the final look. This collaborative and iterative approach ensures that the makeup achieves the desired visual impact and seamlessly integrates with the actor's performance, ultimately contributing to the authenticity and storytelling prowess of the character portrayal in the final production.

The successful execution of character transformations through special effects makeup relies on the expertise, creativity, and collaboration of makeup artists, sculptors, prosthetic designers, and the rest of the production team. When done effectively, special effects makeup can bring characters to life and enhance the storytelling in film and other forms of entertainment.

E. Choreography and Dance Sequences

Intricate Choreography

In the vibrant world of Indian cinema, the inclusion of elaborate dance sequences is a hallmark, and choreographers hold a pivotal role in shaping these visually enchanting and culturally significant performances. Collaborating closely with directors and actors, choreographers infuse their work with artistic creativity, drawing inspiration from rich cultural influences that span centuries and regions. These dance experts employ their technical prowess to meticulously craft every step, gesture, and expression, ensuring that each sequence is not just a visual spectacle but a narrative tool that enhances storytelling, evokes emotions, and resonates deeply with audiences. With a fusion of tradition and innovation, Indian cinema's dance choreography remains an integral and mesmerizing aspect of the cinematic experience, serving as a reflection of the country's diverse and vibrant cultural heritage. Here are some different techniques used to develop intricate choreography in Indian movies:

Choreography in Storytelling: Enhancing Narrative and Emotion through Dance Sequences

Choreography in the context of performing arts, particularly in dance and theater, plays a pivotal role as it is intricately intertwined with the overarching storyline and the multifaceted evolution of characters. Choreographers function as vital collaborators, working in tandem with directors and scriptwriters to meticulously craft dance sequences that seamlessly meld with the narrative fabric, thus effectively transcending mere physical movements into powerful conduits of emotional expression and storytelling. Through their artistic vision and technical expertise, choreographers ensure that each dance performance not only serves as an aesthetically captivating spectacle but also serves as a dynamic vehicle for conveying nuanced emotions, elucidating key plot developments, and providing a deeper insight into the characters' inner worlds. In essence, choreography becomes a storytelling tool, enhancing the viewer's engagement and understanding of the unfolding drama, while also enriching the overall theatrical experience.

Indian Dance Choreography: Weaving Cultural Heritage into Storytelling

Indian dance choreography is a tapestry woven from the vibrant threads of a profound cultural legacy, encompassing a diverse array of classical dance forms such as Bharatanatyam, Kathak, Odissi, and Kathakali, as well as a multitude of regional folk dances. Choreographers adeptly weave these rich influences into their creative process, imbuing their sequences with authenticity and cultural resonance. They draw upon the intricate hand gestures (mudras), facial expressions (rasas), and rhythmic footwork inherent in classical styles, infusing their choreography with timeless grace and intricate storytelling techniques. Simultaneously, they pay homage to the diverse folk traditions of India, incorporating their distinctive movements, costumes, and regional narratives into their work, thereby creating a harmonious synthesis that celebrates the nation's cultural kaleidoscope. In this way, Indian dance choreography becomes a dynamic platform for the preservation and evolution of tradition, while also embracing innovation and cross-cultural influences, offering audiences a captivating glimpse into the multifaceted tapestry of India's artistic heritage.

Collaborative Harmony: Choreographers and Music Directors Crafting Dance Sequences

Choreographers engage in a crucial creative partnership with music directors, working closely to craft original songs or curate fitting music tracks that harmoniously complement dance sequences. The synergy between music and movement is pivotal, as the rhythm, melody, and lyrics of the chosen music serve as the guiding forces shaping the style and tempo of the choreography. Whether it's a stirring classical composition or a contemporary hit, the music's emotional nuances, tempo fluctuations, and thematic resonance influence the choreographer's decisions, helping to convey mood, narrative depth, and the overall impact of the performance. This symbiotic relationship between choreography and music not only enhances the aesthetic appeal of the dance but also establishes a powerful emotional connection with the audience, creating a dynamic fusion of auditory and visual artistry that elevates the performance to a captivating and immersive experience.

Precision in Motion: The Rigorous Training and Rehearsals of Dancers

Dancers embark on an arduous journey of rigorous training, dedicating themselves to the mastery of specific dance styles and techniques. This rigorous preparation forms the foundation of their ability to execute choreography with precision and artistry. Choreographers, in turn, lead the dancers through painstakingly detailed rehearsals that serve multiple crucial purposes. These sessions are instrumental in refining individual movements, fostering collective synchronization among performers, and upholding a uniformity of style and execution. Through relentless practice and meticulous guidance, choreographers transform dancers into cohesive and polished ensembles, ensuring that each step, gesture, and expression harmoniously coalesces to bring their creative vision to life. This disciplined and collaborative process is the crucible in which dance performances evolve from mere steps and movements into awe-inspiring expressions of skill, passion, and artistic expression.

Blocking and Spatial Arrangement in Dance Choreography: Crafting Dynamic Stage Presence

Choreographers meticulously orchestrate the spatial arrangement of dancers within the performance's set or stage, a strategic process encompassing the delineation of positions, formations, and pathways that optimally highlight the choreographed dance. This multifaceted task involves choreographers crafting intricate group formations that not only maximize visual impact but also convey narrative elements and thematic depth. Furthermore, they craft poignant solo moments that spotlight individual dancers and their unique abilities, while also integrating interactions between dancers that evoke emotional resonance and enhance storytelling. The choreographer's spatial design is an artful and strategic endeavor that transforms the performance space into a canvas where movement and expression converge, creating a captivating visual spectacle that complements and amplifies the essence of the dance, captivating audiences and enhancing the overall artistic experience.

Visual Synergy: Collaborative Artistry in Dance Costume and Makeup Design

Choreographers collaborate closely with costume designers and makeup artists to create visually captivating looks that complement the dance style and overall aesthetic. This collaborative effort goes beyond appearance, involving storytelling through clothing and makeup. Costumes are designed to allow unrestricted movement while reflecting artistic and cultural motifs. Makeup enhances facial expressions to match the dance's emotional tone. In some cases, these choices are elaborate and culturally significant, becoming integral to the narrative and transporting audiences to specific time periods or cultural contexts. This collaboration transcends aesthetics, contributing deeply to the immersive artistic experience of the performance.

Prop Choreography: Elevating Dance Sequences with Visual Elements

In certain dance sequences, choreographers incorporate the use of props such as fans, scarves, swords, or other accessories, which serve to add an extra layer of complexity and visual intrigue to the choreography. These props become extensions of the dancers' bodies and expressions, enhancing the storytelling and thematic depth of the performance. Choreographers take on the responsibility of meticulously integrating these props into the routine, ensuring they are seamlessly and skillfully manipulated by the dancers. This involves not only teaching dancers how to handle the props with precision but also choreographing movements that synchronize harmoniously with the prop's presence, amplifying the overall aesthetic impact. The successful incorporation of props into the dance adds depth, symbolism, and artistic flair, transforming the performance into a multidimensional sensory experience that captivates and engages the audience.

Expressive Narration: The Art of Symbolic Gestures and Facial Expressions in Indian Dance

Indian dance is renowned for its ability to convey intricate stories, emotions, and thematic elements through the eloquent use of symbolic gestures and facial expressions. Choreographers play a pivotal role in guiding dancers to master these expressive techniques, known as mudras (hand gestures) and abhinaya (facial expressions). Mudras are a sophisticated language of hand and finger movements, each with its own meaning, and when combined in sequences, they convey intricate narratives and emotions. Abhinaya involves the art of using the face, eyes, and body to express a wide range of sentiments, from joy and love to sorrow and anger. Choreographers work with dancers to ensure that these gestures and expressions are not only technically precise but also emotionally resonant, enhancing the storytelling aspect of the performance. Through their expertise, choreographers empower dancers to transform movements into powerful tools of communication, making Indian dance not just a visually captivating art form but also a profound means of conveying complex narratives and emotions to the audience.

Rhythmic Precision: The Mastery of Intricate Footwork in Indian Dance

Intricate footwork stands as a defining hallmark within numerous Indian dance forms, and choreographers place significant emphasis on crafting these elaborate patterns and rhythms generated by the dancers' feet. This intricate footwork, which is a fusion of technique, precision, and artistic expression, often demands meticulous timing and impeccable coordination. Choreographers meticulously design sequences where each step and movement, whether it be the delicate taps of Kathak, the energetic stomps of Bharatanatyam, or the graceful glides of Odissi, serves both an aesthetic and narrative purpose. Through their expertise, choreographers guide dancers to execute these intricate footwork sequences with remarkable dexterity, creating an auditory and visual spectacle that not only showcases the dancers' technical prowess but also adds depth, complexity, and a rhythmic vibrancy to the performance, further enriching the audience's experience.

Time Manipulation in Dance: Slow-Motion and Fast-Motion Techniques for Dramatic Effect

Choreographers occasionally employ the creative techniques of slow-motion and fast-motion to introduce dramatic and stylized effects into a dance sequence. These innovative tools serve to manipulate time and pace, allowing choreographers to add layers of artistic depth and visual interest to their choreography. Slow-motion can be utilized to accentuate the intricacy of movements, showcasing the dancers' control and grace in exquisite detail while imbuing the sequence with an ethereal quality. Conversely, fast-motion can inject energy and excitement into the performance, creating a sense of urgency and dynamism. The strategic use of these techniques involves careful planning and precise execution, and when integrated seamlessly, they not only add a unique and captivating dimension to the choreography but also provide the audience with a heightened sensory experience, elevating the overall impact of the dance sequence.

Capturing Dance on Film: The Art of Camera Angles and Shots in Choreography

Filmmakers employ a variety of camera angles and shots to effectively capture the intricate nuances of choreography in a dance sequence. Wide shots are employed to provide a comprehensive view of the performance, showcasing the grandeur of group formations, the spatial dynamics, and the synchronization of the dancers in relation to the set or stage. These shots are instrumental in conveying the overall aesthetic and visual impact of the choreography. In contrast, close-ups are utilized to zoom in on individual dancers, emphasizing their expressions, hand movements; and footwork, thus offering a more intimate and detailed perspective. These close-ups not only accentuate the technical finesse and emotional depth of the performers but also provide a means of connecting with the audience on a more personal level, enabling viewers to appreciate the subtleties and artistry of the dance. The careful orchestration of these camera angles and shots is essential in bringing out the full spectrum of the choreography's beauty and complexity on the cinematic canvas.

Seamless Integration: Enhancing Dance Sequences in Post-Production

In film post-production, skilled editors are crucial for integrating dance sequences seamlessly into the movie. They synchronize choreography with the film's narrative and pacing, ensuring smooth transitions in and out of the dance. Editors can also enhance the aesthetic and mood of the dance with visual effects and color grading. These enhancements range from subtle adjustments to dramatic effects that amplify the choreography's artistic and emotional impact. Editors play a significant role in harmoniously merging dance and film, ensuring the sequences complement the storyline and stand as visually compelling elements within the cinematic narrative.

Audience-Centric Choreography: Crafting Dance Sequences for Engagement and Connection

Choreographers aspire to captivate the audience through a multifaceted approach that encompasses captivating dance movements, compelling storytelling, and establishing a deep emotional connection. They are acutely attuned to the preferences and expectations of the target audience, recognizing that the success of their choreography hinges on resonating with the spectators. Choreographers meticulously craft movements that are not only technically impressive but also visually engaging, aiming to enrapture the viewers with the sheer artistry of the dance. Simultaneously, they weave a narrative thread throughout the choreography, allowing the audience to follow a storyline or thematic development through the movements. Crucially, choreographers infuse the dance with genuine emotion, striving to evoke a visceral response in the audience, whether it be joy, sorrow, or awe. By understanding and catering to the audience's desires, choreographers create performances that leave a lasting impact, forging a profound connection between the dancers and those who witness their artistry.

Fusion Choreography: Bridging Traditional Indian Dance with Modern Innovation

Certain choreographers engage in the innovative practice of fusion, where they skillfully amalgamate traditional Indian dance styles with contemporary or global dance forms, resulting in a distinctive and modern interpretation of dance sequences. This creative process involves a delicate balancing act, as choreographers strive to retain the essence of the traditional styles while infusing them with contemporary influences. The fusion of these diverse elements not only breathes new life into classical Indian dance but also creates a bridge between cultures, offering a fresh perspective that resonates with modern audiences. These choreographers draw upon their deep understanding of both the classical and contemporary dance vocabularies to craft performances that are both artistically compelling and culturally enriching, exemplifying the ever-evolving nature of dance as a dynamic and transformative art form.

Cinematic Brilliance: Choreography in Indian Movies Amplified by Visual Elements

Choreography in Indian movies frequently transcends the boundaries of traditional stage performances, seamlessly integrating cinematic elements such as camera movement, special effects, and dynamic lighting to elevate the visual impact of the dance sequences. Directors and choreographers collaborate closely to choreograph dance routines that are not only artistically compelling but also optimized for the cinematic medium. Camera movement, for instance, enables filmmakers to capture dance sequences from multiple angles, enhancing the viewer's perspective and allowing for dynamic and immersive shots. Special effects can be employed to add a layer of magic and spectacle to the performance, enhancing the choreography's visual allure. Dynamic lighting, on the other hand, sets the mood, accentuates movements, and adds depth to the visual composition, underscoring the emotional and narrative dimensions of the dance. This fusion of dance and cinema creates a captivating synergy, where choreography becomes an integral component of the storytelling process, engaging the audience on both an artistic and cinematic level, resulting in a visually stunning and emotionally resonant cinematic experience.

Indian cinema's enchanting choreography is a masterpiece born from the harmonious fusion of various artistic techniques and creative elements. Talented choreographers, with their profound knowledge of diverse dance forms and a strong artistic vision, collaborate closely with a team of highly skilled and dedicated dancers to transform their ideas into reality. Through meticulous planning and execution, choreographers infuse these sequences with expressive movements, symbolic gestures, precise footwork, and storytelling elements. It's within these intricacies that the dance sequences acquire their artistic depth and cultural richness.

The collaborative effort extends to the incorporation of cinematic elements, including innovative camera work, special effects, and dynamic lighting, which collectively elevate the visual appeal and narrative significance of the choreography. These cinematic techniques allow the dance performances to transcend the stage, creating an immersive experience that captivates audiences with both its artistic prowess and emotional depth. The result is a magical and captivating dance sequence, one of the defining characteristics of Indian cinema. These sequences not only showcase the mastery of the choreographers and dancers but also resonate deeply with audiences, underscoring the unique fusion of art, culture, and storytelling that defines Indian cinema.

Visual Spectacle

Dance sequences in Indian films are nothing short of visual extravaganzas, characterized by their vibrant costumes, dynamic camera movements, and intricate choreography. They transcend the boundaries of storytelling and become captivating spectacles in their own right, adding a layer of entertainment value that complements the film's narrative. Renowned for their grandeur, these sequences are a fusion of artistic expression and technical excellence, often showcasing a range of dance styles and cultural influences. Through meticulously crafted movements and visually stunning presentations, choreography in Indian cinema transforms into an unforgettable visual treat, contributing significantly to the overall cinematic experience and leaving audiences spellbound by the sheer creativity and energy on display. Here are different types of techniques used to develop choreography and dance sequences with a focus on visual spectacle in Indian movies:

The Grand Spectacle: Ensemble Cast and Intricate Choreography in Indian Film Dance Sequences

In Indian cinema, dance sequences often unfold as grand spectacles that showcase the artistry and coordination of a large ensemble cast, which typically includes not only the main performers but also background dancers. This ensemble approach is employed to create a visually striking and awe-inspiring spectacle. Choreographers meticulously craft intricate formations and meticulously synchronized movements that involve every member of the cast, achieving a breathtaking visual harmony. Whether it's a vibrant Bollywood dance number or a classical dance sequence, the sheer scale and precision of these performances contribute to the cinematic magic, adding layers of complexity, depth, and grandeur to the choreography. The unity of the ensemble cast, combined with the choreographer's vision, results in dance sequences that leave a lasting impact, captivating audiences with their sheer scale and breathtaking coordination.

Harmonizing Artistry: The Collaboration Between Choreographers and Costume Designers in Indian Dance

Choreographers engage in a collaborative process with costume designers to craft ornate and visually captivating costumes that serve as an integral element of dance performances, enhancing their overall visual appeal. These costumes are meticulously designed to complement and accentuate the choreography, often drawing inspiration from a wide spectrum of sources. They can be rooted in traditional attire, paying homage to cultural heritage and dance traditions, or they may incorporate historical references, imbuing the dance with a sense of time and place. Alternatively, choreographers and costume designers might opt for a contemporary fashion-forward approach, reflecting current trends and styles. Regardless of their inspiration, these costumes are strategically chosen to align with the thematic, emotional, and aesthetic goals of the dance sequence, making them an essential component of the storytelling and artistic expression within the performance.

The Majestic Backdrops: Scenic Beauty and Ambiance in Dance Sequences

Dance sequences in Indian cinema are frequently elevated by opulent and picturesque settings that serve as backdrops to the performances, transporting viewers into a world of visual splendor. These locations span a wide spectrum, ranging from majestic palaces and ancient temples to pristine natural landscapes and bustling urban cityscapes. In addition to the choice of location, meticulous attention is paid to set design, with elaborate props, decorations, and dynamic lighting schemes being meticulously orchestrated to amplify the visual impact. These carefully curated environments are not only visually captivating but also play a significant role in enhancing the mood, narrative depth, and emotional resonance of the dance sequences, transforming them into immersive and cinematic experiences that leave a lasting impression on the audience.

Enchanting Visual Magic: Enhancing Dance Sequences with Post-Production Wizardry

In filmmaking, dance sequences are often elevated through the application of visual effects and post-production techniques, a process that infuses the performances with an added layer of artistry and cinematic magic. These techniques encompass a wide array of possibilities, from seamlessly integrating digital elements like fantastical backgrounds or visual enhancements to the dancers themselves, to enhancing lighting effects that emphasize the mood and atmosphere of the choreography. Furthermore, filmmakers can employ post-production to create surreal and otherworldly visuals, allowing the dance to transcend the boundaries of reality and venture into the world of the extraordinary. These enhancements, when judiciously applied, contribute to the overall aesthetic and emotional impact of the dance sequences, elevating them from captivating performances to mesmerizing cinematic spectacles that engage and transport the audience into a world of enchantment and wonder.

Dance on the Edge: Adding Thrills and Awe with Acrobatic Moves and Daring Stunts

Choreographers often infuse dance routines with acrobatic movements, flips, and daring stunts to inject an exhilarating and awe-inspiring dimension into the performance. These physically demanding and high-energy maneuvers not only showcase the exceptional athleticism and skill of the dancers but also contribute significantly to the overall spectacle of the dance sequence. Whether it's gravity-defying leaps, intricate tumbling, or breathtaking aerial feats, these acrobatic elements add an element of excitement, suspense, and surprise, holding the audience in rapt attention. Furthermore, they provide a dynamic contrast to the more traditional dance movements, creating a visually captivating juxtaposition that heightens the impact of the choreography. The incorporation of acrobatics not only pushes the boundaries of what's possible in dance but also amplifies the emotional and visual resonance of the performance, leaving viewers in a state of exhilaration and awe.

Elevating the Dance: Innovative Camera Techniques in Cinematography for Dynamic Dance Sequences

Cinematographers and directors employ innovative camera techniques like crane shots, aerial shots, and drone shots to infuse dance sequences with a dynamic visual dimension that goes beyond the conventional. These techniques allow for capturing the choreography from unique and striking angles, providing viewers with a fresh perspective that amplifies the visual impact of the dance. Crane shots, with their sweeping movements and vertical reach, offer a sense of grandeur, emphasizing the scale and intensity of the performance. Aerial shots, on the other hand, provide an expansive view that showcases intricate formations and synchronized movements, offering an immersive bird's-eye view of the dance. Drone shots take this a step further, enabling fluid and dynamic tracking of the dancers, offering a sense of intimacy and connection with the performers while simultaneously highlighting the beauty of the choreography. These innovative camera techniques add depth, excitement, and visual interest to the dance, making it a cinematic spectacle that engages the audience on a whole new level.

Capturing the Essence: Slow-Motion and Freeze Frames in Dance Sequences for Enhanced Appreciation

Slow-motion sequences and freeze frames are cinematic tools employed to draw the audience's attention to pivotal moments within a dance sequence, granting viewers the opportunity to savor and fully appreciate the intricate movements and nuanced expressions of the performers. Slow motion, by decelerating the pace of the dance, accentuates the grace, precision, and artistry of each movement, highlighting the beauty of the choreography. Freeze frames, on the other hand, momentarily halt the action, affording the audience a close-up and intimate view of a specific pose or facial expression, enabling a deeper emotional connection with the dancer and the performance. These techniques not only serve as a means of emphasizing the technical skill and storytelling within the dance but also create a mesmerizing visual effect that adds layers of depth and appreciation to the overall choreography, making it a visually captivating and emotionally resonant experience for the audience.

Illuminating Artistry: Collaborative Choreographer-Lighting Designer Duets for Mesmerizing Dance

Choreographers collaborate closely with lighting designers to craft dynamic lighting schemes that play a pivotal role in enhancing the mood and aesthetics of a dance performance. This collaboration is essential for creating an immersive and visually compelling experience. Lighting designers use a diverse range of tools, including coloured lights, spotlights, and moving lights, to orchestrate the interplay of light and shadow, thus infusing the choreography with a captivating visual dimension. Coloured lights can evoke different emotions and thematic nuances, altering the atmosphere of the performance space. Spotlights highlight specific dancers or moments within the choreography, drawing the audience's focus and emphasizing key elements. Moving lights add kinetic energy and dynamic visual effects, enhancing the overall dynamism of the dance. Through this meticulous attention to lighting, choreographers and designers craft a synergy where light becomes an integral component of the storytelling, amplifying the emotional and artistic resonance of the performance while creating a visually stunning and evocative spectacle for the audience.

Dance as Visual Narration: The Role of Choreography in Storytelling Within Films

In filmmaking, dance sequences serve as a potent narrative device, seamlessly woven into the film's storyline to convey a wide array of emotions, facilitate character development, or advance the plot in a visually compelling manner. Choreography transcends mere aesthetic expression to become a powerful storytelling tool, as each movement and gesture is infused with intention and meaning. Through dance, characters can reveal their innermost emotions and desires, engage in interpersonal dynamics, or undergo transformative journeys, all without the need for explicit dialogue. Whether it's a passionate romantic duet, a lively group dance celebrating a victory, or a somber solo expressing profound sorrow, choreography communicates the unspoken and transcends language, creating a sensory and emotional connection between the characters and the audience. This integration of dance into the narrative not only enriches the storytelling but also elevates the cinematic experience, making it a potent and evocative form of visual storytelling.

Cultural Fusion in Choreography: Blending Traditions for a Visually Enriching Dance Experience

Choreographers often embark on a creative journey where they blend diverse dance styles, seamlessly marrying traditional and contemporary elements, to craft a visually captivating fusion that transcends cultural and aesthetic boundaries. This artistic endeavor brings an enriching depth to the choreography, making it a dynamic and multicultural tapestry of movement. By amalgamating styles, choreographers not only pay homage to cultural traditions but also infuse the dance with fresh vitality and relevance, allowing it to resonate with modern audiences. Whether it's the fusion of classical Indian Bharatanatyam with contemporary hip-hop, or the integration of traditional African dance with modern ballet, this blending of styles adds layers of complexity and visual interest to the choreography, creating a unique and captivating dance experience that celebrates the diversity and universality of dance as an art form.

Dance as Language: Symbolism and Themes in Indian Cinema Choreography

In Indian cinema, dance sequences are not just artistic interludes but integral components of the narrative, often laden with profound symbolic meanings and thematic elements. Choreographers meticulously craft movements and gestures that serve as a visual language, allowing characters to convey messages, emotions, and themes relevant to the storyline without relying on verbal communication. Each step, gesture, and expression is imbued with intention, adding layers of depth to the narrative. These sequences can convey a wide array of emotions, from love and longing to defiance and resilience, and they often serve as pivotal moments of character development. Beyond individual emotions, dance sequences can also explore broader societal themes, cultural traditions, and historical contexts. Through this fusion of movement and storytelling, choreographers play a pivotal role in making dance an evocative and impactful tool for narrative expression within Indian cinema, captivating audiences and enriching the cinematic experience with layers of meaning and emotion.

Propel the Performance: The Artful Integration of Props in Choreography

Choreographers skillfully incorporate a wide array of props, ranging from umbrellas and scarves to veils and traditional instruments, into their choreography to infuse dance sequences with both visual interest and profound cultural significance. These props become integral extensions of the dancers' expressions, serving multiple purposes within the performance. They add a layer of visual enchantment, creating captivating and dynamic visual effects as they interact with the movements of the dancers. Furthermore, these props carry cultural and symbolic weight, often representing traditions, narratives, or themes relevant to the dance. For example, a traditional instrument like a tabla drum might accompany a classical Indian dance, enhancing the cultural authenticity and rhythm of the performance. Scarves or veils can be used to accentuate the grace and elegance of movements or to symbolize emotions like mystery or romance. By skillfully integrating props into choreography, dancers and choreographers create a multi-dimensional dance experience that combines aesthetics, culture, and storytelling, captivating audiences and conveying intricate layers of meaning.

The Art of Emotional Connection: Expressive Storytelling and Close-Ups in Dance Performances

Facial expressions and emotive storytelling through dance are paramount elements, extensively emphasized by choreographers to forge a deep emotional connection with the audience. Within dance sequences, performers use their faces as canvases to convey a wide spectrum of feelings, from joy and love to sadness and anger, ensuring that emotions are not only expressed through movements but also etched onto their visages. These expressive faces become powerful tools for storytelling, allowing characters to communicate their innermost thoughts and experiences. Furthermore, close-up shots, often captured by cinematographers, zoom in on the dancers' faces, capturing the nuances of their expressions in exquisite detail. These close-ups serve as emotional windows, inviting the audience to intimately connect with the performers and become immersed in the narrative and emotional journey of the dance. This emphasis on facial expression and close-ups not only enhances the storytelling within the dance sequence but also elevates it to an art form that resonates deeply with the viewer on a visceral and emotional level, forging a powerful connection between the performers and the audience.

Dance as Poetry: The Power of Repetition and Variation in Choreography

Choreographers employ a delicate interplay of repetition and variation in their craft, weaving dance motifs and movements into intricate patterns and rhythms that captivate the eye and engage the audience. Repetition serves as a foundational element, introducing familiar movements or sequences that establish a thematic or structural framework within the choreography. It provides a sense of continuity and recognition for the viewers. However, it is the artful use of variation that breathes life and creativity into the dance. Choreographers introduce subtle or dramatic alterations in timing, direction, intensity, or style, infusing each repetition with unique nuances that surprise and delight the audience. These variations create a dynamic visual narrative, inviting viewers to witness the evolution and transformation of the dance in real-time. Through this interplay of repetition and variation, choreographers not only showcase their technical mastery but also tell stories, evoke emotions, and engage the audience in a mesmerizing dance experience that celebrates the beauty of movement and rhythm.

Spectacle in Numbers: Choreographing Mass Dance Sequences for Grandeur and Precision

Certain dance sequences in cinema feature expansive crowds or audiences within the film, contributing to the grandeur and visual spectacle of the performance. These scenes are meticulously choreographed to maintain synchronization and precision among the large number of participants. Choreographers orchestrate the movements of both the central performers and the surrounding crowds to create visually impressive formations and patterns that accentuate the scale and energy of the dance. These sequences often serve to underscore the significance of the moment within the film's storyline, emphasizing communal celebrations, cultural events, or moments of unity. The careful synchronization of such massive crowds not only adds to the visual spectacle but also showcases the choreographer's ability to harmonize a multitude of performers into a seamless and visually striking display of collective artistry, leaving a lasting impression on the audience.

Quick Costume Transformations: Enhancing Visual Variety in Dance Sequences

Dancers occasionally undergo rapid costume changes within a dance sequence, a technique employed to showcase a diverse array of looks and introduce visual variety. These quick costume changes are seamlessly integrated into the choreography, adding a dynamic and transformative element to the performance. They serve multiple purposes, allowing dancers to convey different facets of their characters or emotions, signal transitions within the narrative, or symbolize transformations in the storyline. These costume changes not only create an aesthetic feast for the audience but also emphasize the versatility and skill of the performers, as they must execute these changes swiftly and flawlessly, often behind the scenes. In doing so, dancers not only enhance the visual appeal of the dance but also contribute to the storytelling and artistic depth of the performance, making quick costume changes a captivating and integral component of the choreographic artistry.

The synergy of these techniques harmoniously converges to give rise to the visually spectacular dance sequences that have become a defining hallmark of Indian cinema. In these collaborative endeavors, choreographers, dancers, and filmmakers unite their talents and expertise to craft unforgettable moments that effortlessly captivate audiences with their sheer visual splendor. Through the meticulous coordination of movements, the infusion of cultural and emotional depth, the utilization of innovative camera work, the incorporation of props and costumes, and the application of post-production enhancements, these sequences transcend mere performances to become immersive cinematic spectacles. These moments in Indian cinema not only showcase the technical prowess of the artists but also celebrate the rich tapestry of cultures and traditions that dance embodies. The result is a sensory feast that leaves a lasting imprint, captivating audiences with the breathtaking beauty, emotion, and artistry of these iconic dance sequences.

F. Location Scouting and Natural Landscapes

Location scouting and natural landscapes play a crucial role in filmmaking, as they contribute significantly to the visual storytelling and overall aesthetic of a film. In India, with its diverse geography and rich cultural heritage, filmmakers have access to a wide range of scenic locations that can enhance the cinematic experience. Here, we'll explain in detail the importance of location scouting and how scenic locations in India contribute to the visual appeal of films:

Location Scouting

Scenic Locations: Narrative Extensions That Immerse the Audience in Film Worlds

Scenic locations are not merely backdrops in filmmaking; they serve as an integral extension of the film's narrative, offering a visual language that communicates context, atmosphere, and a tangible sense of place. These locations play a vital role in enveloping the audience within the story's world, allowing them to immerse themselves fully in the narrative's unfolding drama. The choice of location contributes to the film's overall tone, helping to set the mood and evoke specific emotions. Whether it's a sprawling desert landscape evoking a sense of isolation and hardship or a lush, tropical paradise invoking romance and adventure, scenic locations become silent storytellers, aiding in character development and plot progression. They add layers of authenticity to the film, grounding it in a physical and cultural reality that resonates with viewers. In essence, scenic locations are not just picturesque backgrounds but active participants in the storytelling process, enriching the cinematic experience by providing a visual and emotional context that deepens the audience's connection to the narrative.

Cultural and Historical Significance: India's Landscapes Enriching Film Narratives

India's diverse landscapes serve as more than just picturesque settings; they are repositories of cultural and historical significance, deeply interwoven with the nation's rich heritage. Filming in locations like ancient temples, opulent palaces, and revered heritage sites offers filmmakers a unique opportunity to infuse depth and authenticity into their narratives. These sites provide a tangible link to India's storied past, acting as visual anchors that connect the storyline to the country's traditions and history. Whether showcasing the grandeur of a majestic fort or the spiritual aura of a centuries-old temple, these locations become pivotal elements in the storytelling process. They not only lend a sense of time and place to the narrative but also evoke emotions, symbolize cultural themes, and facilitate character development. In essence, India's culturally significant landscapes are more than just backgrounds; they are storytellers in their own right, adding layers of cultural and historical resonance to the cinematic experience, making it a profound and immersive journey through time and tradition.

Setting the Cinematic Mood: How Location Choices Influence Film Tone and Atmosphere

The selection of a filming location is a powerful tool that directors and filmmakers use to sculpt the mood and tone of a film, providing a visual and emotional context that profoundly influences the audience's perception and engagement with the narrative. The contrast between serene natural landscapes like the Himalayan mountains and bustling city streets exemplifies this impact. The Himalayas, with their majestic peaks and tranquil vistas, convey a sense of peace, spirituality, and introspection. These landscapes serve as a canvas for stories of introspection, self-discovery, or enlightenment, setting a contemplative and serene tone. In contrast, the dynamic energy and chaos of bustling city streets can evoke a feeling of vitality, urgency, or freneticism. These urban backdrops become ideal settings for narratives centered around ambition, fast-paced lifestyles, or the complexity of modern living. In both cases, the choice of location becomes an essential element in conveying the film's emotional and thematic nuances, effectively becoming a visual language that communicates the desired mood, leaving a lasting impression on the audience.

India's Diverse Geography: A Palette of Cinematic Backdrops for Varied Storytelling

India's vast geographical diversity is a treasure trove for filmmakers, offering an expansive palette of visual backdrops that span from the arid deserts of Rajasthan to the lush, verdant forests of Kerala, and everything in between. This remarkable diversity provides a rich canvas for storytelling, allowing filmmakers to craft narratives that traverse different climates, terrains, and cultural contexts within the same country. The arid landscapes of Rajasthan can set the stage for tales of valor, epic battles, or romantic sagas amidst the grandeur of historical palaces and forts. In contrast, the emerald forests of Kerala provide a backdrop for stories woven with themes of nature, mysticism, and the harmony of life. The Himalayan ranges offer cinematic possibilities for narratives exploring spiritual journeys, while the bustling cityscapes of Mumbai or Delhi can depict the fast-paced, urban narratives of contemporary life. This geographical diversity not only enriches the visual appeal of Indian cinema but also lends authenticity and cultural richness to narratives, making India a compelling and versatile canvas for filmmakers to paint their stories upon.

Authenticity and Realism: The Impact of Filming in Real Locations on Cinematic Storytelling

Filming in authentic, real-life locations is a time-honored practice in filmmaking that adds an invaluable layer of authenticity and realism to a film. It enables filmmakers to immerse their audience in genuine cultural and environmental elements, fostering a sense of believability that enriches the storytelling. When scenes unfold in actual locations, viewers can tangibly connect with the cultural nuances, architectural intricacies, and natural landscapes that form the backdrop of the narrative. This connection enhances the emotional resonance of the film, making it more convincing and relatable. Whether it's the bustling streets of a historical city, the serene landscapes of a countryside village, or the vibrant markets of a bustling metropolis, these real locations serve as cultural and sensory touchpoints that breathe life into the narrative. They become integral characters in the story, shaping the characters' interactions and experiences, and ultimately contributing to a cinematic journey that feels authentic and deeply rooted in the real world.

Epic Backdrops: The Grandeur of India's Scenic Locations in Cinematic Spectacles

India's scenic locations possess a unique ability to exude grandeur and scale, elevating the cinematic experience to awe-inspiring heights. Films shot against majestic backdrops like the iconic Taj Mahal or the resplendent Jaipur City Palace create a profound sense of awe and wonder. These architectural marvels, steeped in history and cultural significance, not only serve as breathtaking visual spectacles but also imbue the storytelling with an unparalleled sense of grandeur. The sheer scale and opulence of such locations amplify the impact of the narrative, evoking a sense of reverence and admiration. Whether capturing a romantic rendezvous against the backdrop of the Taj Mahal's ethereal beauty or weaving tales of regal splendor within the walls of the Jaipur City Palace, these locations become integral components of the cinematic experience. They inspire awe, evoke emotions, and transport the audience into a world of visual splendor and historical richness that lingers long after the credits roll.

Character Development Through Location: How Environments Shape Cinematic Personas

The choice of location in filmmaking is a subtle yet powerful tool that extends beyond aesthetics; it significantly influences the development of characters within the narrative. A character's background, upbringing, and lifestyle can seamlessly be reflected in the environment they inhabit, creating a dynamic synergy that adds profound depth to their portrayal. For example, a character raised in the serene countryside may exhibit qualities of simplicity, closeness to nature, and a slower pace of life, all of which are subtly conveyed by their surroundings. In contrast, a character rooted in a bustling urban setting might embody traits of ambition, sophistication, and a fast-paced lifestyle mirroring the chaos of the cityscape. These environmental cues not only offer insights into a character's past but also influence their present actions and choices. As a result, the location becomes a narrative device, enriching character development and adding layers of authenticity to their journey, making it a vital element in crafting multi-dimensional, relatable personas within the cinematic landscape.

Versatile Scenic Locations: Adapting India's Landscapes to Diverse Film Genres

India's scenic locations boast an unparalleled versatility that makes them a coveted asset in the world of filmmaking. These diverse landscapes, spanning from the arid deserts of Rajasthan to the misty tea plantations of Darjeeling, offer a wide array of backdrops that can be seamlessly adapted to suit a broad spectrum of film genres. The grandeur of historical monuments and palaces can transport audiences to bygone eras in epic historical dramas, while the tranquil beauty of natural landscapes can create picturesque settings for romantic narratives. The bustling streets of metropolitan cities can provide the perfect stage for contemporary dramas or fast-paced action sequences, while serene rural villages offer authenticity to heartwarming stories of simplicity and connection. This versatility of Indian locations empowers filmmakers to push the boundaries of creativity and genre, allowing them to craft narratives that resonate with a global audience, making India a treasure trove of cinematic possibilities that can cater to a diverse array of storytelling needs.

Visual Contrasts: Utilizing India's Locations to Convey Diverse Story Elements

India's locations are a cinematographer's dream, offering striking visual contrasts that can be masterfully harnessed to convey diverse facets of a story. One of the most vivid examples of this contrast is found in the bustling streets of Mumbai, where the relentless energy, vibrant colours, and sheer chaos create an atmosphere of urgency and kinetic motion. These urban landscapes become a canvas for narratives of ambition, modernity, and the relentless pace of life. In stark contrast, Kerala's tranquil backwaters with their serene canals, lush greenery, and timeless stillness evoke a sense of peace, harmony, and timelessness. These natural landscapes become the backdrop for stories of introspection, connection with nature, and the gentle passage of time. The deliberate use of such contrasts allows filmmakers to juxtapose and accentuate different facets of a story, underscoring the yin and yang of human experiences, creating a visual language that engages the audience on a profound emotional level, and ultimately enriching the narrative with layers of complexity and depth.

Beyond Beauty: Navigating Logistical Challenges When Filming in India's Scenic Locations

While India's scenic locations offer unparalleled visual appeal, filmmakers often grapple with a host of logistical challenges that must be meticulously addressed. Obtaining permits for shooting at iconic landmarks or protected areas can be a complex bureaucratic process, requiring patience and negotiation skills. Ensuring access to remote or delicate locations demands careful logistical planning, including transportation, equipment, and crew accommodation. The availability of infrastructure such as electricity, water, and facilities for the cast and crew can vary greatly between locations, necessitating adaptable production strategies. Weather conditions, ranging from the scorching heat of deserts to the monsoon rains of tropical regions, can disrupt schedules and require contingency plans. All these logistical challenges emphasize the significance of thorough planning, coordination, and local expertise. By addressing these challenges effectively, filmmakers can unlock the full potential of India's scenic locations and transform them into the captivating backdrops that enrich cinematic storytelling.

Cinematic Tourism Boost: The Impact of Filming in Scenic Locations on Local Economies

Filming in scenic locations holds the dual power of not only creating cinematic magic but also boosting local tourism and economies. When popular film locations are featured prominently on the silver screen, they often become sought-after tourist attractions. Visitors are drawn to these locales, eager to witness the real-life settings of their favorite movies, leading to a surge in tourism. This influx of tourists bolsters the local economy by creating jobs in the hospitality, transportation, and service industries. Businesses catering to tourists, such as hotels, restaurants, souvenir shops, and tour operators, flourish in the wake of film-induced tourism. Additionally, the increased visibility of a region through films can foster a sense of pride among the local community, encouraging them to invest in and preserve their cultural and natural heritage. In essence, the symbiotic relationship between filmmaking and tourism is a win-win, with films benefiting from captivating locations and local economies reaping the rewards of increased visitor traffic, ultimately creating a positive impact that extends well beyond the silver screen.

In Indian filmmaking, meticulous location scouting and the thoughtful choice of scenic backdrops are essential processes that significantly shape a film's visual narrative and overall impact. Filmmakers collaborate closely with location scouts and production teams to find settings that seamlessly align with the storyline, infusing it with cultural authenticity and visual splendor. Whether it's the grandeur of historical monuments, the serenity of natural landscapes, or the vibrancy of urban settings, each chosen location contributes to the film's immersive quality, transporting the audience deep into the heart of the narrative. These locations also play a pivotal role in character development, enabling personas to interact with their environment in a meaningful way. Beyond their artistic significance, these film locations often become tourist attractions, providing economic benefits to local communities. In essence, location scouting and selection are critical aspects of the filmmaking process, pivotal in creating captivating, culturally resonant, and visually striking cinematic experiences.

Authenticity in location scouting

Authenticity in location scouting and the use of natural landscapes in filmmaking are essential for creating a genuine and immersive cinematic experience. These authentic settings not only add depth and cultural context to the story but also enhance its believability, helping filmmakers forge a profound connection with their audience. The choice of real locations brings a tangible, relatable quality to the narrative, allowing viewers to immerse themselves fully in the world depicted on screen. This connection extends beyond visual aesthetics, as it taps into the emotional and sensory aspects of storytelling. Authentic locations provide a rich tapestry of sights, sounds, and textures that resonate with viewers, drawing them deeper into the story and fostering a lasting connection. Ultimately, authenticity in location scouting and the embrace of natural landscapes enrich the cinematic journey, making it a more genuine and profound experience for both filmmakers and audiences. Here's a detailed explanation of how authenticity is crucial in this context:

Realism and Believability: The Role of Real Locations in Immersive Filmmaking

Filmmakers are perpetually driven to construct a world on screen that is both believable and immersive, and one of the most potent tools at their disposal is the choice to shoot on location. This decision provides a tangible and authentic backdrop that allows viewers to not merely witness but fully immerse themselves in the story's universe. Authentic settings have the remarkable ability to suspend disbelief, blurring the line between reality and fiction, and in doing so, they become an invaluable conduit for drawing the audience deeper into the narrative. When viewers recognize real locations, whether it's the streets of a bustling city or the serene beauty of a natural landscape, they establish an immediate and relatable connection with the story and its characters. This connection transcends the screen, resonating on a profound emotional level, and creates an authentic cinematic experience that lingers long after the credits roll. In essence, the choice to shoot on location becomes the cornerstone upon which the immersive world of cinema is built, a world where stories come alive and captivate the hearts and minds of audiences.

Cultural and Environmental Context: The Significance of Authentic Locations in Filmmaking

The utilization of authentic locations in filmmaking is not merely an aesthetic choice but a powerful narrative tool that offers a rich cultural and environmental context. These locations serve as windows into the lives of the people who inhabit them, the very landscapes that shape their daily existence, and the challenges they confront. This inherent authenticity provides audiences with a nuanced and immersive understanding of the characters and the world they inhabit. It grants viewers insight into the customs, traditions, and way of life of the on-screen individuals, fostering a deeper connection and empathy with their experiences. Furthermore, the environmental context, whether it's the starkness of a desert or the lushness of a tropical forest, becomes an integral element in character development, as it influences their decisions, aspirations, and the obstacles they encounter. In essence, authentic locations act as storytellers themselves, weaving a complex tapestry that enriches the narrative, offering viewers a profound and insightful cinematic experience.

Fostering Emotional Connection: The Impact of Recognizable Locations in Filmmaking

The recognition of real locations by viewers not only enhances the cinematic experience but also nurtures a potent emotional connection to the story and its characters. Familiarity with these settings, whether it's a bustling city street or a quaint countryside village, creates a sense of relatability that resonates deeply with the audience. This connection enables viewers to effortlessly immerse themselves in the experiences and emotions portrayed on screen, as they can draw parallels between the fictional world and their own real-life encounters. Real locations become a bridge between the narrative and the viewer's personal experiences, fostering empathy and emotional resonance. The authenticity of these settings makes the characters and their journey feel more genuine and tangible, elevating the storytelling to a level where it becomes a shared and profound human experience.

Historical Authenticity: The Role of Real Locations in Period Filmmaking

Period films, historical dramas, and biopics hinge on the precise recreation of bygone eras, and authentic locations play a pivotal role in achieving this historical accuracy. Filming in real historical settings or meticulously crafted, historically faithful locations is paramount to transporting the audience to a specific time and place. The authenticity offered by these settings becomes a cornerstone for conveying the nuances of the era, from architectural details to the social customs and lifestyle of the period. This meticulous attention to historical accuracy provides viewers with a genuine sense of time and place, allowing them to step back in history and immerse themselves in the world of the characters. The use of authentic locations is akin to opening a portal to the past, a testament to the meticulous dedication of filmmakers in their pursuit of storytelling excellence, and it plays a pivotal role in enhancing the authenticity and impact of period-based narratives.

Cultural Collaboration: The Importance of Authentic Locations and Local Communities in Filmmaking

The choice of authentic locations in filmmaking often necessitates a profound collaboration with local communities, which is founded upon a fundamental respect for their traditions and customs. This cultural sensitivity is not only a matter of ethical filmmaking but also a crucial element in achieving an authentic portrayal of the setting and its people. Filmmakers engage with local communities to gain insights into the unique cultural fabric of the location, fostering a deeper understanding that permeates every frame of the film. This collaborative approach enriches the narrative with an authenticity that extends beyond mere aesthetics, allowing characters to interact with their surroundings in a genuine and respectful manner. The local customs, traditions, and even the participation of community members as extras or consultants become integral components of the storytelling process, ensuring that the film resonates with a global audience while honoring the identity and heritage of the communities portrayed. In essence, cultural sensitivity and collaboration with local communities serve as the bedrock of authenticity in location-based filmmaking, nurturing narratives that are both respectful and genuine.

Sustainable Filmmaking: The Eco-Friendly Benefits of Shooting on Authentic Locations

Shooting on location holds an environmental advantage by reducing the necessity for elaborate set construction, ultimately lessening the environmental footprint of filmmaking. This approach aligns harmoniously with the burgeoning emphasis on sustainable and eco-friendly production practices in the film industry. By utilizing existing, real-world locations, filmmakers can harness the inherent beauty and authenticity of the environment without the resource-intensive process of constructing elaborate sets, which often require large amounts of materials, energy, and transportation. The result is a more environmentally responsible approach that minimizes waste, energy consumption, and carbon emissions, all while preserving the natural landscapes and heritage sites featured in the film. This growing commitment to eco-conscious filmmaking underscores the industry's recognition of its role in environmental conservation and sustainability, making location shooting a conscientious choice that aligns with the global movement toward a greener, more responsible future for film production.

Unmatched Beauty: The Aesthetic Value of Natural Landscapes in Filmmaking

Natural landscapes hold an innate beauty and aesthetic allure that transcends anything that can be artificially replicated in a studio. Authentic locations, whether they are vast desert vistas, lush forests, serene lakesides, or majestic mountain ranges, offer filmmakers an exquisite canvas that elevates the visual appeal of their films. The organic grandeur of these settings infuses the cinematography with a breathtaking quality that captivates the audience's senses. The interplay of light and shadow, the vibrancy of natural colours, and the dynamic shifts in weather and terrain create a visual tapestry that is impossible to emulate in a controlled studio environment. The authenticity of these natural landscapes enriches the storytelling, becoming an integral part of the narrative's emotional impact. Each scene set against such backdrops becomes a work of art, imbued with a mesmerizing beauty that lingers in the minds of viewers long after the credits roll, reminding them of the power and magnificence of the natural world.

Location Character: Shaping the Identity and Atmosphere of a Film

Every location possesses a distinctive character and ambiance, whether it's the vibrant hustle and bustle of an urban metropolis, the serenity of a quaint rural village, or the awe-inspiring presence of a natural wonder. This inherent character of each location transcends mere scenery, becoming an essential component of the film's identity and atmosphere. It infuses the narrative with a sense of place and authenticity, contributing to the overall mood and emotional resonance of the story. The character of a location influences not only the visual aesthetics but also the behaviors and interactions of the characters, shaping their development and the dynamics of the plot. From the evocative ambiance of a historic landmark to the untamed beauty of a rugged wilderness, each location brings its own unique essence to the cinematic experience, leaving an indelible mark on the storytelling canvas.

Rich Details: How Authentic Locations Enhance Scene Depth in Filmmaking

Authentic locations are treasure troves of subtle details that enrich the cinematic experience by adding depth and nuance to each scene. These nuanced elements may include the architectural intricacies of buildings, which not only provide visual authenticity but also offer insights into the historical or cultural context of a location. The foliage of trees and the surrounding natural environment contribute to the atmosphere, reflecting the climate and geographical setting in which the story unfolds. Even seemingly mundane details like street signs, local businesses, or street art infuse authenticity into the narrative, grounding it in the reality of the location. These subtle but essential details create a multi-dimensional backdrop that not only enhances the believability of the story but also offers viewers a richer, more immersive experience, where every frame tells a deeper story beyond the central plot, making the film world feel more vivid and authentic.

Engaging the Senses: How Authentic Locations Heighten the Cinematic Experience

Authenticity in location choices transcends visual aesthetics and engages the audience on a sensory level, creating a more profound and immersive cinematic experience. The sights, whether it's the stunning natural landscapes, historical architecture, or vibrant city streets, offer a visual feast that captures the eye. The soundscape of real locations, from the hum of a bustling market to the rustling of leaves in a forest, adds an auditory layer that envelops viewers in the film's world. Even the textures of authentic settings, be it the rough-hewn stones of ancient ruins or the softness of a sandy beach, can be felt vicariously. These sensory elements combine to create a multisensory tapestry that resonates deeply with the audience, making the film world tangible and evoking a range of emotions. In this way, authenticity enhances the overall viewing experience, allowing viewers to not just watch but to truly feel and immerse themselves in the story unfolding before them.

Cost-Effective Filmmaking: The Advantages of Utilizing Existing Locations

Shooting on location often proves to be a cost-effective alternative to constructing elaborate sets, particularly when filmmakers discover that the existing locations closely align with their creative vision. Building and designing intricate sets can be a resource-intensive process, requiring substantial budgets, time, and manpower. However, when filmmakers identify real-world locations that authentically capture the essence of their narrative, they can leverage these settings to their advantage. Utilizing existing locations can significantly reduce production costs, as it eliminates the need for constructing and dismantling sets, transporting materials, and maintaining large-scale production crews. This cost-saving approach allows filmmakers to allocate resources to other essential aspects of their project, such as talent, post-production, or marketing. Ultimately, the choice to shoot on location, when viable, not only streamlines the production process but also aligns with budgetary considerations, making it a practical and efficient option for realizing the director's creative vision.

Real-World Locations: Enhancing Films Through Authenticity and Inspiration

Authentic locations offer numerous advantages that can greatly enhance a film's narrative. Beyond their visual appeal, real-world settings bring unique elements, challenges, and opportunities that are difficult to replicate in a studio or manufactured environment. These locations might possess inherent quirks, architectural features, or historical significance that can become integral to the plot or thematic elements, adding complexity to the storytelling. Additionally, the challenges presented by working in authentic locations, such as dealing with unpredictable weather or adapting to existing structures, can inspire creative problem-solving and lead to innovative and memorable cinematic moments. Lastly, these settings often provide opportunities for spontaneous and genuine interactions with the environment and local culture, enriching character development and adding depth to the story. In essence, the authenticity of locations not only anchors the film in reality but also serves as a wellspring of narrative inspiration, making the storytelling more layered and multifaceted.

Real-World Locations: Enhancing Immersion and Emotional Impact in Filmmaking

The use of authentic locations can significantly enhance a film's sense of immersion and emotional impact, as audiences can relate to the real-world settings. These locations create a deep sense of place and time, which resonates with viewers, helping them to connect with the story on a more profound level. The challenges and limitations of authentic locations often necessitate creative solutions, pushing filmmakers to think outside the box and craft inventive scenes that add depth and authenticity to the narrative. This approach ultimately leads to a richer and more multifaceted storytelling experience, where the locations themselves become essential characters in the film, influencing the plot, character development, and the overall emotional resonance of the story.

Timeless Appeal: The Enduring Allure of Films Shot in Authentic Locations

Films shot in authentic locations possess a timeless quality that resonates with audiences across generations. By capturing the essence of a specific place and time, these films transcend the constraints of their era of production and become enduring classics. The authenticity of these settings immerses viewers in a world that feels genuine and rooted in reality, allowing them to connect with the characters and stories on a deeper level. As a result, these films continue to be relevant and emotionally resonant over the years, serving as cultural touchstones that evoke nostalgia and a sense of timelessness. Whether set in a historical period or a contemporary locale, the authenticity of the locations ensures that these films remain a testament to the enduring power of storytelling and the lasting impact of cinema on our collective consciousness.

G. Costume and Colour Palette

Colour Symbolism

This collaborative effort helps create a visually cohesive and emotionally resonant cinematic experience for the audience. Colours are not just aesthetically pleasing but also serve as a language that communicates subtext, foreshadows events, and symbolizes deeper meanings. Whether it's the bold, passionate reds of a character in love or the cool, desaturated blues that evoke melancholy, colour symbolism engages viewers on a subconscious level, encouraging them to analyze and interpret the visual cues woven into the film's fabric. Through this intricate use of colour, filmmakers enhance the audience's connection with the story, allowing them to delve deeper into the narrative's emotional and thematic layers. Here's a detailed explanation of how colour symbolism is used in film:

Exploring the Emotional Power of Colours in Filmmaking: Leveraging Warm and Cool Tones to Elicit Viewer Reactions

Colours play a pivotal role in evoking emotional responses from viewers in filmmaking. The psychology of colour has long established that warm colours like red and orange can stir feelings of passion, love, and even danger, heightening tension and excitement in the narrative. Conversely, cool colours like blue and green often convey a sense of calmness, tranquility, or sadness, which can be harnessed to create moments of reflection or contemplation within the story. Filmmakers are keenly aware of these emotional associations and strategically employ them to elicit specific reactions from the audience. For instance, a vibrant red in a scene might signify intense love or impending danger, immediately grabbing the viewer's attention and enhancing their engagement with the unfolding plot. In contrast, a serene blue backdrop could establish a peaceful atmosphere, providing a sense of relief or contrast in a story filled with emotional highs and lows. Thus, the careful selection and manipulation of colours become a powerful tool for filmmakers in shaping the audience's emotional journey through the film.

The Art of Character Development: How Costume Designers Use Colours to Convey Personality and Story Arcs

Costume designers wield colour as a significant tool in character development within the area of filmmaking. They meticulously choose colours for characters' clothing that align with their personality traits and narrative arcs. This selection process involves a deep understanding of colour psychology and storytelling nuances. For instance, a character donned in vibrant, bold colours like red or yellow might immediately appear confident, assertive, or extroverted, signifying strength and dynamism. Conversely, a character draped in muted, neutral tones such as grays or earthy browns can convey introversion, modesty, or reserve, reflecting a quieter disposition. These carefully curated costume choices serve as a visual shorthand for character traits, allowing audiences to quickly grasp key aspects of a character's personality or emotional journey before a single word is spoken. In this way, costume designers not only contribute to the aesthetic appeal of a film but also play a pivotal role in enhancing character depth and narrative development through the language of colour.

Colour Symbolism in Film: Foreshadowing and Theme Exploration Through Visual Motifs

Colours in filmmaking extend beyond aesthetics; they are potent symbols and foreshadowing tools that can enrich the narrative on multiple levels. A recurring colour can become a visual motif, weaving through the story to represent specific themes, emotions, or impending events. Take the example of the colour red, often used to symbolize impending danger or inner turmoil. When red appears throughout the film, it can create a sense of unease or foreboding, alerting the audience to potential conflicts or crises. This visual consistency primes the viewers' subconscious, making them attuned to the impending narrative developments. In essence, colour becomes a language within the film, allowing filmmakers to communicate complex ideas and evoke emotional responses without explicit dialogue or exposition, enhancing the depth and richness of the storytelling experience.

Colour Contrast in Film: Portraying Character Conflict and Isolation through Visual Choices

Colour choices in filmmaking serve as a powerful means to accentuate contrasts and conflicts within the narrative. When a character's attire starkly contrasts with their environment or the clothing of other characters, it becomes a visual representation of their separation or opposition from the world around them. This deliberate choice of colour not only sets the character apart but also underscores their uniqueness, inner turmoil, or discord with their surroundings or peers. For instance, a character wearing dark, somber tones in a brightly lit and colourful world might signify their emotional isolation or internal conflict, visually isolating them from their surroundings. Conversely, a character dressed in vibrant colours within a predominantly monochromatic setting can symbolize rebellion or a desire to stand out. These visual contrasts not only provide depth to the characters but also enhance the audience's understanding of the dynamics and tensions within the story, all conveyed through the language of colour.

Setting the Tone: How Film Colour Palettes Shape Mood and Atmosphere

The overarching colour palette of a film plays a pivotal role in shaping its mood and atmosphere, wielding a subtle yet profound influence on the audience's emotional engagement. Warm, inviting colours such as soft yellows, oranges, or warm reds have the power to create a sense of cosiness, intimacy, and emotional connection within the narrative. These hues can make the viewer feel welcomed into the world of the story, fostering a sense of warmth and familiarity. In contrast, cool, desaturated colours like blues, grays, or muted greens can establish a more detached, melancholic, or contemplative tone. These colours have the ability to evoke a sense of distance, isolation, or introspection, mirroring the emotional landscape of the characters or the overarching themes of the film. The carefully orchestrated use of colour in the palette, in conjunction with other cinematic elements, enables filmmakers to set the stage for the emotional journey they want the audience to embark upon, thus enhancing the overall impact and resonance of the story.

Enhancing Visual Storytelling: The Power of Colour Symbolism in Film

Color symbolism is a powerful cinematic tool for nuanced storytelling through visual cues. A character's wardrobe color can represent emotional changes or character development. For instance, transitioning from neutral to vibrant colors may symbolize growing confidence, while shifting from cheerful to somber hues conveys sadness or disillusionment. These color shifts enrich the storytelling, connecting the audience emotionally with the narrative and adding depth and resonance to the overall experience. In essence, color symbolism enhances the narrative by adding subtext, making it more engaging and compelling for viewers.

Cultural and Historical Significance of Colours in Film: Authenticity and Contextual Resonance

Colours are not only vehicles for emotional and thematic expression but also carry profound cultural and historical connotations. Costume designers and art directors delve into these associations when meticulously selecting colours for a film's costumes and sets to ensure authenticity and resonance with the chosen setting and time period. Whether it's the regal purples of royalty in a period piece, the earthy tones of a rustic rural landscape, or the vibrant hues of a specific cultural celebration, colours can transport the audience into a specific historical or cultural context. This attention to detail not only enhances the visual authenticity of the film but also allows viewers to connect more deeply with the characters and story, immersing them in a world that feels both believable and richly textured. In doing so, filmmakers harness the cultural and historical power of colours to evoke a sense of time and place, enriching the narrative with layers of meaning and resonance.

Seamless Collaboration: The Crucial Role of Costume Designers and Art Directors in Maintaining Visual Cohesion in Film

The collaboration between costume designers and art directors is pivotal in maintaining a seamless and consistent colour palette throughout a film. This unity of vision ensures that colours remain harmonious and purposeful, reinforcing the film's overarching themes and narrative continuity. The deliberate repetition of specific colours or colour schemes throughout the film serves as a visual thread that ties together various scenes and character arcs. This cohesion not only enhances the aesthetic appeal but also keeps the audience engaged in the narrative by providing a visual anchor that subtly communicates subtext and motifs. When viewers see a consistent colour palette, it becomes a silent guide, directing their attention and emotions, while also deepening their connection with the story's unfolding themes. The careful orchestration of colours in this collaborative effort elevates the film's storytelling, making it a visually resonant and immersive experience for the audience.

Subtle Colour Symbolism: Unveiling Layers of Meaning in Film through Nuanced Visual Choices

Colour symbolism in storytelling often operates at a level of subtlety that might elude immediate notice but contributes significantly to the narrative's richness. These nuanced colour choices add layers of meaning and depth to the storytelling, enhancing the audience's experience upon closer examination. For instance, a character's clothing may subtly shift in shade as their emotional journey progresses, reflecting their evolving personality or inner conflicts. Background colours, lighting choices, or prop colours may be carefully orchestrated to create subliminal associations or connections between characters, themes, or story elements. These meticulously crafted details function as a visual language that communicates on a subconscious level, making the storytelling more intricate and immersive. The beauty of these subtleties lies in their capacity to engage viewers on multiple levels, encouraging them to unravel the hidden symbolism and enriching their appreciation of the narrative's complexity and depth.

Colour Subtext and Character Arcs: How Visual Changes Reflect Deeper Narrative Elements in Film

Colours serve as a silent yet powerful tool for conveying subtext and subplot details in filmmaking. One compelling example is the use of colours to depict character transformations. A character's association with a particular colour that gradually shifts throughout the film can be a visual metaphor for their evolving character arc. For instance, a character who starts the story in muted, somber tones but gradually transitions to brighter, more vibrant colours may symbolize a journey from darkness to enlightenment, from insecurity to self-confidence. This subtle colour progression not only mirrors the character's inner transformation but also allows the audience to vicariously experience their growth. These nuanced colour shifts serve as a visual narrative within the larger story, deepening the viewer's emotional connection and understanding of the character's development, often revealing layers of meaning that unfold with each visual cue.

Genre and Style in Film: The Role of Distinct Colour Palettes in Visual Storytelling

Colours play a pivotal role in distinguishing and defining the visual identities of different film genres and styles. Each genre, from film noir to romantic comedy, employs a distinct colour palette that becomes a hallmark of its storytelling aesthetic. In film noir, for example, the heavy reliance on dark, moody colours such as deep blacks, shadowy grays, and stark contrasts between light and dark creates an atmosphere of mystery, suspense, and moral ambiguity. These colours reflect the genre's themes of crime, intrigue, and complex characters. Conversely, in a romantic comedy, the use of bright and cheerful hues, such as pastel pinks, vibrant reds, and sunny yellows, fosters an atmosphere of love, humor, and optimism. These colours mirror the genre's emphasis on romance, lightheartedness, and feel-good narratives. By carefully selecting and manipulating colours in line with genre conventions, filmmakers not only establish a visual identity for their films but also set the tone and expectations for the audience, enhancing the overall cinematic experience.

The Subconscious Power of Colour Symbolism: Engaging Audiences in Visual Interpretation of Film

The subtle and often subliminal language of colour symbolism in film greatly enhances audience engagement by tapping into viewers' subconscious understanding of these visual cues. Colours convey emotions, themes, and character traits without the need for explicit dialogue or narration. Audiences, even without consciously realizing it, pick up on these colour associations, which enrich their overall experience and encourage a deeper level of engagement. As viewers become attuned to the colours' symbolic meanings, they find themselves actively analyzing and interpreting the visual cues woven into the narrative. This process of visual decoding not only adds layers of depth to the storytelling but also fosters a sense of active participation in the film. As viewers uncover the meaning behind the colours, they develop a more profound connection with the characters and themes, ultimately immersing themselves more fully in the cinematic world and narrative, making it a truly engaging and emotionally resonant experience.

Cultural Significance

Cultural significance in costume and set design is vital in filmmaking, creating a deeper connection between the story, characters, and the audience. Costumes that reflect a specific time or culture enhance authenticity and relatability. Incorporating cultural elements in set design provides context and depth to the characters' world, aiding in understanding their motivations. Attention to cultural detail fosters respect and inclusivity, making the storytelling experience more immersive, engaging, and resonant for viewers, enhancing the overall quality and impact of the film.

Fostering Authenticity: The Role of Cultural Elements in Costume and Set Design

Integrating cultural elements and symbols into costume and set design is a pivotal cinematic technique that goes beyond aesthetics; it serves as a storytelling mechanism, enriching the viewer's experience. By meticulously infusing these elements, such as clothing styles, architectural details, and symbolic artifacts, filmmakers create a visual language that transports the audience to a specific temporal, geographic, or cultural milieu. This attention to detail not only ensures a visually convincing portrayal but also invites the audience to emotionally invest in the narrative. It enables viewers to genuinely believe that the characters and settings are intricately intertwined with a particular cultural, historical, or geographical context, fostering a deeper connection between the cinematic world and the audience's own cultural sensibilities, ultimately enhancing the film's authenticity and resonance.

Cultural Immersion through Costume and Set Details: Enhancing Audience Engagement in Film

The incorporation of cultural details in costumes and sets is a powerful storytelling tool that serves to immerse the audience in the film's world. It goes beyond mere aesthetics, as it enables viewers to instantly connect with the narrative on a deeper level. When characters are adorned in clothing that aligns with a particular culture, surrounded by objects that carry cultural significance, or placed in settings that evoke a specific time and place, it lends an air of authenticity and credibility to the story. This immersion allows the audience to suspend disbelief and become emotionally invested in the characters and their journey, as the cultural context not only adds depth to the characters but also enriches the overall narrative, making it more relatable and resonant for viewers, ultimately enhancing their engagement and enjoyment of the film.

Dressing Up the Character: The Significance of Costumes in Character Development

Costumes serve as a vital component of character development in film and storytelling, functioning as a visual language that communicates essential aspects of a character's identity. The attire a character wears, along with accompanying accessories, offers insights into their cultural affiliations, socioeconomic status, religious or ideological beliefs, and personal history. This visual storytelling tool enables the audience to swiftly grasp not just what a character looks like, but who they are and what drives them. Whether it's a protagonist dressed in the regalia of a bygone era to showcase their historical significance or a supporting character adorned in contemporary streetwear to signal their modernity, costumes are an invaluable means of crafting multifaceted, relatable characters and driving the narrative forward through visual cues and symbolism.

The Power of Cultural Symbols in Costume and Set Design: Unveiling Subtext and Symbolism in Film

Cultural symbols and motifs ingeniously integrated into costume and set design serve as potent vehicles for conveying symbolic depth and subtext within a film's narrative. These elements, whether it's the selection of a particular colour palette, the use of intricate patterns, or the inclusion of meaningful objects, have the ability to transcend the surface aesthetics and carry layered meanings. They can subtly communicate themes, emotions, and character arcs, often acting as foreshadowing devices that provide astute viewers with clues about the story's unfolding events. Additionally, these cultural symbols can operate on a subconscious level, resonating with the audience's collective cultural knowledge and enriching the viewing experience by adding nuanced layers of interpretation and understanding to the narrative's subtext.

Celebrating Cultural Diversity in Film: The Role of Authentic Costume and Set Representation

In the contemporary globalized landscape of filmmaking, it's increasingly common to encounter characters from a wide array of cultural backgrounds in movies. Costume designers and set decorators play a pivotal role in ensuring that these portrayals are both accurate and respectful. Their meticulous research and attention to detail extend beyond aesthetics to capture the essence of diverse cultures, promoting authenticity and cultural richness in storytelling. By accurately representing these cultures, filmmakers not only create a more inclusive and diverse cinematic world but also send a powerful message of respect and recognition to global audiences. This approach fosters a sense of cultural appreciation, broadens perspectives, and reinforces the idea that the tapestry of human experiences is vast and multifaceted, ultimately contributing to a more empathetic and interconnected global community.

Storytelling with Cultural Artifacts: The Narrative Power of Set Design

Set designers are masterful storytellers who utilize cultural objects and artifacts as integral elements in weaving narratives within a physical space. These items serve as more than just props; they are conduits for storytelling. An ancient artifact displayed on a character's bookshelf or an heirloom carefully positioned in a scene can imbue the story with layers of meaning and emotion. These objects not only provide historical or cultural context, but they also offer glimpses into a character's personal history, beliefs, or aspirations. They become visual cues that invite the audience to engage in a form of visual storytelling where the presence or absence of such artifacts can convey themes, character motivations, or plot developments, adding a nuanced richness to the narrative that deepens the audience's connection with the story and its characters.

Crafting Immersive Sets: Transforming Spaces with Cultural References

Sets in filmmaking are meticulously crafted to serve as immersive backdrops, often drawing inspiration from real-world cultural references to transport the audience to a distinct sense of place. Through a careful blend of architectural design, decor, lighting, and even auditory elements like music or ambient sounds, sets can recreate the ambiance of a particular cultural environment with remarkable authenticity. For instance, in the case of a restaurant set, every detail, from the choice of furniture and table settings to the colour palette, artwork, and even the culinary choices, can reflect the nuances of a specific cuisine and culture. This level of meticulousness extends beyond aesthetics, as it enables viewers to experience the culture and environment vicariously, fostering a deeper engagement with the narrative by evoking a sensory and emotional connection to the setting. In essence, well-designed sets become integral storytellers, enhancing the film's world-building and narrative resonance.

Authenticity in Historical Films: Unveiling the Craft of Costume and Set Design

Historical films and period pieces are deeply dependent on the meticulous pursuit of cultural authenticity to transport audiences to bygone eras. Costume and set designers undertake rigorous research and attention to detail to ensure a seamless integration of historical accuracy into every visual aspect of the film. This encompasses the selection of clothing styles, fabrics, and accessories that align with the fashion of the chosen historical period, as well as the recreation of architectural and interior design elements to match the architectural norms of the time. Additionally, props, from everyday objects to items of significance, are carefully curated to reflect the historical period's aesthetics and functionality. This commitment to cultural authenticity not only enhances the film's visual appeal but also offers viewers a genuine glimpse into the past, fostering a profound sense of immersion, and allowing them to journey through history while experiencing the cultural and social norms of the chosen era.

Cultural Clashes on Screen: The Role of Costume and Set Design

Cultural differences and clashes serve as compelling narrative devices in many films, often driving the central plot or character conflicts. Costume and set designers play a pivotal role in amplifying these differences by strategically contrasting cultural elements among various characters or groups within the story. Through the careful selection of clothing styles, colours, textures, and accessories, costume designers can visually accentuate the disparities in cultural backgrounds and values. Similarly, set design, including architectural details, decor, and symbolic objects, can reinforce these distinctions and create visual tension. By juxtaposing these cultural elements, filmmakers not only enhance the storytelling but also invite viewers to explore the complexities of cultural diversity, facilitating discussions on identity, tolerance, and the dynamics of human interaction. In doing so, costume and set design become integral tools in conveying the narrative's themes and promoting a deeper understanding of the characters and their cultural contexts.

Visual Storytelling Through Costume and Set Design: Illuminating Cultural Contexts and Characters

Costume and set design are indispensable components of visual storytelling in film, as they serve as powerful tools for reinforcing cultural contexts and character backgrounds. Through the strategic selection of clothing, accessories, and props, costume designers can provide immediate visual cues about a character's identity, background, and even their emotional state. Similarly, set design, including architectural details, furnishings, and decor, can establish the time, place, and cultural milieu in which the story unfolds. These elements work in harmony to create a cohesive visual narrative that enhances the audience's understanding of the characters and the broader context of the story. By offering viewers these visual cues, costume and set design not only enrich the storytelling experience but also facilitate a deeper connection between the audience and the narrative, making it easier for viewers to empathize with the characters and immerse themselves in the story's world.

Cultural Influence on Film Atmosphere: The Power of Set Design

Cultural elements wield a profound influence over the overarching atmosphere and mood of a film, providing a nuanced layer of emotional resonance. Filmmakers deftly employ cultural cues, such as set design, to create immersive environments that evoke specific emotions or atmospheres. For instance, in the context of a cultural celebration scene, a set adorned with vibrant and colourful decorations, traditional symbols, and cultural artifacts can instantly convey a sense of festivity, joy, and unity. The colours, patterns, and textures used in the set design align with the cultural norms associated with the celebration, effectively transporting the audience into the heart of the event and imbuing the scene with the authentic spirit and energy of the culture being depicted. In this way, cultural elements become not only visual aesthetics but also powerful tools for shaping the audience's emotional response, thus contributing significantly to the film's overall impact and storytelling.

Films as Mirrors and Windows: Cultural Representation and Awareness in Cinema

The accurate representation of one's own culture or familiar cultural references in a film is a powerful catalyst for audience connection and relatability. When viewers see elements of their own culture authentically portrayed on screen, it elicits a deep sense of resonance and validation, forging an immediate emotional connection between the audience and the narrative. This connection can stem from shared experiences, values, or traditions, enhancing the viewers' ability to empathize with the characters and their journey. Conversely, when films delve into unfamiliar cultures, it presents an invaluable opportunity for viewers to broaden their horizons and gain insight into different ways of life, traditions, and perspectives. Such cinematic exploration fosters cultural awareness, encourages empathy, and promotes a richer understanding of the diversity of the human experience, ultimately serving as a bridge between cultures and societies, nurturing tolerance, and expanding the audience's worldview. In both cases, film serves as a potent medium for cultural exchange, offering viewers a platform for self-recognition and cultural enrichment.

H. Special Visual Elements

Slo-Mo and Fast-Mo

Slow-motion (slo-mo) and fast-motion (fast-mo) techniques are essential tools in filmmaking that allow directors and cinematographers to manipulate time and motion for dramatic, emotional, comedic, or stylistic purposes. When used thoughtfully and in context, these techniques can significantly enhance the storytelling and visual impact of a film. Slow-motion, for example, can intensify the drama and detail of a moment, heightening emotions and emphasizing crucial elements. Conversely, fast-motion can compress time, adding energy and urgency to scenes or conveying surreal and fantastical atmospheres. The interplay between these techniques can create powerful visual contrasts, while each technique, on its own, offers filmmakers a versatile palette for creative expression and narrative enhancement. Below is a detailed explanation of how slo-mo and fast-mo are used in filmmaking:

Slow-Motion (Slo-Mo):

Enhancing Action Sequences with Slow Motion: Amplifying Drama and Detail

Slow-motion (slo-mo) is a widely employed technique in filmmaking, particularly in action sequences, as it serves to accentuate the drama and intensity of pivotal moments. By significantly reducing the speed of motion, slo-mo stretches out time, allowing viewers to savor every detail of the action, from the subtle nuances of facial expressions to the intricate choreography of physical movements. This deliberate manipulation of time not only heightens the visual spectacle but also deepens the emotional engagement of the audience, as it offers a more immersive and contemplative perspective on the scene. Consequently, slo-mo enhances the impact of action sequences by granting viewers the opportunity to fully absorb and appreciate the intricacies of the action, making it a valuable tool for creating memorable, adrenaline-pumping cinematic moments.

Emotional Depth Through Slow Motion: Amplifying Feelings in Film

Slow-motion (slo-mo) is an indispensable tool in filmmaking for conveying heightened emotions within a scene. By decelerating a character's movements or expressions, this technique magnifies their emotional states, allowing the audience to intimately connect with their feelings. This deliberate manipulation of time grants viewers the opportunity to delve deeply into the emotional nuances of a moment, whether it's a tear rolling down a character's cheek or the intense determination in their eyes. As time stretches, so does the emotional impact, intensifying the audience's empathy and connection with the character's inner world. This heightened emotional resonance not only makes scenes more poignant but also enables viewers to experience the narrative on a profoundly emotional level, forging a stronger bond between the audience and the characters, and ultimately enhancing the storytelling's emotional depth and impact.

Capturing Intimate Details: Slow-Motion's Role in Highlighting Moments

Slow-motion (slo-mo) is a cinematic technique that excels at accentuating specific details or objects within a scene, often harnessing its power to amplify the emotional resonance or thematic elements of a moment. In a love story, for instance, slo-mo can be deployed to draw attention to the minutiae of a scene, such as a raindrop slowly descending onto a character's face. By stretching the passage of time, this technique transforms what might be a fleeting and easily overlooked event into a profound and visually arresting experience. The languid descent of the raindrop becomes a symbol of the heightened emotions and romantic atmosphere, enabling the audience to immerse themselves in the subtleties of the moment, deepening their connection to the characters' emotions and the overarching themes of the narrative. In this way, slo-mo becomes a potent artistic tool, enabling filmmakers to imbue even the smallest details with significance, enriching the visual storytelling and the audience's engagement with the story.

Elevating Cinematic Beauty: The Artistry of Slow Motion in Visual Storytelling

Slow-motion (slo-mo) is an indispensable cinematic technique that goes beyond storytelling and emotional impact—it's also a powerful tool for enhancing the sheer visual beauty of a shot. By drastically reducing the speed of motion, slo-mo transforms ordinary movements into graceful, poetic sequences. This technique captures the intricate details and nuances of actions, rendering them in a manner that feels more cinematic and aesthetically pleasing. Whether it's the gentle fluttering of a butterfly's wings, the delicate swirl of a dancer's dress, or the mesmerizing ripple of water droplets, slo-mo transforms these elements into mesmerizing visual poetry. It elevates the mundane into the sublime, allowing filmmakers to craft moments of breathtaking beauty that linger in the viewer's memory long after the film has concluded. In this way, slo-mo becomes a vital tool for not only storytelling but also for the pure artistry of filmmaking, contributing to the creation of unforgettable, visually stunning sequences.

Stretching Time: The Narrative Impact of Slow Motion in Film

Slow-motion (slo-mo) in filmmaking serves as a remarkable time-manipulation technique that skillfully extends the duration of a moment, providing filmmakers with a tool to stretch a brief instant into a more extended and impactful sequence for storytelling purposes. By dramatically reducing the speed of motion, slo-mo elongates time, allowing viewers to experience every fraction of a second in rich detail. This technique is particularly useful when filmmakers aim to delve deeper into the emotional or thematic aspects of a scene, emphasizing the significance of a particular moment. It grants characters and events more breathing space, allowing for heightened emphasis on facial expressions, actions, and reactions. In this way, slo-mo transforms a mere moment into a powerful narrative device, enabling filmmakers to extract maximum emotional or thematic resonance from that fraction of time and, ultimately, enhancing the storytelling's depth and impact on the audience.

The Art of 'Bullet Time': Dynamic Visual Storytelling Through Slow-Motion Multicam Techniques

The "bullet time" effect, made famous by films such as "The Matrix" or in "Ra.One," is a cinematic technique that revolutionized action sequences. It entails capturing a scene from numerous angles using slow-motion photography to freeze moments in time. By doing so, it enables the camera to move around the action in a circular or semi-circular path, offering multiple perspectives within a single shot. This results in a visually stunning and dynamic sequence where characters and objects appear to move in an almost surreal and three-dimensional manner. The technique not only adds a mesmerizing visual element but also allows for intricate choreography and precise timing, making it particularly effective for high-intensity action scenes and enhancing the overall cinematic experience for the audience.

Enhancing Combat Choreography: The Martial Arts of Slow-Motion Filmmaking

Slow-motion is a fundamental cinematic technique frequently deployed in martial arts and combat scenes to illuminate the intricacies of choreography and the extraordinary skill of fighters. By significantly reducing the speed of motion, it prolongs the duration of each movement, affording viewers an opportunity to scrutinize every subtle detail of the action. In martial arts sequences, this technique highlights the precision, agility, and artistry of the combatants, from the fluidity of their movements to the calculated strikes and defensive maneuvers. Slow-motion not only elevates the spectacle of the combat but also immerses the audience in the mastery of the fighters, amplifying their physical prowess and the overall impact of the scene. This heightened appreciation for the action enriches the audience's connection to the characters and their combat skills, making slow-motion an indispensable tool for crafting captivating and visually immersive martial arts sequences.

Unleashing Creative Vision: The Artistry of Slow Motion in Visual Storytelling

Slow-motion (slo-mo) is an artistic and narrative device often utilized by filmmakers to expand their creative horizons and experiment with visual storytelling. By manipulating the speed of motion, slo-mo offers filmmakers a canvas to craft scenes with a heightened sense of aesthetics and emotional depth. It enables them to explore the minutiae of a moment, unveiling hidden layers of meaning and subtleties that might be missed in real-time. Whether it's capturing the delicate flutter of a butterfly's wings, the gentle fall of a raindrop, or the profound impact of a character's expression, slo-mo amplifies the significance of these elements. It encourages viewers to contemplate the scene's emotional resonance and thematic subtext, thereby enriching the storytelling experience. Filmmakers can use slo-mo to transform ordinary moments into extraordinary visual poetry, pushing the boundaries of creativity and offering audiences a deeper and more profound connection with the narrative and its underlying themes.

Syncing Sound and Vision: The Art of Slow Motion in Music Videos

In music videos, slow-motion (slo-mo) is a commonly employed technique that serves to harmonize the visual storytelling with the rhythm and tempo of the music, resulting in a seamless and captivating audio-visual fusion. By carefully choreographing the slow-motion sequences to align with the beats, melodies, and emotional cadence of the music, filmmakers achieve a synchronized harmony that elevates the overall impact of the video.

This technique allows for the accentuation of key moments, enhancing the emotional resonance and thematic elements of the song. It enables viewers to not only hear but also feel the music, as the languid movements and meticulously timed visuals create a sensory experience that deepens their connection to the song's narrative or mood. Ultimately, slo-mo in music videos transforms the medium into a powerful art form that can convey complex emotions, storytelling, and artistic expression in a uniquely captivating and immersive way.

Fast-Motion (Fast-Mo)

Comedy in Motion: The Role of Fast Motion in Creating Humorous Scenes

Fast-motion (fast-mo) is a comedic technique frequently utilized in film and television to generate humor by exaggerating movement and action. By accelerating the speed of motion, this technique imparts a sense of frantic energy to characters and events, making them appear comically exaggerated or over-the-top in their actions. It distorts the perception of time, causing characters to move swiftly and often in a chaotic manner, which can be inherently humorous. Fast-mo creates a sense of urgency and frenzy that contrasts with the normal pacing of the scene, leading to unexpected and amusing outcomes. It has been a staple of physical comedy, slapstick routines, and comedic chase sequences, enhancing the comedic timing and absurdity of the situations. In essence, fast-mo is a versatile comedic tool that adds a dynamic and playful element to humorous storytelling, eliciting laughter by pushing the boundaries of physicality and exaggeration.

Speeding Through Time: The Cinematic Utility of Fast-Motion Sequences

Fast-motion (fast-mo) is a cinematic technique employed to compress time, enabling filmmakers to depict lengthy sequences of events within a shorter duration. By increasing the speed of motion, fast-mo condenses time and accelerates the narrative, effectively bypassing extended processes, routines, or transitions that might otherwise be time-consuming to portray in real-time. This technique is especially valuable in illustrating the passage of time, showcasing transformations, or highlighting sequences where efficiency or rapid progression is essential to the storytelling. Whether it's depicting the construction of a building, the growth of a plant, or a character's journey, fast-mo serves as a cinematic shortcut, offering a concise yet visually engaging way to communicate the essence of these events without dwelling on the minutiae, thereby enhancing the pacing and efficiency of the narrative.

Injecting Energy and Urgency: The Dynamic Impact of Fast-Motion in Film

Fast-motion (fast-mo) is a cinematic technique employed by filmmakers to inject scenes with a burst of energy and an intense sense of urgency. By increasing the speed of motion, fast-mo creates a dynamic and lively atmosphere within a scene, making characters and events appear more vibrant and active. This acceleration of motion propels characters into action, whether it's characters moving rapidly through their environment, frenetic activities, or quick-paced dialogue exchanges. The technique amplifies the impression of liveliness and dynamism, imbuing the scene with a heightened sense of excitement and anticipation. Filmmakers often use fast-mo during action sequences, chase scenes, or moments of exhilaration, as it intensifies the audience's engagement with the story and adds a palpable sense of motion and vitality, making the overall viewing experience more exhilarating and memorable.

Beyond Reality: Fast-Motion's Role in Crafting Surreal and Fantastical Cinematic Worlds

Fast-motion (fast-mo) in filmmaking serves as a powerful artistic tool that can imbue scenes with a surreal or dreamlike quality. By accelerating the speed of motion, this technique distorts the perception of time and reality, transforming the ordinary into the extraordinary. Filmmakers often employ fast-mo to depict altered states of consciousness, dream sequences, or fantastical elements within the narrative. In these instances, characters and objects move with an otherworldly swiftness, defying the laws of physics and creating a sense of unreality. This surreal quality not only adds a layer of visual fascination but also allows filmmakers to delve into the psyche of characters, exploring their inner thoughts, fears, or desires through the lens of the fantastical. Fast-mo serves as a portal into the imagination, transporting viewers into a world where the boundaries of reality blur, and the extraordinary becomes possible, enriching the storytelling by delving into the subconscious and expanding the narrative's creative horizons.

Swift Transitions: Using Fast-Motion in Montage and Time Passage Sequences

Fast-motion (fast-mo) is a versatile cinematic technique often utilized in transitions and montage sequences to efficiently convey the passage of time or the completion of tasks. By accelerating the speed of motion, fast-mo condenses what might be an extended period into a brief, engaging sequence. In transition scenes, it can swiftly transport the narrative from one point in time to another, making the temporal shift seamless and concise. In montage sequences, fast-mo efficiently communicates the accomplishment of tasks, showing characters progressing through a series of actions or events rapidly and effectively. Whether it's a training montage, a journey, or the progression of a day, fast-mo streamlines storytelling, maintaining audience engagement while avoiding unnecessary narrative drag. This technique's efficiency lies in its ability to succinctly convey the passing of time or the completion of tasks, ensuring that the audience remains connected with the overarching narrative without becoming mired in minutiae.

Accelerating Time: The Art of Time-Lapse with Fast Motion in Film

Fast-motion (fast-mo) is a fundamental technique in time-lapse sequences, where it plays a crucial role in condensing extended periods—ranging from hours and days to even years—into a matter of seconds or minutes. This technique allows filmmakers to offer viewers a unique and often awe-inspiring perspective on long-term changes or events, such as the blooming of flowers, the construction of a building, or the changing seasons. By significantly accelerating the speed of motion, fast-mo provides a compact yet visually engaging representation of the passage of time, emphasizing the transformative and dynamic aspects of the subject matter. Time-lapse sequences not only captivate the audience with their visual spectacle but also convey a profound sense of the world's continuous evolution, offering viewers a fresh and insightful perspective on the subtleties of change and growth that might otherwise go unnoticed in the flow of everyday life.

Contrasting Realities: The Dynamic Interplay of Fast-Motion and Slow-Motion in Film

The strategic use of fast-motion and slow-motion in the same film serves as a potent tool for filmmakers to create compelling visual contrasts and accentuate the differences between two scenes or moments. By employing fast-motion, they can convey a sense of speed, urgency, or even chaos, making one scene appear dynamic and lively. In contrast, the implementation of slow-motion in another scene imparts a contemplative, dramatic, or emotionally charged quality, inviting viewers to delve deeper into the subtleties of the moment. This juxtaposition of visual styles can accentuate the disparities in pacing, mood, and thematic significance between the two scenes. Whether it's transitioning from a frenetic action sequence to a poignant emotional revelation or highlighting the contrast between a character's ordinary life and extraordinary experiences, the combination of fast and slow-motion enhances storytelling by offering viewers a nuanced and visually stimulating experience, thereby deepening their engagement with the narrative's emotional and thematic layers.

Graphic Design

Graphic design and animation are essential tools in filmmaking, enhancing storytelling and the cinematic experience. They provide visual context, emphasize themes, and engage the audience. Collaboration between filmmakers, graphic designers, animators, and visual effects artists is crucial. These elements serve various purposes, such as translating on-screen text for wider accessibility, creating visual metaphors for abstract concepts, and adding depth to the narrative. They seamlessly blend with live-action footage, immersing viewers in the filmmaker's world. Ultimately, graphic design and animation expand creativity, enrich storytelling, and deepen the audience's connection to the narrative.

Enhancing Multilingual Films: The Role of Graphic Design and Animation in On-Screen Text Translation

In multilingual films or scenes set in foreign locales, graphic design and animation emerge as indispensable tools for bridging language barriers and fostering viewer comprehension. They are deployed to visually translate on-screen text, ensuring that the audience can grasp the significance of written information, whether it be street signs, crucial documents, or subtitles. This strategy not only facilitates linguistic accessibility but also enriches the immersive quality of the cinematic experience, seamlessly integrating translations into the visual narrative without breaking the flow of the film. Through carefully designed graphics and animations, filmmakers create a harmonious synergy between languages and visuals, allowing the audience to navigate different linguistic landscapes effortlessly and enhancing their overall engagement with the story, regardless of their language proficiency.

Simplifying Complexity: The Power of Visual Metaphors through Graphics and Animation

Graphics and animations serve as powerful storytelling devices, particularly when used to craft visual metaphors that simplify intricate concepts or evoke profound emotions. These metaphors act as bridges between the abstract and the tangible, rendering complex ideas more accessible to the audience. By harnessing the visual language of animation, filmmakers can transform challenging notions into intuitive, relatable images. For instance, the incorporation of an hourglass animation becomes a potent symbol for the inexorable passage of time or the looming specter of impending deadlines, instantly resonating with viewers. These visual metaphors transcend linguistic and cultural barriers, engaging the audience on a visceral level, and enabling them to connect with the underlying themes or emotions of the narrative in a profoundly evocative and memorable manner.

Visual Storytelling: Graphics and Animation as Narrative Devices

Graphics and animations within the area of filmmaking function as indispensable storytelling devices, offering a visual medium through which context, backstory, or exposition can be efficiently conveyed. These elements act as narrators themselves, elucidating intricate details that might otherwise be cumbersome to explain through dialogue or traditional means. They become instrumental in delivering historical information, visualizing complex scientific concepts, or portraying pivotal events from a character's past. Whether it's illustrating the rise and fall of an ancient civilization, elucidating the inner workings of a scientific experiment, or delving into a character's memories through a poignant animated flashback, graphics and animations deftly enrich the narrative tapestry, offering audiences a comprehensive understanding of the story's foundations and intricacies while enhancing the visual storytelling in a visually compelling and engaging manner.

Crafting Imaginary Worlds: The Role of Graphic Design and Animation in Sci-Fi and Fantasy World-Building

Within the realms of science fiction and fantasy genres, graphic design and animation play pivotal roles in the art of world-building, acting as architects of imagination. They breathe life into fictional realms by crafting unique symbols, logos, and interfaces for futuristic or otherworldly societies and technologies. These bespoke visual elements serve as a bridge between the viewers and the intricately woven tapestry of these fantastical worlds, imbuing them with distinct visual identities. Through the creation of alien alphabets, futuristic user interfaces, and emblematic logos, graphic designers and animators seamlessly integrate the audience into the fabric of these fictional settings, allowing them to navigate and comprehend the societal structures, technologies, and cultural nuances that define these imaginative universes. In this way, graphic design and animation transcend mere aesthetic embellishments, becoming conduits for immersion and engagement, enabling viewers to explore and embrace the intricacies of the fantastical realms envisioned by filmmakers.

Visualizing Knowledge: Graphics and Animations in Educational Filmmaking

Filmmakers employ graphics and animations as potent visual aids to facilitate the audience's comprehension of intricate and multifaceted subjects, a practice particularly prevalent in the domains of documentaries and educational films. These dynamic visuals serve as bridges between complex data or concepts and the viewers, rendering abstract or intricate information more accessible and engaging. Through the artful animation of charts, graphs, and diagrams, filmmakers can visually distill intricate data, theories, or historical events into digestible and compelling narratives. This approach not only augments the audience's understanding but also fosters a deeper connection with the subject matter. It transforms educational films into immersive learning experiences, empowering viewers to engage with the material in a meaningful and memorable way, ultimately enhancing their grasp of the complex topics at hand.

Character Depth and Development: The Role of Graphics and Animation in Revealing Backstories and Inner Worlds

Graphics and animations wield the power to enrich a character's depth and backstory, functioning as narrative tools that offer invaluable insights into their personality, motivations, and inner conflicts. Filmmakers often utilize these visual elements to delve into a character's psyche or past, employing animated flashback sequences or visual representations of their inner thoughts as windows into their emotional landscapes. By visually conveying pivotal memories, traumatic experiences, or profound moments from a character's past, these animations breathe life into their backstory, allowing the audience to empathize with their struggles and aspirations. Similarly, by visually externalizing a character's inner turmoil or thoughts through graphics and animations, filmmakers unveil the complexities of their motivations and conflicts, fostering a deeper connection between the audience and the character. In this way, graphics and animations emerge as integral storytelling devices that illuminate the intricacies of a character's journey, enriching the narrative tapestry and deepening the emotional resonance of the film.

Seamless Transitions: Elevating Cinematic Storytelling with Creative Graphics and Animations

Creative transitions employing graphic elements and animations serve as seamless bridges between scenes or time periods, elevating the art of film editing by infusing it with innovation and style. These transitions transcend the conventional cuts and fades, adding a distinctive and artistic dimension to the film's visual narrative. Through the skillful integration of graphics and animations, filmmakers can evoke emotions, establish thematic connections, or emphasize narrative nuances during these transitional moments. Whether it's a change in location, the passage of time, or a shift in perspective, these visually captivating transitions captivate the audience's attention and contribute to the overall cinematic experience. They are a testament to the collaborative synergy between filmmakers and graphic designers, who harness the power of visual storytelling to craft unforgettable and artistically enriched transitions that linger in the viewer's memory long after the film has ended.

Elevating Visual Effects: The Role of Complex Computer Graphics and Animations in Filmmaking

Complex computer-generated graphics (CGI) and animations are integral components of modern filmmaking, primarily deployed in visual effects (VFX) and CGI sequences. These sophisticated digital tools empower filmmakers to realize breathtaking and fantastical visions that would be nearly impossible to capture through practical means. Whether crafting lifelike creatures, constructing otherworldly environments, or orchestrating gravity-defying action sequences, CGI and VFX bring a sense of awe and wonder to the screen. They erase the boundaries of the possible, opening doors to previously unattainable cinematic feats. With the mastery of CGI and animation, filmmakers can transport audiences to unimaginable realms, evoke visceral emotions, and amplify the storytelling experience, ultimately pushing the boundaries of cinematic artistry to new frontiers.

Setting the Tone: The Impact of Graphic Design and Animation in Film Title Sequences and Credits

Graphic design and animation wield a substantial influence in the crafting of captivating title sequences and credits, which serve as essential components of a film's aesthetic and narrative. These sequences serve a dual purpose: they not only introduce the cast and crew but also set the tone and establish the visual identity of the entire film. Through artful design and animation, filmmakers can convey thematic nuances, foreshadow narrative elements, and immerse the audience in the stylistic universe of the film. These sequences are akin to the overture of a symphony, providing a sneak peek into the upcoming cinematic journey while invoking a sense of intrigue and anticipation. By artfully combining typography, graphics, and animations, filmmakers can create unforgettable title sequences that resonate with viewers long after the film has concluded, leaving an indelible mark on the audience's cinematic experience.

Branding the Cinematic Universe: The Role of Graphic Design in Real and Fictional Product Placement

In select instances, films integrate genuine or fictional brands and products into their narratives, and graphic designers become key contributors in this endeavor. These designers are tasked with meticulously crafting logos, packaging, and advertising materials, lending an air of authenticity and familiarity to the cinematic world. Whether it's showcasing a character sipping a well-known soft drink or presenting a futuristic gadget with a carefully designed brand, these elements serve to anchor the film in a recognizable reality, enhancing the viewer's immersion. This practice creates a sense of believability within the film's universe, reinforcing the notion that the characters and events are occurring within a tangible and relatable context, even if that context involves fictional brands. Through the skillful work of graphic designers, these visual elements not only contribute to the realism of the film's world but also add layers of depth and cultural resonance to the narrative, enriching the overall storytelling experience.

Visual Aesthetics in Film: How Graphics and Animations Shape Mood and Atmosphere

In video games and virtual reality, graphic design and animation are crucial for narrative shaping and user engagement. They create interactive interfaces, character animations, and immersive environments, conveying information, guiding players, and evoking emotions. In virtual reality, they enhance immersion. Through innovation, developers and VR creators craft compelling narratives, empower player agency, and elevate interactive storytelling to new heights.

Unleashing Creativity: Graphic Design and Animation as Artistic Expression in Film

Filmmakers and graphic designers harness the expressive potential of graphic design and animation as a captivating artistic medium, effectively transcending the boundaries of traditional storytelling. In the area of artistic and experimental films, these visual elements become potent tools for pushing creative boundaries and provoking emotional responses. Unconventional or avant-garde styles, characterized by abstract forms, non-linear narratives, and unconventional visuals, enable filmmakers to challenge the norms of conventional cinema. These avant-garde graphic designs and animations often eschew straightforward storytelling in favor of abstract, symbolic, or surreal representations, resulting in an immersive and thought-provoking visual experience. Through this medium, filmmakers can craft films that delve into the subconscious, explore existential questions, or elicit profound emotional responses, effectively pushing the boundaries of cinematic expression while inviting audiences to engage in a unique and often transformative artistic encounter.

Dynamic Storytelling: The Role of Graphic Design and Animation in Interactive and Immersive Media

In interactive and immersive media, including video games and virtual reality experiences, graphic design and animation serve as pivotal instruments for shaping the narrative and orchestrating a dynamic and engaging user experience. These visual elements play a multifaceted role, transcending mere aesthetics to become critical components of the storytelling process. Graphic design and animation are harnessed to create not only stunning visuals but also interactive interfaces, character animations, and environmental designs that seamlessly draw players into the narrative. They act as conduits for conveying vital information, guiding players through intricate game worlds, and evoking emotional responses. In virtual reality, these elements achieve a heightened level of immersion, allowing users to explore and interact with the digital environment in a way that feels visceral and lifelike. Through innovative graphic design and animation, video game developers and creators of virtual reality experiences are able to craft compelling narratives, foster player agency, and elevate the overall user engagement to unparalleled heights, thus reshaping the landscape of interactive storytelling and entertainment.

I. Virtual Production Techniques

The advent of virtual production techniques has brought about a transformative wave in the landscape of Indian cinema, redefining how visuals are conceived and executed. This innovative approach fuses the realms of physical filmmaking with cutting-edge technology to craft immersive and visually stunning cinematic experiences. It involves the utilization of real-time rendering, digital backdrops, and virtual sets, allowing filmmakers to seamlessly blend live-action with computer-generated elements.

Virtual production is a revolutionary filmmaking technique that blends real-time CGI and virtual environments with live-action filming. It provides filmmakers with unprecedented creative freedom, cost efficiency, and realism, making it a powerful tool for creating visually stunning and immersive cinematic experiences. However, it also comes with technical challenges and requires a learning curve for filmmakers and crew members. As technology continues to advance, virtual production is likely to become an even more prominent and influential aspect of the filmmaking industry. This approach empowers filmmakers to push the boundaries of storytelling, offering endless possibilities for creating cinematic worlds and narratives that were once thought to be unattainable. Here's a detailed explanation of virtual production for movies:

Components of Virtual Production

Crafting Cinematic Worlds: The Power of Advanced CGI Techniques in Virtual Set Design

In contemporary filmmaking, the creation of virtual sets, locations, and backgrounds through advanced CGI techniques has revolutionized the storytelling landscape. Filmmakers can now conjure highly detailed and dynamic environments that were once unimaginable. These digital constructs afford unparalleled versatility in storytelling, as they can seamlessly transition from the sprawling landscapes of fantasy realms to the intricate intricacies of futuristic cityscapes, all with an astonishing level of detail and realism. This flexibility enables filmmakers to push the boundaries of cinematic narratives, taking audiences on immersive journeys across time and space or immersing them in fantastical realms that defy the constraints of the physical world. Moreover, the advent of CGI has also democratized storytelling, making it possible for independent filmmakers to bring their creative visions to life with a level of visual fidelity and artistic expression that was once the exclusive domain of major studios. Ultimately, CGI-enhanced virtual environments have become a transformative force in modern filmmaking, offering boundless creative possibilities and enhancing the cinematic experience for audiences worldwide.

Real-Time CGI Rendering: Enhancing Immersion in Filmmaking Through Interactive Virtual Environments

The backbone of modern filmmaking's immersion into virtual environments lies in the formidable power of computer systems and cutting-edge software. These technological marvels render complex virtual environments in real time, a feat that was once reserved for post-production processes. This real-time rendering capability allows actors and filmmakers to step into these digital realms and interact with the virtual elements while they are in the midst of shooting. It fundamentally transforms the filmmaking process, as it grants immediate visual feedback on how the virtual elements integrate with the live action, lighting, and camera angles. This not only streamlines production but also elevates the sense of immersion for both the actors and the audience. It enables performers to react organically to their surroundings, enhancing the authenticity of their performances, and provides directors with unprecedented creative control over the virtual elements. As a result, the synergy between powerful computer systems, real-time rendering, and filmmaking serves as a catalyst for a new era of cinematic storytelling, where the boundaries between reality and the digital realm are seamlessly blurred, offering audiences a richer and more immersive viewing experience.

Bringing Virtual Characters to Life: Motion Capture Suits and Real-Time Animation in Filmmaking

In modern filmmaking and the creation of immersive virtual environments, actors frequently don motion capture suits adorned with an array of sensors designed to meticulously track their movements and facial expressions. These sensors capture an extensive range of data, from the subtlest gestures to nuanced facial nuances, with remarkable precision. This wealth of real-time data serves as the foundation for animating virtual characters or creatures within the digital realm. As actors perform, their movements and expressions are instantaneously translated into the digital domain, enabling the virtual characters to mimic their every action and emotion. This technology has ushered in a new era of cinematic storytelling, where the line between the physical and digital worlds is blurred, and the performances of actors breathe life into fantastical beings and characters in real time, fostering a deeper connection between the audience and the cinematic narrative.

Immersive Realism: Utilizing Large LED Screens for Real-Time Virtual Set Integration in Filmmaking

In the contemporary landscape of filmmaking, large LED screens or walls have emerged as game-changing tools, serving as practical sets that enhance the immersive experience for actors and elevate the overall production quality. These screens are not just static backdrops but dynamic canvases that display the virtual environments in real time. They are often synchronized with the camera's movements and angles, ensuring that the actors perform against realistic backgrounds and lighting conditions that seamlessly integrate with the digital elements. This approach transforms the traditional green screen approach, providing actors with tangible reference points and allowing them to react organically to the virtual surroundings. The result is a heightened level of authenticity in performances, as actors can physically interact with their digital surroundings, casting convincing shadows and reflections, and responding to dynamic changes in lighting. This innovative use of LED screens not only streamlines post-production efforts but also revolutionizes the filmmaking process, fostering a more immersive and responsive environment that ultimately enriches the cinematic experience for both the cast and the audience.

Virtual Cameras: Capturing Cinematic Magic Within Virtual Environments in Real Time

In the world of crafting cinematic worlds within virtual environments, filmmakers employ virtual cameras as indispensable tools for capturing the scenes with precision and creativity. These virtual cameras are meticulously synchronized with the virtual world, mirroring the movements and angles of the physical camera used during filming. They provide a live feed of the composited shot, allowing directors and cinematographers to orchestrate the framing and composition in real time within the digital landscape. This innovation not only streamlines the post-production process but also offers filmmakers unprecedented creative control. They can experiment with camera movements, angles, and focal lengths, all while observing how the virtual elements blend seamlessly with the live-action footage. This dynamic interaction between the virtual camera and the digital world enables filmmakers to achieve a level of visual cohesion and storytelling finesse that was once challenging to attain. It empowers directors to make on-the-fly adjustments, fostering a more responsive and creatively fluid filmmaking process that ultimately enhances the storytelling and visual impact of the final cinematic product.

Benefits of Virtual Production

Unleashing Creativity: The Transformative Power of Virtual Production in Filmmaking

Creative freedom is a cornerstone of virtual production, empowering filmmakers to explore new horizons in storytelling. Unlike traditional filmmaking, where location constraints and post-production limitations often restrict creative choices, virtual production offers a dynamic and liberating platform for filmmakers. They can swiftly iterate on scenes, manipulate virtual environments, and experiment with diverse settings, all while maintaining complete creative control. This real-time adaptability enables filmmakers to bring their visions to life with unparalleled precision, fostering a fluid and immersive cinematic experience. Whether it involves creating otherworldly landscapes or fine-tuning lighting and camera angles on the fly, virtual production liberates filmmakers to push the boundaries of their creativity and deliver cinematic masterpieces that were once considered unattainable.

Transforming Film Economics: The Cost Efficiency Revolution of Virtual Production

Cost efficiency is a fundamental advantage of virtual production that fundamentally transforms the economics of filmmaking. While the initial setup, including the investment in advanced technology and skilled personnel, can be substantial, virtual production offers substantial long-term savings. Filmmakers can shoot intricate scenes without the need for elaborate practical sets, costly location scouting, or extensive post-production visual effects (VFX) work. The real-time rendering of digital elements and virtual environments eliminates the need for extensive VFX work in post-production, which can be both time-consuming and expensive. Additionally, the ability to swiftly iterate and experiment with scenes reduces on-set production time, minimizing labor costs and resource expenditures. Ultimately, virtual production's cost efficiency streamlines the filmmaking process, enabling filmmakers to allocate resources more strategically, reduce the reliance on physical set construction and post-production VFX, and deliver high-quality cinematic experiences within budget constraints.

Beyond Belief: Elevating Cinematic Realism with Virtual Production

Realism in virtual production is key for immersive cinematic experiences. Meticulously crafted virtual environments replicate historical, fantastical, or futuristic settings with precision. It goes beyond aesthetics, seamlessly integrating live-action footage with digital elements for convincing actor-environment interaction. This heightened realism suspends the audience's disbelief, drawing them into the narrative. From ancient civilizations to otherworldly dimensions or futuristic worlds, virtual production sets a new standard for cinematic authenticity, enhancing immersion and engagement.

Unleashing Creative Freedom: The Dynamic Flexibility of Virtual Production

Flexibility is a defining feature of virtual production, offering filmmakers unprecedented control over their creative vision. In virtual environments, filmmakers can effortlessly manipulate lighting conditions, weather patterns, and the time of day, allowing for real-time adjustments that would be exceedingly challenging to achieve on practical sets. This dynamic control fosters a level of precision and adaptability that is unparalleled in traditional filmmaking. Filmmakers can experiment with different moods, atmospheres, and visual aesthetics, all while maintaining complete creative autonomy. Whether it involves transforming a daytime scene into a moonlit night or orchestrating the perfect storm, virtual production empowers filmmakers to bring their visions to life with unparalleled flexibility, elevating the art of storytelling to new heights.

Transforming Performances: The Real-Time Interactivity of Virtual Production

Interactivity is a groundbreaking aspect of virtual production that reshapes the dynamics of filmmaking. With virtual environments, actors have the unique opportunity to interact seamlessly with digital elements and characters in real time. This level of engagement leads to more authentic and natural performances, as actors can respond to their surroundings and virtual co-stars in a lifelike manner. The ability to physically interact with virtual objects, whether it's handling a digital prop or engaging in combat with a CGI creature, brings a tangible dimension to the acting process. This interactivity not only enhances the actors' performances but also deepens the audience's immersion, as they witness genuine reactions and interactions between the live-action and virtual elements. In essence, virtual production elevates the art of filmmaking by fostering a dynamic synergy between actors and their digital surroundings, resulting in more compelling and convincing cinematic experiences.

Sustainability in Cinema: Reducing the Environmental Footprint Through Virtual Production

Virtual production offers a promising solution to reduce the environmental footprint of filmmaking. By significantly minimizing the reliance on extensive physical sets and location shoots, this innovative approach contributes to a more sustainable film industry. Traditional filmmaking often generates substantial waste and consumes resources such as timber, construction materials, and energy for transportation and on-set operations. In contrast, virtual production reduces the demand for these resources, curbing environmental degradation. Additionally, the lower reliance on travel and logistics associated with location shoots can decrease greenhouse gas emissions and air pollution. By embracing virtual production, the film industry takes a step toward a more environmentally responsible and eco-conscious approach to filmmaking, aligning with global efforts to combat climate change and reduce its ecological impact.

Applications of Virtual Production

Unleashing Imagination: The Power of Virtual Production in Science Fiction and Fantasy Filmmaking

Virtual production excels in the realms of science fiction and fantasy filmmaking, where the creation of otherworldly and imaginative settings is paramount. Filmmakers in these genres can leverage the power of virtual environments to bring to life alien landscapes, fantastical realms, and futuristic cityscapes with unparalleled creativity and precision. The flexibility of virtual production allows for the seamless integration of extraordinary elements such as alien creatures, advanced technologies, and magical phenomena. Directors can explore uncharted territories, pushing the boundaries of visual storytelling to craft immersive and visually stunning cinematic worlds that transport audiences to the far reaches of their imaginations. Whether it's traversing distant galaxies, unveiling mythical realms, or envisioning dystopian futures, virtual production serves as an indispensable tool for translating the fantastical into breathtaking cinematic realities.

Resurrecting the Past: Virtual Production's Role in Historical Filmmaking

Virtual production is a valuable asset for historical filmmaking, allowing filmmakers to recreate intricate and historically accurate settings and landmarks. This approach significantly reduces the cost and logistical challenges associated with shooting in real historical locations, which often require extensive permissions, restoration efforts, and travel expenses. With virtual environments, filmmakers can meticulously reconstruct period-specific architecture, landscapes, and iconic landmarks, ensuring an authentic visual representation of historical eras. Whether it's transporting viewers to ancient civilizations, reimagining historical events, or reviving long-lost settings, virtual production offers a cost-effective and efficient means to bring history to life on the silver screen, all while maintaining the integrity of the past and enhancing the storytelling potential of historical films.

Redefining Action and Visual Effects: The Power of Virtual Production

Virtual production serves as a game-changing tool for action-packed films and those reliant on intricate visual effects. This approach excels in seamlessly integrating complex action sequences and visual effects into live-action scenes, ensuring that actors interact convincingly with CGI elements. Whether it involves high-stakes battles, gravity-defying stunts, or encounters with fantastical creatures, virtual production bridges the gap between the real and the digital. Actors can perform against green screens or LED walls, with the virtual elements dynamically incorporated in real time. This immersive approach not only enhances the authenticity of performances but also streamlines post-production processes, as many visual effects can be captured during the initial shoot. As a result, filmmakers can achieve breathtaking action sequences and breathtaking visual effects with a level of seamlessness that elevates the cinematic experience and sets new standards for action and visual effects-driven films.

Revolutionizing Animation: The Creative Power of Virtual Production

Virtual production techniques are a transformative asset in animation and cartoons, where they enhance the efficiency and creative possibilities of animation pipelines. Traditionally, animation involved a lengthy process of hand-drawn or computer-generated frame-by-frame rendering. However, virtual production streamlines this workflow by allowing animators to work within virtual environments in real time. Animators can manipulate digital characters, objects, and settings with ease, achieving dynamic and lifelike movements. The level of control and interactivity offered by virtual production not only accelerates animation production but also opens up new avenues for creative experimentation. This approach benefits both traditional 2D animation and 3D CGI, enabling animators to focus on refining character performances and storytelling while expediting the production timeline. Ultimately, virtual production empowers animators to push the boundaries of creativity, resulting in visually stunning and emotionally resonant animated films and television shows.

Challenges of Virtual Production

Investing in the Future: The Initial Costs of Virtual Production

The initial investment required for setting up a virtual production stage can be substantial, encompassing the acquisition of high-end equipment and software licenses. Building a virtual production environment entails procuring cutting-edge hardware such as powerful computers, motion capture systems, high-resolution LED screens or walls, and advanced cameras. Additionally, software licenses for 3D modeling, real-time rendering, motion capture, and virtual production software must be secured. Furthermore, skilled personnel, including virtual production supervisors, technical directors, and animators, are essential to the success of the venture, adding to the initial cost. While this upfront expenditure can be significant, it is important to recognize that virtual production offers long-term benefits, including cost savings in other areas such as set construction and post-production visual effects. Ultimately, the initial investment serves as a critical foundation for unlocking the full potential of virtual production, revolutionizing the filmmaking process, and enhancing storytelling capabilities.

Navigating the Learning Curve: Building Technical Expertise in Virtual Production

The adoption of virtual production introduces a need for technical expertise among filmmakers and crew members as they navigate new technologies and workflows. This transition requires a learning curve as professionals adapt to the intricacies of virtual production tools, real-time rendering, motion capture systems, and virtual cameras.

Cinematographers, directors, and art departments must gain proficiency in collaborating within the virtual environment, adjusting to the nuances of shooting against green screens or LED walls, and understanding the capabilities and limitations of virtual production software. Additionally, virtual production supervisors and technical directors play a pivotal role in guiding the crew through the intricacies of the process. While the adjustment may present initial challenges, the investment in technical expertise ensures that the creative potential of virtual production can be fully harnessed, ultimately leading to more innovative and immersive storytelling in filmmaking.

Beyond the Uncanny Valley: Striving for Realism in Virtual Production

One of the challenges in virtual production lies in achieving a high level of realism, especially concerning virtual environments and characters. While technology has advanced significantly, achieving photorealism remains a complex endeavor. There's a constant push to bridge the gap between the virtual and the real, but there's a risk of encountering the "uncanny valley" phenomenon, where virtual characters appear unsettlingly close to being human but not quite there. This can lead to audience discomfort and a loss of immersion if not executed correctly. Striking the right balance to avoid the uncanny valley and create convincing virtual elements that seamlessly integrate with live-action components requires meticulous attention to detail in areas such as texture, lighting, and animation. Overcoming this challenge is essential for virtual production to fulfill its potential in delivering visually stunning and emotionally resonant cinematic experiences.

Balancing Act: Navigating the Challenges of Physical Interactions and Practical Effects in Virtual Production

Virtual production, despite its myriad advantages, has its limitations, particularly when it comes to physical interactions and practical effects. In a virtual environment, creating realistic physical interactions, such as characters touching or manipulating objects, can be challenging to execute convincingly. Practical effects, like explosions, pyrotechnics, or intricate mechanical contraptions, may require traditional on-set techniques. Additionally, the tactile qualities of real-world props and materials can be difficult to replicate virtually, impacting the authenticity of certain scenes. Filmmakers must carefully balance the use of virtual and physical elements to ensure the seamless integration of both, leveraging the strengths of each approach to deliver a compelling and immersive cinematic experience.

Unleashing Creative Freedom: The Impact of Virtual Production on Indian Cinema's Spectacle and Storytelling

Virtual production has ushered in a new era of creative freedom and innovation in Indian cinema, a realm known for its penchant for grandeur and spectacle. With its boundless capabilities, this technology enables filmmakers to recreate historically accurate settings with an unparalleled level of detail. Whether it's transporting the audience to a bygone era or immersing them in the vibrant tapestry of a fantasy world, virtual production offers limitless possibilities in terms of setting and world-building, allowing for storytelling that was previously unattainable. The integration of visual effects, once constrained by budgetary limitations, is now carried out with greater ease and precision. This not only enhances the visual spectacle and artistic integrity of Indian cinema but also accelerates the production process, offering filmmakers more creative control and efficiency. As Indian cinema continues to evolve and diversify, virtual production stands as a transformative tool that empowers filmmakers to push the envelope of storytelling and visual aesthetics, promising audiences even more captivating and immersive cinematic journeys that celebrate the limitless possibilities of storytelling and filmmaking.

Beyond Visual Enhancements: The Evolution of Indian Cinema Through Virtual Production

This technology's impact on Indian cinema extends beyond enhancing visual aesthetics. It redefines the boundaries of creativity, allowing filmmakers to venture into uncharted territory, experiment with narrative structures, and create cinematic worlds that challenge the limits of imagination. As grandiosity and spectacle have been integral to Indian cinema's identity, virtual production helps filmmakers to take these elements to even greater heights. While it complements the traditional aspects of filmmaking, it also encourages the industry to evolve by embracing cutting-edge technology. In the dynamic landscape of Indian cinema, virtual production serves as a game-changer, enabling storytellers to craft immersive narratives that seamlessly weave historical accuracy and fantastical elements while delighting audiences with visual splendor and narrative depth. It celebrates the boundless possibilities of cinematic storytelling and ensures that Indian cinema continues to captivate and inspire viewers worldwide.

CHAPTER - 04

4. The Role of Auditory Elements in Indian Cinema

Auditory elements constitute a cornerstone of Indian cinema, wielding immense influence in elevating the cinematic experience to new heights and eliciting a profound emotional connection with the audience. Indian filmmakers harness a diverse array of auditory techniques, including music, sound effects, dialogue delivery, and ambient sounds, to craft immersive soundscapes that seamlessly complement and enhance the visual storytelling. Music, in particular, holds a special place in Indian cinema, with carefully composed songs and background scores serving as powerful narrative tools that can evoke a wide spectrum of emotions and propel the storyline forward. Sound effects and ambient sounds add depth and authenticity to on-screen environments, transporting viewers into the heart of the narrative. Additionally, dialogue delivery and vocal performances are often accentuated to convey the nuances of character emotions and motivations. In sum, the intricate marriage of auditory elements with visual storytelling is a hallmark of Indian cinema, enabling filmmakers to immerse audiences in rich, multi-sensory experiences that resonate on both emotional and artistic levels. Here's how auditory elements are treated in Indian cinemas:

A. Music and Songs

The Significance of Original Soundtracks in Indian Cinema

Original Soundtracks (OSTs) in Indian cinema hold a pivotal role as storytelling tools, adding layers of emotional depth, thematic richness, and cultural resonance to films. Comprising a collaborative effort involving music directors, lyricists, playback singers, and composers, these OSTs contribute to the film's narrative and overall cinematic experience. Indian film music, known for its diversity and emotional impact, enjoys global acclaim for its ability to encapsulate the essence of a film's story and characters. It serves as an integral and cherished element of the cinematic journey, fostering a profound connection between the audience and the narrative. OSTs in Indian cinema have the power to evoke a wide range of emotions, from joy to sorrow, and have a lasting impact, making them a cultural and artistic treasure of the industry.

Harmonizing Narratives: The Integral Role of Songs and Music in Indian Cinema

In Indian cinema, songs and music serve as indispensable components of the storytelling process, distinguishing it from its Western counterparts. Unlike Western films, where songs are typically relegated to standalone musical interludes or credits sequences, Indian cinema seamlessly weaves songs and musical sequences into the very fabric of the narrative. These musical moments transcend mere entertainment, acting as emotional anchors that reinforce character development, evoke deep-seated feelings, and advance the plot. Whether expressing love, joy, sorrow, or even social commentary, Indian film songs resonate with audiences on a profound level, enhancing the overall cinematic experience by engaging both the auditory and visual senses in a harmonious fusion of storytelling and music. This unique approach not only sets Indian cinema apart but also underscores the power of music to enrich and elevate the cinematic narrative.

Maestros Behind the Melodies: The Influence and Significance of Music Directors in Indian Cinema

Music directors occupy a pivotal and revered role in the Indian film industry. They are the creative architects behind the film's musical tapestry, tasked with composing both the memorable songs and the evocative background score. Collaborating closely with the director, they play a crucial part in synchronizing the music with the film's emotional depth and thematic essence. Music directors possess the ability to translate the director's vision into musical expressions that resonate deeply with the audience, enhancing the overall cinematic experience. Their influence extends beyond just the composition; they often scout for talented playback singers, lyricists, and instrumentalists, curating a harmonious ensemble that brings their musical vision to life. Their work can have a profound impact, shaping the way audiences connect with the narrative, characters, and the film's cultural and emotional nuances, making them indispensable and celebrated figures in the world of Indian cinema.

Melodic Narratives: The Thematic Significance of Songs in Indian Cinema

In Indian cinema, every song holds a distinct and essential thematic purpose. These musical interludes transcend mere entertainment; they are powerful tools for conveying the complex spectrum of human emotions within the narrative. Whether it's the exuberant expression of love, the poignant articulation of sorrow, the jubilant celebration of life's moments, or the tense confrontation of conflict, songs serve as emotive bridges that connect the audience with the characters' innermost feelings and the overarching storyline. They don't just stand as standalone performances but are intricately woven into the fabric of the plot, propelling character development and enhancing the audience's engagement. In Indian cinema, songs are not interruptions but integral elements that breathe life into the narrative, making them an indispensable and memorable aspect of the storytelling process.

Harmonizing Diversity: The Multifaceted Musical Styles of Indian Cinema

Indian cinema stands as a vibrant tapestry of musical diversity, offering a vast spectrum of styles that range from classical and folk to contemporary and fusion. The selection of a particular musical style is a nuanced decision, intricately tied to the film's genre, setting, and the emotional resonance it seeks to create. Classical music, deeply rooted in tradition, often finds its place in historical or emotionally intense narratives, adding a timeless and evocative quality to the storytelling. Folk music, on the other hand, connects the audience with regional flavors and cultural richness, making it a choice for films celebrating India's diverse heritage. Contemporary and fusion styles adapt to the modern cinematic landscape, allowing for innovative and experimental soundscapes that align with contemporary narratives. These musical choices are more than just background; they serve as a narrative language that enhances the overall cinematic experience, offering a rich tapestry of sound to complement and enrich the film's thematic essence.

Songs of the Soul: The Poetic Narratives within Indian Film Music

Indian film songs are a unique and profound form of artistic expression that goes beyond mere music. They serve as lyrical storytelling devices, imparting additional layers of meaning, depth, and emotion to the cinematic narrative. The lyrics of these songs are meticulously crafted, with a keen focus on synchronization with the film's storyline and the development of its characters. Each verse is a poetic masterpiece, carefully chosen to reflect the characters' inner thoughts, desires, and conflicts, offering audiences a window into their psyche. These lyrical compositions not only enhance the viewer's connection with the film but also contribute to its cultural and emotional resonance, making them an indispensable part of the Indian cinematic experience. Through poignant verses and evocative words, Indian film songs transcend their musical elements, becoming vessels for storytelling and emotional revelation.

Elevating Emotions: The Impact of Original Soundtracks on Cinematic Storytelling

Original Soundtracks (OSTs) in Indian cinema are meticulously designed to serve as powerful tools for enhancing the emotional resonance of a film. These songs, meticulously composed and expertly arranged, are strategically placed within the narrative to intensify the audience's connection with the characters and their experiences. Whether it's the haunting melody that underscores a moment of profound sorrow, the uplifting tune that accompanies a joyous celebration, or the pulsating rhythm that amplifies a thrilling action sequence, OSTs are carefully crafted to heighten the viewer's emotional engagement. They act as conduits for empathy, allowing the audience to not only witness but deeply feel the characters' joys, sorrows, triumphs, and tribulations. In this way, original soundtracks transcend their musical role to become integral components of the storytelling process, elevating the overall cinematic experience and leaving a lasting impact on the audience.

Musical Characterization: The Role of Songs in Indian Films' Character Development

Songs in Indian films serve as potent tools for character development, offering viewers a window into the intricate facets of a character's psyche. These musical interludes offer a unique lens through which we can peer into their inner thoughts, desires, and conflicts. A character's choice of song or musical style is more than a simple artistic preference; it's a narrative device that can reveal a wealth of information about their personality and background. Whether it's a melodious love ballad that hints at a character's romantic yearnings, a somber tune that delves into their inner struggles, or an energetic dance number that showcases their exuberance, these musical choices become extensions of the character's identity, enriching their depth and complexity. Through the medium of song, Indian cinema masterfully intertwines music and character, allowing the audience to forge a deeper connection with the individuals at the heart of the story, making the characters not just players on the screen but emotionally resonant figures in the viewers' hearts and minds.

Cultural Cadence: The Integration of Traditional Music and Dance in Indian Film Soundtracks

Indian cinema frequently draws inspiration from the nation's rich and diverse cultural heritage, often weaving traditional music and dance forms seamlessly into its soundtracks. This incorporation serves as more than just a nod to tradition; it infuses the storytelling with authenticity and cultural depth. From classical ragas and folk tunes to intricate classical dance forms like Kathak, Bharatanatyam, or Odissi, these elements offer a vivid glimpse into India's multifaceted cultural tapestry. They not only provide a sensory treat for the audience but also contribute to the narrative's authenticity, enriching the film's setting, characters, and themes. Whether it's a devotional bhajan enhancing a spiritual moment, a folk melody capturing the essence of a rural backdrop, or a lavishly choreographed classical dance sequence, these cultural elements elevate the cinematic experience by resonating with both Indian and international audiences, making Indian films a window into the nation's vibrant cultural heritage.

Echoes of Legends: Iconic Playback Singers in Indian Cinema

Indian cinema boasts a remarkable lineage of iconic playback singers who have lent their voices to legendary actors, becoming indelible figures in the industry's history. These vocal virtuosos are celebrated for their exceptional talent, distinct vocal styles, and the ability to infuse unparalleled emotion into their renditions. From Lata Mangeshkar's mellifluous melodies to Kishore Kumar's versatile and soul-stirring performances, and from Asha Bhosle's dynamic range to the unique depth of Mohammed Rafi's voice, each playback singer has brought a distinctive flavor to the songs they've sung. Their contributions extend beyond the songs themselves; they've become cultural icons, elevating the cinematic experience and imprinting their names in the annals of Indian music history. These legendary playback singers have transcended generations, leaving an indomitable legacy that continues to inspire and influence contemporary artists and shape the soundscape of Indian cinema.

Chart-Toppers Beyond the Silver Screen: The Enduring Success of Indian Film Songs

Successful film songs in Indian cinema possess an extraordinary ability to transcend the silver screen and etch themselves into the collective consciousness of the nation. Often characterized by catchy tunes, poignant lyrics, and emotionally resonant melodies, these songs become chart-topping hits and enjoy enduring popularity that spans years, sometimes even decades. Their appeal extends far beyond the confines of the movie theater, permeating everyday life. From radio airwaves to wedding celebrations, from cultural events to social gatherings, these iconic tunes become part of the fabric of Indian society. They contribute significantly to a film's commercial success, attracting audiences and boosting box office revenues. Moreover, these songs serve as a cultural touchstone, eliciting nostalgia, evoking emotions, and fostering a sense of unity among diverse communities. They are celebrated not just as musical compositions but as timeless cultural treasures that continue to resonate with audiences across generations, reaffirming the profound and lasting impact of Indian film music.

Melodic Excellence: Honoring Outstanding Soundtracks and Songs in the Indian Film Industry

Outstanding original soundtracks (OSTs) and songs hold a special place of recognition and celebration within the Indian film industry. These musical achievements are honored through a variety of prestigious national and regional awards. Awards for the best music direction and playback singing are a testament to the exceptional talent and artistry of the composers, music directors, lyricists, and playback singers who breathe life into Indian cinema's musical landscape. The recognition not only acknowledges their artistic contributions but also underscores the profound impact of music on the overall cinematic experience. These awards ceremonies serve as a platform to applaud the creativity and innovation in film music, further highlighting its significance in Indian culture and storytelling.

Resonating Beyond Cinema: The Enduring Impact of Iconic Indian Film Songs on Pop Culture

Iconic film songs in Indian cinema possess an enduring and pervasive influence on the nation's pop culture landscape. These musical gems transcend their original context, becoming timeless classics that continue to capture the hearts and minds of generations. They are not confined to the film industry alone but permeate various facets of Indian society, from television shows to reality competitions, and even advertising campaigns. These songs are frequently covered by emerging artists and remixed into contemporary compositions, ensuring their relevance in today's music scene. Moreover, they serve as a source of inspiration for choreographers, fashion designers, and even meme creators, attesting to their profound and multifaceted impact. The resonance of these iconic songs is a testament to their enduring quality and the indelible mark they have left on Indian pop culture, showcasing the timeless power of music to shape and reflect the cultural zeitgeist.

Harmonizing the World: The Global Appeal of Indian Film Music

Indian film music, with its irresistible melodies and deep emotional resonance, has transcended geographical borders to garner a dedicated and diverse global fan base. What sets Indian film music apart is its ability to evoke a wide range of emotions, making it universally relatable. Whether it's the infectious rhythms of a dance number, the soul-stirring melody of a love song, or the poignant lyrics of a melancholic tune, these compositions resonate with listeners around the world. International audiences have not only embraced Indian film music but have also actively participated in its appreciation, with cover versions, dance tributes, and collaborations becoming increasingly popular. The music's global appeal is a testament to its universality and the capacity of art to transcend linguistic and cultural barriers, uniting people through the sheer power of melody and emotion.

Playback Singing

Playback singing is a distinctive and widely celebrated aspect of Indian cinema, particularly in Bollywood and other regional film industries in India. It involves professional playback singers lending their voices to actors, who then lip-sync to the recorded vocals during song sequences in films. Playback singing has played a significant role in enhancing the emotional impact and musical richness of Indian cinema. Here's a detailed explanation of playback singing in Indian cinema:

Unsung Heroes: The Vital Role of Playback Singers in Indian Cinema

Playback singers in the Indian film industry are remarkable artists who provide the voices for on-screen actors, showcasing exceptional vocal talent and emotional depth. They possess versatility and adaptability to convey a wide range of emotions through their singing across various musical genres. Despite often working in the background, these singers are the emotive voices of characters, forming a profound connection with audiences. Their contributions are at the heart of the enchantment that Indian film music brings to the silver screen, making them the true unsung stars of the industry.

The Vocal Virtuosos: Celebrating the Mastery of Playback Singers in Indian Film Music

Playback singers are revered for their remarkable vocal abilities, which are the bedrock of their success in the world of film music. Their exceptional vocal talent is characterized by their innate ability to deliver impeccable performances. They have honed their voices to possess a remarkable range and control, allowing them to effortlessly handle intricate melodies that span multiple octaves. Their mastery of pitch and tone ensures that they can interpret and express the nuances of a song with impeccable accuracy. This skill is particularly crucial in Indian film music, which often features complex and melodically rich compositions. Whether it's hitting high notes with crystal clarity or navigating the depths of lower registers with resonance, playback singers consistently demonstrate their vocal dexterity. Their ability to execute these technical feats with precision and finesse is a testament to their dedication, training, and the extraordinary depth of their talent, making them the backbone of Indian film music.

Versatility Unveiled: The Multifaceted Talent of Playback Singers in Indian Film Music

Playback singers in the Indian film industry are celebrated for their remarkable versatility, seamlessly adapting their singing style to a wide range of musical genres. They excel in classical, folk, pop, and contemporary music, demonstrating a deep understanding of diverse musical traditions and an ability to convey the intended emotions, whether it's timeless romance or high-energy rhythms. This extraordinary versatility equips them to meet the diverse musical demands of the industry, transcending genre boundaries and ensuring that their voices remain an indispensable element of Indian cinema's rich musical tapestry.

The Heartfelt Harmonies: Playback Singers as the Emotion Conduits of Indian Film Music

Playback singers in Indian film music possess a remarkable ability to convey a wide range of emotions through their singing, making them the authentic voice of on-screen characters. They can express joy, sorrow, or energy with an innate capacity to channel the emotions of lyrics and melodies. Their vocal expressions complement on-screen performances, adding depth and resonance to the characters' feelings. This ability to connect with a song's emotional core and convey it with sincerity and intensity is what makes them indispensable to film music, bringing characters and their emotions to life in a deeply resonant way.

Harmonizing with the Silver Screen: The Precision and Professionalism of Playback Singers in Indian Cinema

Synchronization with actors is a critical aspect of a playback singer's craft in Indian cinema. These skilled vocalists must meticulously align their singing with the lip movements, expressions, and body language of the actors on screen. This synchronization demands a high level of precision and professionalism to ensure that the song appears seamlessly integrated into the film's narrative. Playback singers must not only match the timing of their vocals with the actors' lip-sync but also mirror the emotional nuances and intensity of the characters at that particular moment in the story. This synchronization process involves careful rehearsals and a keen understanding of the script and the characters' motivations. The success of this coordination lies in making the audience believe that the actor is singing the song themselves, creating a cohesive cinematic experience where the music feels like an organic extension of the narrative. This level of professionalism and attention to detail is what elevates the role of playback singers to an indispensable part of the Indian film industry.

The Diligent Pursuit of Excellence: Professionalism and Discipline in the Life of a Playback Singer in Indian Cinema

Professionalism and discipline are the cornerstones of a playback singer's career in Indian cinema. These artists adhere to a strict regimen of training, practice, and vocal care to ensure the maintenance of their vocal quality and consistency. Their vocal cords, akin to their primary instruments, require meticulous care and conditioning. This involves daily vocal exercises, warm-ups, and practices that strengthen their range, pitch, and control. Additionally, playback singers are known to maintain a disciplined lifestyle, encompassing dietary restrictions, regular exercise, and sufficient rest to preserve their vocal health. They also stay updated with evolving musical styles and industry trends, constantly honing their skills to remain relevant in the ever-changing world of film music. This unwavering commitment to their craft and the high level of professionalism they exhibit contribute significantly to their enduring success and reputation as vocal virtuosos in the Indian film industry.

The Iconic Role of Playback Singers in Indian Cinema: Shaping On-Screen Personas and Cultural Legacy

Playback singers in the Indian film industry play a unique and revered role that extends beyond the boundaries of a conventional musical career. They have achieved an almost iconic status, with many of these talented vocalists acquiring a dedicated and passionate fan base. What sets these singers apart is their ability to transcend being mere musicians, becoming integral to the cinematic experience and cultural fabric of India. One of the most intriguing aspects of this phenomenon is how certain playback singers' voices have become synonymous with specific actors. This connection is a powerful one, as it contributes significantly to the on-screen personas of these stars. When a particular actor consistently pairs with a playback singer, it not only enhances the emotional depth and impact of their performances but also creates an enduring bond between the two artists, with their careers often intertwined.

Playback Singers in Indian Cinema: The Timeless Icons Shaping Cultural and Cinematic Legacies

The recognition and stardom enjoyed by playback singers reflect their extraordinary talent and their profound influence on the world of Indian entertainment. Their voices serve as the emotional anchors of films, infusing life into the characters and storylines. Audiences develop a deep connection with these singers, and their songs transcend generations, becoming timeless classics. Playback singers have, in a way, become cultural icons, celebrated not just for their vocal prowess but also for their role in shaping the Indian cinematic experience. Their contributions to Indian cinema are immeasurable, and they continue to be revered and cherished figures who have left an indelible mark on the nation's cultural landscape.

Advantages of Playback Singing

Playback singing is an indispensable and distinctive facet of Indian cinema, intricately woven into the fabric of filmmaking. It operates as a vital cog in the wheel of cinematic storytelling, with playback singers working in tandem with music directors, lyricists, and composers to craft songs that not only complement the narrative but also stir the deepest of emotions in the audience. These gifted artists possess a remarkable ability to convey a wide spectrum of feelings through their renditions, making the songs an emotional anchor for the characters and the storyline. Whether it's the infectious joy of a celebratory tune or the heart-wrenching pathos of a poignant ballad, playback singers infuse their performances with unparalleled versatility, ensuring that the music remains relatable and resonant. Their collaborative efforts extend beyond the recording studio, leaving an indelible mark on Indian cinema's musical richness and emotional depth, endowing it with a timeless legacy that continues to captivate audiences across generations.

The Artistry of Playback Singers: Technical Prowess and Emotional Resonance

Playback singers are revered for their exceptional vocal quality, which is a hallmark of their artistry in the world of music. Their voices possess a rare combination of technical prowess and emotional depth, allowing them to deliver performances that are both technically flawless and emotionally resonant. These singers have undergone rigorous training to develop their vocal range, control, and precision, enabling them to hit high and low notes with remarkable accuracy. Their ability to maintain pitch and tone consistency throughout a song ensures a polished and enjoyable listening experience. Moreover, their capacity to infuse their renditions with genuine emotion adds a layer of depth to the music, making it emotionally charged and relatable. In essence, playback singers elevate the quality of the songs they perform, enhancing their overall impact on the audience and making them indispensable to the world of Indian film music.

The Pursuit of Vocal Consistency: Playback Singers and the Standard of Excellence in Film Music

Consistency is a hallmark of playback singers in the world of music, and it plays a pivotal role in maintaining the high standard of quality for a film's soundtrack. These skilled vocalists are known for delivering performances that are consistently top-notch, ensuring that the songs maintain a polished and professional standard throughout the film. This reliability is particularly crucial in Indian cinema, where songs often form integral parts of the storytelling process. Playback singers undergo rigorous training and practice to maintain their vocal consistency, ensuring that their pitch, tone, and delivery remain impeccable from start to finish. This dedication to maintaining a consistent level of excellence contributes significantly to the overall quality and impact of the music in a film, making playback singers indispensable assets in the world of Indian film music. Their ability to provide a reliable and polished vocal track adds depth and resonance to the cinematic experience, allowing the audience to fully immerse themselves in the emotional journey of the characters.

Versatility in Song: The Multifaceted Talent of Playback Singers in Indian Cinema

Playback singers in Indian music are defined by their remarkable versatility. They can adapt their singing styles to suit a wide range of actors and characters, making them essential to Indian cinema. Their versatility spans various musical genres, from classical to contemporary, allowing them to seamlessly transition between different styles while tailoring their performances to match on-screen characters. This adaptability ensures technically proficient and emotionally resonant songs, enriching the cinematic experience by making music integral to character development and storytelling, transcending genre boundaries, and adding depth to the narrative.

The Emotion Enchanters: Playback Singers and the Power of Emotional Expression in Film Music

Playback singers hold a crucial role in elevating the emotional impact of songs within the context of Indian cinema. Their exceptional talent lies in their ability to convey a wide spectrum of emotions through their singing, making their performances a poignant and resonant force. Whether it's the exuberance of a romantic melody that radiates love, the infectious joy of a celebratory tune, the poignant melancholy of a soul-stirring ballad, or the fervent longing expressed in a song, playback singers bring these emotions to life with extraordinary depth and authenticity. Their emotive renditions complement the on-screen performances of actors, enriching the audience's connection with the characters and the storyline. By infusing their singing with genuine feeling and nuance, playback singers play a pivotal role in making the songs a powerful tool for storytelling, imbuing them with a sense of universality and emotional resonance that transcends language and culture, making them an indispensable element of Indian film music.

The Art of Lip-Sync: Playback Singers and the Synchronization of Music and Performance in Indian Cinema

In Indian cinema, actors typically do not perform live singing during song sequences; instead, they rely on the practice of lip-syncing to pre-recorded playback singer vocals. This strategic approach serves multiple purposes. Firstly, it allows actors to concentrate fully on their performance, enabling them to convey the required emotions, expressions, and choreography with precision. Secondly, by using playback singers, the songs maintain a consistent and flawless quality, as these vocalists are highly trained professionals who can deliver technically impeccable and emotionally charged renditions. Additionally, this method ensures that the music is of the highest standard, enhancing the overall cinematic experience. Ultimately, this division of labor between actors and playback singers allows for a seamless fusion of compelling on-screen performances and outstanding musical compositions, solidifying the role of playback singers as indispensable contributors to Indian film music.

Harmonizing Diversity: The Vast Spectrum of Playback Singers in Indian Cinema

Indian cinema takes pride in its diverse array of playback singers, each possessing a distinct vocal style, range, and artistic essence. This rich tapestry of vocal talent grants filmmakers the flexibility to select the perfect singer for a particular song, thereby ensuring a vast spectrum of musical styles in Indian films. Whether it's the mellifluous and timeless quality of Lata Mangeshkar, the charismatic versatility of Kishore Kumar, the evocative depth of Asha Bhosle, or the dynamic range of Mohammed Rafi, each singer brings their unique signature to the songs they perform. This diversity allows filmmakers to craft songs that align seamlessly with the film's narrative, character personalities, and emotional nuances. Consequently, the myriad vocal styles available enrich the cinematic experience, offering audiences a captivating array of musical experiences that cater to a wide range of tastes, moods, and storytelling requirements. The diversity of playback singers is a testament to the inclusivity and artistic richness of Indian cinema's musical landscape.

Legends of Playback Singing: The Enduring Impact of Iconic Voices in Indian Cinema

Over the decades, Indian cinema has been graced by the emergence of legendary playback singers who have made an enduring impact on the industry and achieved iconic status. The likes of Lata Mangeshkar, Kishore Kumar, Asha Bhosle, and numerous others have transcended mere artists to become cultural icons. Their extraordinary vocal talents, versatility, and emotive depth have not only shaped the landscape of Indian film music but have also left an indelible mark on the hearts and minds of audiences across generations. These luminaries have lent their voices to countless memorable songs that have become timeless classics, deeply embedded in the fabric of Indian culture. Their legacy extends far beyond their individual careers, as they continue to inspire and influence contemporary artists, aspiring playback singers, and music enthusiasts worldwide, underscoring their profound and lasting impact on the world of Indian cinema and music.

Versatility Unleashed: Playback Singers and the Diverse Musical Palette of Indian Cinema

Playback singers in Indian cinema possess a remarkable ability to traverse an expansive spectrum of musical genres, ranging from classical and semi-classical to folk, pop, rock, and fusion. This unparalleled diversity in their repertoire provides Indian cinema with a vast canvas to explore and experiment with an array of musical styles. It empowers filmmakers to tailor the music to suit the thematic essence, narrative requirements, and character personalities of their films. Whether it's the exquisite intricacies of classical ragas and the timeless appeal of folk melodies, the vibrant rhythms of pop and rock, or the innovative fusion of traditional and contemporary elements, playback singers adeptly navigate these musical terrains. This dynamic versatility ensures that Indian cinema continually evolves its musical expressions, adapts to changing tastes, and remains a cultural powerhouse that can both honor tradition and embrace innovation in the world of film music. The range and adaptability of playback singers are essential components that contribute to the ever-evolving musical landscape of Indian cinema.

Harmonizing the Lyrics: Playback Singers and Lyricists Crafting Impactful Songs in Indian Cinema

Playback singers collaborate closely with lyricists to ensure the seamless integration of lyrics with the film's narrative and character development. This collaboration is a critical aspect of creating impactful songs in Indian cinema. The lyrics are not just words set to music; they are an integral part of storytelling. Playback singers work hand in hand with lyricists to understand the emotional nuances, thematic context, and character motivations within a song. This collaboration allows them to infuse their renditions with the appropriate emotional depth and resonance, ensuring that the audience connects deeply with the characters' feelings and the overall narrative. The singer's interpretation plays a pivotal role in conveying the lyrical message effectively, adding another layer of artistry to the song. In essence, the partnership between playback singers and lyricists is a harmonious synergy that brings the magic of Indian film music to life, making it an essential and cherished component of the cinematic experience.

Playback Singers in Indian Cinema: Elevating Character Development through Emotive Renditions

In the Indian film industry, songs play a crucial role in character development, and playback singers are essential for this process. Their emotive performances breathe life into on-screen characters, establishing their personalities and emotional journeys. Whether it's the passion of a romantic ballad, the introspection of a soliloquy, or the infectious energy of a dance number, the singer's rendition connects the audience with the character's inner thoughts and emotions. This connection fosters a deeper bond between the audience and the characters, enhancing their understanding of motivations, desires, and conflicts, making them more vivid and relatable within the cinematic narrative. In essence, songs are a vital part of character development, infusing depth and emotion into the fictional personas, bringing the audience closer to their hearts.

The Harmonious Collaboration: Playback Singers and Film Composers Crafting Emotional Narratives in Indian Cinema

Moreover, the collaboration between playback singers and film composers is a dynamic process that involves interpreting the character's psyche and the emotional nuances of a particular scene. These singers possess the remarkable ability to convey the innermost feelings and struggles of the characters, translating them into the lyrics and melodies they perform. This synergy between music, lyrics, and vocal delivery is a testament to the artistry of playback singers and their contribution to the holistic storytelling experience in Indian cinema. The emotional depth and connection forged through these songs elevate the entire cinematic narrative, making it an immersive and enriching journey for the audience, and showcasing the profound impact of playback singers in shaping the characters and their stories. Their role goes beyond just providing a voice; they become storytellers in their own right, conveying the heart and soul of the characters, and by extension, the culture and emotions that define Indian cinema.

Captivating the Stage: Playback Singers' Enchanting Live Performances

Successful playback singers often extend their talents beyond the recording studio and grace the stage with live performances in concerts and musical events. These live shows are eagerly anticipated by fans and serve as a platform for the singer to showcase their vocal prowess, stage presence, and charismatic connection with the audience. The energy and excitement generated during these performances are electric, as fans get to witness their favorite playback singers interpreting beloved songs in a dynamic and interactive setting. These concerts not only provide a rare opportunity for fans to experience the magic of their favorite songs in a live environment but also demonstrate the singer's versatility as they navigate diverse musical genres and emotional depths on stage. These performances are a testament to the enduring appeal and star power of playback singers, underscoring their ability to captivate and enthrall audiences not only through their recorded music but also through their compelling live shows.

Song Placement

Song placement in films, especially within the context of Indian cinema, is a multifaceted and dynamic storytelling tool. It serves as a bridge between the narrative and the audience's emotions, providing a unique avenue for character development, plot progression, and entertainment. These songs are meticulously crafted, with an emphasis on lyrics, composition, choreography, and visual aesthetics, ensuring that they seamlessly integrate into the film's overarching narrative and thematic framework. Whether it's the effervescent celebration of love in a romantic melody or the high-energy rhythms of a dance sequence, songs enhance the audience's connection with the characters, allowing them to experience their emotions, dreams, and aspirations on a profound level. Moreover, songs serve as a universal language, transcending linguistic and cultural boundaries, making them an essential and memorable component of the cinematic experience. Here's a detailed explanation of song placement in films:

Harmonizing Emotions: The Potent Role of Songs in Storytelling

Emotional expression in storytelling is artfully conveyed through songs, which serve as powerful vehicles for amplifying the depth of characters' emotions and setting the mood of a scene. These melodic compositions transcend mere words and allow characters to immerse themselves in a sea of emotions, whether it's the tender intimacy of a romantic duet that speaks volumes about love's passion, a soulful melody that delves into the complexities of inner turmoil and reflection, or an infectious, upbeat track that effortlessly captures the jubilant spirit of a moment. Songs wield the remarkable ability to intertwine lyrics and melodies, creating a harmonious synergy that resonates deeply with audiences, stirring their own emotions, and forging a profound connection between the story's narrative and the human experience.

Songs as Mirrors: Unveiling Character Depths in Narrative Development

Character development within a narrative is intricately woven through the transformative power of songs, as they serve as windows into a character's psyche, history, and emotional evolution. The selection of a particular song, its lyrics, and the character's interpretation of it become a compelling means to unveil the intricate layers of their personality, their past experiences, and the tumultuous journey of their emotions. Whether through a haunting ballad that unveils hidden vulnerabilities, a defiant anthem that reflects their strength and determination, or a nostalgic tune that harks back to their formative years, songs become poignant mirrors that reflect the innermost thoughts, desires, and motivations of these fictional beings. In doing so, songs not only deepen our understanding of the character but also establish a profound and lasting connection between the audience and the narrative, making character development a harmonious symphony of emotion and storytelling.

Melodic Narratives: Songs as Catalysts for Plot Advancement and Emotional Retrospection

Narrative advancement finds a captivating ally in songs, as they serve as dynamic tools to propel the plot forward by delivering vital information or contextualizing key events. In the storytelling tapestry, a well-placed song sequence can act as a narrative linchpin, drawing viewers or readers into a crucial moment of the past through a mesmerizing flashback. These sequences unfold like lyrical time capsules, recounting pivotal past events with vivid emotion and detail, thereby enriching the storyline's tapestry. Whether it's a haunting ballad that unveils the origin of a protagonist's trauma or a celebratory anthem that narrates the historical turning point of a community, songs act as sonic storytellers, transcending the boundaries of time and space to intricately weave together the threads of a narrative, ensuring that essential plot elements are delivered in a melodious and memorable manner.

Entertainment Extravaganza: The Joyful Impact of Songs in Storytelling

Beyond their narrative roles, songs serve as a vibrant source of entertainment, infusing a burst of joy and delight into the audience's experience. These musical interludes bring the narrative to life with energetic dance numbers that set the stage ablaze, catchy tunes that linger in the viewer's memory long after the credits roll, and visually stunning sequences that captivate the senses. They elevate the overall entertainment quotient, transforming a passive viewing experience into an active engagement with the story. Through the magic of song and dance, viewers are transported to a realm where emotions are expressed with exuberance and storytelling takes on a vivacious and dynamic form, fostering a sense of enjoyment that resonates deeply with the audience and leaves an indelible mark on their cinematic or literary journey.

Harmonizing Culture: The Cultural Significance of Songs in Indian Cinema

In Indian cinema, songs bear profound cultural significance, acting as vibrant mirrors reflecting the diverse traditions and celebrations that define the tapestry of the nation. These musical interludes go far beyond mere entertainment, serving as conduits for the exploration of regional music and dance forms that hold a deep-rooted place in the hearts of audiences. Whether it's the exuberant energy of a Punjabi Bhangra or the graceful expressions of classical Kathak, songs encapsulate the essence of India's rich and multifaceted cultural heritage. They become platforms for the celebration of festivals, rituals, and customs, allowing filmmakers to pay homage to the mosaic of cultures that make up the Indian subcontinent. These cinematic musical journeys not only entertain but also educate, fostering a sense of pride and appreciation for the nation's cultural diversity while transcending linguistic and geographical boundaries to unite viewers in their shared appreciation of the Indian artistic legacy.

Diverse Melodies: The Multifaceted World of Songs in Cinema

In the world of cinema, musical variety reigns supreme, as films strategically incorporate a spectrum of songs to cater to diverse tastes and genres. This musical tapestry is carefully woven with romantic ballads that tug at the heartstrings, dance numbers that ignite the senses with infectious energy, melancholic melodies that resonate with sorrow and introspection, and devotional hymns that connect with the spiritual dimensions of the narrative. Such diversity ensures that the audience embarks on a multifaceted musical journey, resonating with the myriad emotions and themes threaded throughout the film's narrative. These songs become more than just auditory accompaniments; they are emotional anchors, expertly crafted to evoke empathy, elation, or reflection, thereby enriching the viewer's cinematic experience by offering a comprehensive and dynamic soundscape that mirrors the complexities of human emotions and storytelling.

Sensational Spectacles: The Visual Splendor of Song Sequences in Cinema

Song sequences within films transcend mere auditory experiences to become breathtaking visual spectacles, where elaborate choreography, vibrant and meticulously designed costumes, and mesmerizing set pieces converge to elevate the film's visual appeal to extraordinary heights. These sequences are choreographed with precision and artistic flair, transforming the screen into a canvas where movement, colour, and emotion blend seamlessly. Characters become dancers, their every step a brushstroke of expression, while the sets become immersive worlds that transport the audience to new realms. These visual extravaganzas not only enchant the senses but also etch indelible memories, serving as the film's iconic moments that linger long after the credits roll. They are the epitome of cinematic artistry, where storytelling transcends words and melodies to create a symphony of visual delight, ensuring that the audience is not only emotionally moved but also visually captivated.

Songs as Mood Architects: Enhancing Cinematic Atmosphere and EmotionsTop of Form

Songs wield a remarkable ability to serve as mood enhancers within the cinematic landscape, elevating the emotional atmosphere and atmosphere of a film with finesse. Through the harmony of music, lyrics, and visuals, they become atmospheric catalysts, capable of transforming a scene's ambiance with profound impact. Whether set against a picturesque backdrop, they infuse a romantic or dreamy aura into the narrative, invoking a sense of longing and enchantment. Conversely, in a tense or suspenseful context, a haunting melody can ratchet up the suspense and anticipation, leaving the audience on the edge of their seats. These musical choices, carefully tailored to the storyline, have the power to amplify the emotional resonance of the film, drawing viewers deeper into its world and heightening their engagement with the characters' experiences. Thus, songs become the sonic architects of mood, constructing and sculpting the cinematic landscape to evoke a wide spectrum of emotions, from euphoria to melancholy, and from excitement to contemplation.

Iconic Songs: The Timeless Symbols of Cinematic Legacy

Cinematic iconography is profoundly shaped by the indelible mark left by iconic songs and their accompanying sequences, which become integral components of a film's cultural and historical legacy. These musical masterpieces often transcend their role as mere audiovisual elements to become enduring symbols, inseparably linked to particular actors, characters, or pivotal moments in film history. Such songs are not merely heard but etched into the collective memory, becoming cultural touchstones that evoke nostalgia and emotion. They breathe life into characters, immortalize performances, and define eras within the cinematic landscape. These musical gems wield the power to transcend time and generation, their notes and visuals transcending language and culture to connect with audiences on a universal and profound level, ensuring their enduring status as cinematic treasures and icons.

Songs as Emotional Bridges: Forging Deep Audience Connections in Cinema

Audience engagement in cinema is artfully achieved through well-placed songs that act as emotional conduits, forging a deep and resonant connection between viewers and the characters they're following. These musical interludes have the unique ability to transcend the boundaries of the screen, eliciting a visceral response from the audience by immersing them in the characters' emotions and experiences. Memorable songs, in particular, possess the power to linger in the collective consciousness long after the film's release, creating an enduring cultural impact. These tunes become more than just aural companions to the narrative; they take on lives of their own, influencing fashion, language, and even societal norms. Audiences find themselves humming these melodies, dancing to their beats, and, most importantly, reliving the film's emotions. In this way, songs not only enrich the cinematic experience but also become timeless markers of cultural significance, binding generations together through the shared emotions and memories they evoke.

Musical Artistry in Film: Spotlight on Playback Singers, Music Directors, and Composers

Song placement within films serves as an invaluable platform for the showcase of musical talent, spotlighting the prowess of playback singers, music directors, and composers whose contributions are integral to a film's success. Playback singers, with their melodious and emotive voices, breathe life into the characters, lending them a unique vocal identity that resonates deeply with the audience. The music director, as the creative maestro behind the scenes, orchestrates the entire sonic landscape, skillfully weaving melodies that harmonize with the narrative's emotions. Composers infuse the film with memorable tunes that linger in the hearts and minds of viewers, enhancing the overall impact. Together, these artists craft a symphony that transcends the screen, evoking emotions and enhancing storytelling. Their talents are instrumental in elevating the film's emotional depth and making it resonate with audiences, ultimately adding a layer of artistry and enchantment to the cinematic experience that would be incomplete without their remarkable contributions.

Striking the Right Chord: Songs as Pre-release Marketing Marvels in Film Promotion

In film promotion and marketing, songs play a pivotal role as powerful tools for generating buzz and anticipation before a film's release. The release of music videos and audio tracks becomes a strategic maneuver to captivate and engage the audience. These pre-release musical offerings not only provide a tantalizing glimpse into the film's soundtrack but also serve as alluring teasers, offering a sneak peek into the visual and auditory splendor that awaits viewers. The synergy between music and visuals in these promotional materials creates a captivating spectacle that ignites curiosity and excitement. Furthermore, these songs often become anthems associated with the film, cultivating a dedicated fanbase and boosting the film's visibility. Thus, songs wield their promotional power to not only tantalize the senses but also to effectively create a groundswell of interest and enthusiasm, making them indispensable assets in the film industry's marketing arsenal.

Indian Cinema's Timeless Tradition: Songs as the Heartbeat of the Cinematic Experience

In the landscape of Indian cinema, songs have evolved to become a cherished and intrinsic part of the cinematic experience, aligning with a deep-seated tradition that resonates with the expectations of audiences. Over the years, this cultural phenomenon has ingrained itself in the collective psyche of moviegoers, creating an enduring bond between music and storytelling. Indian audiences have come to expect not just songs, but an entire spectrum of emotions, storytelling, and cultural richness conveyed through these musical interludes. It has become a tradition that transcends linguistic, regional, and generational boundaries, uniting diverse audiences in their shared anticipation of the emotional depth and artistic expression that songs bring to films. As a result, song placement in Indian cinema has transcended the realm of mere entertainment, evolving into a cultural legacy that continues to enchant and captivate, making it an integral and cherished aspect of the cinematic journey for generations of movie enthusiasts.

Lyrical Depth

Lyrical depth is a hallmark of Indian song lyrics, which explore themes like love, longing, philosophy, and social commentary with profound poetry and emotional content. This depth, combined with emotive music and powerful vocal performances, contributes to the enduring appeal of Indian music globally. Indian song lyrics connect deeply with listeners, evoking strong emotions and resonating with the human experience. Whether conveying love's joys or sorrows, these lyrics enrich the nation's musical tapestry and transcend borders and cultures to create a lasting impact on the global music scene. This fusion of profound lyrics with emotive music is a treasure trove of artistic expression and a source of cultural pride.

Indian Song Lyrics: A Tapestry of Poetic Richness and Cultural Significance

Indian song lyrics are renowned for their profound poetic richness, and they serve as a testament to the literary artistry deeply embedded in the culture. Songwriters and lyricists weave intricate tapestries of language, employing a myriad of literary devices, including intricate rhyme schemes, metaphors, allegories, and allusions, to craft verses that transcend the boundaries of mere entertainment. These poetic compositions elevate the songs beyond their melodic elements, resonating with audiences on both emotional and intellectual levels. Each song becomes a lyrical journey, conveying profound emotions, philosophical musings, and cultural nuances. These verses are not only meant to be heard but also to be savored, contemplated, and cherished, enriching the audience's experience by adding layers of depth and meaning to the narrative. In this way, Indian song lyrics stand as a testament to the enduring tradition of poetry in the subcontinent, leaving an indelible mark on the hearts and minds of those who engage with them.

The Profound Emotional Resonance of Indian Song Lyrics: A Journey Through the Spectrum of Human Sentiment

The emotional resonance of Indian song lyrics is a testament to their profound lyrical depth. These verses possess a unique ability to evoke a rich spectrum of emotions with unparalleled intensity and sensitivity. Whether it's the palpable ardor of love, the infectious euphoria of joy, the heart-wrenching ache of sorrow, the wistful nostalgia of bygone days, the fiery fervor of anger, or the profound depths of existential contemplation, Indian songs have a lyrical composition for every human sentiment. The power of these verses lies in their ability to encapsulate the nuances of the human experience, transcending language barriers to touch the hearts and souls of listeners. They become a source of solace, catharsis, and celebration, forging an emotional connection between the audience and the narrative that is deeply resonant and enduring, making Indian song lyrics an unparalleled vehicle for the expression of the most intricate and universal facets of human emotion.

Love and Romance in Indian Song Lyrics: A Timeless Exploration of Passion, Longing, and Heartache

Love and romance stand as enduring pillars in Indian song lyrics, serving as a timeless and ubiquitous theme that has captivated audiences for generations. These verses, rich in emotional depth and poetic flourish, intricately explore the multifaceted nature of love. They narrate the ecstasy of newfound love, where hearts entwine with joyous abandon, and the world is bathed in the hues of passion. Conversely, they also delve into the poignant pain of unrequited affection, where love's longing is juxtaposed with the ache of separation. These songs, often accompanied by evocative melodies and expressive vocals, become anthems of the heart, resonating with listeners' personal experiences and emotions. Whether celebrating the intoxicating highs or lamenting the heart-wrenching lows of love, Indian love songs navigate the labyrinth of human relationships with nuance and sensitivity, making them enduring favorites that continue to enchant and evoke profound emotions in audiences worldwide.

Longing and Separation in Indian Song Lyrics: A Melodic Exploration of Love's Bittersweet Ache

Themes of longing and separation are exquisitely explored in numerous Indian songs, where verses become poignant vessels for conveying the profound ache of being distanced from a beloved. These musical narratives encapsulate the essence of yearning, painting a vivid emotional landscape where love is tinged with the bittersweet hues of distance and separation. The lyrics, often accompanied by haunting melodies and soul-stirring vocals, evoke a profound sense of melancholy, resonating with the deep and universal human experience of longing for someone who is physically or emotionally distant. These songs become cathartic outlets for those grappling with separation, offering solace and companionship in shared emotional turmoil. In the intricate tapestry of Indian songwriting, longing and separation form an integral thread, weaving together a symphony of emotions that capture the essence of love's enduring, poignant, and sometimes heartbreaking journey.

Indian Song Lyrics: Exploring the Philosophical and Existential Depths of the Human Psyche

Indian song lyrics extend far beyond matters of the heart, transcending into a realm of profound philosophical and existential exploration. These songs serve as lyrical portals to the contemplative depths of the human psyche, delving into the intricacies of existence, spirituality, and the quest for meaning in life. Through intricate metaphors, allegorical narratives, and deeply introspective verses, they invite listeners on a philosophical journey that traverses the complexities of the human condition. These songs become thought-provoking meditations, stirring the intellect and encouraging introspection, often offering profound insights into the mysteries of existence. In this manner, Indian song lyrics become more than just musical compositions; they become poetic vessels for the dissemination of age-old wisdom, inviting audiences to ponder life's grand questions and seek solace in the beauty of lyrical contemplation.

Indian Song Lyrics: Celebrating the Majesty of Nature through Poetic Odes

Indian songwriters possess a remarkable propensity for drawing profound inspiration from the awe-inspiring canvas of the natural world. Their verses serve as poetic odes to the beauty that envelops us, with lyrics that intricately weave the splendor of landscapes, the ebb and flow of seasons, and the magic of natural phenomena into the fabric of their compositions. These songs forge a powerful connection between human emotions and the majesty of the environment, transforming the act of listening into a sensory journey through the wonders of nature. As listeners are transported to lush meadows, serene riversides, or misty mountain peaks through the evocative imagery of song, they experience a profound sense of harmony with the world around them. Indian songs that celebrate nature's beauty not only evoke admiration for the physical world but also evoke a deeper, spiritual connection, reminding us of our place within the grand tapestry of the natural world and the indomitable power of lyrical expression to capture its ineffable allure.

Indian Songs as Cultural Tapestries: Weaving History, Tradition, and Folklore into Lyrical Narratives

Indian songs serve as cultural tapestries, intricately weaving together a rich tapestry of cultural and historical references, as well as echoes of folklore and tradition, within their lyrical narratives. These references become poignant signposts in the storytelling, offering valuable cultural context and historical depth to the song's thematic and emotional elements. They act as a bridge between the past and present, fostering an appreciation for the heritage, traditions, and legacies that shape Indian culture. Whether it's celebrating a festival, narrating a historical event, or paying homage to a cultural icon, these songs become more than just melodic compositions; they are living embodiments of India's diverse and multifaceted cultural identity. In doing so, they enrich the cinematic or musical experience by not only evoking emotions but also fostering a deeper understanding and connection to the cultural heritage that they so beautifully encapsulate.

Indian Songs as Catalysts for Social Commentary and Change: Spotlighting Contemporary Issues Through Lyrical Narratives

Within the arena of Indian songs, there exists a profound avenue for social commentary and the exploration of contemporary issues. These lyrical narratives transcend the confines of melody and rhythm to become powerful platforms for addressing pressing societal concerns such as inequality, injustice, and prevailing norms. By weaving compelling verses that resonate with the collective consciousness, these songs serve as catalysts for social awareness and change. They provide a poignant mirror to the challenges and disparities faced by society, provoking thought and igniting conversations that often lead to transformative action. Through their emotive storytelling, they not only entertain but also inspire, harnessing the emotive power of music to spotlight issues that might otherwise remain hidden or ignored. In this way, these songs become more than just artistic expressions; they become a vital force in challenging the status quo, advocating for change, and shaping the social discourse of the nation.

Indian Song Lyrics: A Spiritual Journey Across Faiths and Traditions

India's kaleidoscope of religious and spiritual traditions finds eloquent expression through song lyrics that serve as profound channels for devotion, spiritual awakening, and the quest for enlightenment. These lyrical compositions traverse the spectrum of faith, from the fervent devotion of bhajans and kirtans that resonate in Hindu temples to the Sufi qawwalis that channel mystical devotion within Islam. Whether it's the mystical poetry of Rumi, Kabir, or the Bhakti and Sufi saints, or the serene hymns of the Guru Granth Sahib in Sikhism, these songs become vessels for spiritual transcendence, nurturing a deep connection between the human soul and the divine. They carry the essence of faith and the yearning for spiritual growth, uniting diverse religious communities through the universal language of music and devotion. These devotional and spiritual themes in Indian song lyrics transcend religious boundaries, offering a transcendent experience that resonates with individuals seeking solace, inner peace, and a deeper connection with the divine.

India's Linguistic Mosaic: Celebrating Diversity Through Lyrical Expression in Different Languages and Traditions

India's lyrical landscape is a testament to the nation's extraordinary linguistic diversity, with each region and language boasting its own rich poetic traditions that contribute to the depth and variety of song lyrics. From the poetic verses of Tamil Sangam poetry to the classical elegance of Sanskrit shlokas, the poignant ballads of Bengali Baul songs to the rhythmic beauty of Punjabi folk lyrics, India's linguistic tapestry is an endless source of inspiration for songwriters. This diversity not only adds a rich tapestry of melodies but also imbues each song with a distinct cultural identity, capturing the nuances of regional traditions, customs, and emotions. In doing so, these songs become cultural ambassadors, celebrating India's kaleidoscope of languages and traditions while fostering an appreciation for the nation's linguistic diversity and the enduring power of lyrical expression to connect people across geographical and linguistic boundaries.

The Symbiotic Harmony of Lyrics and Music: Crafting an Immersive and Emotionally Resonant Musical Experience

The synergy between lyrics and music in songwriting creates a harmonious and immersive musical experience that elevates the depth of lyrical expression. This collaboration is a delicate dance where the composition and melody become integral partners to the words, enriching the narrative with emotional resonance. The music not only complements but also amplifies the sentiments conveyed in the lyrics, adding layers of depth and nuance. Whether it's the haunting melancholy of a sad song accentuated by a mournful melody, the exuberant celebration of joy matched with an upbeat composition, or the introspective introspection of philosophical verses underscored by a contemplative tune, this partnership between lyrics and music captures the essence of the narrative with unparalleled precision. Together, they create a holistic musical journey, where the combined effect transcends mere words and melodies, touching the very soul of the audience and leaving an indelible mark on their hearts and minds.

Playback Singers: The Emotive Interpreters Who Breathe Life into Lyrical Narratives

Playback singers are the virtuosic interpreters who breathe life into song lyrics through their emotive vocal renditions, making them a pivotal component of the lyrical narrative. Their extraordinary talent lies in their ability to not just sing the words but to convey the profound emotions, subtle nuances, and intricate layers of meaning embedded within the lyrics. Whether it's the tender quiver in their voice that evokes heartache in a melancholic ballad or the soaring crescendo that ignites passion in a romantic melody, playback singers become the vessels through which the emotional essence of the song is channeled. Their artistry transcends the boundaries of language and culture, forging an emotional connection between the listener and the lyrical narrative that is immediate and profound. It is their interpretive skill that adds depth and resonance to the song's impact, making the lyrical journey a transcendent and unforgettable experience for audiences worldwide.

Lyrical Depth: Forging a Profound Connection Between Music and the Human Experience

Lyrical depth is a paramount factor in forging a powerful and enduring connection between the audience and a song. When lyrics are imbued with substance, meaning, and emotional authenticity, they have the remarkable ability to resonate with listeners on a profound level. Meaningful verses have the capacity to evoke empathy, spark nostalgia, or ignite introspection, creating a sense of shared experience that transcends the boundaries of the individual. Such songs become mirrors to the listener's own emotions, experiences, and memories, providing a soundtrack to their lives and leaving an indelible impression that endures long after the music fades. This emotional resonance transforms a song from mere auditory entertainment into a vessel for human connection, making it a treasured and cherished part of the listener's personal journey, and highlighting the transformative power of lyrical expression to touch hearts, inspire, and provoke thought.

Musical Instruments and Cultural Significance

"Instrumentation" in film music refers to the process of carefully selecting and utilizing various musical instruments to compose and arrange the soundtrack of a film. In the vibrant landscape of Indian cinema, this choice of musical instruments becomes a pivotal element in conveying not only the emotional depth of a scene but also the cultural and regional context of the story. India's diverse linguistic, geographical, and cultural tapestry is beautifully mirrored through its music, and the instrumentation chosen for a film score can accentuate this diversity. Moreover, Indian cinema often incorporates cultural music forms that are deeply rooted in tradition, including folk music, classical compositions, and regional styles, which serve to celebrate and showcase the country's rich and multifaceted cultural heritage. These musical choices are not only artistic but also profoundly symbolic, contributing to the narrative's authenticity and emotional resonance while fostering a sense of unity in diversity that is a hallmark of Indian culture and cinema. Here's a detailed explanation of how instrumentation and cultural music contribute to Indian film music:

Instrumentation in Indian Film Music

Reflecting Cultural and Regional Context: Harmonizing the Past and Present, Exploring India's Diverse Musical Instruments in Film Scores

India's rich musical heritage encompasses a wide array of traditional and regional musical instruments that hold deep cultural significance. The choice of instruments in Indian film music is a dynamic and diverse process, influenced by factors such as the geographical location, cultural context, and the specific time period depicted in the film's narrative. For instance, in a Bollywood film set in northern India, one might hear the resonant sounds of the sitar or the vibrant beats of the tabla, both quintessential to North Indian classical and folk music. Conversely, a film set in the southern state of Tamil Nadu might feature instruments like the mridangam or veena, which are prominent in the region's classical traditions. Moreover, historical films may incorporate period-specific instruments, creating a sonic tapestry that transports the audience to a different era. This rich diversity of instruments not only adds authenticity to the film's cultural portrayal but also enriches the musical landscape of Indian cinema, ensuring that each film's score is a unique fusion of traditional and contemporary musical elements. For example:

North Indian Cinema's Musical Tapestry: The Sitar, Tabla, Harmonium, and Sarod in Film Music

In North Indian cinema, a distinctive selection of musical instruments takes center stage in film music compositions. Among these, the sitar, tabla (a hand-drum), harmonium, and sarod are prominently featured. These instruments are deeply rooted in the classical and semi-classical music traditions of North India, and their inclusion in film music compositions reflects the region's rich musical heritage. The sitar, with its melodic and resonant strings, lends a soulful and captivating quality to compositions, often used to evoke emotional depth and beauty. The tabla, a percussion instrument, provides rhythmic intricacy and dynamic beats, infusing energy and vitality into the music. The harmonium, a portable keyboard instrument, adds harmonic and melodic textures, enhancing the overall musical arrangement. The sarod, with its complex tonalities and expressive capabilities, offers a unique sonic character that enriches the emotional palette of film scores. Together, these instruments form the backbone of North Indian cinema's musical identity, creating a cultural and musical resonance that is both distinctive and enduring.

In the Vibrant world of South Indian Cinema: The Distinctive Ensemble of Musical Instruments Shaping Film Music Compositions

In the vibrant world of South Indian cinema, a distinctive ensemble of musical instruments takes the spotlight in film music compositions, reflecting the region's deep-rooted Carnatic music tradition. Among these instruments, the mridangam (a South Indian drum), veena (a plucked string instrument), nadaswaram (a double-reed wind instrument), and ghatam (a clay pot drum) are particularly prominent. The mridangam contributes rhythmic complexity and resonance, providing a foundational beat that underpins the music's intricate rhythms. The veena adds a melodic and soulful dimension, offering a vast tonal range and emotional expressiveness to compositions. The nadaswaram, with its distinctive timbre and ornate melodies, plays a pivotal role in festive and celebratory musical contexts. The ghatam, a percussive clay pot drum, contributes earthy and rhythmic textures, adding a unique sonic flavor. Together, these instruments not only form the backbone of South Indian cinema's musical identity but also embody the rich cultural and musical tapestry of the region, infusing each film's score with authenticity and regional flavor.

Unveiling Regional Indian Cinema: The Musical Tapestry of Bengali and Marathi Films

In regional Indian cinema, such as Bengali or Marathi cinema, a unique selection of instruments often takes prominence, reflecting the distinct musical and cultural traditions of those regions. For instance, in Bengali cinema, the santoor, a dulcimer-like instrument with strings that are struck with mallets, is frequently featured. The santoor's melodious and evocative tones align with the nuanced and emotive storytelling of Bengali cinema, adding depth and poignancy to its musical compositions. On the other hand, in Marathi cinema, the dholki, a double-headed hand-drum, is a prominent instrument. Its rhythmic and percussive qualities infuse Marathi film music with vibrant energy, particularly in celebratory and folk music contexts. These region-specific instruments not only contribute to the authenticity of the film's cultural portrayal but also showcase the diversity of India's musical heritage, ensuring that each regional cinema has its unique and resonant musical identity.

Instrumental Alchemy in Film Music: Crafting Mood and Atmosphere Through Sound

The tonal quality and timbre of each musical instrument are distinctive, and filmmakers harness these inherent qualities to craft the mood and atmosphere of a scene. In film music composition, instruments become the palette from which emotions and sentiments are painted. For instance, the soft, melodic tones of the flute can be employed to evoke a sense of romance, serenity, or nostalgia, its ethereal qualities creating an ambiance of tenderness or longing. Conversely, the tabla's intricate rhythmic patterns, with their dynamic and percussive timbre, can infuse a dance sequence with vibrant energy and excitement, setting a lively and infectious tempo that compels the audience to move along with the rhythm. Whether it's the resonant and emotive strains of a violin for a melancholic moment or the thundering drums of a war sequence, the choice of instruments becomes a powerful tool for filmmakers to convey emotions, establish atmosphere, and enhance the overall narrative impact of a scene, contributing to the rich tapestry of film music.

The Emotional Power of Instrumentation in Film Music: Crafting Authentic Feelings and Resonance

The choice of instrumentation in film music wields a profound emotional impact on the audience, becoming a direct conduit for eliciting and intensifying emotions. Each instrument possesses a unique emotional resonance, and filmmakers strategically leverage this quality to communicate feelings and sentiments. For example, the hauntingly resonant notes of the sarangi, with their melancholic and soulful timbre, have the power to evoke profound sorrow, longing, or introspection. On the other hand, the vibrant and rhythmic beats of the dhol drum, with their infectious and celebratory quality, serve as a musical embodiment of joy, festivity, and exuberance. These instruments become emotional touchpoints in a film, enabling viewers to connect deeply with the characters' experiences and the narrative's thematic layers. Whether it's the tender strains of a flute during a romantic confession or the thunderous percussion of war drums during a climactic battle, the choice of instrumentation is a pivotal element in evoking and amplifying the emotional impact of a scene, leaving a lasting impression on the audience.

Cultural Music in Indian Film Music

Instrumentation and the integration of cultural music are vital components of Indian film music, shaping the essence of cinematic storytelling. The choice of musical instruments is an art form in itself, intricately weaving cultural and regional nuances into the film's narrative. Each instrument, whether the flute or tabla, adds emotional and tonal qualities, painting the mood of a scene. Additionally, the inclusion of cultural music, like folk and traditional elements, celebrates India's diverse musical heritage, connecting with viewers emotionally and culturally. This fusion of music and culture defines Indian cinema, providing a unique and immersive experience that entertains, educates, and transcends cultural boundaries, fostering a deeper appreciation of India's multifaceted artistic traditions.

Celebrating India's Cultural Diversity through Folk and Traditional Music in Cinema

Indian cinema, known for its celebration of cultural diversity, frequently incorporates folk and traditional music into its soundtracks as a means of honoring the nation's profound cultural richness. The varied regions of India boast their own distinct musical traditions, and filmmakers adeptly weave this diversity into their cinematic narratives. By doing so, they establish a cultural resonance that connects with audiences hailing from different backgrounds and linguistic regions. For instance, a Bollywood film set in rural Punjab may feature the energetic rhythms of Bhangra music, infusing the narrative with the lively spirit of Punjabi folk celebrations. Conversely, a South Indian film might embrace the soul-stirring melodies of classical Carnatic music to evoke the region's cultural authenticity. By incorporating these indigenous musical elements, Indian cinema not only enriches its storytelling but also pays homage to the diverse tapestry of India's musical heritage, fostering a deep sense of cultural pride and unity among its viewers.

Folk Music in Indian Cinema: A Cultural Homage and Narrative Authenticity

The inclusion of folk music in Indian cinema carries immense cultural significance as it taps into the deep-rooted heritage and traditions of diverse regions across the country. Filmmakers who incorporate folk elements into their soundtracks pay a profound homage to the local customs and practices, connecting the narrative with the genuine authenticity of the setting and characters. Whether it's the rustic melodies of Rajasthan echoing through the sand dunes, the spirited rhythms of Maharashtra's Lavani dance, or the ethereal sounds of Assam's Bihu celebrations, folk music becomes a bridge that transports the audience directly into the heart of the culture being depicted on screen. It serves as a testament to the enduring cultural legacies of India's various regions, fostering a deeper understanding and appreciation for the richness and diversity of the nation's cultural tapestry. Moreover, the integration of folk music in film underscores the role of cinema as a custodian of cultural heritage, preserving and celebrating the traditions that make India a mosaic of unique cultural identities.

Enhancing Storytelling: Folk and Traditional Music in Indian Cinema, Weaving Culture and Storytelling

Folk and traditional music in Indian cinema are not only expressions of culture but also potent storytelling tools that enrich the narrative context. Filmmakers judiciously employ these musical traditions to deepen the storytelling process. For instance, a song rooted in the Baul music tradition of West Bengal can be strategically used to emphasize the spiritual or philosophical journey of a character. The hauntingly poetic lyrics and melodic nuances inherent in Baul music infuse the character's arc with profound depth and meaning, unraveling their inner struggles, aspirations, or quest for enlightenment. Such musical choices transcend mere entertainment, becoming a means of imparting subtext, metaphor, and emotional resonance to the narrative. By weaving folk and traditional music into the storytelling fabric, Indian cinema leverages these musical traditions as a conduit for exploring the intricate tapestry of human emotions, beliefs, and experiences, resulting in a more profound and immersive cinematic journey for the audience.

Traditional Music in Film: Guiding the Narrative Through Cultural Signposts

Traditional music serves as cultural signposts within the narrative, effectively guiding the audience toward a deeper understanding of characters and the cultural backdrop of a specific region. Filmmakers strategically use traditional music to underline a character's roots or to emphasize the cultural context of a particular locale. For example, a character's arrival in a vibrant Rajasthan setting may be accompanied by the resounding strains of traditional Rajasthani folk music, immediately establishing their connection to the region and its distinctive cultural heritage. Similarly, a scene set in the tranquil backwaters of Kerala may incorporate the melodious notes of classical Carnatic music, creating an atmosphere that resonates with the cultural authenticity of the place. These musical choices function as cultural cues, offering viewers valuable insights into the characters' backgrounds and the cultural milieu in which the story unfolds, thereby enhancing the overall narrative depth and cultural richness of the cinematic experience.

Nurturing Nostalgia: The Profound Impact of Traditional and Folk Music in Indian Cinema

Traditional and folk music in Indian cinema possess a remarkable power to elicit nostalgia and create a deep emotional connection with the audience. These musical genres often incorporate melodies, rhythms, and tunes that have been an integral part of India's cultural heritage for generations. When viewers encounter these familiar musical elements in a film, it can trigger a strong sense of nostalgia, transporting them to past memories and experiences associated with the music. This emotional resonance not only heightens the audience's immersion in the film but also imparts an aura of authenticity to the storytelling, as it mirrors the real-life experiences and cultural legacy of the people. Whether it's the soulful strains of a bhajan (devotional song) from a character's childhood or the rhythmic beats of a traditional folk dance, the inclusion of traditional and folk music engenders a feeling of familiarity that bridges the gap between the cinematic world and the audience's own cultural identity. Consequently, it results in a more relatable and emotionally resonant cinematic experience.

Traditional and Folk Music in Indian Cinema: A Resonating Ode to Cultural Preservation and Global Celebration

Furthermore, traditional and folk music in Indian cinema serves as a conduit for cultural preservation and celebration. It offers a platform for the rich and diverse musical traditions of India to be showcased and celebrated on a global stage. The inclusion of these musical forms not only adds depth to the narrative but also helps preserve and propagate the country's cultural heritage. It allows audiences, both within and outside India, to gain a deeper understanding of the nation's diverse musical traditions and the cultural context in which they are embedded. This not only fosters a sense of cultural pride but also helps bridge generational and geographical gaps, ensuring that these cherished musical traditions continue to thrive and evolve within the contemporary cinematic landscape. In this way, traditional and folk music in Indian cinema serves as a powerful medium for cultural expression, preservation, and connection.

Traditional Indian Music in Cinema: A Universal Language of Emotion and Culture

Traditional Indian music, while deeply rooted in the country's rich cultural tapestry, possesses a universal appeal that transcends geographical boundaries. Its melodies and rhythms, often characterized by their timeless and emotive qualities, possess a remarkable ability to resonate with audiences worldwide. The intricate interplay of instruments, the emotive power of vocals, and the deep spirituality often embedded in traditional compositions create a musical language that speaks to the human soul, regardless of cultural background. Consequently, when Indian cinema incorporates traditional music into its soundtracks, it not only celebrates India's musical heritage but also introduces global audiences to the enchanting and evocative world of Indian music. The universal appeal of this music fosters cross-cultural appreciation, encouraging viewers from diverse backgrounds to connect with and embrace India's rich artistic traditions, thereby strengthening the global cultural dialogue.

B. Sound Effects

Foley Artistry

Foley artistry is a critical and highly specialized aspect of filmmaking that enhances the auditory experience of a film. Foley artists use their expertise to meticulously create and synchronize sound effects, ensuring that the audience is fully immersed in the world of the film. This attention to detail and dedication to realism contribute significantly to the overall quality and impact of a movie's audio track. Foley artists are skilled in recreating a wide range of sounds that may not have been adequately captured during filming, such as footsteps on different surfaces, the rustling of clothing, or the clinking of glasses. They use various props and surfaces to mimic these sounds and precisely match them to the corresponding actions on screen. The meticulousness of their work extends to timing and spatial accuracy, as they carefully synchronize the sound effects with the actors' movements to create a seamless and immersive auditory experience. This level of craftsmanship not only enhances the realism of a film but also adds depth and emotional resonance to the storytelling, making Foley artistry an indispensable part of the cinematic process. Here's a detailed explanation of Foley artistry in film production:

Foley Artists: The Unseen Architects of Cinematic Soundscapes

The role of Foley artists in filmmaking is absolutely crucial and often overlooked, as they are the unsung heroes responsible for meticulously crafting and recording sound effects in a controlled studio setting. These highly skilled professionals collaborate closely with the film's sound designer and editor to enhance the auditory dimension of the cinematic experience. Whether it's the subtle rustling of clothing, the crunch of footsteps on gravel, the clinking of glassware, or the dramatic thud of a punch landing, Foley artists expertly re-create these sounds in a synchronized and hyper-realistic manner, ensuring that the film's audio is as compelling and immersive as its visuals. Their creative ingenuity extends to recreating sounds that might not have been adequately captured during the initial on-set recording, bringing a level of authenticity and emotional resonance to the film that would be impossible to achieve otherwise. In this collaborative effort, Foley artists are instrumental in shaping the auditory landscape of the movie, turning it into a visceral and multisensory experience for the audience.

Foley Artistry: The Precise Synchronization of Sound and Image in Filmmaking

The essence of Foley artistry lies in its relentless pursuit of realism and synchronization with on-screen actions. Foley artists meticulously watch the film multiple times, immersing themselves in the subtleties of every scene and character movement. Their craft requires an acute sense of timing and an innate ability to recreate sounds that mirror the exact nuances of the actions performed on-screen. Whether it's the delicate swish of a character's clothing, the gentle patter of raindrops, or the thunderous impact of a dramatic moment, Foley artists painstakingly time their sound effects to align with the precise moments and intensity of the visuals. This meticulous attention to detail ensures that the auditory and visual elements of the film merge seamlessly, creating an immersive and authentic cinematic experience that allows audiences to suspend disbelief and become fully engrossed in the narrative world. In this way, Foley artistry becomes an essential bridge between the tangible and the perceived, forging a connection that enhances the film's emotional impact and contributes significantly to its overall realism and sensory appeal.

Foley Artistry: Crafting Custom Sound Effects for Cinematic Realism

Foley artists are masters of ingenuity, constantly exploring and inventing ways to create custom sound effects that precisely match the on-screen actions. They employ a vast array of props and materials to achieve the desired auditory result, crafting sounds that are unique to each scene. For instance, they might use an assortment of shoes and surfaces to replicate the distinct quality of footsteps on various terrains, whether it's the crunch of gravel underfoot, the resonance of steps on wooden floors, or the muffled echo of movement on concrete surfaces. These artists are akin to sonic magicians, drawing upon their deep understanding of acoustics, materials, and the physics of sound to craft the perfect auditory accompaniment to the visual storytelling. In doing so, they breathe life into the film's audio, allowing audiences to feel every footfall, rustle of clothing, or clinking of objects, creating a sensory tapestry that enriches the cinematic experience and immerses viewers in the world of the story.

Foley Artistry: Elevating Cinematic Realism Through Everyday Sound Recreation

Foley artists possess a remarkable skill for recreating the tapestry of everyday sounds that are essential for a film's realism. Their expertise extends to capturing the mundane yet crucial auditory details of daily life, such as the subtle rustling of clothing as characters move, the precise clinking of cutlery during a meal, the distinct jingling of keys as they're handled, and the evocative creaking and squeaking of doors as they swing open or shut. These seemingly ordinary sounds are meticulously crafted by Foley artists, who utilize an array of props and techniques to ensure that every auditory element is perfectly synchronized with the on-screen action. Through their artistry, these professionals elevate the film's authenticity by infusing it with the rich and immersive soundscape of the real world, allowing viewers to not only see but also hear and feel the subtle nuances that make the cinematic experience vivid and true to life.

Foley Artistry: Crafting Character Movement Soundscapes for Cinematic Authenticity

The artistry of Foley extends its meticulous touch to character movement within a film. Foley artists are keenly attuned to the subtleties of on-screen actions, paying close attention to the nuances of character and object movement. With an astute understanding of how sound complements visuals, they recreate the swish of clothing as characters make their way through a scene, the precise handling of props that adds tactile realism to the action, or the gentle rustling of leaves as a character interacts with their environment. These artists become choreographers of sound, synchronizing their craft with the intricacies of the characters' physicality, bringing an authentic auditory dimension to each moment. In this way, Foley artists become silent collaborators in the storytelling process, ensuring that the audience is not only immersed in the visual narrative but also intimately connected with the auditory subtleties that breathe life into the characters and their world.

Foley Artistry: Constructing Cinematic Environments Through Authentic Soundscapes

The artistry of Foley extends its reach beyond individual actions to craft a comprehensive auditory environment that aligns seamlessly with the film's setting and atmosphere. Foley artists have a keen ability to replicate the ambient sounds that define a particular location, whether it's the bustling streets of a vibrant city with honking horns and chattering pedestrians, the serene tranquility of a forest with chirping birds and rustling leaves, or the comforting hum of a busy café filled with clinking cups and hushed conversations. Through their meticulous work, they become sonic architects, constructing a sonic backdrop that mirrors the visual world on screen. This not only enhances the film's realism but also engrosses the audience in the immersive experience, ensuring that the auditory environment is as authentic and evocative as the visual one. The subtlety and precision with which Foley artists craft these environmental ambiances play a pivotal role in enhancing the film's sensory richness and emotional impact.

The Emotional Artistry of Foley Sound Effects: Enhancing Character Emotions in Film

The power of Foley sound effects to influence the emotional impact of a scene cannot be overstated. It is in the subtlety of their craft that Foley artists wield a profound influence over the audience's emotional connection with the characters. Through meticulously timed and executed sound effects, they can capture the essence of a character's emotions with striking precision. A sigh can convey a deep sense of weariness or resignation, a sharp intake of breath can signify surprise or anticipation, and the gentle touch of a hand can evoke tenderness and intimacy. These nuanced auditory cues not only complement the actors' performances but also enhance them, adding layers of depth to the characters' emotional journeys. It is in these delicate details that Foley artists excel, creating a sensory landscape that resonates with the audience's own feelings and experiences, making them active participants in the narrative's emotional tapestry. In this way, Foley sound effects become a powerful tool for filmmakers to communicate, evoke, and intensify the emotional impact of a scene, ensuring that the audience is fully immersed in the characters' world and their emotional states.

Foley Artistry: Mastering Suspense and Drama through Sonic Tension

Foley artists are masters of enhancing the suspense and drama within a film, wielding their craft like virtuosos of tension. During suspenseful or mysterious scenes, they become architects of anxiety, introducing tension-building sounds that send shivers down the audience's spine. The subtle creak of a floorboard or the eerie whisper of a distant voice takes on a profound significance, adding layers of anticipation and intrigue to the narrative. These auditory cues are strategically placed to heighten the audience's sense of unease and anticipation, fostering an atmosphere of uncertainty and mystery that keeps viewers on the edge of their seats. It is in these moments of auditory manipulation that Foley artists become integral to the storytelling process, using sound to craft an emotionally charged atmosphere that amplifies the suspense and drama of a film, ensuring that audiences are fully immersed in the gripping narrative and its pulse-pounding moments.

Foley Artistry: Bridging the Real and the Digital in Cinematic Visual Effects

Foley artistry is a crucial companion to visual effects (VFX) in filmmaking. In scenes with CGI characters or objects, Foley artists create sound effects to make interactions appear realistic. Whether it's footsteps of a CGI monster or futuristic gadget noises, Foley sound effects seamlessly blend with the visual spectacle. These sounds enhance the believability of VFX, immersing the audience in imaginative worlds. The synchronization between Foley and VFX is a testament to the collaborative nature of filmmaking, where sound enhances the visual and emotional impact of the cinematic experience.

Foley Artists: Guardians of Sound Quality in Cinematic Storytelling

Foley artists are unwavering guardians of sound quality in the filmmaking process, meticulously crafting auditory elements that are not only of high quality but also seamlessly align with the film's visual storytelling. They approach their craft with unrelenting precision, continuously refining their techniques to ensure that every sound effect resonates authentically with the on-screen action. This dedication to detail extends to their extensive collection of sound props and materials, meticulously chosen to replicate a wide spectrum of sounds with accuracy and realism. These artists are both creators and curators, amassing a treasure trove of auditory resources that allows them to bring even the most complex and fantastical scenes to life. In doing so, they become the guardians of sound quality, ensuring that every rustle, footstep, or whisper contributes to the film's sensory richness and emotional resonance. This unwavering commitment to excellence makes Foley artists indispensable partners in the quest for cinematic perfection, where sound quality becomes a critical element in the seamless fusion of visual and auditory storytelling.

Foley Artists: Precision Recording Techniques for Cinematic Sound Excellence

Foley artists employ highly specialized recording techniques in their craft, working within a meticulously soundproof studio environment that allows them to capture every sound with pristine clarity. Equipped with specialized microphones and high-quality recording equipment, they create a controlled and isolated acoustic space where every auditory nuance can be captured without interference. Typically, Foley artists work in pairs, with one artist performing the actions while the other operates the recording equipment. This collaborative approach ensures that the timing and synchronization between the on-screen actions and the corresponding sound effects are impeccable. As the performing artist meticulously mimics the actions of the characters, their partner captures these sounds with precision, adjusting microphone placement and recording settings to capture the desired audio quality. It is this synergy between the two artists and the advanced recording technology that enables Foley to deliver sound effects of exceptional clarity and authenticity, enriching the auditory dimension of the film and elevating the overall cinematic experience.

The Culmination of Foley Artistry: Integrating Sound Effects into the Film's Post-Production Audio

The post-production phase of filmmaking marks the culmination of Foley artistry, as Foley artists collaborate closely with sound editors and mixers to seamlessly integrate the meticulously crafted sound effects into the film's overarching audio track. This collaborative effort is characterized by meticulous attention to detail, as the Foley artists work to ensure that every sound aligns perfectly with the on-screen actions and the overall auditory landscape. Sound editors refine and manipulate the recorded Foley effects, adjusting volume levels, fine-tuning frequencies, and adding spatial depth to achieve the desired auditory impact. The mixers then layer these sounds alongside dialogue, music, and other sound elements to create a harmonious auditory experience. This intricate process of integration and refinement is essential in ensuring that the Foley sound not only enhances the visual storytelling but also seamlessly blends with other auditory components to create a cohesive and immersive sonic tapestry that captivates and envelops the audience. In this final stage of post-production, Foley artists play a vital role in shaping the film's auditory identity, contributing to its emotional resonance and sensory richness.

Creating Cinematic Ambiance in Indian Cinema

Ambience in Indian cinema is a multifaceted tool that encompasses location, sound design, and visual aesthetics. It serves to immerse audiences in the diverse and evocative settings of Indian films, enhancing the narrative's texture and contributing to the emotional resonance of the cinematic experience. Whether through the cacophony of a bustling city or the serene tranquility of nature, ambience is a powerful storytelling device that helps transport viewers into the heart of the film's world. In Indian cinema, the choice of locations is often a deliberate and integral part of storytelling, with each location contributing to the mood, atmosphere, and cultural context of the narrative. Sound design, including ambient sounds like street noises, wildlife, or even the subtle rustling of leaves, is meticulously crafted to complement the visual elements and evoke emotional responses from the audience. Furthermore, visual aesthetics, such as lighting and set design, work in harmony with ambience to create a sensory-rich experience that resonates deeply with viewers. This synergy between location, sound, and visuals not only adds authenticity to the film's world but also enriches the storytelling, making ambience an indispensable aspect of Indian cinema's narrative toolbox.

Strategic Location Selection for Authentic Ambience in Indian Cinema

One of the primary ways Indian filmmakers use ambience is by carefully selecting filming locations that reflect the story's intended setting. For instance, if a film is set in a rural village in the heart of India, the choice of a real village as the backdrop adds authenticity to the narrative. This location choice not only provides visual cues but also introduces ambient sounds that are unique to that environment, such as the chirping of crickets or the rustling of leaves. These sounds become an integral part of the film's atmosphere, immersing the audience in the world being depicted. The choice of authentic locations also extends to urban settings, historical periods, and specific cultural contexts, all of which contribute to the overall ambience and mood of the film. By selecting locations that align with the story's setting, Indian filmmakers enhance the sensory experience of the audience, making the film more emotionally resonant and immersive. This attention to detail in location selection showcases the significance of ambience in Indian cinema as a tool for storytelling and world-building.

Crafting Cinematic Atmosphere Through Sound Design in Indian Cinema

Sound design is a crucial aspect of creating ambience in Indian cinema. Sound designers work meticulously to capture and recreate ambient sounds that resonate with the story's setting. This involves recording or adding sounds like street noise, bird chirping, or traffic, depending on the scene's requirements. These sounds are strategically placed in the film's audio mix to enhance the viewer's sensory experience. For example, the honking of horns in a chaotic street scene or the call of a distant peacock in a serene countryside setting can evoke a strong emotional response from the audience. Sound designers not only focus on capturing the sounds themselves but also pay careful attention to the spatial placement and timing of these sounds, ensuring they align seamlessly with the on-screen visuals. This level of precision in sound design helps create a more immersive and believable environment for the audience, enriching the overall cinematic experience. It is through sound design that filmmakers can transport viewers to different worlds, eras, and emotional landscapes, making it an indispensable element of Indian cinema's storytelling toolkit.

Visual Aesthetics and Ambiance: The Symbiosis in Indian Filmmaking

The visual aesthetics of a film, including its colour palette and overall look, complement the ambience created by location and sound. Indian filmmakers are known for their vivid and vibrant visuals, and these visuals often align with the ambient elements of a scene. For instance, the rich and colourful attire and decorations in a traditional Indian wedding scene not only add to the visual appeal but also contribute to the overall ambience, creating a sense of celebration and festivity. Similarly, the choice of lighting, whether it's the warm and soft glow of oil lamps during a cultural festival or the stark and moody lighting in a suspenseful sequence, plays a crucial role in setting the tone and enhancing the ambience of the film. Furthermore, the visual aesthetics extend to set design, props, and costume choices, all of which work in harmony to create a sensory-rich experience for the audience. The meticulous attention to visual detail in Indian cinema ensures that the look of a film aligns with its narrative and contributes to the overall mood and atmosphere, making it an integral part of the storytelling process.

Beyond Background Noise: The Artful Use of Ambience in Indian Cinema

Ambience in Indian cinema goes beyond mere background noise; it weaves into the fabric of the narrative. Whether it's the bustling chaos of a crowded marketplace, the serene silence of a rural village, or the echoing footsteps in an empty mansion, these ambiances add depth to the storytelling. They set the stage for the characters' journeys and emotional arcs, enhancing the audience's understanding of the characters' experiences and motivations. The sounds and visuals associated with these ambiances become symbolic and often serve as storytelling cues. For instance, the sound of rain against a window may evoke feelings of melancholy or nostalgia, while the vibrant colours and music of a street festival can signify joy and celebration. The careful integration of ambience into the narrative creates a more immersive and emotionally resonant cinematic experience, allowing viewers to connect with the characters and their surroundings on a deeper level. It is through the artful use of ambience that Indian filmmakers elevate their storytelling, making ambience an integral part of the storytelling process and a powerful tool for conveying emotions and context in their films.

The Diverse Palette of Ambiance in Indian Cinema: Harnessing Culture and Geography for Emotional Resonance

The rich tapestry of Indian culture and geography offers a plethora of ambient possibilities. Filmmakers skillfully harness these elements to evoke specific emotions in the audience. For instance, the use of ambient sounds and visuals can evoke nostalgia for one's hometown, create suspense in a thrilling chase sequence, or set a romantic mood during a love story. In this way, ambience becomes an integral aspect of storytelling in Indian cinema, helping to convey the intended emotional tone and atmosphere of a scene. The diverse regions of India, with their distinct landscapes, traditions, and lifestyles, provide a treasure trove of ambience options that allow filmmakers to transport viewers to various corners of the country, each with its own unique ambience and cultural resonance. Whether it's the bustling streets of Mumbai, the serene backwaters of Kerala, or the mystical landscapes of Rajasthan, the careful selection and incorporation of ambient elements enable filmmakers to paint a vivid and immersive picture of the story's world, deepening the audience's connection with the narrative and its emotional landscape.

C. Action Sequences

Impactful sound effects are essential for enhancing high-energy action sequences in films. They contribute to realism, build tension and excitement, aid in characterization and storytelling, and immerse the audience in the action. When done effectively, these sound effects elevate the overall cinematic experience and leave a lasting impression on viewers, making action sequences memorable and exhilarating. High-energy action sequences are a staple in many films, and they rely heavily on impactful sound effects to create an immersive and thrilling experience for the audience. These sequences often involve intense physical combat, explosions, gunfire, and other dynamic elements. Sound designers meticulously craft each sound effect to match the visual cues on screen, ensuring that the audience not only sees but also feels the impact of each punch, explosion, or gunshot. The thunderous roar of an explosion, the sharp clang of a sword, or the bone-crushing impact of a fight move all add a visceral layer to the action, engaging the audience's senses and heightening their emotional involvement in the scene. This auditory dimension of action sequences is not only about creating a realistic portrayal but also about enhancing the storytelling and characterization. The sounds associated with action can convey the power and prowess of the characters, their struggles, and their triumphs, adding depth to their personas. Moreover, impactful sound effects help build tension and excitement, keeping the audience on the edge of their seats throughout the sequence. The rush of adrenaline, the heart-pounding beats, and the immersive experience created by these sound effects make action sequences come alive, leaving a lasting impact and making them a defining element of the cinematic experience. Here's a detailed explanation of how impactful sound effects enhance action sequences in film:

Sound Effects in Action Sequences: Elevating Realism, Intensity, and Emotional Engagement

The inclusion of sound effects like punches, kicks, and body impacts in hand-to-hand combat or physical confrontations is a pivotal element in the world of film and television. These sounds serve as a crucial layer of realism, allowing the audience to not only witness but also feel the force and intensity of each blow exchanged during the action sequences. When executed effectively, these sound effects can bridge the gap between the fictional world of the story and the viewer's sensory experience, making the action on-screen more believable and emotionally engaging. The impact of a punch or a kick becomes tangible, heightening the audience's visceral response and immersing them in the heart-pounding intensity of the action. This auditory dimension adds depth to the choreography and elevates the overall cinematic experience, transforming fight sequences into dynamic and riveting encounters that leave a lasting impression.

The Art of Explosive Sound: Crafting Intensity and Immersion in Action Sequences

In action sequences, explosions are a quintessential element, and their auditory depiction plays a pivotal role in crafting a visceral and immersive experience for the audience. The sound of an explosion, when meticulously crafted, goes beyond being a mere auditory accompaniment; it becomes a conduit for conveying the overwhelming destructive power and imminent danger of the event. The deep, resonant rumble, coupled with shockwave-like sound effects, not only reverberate through the cinema's sound system but also through the viewer's senses. These meticulously engineered sounds transport the audience right into the heart of the chaos, creating a sensory landscape where the deafening roar of the explosion is not just heard but felt. It's this auditory dimension that adds a layer of intensity and urgency to the on-screen mayhem, making viewers instinctively grasp the magnitude of the danger unfolding before them. In this way, the sound of explosions becomes an art form, transforming action sequences into pulse-pounding and heart-racing encounters that leave audiences on the edge of their seats, fully immersed in the cinematic spectacle.

Shots Fired: Crafting Authentic and Impactful Gunfire in Action Scenes

Gunfire, a staple in action scenes, serves as a classic element that not only heightens excitement but also conveys the imminent danger and urgency of the situation. In crafting the sound of gunfire, sound designers meticulously attend to detail, recognizing that different firearms produce distinct and recognizable sounds. The choice of weaponry in a scene is matched with precision, ensuring that the auditory portrayal aligns seamlessly with the visual depiction. Whether it's the sharp crack of a handgun, the thunderous roar of a shotgun, or the rhythmic staccato of an automatic rifle, these auditory cues provide vital contextual information to the audience. They help viewers understand the nature of the threat, the intensity of the firefight, and the dynamics of the action, all while amplifying the emotional impact of the scene. This level of authenticity in sound design transforms gunfights into heart-pounding spectacles, where the auditory dimension not only complements but elevates the visual storytelling, making the danger and urgency palpable to the audience.

Building Tension and Excitement: The Art of Dynamic Sound Design and Rhythmic Timing in Action Sequences

Dynamic sound design in action sequences is a masterful tool for building tension and excitement in filmmaking. It operates as a living, breathing entity that responds to the ebb and flow of the action. As the intensity of the action sequences escalates, the sound effects seamlessly follow suit, amplifying in volume and intensity. This dynamic interplay between visual and auditory elements creates a palpable sense of danger and adrenaline that courses through the audience's veins. The auditory landscape mirrors the rising stakes, with each punch, gunshot, or explosion becoming not just a sound but a pulse-pounding experience. This synergy between the action on screen and its auditory counterpart transforms the scene into a sensory rollercoaster ride, with the auditory dimension heightening the emotional engagement, making viewers feel every jolt, every impact, and every heartbeat of the action. In this way, dynamic sound design becomes a vital element in the art of storytelling, enhancing the cinematic experience and leaving audiences on the edge of their seats, fully immersed in the pulse-pounding intensity of the action.

The Dance of Sound: Rhythmic Timing in Action Sequence Sound Effects

Rhythmic timing in sound effects is a subtle yet pivotal component in crafting the pacing and emotional resonance of action sequences. When meticulously choreographed to sync seamlessly with on-screen action, sound effects become a silent partner in guiding the audience through the narrative's ebb and flow. Quick, rhythmic sounds, akin to a percussive beat, can harmoniously match the tempo of a fast-paced fight scene, infusing it with energy and precision. In contrast, sudden, loud bursts of sound can jolt the audience, accentuating surprise or shock moments with a visceral intensity that reverberates through the senses. This delicate dance between visual and auditory elements enhances the scene's pacing, amplifies its emotional impact, and ensures that viewers are not merely passive observers but active participants in the cinematic experience. The rhythm of sound effects becomes a narrative tool, shaping the sequence's cadence and emotional dynamics, and leaving a lasting imprint on the audience's sensory memory.

Characterization and Storytelling: The Role of Sound Effects in Character Differentiation and Plot Advancement in Action Sequences

Sound effects in action sequences are not just auditory embellishments; they serve as a subtle yet potent tool for character differentiation and development. In these high-stakes confrontations, the sound of each character's actions becomes a sonic signature, reflecting their unique traits and motivations. The distinctiveness in the sound of a hero's punch, for instance, may convey a sense of valor and righteousness, while that of a villain could evoke menace and ruthlessness. This nuanced auditory portrayal not only adds depth to the characters but also invites the audience to emotionally invest in their favorites. Through sound, viewers can form a sonic connection with the characters, rooting for them with each resonating punch or kick. This auditory dimension becomes a powerful narrative tool, enhancing the characterization and allowing audiences to become emotionally entangled in the struggle between heroes and villains, making the action sequences not just a spectacle but a character-driven journey that leaves a lasting impression.

Sounding the Story: The Narrative Significance of Sound Effects in Film

Sound effects in film are not limited to mere embellishments but serve as a critical storytelling tool, often conveying essential plot points that propel the narrative. The sound of a ticking bomb or the ominous charging of a weapon can serve as auditory omens, signaling impending danger and injecting a sense of urgency into the storyline. These auditory cues function as narrative signposts, helping the audience understand the stakes and the evolving plot, even without relying solely on dialogue or visual cues. The tension and anticipation evoked by these sounds create a heightened sense of engagement, driving the narrative forward and leaving viewers on the edge of their seats as they follow the story's twists and turns. In this way, sound effects become storytellers in their own right, weaving an auditory narrative that complements and enriches the visual and thematic elements of the film, making the storytelling experience multi-dimensional and unforgettable.

The Immersive Power of Sound Effects in Film: Crafting Emotional Journeys Through Auditory Mastery"

Impactful sound effects serve as the linchpin for audience immersion in the world of film, transcending the role of mere auditory elements to become immersive conduits into the cinematic experience. These sounds go beyond simple embellishments; they are the keys to unlocking the viewer's senses and transporting them directly into the heart of the action. By seamlessly complementing the visuals, sound effects create a sensory tapestry that envelops the audience, making them feel like active participants rather than passive observers. The deafening roar of an explosion, the visceral crunch of a bone-crushing punch, or the nerve-racking rattle of gunfire doesn't just resonate in the theater; it reverberates through the viewers, engaging them on a visceral and emotional level. This immersive auditory dimension enhances the film's impact, forging an unbreakable connection between the audience and the narrative, ensuring that the cinematic world becomes more than just images on a screen-it becomes an unforgettable, multisensory journey that transcends the boundaries of fiction.

The Emotional Orchestration of Action: Sound Effects as Catalysts in Cinematic Engagement

Sound effects in action sequences are masterful architects of emotional impact, capable of evoking a wide spectrum of feelings within the audience. Whether it's the adrenaline-pumping excitement of a high-octane chase, the visceral fear induced by a looming threat, or the nail-biting tension of a suspenseful confrontation, these auditory elements are conduits for emotional engagement. They become the emotional compass, guiding the audience through the character's experiences and the narrative's twists and turns. The precisely crafted sound of action sequences is a symphony of emotion, allowing viewers to not only witness but also feel the pulse-pounding heartbeats of the story. In doing so, sound effects become catalysts for empathy, forging an emotional connection between the audience and the characters on screen. This emotional resonance amplifies the cinematic experience, making it a journey of not just visual but also visceral storytelling, where every sound is a thread in the tapestry of emotions that immerses and captivates the audience.

D. Dialogues and Voice Acting

Dialogues

These dialogues have a multifaceted purpose, as they not only advance the plot but also provide cultural commentary and reflect the diverse linguistic landscape of India. They can be humorous, poignant, or thought-provoking, depending on the context and character. The dramatic delivery of dialogues intensifies their impact, allowing actors to convey a wide range of emotions effectively. Whether it's the iconic one-liners that become part of popular culture or the emotionally charged exchanges that resonate deeply with viewers, dialogues have the power to engage, entertain, and leave a lasting impression on audiences, enhancing the overall cinematic experience. Here's a detailed explanation of the importance of dialogues in Indian cinema:

Character Development: The Multifaceted Role of Dialogues in Character Development and Narrative Depth

Dialogues serve as a vital tool for conveying the intricacies of a character's personality, beliefs, and values within a narrative. Through the words they choose and the manner in which they articulate them, characters offer profound glimpses into their underlying motivations and backgrounds. This can be exemplified by observing the way in which characters employ distinct vocabularies, accents, and tones, each of which is indicative of their unique upbringing, educational experiences, and social standing. Such linguistic nuances illuminate the depth of a character's identity and, in turn, enhance the audience's comprehension of their role within the story, thereby adding depth and authenticity to the narrative.

Dialogue Dynamics: Illuminating Character Evolution in Film

Dialogues serve as a dynamic instrument in depicting a character's evolution and growth within the context of a film. As the story unfolds, subtle shifts in a character's speech patterns, such as progressing from hesitancy to confidence or transitioning from cynicism to hopefulness, are instrumental in signifying their profound transformation over time. These changes in dialogue mirror the character's evolving mindset, emotional journey, and newfound perspectives, allowing the audience to witness their personal growth and development throughout the narrative. It's through these linguistic transformations that characters transcend their initial limitations and evolve into more complex and relatable beings, enriching the storytelling experience and deepening the audience's emotional connection to the narrative.

The Dual Essence of Dialogues in Indian Cinema: Comic Relief and Memorable Character Quirks

Dialogues play a pivotal role in Indian cinema as a potent source of comic relief. Whether in the context of lighthearted comedies or even intense dramas, the art of delivering comedic dialogues with impeccable timing and clever wit has become an integral part of the cinematic experience. These well-crafted humorous exchanges have the remarkable ability to alleviate tension within the storyline, engage the audience's emotions, and elevate the overall entertainment quotient of the film. Such moments of levity offer viewers a much-needed respite from the often complex or intense narrative, creating a delightful contrast that not only generates laughter but also fosters a deeper connection between the audience and the characters. In this way, comedic dialogues serve as a vital tool for both storytelling and audience engagement in Indian cinema.

Quirks and Catchphrases: Crafting Iconic Characters Through Distinct Dialogue in Indian Cinema

In Indian cinema, character quirks embodied through distinct speech patterns, eccentricities, or memorable catchphrases play a significant role in creating iconic and unforgettable characters. These idiosyncratic dialogues become synonymous with particular individuals onscreen, contributing to their enduring charm and memorability. Viewers form a strong emotional bond with characters who possess such quirks, as these distinctive linguistic elements not only differentiate them but also provide a window into their personas. These traits can range from a character's endearing quirks that evoke laughter to poignant catchphrases that resonate with deeper themes in the narrative, all of which elevate the character's impact and contribute to the rich tapestry of Indian cinema.

Emotional Resonance: The Significance of Dialogues in Indian Cinema

Dialogues in Indian cinema are a potent tool for delivering emotions, transcending language barriers to connect with audiences on a profound emotional level. Well-crafted and emotionally charged dialogues have the remarkable ability to convey a wide spectrum of feelings, from love and grief to anger and joy, eliciting a genuine response from viewers. Through these words and the nuanced expressions of the characters delivering them, the audience is transported into the emotional landscape of the narrative. Viewers become emotionally invested in the story, forging a deep connection with the characters and their experiences. In this way, dialogues serve as a bridge between the on-screen world and the audience's hearts, making Indian cinema a powerful medium for evoking genuine and relatable emotions.

Transcendent Lines: The Impact and Endurance of Iconic Movie Dialogues

In the world of cinema, certain dialogues transcend the confines of the screen to become iconic, leaving an indelible mark on the collective memory of audiences. These memorable quotes possess the remarkable ability to encapsulate profound emotions, themes, or pivotal moments in a film's narrative. They resonate with viewers on a deep and personal level, often becoming part of popular culture and everyday conversation. Fans eagerly quote these lines, celebrating their wit, wisdom, or emotional resonance, and in doing so, these dialogues extend the film's impact far beyond its release date. Such memorable quotes not only serve as a testament to the power of well-crafted writing and exceptional delivery but also underscore the enduring influence of cinema in shaping culture and society.

The Theatrical Power of Dialogues in Indian Cinema: Intensity, Confrontation, Exaggeration, and Exuberance

Indian cinema is renowned for its penchant for dramatic confrontations, and dialogues play an indispensable role in these high-stakes scenes. Whether it's a heated verbal exchange, a tense face-off between rivals, or a heartfelt declaration of love, the delivery of dialogues with dramatic flair serves as the linchpin in elevating the intensity and impact of these pivotal cinematic moments. The meticulously crafted dialogues, often laden with emotional depth and powerful rhetoric, not only heighten the tension within the narrative but also amplify the emotional resonance, drawing viewers deeper into the characters' experiences. Through their words and expressions, actors convey a range of emotions, from anger and defiance to passion and vulnerability, creating a captivating and immersive experience that has become a hallmark of Indian cinema.

Exaggerated Dialogue Delivery in Indian Cinema: Amplifying Emotions and Theatrical Flair

Indian cinema frequently embraces a unique style of dialogue delivery characterized by exaggeration and exuberance. In many films, characters express their emotions in a larger-than-life manner, amplifying their feelings through extravagant speech and dramatic gestures. This penchant for over-the-top dialogue delivery adds to the grand spectacle and melodramatic flair often associated with Indian cinema. It allows emotions to be magnified and intensified, creating a heightened cinematic experience where passion, love, anger, and other sentiments are vividly portrayed. This exaggeration not only contributes to the entertainment value of the films but also serves as a reflection of the vibrant and expressive cultural milieu in which Indian cinema thrives, captivating audiences with its theatricality and emotional resonance.

Dialogue Dynamics: The Role of Film Dialogues in Shaping Social Discourse in Indian Cinema

Indian cinema has long served as a powerful reflection of the societal landscape, and the role of dialogues within films is integral to this function. Filmmakers, in their pursuit of storytelling, have consistently used dialogues to address and comment upon prevalent social issues and cultural values. These dialogues become a potent vehicle for raising awareness and sparking discussions around a multitude of topics, ranging from gender equality, societal norms, and political matters to economic disparities and more. Through carefully crafted verbal exchanges, Indian cinema not only entertains but also presents thought-provoking insights and diverse perspectives, enabling a nuanced exploration of real-world challenges and dilemmas. In this sense, dialogues transcend their role as mere lines of script; they become a platform for conveying essential messages, igniting social consciousness, and instigating change. This makes Indian cinema not just a source of entertainment but a significant force for reflecting and influencing the society it represents.

The Ripple Effect: How Film Dialogues in Indian Cinema Transcend Screens to Influence Society

The impact of dialogues in Indian cinema goes beyond the screen. It permeates society, generating dialogue, debate, and, in some cases, even real-world action. Memorable film dialogues often become part of popular culture and public discourse. They have the potential to shape public opinion, challenge prevailing norms, and galvanize movements for social change. In this way, Indian cinema, through its powerful dialogues, bridges the gap between fiction and reality, transforming entertainment into a dynamic medium for societal reflection and transformation. The influence of these dialogues is profound, as they encourage audiences to think critically, question the status quo, and consider alternative perspectives, thus cementing the role of Indian cinema as a mirror that not only reflects but also shapes the society it engages with.

Song Lyrics and Musical Integration: How Song Lyrics Serve as Narrative and Emotional Extensions in Indian Cinema

In Indian cinema, the integration of songs into the storytelling process serves as a unique and compelling narrative and emotional extension. The lyrics of these songs often contain dialogues that seamlessly extend the narrative by providing additional context, advancing character development, or conveying critical plot points. Moreover, these musical sequences serve as a conduit for characters to express their deepest emotions and innermost thoughts, transcending the limitations of spoken language. Through melodious tunes, captivating choreography, and visually stunning cinematography, these song sequences evoke a range of emotions in the audience, from joy and romance to sorrow and introspection. In this way, songs in Indian cinema become a dynamic and integral part of the storytelling, enhancing the overall impact of the film by forging a powerful connection between the characters and the viewers and adding depth and dimension to the narrative.

Voice Acting

Voice actors must not only convey the spoken dialogue but also capture the essence of the original performance, maintaining synchronization with the characters' lip movements and expressions. This synchronization ensures that the emotional nuances and dramatic impact of the scenes are preserved in the dubbed version. Additionally, voice actors often play a crucial role in adapting the content culturally, making it relatable to the target audience. The ability to effectively convey a character's personality, emotions, and nuances through voice acting is a skill that requires both technical proficiency and an understanding of the original performance. Overall, well-executed voice acting is indispensable for creating a seamless and compelling cinematic experience, enabling films to transcend language barriers and resonate with diverse audiences worldwide. Here's a detailed explanation of the significance of voice acting in film:

Dubbing in Film: Multilingual Accessibility and Cultural Preservation

In today's interconnected and globalized world, the reach of films extends far beyond their country of origin, often targeting diverse audiences with varying linguistic backgrounds and cultural contexts. Dubbing serves as a crucial tool for filmmakers to bridge these linguistic barriers and ensure that their content reaches a broader and more inclusive viewership. Through the process of dubbing, the original dialogue is translated and replaced with voiceovers in different languages, enabling audiences who may not understand the film's original language to fully engage with the narrative and its emotional nuances. This practice not only enhances a film's accessibility but also promotes cross-cultural appreciation and understanding, allowing stories to resonate with people from diverse linguistic backgrounds and fostering a sense of global cinematic community.

Preserving Cultural Context in Dubbing: The Art of Skilled Voice Actors

Preserving cultural context in dubbing is a nuanced art that goes beyond mere translation. It involves skilled voice actors who possess a deep understanding of both the source and target cultures. These actors must not only convey the literal meaning of the words but also capture the underlying cultural nuances, emotional subtleties, and social context of the original dialogue. By doing so, they ensure that the essence and authenticity of the film are retained across languages. This level of expertise is vital because it allows viewers from different cultural backgrounds to fully grasp the intricacies of the narrative, humor, social commentary, and even the historical references embedded in the film. Effective cultural preservation in dubbing enriches the viewer's experience, facilitating a deeper connection with the story and characters, and exemplifies the importance of skilled voice actors in bridging linguistic and cultural gaps in the world of cinema.

The Art of Voice Acting: Conveying Emotions and Character Identification in Film and Animation

Voice actors play a pivotal role in bringing characters to life by imbuing them with a rich tapestry of emotions, personality traits, and depth. Their mastery of tone, cadence, and timbre allows them to seamlessly convey a spectrum of emotions, from the infectious joy of a character's laughter to the profound sorrow of their tears or the fiery intensity of their anger. It is through the skilled artistry of voice acting that audiences can forge a genuine connection with the characters and empathize with their emotional journeys. The authenticity and quality of voice acting serve as a bridge, allowing viewers to invest themselves emotionally in the narrative, making it a fundamental element in the cinematic experience.

Voice Acting and Character Identification: Forging a Deeper Connection

Strong voice acting plays a pivotal role in creating character identification within storytelling. When viewers not only see but also hear a character's voice, a powerful connection is established. This auditory connection, when skillfully executed, allows audiences to delve deeper into the character's psyche, feel their emotions, and relate to their experiences. As viewers empathize with the character's emotions and struggles, their attachment to both the character and the overarching narrative strengthens significantly. This heightened sense of connection enhances the overall viewing experience, making it more immersive and emotionally resonant. Well-crafted voice acting, by making characters relatable and memorable, ensures that the audience remains engaged, empathetic, and invested in the story's unfolding, enriching the cinematic journey.

Precision in Voice Acting: Lip Sync and Timing for Visual and Narrative Cohesion

Synchronizing dialogue delivery with on-screen lip movements is an indispensable aspect of voice acting in film and animation. This meticulous process, known as lip sync, is pivotal for upholding the film's visual realism and maintaining the illusion of a seamless integration between the spoken words and the characters' on-screen performances. Achieving precise lip sync entails an intricate coordination between the timing and articulation of the voice actor's delivery and the animated or recorded movements of the character's lips. When executed with precision, accurate lip sync enhances the authenticity of the character's speech, fostering a sense of believability and immersion for the audience. It ensures that the dialogue flows naturally within the visual context, making the characters' interactions appear organic and true to life, ultimately enriching the cinematic experience.

Timing and Pacing in Voice Acting: Preserving the Essence of Performance

In voice acting, the importance of matching the timing and pacing of the original performance cannot be overstated. It goes beyond merely translating words; it's about capturing the essence of a character's delivery in terms of when they speak, how fast they speak, and when they pause for emphasis. This synchronization is critical for conveying the intended emotional impact of a scene, whether it's delivering a punchline in a comedic moment, building suspense in a thriller, or heightening the drama in a poignant exchange. When voice actors master the art of timing and pacing, they align their delivery with the director's vision, ensuring that the narrative unfolds in a way that engages the audience and elicits the desired emotional responses. This level of precision elevates the quality of the dub and enhances the overall viewer experience, preserving the integrity of the original performance while making it accessible to a broader audience.

Casting and Characterization: The Crucial Role of Casting and Consistency in Voice Acting

The process of casting the right voice actor is a pivotal decision in the world of dubbing and animation. It involves a careful consideration of multiple factors beyond age and gender, including the character's personality, quirks, and distinctive traits. The chosen voice actor must not only vocally align with the character's physical attributes but also possess the ability to embody their essence. When done effectively, this selection can bring a character to life in a way that makes them utterly captivating and relatable. A well-matched voice actor infuses the character with depth, authenticity, and emotional resonance, elevating the overall quality of the dub and forging a strong connection between the audience and the characters. This harmonious match between the character's visual and vocal representation is instrumental in making the narrative more immersive, engaging, and compelling for viewers.

Consistency in Voice Acting: Maintaining Character Authenticity in Film Series

Consistency in voice acting is of paramount importance, particularly in film series or franchises. Audiences often develop a deep familiarity with and attachment to the voices of specific characters over the course of multiple installments. When voice actors change, it can disrupt the viewer's connection to the narrative, creating a sense of discontinuity and potentially diminishing the immersive experience. Consistent voice acting not only maintains the authenticity of the characters but also upholds the narrative's integrity, ensuring that viewers can seamlessly transition from one installment to the next while retaining their emotional investment in the story. This continuity strengthens the overall cohesion of the series or franchise, allowing for a more immersive and enjoyable viewing experience while preserving the audience's connection to the beloved characters they've come to know and love.

Cultural Adaptation in Dubbing: Ensuring Relevance and Authenticity in Translated References

During the dubbing process, adapting cultural references is a delicate and essential task. Voice actors and translators may encounter references in the original script that wouldn't resonate with the target audience due to differences in culture, geography, or time period. To bridge this gap, skilled voice actors, along with knowledgeable translators, must carefully replace or reinterpret these references while preserving the humor, context, or emotional impact of the original dialogue. This adaptation requires a nuanced understanding of both the source and target cultures to ensure that the new references feel natural and seamless within the narrative. When executed successfully, these adapted cultural references not only maintain the intended tone and depth of the scene but also make the content more relatable and enjoyable for the audience, allowing the story to transcend cultural boundaries while still being faithful to its essence.

The Dual Dimensions of Voice Acting: Technical Proficiency and Artistic Excellence

Technical expertise is a fundamental requirement for voice actors, as it encompasses the skills and knowledge necessary to deliver clear and high-quality audio in their performances. This proficiency ensures that the dialogue they convey is not only audible but also easily comprehensible to the audience. Voice actors must have a good grasp of microphone techniques, sound recording equipment, and vocal control to eliminate unwanted noise, distortion, or inconsistencies in their recordings. Moreover, they need to maintain proper vocal projection, enunciation, and articulation to ensure that every word and nuance is accurately conveyed to the listener. This technical prowess is critical for maintaining the overall audio quality of a production, ensuring that the audience can fully engage with the narrative and connect with the characters without any impediments, ultimately enhancing the viewer's experience.

Voice Acting as an Art Form: The Profound Impact of Skilled Actors on Character Portrayal

Voice acting is far more than a technical skill; it is a nuanced art form that hinges on the talent and creativity of proficient actors. Exceptional voice actors are not just voices behind the characters; they are the embodiment of those characters. Their unique ability lies in infusing their performances with depth, nuance, and authenticity, which ultimately enhances the overall quality of the dub. Through their artistic delivery, they breathe life into the animated or foreign-language characters, granting them emotions, quirks, and distinctive personalities that might otherwise be lost in translation. These skilled professionals are masters of vocal inflection, tone, and expression, allowing them to convey a wide spectrum of emotions and subtle nuances that deeply resonate with the audience.

Enriching Characters, Enchanting Audiences: The Artistic Mastery of Voice Actors in Dubbing

It's through this artistic prowess that voice actors add layers of complexity to the characters they portray, making them more relatable, compelling, and memorable. Their contributions can't be understated, as they act as conduits for the audience to connect with and understand the characters' inner thoughts and feelings. In essence, voice actors possess the power to transform the dubbing process from a mere technical task into a form of artistry that enriches the viewer's experience and amplifies the narrative's impact. Their work transcends the screen, with their performances lingering in the minds of the audience long after the credits roll, showcasing the profound influence of voice acting on the world of entertainment.

E. Sound Design

Emotional resonance

"Emotional resonance" in the context of sound design is the practice of using various auditory elements, including soundscapes and atmospheric sounds, to evoke specific emotions in the audience and enhance their emotional connection to characters and situations in a film. Here, we'll focus on the role of atmospheric sound in achieving emotional resonance:

Crafting Atmosphere through Sound: The Art of Audio Design in Film

Atmospheric sound is a crucial element in audio design, utilized to craft the mood and atmosphere within a scene, particularly in the context of film. It involves the deliberate incorporation and manipulation of various auditory components, including background noises, environmental sounds, and ambient audio. These elements serve as a sonic tapestry that envelops the audience and immerses them in the world of the story. Sound designers, who play a pivotal role in this process, approach their work with meticulous attention to detail. They carefully choose and manipulate these sounds, ensuring that they align with the emotional tone and narrative intention of a specific moment in the film.

Strategic Selection of Atmospheric Sounds in Film: Crafting Mood and Emotion

The selection of atmospheric sounds in the area of audio design for film is far from arbitrary; it is a meticulous and artful process. Sound designers undertake this task with a keen eye for creativity and a strategic approach, taking into account a myriad of factors that collectively contribute to crafting the desired mood and atmosphere within a scene.

They consider essential elements such as the specific setting, the time period in which the story unfolds, the complex emotions of the characters, and the overarching narrative arc. This holistic approach enables them to make informed choices about which sounds will be most effective in conveying the intended emotional resonance. For instance, in a suspenseful scene rife with tension, these skilled professionals may strategically incorporate subtle yet eerie background noises like creaking floorboards or distant, ominous footsteps. Such additions serve to heighten the suspense, enveloping the audience in an atmosphere of apprehension and anticipation. In stark contrast, for a tranquil outdoor scene where peace and serenity are the dominant emotions, sound designers might opt for the soothing sounds of chirping birds and the gentle rustling of leaves. In doing so, they create an auditory backdrop that lulls the audience into a state of calm and harmony, reinforcing the desired emotional response and contributing significantly to the immersive power of cinematic storytelling.

Sculpting Atmospheres: The Art of Sound Manipulation in Film

Manipulating these sounds is equally important. Sound designers use various techniques, such as equalization, reverb, and volume adjustments, to precisely control the characteristics of each sound. For instance, they can make a rainstorm sound distant and soft or close and intense, depending on the scene's requirements. This level of control allows them to shape the emotional backdrop with precision. By carefully adjusting the spatial qualities of sounds, they can create a sense of depth and immersion, making the audience feel as though they are truly part of the on-screen world. Additionally, sound designers work on layering sounds, blending them seamlessly to achieve the desired auditory landscape. These manipulations are crucial in conveying the intended mood, atmosphere, and emotional resonance within a scene, showcasing the artistry behind sound design in cinema. Atmospheric sound is a powerful storytelling tool that enriches the viewer's experience by immersing them in a carefully crafted auditory environment. It complements the visual aspects of a film, enhancing the audience's emotional engagement and connection to the narrative, making it an integral part of the cinematic art form.

Setting the Mood and Atmosphere: The Emotional Spectrum of Rainfall, A Cinematic Exploration

Rainfall, as a classic example of atmospheric sound, possesses the remarkable ability to establish and manipulate mood through its auditory qualities. The melodic patter of raindrops cascading onto different surfaces is a sensory experience that transcends mere meteorological phenomena. A gentle rain, with its soft, rhythmic percussion, often invokes a sense of serenity, tranquility, or even a poignant melancholy, as it gently weaves its way into our auditory landscape. In contrast, a torrential downpour, with its relentless and chaotic assault, can swiftly usher in feelings of tension, anxiety, or an overwhelming intensity, underscoring the profound impact of ambient soundscapes on our emotional states and the power of nature's symphony to resonate with our innermost feelings and perceptions.

The Dramatic Resonance of Thunder: An Emotional Catalyst in Storytelling

The resonant rumble of thunder carries with it a potent association with moments of dramatic significance. Its deep, rolling cadence frequently serves as a symbol of impending danger, heightened excitement, or visceral fear in various contexts. Thunder becomes an invaluable tool in the hands of storytellers and filmmakers, enabling them to amplify the emotional impact of a scene, particularly during suspenseful or climactic sequences where tension is at its zenith. The abrupt and unpredictable nature of thunderclaps mirrors the sudden twists and turns of a plot, further intensifying the viewer or reader's engagement with the narrative. In this way, thunder, as both a natural phenomenon and a metaphorical device, underscores its pivotal role in shaping the emotional landscapes of stories and evoking profound sensations of anticipation, excitement, or dread in the audience or reader.

The Desolate Symphony of Wind: Crafting Isolation and Eeriness in Storytelling

The haunting sound of wind as it rustles through trees or mournfully howls in the distance possesses a unique capacity to evoke a vivid sense of isolation, eeriness, or desolation. Often harnessed by creators to set the atmospheric tone, this elemental auditory force becomes a crucial tool in crafting scenes that depict desolate landscapes, haunted settings, or poignant moments of solitude. The eerie, otherworldly quality of the wind's whispering or wailing amplifies the sense of abandonment and remoteness, enveloping the environment with an unsettling ambiance that resonates with the audience or reader. Whether it's the forlorn moan of wind through barren branches in a bleak forest, the desolate howl across a barren plain, or the solitary gusts that accompany a character's introspective journey, the sound of wind is a masterful storyteller's asset, capable of painting emotional landscapes that convey isolation, unease, or a profound sense of abandonment in the narrative.

The Symbiotic Harmony of Character Emotions and Atmospheric Sounds in Storytelling

Atmospheric sounds wield a remarkable narrative power by serving as a mirror to the emotional states of characters within a story. When skillfully employed, they can accentuate and amplify these emotions, forging a deep connection between the audience and the characters. For example, when a character grapples with isolation and loneliness, the haunting, mournful howl of the wind outside their window can resonate in harmony with their internal turmoil, effectively externalizing their emotional journey. This synchronization between sound and character emotions not only heightens the audience's empathy but also immerses them more profoundly in the character's experience, fostering a stronger bond and a heightened emotional resonance with the narrative. In essence, atmospheric sounds become a powerful tool in the storyteller's arsenal, enabling the audience to feel, rather than just observe, the characters' innermost struggles and emotions, enriching the storytelling experience.

Amplifying Narratives: The Transformative Role of Atmospheric Sounds in Storytelling

The strategic deployment of various atmospheric sounds holds the power to profoundly enhance the impact of different narrative situations. When skillfully employed, these sounds become not only auditory cues but also emotional amplifiers. In the context of storytelling, consider a serene rainfall during a romantic scene: the gentle patter of raindrops can function as a subtle yet potent backdrop, accentuating the emotions of love and tenderness, enveloping the moment in an aura of intimacy and vulnerability. Conversely, the inclusion of a thunderstorm during a pivotal moment of conflict adds layers of tension and drama to the narrative canvas. The booming thunder, crackling lightning, and torrential rain can serve as a metaphorical storm brewing within the characters' internal worlds, intensifying the external conflict and raising the stakes. In this way, atmospheric sounds, as auditory companions to storytelling, wield a versatile and evocative tool that enriches the narrative experience by harmonizing with and elevating the emotional contours of the scenes they accompany.

Symbolic Soundscapes: Elevating Narrative Depth through Atmospheric Sound Design

Sound designers possess a powerful tool in the form of atmospheric sound, which they can wield symbolically to imbue narratives with deeper layers of meaning. This approach enables them to elevate storytelling beyond the literal and into metaphor and emotion. For instance, the sound of rain can be harnessed to symbolize cleansing or renewal, its rhythmic patter mirroring the idea of washing away the old and bringing forth the new. Similarly, a howling wind can serve as a sonic representation of the chaos or turbulence within a character's life, evoking a sense of inner turmoil or external upheaval. These symbolic uses of sound operate as a subtextual language, enriching the narrative tapestry with subtle, emotionally charged nuances that resonate with the audience on a profound level. As a result, sound design becomes a means of crafting a more immersive and emotionally resonant storytelling experience, where the auditory landscape becomes a canvas for conveying intricate layers of meaning and enhancing the audience's engagement with the narrative.

Immersive Cinematic Worlds: The Transformative Role of Atmospheric Sound

Atmospheric sound serves as a crucial tool in cinematic immersion, effectively transporting the audience into the world of the film. When meticulously crafted, it forges a seamless auditory environment that harmonizes with the visuals and emotional tone of the narrative. This synchronization enhances the viewers' engagement on multiple levels, allowing them to not only see but also feel the story. Whether it's the subtle rustling of leaves in a serene forest, the bustling cacophony of a vibrant city, or the eerie silence of a desolate wasteland, the auditory landscape amplifies the authenticity of the setting, making it more tangible and immersive. Moreover, by mirroring the emotional nuances of the characters and plot, atmospheric sound helps viewers connect more deeply with the story, as the sonic cues trigger visceral responses and emotional resonance. In this way, atmospheric sound functions as an indispensable conduit between the audience and the cinematic world, facilitating a richer, more immersive viewing experience that transcends mere visual storytelling.

The Harmonious Convergence of Sight and Sound: The Role of Atmospheric Sound in Cinematic Immersion

Atmospheric sound plays a pivotal role in enhancing the authenticity and completeness of a cinematic scene by harmoniously complementing its visual elements. It serves as a bridge, seamlessly connecting what the audience observes with what they hear, thereby cultivating a more immersive and comprehensive cinematic experience. This synergy ensures that the sensory elements of a scene align perfectly, reinforcing the audience's suspension of disbelief and allowing them to fully immerse themselves in the narrative world. Whether it's the gentle chirping of birds in a sun-drenched meadow, the bustling chatter of a crowded marketplace, or the eerie silence of a moonlit graveyard, atmospheric sound transforms a scene into a multi-sensory tapestry, enabling viewers to not only witness but also emotionally engage with the story, transcending the boundaries of visual storytelling and fostering a deeper connection with the cinematic universe.

F. Background scores

Background scores are a fundamental and intricate element of the filmmaking process, wielding the power to amplify the emotional impact and narrative depth of a film. These scores are like the unseen hands that guide the viewer's emotions throughout the cinematic journey. Whether through dramatic crescendos to heighten tension during a suspenseful sequence, tender melodies to infuse a romantic moment with warmth, or leitmotifs that symbolize characters or themes, background scores serve as sonic storytellers. They collaborate with the visual elements on screen, harmonizing with every shot and scene to enhance the audience's connection with the characters and the unfolding narrative. Moreover, these musical compositions are key in structuring the film's emotional trajectory, guiding the viewer through the highs and lows of the story. Through their expertly crafted melodies and synchronized timing, background scores provide a multisensory experience that transcends mere visual storytelling, leaving a profound and lasting emotional imprint on the audience, making them an indispensable component of the cinematic art form.

Background Score: Emphasizing Key Moments:

"Emphasizing key moments" in filmmaking refers to the practice of using background scores, or musical compositions, to draw the audience's attention to pivotal and emotionally significant moments in the film. These musical scores are meticulously crafted to enhance the overall impact of the scene and create a more immersive and emotionally resonant cinematic experience. Whether it's intensifying the drama of a climactic confrontation, heightening the suspense of a thrilling sequence, or enhancing the romance in a tender moment, the choice of music serves as a powerful tool for filmmakers to guide the audience's emotions and ensure that the essence of these crucial scenes is deeply felt and remembered.

Creating Emotional Impact: The Transformative Role of Background Scores, Elevating Emotion and Impact in Storytelling

Background scores serve as powerful tools in elevating the dramatic impact of a scene, acting as sonic architects of emotion. During pivotal moments in a narrative, such as when a character stands at the precipice of a life-altering decision, confronts a formidable adversary, or undergoes a profound turning point, the musical accompaniment can artfully underscore the gravity and emotional depth of the situation. Through carefully composed melodies, harmonies, and rhythms, the score can evoke a spectrum of emotions, ranging from suspense and tension to triumph and catharsis. This emotional resonance pulls the audience deeper into the narrative, forging a profound connection between viewers and the characters they're observing. It heightens the intensity of the experience, immersing the audience in the characters' emotional journey and imbuing the story with a lasting impact that lingers far beyond the final frame, making the role of background scores in storytelling nothing short of transformative.

Architects of Suspense: The Role of Background Scores in Crafting Tension and Anticipation

In scenes fraught with suspense and tension, such as thrilling chases or moments steeped in mystery and anticipation, background scores become indispensable tools for manipulating the audience's emotional state. Composers deftly employ a blend of instruments, tempo, and dynamics to craft a sonic landscape that engenders a palpable sense of unease and anticipation. The careful selection of instruments, often featuring dissonant chords and eerie harmonies, creates an unsettling auditory atmosphere, while the tempo, whether quickening or slowing, heightens the viewer's heart rate and reinforces the feeling of imminent danger or intrigue. Gradually escalating dynamics, from soft and subtle to loud and intense, mirror the rising tension onscreen, effectively keeping the audience on the edge of their seats and intensifying their emotional investment in the unfolding narrative. In this way, background scores in suspenseful sequences are not mere auditory accompaniments; they are skillful architects of tension, enhancing the overall cinematic experience by immersing the viewer in a state of anxious anticipation.

Elevating Romance: The Transformative Role of Background Scores in Cinematic Love Stories

In cinematic storytelling, background scores assume a pivotal role in accentuating the emotional resonance of romantic and tender moments. They become the sonic conduits of love, imbuing these scenes with a profound sense of intimacy and emotion. Composers skillfully craft gentle melodies and soothing harmonies, often employing instruments like strings or piano to evoke a sense of timelessness and vulnerability. This musical backdrop not only enhances the romantic atmosphere but also serves as an emotional anchor, allowing viewers to feel the depth of the characters' emotions. When executed masterfully, the right musical composition can elevate a love confession or a heartfelt gesture to a level of poignancy that lingers in the hearts and memories of the audience, underscoring the transformative power of background scores in eliciting profound emotional connections between viewers and the characters they're invested in.

Harmonizing Character Journeys: The Dynamic Role of Background Scores in Storytelling

Background scores in film and storytelling are dynamic companions to character arcs, intimately tracing the emotional evolution of characters as they grapple with challenges and transformations. The music serves as a sonic mirror to the characters' inner worlds, adapting in tone and intensity to reflect their changing circumstances and emotional states. As characters grow and confront obstacles, the score's evolution parallels their own, enhancing their narrative arcs. This symbiotic relationship between character development and music invites the audience to form a deeper connection with the characters by directly engaging with their emotional journeys. Subtle shifts in the score can communicate a character's internal turmoil, resilience, or triumph, enriching the storytelling experience and fostering a profound empathy between the audience and the characters as they collectively navigate the twists and turns of their narrative paths.

Harmonizing Narratives: The Synchronicity of Film Scores and Story Structure

Film scores are intricately designed to synchronize with the overarching narrative structure of a film, representing a collaborative effort between composers and directors. The score is meticulously orchestrated to align with the rise and fall of the story's dramatic arc, strategically punctuating the narrative's key elements: the rising action, climax, and resolution. As the visual storytelling unfolds, the music serves as a guidepost, subtly directing the audience's emotional journey and helping them navigate the narrative terrain. By skillfully signaling transitions and emotional cues, the score communicates to the audience where they are in the storytelling process and what emotions to anticipate, thereby enhancing the overall impact and coherence of the cinematic experience. This synergy between music and narrative structure underscores the critical role of film scores in shaping the audience's engagement and comprehension of the story, making them an indispensable component of the cinematic storytelling apparatus.

Visual-Music Synchronization: Elevating Cinematic Storytelling through Harmonious Integration

In cinematic storytelling, the art of visual-music synchronization is a cornerstone of creating a harmonious and immersive audio-visual experience. Background scores are meticulously orchestrated to align with the visual elements and cinematography of a film, forging a symbiotic relationship between what is seen and what is heard. This synchronization involves well-timed musical cues that strategically accentuate specific shots, camera movements, and editing choices. For instance, a dramatic soaring crescendo may accompany a breathtaking landscape shot, intensifying its visual impact and eliciting an emotional response from the audience. This alignment between music and visuals not only amplifies the sensory engagement but also adds depth and dimension to the storytelling, elevating the overall cinematic experience by seamlessly merging the auditory and visual realms into a cohesive narrative tapestry.

The Power of Music in Film: Shaping Mood and Enhancing Emotional Atmosphere

The art of selecting music in filmmaking holds immense power in shaping the mood of a scene. The choice of music, whether it's a haunting and foreboding orchestration for a horror film or a vibrant and energetic score for an action sequence, acts as a potent mood enhancer. It intricately weaves itself into the fabric of the visual elements, working hand-in-hand to establish a specific emotional atmosphere. The music becomes an emotional compass, guiding the audience's feelings and reactions, ultimately enhancing their immersion in the narrative. A well-matched score can elevate tension in suspenseful moments, infuse romance with warmth and tenderness, or inject energy and excitement into action sequences. By seamlessly harmonizing with the visual storytelling, music becomes a vital conduit for the audience's emotional journey, fostering a deeper connection with the narrative and amplifying the overall impact of the film.

The Timeless Impact of Film Music: Melodies That Echo in Memory

Music's ability to evoke potent emotions and leave a lasting imprint on the audience's psyche is a testament to its profound impact in filmmaking. Memorable musical motifs or themes, strategically associated with pivotal moments in the narrative, transcend the boundaries of the screen to become integral components of the film's emotional resonance. These musical cues serve as emotional triggers, triggering a rush of feelings and memories long after the movie has ended. Viewers often find themselves recalling these melodies when reminiscing about the film, as they are intricately woven into their personal connection with the story and its characters. In this way, music transcends its role as a mere auditory backdrop and becomes an enduring emotional thread that binds viewers to the film, enhancing its cultural and emotional significance in their lives.

The Indelible Legacy of Iconic Film Scores: Sonic Signatures of Cinematic Identity

Iconic film scores have the remarkable capacity to become inextricably linked with the films they accompany, forging a unique and enduring cinematic identity. Consider the infamous "Jaws" theme, which instantly evokes fear and suspense, or the epic resonance of the "Star Wars" theme that embodies grand adventures in a galaxy far, far away. These scores transcend their role as mere musical accompaniments to become integral facets of the film's identity. They resonate deeply within popular culture and the collective consciousness, serving as sonic touchstones that symbolize the essence of the movies they are associated with. These memorable compositions not only enhance the emotional impact of the films but also contribute significantly to their cultural significance, making them a vital part of cinematic history and an indelible aspect of the audience's connection to the stories they tell.

Musical Leitmotifs

They act as a sonic storytelling tool, allowing the audience to subconsciously connect with characters and their journeys on a deeper level. When a character's leitmotif resurfaces, it triggers associations with that character's personality, struggles, or story arc. Additionally, leitmotifs can convey emotions and thematic elements, providing a musical language that enriches the storytelling. Composers carefully craft these motifs to match the character's personality or the essence of the idea they represent, ensuring a seamless integration with the visual narrative. As a result, musical leitmotifs enhance character development, reinforce narrative themes, and create a more immersive and emotionally resonant cinematic experience. They leave a lasting impression on the audience, contributing to the overall impact and artistry of the film. Here's a detailed explanation of how musical leitmotifs work in film:

Enriching Character Development: The Role of Leitmotifs in Filmmaking

In filmmaking, individual characters often have their own distinctive musical themes or leitmotifs, a technique that enriches character development and storytelling. These musical motifs serve as sonic signatures, encapsulating the essence of each character, conveying their personality traits, and tracing their emotional arcs throughout the narrative. For instance, a hero may be accompanied by a heroic and uplifting theme, reflecting their courage and nobility, while a villain's leitmotif might be sinister and foreboding, signaling their malevolent intent. These musical identities not only deepen the audience's connection with the characters but also provide a narrative shorthand, allowing viewers to instantly recognize and connect with a character's presence and emotional state. The use of character-specific themes enriches the storytelling experience, adding layers of depth to character development and enhancing the overall emotional resonance of the film.

Creating Sonic Bonds: The Continuity and Emotional Resonance of Character-Specific Musical Motifs in Film

The use of consistent musical motifs associated with specific characters in a film or narrative provides a crucial layer of continuity and emotional resonance. These motifs are thoughtfully woven into the soundtrack, ensuring that they play whenever their respective characters appear on screen. This steadfast association forms a sonic bond between the characters and their music, allowing the audience to swiftly and intuitively identify each character and deeply connect with them throughout the storytelling. This auditory reinforcement not only solidifies the characters' presence but also underscores their importance in the narrative, guiding the viewers' emotional engagement and heightening their immersion in the story. By consistently aligning music with characters, storytellers enhance the overall cohesiveness of the narrative, enabling the audience to establish meaningful connections with the characters and their individual journeys within the larger storytelling tapestry.

Musical Leitmotifs: Mirrors of Emotion in Character Development

Musical leitmotifs are powerful tools for conveying the emotional depth and evolution of characters in a narrative. These motifs adapt and transform to mirror characters' emotional states. For instance, sadness is expressed with a melancholic arrangement, while triumph is underscored by a celebratory orchestration. Leitmotifs directly translate characters' emotions into music, deepening the audience's connection by allowing them to experience the characters' feelings through music. This adds emotional nuance to character development, enhancing understanding of their internal struggles, growth, and victories within the narrative.

Unlocking Character Subtext: The Subliminal Power of Leitmotifs in Storytelling

Leitmotifs in film and storytelling hold a multifaceted role in conveying character subtext, providing a rich layer of complexity to character development. These motifs extend beyond the surface to reveal the intricate inner workings of characters, even when their outward demeanor suggests otherwise. For instance, a seemingly confident character may have a theme that, when played with subtlety or nuanced variation, unveils their hidden vulnerability or inner turmoil. This subtextual use of leitmotifs allows the audience to delve deeper into the character's psyche, unraveling the layers of their emotional landscape and motivations. It transforms the music into a subliminal language, conveying nuances of the character's thoughts and feelings that may not be explicitly expressed in dialogue or actions. This added depth enhances the audience's engagement with the character, making them more relatable, complex, and multidimensional, and ultimately enriching the storytelling experience by inviting viewers to explore the subtextual depths of the narrative.

Harmonizing Growth: The Evolution of Leitmotifs in Character Development

Character development in storytelling is often intricately intertwined with the evolution of leitmotifs, creating a profound musical reflection of a character's growth and transformation. These motifs adapt and change in tandem with the character's journey, serving as auditory markers of their development and the challenges they face. For instance, a character's leitmotif may undergo subtle or dramatic alterations to signify their evolving personality, beliefs, or circumstances. These changes can coincide with pivotal moments in the narrative, marking turning points or character arcs. A shift in the musical motif might denote the character's inner turmoil, resilience, or newfound resolve. This musical evolution acts as a sonic companion to the character's narrative arc, allowing the audience to bear witness to their transformation and empathize with their trials and triumphs. In this way, leitmotifs become an integral facet of character-driven storytelling, enhancing the audience's understanding of the characters' inner worlds and amplifying their emotional connection to the narrative.

Musical Foreshadowing and Symbolism: The Power of Leitmotifs in Storytelling

Leitmotifs, with their reappearance and subtle variations, serve as powerful tools for foreshadowing and symbolism within a narrative. These recurring musical themes can act as foreshadowing agents, hinting at future events or developments in the story. For instance, a love theme that resurfaces at various points in the narrative can symbolize the enduring and timeless nature of a romantic relationship, subtly hinting at its importance in the unfolding plot. Additionally, leitmotifs can be employed to symbolize thematic elements, offering deeper layers of meaning to the narrative. In this way, music becomes a symbolic language, enriching the storytelling experience by infusing it with subtext and thematic resonance. This use of leitmotifs not only engages the audience on an intellectual level but also heightens their emotional connection to the story, making it a compelling tool for narrative depth and complexity.

Harmonies and Discord: The Role of Leitmotifs in Interpersonal Dynamics of Film

The interplay of musical leitmotifs in films with intricate character relationships adds a layer of depth and complexity to the storytelling. When two characters share a significant connection, their respective leitmotifs might interact and overlap, symbolizing the fusion of their emotional worlds. This blending or harmonizing of themes signifies their bond, whether it's a romantic partnership, a deep friendship, or a complex alliance. Conversely, in conflict situations or moments of tension, the clashing of leitmotifs can create a discordant and dramatic musical landscape, mirroring the conflict and emotional discord between the characters. This dynamic use of leitmotifs becomes a sonic reflection of the intricate dynamics at play within the narrative, enhancing the audience's understanding of the characters' relationships, alliances, and conflicts, and amplifying the emotional impact of their interactions onscreen. It underscores the notion that music is not just a passive accompaniment but an active storyteller that shapes and enriches the narrative experience.

Musical Evolution of Relationships: Leitmotifs as Emotional Barometers in Narrative

The evolution of relationships within a narrative is often artfully conveyed through the nuanced changes in the musical interplay between characters. As relationships progress, the emotional dynamics and connections between characters can undergo transformation, and this metamorphosis is reflected in the leitmotifs associated with them. For instance, the transition from initial animosity to friendship or romantic involvement may be accompanied by subtle or pronounced shifts in the way their respective musical motifs are presented within the score. These changes may signify the softening of hostilities, the deepening of understanding, or the emergence of affection. As characters grow closer or more distant, their musical interaction becomes a narrative thread that guides the audience's perception of their evolving dynamics. This musical evolution enhances the emotional depth and realism of the storytelling, allowing viewers to emotionally invest in the progression of relationships and fostering a deeper connection with the characters' personal journeys within the narrative.

Unforgettable Melodies: The Enduring Impact of Leitmotifs in Cinematic Memory

Well-crafted leitmotifs possess a remarkable capacity for memorability, often becoming indelibly etched in the minds of the audience and synonymous with the characters they represent. These musical motifs serve as distinctive auditory signatures, encapsulating the essence and emotional journey of each character. As a result, viewers may find themselves recalling these musical cues long after the film has concluded, evoking vivid memories of the story and its characters. This enduring musical connection deepens the emotional resonance of the narrative, allowing the audience to carry the essence of the film with them, even beyond the confines of the screen. The memorability of leitmotifs enriches the overall cinematic experience by creating lasting impressions, nurturing a strong emotional connection between viewers and the characters, and contributing to the enduring cultural significance of the film.

Elevating the Cinematic Experience: The Transformative Power of Musical Leitmotifs

The inclusion of musical leitmotifs in a film significantly enhances the viewing experience by adding a profound layer of storytelling that transcends mere dialogue and visuals. These recurring musical themes become a parallel narrative, intricately woven into the emotional fabric of the story. They act as emotional cues, guiding the audience's emotional responses and heightening their immersion in the narrative. The music serves as a bridge that connects viewers with the characters, their inner worlds, and their emotional journeys, fostering a deeper sense of empathy and engagement. This immersive quality transforms the act of watching a film into a holistic sensory experience, where the auditory and visual elements combine to create a powerful and lasting impact on the audience. In this way, musical leitmotifs contribute significantly to the overall richness and emotional resonance of the cinematic journey, elevating it to a level of depth and immersion that goes beyond the sum of its parts.

Silence and Pause

Silence can serve as a canvas for amplifying emotional intensity. By juxtaposing a quiet scene with what has been a cacophony of sound, filmmakers can accentuate the gravity of a moment, making it stand out in stark relief. The absence of dialogue or music can draw the audience's attention to the characters' facial expressions, body language, and the subtleties of their interactions, inviting viewers to delve deeper into the characters' emotional states and motivations. In essence, silence becomes a shared space where the audience and the characters intersect on an emotional level, fostering a more profound connection between the viewer and the narrative. It allows the audience to fill in the emotional blanks with their own interpretations and experiences, making the storytelling experience more personal and resonant. In the hands of a skilled filmmaker, silence becomes a dynamic storytelling tool, capable of evoking a wide range of emotions and leaving a lasting impression on the audience. Here's a detailed explanation of how the absence of sound can create emotional impact in film:

Unveiling Inner Turmoil: The Narrative Power of Silent Moments in Film

Moments of silence within a film hold a distinct narrative power by compelling the audience to focus on a character's inner turmoil, conflicts, or emotional struggles. In these instances, the absence of dialogue and background noise serves as a deliberate choice to heighten the viewer's connection to the character's internal world. By stripping away external distractions, the audience becomes acutely attuned to the character's thoughts, emotions, and psychological state. For example, a silent close-up shot of a character's face can become a canvas for conveying their inner turmoil through subtle facial expressions, micro-expressions, and body language. The power of these silent moments lies in their ability to reveal the depth of a character's emotional journey, allowing viewers to intimately connect with their innermost thoughts and feelings. This narrative device engages the audience on a visceral level, inviting them to empathize with the character's struggles and fostering a deeper emotional connection to the story.

Building Suspense: The Artful Use of Silence in Anticipation of Pivotal Plot Moments

Silence within a narrative serves as a potent tool for building anticipation and tension, particularly in the lead-up to significant events or revelations in the plot. When used strategically, the absence of sound becomes a powerful auditory vacuum that amplifies the audience's awareness of an impending moment of great importance. This heightened awareness fosters a sense of suspense and emotional investment, as viewers become acutely attuned to the gravity of what is about to unfold. The silence becomes a palpable void, almost like a held breath, where the audience's collective anticipation is intensified. This artful use of silence creates a dynamic interplay between sound and silence, allowing filmmakers to manipulate the audience's emotions and engagement with the narrative, ensuring that pivotal moments are met with an even greater impact and resonance.

Silent Dialogues: Enhancing Emotional Depth Through Dramatic Pauses in Film

Dramatic pauses and the use of silence within dialogue-driven scenes serve as powerful cinematic devices to underscore a character's emotional state or the significance of their words. These strategic pauses act as temporal vacuums, punctuating the dialogue and allowing the audience to immerse themselves in the emotional landscape of the characters. Whether conveying hesitation, grief, shock, or anger, these pauses create space for the audience to absorb and empathize with the emotions portrayed on screen. They become moments of profound connection between the characters and the viewers, as the silence heightens the impact of the spoken words and allows the audience to share in the characters' experiences and feelings. This narrative technique transforms dialogue into a multi-dimensional exchange of not just words but also emotions, fostering a deeper engagement with the story and its characters.

Silent Impact: Enhancing Emotional Intensity in Critical Story Scenes

Critical scenes in storytelling, such as a character's decision to confront a long-standing fear, a shocking revelation, or a moment of personal realization, are frequently enriched by the deliberate use of silence. In these pivotal moments, the absence of sound becomes a powerful tool for amplifying the emotional intensity of the scene. The silence serves as a canvas upon which the audience's heightened emotional responses can unfold. It creates a profound contrast to the events taking place, emphasizing their significance and allowing viewers to absorb the full weight of the moment. This auditory vacuum becomes a moment of suspended anticipation, immersing the audience in the character's experience and eliciting a more visceral and memorable reaction. By using silence strategically in these impactful scenes, storytellers can elicit a deeper emotional connection with the audience, making these moments resonate long after the story has concluded.

From Noise to Silence: Using Cinematic Contrast to Spotlight Moments of Significance

The deliberate contrast between sound and silence serves as a highly effective cinematic technique for drawing attention to specific moments or characters within a narrative. When the storytelling context involves a sudden shift from a noisy or chaotic environment to silence, it creates a stark and abrupt change that immediately captures the audience's focus. For instance, a bustling party abruptly falling silent when a character enters can symbolize their significance in the narrative or signal a pivotal turning point in the story. This auditory juxtaposition functions as a narrative spotlight, highlighting the character or event in question and emphasizing its importance. By exploiting this contrast between sound and silence, filmmakers not only steer the audience's attention but also imbue the scene with a heightened sense of drama and significance, making it a memorable and impactful moment within the narrative.

Silence as Symbolism: Conveying Profound Meaning in Storytelling

Silence in storytelling transcends mere absence of sound; it can hold profound symbolic meaning. Deliberate use of silence can serve as a potent storytelling device to convey complex concepts. It can symbolize emptiness, highlighting the void within a character's life or their emotional landscape. Silence can evoke feelings of isolation, underscoring a character's detachment from their surroundings or their struggle to connect with others. In this way, silence becomes a universal language that communicates deeper layers of meaning and emotion. It invites the audience to interpret and reflect upon the narrative on a symbolic level, fostering a more profound engagement with the characters' inner worlds and the overarching themes of the story. This symbolic use of silence elevates the storytelling experience by inviting viewers to contemplate the nuanced subtext of the narrative, making it a powerful tool for conveying complex emotions and ideas.

Character Revealed: The Power of Silence for Introspection and Decision-Making in Narrative

Moments of silence within a narrative serve as poignant opportunities for characters to engage in reflection, introspection, or to make pivotal decisions. These silent interludes offer a window into the character's inner world, inviting the audience to share in their thoughts, emotions, and motivations. As the character navigates the stillness, their facial expressions, body language, and the subtleties of their actions become the primary means of communication, revealing the intricacies of their internal struggles and decision-making processes. These moments enable viewers to forge a more profound connection with the character, as they are granted intimate access to their innermost thoughts and emotions. This narrative device fosters empathy and understanding, allowing the audience to invest more deeply in the character's journey and the broader storytelling, making it a powerful tool for character development and audience engagement.

Sound and Silence: Signifying Character Transformation in Narrative

The transformation of a character's journey within a narrative can be powerfully accentuated through the strategic use of silence as a narrative device. The transition from silence to speech, or vice versa, serves as a symbolic marker of personal growth and transformation. For example, a character who initially presents as introverted and reserved but later finds their voice and the confidence to express themselves undergoes a profound shift in their character arc. This transition can be highlighted through the deliberate use of silence, showcasing their initial hesitancy or inner turmoil and contrasting it with their eventual ability to communicate and assert themselves. The moments of silence that bookend this transformation become pivotal in conveying the character's evolution, allowing the audience to witness their journey and growth firsthand. This narrative technique adds layers of depth and complexity to character development, making it a compelling tool for storytelling that resonates with the audience on an emotional level.

Inviting Engagement: The Transformative Power of Silence in Audience Participation

Silence in storytelling acts as an invitation to active audience engagement, a subtle yet powerful call to viewers to participate more actively in the narrative experience. In moments of silence, the absence of dialogue and background noise compels the audience to focus on visual and emotional cues, encouraging them to read between the lines and interpret the characters' thoughts and feelings through non-verbal communication, facial expressions, and body language. This heightened attention to detail not only fosters a deeper connection with the characters but also immerses viewers more fully in the narrative. Silence becomes a shared moment of introspection, a collaborative experience where the audience is encouraged to actively participate in unraveling the story's subtext and emotional nuances. In this way, silence transforms from a passive element into an interactive tool that enriches the audience's understanding and emotional investment in the narrative, ultimately leading to a more profound and immersive viewing experience.

Silence as an Open Canvas: Fostering Personal Interpretation and Emotional Resonance in Narrative

The absence of sound within a narrative creates a unique space for open interpretation, where viewers are invited to engage with the story on a more personal and subjective level. In moments of silence, the lack of explicit auditory cues allows audiences to project their own emotions, experiences, and perspectives onto the characters and scenes, making the emotional impact of the narrative highly relatable and deeply personal. This open canvas for interpretation fosters a sense of universality, where viewers can see reflections of their own lives, thoughts, and feelings within the storytelling. Silence becomes a powerful catalyst for emotional resonance, creating a more intimate and empathetic connection between the audience and the narrative as they actively contribute to the meaning and depth of the story. It encourages viewers to find their own emotional resonance within the silence, making the storytelling experience more personal, memorable, and emotionally enriching.

G. Sound Mixing and Dolby Atmos

Immersive sound technologies, exemplified by innovations like Dolby Atmos, have indeed ushered in a paradigm shift in the way audiences perceive and engage with cinema. Unlike traditional audio systems, these technologies enable sound engineers to meticulously control the placement and movement of audio elements within a three-dimensional sound space. This precision in sound placement allows for a more authentic and emotionally resonant audio experience. When used effectively, immersive sound can transport viewers into the heart of the narrative, whether it's the echo of footsteps in a haunted house, the thunderous roar of a racing car, or the whisper of a character's inner thoughts. By enveloping the audience in a multidimensional audio environment, immersive sound transcends the boundaries of the screen and speakers, forging a deeper connection between viewers and the cinematic world. It doesn't just complement storytelling; it becomes an integral part of it, immersing audiences in the film's emotional core. In theaters, where this technology is most pronounced, the impact is even more pronounced, as it can elevate the entire cinematic experience to new heights, making it a sensory journey that transcends the visual and auditory to create a truly unforgettable encounter with storytelling. Here's a detailed explanation of how immersive sound works in the context of Dolby Atmos and its impact on cinematic experiences:

Dolby Atmos Technology: A Paradigm Shift in Cinematic and Home Entertainment Audio

Dolby Atmos represents a cutting-edge audio technology that revolutionizes the way sound is experienced in the cinematic and home entertainment realms. Departing from the traditional channel-based audio systems where sounds are assigned to fixed channels like left, right, center, and surround speakers, Dolby Atmos introduces the concept of object-based audio. In this innovative approach, sound engineers have the flexibility to assign audio objects to precise locations within a three-dimensional space. These audio objects are not confined to predefined channels but are treated as independent entities with their own positional data. This dynamic spatial awareness enables a more immersive and lifelike sound experience, as sound can move freely in any direction, including overhead, creating a captivating audio environment that complements the visual aspect of storytelling in unprecedented ways. It's a technology that offers greater precision and versatility in sound design, providing filmmakers with a powerful tool to craft richer, more immersive audio experiences for audiences.

Dolby Atmos: Elevating the Audio Experience with Vertical Sound Channels

A standout feature of Dolby Atmos is the integration of height channels, a significant departure from conventional audio systems. In traditional setups, sound is typically distributed through horizontal channels, but Dolby Atmos introduces the concept of vertical or overhead channels. This means that audio engineers can direct sound from speakers positioned above the audience, expanding the audio canvas to include the dimension of height. By doing so, Dolby Atmos creates a profoundly immersive and lifelike audio experience. The addition of sounds from overhead sources adds a new layer of depth and dimension to the soundstage, enhancing the sense of realism and enveloping the audience in a more convincing and captivating audio environment. This technology allows for precise sound placement both horizontally and vertically, enabling filmmakers to craft audio experiences that mirror the complexity and subtleties of the real world, further intensifying the emotional impact of the storytelling.

Dolby Atmos Precision: Creating Realistic Three-Dimensional Soundscapes

Dolby Atmos empowers sound engineers with the ability to achieve unparalleled precision in sound placement within a three-dimensional space. This level of accuracy enables the creation of a sonic environment that closely mirrors the natural world, resulting in an exceptionally realistic audio experience. For instance, in a Dolby Atmos system, sound objects can be positioned with such precision that raindrops can be perceived as falling from above, creating an authentic sense of rain showering down on the listener. Similarly, the technology allows for the simulation of a helicopter flying overhead, with the sound moving seamlessly from one speaker to another, delivering a truly immersive auditory sensation. This capability to recreate the subtleties of real-world sound and precisely place audio objects within a three-dimensional audio canvas enhances the storytelling by immersing the audience in a lifelike and emotionally resonant soundscape that complements the visual narrative.

Dolby Atmos technology: Creating a 360-Degree Audio Experience for Total Immersion

Dolby Atmos technology offers a transformative audio experience by delivering sound from every conceivable direction, including not only the traditional horizontal plane but also from above and below the audience. This revolutionary approach creates a 360-degree soundstage that envelops the viewers in a three-dimensional audio environment. It goes beyond conventional audio systems, making the audience feel as though they are not merely watching a movie but fully immersed in it. Sounds come from all around, enhancing the perception of depth, dimension, and movement within the audio landscape. Whether it's the rustling of leaves overhead, the rumble of thunder surrounding the viewer, or the footsteps of a character approaching from behind, Dolby Atmos elevates the cinematic experience by making the audience an integral part of the narrative, intensifying emotional engagement and delivering a level of immersion that was previously unattainable with traditional audio technologies.

The Emotional Impact of Immersive Sound: How Dolby Atmos Enhances the Cinematic Experience

Immersive sound technology, such as Dolby Atmos, plays a pivotal role in elevating the emotional impact of a film. By delivering sound with remarkable precision and realism, it brings the auditory elements of a movie to life in a way that deeply resonates with the audience's senses and emotions. Whether it's the thunderous roar of a spaceship taking off, the delicate rustling of leaves in a tranquil forest, or the emotionally charged dialogue between characters, immersive sound enhances the storytelling by creating an authentic and immersive auditory experience. This heightened level of realism not only immerses viewers more deeply in the narrative but also intensifies emotional engagement. Audiences can feel the adrenaline rush during action sequences, the tension in suspenseful moments, or the warmth in heartfelt conversations, all of which contribute to a more profound and emotionally resonant cinematic journey that lingers long after the credits roll.

Seamless Scene Transitions: Enhancing Cinematic Flow with Dolby Atmos Immersive Sound

Immersive sound technology, such as Dolby Atmos, serves as a powerful tool in facilitating seamless scene transitions in filmmaking. As the audience follows the narrative from one location to another, immersive sound enables the audio to transition with a level of fluidity and precision that enhances the overall cinematic experience. Sounds can seamlessly pan from one set of speakers to another, mirroring the movement and shift in the visual narrative. This cohesive audio continuity not only maintains the audience's engagement but also contributes to the overall coherence of the storytelling. Whether it's the gradual fading of music as characters exit a party or the gradual immersion into a new environment through the subtlety of background sounds, immersive sound technology aids in ensuring that the transitions between scenes are not only smooth but also enhance the narrative flow, creating a more immersive and captivating viewing experience.

Audience Engagement: The Role of Immersive Sound in Sustaining Viewer Engagement

Immersive sound technology, offering a multidimensional auditory experience, is vital for maintaining audience engagement throughout a film. It envelops viewers in a three-dimensional soundscape, enhancing immersion and emotional connection with the narrative and characters. Whether through spatial audio in action scenes, subtle background sounds, or dynamic audio interplay, it consistently captivates audiences, keeping them fully invested in the cinematic journey. This technology not only enhances the viewing experience but also underscores its importance in holding viewers' attention and creating a profound and memorable cinematic impact.

Elevating Suspense and Thrills: The Impact of Immersive Sound in Action and Horror Films

Immersive sound technology, especially in genres like action and horror, intensifies suspense and thrills in films. Precise sound placement, whether stealthy footsteps or sudden jump scares, creates an electrifying cinematic experience. Multidimensional audio allows for precise orchestration, capitalizing on the audience's sensitivity to sound in suspenseful or terrifying moments. The result is a sensory assault that keeps viewers on the edge of their seats, amplifying the emotional impact of the narrative. Whether it's the thunderous approach of a threat or the eerie creaking of a haunted house, immersive sound not only heightens intensity but also ensures maximum impact, immersing the audience in a visceral and unforgettable cinematic journey.

The Unmatched Cinematic Immersion: The Impact of Immersive Sound Technologies in Movie Theaters

Immersive sound technologies like Dolby Atmos shine in movie theaters, providing an unmatched cinematic experience hard to replicate at home. The combination of top-notch visuals and immersive sound creates a sensory symphony, elevating the film's enjoyment. The precision and scale of theater sound systems, along with technologies like Dolby Atmos, immerse the audience deeply in the narrative. Whether it's thunderous explosions, intimate dialogue, or sweeping musical scores, the theater becomes a hub of cinematic immersion. This experience not only enriches storytelling but offers a unique emotional and sensory journey exclusive to the theater, highlighting its enduring role as a communal space for transcendent storytelling.

The Home Theater Revolution: Bringing Immersive Sound Technologies to Your Living Room

Immersive sound technologies, initially designed for theaters, are now adapted for home theater systems, offering a similar level of audio immersion at home. Advancements in soundbar tech, specialized speakers, and audio processing allow viewers to replicate cinematic sound quality. Whether it's the powerful bass of an action scene or precise spatial audio in a thriller, home theaters provide a immersive experience, bridging the gap between cinema and home. This offers viewers the chance to fully immerse themselves in their favorite films without leaving their homes, reshaping the landscape of home entertainment.

CHAPTER - 05

5. The Art of Editing in Indian Cinema

Editing in Indian cinema is a fundamental and intricate element, with a pivotal role in shaping the overall narrative, pacing, and emotional impact of the film. Indian filmmakers skillfully employ a diverse range of editing techniques to craft engaging and immersive storytelling experiences. These techniques encompass both traditional and innovative methods, such as the use of montage sequences to condense time or convey complex emotions, jump cuts to add a dynamic and unconventional visual style, and intricate parallel editing to build tension or contrast multiple storylines effectively. Moreover, editing in Indian cinema often integrates seamlessly with music, dance, and elaborate choreography, enhancing the cinematic experience and contributing to the rich cultural tapestry of Indian storytelling. Whether it's the high-energy song-and-dance sequences of Bollywood or the nuanced storytelling of regional cinema, editing is the glue that binds together the various elements of Indian cinema, elevating it to a powerful and emotionally resonant art form. Here's how editing elements are treated in Indian cinemas:

A. Narrative Structure

Narrative structure in Indian cinema is a dynamic and multifaceted element that encompasses a rich tapestry of storytelling approaches. Indian filmmakers, spanning Bollywood, Tollywood, Kollywood, and other regional industries, employ diverse narrative structures to engage audiences and convey their stories effectively. Traditional linear storytelling is prevalent, where narratives progress chronologically from start to finish, but Indian cinema often showcases an intricate blend of flashbacks, nonlinear storytelling, and parallel narratives. Flashbacks are frequently used to provide backstory or reveal character motivations, while nonlinear storytelling adds complexity and intrigue. Parallel narratives deftly intertwine multiple storylines, building tension or emphasizing thematic connections. Indian cinema is also renowned for its emotional depth and thematic richness, which are seamlessly integrated into the narrative structure. Whether it's the larger-than-life sagas of Bollywood, the realistic and socially conscious tales of regional cinema, or the genre-bending experiments of emerging filmmakers, the narrative structure serves as a versatile canvas upon which Indian cinema paints its stories, reflecting the diverse cultural, social, and emotional landscapes of the Indian subcontinent.

B. Linear and Non-Linear Storytelling

Indian cinema exhibits a versatile narrative toolbox by employing both linear and non-linear storytelling techniques, each carefully selected to serve distinct cinematic objectives. Linear storytelling, with its chronological progression, provides a clear and straightforward narrative structure, ideal for conveying straightforward tales and character journeys, ensuring that the audience effortlessly follows the story's flow. In contrast, non-linear storytelling disrupts this chronological order, intentionally jumbling events, timelines, or perspectives to foster intrigue and suspense. This technique is adept at weaving intricate narratives, showcasing unique viewpoints, and challenging conventional storytelling norms. Filmmakers choose between these approaches based on their creative vision and the specific needs of their narrative; linear storytelling for clarity and simplicity, and non-linear storytelling to heighten engagement, complexity, and thematic exploration. This dynamic blend allows Indian cinema to cater to a diverse range of genres and storytelling demands, captivating audiences with a rich array of cinematic experiences.

Linear Storytelling:

Linear Storytelling in Indian Cinema: The Traditional Narrative Structure

Linear storytelling, the foundational and most traditional narrative structure in Indian cinema, adheres to a straightforward chronological order. In this narrative approach, events are presented in a linear fashion, aligning with the flow of time. The story initiates from its starting point and unfolds progressively, following a clear and uninterrupted sequence of events. This linear structure is characterized by its simplicity and accessibility, making it easy for audiences to follow the narrative's progression and character development. It allows for a clear cause-and-effect relationship between events, making it ideal for storytelling that seeks to convey a direct and comprehensible narrative. In this way, linear storytelling serves as a foundational framework in Indian cinema, offering a coherent and easily digestible narrative structure that accommodates various genres and storytelling objectives.

Straightforward Storytelling: The Allure of Linear Narratives in Classic Indian Cinema

Linear storytelling, favoured for its clarity and simplicity, is a narrative structure that prioritizes straightforward storytelling without complex temporal shifts or non-linear elements. It is often the preferred choice in Indian cinema, particularly in classic Bollywood films, especially those belonging to genres like romantic dramas or family sagas. This narrative approach ensures that the audience can easily follow the plot and character development without confusion. Events are presented in a sequential and cause-and-effect manner, mirroring the passage of time, making it accessible to a broad range of viewers. The linear structure is especially effective in films where emotional engagement and relatability are paramount, as it allows the audience to connect with the characters and their journeys in a direct and comprehensible manner, ultimately enhancing the emotional impact of the storytelling.

Classic Bollywood: Linear Storytelling in 'Dilwale Dulhania Le Jayenge' and 'Kabhi Khushi Kabhie Gham'

Movies such as "Dilwale Dulhania Le Jayenge" and "Kabhi Khushi Kabhie Gham" serve as prime examples of linear storytelling within the world of Indian cinema. In these iconic films, the narrative unfolds in a straightforward and chronological manner, mirroring the natural progression of events in the characters' lives. There are no major temporal disruptions or non-linear elements, making it easy for viewers to follow the story's development from start to finish. This narrative structure aligns perfectly with the genre of family dramas and romantic tales, as it allows for a clear depiction of character relationships, emotional arcs, and the evolution of familial bonds over time. The linear storytelling approach in these films not only enhances clarity and accessibility but also resonates deeply with audiences, contributing to the enduring popularity and cultural significance of these cinematic classics.

Non-Linear Storytelling:

Exploring the Intricacies of Non-Linear Storytelling: Disrupting Chronological Order in Film Narratives

Non-linear storytelling, in stark contrast to its linear counterpart, intentionally disrupts the conventional chronological order of events within a narrative. This narrative technique involves presenting the story in a fragmented or non-sequential manner, often featuring events that jump back and forth in time. The deliberate use of temporal disruptions adds a layer of intrigue and complexity to the storytelling, challenging the audience to piece together the puzzle of the narrative and draw connections between disparate moments. This approach allows filmmakers to explore themes of memory, perception, and the subjective nature of truth, as well as create suspense, surprise, and a sense of mystery within the narrative structure. By subverting the traditional flow of time, non-linear storytelling offers a dynamic and unconventional approach to filmmaking that can be particularly effective in genres such as psychological thrillers, mysteries, and narratives that explore the multifaceted nature of human experience.

Unlocking the Allure of Non-Linear Storytelling: Crafting Mystery and Suspense Through Narrative Disruption

Non-linear storytelling is a narrative technique prized for its ability to captivate and intrigue audiences by intentionally revealing information in a non-sequential fashion. By presenting events out of chronological order, this approach creates a sense of mystery and suspense within the narrative. Audiences are kept on their toes as they piece together the fragmented storyline, drawing connections between past and present moments. This technique is particularly effective in genres such as thriller, suspense, and mystery, where the element of surprise and the gradual unveiling of key plot details are essential to keeping viewers engaged. Non-linear storytelling, with its inherent complexity and unpredictability, fosters a heightened sense of curiosity, encouraging viewers to actively participate in deciphering the narrative puzzle, making it a valuable tool in crafting gripping and intellectually stimulating cinematic experiences.

Exploring the Depths of Character: Non-Linear Storytelling's Profound Insight into the Human Psyche

Non-linear storytelling serves as a creative canvas for filmmakers to explore unique perspectives and delve into the inner workings of characters' minds by presenting their experiences in a non-sequential manner. This narrative technique enables a deeper exploration of character motivations, emotions, and personal growth, as viewers gain insights into the complex interplay of past and present events shaping a character's psyche. By unraveling the narrative threads in a non-linear fashion, filmmakers can intricately portray the subjective nature of memory and perception, illustrating how the characters' past experiences continue to influence their present choices and actions. This approach adds layers of depth and complexity to character development, fostering a more profound and multi-dimensional understanding of the protagonists and their evolving journeys, which can be particularly impactful in character-driven dramas and psychological narratives.

Indian Cinema's Artful Embrace of Non-Linear Storytelling: A Case Study of 'Dil Se' and 'Rang De Basanti

Indian cinema has embraced non-linear storytelling as a narrative device, and exemplary instances can be found in films like "Dil Se" directed by Mani Ratnam and "Rang De Basanti." In "Dil Se," a complex love story unfolds amidst the backdrop of political turmoil, and the non-linear structure enhances the emotional depth of the characters by interweaving their past and present experiences. This approach reflects the intricacies of human emotions and memories, highlighting how the characters' pasts continue to shape their lives. Similarly, "Rang De Basanti" skillfully employs non-linear storytelling to convey a potent message about social and political activism by juxtaposing events from India's freedom struggle with the contemporary lives of its characters. The use of temporal disruptions in these films not only adds layers of complexity to the narratives but also serves as a powerful storytelling tool, allowing filmmakers to explore the profound connections between past and present, personal and political, and love and activism.

C. Flashbacks and Flash-forwards

Flashbacks:

Unveiling the Past: The Narrative Significance and Creative Potential of Flashbacks in Storytelling

A flashback is a narrative device employed in storytelling where the chronological timeline of a story is momentarily interrupted to depict events that occurred in the past. These past events are often chosen for their relevance to the current storyline, serving various narrative purposes such as providing essential context, explaining character motivations, or revealing critical information that aids in the audience's comprehension of the overarching plot. Flashbacks are a powerful tool for filmmakers and writers, as they allow for the exploration of characters' backgrounds, the unveiling of hidden secrets, and the gradual unfolding of a character's emotional and psychological development. By seamlessly weaving the past into the present narrative, flashbacks contribute depth, complexity, and a sense of completeness to the overall storytelling experience, providing audiences with a richer and more nuanced understanding of the characters and their journeys.

Unearthing Character Depths: The Role of Flashbacks in Crafting Rich and Multifaceted Personalities in Storytelling

Flashbacks serve as a potent narrative device to delve into the intricate process of character development within storytelling. They are often used to provide the audience with glimpses into a character's past, allowing for a deeper understanding of their motivations, emotional scars, or pivotal life experiences that have shaped their current persona. By exploring these formative moments or traumas through flashbacks, filmmakers and writers offer insights into why characters behave, think, or make decisions in specific ways in the present. This approach adds layers of complexity to the characters, making them more relatable and multidimensional, as viewers can empathize with their past struggles and triumphs, ultimately forging stronger connections with the narrative's protagonists and antagonists alike. In essence, flashbacks are a vital tool for unravelling the intricate web of human psychology and emotions, enhancing the overall storytelling experience.

Elevating Plot Dynamics: The Role of Flashbacks in Unveiling Crucial Details and Enhancing Narrative Engagement

Flashbacks are a narrative tool that serves to enhance the overall plot of a story by providing crucial backstory and revealing hidden details that are essential for the audience's comprehension of the main narrative. These glimpses into the past often contain information, events, or relationships that are integral to the central storyline. By strategically deploying flashbacks, filmmakers and writers can unravel mysteries, clarify ambiguous situations, and connect seemingly unrelated plot points. This not only deepens the audience's engagement with the story but also adds a layer of intrigue and complexity, as viewers become actively involved in piecing together the puzzle of the narrative. Whether it's unlocking the secrets of a character's past or shedding light on a pivotal historical event, flashbacks contribute to plot development by providing the essential context needed to make sense of the unfolding events in the present storyline, thereby enriching the storytelling experience.

Eliciting Emotions Through Flashbacks: The Power of Past Experiences in Connecting Audiences to Characters

Flashbacks are a powerful storytelling device renowned for their ability to evoke emotions within the audience. By showcasing pivotal moments from a character's history or past experiences, they effectively tug at the viewer's heartstrings, compelling them to empathize or sympathize with the character on a profound level. These glimpses into the character's emotional journey, whether it be moments of joy, sorrow, love, or trauma, enable viewers to connect with the character's humanity and vulnerabilities. This emotional resonance not only deepens the audience's engagement with the story but also reinforces their investment in the character's development and arc. As viewers witness the highs and lows of a character's past through flashbacks, they forge a stronger emotional bond with the narrative, experiencing the character's triumphs and tribulations as if they were their own, thus heightening the overall emotional impact and resonance of the storytelling.

Fanning the Flames of Anticipation: Using Flashbacks for Effective Foreshadowing in Storytelling

Flashbacks serve as a dynamic narrative tool, not only delving into a character's past but also allowing for effective foreshadowing within storytelling. Filmmakers and writers employ flashbacks to hint at or tease future events, creating an air of anticipation and suspense. These glimpses into the past may contain subtle clues, cryptic imagery, or enigmatic dialogues that offer viewers tantalizing hints about forthcoming plot developments or revelations. By strategically using flashbacks for foreshadowing, storytellers engage the audience's curiosity and intrigue, inviting them to actively speculate about how these past events might connect to or influence the unfolding narrative. This narrative technique adds an extra layer of complexity to the storytelling, encouraging viewers to invest themselves more deeply in the plot as they eagerly await the fulfillment of the foreshadowed events, ultimately enhancing the overall sense of anticipation and excitement in the story.

Emotional Storytelling and Character Development Through Flashbacks in Indian Cinema: A Case Study of 'Kabhi Khushi Kabhie Gham'

In Indian cinema, flashbacks are frequently employed as a narrative device to delve into character backgrounds and motivations, offering viewers valuable insights into the complexities of the characters and their relationships. An illustrative example can be found in the Bollywood classic "Kabhi Khushi Kabhie Gham." In this film, flashbacks are strategically utilized to unveil the underlying reasons behind familial conflicts and estrangements within a wealthy Indian family. These flashbacks take the audience on a journey into the past, shedding light on pivotal moments, misunderstandings, and emotional upheavals that have shaped the characters' present-day personas and strained family bonds. By weaving the past into the present narrative through these flashbacks, the film not only adds depth and nuance to the characters but also imbues the overarching story with a poignant sense of nostalgia and redemption. As a result, flashbacks in Indian cinema serve as a vital tool for character development and emotional storytelling, enriching the viewer's understanding and connection to the narrative.

Flashforwards:

Propelling the Plot Forward: The Narrative Significance of Flashforwards in Storytelling

A flashforward is a narrative device that propels the audience into the future, revealing events yet to occur. Storytellers use this to create anticipation and suspense, engaging viewers by hinting at what's to come. It piques curiosity and invites audiences to consider how future events will unfold and impact the characters. Flashforwards also allow for exploring alternative scenarios and potential outcomes, adding complexity to the narrative and prompting viewers to ponder various story trajectories. This technique infuses storytelling with foresight and intrigue, enhancing engagement by offering hints of what lies ahead.

Heightening Anticipation and Engagement: The Art of Foreshadowing Through Flashforwards in Storytelling

Flashforwards serve as a potent tool for foreshadowing within storytelling, as they grant storytellers the ability to provide tantalizing hints and clues about future developments, thus building anticipation and maintaining the audience's active engagement. By presenting glimpses of events that have yet to unfold, flashforwards introduce an air of mystery and intrigue, encouraging viewers to piece together the narrative puzzle and speculate about how these future occurrences will come to fruition. This narrative technique not only heightens the audience's curiosity but also fosters a deeper connection to the story as they become emotionally invested in uncovering the significance of these foreshadowed events. Ultimately, flashforwards amplify the sense of anticipation and suspense within the narrative, enhancing the overall storytelling experience by keeping the audience eagerly awaiting the eventual realization of the hinted outcomes.

Unveiling the Future: Cultivating Suspense Through Flashforwards in Storytelling

Flashforwards serve as a powerful narrative tool for building suspense by offering a glimpse of an upcoming event that leaves the audience curious and speculating about its unfolding and significance. This deliberate withholding of context creates tantalizing uncertainty, sparking questions about the circumstances, motivations, and consequences surrounding the depicted future event. Viewers become deeply engaged in the narrative, actively theorizing and speculating about the plot, characters, and their fates, intensifying the overall suspense and anticipation in the storytelling. In essence, flashforwards act as a catalyst, fueling intrigue and suspense, motivating the audience to unravel the mysteries of the future event.

Character Evolution Across Time: Exploring Character Development Through Flashforwards in Storytelling

Flashforwards are versatile tools for character development in storytelling. They show how characters evolve over time, offering glimpses into their future trajectories. By contrasting a character's present with their future self or circumstances, flashforwards reveal the effects of growth, choices, or external factors on their development. This can be powerful when the character's future self represents a significant change, reflecting the evolution of their personality, values, or relationships. Flashforwards also delve into character motivations, aspirations, and decision consequences, enhancing the audience's understanding of the characters and fostering a deeper emotional connection as viewers witness their personal journeys unfold over time.

Shaping Destiny: The Impact of Flashforwards in Indian Cinema - A Case Study of 'Dil Chahta Hai

In Indian cinema, flashforwards are strategically used to provide a glimpse into the future trajectories of characters, creating a dramatic impact. The film "Dil Chahta Hai" offers a notable example, employing a well-placed flashforward scene to reveal the lives of central characters several years ahead. This narrative choice hints at character growth, conflict resolution, and relationship evolution. By contrasting present struggles and aspirations with future circumstances, the flashforward adds depth to character arcs, builds anticipation for their personal journeys, and elevates emotional engagement in the narrative. This showcases how flashforwards in Indian cinema enhance storytelling by infusing dramatic tension and intrigue, ultimately enriching the cinematic experience for the audience.

Combination of Flashbacks and Flashforwards:

In Indian cinema, the combination of flashbacks and flashforwards creates a rich storytelling experience. Flashbacks delve into characters' pasts, enriching the audience's emotional connection to the narrative. On the other hand, flashforwards propel the story into the future, generating anticipation, suspense, and curiosity about upcoming events or character changes. When interwoven, these temporal shifts create a captivating narrative tapestry, deepening character development and adding mystery to plotlines by revealing crucial information at the right moments. This approach elevates Indian cinema to an art form that engages, enlightens, and emotionally resonates with viewers. The Bollywood film "Ghajini," directed by A.R. Murugadoss, exemplifies this technique, depicting the protagonist's short-term memory loss through a mix of flashbacks and flashforwards.

Unraveling Sanjay's Past: The Role of Flashbacks in Character Development and Context Building in 'Ghajini'

Through flashbacks, the audience gains insight into Sanjay's past, including his life before the incident that led to his memory loss. These flashbacks reveal his relationships, career, and personality, helping the audience understand the stark contrast between his past and present self. These glimpses into his past serve as a foundation for character development and provide context for his current predicament.

Forging Ahead: The Use of Flashforwards to Illuminate Sanjay's Quest for Truth and Justice in 'Ghajini'

Simultaneously, the film employs flashforwards to portray Sanjay's efforts to uncover the truth about his condition and seek revenge against those who harmed him. These flashforwards offer a glimpse into the future, showcasing his determination, resourcefulness, and the obstacles he faces in his quest for justice. They also create a sense of anticipation as viewers wonder how these future events will unfold and intersect with the present.

Fragmented Narratives: Crafting Emotional Resonance through the Interplay of Flashbacks and Flashforwards in 'Ghajini'

The combination of flashbacks and flashforwards in "Ghajini" effectively mirrors the fragmented nature of Sanjay's memory. It places the audience in a position similar to the protagonist, experiencing moments of confusion and disorientation. As the narrative alternates between past and future events, viewers are challenged to piece together the puzzle of Sanjay's life and his pursuit of vengeance. This complex narrative structure not only adds depth to the storytelling but also keeps the audience engaged and emotionally invested in Sanjay's journey. It underscores the impact of his memory loss on his character, relationships, and motivations, making "Ghajini" a compelling and emotionally resonant film that uses a combination of flashbacks and flashforwards to explore the complexities of memory, identity, and revenge.

D. Pacing and Rhythm

Pacing and rhythm in Indian cinema are fundamental elements that play a crucial role in shaping the overall cinematic experience. Indian filmmakers, across various film industries including Bollywood, Tollywood, Kollywood, and others, meticulously employ a wide range of pacing techniques to control the narrative flow, engage the audience, and evoke emotions. These techniques encompass both traditional and innovative methods, such as the use of montage sequences to condense time and convey complex emotions effectively, jump cuts to infuse dynamism and unconventional visual styles, and intricate parallel editing to build tension or contrast multiple storylines seamlessly. The concept of "masala" filmmaking, often associated with Bollywood, combines various cinematic elements, including action, romance, drama, and music, in a way that requires skillful pacing transitions between these different narrative facets. Moreover, the integration of music, dance, and choreography into Indian cinema adds another layer to the rhythm and pacing, contributing to the cultural richness and emotional resonance of the storytelling. Whether it's the vibrant and high-energy song-and-dance sequences of Bollywood or the more subtle and realistic storytelling of regional cinema, pacing and rhythm serve as the invisible hands guiding the audience through the narrative journey, making Indian cinema a powerful and captivating art form that transcends linguistic and cultural boundaries.

E. Song and Dance Sequences

In Indian cinema, the inclusion of song and dance sequences is a hallmark tradition that editors skillfully navigate to ensure they become an integral part of the storytelling. These sequences serve not only as entertainment but also as a means to convey emotions, relationships, and narrative progress. Editors must meticulously integrate these moments into the film's pacing, so they feel organic and harmonious with the overall narrative flow. When executed effectively, song and dance sequences elevate the cinematic experience, allowing audiences to connect on a deeper level with the characters and their emotional journeys. These sequences are more than just visual spectacles; they are tools for enhancing storytelling, making Indian cinema a unique and immersive cinematic experience for viewers. Let's explore the use of song and dance sequences in Indian cinema in detail, including how editors work to integrate them seamlessly into the narrative:

Song and Dance Sequences in Indian Cinema: The Cultural and Narrative Significance of Song and Dance Sequences in Bollywood Cinema

Song and dance sequences hold a profound and multifaceted significance within Indian cinema, notably in the vibrant world of Bollywood. These musical interludes not only provide a distinctive cultural identity but also play several pivotal roles in the narrative and aesthetics of the films. They serve as a means of emotional expression, advancing the storyline, and character development, allowing characters to convey their innermost feelings and struggles through music and choreography. Furthermore, these sequences contribute to the entertainment quotient, captivating audiences with their colourful costumes, intricate dance moves, and melodious tunes, making Bollywood films globally renowned for their exuberant and visually captivating musical numbers. In essence, song and dance have become an inseparable and celebrated component of Indian cinema, encapsulating the essence of storytelling, culture, and entertainment, and have left an indelible mark on the cinematic landscape.

Harmonizing Emotions: The Expressive Power of Songs in Indian Cinema

In Indian cinema, songs play a pivotal role in the expression of emotions, functioning as a powerful conduit for characters to convey their innermost feelings. These musical interludes offer a heightened and emotive dimension that transcends mere dialogue, allowing characters to immerse themselves in the spectrum of human emotions. Love is professed with melodious serenades amidst picturesque landscapes, joy is celebrated with exuberant dance numbers, sorrow finds solace in soulful ballads, and even anger finds its voice through intense musical performances. Through the fusion of evocative lyrics, soul-stirring melodies, and expressive choreography, songs become a deeply ingrained and evocative tool for storytelling, evoking empathy and connecting the audience to the characters' emotional journey, thus enriching the cinematic experience.

Sensory Extravaganza: The Entertainment Value of Song and Dance Sequences in Indian Cinema

Song and dance sequences in Indian cinema constitute a significant source of entertainment, offering a captivating blend of audiovisual delights that resonate with audiences across the globe. These sequences are characterized by catchy tunes that linger in the memory, intricate and energetic choreography that showcases the dancers' skill and agility, vibrant and ornate costumes that add a visual spectacle, and the utilization of breathtaking locations that transport viewers to exotic and fantastical worlds. This amalgamation of elements creates a sensory feast that transcends the confines of the screen, inviting the audience to immerse themselves in a world of joy and escapism. Through their sheer exuberance and artistic excellence, these sequences contribute significantly to the overall entertainment value of Indian cinema, making it a globally recognized and cherished form of cinematic expression.

Cultural Tapestry in Motion: The Significance of Song and Dance Sequences in Reflecting India's Rich Heritage in Cinema

Song and dance sequences in Indian cinema carry profound cultural significance, serving as a vibrant tapestry that reflects the country's diverse and rich heritage. They frequently integrate traditional music and dance forms, showcasing the kaleidoscope of India's cultural traditions, from classical Kathak and Bharatanatyam to folk dances like Bhangra and Garba. These sequences become a celebration of India's artistic legacy, bridging the gap between past and present, and often infusing modern narratives with a timeless cultural essence. They not only preserve and promote these ancient art forms but also contribute to the preservation of regional and linguistic diversity by incorporating various styles and languages. In doing so, they offer audiences a window into India's multifaceted cultural identity, making Indian cinema a repository of the country's artistic and cultural wealth, while also fostering a sense of pride and connection among viewers.

Seamless Integration: The Vital Role of Editors in Balancing Song and Dance Sequences with Narrative in Indian Cinema

Editors wield a pivotal role in the art of seamlessly integrating song and dance sequences into the narrative fabric of a film. Their objective is to orchestrate a harmonious coexistence between these musical interludes and the overarching storyline, ensuring that the transitions between the two are fluid and unobtrusive. This involves meticulous synchronization of the music and choreography with the plot's emotional beats and character development, as well as maintaining consistency in tone and pacing. Editors must adeptly navigate the challenge of balancing entertainment value with narrative coherence, allowing these sequences to enhance the storytelling rather than disrupt it. By skillfully crafting the rhythm and structure of these musical moments, editors contribute significantly to the overall impact of Indian cinema, enabling audiences to be engrossed in both the story's emotional journey and the sensory delight of song and dance.

Contextual Significance: The Art of Integrating Song Sequences into the Narrative by Film Editors in Indian Cinema Top of Form

The contextual relevance of song sequences within Indian cinema is paramount, and editors play a crucial role in ensuring that these musical interludes are intricately woven into the narrative fabric. These sequences are not isolated moments of entertainment but are intricately linked to the storyline and character development, often serving as vehicles for emotional expression. Editors meticulously craft the placement of songs to align with the plot's progression, ensuring that the lyrics, music, and choreography resonate with the characters' emotions and the narrative's thematic arc. This requires a deep understanding of the film's thematic intent and the characters' motivations at a given moment, as well as a keen sense of pacing to maintain a cohesive flow. By anchoring the songs within their respective contexts, editors elevate the storytelling experience, making these sequences not only visually and musically captivating but also emotionally resonant and integral to the overall cinematic journey.

Harmonizing Pacing and Rhythm: The Editorial Craft in Shaping the Cinematic Experience

Pacing and rhythm are fundamental elements that editors meticulously manage to enhance the overall cinematic experience. The strategic placement of song sequences is instrumental in modulating the film's tempo and emotional cadence. Editors take into account the movie's overarching structure and storyline, utilizing songs strategically to provide viewers with respites from intense or dramatic scenes, offering moments of reflection or emotional release. Conversely, songs can be employed to build anticipation or accentuate climactic moments by utilizing their inherent musicality to heighten tension or excitement. By deftly orchestrating the ebb and flow of these sequences within the film, editors contribute significantly to the audience's engagement, ensuring that the pacing and rhythm are finely tuned to create a cohesive and emotionally resonant storytelling experience.

Visual Continuity: The Editor's Role in Creating Seamless Transitions Between Narrative and Song Sequences

Visual continuity plays a vital role in the seamless integration of song sequences within a film, and editors are tasked with meticulous attention to detail in this regard. They must ensure that transitions between narrative scenes and musical interludes are visually smooth and coherent. This involves coordinating camera angles, lighting schemes, and costumes to maintain a consistent aesthetic throughout the film. Editors strive to create a sense of visual harmony, so the audience is not abruptly pulled out of the narrative's world when a song begins but instead experiences a natural and immersive flow from one scene to the next. This continuity not only enhances the film's overall polish and professionalism but also reinforces the emotional and narrative connections between the characters and their surroundings, enriching the viewer's cinematic journey.

Preserving Emotional Continuity: The Editorial Art of Seamlessly Integrating Song Sequences into Film Narratives

Editors play a pivotal role in preserving the emotional flow of a film, particularly when integrating song sequences into the narrative. Their skill lies in ensuring that these musical interludes do not disrupt the audience's emotional connection to the story. Editors strike a delicate balance between storytelling and entertainment, carefully crafting the placement and duration of song sequences so that they enhance rather than interrupt the narrative's emotional arc. This involves seamlessly transitioning from dialogue-driven scenes to musical numbers while maintaining the film's emotional continuity, thus preventing jarring shifts in tone or sentiment. By orchestrating this harmonious coexistence, editors ensure that viewers remain deeply engaged in the plot, experiencing a cohesive and emotionally resonant cinematic journey that seamlessly blends storytelling with entertainment.

Balancing Act: Editors' Role in Determining the Duration of Song Sequences for Pacing and Narrative Cohesion

The duration of a song sequence is a crucial aspect that editors carefully assess to maintain the film's overall pacing and narrative cohesion. Editors possess the ability to make precise decisions regarding the length of these sequences, whether it involves trimming them down for brevity or extending them for added depth, all in service of the film's rhythm and storytelling demands. This entails a keen understanding of the narrative's ebb and flow, ensuring that songs neither overstay their welcome nor feel rushed. By skillfully managing the length of song sequences, editors contribute significantly to the film's overall balance and emotional impact, allowing these musical interludes to enhance the storytelling rather than detract from it. This expertise ensures that the audience's engagement remains consistently aligned with the film's intentions and cinematic experience.

Example of Musical Milestone: The Iconic 'Tujhe Dekha To' Song in 'Dilwale Dulhania Le Jayenge' - A Celebration of Love in Bollywood Cinema

In the iconic Bollywood film "Dilwale Dulhania Le Jayenge," the song "Tujhe Dekha To" stands as a pivotal and emotionally charged moment in the unfolding love story between the two central characters, Raj and Simran. This song is masterfully integrated into the narrative, serving as a powerful expression of their burgeoning affection. Against the backdrop of the scenic Swiss countryside, the song encapsulates the essence of their deepening connection, with lush lyrics and evocative music underscoring the palpable chemistry between the characters, played by Shah Rukh Khan and Kajol. The sequence beautifully combines elements of romance, visual splendor, and stirring music to encapsulate the transformative and indelible impact of love, making it an enduring and iconic moment in Indian cinema that resonates with audiences of all generations.

Harmonious Fusion: The Integration of Song Sequences as Narrative and Cultural Expressions in 'Lagaan

In the epic Bollywood film "Lagaan," the song sequences serve as an integral and harmonious part of the narrative, exemplifying the exceptional storytelling and artistic prowess of Indian cinema. These musical interludes, frequently featuring elaborate dance routines, are skillfully interwoven into the storyline. They do more than just entertain; they vividly depict the villagers' arduous struggle against colonial oppression, their unwavering unity, and their indomitable determination to triumph over adversity through cricket. The songs not only celebrate the spirit of resilience and hope but also act as a powerful tool for character development, emotional expression, and thematic reinforcement. This seamless integration of music, dance, and storytelling in "Lagaan" elevates the cinematic experience, making it a compelling testament to the cultural and narrative richness that song sequences can bring to Indian cinema.

F. Montages

Montages serve as a powerful cinematic device for compressing time and efficiently conveying character development or plot progression. By seamlessly editing together a series of shots or scenes, often accompanied by evocative music, montages condense significant moments or actions into a succinct sequence. This technique not only accelerates the narrative but also allows filmmakers to convey complex information, emotional transformations, or character growth in a visually compelling and emotionally resonant manner. Montages harness the synergy of visuals and music to evoke specific emotions, making them a versatile and effective storytelling tool in filmmaking. Whether it's showcasing a training regimen, illustrating a character's evolving relationships, or highlighting a pivotal transformation, montages enhance the audience's engagement and understanding, contributing to a more immersive cinematic experience.

Montages in Filmmaking:

Montage Mastery: The Art of Condensing Time, Emotions, and Themes in Cinema

A montage is a powerful cinematic technique that compresses time, conveys information, and evokes specific emotions or themes through the seamless editing of a series of short shots or scenes. These sequences are expertly intercut to create a succinct and visually impactful narrative device. Often synchronized with music, montages utilize a diverse range of visuals, including images, clips, or even animations, to craft a concise yet compelling storytelling experience. This technique can condense lengthy periods into mere minutes, illustrate character development, or underline key plot points, making it a versatile tool in a filmmaker's arsenal for conveying complex ideas, emotions, and narratives with brevity and impact.

Time Unveiled: The Art of Condensing Narratives with Montages in Cinema

Montages are a cinematic tool primarily employed for time compression. They enable filmmakers to efficiently convey a series of events, actions, or developments that unfold over an extended duration in a compact and visually engaging format. By juxtaposing and intercutting a sequence of short shots or scenes, montages condense time, eliminating the need for protracted, linear storytelling. This compression not only serves to advance the narrative efficiently but also maintains the audience's engagement, providing a dynamic and concise overview of character growth, skill acquisition, or the passage of time within the storyline. Whether it's a training montage in a sports film, a romantic montage capturing a budding relationship, or a sequence illustrating a character's transformation, montages are a powerful cinematic device for conveying complex temporal elements in a succinct and captivating manner.

Efficiency in Storytelling: The Role of Montages in Condensing Narrative Elements and Maintaining Engagement

Montages are an efficient storytelling technique that serves to convey information or depict developments in a succinct and time-effective manner, especially when the alternative would be a lengthy and potentially monotonous real-time depiction. This efficiency is particularly valuable for showcasing character growth, skill acquisition, or the passage of time within a narrative. Instead of dedicating significant screen time to these processes, montages allow filmmakers to condense these elements into a concise yet impactful sequence. Whether it's a protagonist mastering a new skill, a romantic relationship blossoming over time, or the gradual transformation of a setting or character, montages enable audiences to grasp these essential narrative aspects efficiently, maintaining the pacing and engagement of the story while providing a visually engaging and emotionally resonant experience.

Harmonizing Emotions: The Profound Impact of Montages Through Visuals and Music in Cinema

Montages wield a potent cinematic tool to elicit profound emotional responses from the audience. Through the synergy of carefully selected visuals and music, they create a visceral and resonant impact. The choice of music, with its rhythm, melody, and lyrics, can evoke specific emotions, setting the tone for the montage. When synchronized with imagery that captures pivotal moments, character expressions, or significant events, the emotional resonance intensifies. This combination allows audiences to deeply connect with the characters and the narrative, empathizing with their joys, sorrows, triumphs, and struggles. Whether it's a triumphant training montage, a poignant reflection on a character's journey, or a heartwarming sequence of love and connection, the emotional potency of montages lies in their ability to encapsulate the essence of the story and the characters' experiences, leaving a lasting impact on the viewer's heart and mind.

Visualizing Themes: The Art of Thematic Exploration Through Montages in Cinema

Montages serve as a dynamic cinematic device for thematic exploration within a film. They offer filmmakers the opportunity to delve into and emphasize specific themes or motifs by presenting a series of related visuals or actions in a coherent and visually compelling sequence. This thematic exploration allows for a concentrated examination of ideas, symbols, or concepts that are central to the narrative, amplifying their significance and resonance. By weaving together a montage that features recurring symbols, contrasting elements, or parallel narratives, filmmakers can enrich the viewer's understanding of the overarching themes and messages of the story. Whether it's exploring themes of love, loss, resilience, or societal commentary, montages provide a concise and impactful means to engage the audience in a deeper contemplation of the film's underlying ideas and subtext.

Editing Mastery: Crafting Rhythm, Energy, and Impact in Montages

The editing of a montage is a critical element that significantly influences its impact. It involves the selection, arrangement, and timing of individual shots or scenes to create a specific sense of rhythm and energy. Quick cuts between these shots or scenes generate a dynamic pace that can convey excitement, urgency, or momentum, aligning with the emotional or thematic goals of the montage. Techniques such as cross-cutting, where the montage alternates between different actions or locations, add depth and complexity to the sequence by juxtaposing parallel narratives or contrasting elements. Additionally, match cuts, which enable seamless transitions between shots through visual or thematic connections, enhance the montage's flow and cohesiveness. The art of montage editing lies in its ability to use these techniques judiciously to engage the audience, heighten emotions, and effectively convey information or themes within a condensed yet impactful sequence.

Harmony in Motion: The Impact of Music in Montages on Emotional Resonance and Storytelling

Music is an integral component of montages, wielding a substantial influence on their impact and emotional resonance. The selection of music is a pivotal decision, as it not only sets the overall tone but also enhances the viewer's emotional connection to the sequence. The music chosen often synchronizes intricately with the visuals, creating a powerful synergy where specific beats, rhythms, or lyrics align with the actions, emotions, or themes depicted on screen. This synchronization elevates the viewer's engagement by amplifying the sensory experience, making the montage a dynamic fusion of auditory and visual elements. Whether it's a stirring soundtrack that intensifies the emotional highs and lows of a character's journey or a catchy tune that underscores the exuberance of an achievement, music in montages enhances storytelling and leaves a lasting impression on the audience's senses and emotions.

The Visual Tapestry of Montages: Crafting Narrative Impact Through Thoughtful Visual Selection

Visuals are a cornerstone of montages, and they encompass a wide array of elements, from images and video clips to photographs and even abstract visuals. The selection of these visuals is a deliberate process, with each element chosen to convey the intended message, evoke specific emotions, or underscore particular themes. Filmmakers curate visuals that align with the narrative's goals, character development, or thematic exploration, ensuring that they contribute meaningfully to the montage's overall impact. Whether it's a sequence of fleeting moments capturing a character's growth, a collage of images portraying historical events, or a series of abstract shots symbolizing an emotional journey, the visuals in montages are the building blocks of storytelling, enabling filmmakers to craft a concise and visually engaging narrative that resonates with the audience on multiple levels.

The Art of Character Transformation: Exploring the Training Montage in Cinema

Montages are a cinematic device often harnessed to portray a character's development or transformation throughout a narrative. A classic example is the training montage, where a character's journey from novice to expert, or from self-doubt to confidence, is condensed into a visually engaging sequence. This narrative tool is frequently utilized in genres like sports films or coming-of-age stories to effectively communicate a character's evolution. Through a sequence of meticulously selected shots, viewers witness the character's commitment, perseverance, and progress, experiencing the emotional highs and lows of their journey. The training montage encapsulates the essence of character development, making it tangible and relatable, while also conveying the overarching themes of the narrative, such as dedication, self-discovery, or the pursuit of excellence, in a concise and impactful manner.

Accelerating the Narrative: The Role of Montages in Plot Advancement

Montages are a potent tool for advancing the plot, particularly when there is a necessity to traverse extended periods of time or depict significant transitions within the narrative. A travel montage, for example, efficiently conveys a character's journey across various locations, swiftly bridging geographical gaps and signifying a profound sense of change and progression. By skillfully selecting and sequencing shots, montages compress time and provide viewers with a condensed yet vivid depiction of the plot's unfolding events, ensuring that the story maintains momentum and coherence. Whether it's a character's physical journey, the passage of seasons, the evolution of a relationship, or the unfolding of a complex plan, montages streamline the storytelling process, enabling audiences to grasp the essential plot developments and transitions while maintaining engagement and narrative fluidity.

Nurturing Bonds: Depicting Relationship Evolution Through Montages in Film

Montages serve as a compelling means to illustrate the evolution of relationships between characters, particularly in the context of romantic partnerships or friendships. By crafting a montage, filmmakers can efficiently depict moments where characters bond, grow closer, or experience pivotal moments in their relationships without the need for extensive dialogue or exposition. These sequences often comprise a series of carefully chosen shots that convey shared experiences, laughter, shared meals, intimate gestures, or even conflicts, allowing viewers to witness the emotional journey of the characters' connections. The absence of dialogue in these montages underscores the power of visual storytelling, as the subtleties of body language, expressions, and shared moments speak volumes, deepening the audience's engagement and emotional investment in the characters' relationships, whether they are romantic, platonic, or familial.

Examples:

Memorable Montage: The Journey of Friendship in '3 Idiots' (2009)

One notable example of the effective use of montages in Indian filmmaking is from the movie "3 Idiots" (2009), directed by Rajkumar Hirani. In this film, there is a heartwarming and emotionally impactful montage that encapsulates the journey of the three main characters - Rancho (played by Aamir Khan), Farhan (played by R. Madhavan), and Raju (played by Sharman Joshi) - throughout their years at an engineering college.

The Transformative Montage: Capturing Growth, Friendship, and Self-Discovery Through Visual Storytelling

The montage, set to the song "Give Me Some Sunshine," shows their initial struggles, their budding friendship, and their transformation into confident and self-assured individuals. This montage serves as a poignant narrative device that encapsulates the essence of the film's themes, such as the pursuit of passion over conformity, the importance of genuine friendships, and the value of self-discovery. By efficiently condensing the characters' college years into a few minutes, the montage highlights their journey of personal and academic growth while evoking a range of emotions, from initial hardships and moments of despair to the ultimate triumph of friendship and self-realization. It underscores the power of visual storytelling in conveying complex character development and thematic elements, leaving a lasting emotional impact on the audience and making it a memorable and integral part of the film.

This montage serves as a poignant and integral part of the film, highlighting the central themes of friendship, self-discovery, and the pursuit of one's passions. It not only advances the plot but also emotionally resonates with the audience, making it a memorable and impactful example of montages in Indian filmmaking.

G. The Artful Precision of Editing

Emotional Impact - The Artful Precision of Editing

In Indian cinema, the intricate relationship between timing and emotion stands as a defining characteristic. Editors in Indian films undertake a meticulous and artful endeavor, focusing keenly on the precise timing of cuts, synchronization with music, and the integration of visual elements to amplify and optimize the emotional impact on the audience. Be it a poignant dramatic revelation, a tender and heartwarming romantic interlude, or a nail-biting suspenseful twist, the precision in the timing of edits serves as an indispensable element in sculpting the visceral reactions and intensifying the emotional resonance that Indian films are celebrated for. Let's explore how timing and emotion are intertwined in Indian cinema, and how editors in Indian films carefully time cuts to enhance the emotional impact on the audience:

The Emotional Resonance of Indian Cinema: A Journey Through Heartfelt Storytelling and Cultural Richness

Indian cinema, encompassing Bollywood and various regional film industries, is renowned for its profound commitment to emotional storytelling. These films frequently revolve around themes that are intricately linked to human emotions, such as love, family bonds, relationships, and societal issues. Emotions are at the core of Indian cinematic narratives, and filmmakers skillfully employ storytelling techniques that resonate with viewers on an emotional level. The films often employ melodious songs, expressive dance sequences, and heartfelt dialogues to evoke a wide spectrum of emotions, from joy and laughter to sorrow and empathy. This emphasis on emotional storytelling not only allows audiences to connect deeply with the characters and their journeys but also reflects the cultural richness and emotional depth of Indian storytelling traditions, making Indian cinema a global powerhouse in evoking profound emotional responses from its viewers.

Cultural Context and Emotional Storytelling: Shaping Indian Cinema's Art of Timing and Technique

Cultural context plays a pivotal role in Indian filmmaking, shaping the timing of edits and other cinematic techniques to optimize emotional resonance. Indian films draw heavily from the nation's diverse cultural traditions and values, infusing narratives with elements that are deeply ingrained in the social fabric. Music, with its diverse genres and rhythms,

192

is utilized to set the emotional tone, while dance sequences, ranging from classical forms like Bharatanatyam to vibrant Bollywood choreography, are employed as a means of emotional expression. Symbolism rooted in cultural traditions is deftly incorporated to convey complex emotions, making scenes rich in subtext. Timing of edits is often influenced by the cultural nuances of storytelling, ensuring that emotional beats align with the viewers' cultural sensibilities. This fusion of cultural context with cinematic storytelling results in a profound and culturally resonant emotional experience for audiences, further cementing the importance of culture in the art of Indian filmmaking.

Harmony in Motion: The Transformative Power of Music in Indian Cinema

Music occupies a central and transformative role in Indian cinema, acting as a catalyst for emotional expression and resonance. Songs and background music are meticulously integrated into the narrative to heighten the emotional impact of scenes. The timing of musical cues, whether it's the precise moment when a song begins, the gradual swell of music to underscore a poignant moment, or the delicate fade-out to allow for reflection, is a deliberate and artful process. This synchronization between music and storytelling profoundly influences the audience's emotional journey, amplifying the depth and complexity of the characters' feelings, whether it's love, joy, grief, or despair. Music transcends linguistic and cultural barriers, making it a universal tool for evoking emotions, and in Indian cinema, it serves as a powerful conduit for creating indelible emotional connections between the audience and the narrative, ensuring a deeply resonant and immersive cinematic experience.

How Timing Influences Emotional Impact in Indian Films: Unveiling the Art of Dramatic Reveals

Dramatic reveals or plot twists are a recurring element in Indian cinema, and their execution is a meticulously crafted process. Editors play a vital role in orchestrating these pivotal moments, as their timing and presentation are crucial to ensuring maximum impact. The buildup of tension leading up to these reveals, often achieved through precise editing techniques such as pacing, shot selection, and the interplay of visuals and music, heightens the anticipation and emotional intensity for the audience. Music serves as a powerful ally, enhancing the suspense and accentuating the emotional charge of the revelation. Whether it's the unveiling of a hidden truth, the resolution of a mystery, or the revelation of a character's motivations, the timing and artful editing of these dramatic reveals are essential in captivating the audience, evoking surprise, awe, or even catharsis, and contributing significantly to the overall impact and memorability of Indian films.

Capturing Love's Rhythm: The Artful Timing and Sensuality of Romantic Moments in Indian Cinema

Romantic moments are an intrinsic and cherished aspect of Indian cinema, often forming the heart and soul of the narrative. The timing of cuts during these sequences is meticulously calibrated to capture the nuances of chemistry and passion between characters. Editors skillfully use close-ups to focus on the protagonists' expressions, the exchange of glances that speak volumes, and the tender moments that evoke emotional resonance. Music plays a pivotal role in these scenes, setting the mood and enhancing the emotional connection. The rise and fall of the musical score, synchronized with the characters' movements and dialogue, create a rhythmic dance that mirrors the ebbs and flows of love and desire. These finely tuned elements combine to weave a captivating romantic tapestry, drawing viewers into the emotional intensity and sensuality of the characters' relationships, making them an integral and unforgettable part of Indian cinematic storytelling.

Crafting Emotion: The Role of Timing and Editing in Sentimental Moments of Indian Cinema

Sentimental moments are a cornerstone of Indian cinema, where themes of love, sacrifice, and familial bonds are frequently explored. Editors play a pivotal role in crafting these emotionally charged scenes, leveraging timing to immerse the audience deeply in the sentiments being portrayed. They employ their craft to emphasize the poignancy of these moments – a heartfelt dialogue, a selfless act of sacrifice, or a touching gesture – by judiciously inserting well-timed close-ups or reaction shots. These techniques draw the audience's attention to the raw and genuine expressions of emotion on the characters' faces, allowing viewers to connect intimately with the profound sentiments unfolding on screen. In this way, editors contribute significantly to the audience's emotional engagement, making these sentimental moments a powerful and resonant component of Indian cinematic storytelling.

Harmonizing Art and Rhythm: The Mastery of Editing in Indian Cinema's Musical Extravaganzas

Musical sequences are a hallmark of Indian cinema, celebrated for their grandeur and spectacle. Editors in Indian filmmaking collaborate closely with choreographers and music directors to orchestrate these sequences seamlessly. The timing of cuts is meticulously coordinated with the beat and rhythm of the music, ensuring that the visual elements harmoniously synchronize with the audio. These sequences go beyond mere entertainment; they are designed to evoke a wide array of emotions, whether it's the exuberance of celebration, the fervor of love, or the depth of sorrow. Through synchronized choreography and precise editing, these musical extravaganzas become a sensory delight, captivating the audience with their colourful visuals, intricate dance moves, and melodious tunes. The careful interplay between music, dance, and editing in these sequences is a testament to the artistry of Indian cinema, aiming to transport viewers into a world of emotion, expression, and pure cinematic joy.

Examples:

The Iconic Train Station Scene in 'Dilwale Dulhania Le Jayenge' (DDLJ): The Art of Timing and Emotional Resonance in Indian Cinema"

In the iconic train station scene from "Dilwale Dulhania Le Jayenge" (DDLJ), the art of timing plays a pivotal role in crafting a profoundly poignant moment. As the train is about to depart, the timing is meticulously orchestrated to heighten the emotional impact. The characters, Raj (played by Shah Rukh Khan) and Simran (played by Kajol), exchange intense and heartfelt expressions that communicate their love and longing. The music, a soulful and emotive melody, swells at just the right moment, accentuating the emotional crescendo of the scene. This synchronicity between timing, expressions, and music creates a heartrending tableau, establishing a deep and enduring emotional connection between the protagonists and the audience. It's a moment of reckoning and profound emotion that has become an iconic symbol of love in Indian cinema, demonstrating the power of precise timing in eliciting powerful emotions and enhancing the narrative impact.

Family, Love, and Reconciliation: The Art of Timing and Editing in 'Kabhi Khushi Kabhie Gham' (K3G)

In "Kabhi Khushi Kabhie Gham" (K3G), timing and editing are masterfully employed to underscore the film's central themes of family, love, and reconciliation. The movie hinges on emotional reunions and reconciliations within a fractured family, and the precise timing of cuts during these pivotal moments is instrumental in crafting the film's emotional depth. The well-orchestrated editing allows for a nuanced exploration of complex emotions, highlighting characters' expressions of love, regret, forgiveness, and understanding. Through expertly timed cuts and the interplay of visuals and music, these moments become emotionally charged and resonate deeply with the audience. The artful use of timing and editing in K3G contributes significantly to the film's ability to tug at the heartstrings, making it a classic example of how these elements can elevate a narrative's emotional impact in Indian cinema.

The Pulse of Triumph: Timing and Emotion in the Climactic Cricket Match of 'Lagaan

In the climactic cricket match of "Lagaan," timing becomes a crucial element in heightening the film's emotional impact. As the fate of the characters and the entire village hinges on the pivotal moments of the match, the timing of these instances is meticulously orchestrated to maximize suspense and excitement. The interplay of precise editing, dramatic close-ups, and the rising crescendo of the musical score amplifies the emotional stakes and keeps the audience on the edge of their seats. The climactic timing not only underscores the physical and emotional struggle of the characters but also symbolizes the broader themes of resilience, unity, and the fight against oppression. In this way, the skillful use of timing and music in "Lagaan" transforms the cricket match into a heart-pounding, emotionally charged spectacle, making it one of the most memorable and thrilling sequences in Indian cinema.

H. Close-Ups and Reaction Shots

In Indian cinema, close-up shots and reaction shots are powerful tools for conveying emotions and enriching the narrative's depth and impact. Editors use these shots strategically to capture the nuanced expressions of actors, immersing the audience in the characters' emotional journeys. These intimate visual moments not only provide insight into the characters' innermost feelings but also engage viewers as active participants in the storytelling process. Whether it's a quivering lip, a glistening tear, or a subtle change in gaze, close-ups and reaction shots amplify empathy, forging a deep and immediate connection between the audience and the characters. In Indian cinema, these shots are indispensable instruments, enhancing the storytelling experience by intensifying emotional resonance and making it an integral part of cinematic expression. These shots are characterized by their ability to evoke a sense of cultural and emotional richness and connect viewers with the characters' experiences.

Intimacy and Emotion: The Power of Close-Up Shots in Indian Cinema

Close-up shots are a cornerstone of Indian cinema's cinematographic vocabulary, frequently utilized to establish an intimate and emotive connection between characters and the audience. These shots, tightly framing a character's face, direct the viewer's attention to the nuances of their expressions, the depth of their emotions, and the storytelling conveyed through their eyes. In Indian cinema, where emotions play a central role, close-ups are a powerful tool for conveying the subtleties of feelings such as love, longing, joy, sorrow, or conflict. They enable the audience to delve deep into the characters' inner worlds, fostering empathy and understanding. Whether capturing a tear rolling down a cheek or the twinkle of a smile, close-up shots forge a potent emotional link, intensifying the impact of the narrative and making them an enduring and indispensable technique in Indian cinematic storytelling.

Emotive Signposts: The Role of Reaction Shots in Indian Cinema's Narrative Landscape

Reaction shots in Indian cinema function similarly to their counterparts in international cinema, serving as a crucial tool for storytelling. These shots capture a character's immediate response to a situation, statement, or the actions of another character. They are employed to underscore the emotional impact of a particular moment, offering viewers a glimpse into a character's inner world and their visceral reactions. Reaction shots are instrumental in conveying a character's shock, joy, anger, surprise, or any other emotional state, enhancing the audience's understanding of the narrative and character dynamics. They play a pivotal role in building tension, empathy, and engagement, making reaction shots an essential component of the emotional and narrative palette of Indian films.

Cultural Context and Significance: Emotion as Art, The Role of Close-Up and Reaction Shots in Indian Cinema's Universal Appeal

Indian cinema is celebrated for its emotionally driven storytelling, where themes like love, family, relationships, and societal issues take center stage. The heart of Indian cinema lies in its ability to deeply resonate with the audience's emotions. Close-up shots, with their focus on characters' expressions and eyes, serve as windows into their innermost feelings, allowing viewers to connect intimately with the emotional journeys of the characters. Similarly, reaction shots capture immediate responses, enabling the audience to empathize with characters' joys, sorrows, and conflicts. This emphasis on emotional storytelling, facilitated by these cinematographic techniques, ensures that Indian cinema transcends linguistic and cultural boundaries, forging a universal and enduring emotional connection between the audience and the narratives, making it a distinctive and cherished aspect of Indian cinematic art.

Amplifying the Artistic Embrace: Close-Up and Reaction Shots in Indian Cinema's Musical and Dramatic Spectacle

In Indian cinema, close-ups and reaction shots are vital for enhancing the emotional resonance of music, dance, and dramatic performances. Close-ups tightly frame characters' faces, allowing the audience to deeply connect with the raw emotion and passion conveyed through these artistic expressions. Reaction shots capture characters' responses, reflecting the audience's emotional engagement and enhancing the immersive power of Indian cinema. Whether it's tears of joy during a soul-stirring song or expressions of awe in response to a dramatic monologue, these cinematographic techniques forge a lasting connection between the audience and the musical and dramatic traditions at the heart of Indian cinema.

Character Unveiled: The Depth and Nuance of Close-Up Shots in Indian Cinema

Character depth is a paramount aspect of Indian filmmaking, and close-up shots serve as an indispensable tool for this exploration. Indian filmmakers employ these shots to penetrate the intricacies of characters' emotions and motivations. By zooming in on facial expressions, close-ups create a canvas for nuanced portrayals, allowing viewers to delve into the complex layers of a character's psyche. The subtleties of a quivering lip, a furrowed brow, or a twinkle in the eye become a window into a character's inner world, inviting the audience to connect with them on a profoundly personal level. These shots enable the viewer to not only comprehend a character's external actions but also to empathize with their inner struggles, joys, and conflicts. In the hands of skilled filmmakers, close-up shots become a conduit for character-driven storytelling, enriching narratives with depth and authenticity, and solidifying the emotional bond between the audience and the characters on screen.

Strategic Use of Close-Up Shots and Reaction Shots in Indian Films: In the Heart of Emotion, The Intimacy of Close-Up Shots in Indian Cinema

Close-up shots are strategically harnessed in Indian cinema during intimate and emotionally charged moments, serving as a cinematic technique that enhances the audience's connection with the characters. Whether it's a tender romantic confession, a poignant heartfelt dialogue, or a character's profound realization, these shots offer an intimate perspective that draws viewers deeper into the characters' experiences. By focusing tightly on facial expressions, close-ups bring forth the subtleties of emotions, allowing the audience to intimately witness the vulnerability, sincerity, and authenticity of the characters in these moments. This deliberate use of close-ups heightens the emotional impact, making the audience active participants in the characters' emotional journeys, and thereby intensifying the overall narrative impact and the emotional resonance of these intimate moments in Indian cinema.

Harmonizing Emotions: Close-Up and Reaction Shots in Elevating Musical Sequences of Indian Cinema

Musical sequences are a signature element of Indian cinema, and cinematographic techniques like close-up and reaction shots play a pivotal role in elevating the impact of these sequences. Close-up shots zoom in on the characters' faces, allowing the audience to intimately connect with the emotions conveyed through the lyrics and music. These shots capture the subtlest of expressions, making the audience feel the depth of the characters' sentiments. Reaction shots, on the other hand, shift the focus to the characters' responses, revealing how the musical performances resonate within the story. Whether it's tears of joy, expressions of love, or moments of introspection during a song, reaction shots mirror the audience's emotional engagement. In this way, close-ups and reaction shots work in tandem to transform musical sequences into immersive and emotionally resonant experiences, marking them as a defining and beloved aspect of Indian cinema.

Dramatic Revelations and Emotional Crescendos: The Role of Close-Up and Reaction Shots in Indian Cinema's Narrative Impact

In Indian cinema, editors play a crucial role in orchestrating close-up shots and reaction shots during dramatic revelations or pivotal plot twists. These shots are meticulously timed to enhance the emotional impact of these moments, effectively drawing viewers into the narrative's unfolding drama. Close-up shots zoom in on characters' faces, capturing the raw and genuine expressions that convey shock, awe, or realization, allowing the audience to connect deeply with the characters' emotional states. Reaction shots, in turn, offer a glimpse into how these revelations ripple through the story's fabric, showcasing the characters' immediate responses and emotional turmoil. By employing close-ups and reaction shots in these critical junctures, Indian cinema amplifies the intensity of the narrative, ensuring that viewers are not merely spectators but active participants in the characters' journeys, making these cinematic techniques indispensable for delivering powerful and unforgettable storytelling moments.

Clashes and Confrontations: The Role of Close-Up and Reaction Shots in Amplifying Emotions in Indian Cinema

Close-ups and reaction shots are frequently deployed in Indian cinema during moments of intense conflict and confrontation to intensify the emotional impact of these scenes. Close-ups hone in on the characters' faces, emphasizing the raw and visceral expressions that convey anger, frustration, anguish, or determination. These shots bring viewers face-to-face with the characters' emotional turmoil, making them active participants in the unfolding drama. Simultaneously, reaction shots offer a glimpse into how the confrontations ripple through the narrative, showcasing the characters' immediate responses and the evolving dynamics within the scene. By harnessing these cinematographic techniques during conflict and confrontation, Indian cinema accentuates the emotional intensity of these pivotal moments, ensuring that viewers are not only spectators but deeply engaged in the characters' emotional and dramatic struggles, thereby making these scenes unforgettable and emotionally resonant components of the storytelling.

Examples:

Weaving Emotions: The Role of Close-Up and Reaction Shots in 'Kabhi Khushi Kabhie Gham' (K3G)

In "Kabhi Khushi Kabhie Gham" (K3G), close-up shots and reaction shots are expertly woven into the fabric of the narrative, enhancing the emotional depth of the film. Close-up shots are deployed to capture the rich emotional range of the characters during pivotal moments, allowing viewers to intimately connect with their joys, sorrows, and dilemmas. These shots bring forth the subtleties of their sxpressions, underlining the complexity of their emotions. Concurrently, reaction shots provide insight into the family's collective responses to conflicts and reconciliations, offering a nuanced portrayal of their dynamics and interpersonal relationships. These shots contribute to the creation of a layered emotional tapestry within the film, heightening the audience's engagement and empathy with the characters and their interconnected stories. Through the meticulous use of these cinematographic techniques, "K3G" achieves a profound and enduring impact, making it a classic example of how close-up and reaction shots can elevate emotional storytelling in Indian cinema.

Eyes of Love: The Role of Close-Up and Reaction Shots in 'Dilwale Dulhania Le Jayenge' (DDLJ)

"Dilwale Dulhania Le Jayenge" (DDLJ) masterfully employs close-up shots and reaction shots to enrich its storytelling. Close-up shots are strategically used during romantic scenes to accentuate the palpable chemistry between the film's lead characters, Raj (played by Shah Rukh Khan) and Simran (played by Kajol). These shots focus on their expressive eyes, capturing the depth of their affection and the intensity of their love. In parallel, reaction shots illuminate the family's responses to the burgeoning love story, ranging from surprise and concern to eventual acceptance and support. These shots provide crucial insight into the familial dynamics and emotional evolution within the narrative, reinforcing the central theme of love conquering all obstacles. Through the astute use of close-ups and reaction shots, DDLJ succeeds in creating an enduring and heartfelt cinematic experience, making it a timeless classic and exemplar of how these techniques can enhance emotional storytelling in Indian cinema.

Heartfelt Expressions: The Role of Close-Up and Reaction Shots in 'Bajrangi Bhaijaan

In "Bajrangi Bhaijaan," close-up shots play a pivotal role in conveying the emotional journey of the lead character, Pavan (played by Salman Khan), as he embarks on a heartfelt mission to reunite a lost young girl with her family. These close-up shots focus on Pavan's expressions, his evolving emotional states, and his growing attachment to the child, Munni (played by Harshaali Malhotra). Viewers witness the transformation in his character, from initial curiosity and compassion to unwavering dedication and love. Simultaneously, reaction shots are employed to capture the innocence and vulnerability of Munni, underscoring her emotional connection with Pavan and drawing the audience further into her plight. The juxtaposition of close-up shots of Pavan and reaction shots of Munni creates a deeply empathetic connection between the audience and these two central characters, ultimately underlining the film's core theme of love transcending borders and language barriers, making "Bajrangi Bhaijaan" a poignant and emotionally resonant cinematic experience.

I. Match Cuts in Indian films

Seamless Transitions - Match Cuts in Indian films

Match cuts, a key editing technique, are employed by editors to establish seamless transitions between scenes or shots within a film or video. The concept revolves around connecting two shots by juxtaposing a visual or thematic element present in the first shot with a corresponding or related element in the following shot. This continuity technique serves several crucial purposes in filmmaking. Firstly, it aids in maintaining the narrative flow by smoothly bridging different scenes or locations, helping viewers effortlessly comprehend the progression of the story. Secondly, match cuts can emphasize thematic or symbolic connections between disparate parts of the narrative, reinforcing underlying motifs or themes. Finally, they can evoke emotions or create visual metaphors, enhancing the storytelling by establishing subtle links that resonate with the audience. In essence, match cuts are a fundamental tool for editors to ensure the coherence and impact of a film's narrative, facilitating a seamless and immersive viewing experience. Let's explore match cuts in Indian films, including their purpose, techniques, and how editors use them to create smooth transitions and enhance storytelling:

Match Cuts in Indian Films

Seamless Storytelling: The Art and Significance of Match Cuts in Film Editing

A match cut is a film editing technique that achieves a seamless transition between shots or scenes by juxtaposing a visual or thematic element in one shot with a corresponding element in the following shot. This technique creates a sense of continuity and connection, enhancing the narrative flow and thematic resonance of the film. It can be used to draw parallels between different moments in the story, to symbolize character development or transformation, or to evoke emotions and convey meaning. Match cuts serve as a powerful tool for filmmakers to subtly link disparate elements within their narrative, allowing viewers to make connections and engage more deeply with the story, characters, and themes. Whether it's a match cut that aligns the movement of two characters or one that juxtaposes past and present, this technique adds a layer of complexity and cohesion to the visual storytelling in cinema.

Purpose

Match cuts serve several purposes in Indian films:

Seamless Cinematic Transitions: The Role and Impact of Match Cuts in Film

Match cuts are a fundamental cinematic technique employed to achieve seamless transitions between shots or scenes. Their primary purpose is to make the transition virtually unnoticeable to the audience, ensuring a continuous and fluid narrative flow. By smoothly aligning a visual or thematic element in one shot with a corresponding element in the next, match cuts create an almost invisible link between these segments of the film. This seamless transition helps maintain the story's coherence and emotional rhythm, preventing jarring interruptions that could disrupt the viewer's engagement. As a result, match cuts are an essential tool for filmmakers to ensure that the audience remains immersed in the storytelling, allowing them to experience the narrative as a cohesive and uninterrupted whole.

Visual Metaphors and Symbolism: The Art of Match Cuts in Film Narrative

Match cuts in film serve as a potent means of conveying symbolism and metaphorical connections between various elements, enriching the narrative and adding layers of thematic depth. By juxtaposing similar visual or thematic elements between two shots, filmmakers can draw parallels that carry deeper meaning. For instance, a match cut might connect the opening shot of a rising sun with the closing shot of a character's hopeful face, symbolizing a new beginning and personal growth. Alternatively, it could link the movement of one character with another, reflecting their interconnected destinies. These subtle visual metaphors allow filmmakers to communicate complex ideas and emotions non-verbally, inviting viewers to interpret and engage with the narrative on a deeper level, making match cuts a powerful tool for infusing symbolism and metaphor into cinematic storytelling.

Elevating Emotions: The Impact of Creative Match Cuts on Film's Emotional Resonance

Creatively employed match cuts in film have the capacity to heighten the emotional impact of a scene by accentuating visual or thematic connections between shots, rendering specific moments more indelible in the audience's memory. By seamlessly aligning elements such as gestures, objects, or environments across different shots, filmmakers can evoke a profound sense of continuity and resonance. For example, a match cut that seamlessly transitions from a character's tearful face to a raindrop falling from the sky can magnify the emotional weight of sadness or loss. These visual parallels serve as emotional triggers, amplifying the audience's connection to the characters and the story, and leaving a lasting imprint. In this manner, match cuts become a valuable tool for directors and editors to harness the full emotional potential of their storytelling, leaving viewers with deeply resonant and unforgettable cinematic moments.

Techniques of Match Cuts in Indian Films: Seamless Visual Continuity, The Precision Behind Effective Match Cuts in Film Editing

Visual continuity is a paramount consideration in the art of match cuts. Editors meticulously analyze various visual elements, including shapes, colours, and movements, to orchestrate a flawless match cut. The fundamental objective is to guarantee that these elements align harmoniously between the shots, creating an unbroken visual thread that allows for a seamless transition. This entails a keen eye for detail, as the match cut should make the viewer perceive a sense of uninterrupted progression in the narrative. When executed effectively, the audience is transported effortlessly from one scene to the next, with the visual elements serving as a bridge that preserves the film's visual coherence. Visual continuity, therefore, lies at the heart of the match cut's ability to provide a cohesive and immersive cinematic experience, underscoring the importance of editors' precision in this technique.

Thematic Threads: Exploring the Significance of Match Cuts in Reinforcing Film Themes

Match cuts often serve to establish thematic connections within a film, emphasizing recurring motifs or overarching themes. By strategically aligning thematic elements or motifs between shots, filmmakers can reinforce the underlying messages or ideas of the narrative. For example, in a film that features a recurring motif of circles, a match cut might involve a circular object or shape transitioning seamlessly between scenes. This visual continuity reinforces the thematic thread of unity, completeness, or cyclical nature within the story. Such thematic match cuts not only enhance the storytelling but also encourage viewers to delve deeper into the film's underlying concepts and symbolism, elevating the overall cinematic experience and providing a visual language through which the narrative's themes are expressed and explored.

Harmonizing Sight and Sound: The Integral Role of Audio in Match Cuts for Cinematic Continuity

In match cuts, the role of sound and music is essential, as it complements the visual continuity and contributes to the overall seamless transition between shots. Editors may employ auditory elements, such as sound effects, dialogues, or music, to bridge the gap between scenes and enhance the viewer's sense of continuity. For example, a musical theme initiated in one shot can smoothly flow into the next, maintaining a cohesive auditory experience even as the visuals change. Sound elements can serve as a connective tissue, guiding the audience's perception through the match cut and reinforcing the narrative's emotional or thematic resonance. By aligning both visual and auditory aspects, filmmakers ensure that match cuts are not only visually coherent but also aurally immersive, enriching the storytelling and providing a comprehensive cinematic experience that engages multiple senses.

Examples of Match Cuts in Indian Films:

Symbolism in Motion: The Iconic Match Cut in 'Dilwale Dulhania Le Jayenge' (DDLJ)

In "Dilwale Dulhania Le Jayenge" (DDLJ), the filmmakers employ a striking match cut during the iconic train station scene, when Raj (played by Shah Rukh Khan) lifts Simran's (played by Kajol) hand as she boards a departing train. This poignant moment is seamlessly connected to a shot of a spinning wheel in a potter's shop. The match cut effectively underscores the profound transition occurring in Simran's life, as she leaves behind her family and the life she has known. It symbolizes the turning of the wheel of fate, suggesting that her destiny is in motion and that significant changes lie ahead. This masterful use of a match cut not only provides visual continuity but also conveys a profound thematic message about love, destiny, and the inevitability of change, making it a standout moment in the film and showcasing the storytelling prowess of DDLJ.

Spinning Threads of Resilience: The Thematic Match Cut in 'Lagaan

In "Lagaan," a memorable match cut connects two pivotal elements in the film: the spinning wheel used for spinning cotton yarn and the spinning cricket ball in the climactic match. This transition ingeniously underscores the central theme of spinning, which serves as a common thread throughout the narrative. In the context of daily life in the village, spinning is a symbol of self-sufficiency and resilience as the villagers seek to free themselves from oppressive taxation. In the cricket match, spinning the ball becomes a metaphor for the pivotal moments in the game and the villagers' determination to win against all odds. The match cut artfully weaves these two threads together, emphasizing the thematic continuity and the profound importance of spinning in the film's narrative, ultimately accentuating the film's message of perseverance, unity, and the fight against injustice.

Visualizing Love: The Poignant Match Cut in 'Kabhi Khushi Kabhie Gham' (K3G)

In "Kabhi Khushi Kabhie Gham" (K3G), a profoundly poignant match cut is employed during a pivotal scene where Rahul (played by Shah Rukh Khan) is on the verge of confessing his love to Anjali (played by Kajol). The match cut seamlessly transitions between their faces, accentuating the intense emotional connection between these central characters. This visual transition not only underscores the depth of their feelings but also serves as a symbolic representation of their union and the emotional spark that binds them together. The match cut then proceeds to a flickering lamp, a symbol often associated with the spark of love and the illumination of the heart's desires. This sequence of match cuts is a testament to the film's mastery in conveying emotions and themes through visual storytelling, encapsulating the essence of love and destiny, and solidifying the enduring impact of K3G in Indian cinema.

Match Cuts: Elevating Storytelling in Indian Cinema through Visual Continuity and Symbolism

Match cuts in Indian cinema serve as a versatile and powerful cinematic tool that extends beyond mere aesthetics; they are integral to enhancing storytelling. These cuts play a crucial role in seamlessly transitioning between different elements such as time, space, or thematic motifs, ensuring that the narrative remains cohesive. By juxtaposing shots through visual or thematic links, editors can convey profound layers of meaning and emotion, enriching the viewer's understanding of the story and its characters. Match cuts, when used effectively, transcend the boundaries of individual scenes, creating a unified and immersive cinematic experience. They enable Indian filmmakers to communicate complex ideas, emotions, and symbolism without the need for explicit dialogue or exposition, making them an invaluable asset in crafting compelling and resonant narratives that captivate audiences and leave a lasting impression in Indian cinema.

J. Cross-Cutting in Indian Films

Parallel Narratives: The Impact of Cross-Cutting in Cinematic Storytelling

Cross-cutting, often referred to as parallel editing, is a dynamic and impactful film editing technique employed to narratively alternate between two or more parallel storylines or actions that unfold simultaneously. This technique serves as a potent tool to infuse tension, suspense, and an acute sense of simultaneity into the storytelling. By seamlessly interweaving different narrative threads, cross-cutting enables filmmakers to juxtapose events, character developments, or locations, allowing viewers to perceive multiple layers of the story in real-time. It engenders a heightened engagement as audiences piece together the interconnectedness of these simultaneous events and anticipate their eventual convergence. Cross-cutting, when executed deftly, is a fundamental storytelling device that enhances the film's pacing, emotional resonance, and thematic depth, making it a cornerstone of cinematic storytelling.

Purpose

Cross-cutting serves several key purposes in Indian films:

Suspense Unveiled: The Art of Cross-Cutting in Cinematic Storytelling

Tension and suspense are fundamental outcomes of the film editing technique known as cross-cutting, also referred to as parallel editing. This technique involves alternating between two or more parallel storylines or actions that unfold simultaneously within the narrative. Cross-cutting functions as a powerful tool to elicit anticipation and suspense in storytelling. As the audience toggles between different plotlines or actions, they become deeply engaged in the narrative, eagerly awaiting the point where these elements converge or resolve. The contrasting sequences, often laden with distinct emotional tones or impending conflicts, create a dynamic interplay that intensifies the viewer's emotional investment in the story. Whether it's a thrilling chase scene intertwined with a character's escape or a mounting confrontation between protagonists and antagonists, cross-cutting heightens the stakes, leaving the audience on the edge of their seats and contributing to the overall dramatic impact of the film. This technique has been a cornerstone of cinematic storytelling for decades, showcasing its effectiveness in captivating and holding the viewer's attention.

Exploring Cross-Cutting in Film Editing: Enhancing Narrative Depth and Audience Engagement

Cross-cutting in film editing is a technique that facilitates the comparison and contrast of multiple plotlines, characters, or locations occurring concurrently within the narrative. By seamlessly shifting between these parallel story elements, cross-cutting offers filmmakers a means to emphasize differences or similarities between them, thereby enriching the thematic depth of the film. It allows viewers to draw connections and distinctions between the various facets of the story, often shedding light on overarching themes, character dynamics, or the consequences of divergent choices. This technique invites the audience to engage in a deeper level of storytelling analysis, fostering a greater appreciation for the complexity and intricacy of the narrative. Whether it's juxtaposing a hero's journey with a villain's machinations or contrasting two characters' emotional responses in different settings, cross-cutting serves as a lens through which filmmakers can explore and expand upon the underlying ideas and messages of the film, contributing to a richer and more immersive cinematic experience.

Sustaining Audience Engagement: The Vital Role of Cross-Cutting in Film Editing

Cross-cutting, as a film editing technique, plays a pivotal role in sustaining audience engagement and investment in the various facets of the narrative. By seamlessly alternating between multiple plotlines, characters, or locations that unfold simultaneously, cross-cutting prevents monotony and ensures a consistently high level of interest. It compels viewers to remain actively involved in the story as they follow the parallel developments, eagerly anticipating the connections, resolutions, or conflicts that may arise. This engagement is not only essential for retaining the audience's attention but also for fostering emotional and intellectual connection with the characters and the overarching narrative. It transforms the act of watching a film into a dynamic and participatory experience, with viewers becoming emotionally invested in the outcomes of the multiple storylines. Ultimately, cross-cutting is a storytelling tool that sustains intrigue, intrigue, and curiosity throughout the film, making it a crucial component of cinematic storytelling that keeps audiences captivated from start to finish.

Techniques of Cross-Cutting in Indian Films: The Critical Role of Timing and Rhythm in Cross-Cutting Film Editing

In cross-cutting, the timing and rhythm of cuts are of paramount importance. Editors are tasked with the intricate job of deciding the optimal duration for each segment in order to uphold the tension and flow of the narrative. The pacing of these cuts must strike a delicate balance, ensuring that viewers remain deeply engaged in the parallel storylines without feeling disoriented or overwhelmed. The timing of each switch between different plotlines or actions is orchestrated to enhance the emotional and dramatic impact, creating a synchrony that heightens the overall viewing experience. Editors must have a keen sense of storytelling, rhythm, and visual language to craft cross-cut sequences that maintain coherence, build tension, and sustain the narrative's momentum, making them an indispensable element of cinematic storytelling that requires both precision and artistry.

Harmonizing Narratives: The Crucial Role of Sound and Music in Cross-Cutting Film Editing

Sound and music serve as vital components in the practice of cross-cutting in film. They play a pivotal role in bridging the gap between distinct storylines or actions, elevating the audience's emotional engagement and reinforcing the narrative's continuity. The use of sound encompasses not only dialogue exchanges but also ambient noises and environmental sounds that help establish the mood and context of each parallel narrative. Additionally, music can serve as an auditory thread that connects the disparate elements of the story, enhancing the viewer's sense of cohesiveness and emotional resonance. A well-composed score or a carefully selected soundtrack can accentuate the contrasting emotions or intensify the suspense across multiple plotlines, contributing to a more immersive and cohesive cinematic experience. Ultimately, sound and music in cross-cutting are indispensable tools for directors and editors to guide the audience through the intricate tapestry of parallel narratives, ensuring that they remain fully engaged and emotionally invested in the unfolding story.

Seamless Transitions: The Art of Visual Continuity in Cross-Cutting Film Editing

Visual continuity in cross-cutting is a critical aspect that editors meticulously uphold to create seamless transitions between parallel storylines. This continuity can be achieved through various techniques, including matching shots or employing complementary visuals. Editors closely examine the visual elements in each segment to ensure that they align seamlessly, making the shift between storylines imperceptible to the audience. This might involve maintaining consistent lighting conditions, framing, or visual motifs that link the shots in a way that feels organic and fluid. The goal is to provide viewers with a cohesive and visually harmonious experience as they navigate between different plotlines or actions. By preserving visual continuity, editors facilitate a narrative flow that keeps the audience deeply immersed in the film's multifaceted storytelling, enhancing their overall viewing experience and contributing to the effectiveness of cross-cutting as a storytelling technique.

Examples of Cross-Cutting in Indian Films: "Lagaan" and the Art of Suspense, Masterful Cross-Cutting in the Cricket Match Sequence

In "Lagaan," the extensive use of cross-cutting during the cricket match sequence serves as a masterful example of how this technique can be employed to build tension and suspense. As the high-stakes match unfolds, the film deftly alternates between shots of the cricket action and the emotional reactions of the villagers. This juxtaposition creates a dynamic interplay between the on-field drama and the villagers' hopes, fears, and unwavering determination. The cross-cutting technique not only intensifies the suspense surrounding the outcome of the match but also underscores the profound emotional investment of the characters and the audience alike. It's a powerful tool that immerses viewers in the heart-pounding excitement of the cricket match while simultaneously reminding them of the larger narrative stakes and the villagers' struggle for justice. In "Lagaan," cross-cutting is expertly harnessed to enhance both the dramatic and emotional dimensions of the film, contributing significantly to its enduring impact in Indian cinema.

"Rang De Basanti": Weaving the Past and Present Through Cross-Cutting for Resonant Storytelling

In "Rang De Basanti," cross-cutting is ingeniously deployed during the film's climactic moments, particularly when the modern-day characters reenact historical events from India's freedom struggle. This cross-cutting technique intertwines parallel narratives of the past and the present, creating a powerful juxtaposition that enables the audience to draw thematic connections and experience a profound sense of simultaneity. As the contemporary characters immerse themselves in the roles of their historical counterparts, the cross-cutting between eras blurs the lines of time, showcasing the enduring relevance of the nation's struggle for freedom and its resonance with the challenges faced by the present generation. This technique not only enriches the storytelling by emphasizing the interplay between history and contemporary society but also deepens the emotional impact by highlighting the characters' transformation and their evolving connection to their country's heritage. "Rang De Basanti" effectively demonstrates how cross-cutting can be leveraged to create a resonant and thematically rich narrative structure that engages viewers on multiple levels, making it a standout in Indian cinema.

Unraveling the Mystery: The Role of Cross-Cutting in "Kahaani" for Suspense and Intrigue

In the suspense thriller "Kahaani," cross-cutting emerges as a pivotal cinematic technique employed to craft a palpable sense of urgency and intrigue. The film seamlessly alternates between the actions of its determined protagonist, portrayed by Vidya Balan, as she embarks on a relentless investigation into a mysterious case, and the actions of other characters entangled in the enigmatic plot. This strategic use of cross-cutting generates a constant ebb and flow of suspense, leaving audiences on the edge of their seats as they are plunged into a maze of uncertainty and surprise. The juxtaposition of the protagonist's dogged determination with the actions of other characters not only amplifies the suspense but also serves to heighten the narrative's complexity. As viewers navigate these parallel storylines, they are drawn deeper into the labyrinth of the film's mysteries, resulting in a thrilling and immersive cinematic experience that demonstrates the potent storytelling potential of cross-cutting in the world of suspense thrillers.

Cross-Cutting in Indian Cinema: Crafting Multilayered Narratives and Amplifying Audience Engagement

Cross-cutting is a storytelling technique that holds a significant place in the Indian film industry, much like its use in global cinema. This technique plays a pivotal role in enriching the narrative by deftly constructing tension, suspense, and narrative complexity. By juxtaposing multiple storylines or simultaneous actions in a seamless manner, filmmakers are able to captivate the audience on multiple levels, offering a dynamic and immersive viewing experience. Cross-cutting's versatility is a valuable asset for Indian filmmakers, allowing them to craft narratives that are intricate and multifaceted, which in turn elevates emotional engagement and sustains audience fascination from the beginning to the end of a film. It serves as a dynamic tool that can be employed to heighten suspense in a thrilling mystery, deepen thematic connections in a historical drama, or create a sense of urgency in a suspenseful thriller, thereby remaining an indispensable element in the arsenal of Indian filmmakers. The impact of cross-cutting on Indian cinema is undeniable, contributing significantly to the artistry and impact of storytelling.

Cross-Cutting: Weaving Narratives and Eliciting Emotions in Indian Cinema

One of the remarkable aspects of cross-cutting in Indian cinema is its ability to interweave various narrative threads, creating a rich tapestry of interconnected stories. This technique enables filmmakers to explore complex themes and character dynamics, enriching the storytelling experience. Furthermore, cross-cutting can be a powerful tool in evoking emotional responses from the audience, as it often plays a key role in building tension and suspense, making it a prevalent choice in thrillers and action-packed sequences. In historical dramas, it can help establish parallels between different time periods, providing a deeper understanding of the narrative's context and themes. Overall, cross-cutting remains a vital ingredient in the storytelling recipe of Indian cinema, contributing to the multifaceted and captivating nature of the films, and continuing to be a key feature in the filmmaker's toolbox.

K. Visual Effects and Special Effects Integration

In Indian cinema, particularly when it comes to the incorporation of visual effects (VFX) or special effects into live-action footage, the concept of seamless integration is of paramount importance. Editors assume a pivotal role in this process, serving as the custodians of visual consistency and the architects of an enhanced cinematic experience. The art lies in making sure that the digital elements, whether they involve fantastical landscapes, otherworldly creatures, or breathtaking stunts, harmoniously coexist with the live-action components of the film. This entails meticulous attention to detail, as editors must align the lighting, colour grading, and overall aesthetics to create a fluid transition between the real and the digitally rendered. Furthermore, it's essential that the narrative flow remains unencumbered by the inclusion of these effects, ensuring that the audience remains fully immersed in the story without being distracted by any discrepancies. The end result is a seamless integration that elevates the film, allowing it to transport viewers to captivating and immersive worlds while preserving the visual integrity and consistency that are hallmarks of Indian cinema.

Seamless Integration in Indian Films

The Art and Mastery of Seamless Integration in Filmmaking: Blurring the Line Between Reality and Imagination

Seamless integration in filmmaking represents the art and technique of seamlessly incorporating visual effects (VFX) or special effects into live-action footage to the point where the boundary between the real and the digitally created becomes virtually indistinguishable. This meticulous process strives to achieve a film that maintains visual coherence and consistency, ensuring that the digital and practical elements coexist in perfect harmony. The goal is to immerse the audience in a narrative world where they are unaware of the artifice behind the scenes. Achieving seamless integration requires meticulous attention to detail, encompassing aspects such as lighting, colour grading, and perspective, to create a cohesive visual experience. The end result is a film that transports viewers to fantastical realms, delivers breathtaking spectacles, or seamlessly blends reality and imagination while preserving the film's overall visual integrity – a testament to the artistry and technical prowess of modern filmmaking.

Elevating Indian Cinema: The Role of Seamless Integration in Creating Believable and Immersive Cinematic Worlds

In the context of Indian cinema, the central objective of seamless integration is to elevate storytelling by captivating audiences, immersing them fully in the cinematic universe, and breathing life into imaginative or seemingly impossible elements. Whether the goal is to craft awe-inspiring landscapes, conjure otherworldly creatures, or choreograph heart-pounding action sequences, seamless integration in Indian films serves as the linchpin of believability. It meticulously weaves these elements into the narrative fabric, making them appear not only realistic but also integral to the storytelling process. This meticulous artistry and technical precision ensure that the audience remains engrossed in the film's world, effortlessly suspending disbelief, and allowing them to embrace the extraordinary as an organic extension of the story. Ultimately, seamless integration serves as a bridge between the tangible and the fantastical, enlivening Indian cinema and fostering a deeper connection between the viewer and the narratives that unfold on the screen.

Techniques for Achieving Seamless Integration: The Significance of Pre-Visualization in Achieving Seamless Integration of Visual Effects in Filmmaking

Pre-visualization stands as a pivotal step in the filmmaking process, particularly when incorporating visual effects (VFX) or special effects. Prior to the commencement of production, filmmakers frequently employ pre-visualization techniques such as storyboards and animatics to meticulously plan and conceptualize how the digital elements will seamlessly integrate with live-action scenes. Storyboards provide a visual blueprint, allowing filmmakers to outline the placement, movement, and timing of both practical and digital elements within the frame. Animatics take this a step further by adding rudimentary motion and timing to these visual sketches, essentially creating a dynamic storyboard. By embracing these techniques, filmmakers can gain a comprehensive understanding of how the final shots will unfold, ensuring that digital and live-action elements align flawlessly to serve the narrative's vision. This pre-visualization phase empowers filmmakers to refine their creative choices, streamline production, and minimize surprises during post-production, ultimately facilitating the seamless integration of visual effects or special effects into the cinematic tapestry.

The Essence of Realism: The Role of High-Quality Visual Effects in Achieving Seamless Integration

The attainment of seamless integration heavily relies on the caliber of visual effects (VFX) utilized. The quality of VFX is paramount, and skilled VFX artists harness advanced software and techniques to craft digital elements that are not only highly detailed but also remarkably realistic. These digital components are meticulously designed to align with the lighting, perspective, and physical laws governing the live-action footage. By adhering to these principles, VFX artists ensure that the digital elements appear as organic extensions of the real-world environment, exhibiting convincing interactions with actors and practical set pieces. This commitment to high-quality VFX plays a pivotal role in suspending the audience's disbelief, allowing them to wholeheartedly invest in the cinematic experience and engage with the narrative, regardless of how fantastical or extraordinary the visual elements may be. In essence, it is the dedication to achieving realism and fidelity in visual effects that underpins the achievement of seamless integration in modern filmmaking.

Precision in Motion: The Role of Match-Moving in Achieving Seamless Integration in Filmmaking

Match-moving, also known as motion tracking, serves as a pivotal technology in the pursuit of seamless integration in filmmaking. Its primary function is to guarantee that digital elements harmoniously synchronize with the movements and perspective of the camera and the actors within the live-action scenes. This sophisticated technology enables VFX artists to precisely align the position, scale, and rotation of digital assets with the dynamic and ever-changing real-world environment captured by the camera. By meticulously tracking the camera's movements and the actors' actions, match-moving ensures that the digital components seamlessly follow the same trajectory and adhere to the same spatial relationships as their physical counterparts. This level of precision not only facilitates a convincing interaction between the real and the digital but also guarantees that the audience remains fully immersed in the narrative, unencumbered by any visual inconsistencies that could disrupt the cinematic experience. Match-moving is, therefore, a cornerstone of modern filmmaking, enabling filmmakers to push the boundaries of imagination while maintaining a steadfast commitment to visual realism and coherence.

Crafting Visual Harmony: The Role of Editors in Colour Grading and Lighting Adjustment for Seamless Integration in Filmmaking

Editors play a pivotal role in achieving seamless integration through meticulous colour grading and lighting adjustments. Their task is to meticulously ensure that the colour tones and lighting of digital elements closely align with those of the live-action scenes, thereby creating a harmonious and consistent visual style that transcends the boundaries between the real and the digital. Colour grading involves manipulating the colour palette to match the overall colour scheme and mood of the film, ensuring that digital elements seamlessly blend into the cinematic landscape. Similarly, precise lighting adjustments are made to match the lighting conditions and angles present in the live-action shots, ensuring that shadows, highlights, and reflections align naturally. This commitment to colour and lighting coherence serves to unify the film's visual aesthetics, reinforcing the audience's suspension of disbelief and allowing them to become fully immersed in the narrative without any visual distractions. In essence, the art of colour grading and lighting adjustment in seamless integration is pivotal, shaping the film's overall look and feel while maintaining visual integrity and consistency.

The Art of Compositing: Merging Real and Digital Elements for Seamless Integration in Filmmaking

Compositing represents a crucial phase in the journey toward seamless integration, entailing the intricate process of harmoniously amalgamating distinct visual elements into a single frame. Editors oversee this meticulous process, ensuring that the integration of digital and live-action components is imperceptible to the discerning eye. This attention to detail extends to critical aspects such as shadows, reflections, and depth of field, where editors work diligently to maintain visual consistency and realism. Shadows must fall convincingly, reflections should behave naturally, and the depth of field should correspond seamlessly with the overall aesthetic of the film. In essence, compositing is the art of bringing together the disparate elements of a scene—whether they involve fantastical creatures, mythical landscapes, or awe-inspiring explosions—into a coherent and visually cohesive whole. The result is a frame that seamlessly blends the real and the digital, captivating the audience and allowing them to embrace the narrative without any perceptible visual discontinuities. Thus, compositing emerges as an indispensable tool in the filmmaker's arsenal for crafting a compelling and immersive cinematic experience.

Examples of Seamless Integration in Indian Films: "Baahubali: The Beginning" - A Monumental Achievement in Seamless Integration and VFX Mastery in Indian Cinema

"Baahubali: The Beginning" serves as a monumental example of seamless integration in Indian cinema. This epic film leverages extensive visual effects to craft awe-inspiring landscapes, conjure mythical creatures, and orchestrate epic battles that transport the audience to a mesmerizing world of grandeur and fantasy. The VFX wizardry on display in "Baahubali" is nothing short of remarkable, as digital elements seamlessly meld with live-action footage, creating a vivid and immersive experience for viewers. Whether it's the towering waterfalls, colossal palaces, or awe-inspiring combat sequences, the integration of visual effects not only amplifies the film's spectacle but also enhances its narrative depth, allowing audiences to suspend disbelief and wholly immerse themselves in the mythical universe of "Baahubali," where the fantastical and the real coalesce in harmonious cinematic synergy.

"Krrish 3" - The Role of Seamless Integration in Bringing Superhero Abilities to Life on the Big Screen

"Krrish 3" exemplifies the importance of seamless integration in the context of a superhero film. The narrative revolves around the titular character, Krrish, who possesses an array of superhuman abilities ranging from flight to super strength. To make these powers appear convincing and intrinsic to the film's world, seamless integration plays a pivotal role. Visual effects are meticulously employed to showcase Krrish's extraordinary abilities in a manner that aligns seamlessly with the live-action footage. Whether it's the exhilarating flight sequences through cityscapes or the breathtaking displays of super strength, the VFX ensure that these feats are not only visually striking but also feel completely credible within the film's narrative. The success of "Krrish 3" hinges on the audience's ability to suspend disbelief and fully embrace Krrish's superhuman capabilities as an integral part of the cinematic experience, highlighting the indispensable role of seamless integration in modern superhero storytelling.

"Robot (Enthiran)" - The Transformative Power of Seamless Integration in Bringing Chitti to Life

"Robot (Enthiran)" stands as a testament to the transformative power of visual effects and seamless integration in Indian cinema. The film's core revolves around Chitti, a humanoid robot character brought to life with remarkable VFX wizardry. The success of the character, both in terms of believability and emotional depth, hinges on the film's ability to seamlessly integrate these digital elements with the live-action sequences. Chitti's interactions with the human characters, whether in moments of profound emotion or high-octane action, are brought to life with meticulous attention to detail, ensuring that his presence feels organic and integrated into the narrative fabric. This integration elevates the film beyond the boundaries of conventional storytelling, immersing the audience in a world where the line between the real and the digital is blurred, and the emotional connection with the character becomes deeply resonant. "Robot" exemplifies how seamless integration can transcend technical prowess, becoming a storytelling tool that fosters a profound engagement between viewers and the characters they encounter on screen.

Transforming Indian Cinema: The Impact of Seamless Integration on Storytelling and Visual Spectacle

Seamless integration in Indian films has ushered in a transformative era of storytelling. It has become a cornerstone of modern filmmaking, enabling filmmakers to transcend the limits of imagination and craft visually breathtaking and immersive cinematic experiences. From conjuring mythical realms to orchestrating larger-than-life action sequences and introducing fantastical characters, seamless integration ensures that these extraordinary elements seamlessly coexist within the narrative framework, enhancing rather than distracting from the storytelling. It has redefined the possibilities of Indian cinema, captivating audiences with its ability to seamlessly merge the real and the digital, creating a cinematic tapestry where the boundaries of reality are transcended, and the audience is invited to embark on extraordinary journeys of imagination and emotion. In this way, seamless integration has reinvigorated Indian cinema, making it even more captivating, visually stunning, and narratively compelling.

L. Enhancing Action Sequences in Indian Films

Unleashing the Spectacle: The Significance and Diversity of Action Sequences in Indian Cinema, with a Focus on Bollywood

Action sequences form a prominent and integral component of Indian cinema, particularly in the Bollywood domain. These sequences are characterized by their high-energy, adrenaline-pumping content, which often encompasses intense physical combat, gravity-defying stunts, thrilling chase sequences, and jaw-dropping feats of daring. Beyond being a source of pure cinematic spectacle, these action sequences serve multiple purposes within the narrative. They can propel the plot forward, resolve conflicts, reveal character strengths and vulnerabilities, and even infuse a dose of heroism into the storyline. Additionally, action sequences in Indian cinema frequently incorporate elements of song and dance, seamlessly blending storytelling and entertainment, and showcasing the versatility of Indian filmmaking. With their ability to elicit excitement, suspense, and awe, action sequences have become a signature feature of Indian cinema, drawing audiences into the heart-pounding world of larger-than-life heroes and villains.

Crafting Adrenaline: The Artistry of Editors in Shaping Action Sequences in Indian Cinema

Editors occupy a pivotal role in the crafting of action sequences within Indian cinema. Their contribution extends beyond mere post-production tasks; they are essential architects of the sequences' overall impact. Editors meticulously select shots that capture the essence of the action, ensuring that each frame resonates with energy and intensity. The pacing of the sequence is carefully calibrated to build suspense, intensify the action, and deliver breathtaking climaxes. Editors also employ a repertoire of editing techniques, such as quick cuts, slow motion, and dynamic camera angles, to accentuate the excitement and dynamism of the action. These techniques not only enhance the visual spectacle but also contribute to the emotional engagement of the audience. In essence, editors wield their artistic sensibilities to transform raw footage into pulse-pounding action sequences that leave an indelible mark on the viewer, illustrating their indispensable role in the creation of memorable action moments in Indian cinema.

Rapid Cuts in Action Sequences: The Art of Rapid Cutting in Elevating Action Sequences in Indian Cinema

Rapid cutting is a fundamental editing technique employed to elevate the impact of action sequences in Indian cinema. This technique involves the rapid succession of shots, with each frame enduring only for a fleeting moment. By fragmenting the action into a series of quick shots, editors infuse the sequence with an immediate sense of urgency and tension. The relentless pace keeps the audience on the edge of their seats, intensifying the emotional engagement and adrenaline rush. Rapid cutting not only captures the intricate details of the action but also amplifies the kinetic energy and high-octane dynamics, allowing viewers to immerse themselves fully in the heart-pounding experience of the sequence. It's a technique that embodies the essence of action in Indian cinema, propelling the narrative forward with relentless momentum and enthralling the audience with its sheer intensity.

Crafting Rhythm and Intensity: The Role of Rapid Cutting in Pacing Action Sequences in Indian Cinema

Pacing is a critical element in the orchestration of action sequences within Indian cinema, and rapid cutting plays a pivotal role in achieving the desired rhythm and intensity. The pacing of an action sequence is meticulously calibrated to ensure that it aligns with the narrative's emotional beats and the audience's expectations. Rapid cuts are instrumental in maintaining this pace by injecting constant dynamism into the visuals. By avoiding prolonged shots that may lead to monotony, editors keep the sequence vibrant and engaging. The relentless energy of rapid cutting not only sustains the audience's interest but also heightens their excitement, creating a visceral experience that mirrors the characters' urgency and determination. Consequently, pacing through rapid cutting is an essential aspect of action filmmaking, ensuring that the audience remains fully invested in the sequence from start to finish.

Amplifying Impact: The Art of Rapid Cuts to Highlight Key Moments in Action Sequences in Indian Cinema

Editors leverage rapid cuts to accentuate the impactful moments within action sequences in Indian cinema. This technique allows them to strategically intersperse close-ups of characters' expressions, impactful blows, or pivotal stunts amidst a series of wider shots. By doing so, editors magnify the intensity of these crucial moments, granting them heightened significance and resonance. The rapid succession of such impactful shots not only elevates the visual drama but also enables the audience to emotionally connect with the characters and their struggles on a more profound level. This careful curation of shots ensures that each significant beat within the action sequence is vividly etched in the viewers' memory, contributing to the sequence's overall impact and leaving a lasting impression long after the action has subsided.

Dynamic Visual Flourish: The Role of Rapid Cuts in Introducing Variety to Action Sequences in Indian Cinema

Rapid cuts serve as a crucial tool for introducing visual variety into action sequences within Indian cinema. By swiftly transitioning between different angles, perspectives, and focal points, editors infuse the sequence with a dynamic and ever-evolving visual tapestry. This constant variety not only keeps the audience visually engaged but also prevents desensitization to the action. It allows viewers to appreciate the nuances of the choreography, the impact of each blow, and the intricacies of the stunts from multiple vantage points. The dynamic nature of rapid cuts ensures that no two moments within the sequence feel alike, sustaining the visual stimulation and offering a continuous array of fresh, captivating images. Consequently, visual variety through rapid cutting is an essential element in the success of action sequences, captivating the audience and amplifying their immersion in the thrilling on-screen action.

Creating a Sense of Chaos and Realism: The Role of Rapid Cutting in Simulating Disorder and Excitement in Action Sequences in Indian Cinema

Rapid cutting is a potent tool for simulating chaos and disorientation within action sequences in Indian cinema. It's frequently harnessed to convey the sheer unpredictability of combat scenarios or high-speed chases. By rapidly shifting between shots from varying angles and perspectives, editors recreate the frenetic and often bewildering nature of such situations. This simulation of chaos not only heightens the excitement but also infuses a sense of realism into the sequence. The audience is thrust into the heart of the action, feeling the adrenaline rush and experiencing the challenges and uncertainties faced by the characters. In doing so, rapid cutting contributes to the immersive quality of the sequence, making it a visceral and electrifying encounter that resonates with viewers and amplifies their emotional engagement with the on-screen chaos.

Crafting Realism Through Rapid Cuts: The Art of Making Action Sequences Feel Authentic in Indian Cinema

In action sequences within Indian cinema, a subtle but potent aspiration for realism often underpins the stylized and choreographed nature of these scenes. Rapid cuts serve as a key instrument in achieving this semblance of realism. By rapidly shifting between shots and perspectives, editors can create the illusion that the action is unfolding spontaneously and unscripted. This technique imparts a raw and unpredictable quality to the sequence, making it seem as though the characters are genuinely responding to the dynamic, ever-changing environment. While the action may be meticulously choreographed and rehearsed, the deployment of rapid cuts imparts an organic and unstructured quality that resonates with the audience's desire for authenticity. Consequently, these rapid cuts not only enhance the visual excitement of the sequence but also contribute to the suspension of disbelief, allowing viewers to immerse themselves fully in the high-stakes action while still appreciating its realism.

Examples of Action Sequences: Revving Up the Thrills, How Rapid Cuts Elevate Motorcycle Chase Sequences in "Dhoom 2"

In the "Dhoom 2" film, a prominent installment of the popular "Dhoom" franchise, rapid cuts are strategically employed to amplify the impact of its high-octane action sequences, particularly the motorcycle chases that have become synonymous with the series. These sequences are characterized by their breathtaking speed and agility, and the use of rapid cuts plays a pivotal role in portraying the characters' remarkable feats. By swiftly transitioning between shots that capture the motorcycles' dynamic movements, the characters' reactions, and the various obstacles encountered during the chases, editors create a visually dynamic and pulse-pounding experience for the audience. This technique not only accentuates the thrill of the action but also showcases the characters' prowess, making the sequences exhilarating and memorable while reinforcing the "Dhoom" series' reputation for adrenaline-pumping action.

Unleashing Fury: How Rapid Cutting Empowers Action Sequences in the "Singham" Film Series

In the "Singham" film series, action sequences take center stage, featuring intense hand-to-hand combat and dramatic stunts that define the hero's relentless fight against the villains. Rapid cutting is strategically employed in these sequences to elevate the hero's power and impact. By swiftly transitioning between shots that showcase the hero's formidable martial skills, the villains' reactions, and the high-stakes confrontations, editors heighten the overall intensity and dynamism of these sequences. This technique not only emphasizes the hero's unwavering resolve but also amplifies the physicality and sheer force behind each blow and action. As a result, rapid cutting contributes significantly to the hero's portrayal as a formidable force for justice and intensifies the dramatic impact of the action, making the "Singham" series a hallmark of high-energy Indian cinema.

Precision and Prowess: How Rapid Cutting Enhances Action Sequences in "War"

In the action-packed film "War," rapid cuts are prominently utilized to underscore the precision and skill of the characters, especially in the context of high-octane fight sequences and shootouts. The film is known for its meticulously choreographed action, and rapid cutting plays a pivotal role in accentuating the characters' prowess and the breathtaking choreography. By swiftly transitioning between shots that capture the characters' lightning-fast movements, acrobatics, and calculated maneuvers, editors create a sense of urgency and intensity that permeates these sequences. The rapid cuts not only showcase the physical agility and combat proficiency of the characters but also heighten the adrenaline rush and suspense during these action sequences, making "War" a visually exhilarating cinematic experience that exemplifies the power of rapid cutting in modern Indian action cinema.

Pulsating Action: The Art of Rapid Cuts in Indian Cinema

The use of rapid cuts in action sequences within Indian cinema is a dynamic and highly effective storytelling technique that is instrumental in elevating the excitement and engagement levels of these sequences. Rapid cutting works by creating a pulsating rhythm within the action, effectively propelling the narrative forward and immersing viewers in the sheer intensity of the scenes. Through quick transitions between shots that capture the characters' lightning-fast movements, powerful blows, and intense confrontations, film editors craft action sequences that are not only memorable but also visually striking. This approach has become a defining characteristic of many Indian films, contributing significantly to their entertainment value and enhancing the overall cinematic experience. Rapid cuts inject an electrifying energy into the action, turning it into a visceral and unforgettable spectacle that keeps audiences on the edge of their seats.

Capturing Cinematic Vigor: The Artistry of Rapid Cuts in Indian Action Sequences

The implementation of rapid cuts is a testament to the craftsmanship of Indian filmmakers and their dedication to delivering exhilarating and visually stunning action sequences. These sequences not only serve as thrilling spectacles but also provide a platform for showcasing the physical prowess and choreographic skills of actors and stunt performers. Rapid cuts allow filmmakers to capture and accentuate the speed, agility, and power of the characters, making every punch, kick, and dodge feel immediate and impactful. Furthermore, this technique is not confined to any particular genre; it has found its place in a wide range of Indian films, from high-octane action blockbusters to more nuanced, character-driven narratives, proving its adaptability and enduring relevance in Indian cinema. In essence, the use of rapid cuts in action sequences is an integral part of the cinematic language of Indian films, enhancing their entertainment value and providing audiences with adrenaline-pumping moments that stay etched in their memories.

M. Fade In/Fade Out in Indian Films

Transition Techniques– Fade In/Fade Out in Indian Films

The Art of Transition: Understanding the Significance of Fade-Ins and Fade-Outs in Film Editing

Fade-ins and fade-outs are fundamental film editing techniques employed to create smooth transitions in a narrative. In a fade-in, the screen gradually emerges from complete darkness to reveal an image, serving as an effective way to signal the beginning of a scene, a new chapter, or the start of a film. This technique allows the audience to refocus their attention and prepare for what's to come. Conversely, in a fade-out, an image slowly disappears into darkness, indicating the conclusion of a scene, the end of a chapter, or a transition in time. Fade-outs provide closure, allowing viewers to process the events that have transpired before moving on to the next part of the story. Both fade-ins and fade-outs are subtle yet powerful tools in the filmmaker's arsenal, enhancing the narrative structure and guiding the audience through the storytelling process with a sense of rhythm and coherence.

Purpose

Fade-ins and fade-outs serve several key purposes in Indian films:

Guiding Transitions: The Narrative Significance of Fade-Ins and Fade-Outs in Film Editing

Fade-ins and fade-outs, as film editing techniques, serve as pivotal signals for scene transitions within a cinematic narrative. When a scene begins with a fade-in, it signifies the initiation of a new sequence, effectively guiding the audience's attention to a different location, time frame, or narrative focus. This gradual emergence from darkness to image serves as a visual marker, allowing viewers to mentally adapt to the forthcoming scenario. On the other hand, a fade-out at the end of a scene indicates closure or the conclusion of a particular narrative moment, providing a smooth and gentle transition to the next scene. In this way, these techniques help maintain the narrative's coherence and rhythm, enabling filmmakers to seamlessly traverse various facets of the story, ensuring that changes in location, time, or focus occur with grace and clarity. Fade-ins and fade-outs are integral elements of cinematic storytelling, facilitating the audience's understanding and engagement as they embark on a journey through the multifaceted landscape of the narrative.

Shifting Temporal Realms: The Role of Fade-Ins and Fade-Outs in Conveying Time Transitions in Film

Fade-ins and fade-outs are invaluable tools in conveying temporal shifts within a cinematic narrative. When a scene commences with a fade-in, it can signify a transition from the present to the past, effectively guiding the audience into a flashback sequence. The gradual emergence of an image from darkness gently transports viewers to a different time frame, creating a visual bridge between the two temporal states. Conversely, a fade-out at the end of a scene may indicate a jump in time, moving from the current moment to a future scenario, known as a flashforward. These techniques also prove useful in conveying significant time lapses, allowing the audience to recognize the passing of hours, days, or even years within the story. Whether facilitating flashbacks, flashforwards, or illustrating the passage of time, fade-ins and fade-outs serve as cinematic signposts, ensuring that the audience remains oriented within the narrative's temporal landscape while enhancing the storytelling's depth and coherence.

Evoking Emotions: The Profound Impact of Fade-Ins and Fade-Outs on Cinematic Narrative

Fade-ins and fade-outs possess the unique ability to evoke emotional resonance within a cinematic narrative. When a scene commences with a fade-in, it can engender a sense of new beginnings, renewal, or hope, thereby impacting the emotional tone of the ensuing sequence. Conversely, a fade-out at the scene's conclusion can instill a feeling of closure, reflection, or melancholy, influencing the audience's emotional response to the events that have transpired. These techniques can also heighten anticipation and suspense by leaving certain outcomes or developments to the audience's imagination. In this manner, fades become emotional cues that signal transitions in the story's emotional landscape, enhancing the audience's connection with the characters and events. By harnessing the power of fades, filmmakers can shape the emotional journey of their viewers, intensifying the impact of each narrative beat and contributing to a more profound and memorable cinematic experience.

The Art of Fade-In and Fade-Out Durations in Film Editing: Timing the Transition

The duration of a fade-in or fade-out is a crucial consideration in film editing, as it directly influences the visual and emotional impact of the transition. A shorter and more abrupt fade can create a quick and decisive shift, which may be appropriate for scenes requiring immediate changes in tone or pace. On the other hand, a longer, more gradual fade allows for a smoother and subtler transition, providing the audience with a gentle shift in mood or time without abruptness. Filmmakers strategically choose the duration of these fades to match the narrative's needs and the desired emotional resonance. A shorter fade might be employed for a sudden revelation or moment of tension, while a more extended fade could be used for contemplative or nostalgic sequences, underscoring how the timing of fades is a nuanced art that significantly contributes to the storytelling and visual language of cinema.

Fading into Meaning: The Art of Colour Choices in Film Editing Fades

In film editing, the use of colour in fades provides an additional layer of visual storytelling and symbolism. While the classic fade to or from black is a common choice to signify transitions, editors often employ variations such as fading to white or fading to a specific colour to evoke distinct moods and convey deeper thematic elements. Fading to white can symbolize purity, new beginnings, or a blank slate, while a fade to a particular colour can carry specific emotional or thematic connotations. For instance, a warm, golden fade may evoke feelings of nostalgia or happiness, while a cool, blue fade might suggest tranquility or melancholy. The selection of colours for fades is a deliberate artistic choice that enhances the narrative, enriches the audience's emotional engagement, and communicates subtle layers of meaning within the visual language of cinema.

Harmonizing Senses: Synchronizing Fades with Sound and Music in Film Editing

The synchronization of fades with sound and music is a fundamental aspect of film editing. Editors carefully time fade-ins to coincide with the initiation of music, dialogue, or other audio elements. This synchronization not only ensures a smooth and harmonious transition between the visual and auditory aspects of the film but also adds to the overall cinematic experience. Conversely, fade-outs are used to gradually reduce the volume of music or fade out any ongoing audio, aligning with the end of a scene or sequence. This technique allows for sonically seamless transitions, preventing jarring audio cuts and maintaining the audience's immersion in the film's audio-visual world. It's a testament to the meticulous craftsmanship of film editors, who use fades in conjunction with sound and music to enhance storytelling, emotional resonance, and the overall auditory experience in cinema.

Common Uses in Indian Films: Transitioning with Fades, Shaping Pacing and Structure in Filmmaking

Scene changes in filmmaking are often marked by the use of fades, where a fade-out indicates the conclusion of one scene or sequence, followed by a fade-in to introduce the next. This transition technique serves several critical purposes. Firstly, it helps in maintaining the film's pacing and narrative structure by clearly demarcating different story beats or locations. Secondly, fades can create a momentary pause, allowing the audience to digest the preceding scene's events or emotions before immersing them in a new context. Additionally, the choice of how long the fade lasts can influence the sense of time passing between scenes, whether it's a swift shift to maintain tension or a more leisurely transition to suggest a significant temporal change. Overall, the judicious use of fades in scene changes is a fundamental aspect of film editing that contributes to the overall storytelling and visual rhythm of the film.

Navigating Time with Fades: Transitioning Between Past, Present, and Future in Filmmaking

In filmmaking, fades play a crucial role in navigating temporal shifts, especially when transitioning between the present and past (flashback) or between the present and future (flashforward). When a flashback is introduced, a fade-out can gently blur or fade away the current scene, creating a visual separation from the present timeline. Following this, a fade-in gradually unveils the flashback sequence, transporting the audience to the past events. Conversely, when returning to the present, a fade-out might obscure the flashback, and a fade-in will bring the viewers back to the contemporary narrative. Similarly, for flashforwards, the use of fades ensures clarity by signaling the shift in time while maintaining the audience's engagement with the story. These techniques help in seamlessly transitioning between different temporal contexts, enhancing the storytelling in films by providing insight into characters' backgrounds or future developments while keeping the narrative coherent.

Fades in Filmmaking: Framing and Enhancing Emotional Moments

Fades are a versatile tool in filmmaking, and they can be used to heighten emotional moments within a narrative. When a particularly poignant or impactful scene comes to a close, a gradual fade-out can be employed to allow the audience a moment of reflection on the emotions and themes presented. This deliberate visual transition can help viewers absorb the significance of what they've just witnessed, creating a sense of closure or depth to the emotional experience. On the other hand, a well-timed fade-in can mark the beginning of a crucial event or revelation, signaling to the audience that something momentous is about to happen or that a significant emotional turning point is on the horizon. In both cases, fades contribute to the overall emotional resonance of a film by effectively pacing and framing key emotional beats in the story.

Examples of Fade-ins and Fade-outs in Indian Films

Fades in "Mughal-e-Azam": Conveying Time, Longing, and Emotional Depth

In "Mughal-e-Azam," a timeless classic of Indian cinema, fade-ins and fade-outs play a pivotal role in conveying the grandeur and emotional depth of the epic love story between Anarkali and Prince Salim. These transitions are masterfully used to signify the passage of time, which is central to the narrative as it chronicles the forbidden romance between a courtesan and a prince. The gradual fading in and out of scenes helps evoke a sense of longing and separation, accentuating the emotional resonance of the film. Furthermore, the deliberate and artful use of fades adds to the overall visual and emotional richness of this iconic cinematic masterpiece, underscoring its enduring status in Indian cinema history.

Reflecting on Life's Pivotal Moments: The Role of Fades in "Dil Chahta Hai"

In the modern Bollywood classic "Dil Chahta Hai," fade-outs are employed with a subtle yet effective touch to mark the conclusion of pivotal moments in the lives of three close friends. The fades serve to emphasize the emotional significance of these moments within the narrative, allowing the audience to reflect on the impact they have on the characters' personal journeys and relationships. This editing technique complements the film's contemporary storytelling style, adding depth to the characters and their evolving dynamics, making "Dil Chahta Hai" a relatable and memorable exploration of friendship and growth in the context of urban India.

Cultural and Emotional Journeys: The Use of Fades in "Kabhi Khushi Kabhie Gham" (K3G)

In "Kabhi Khushi Kabhie Gham" (K3G), fades are skillfully utilized to transition between two contrasting worlds: the opulent and modern setting of London and the familiar warmth of India. These fades play a significant role in not only marking the physical shift between these locations but also symbolizing the emotional and cultural differences that drive the narrative. When characters move between these settings, the fades emphasize the stark contrast in their experiences, values, and relationships. This editing technique enhances the film's storytelling by visually reinforcing the central themes of family, tradition, and reconciliation, making it a memorable and emotionally resonant Bollywood classic.

Impact on Indian Film Storytelling: The Significance of Fade-Ins and Fade-Outs in Shaping Indian Cinema

Fade-ins and fade-outs, indispensable tools in Indian cinema, are adeptly employed to enhance storytelling in multifaceted ways. These techniques, characterized by the gradual emergence or disappearance of images, deftly guide the narrative flow, denoting transitions between scenes, temporal shifts, and the commencement or conclusion of key narrative moments. Beyond their functional utility, fade-ins and fade-outs also wield the power of emotional resonance. A scene's closure marked by a fade-out allows the audience to reflect upon its emotional weight, while a well-timed fade-in heralds the onset of pivotal events or emotional turning points, evoking a sense of anticipation and depth. This delicate interplay of visual transitions contributes significantly to the pacing and rhythm of Indian cinema, enhancing the overall cinematic experience by captivating the audience both visually and emotionally.

N. Cutting on Action in Indian Films:

Mastering the Art of Cutting on Action: Enhancing Continuity and Engagement in Film Editing

Cutting on action, or matching on action, is a fundamental film editing technique used to maintain the seamless flow and continuity of an action sequence. Editors strategically make cuts between shots precisely when a character is engaged in a physical action or movement, ensuring that the action appears uninterrupted and visually cohesive. This technique not only enhances the overall fluidity and rhythm of the sequence but also serves to maintain the audience's engagement by creating a sense of immediacy and realism. By aligning the cuts with the character's movements, cutting on action allows for a dynamic and immersive viewing experience, making it a valuable tool in the editor's arsenal for crafting action-packed and visually engaging sequences in film.

Purpose

Cutting on action serves several key purposes in Indian films:

Enhancing Continuity and Realism: The Art of Cutting on Action in Film Editing

Cutting on action is a fundamental film editing technique that enhances the continuity of action sequences. By making cuts precisely at the moment when a character is in the midst of a physical action or movement, editors ensure that the action appears seamless and visually cohesive. This technique contributes to the overall fluidity and rhythm of the sequence, creating a sense of immediacy and realism that keeps the audience engaged. It's particularly effective in maintaining visual continuity, ensuring that the movements of characters and objects flow smoothly from one shot to the next, without any jarring or disjointed transitions. Cutting on action is a valuable tool in crafting action sequences that are not only exciting but also visually coherent and immersive.

Elevating Engagement: Crafting Dynamic Transitions with Cutting on Action in Film Sequences

Cutting on action is a technique that elevates the dynamism and engagement level of film sequences by crafting transitions that are not only visually engaging but also seamlessly connected to the ongoing action. When a cut occurs precisely during a character's physical movement or action, it propels the viewer from one shot to the next with a sense of urgency and excitement. This dynamic transition heightens the overall impact of action sequences, making them more thrilling and immersive. By using this technique, filmmakers can maintain a constant sense of energy and momentum throughout the sequence, ensuring that the audience remains fully engaged in the unfolding action, whether it's a thrilling chase, a fierce fight, or any other physically demanding scenario.

Seamless Storytelling: The Vital Role of Cutting on Action in Clarifying Physical Movements and Actions

Cutting on action serves as a powerful tool in seamless storytelling by ensuring that the audience can effortlessly follow and understand the physical actions and movements of the characters. When the action is synchronized with the cut, it provides a clear and coherent visual narrative. This technique is particularly valuable in action-driven sequences, where the audience needs to comprehend every move and reaction to fully engage with the plot. It prevents any disruptions in the storytelling process, allowing for a more immersive and comprehensible viewing experience. Whether it's a critical fight scene, a daring stunt, or a character's crucial physical response, cutting on action ensures that these moments are presented cohesively and effectively within the larger narrative, contributing to the overall storytelling impact.

Techniques for Cutting on Action

Harmonizing Creativity: The Key Role of Coordination in Executing Cutting on Action in Filmmaking

When employing the cutting on action technique, precise coordination is essential. Filmmakers collaborate closely with actors, directors, and cinematographers to plan and rehearse the scene's physical actions and movements meticulously. This ensures uniform and coherent action across various takes or camera angles. Actors must replicate their actions faithfully to maintain the illusion of seamless motion. Directors guide performers for timing and positioning, while cinematographers capture the action accurately from multiple perspectives. This synchronized effort allows for seamless editing, resulting in a cohesive and visually engaging sequence that enhances the storytelling.

Crafting Cinematic Continuity: The Art of Selecting Camera Angles for Cutting on Action

The choice of camera angles plays a crucial role in the successful application of the cutting on action technique. Editors meticulously select camera angles that provide a comprehensive view of the action from various perspectives, ensuring that the movement or physical activity is effectively conveyed to the audience. These angles are carefully chosen to facilitate seamless transitions between shots during the editing process.

Cinematographers work closely with the director and editor to capture the action from angles that not only capture the required movement but also maintain visual consistency between shots. By using a combination of wide, medium, and close-up shots, the camera angles enhance the overall continuity of the action sequence, allowing for dynamic and uninterrupted transitions that keep the audience engaged and immersed in the narrative.

Precise Timing: The Key to Seamless Transitions in Cutting on Action

The timing of a cut when employing the cutting on action technique is of paramount importance. Editors meticulously select the precise moment when the physical action or movement reaches its zenith or when it naturally aligns with the desired visual continuity for transitioning to the next shot. This careful synchronization ensures that the cut appears seamless and logical to the audience, maintaining the flow and rhythm of the action sequence. The timing is often fine-tuned during the editing process to achieve the most dynamic and coherent transitions between shots, enhancing the overall impact and engagement of the action sequence.

Mastering Motion Continuity: Achieving Seamless Character Movement in Film Editing

Motion continuity is a vital principle in filmmaking and editing, ensuring that a character's movement appears seamless and coherent across different shots or angles within a scene. To achieve this, it's essential to maintain consistency in both the speed and direction of the character's movement from one shot to another. By doing so, filmmakers create the illusion of a continuous and fluid motion, even though the action is often captured from various perspectives and takes. This consistency in speed and direction prevents jarring disruptions and allows the audience to follow the character's movement smoothly, contributing to a more immersive and believable cinematic experience. Whether it's a character walking, running, or engaging in any physical activity, motion continuity is crucial for preserving the visual integrity of a scene and keeping the audience engaged in the narrative.

Examples of Cutting on Action in Indian Films: Dhoom 2, Revving Up Excitement with Cutting on Action in Motorcycle Chase Sequences

In the motorcycle chase sequences of "Dhoom 2," the film employs the cutting on action technique extensively to create a visually thrilling and dynamic experience. As characters perform daring stunts, jump obstacles, and engage in high-speed chases, the editing seamlessly transitions between shots. This technique ensures that the audience perceives the action as a continuous, fluid motion, even though it involves complex maneuvers and various camera angles. By cutting on action during these sequences, the film maintains a sense of momentum and excitement, immersing viewers in the heart-pounding chase and enhancing the overall cinematic impact of these adrenaline-pumping moments.

Chennai Express: Elevating the Thrill Factor with Cutting on Action in the Train Station Chase

In the film "Chennai Express," there is a scene where the characters find themselves in a high-energy chase through a bustling train station. The cutting on action technique is skillfully utilized in this sequence to convey the urgency and excitement of the chase. As the characters sprint, jump, and navigate through various obstacles, the editing involves quick cuts between shots. These rapid transitions maintain the sequence's fast-paced momentum, immersing the audience in the heart-pounding pursuit. Cutting on action ensures that the physical movements of the characters appear seamless and dynamic, creating a sense of continuity and exhilaration throughout the scene, ultimately enhancing the audience's engagement and the overall impact of this thrilling cinematic moment.

Crafting Cinematic Spectacles: Cutting on Action in the Epic Battle Scenes of 'Baahubali: The Beginning

In the epic battle scenes of "Baahubali: The Beginning," cutting on action is a pivotal editing technique employed to capture the fluidity and grandeur of the combat sequences. The film's extensive action choreography involves elaborate sword fights, arrow volleys, and acrobatic maneuvers performed by the characters. Cutting on action is executed with precision, ensuring that transitions between shots take place precisely during moments such as a character swinging a sword, releasing an arrow, or executing a dynamic acrobatic move. This meticulous editing approach creates a visually seamless spectacle, making the battles appear as one continuous and dynamic motion. As a result, the audience is fully immersed in the intensity of the action, and the technique significantly contributes to the film's epic scale and impact.

Seamless Continuity and Engagement: The Significance of Cutting on Action in Indian Cinema

Cutting on action is a fundamental editing technique that enhances the visual continuity and engagement of action sequences in Indian films. It ensures that physical actions and movements by characters are conveyed seamlessly to the audience, creating a dynamic and immersive viewing experience. By maintaining the flow of the action, this technique contributes to the storytelling by allowing filmmakers to effectively communicate character actions, emotions, and the progression of the plot. In essence, cutting on action is a critical tool that ensures the audience remains fully engaged in the on-screen action, making it a hallmark of many thrilling and visually dynamic sequences in Indian cinema.

O. Wipe and Dissolve Transitions in Indian Films

Creating Cinematic Bridges: The Art of Wipe Transitions in Film Editing

Wipe transitions are a fundamental film editing technique used to smoothly transition from one shot to another. In this process, the first shot gradually gives way to the second shot as if a wiping motion is occurring across the screen. This wiping action serves as a visual bridge between two scenes or shots, aiding in the seamless progression of the narrative. The flexibility of wipe transitions allows editors to choose from various shapes for the wipe effect. It can be a simple straight line, creating a clean and straightforward transition. Alternatively, it can be a diagonal line, adding a dynamic and visually engaging element to the switch between shots. Furthermore, editors can customize the shape of the wipe transition to fit the specific context or style of the project. Regardless of the chosen shape, the wipe motion consistently moves from one edge of the frame to the opposite, ensuring a smooth and cohesive visual flow in the final film or video.

Dissolve Transitions: Mastering the Art of Dissolve Transitions in Film Editing

Dissolve transitions are a widely used film editing technique that facilitates a smooth and gradual shift from one shot to another. This transition is achieved by fading out the first shot while, simultaneously, fading in the second shot. The key feature of a dissolve transition is that there is a brief moment when both shots partially overlap, creating a visual blend of the two images. This overlapping period, often referred to as the "cross-dissolve" or "crossfade," serves to seamlessly connect the two shots. It offers a subtle and artistic way to signify the passage of time, change in location, or a thematic link between the two scenes. Dissolve transitions are highly versatile and can be adjusted in terms of duration and opacity, allowing editors to fine-tune the level of blending and the overall feel of the transition. This technique is commonly employed in storytelling to convey a sense of continuity and visual harmony between different parts of a film or video production.

Purposes and Applications of Wipe and Dissolve Transitions: Visual Poetry in Motion:

Stylistic choices in Indian cinema encompass the deliberate utilization of wipe and dissolve transitions as artistic tools, enriching their films with a unique visual language that plays a pivotal role in shaping the movie's aesthetic. Wipe transitions, characterized by their dynamic shapes and directions, infuse energy and thematic resonance into scenes, elevating storytelling by visually conveying emotions and subtext. In contrast, dissolve transitions emphasize continuity, facilitating seamless connections between scenes, and often serving as a means to denote the passage of time or establish thematic links. These transition techniques, carefully selected and tailored to fit the film's context, contribute significantly to the overall visual appeal of Indian cinema, making it a powerful storytelling device and a defining element of its cinematic identity.

Visual Signifiers of Meaning: Exploring Thematic Depth through Wipe and Dissolve Transitions in Filmmaking

Thematic significance in filmmaking is harnessed through the strategic deployment of wipe and dissolve transitions to accentuate particular themes or motifs within a film's narrative. These transitions become a visual language that conveys deeper meanings to the audience. For instance, a heart-shaped wipe transition elegantly underscores romantic elements in a storyline, invoking feelings of love and passion, while a dissolve from one character's face to another signifies a profound emotional bond or connection, allowing the audience to discern the intricate relationships and sentiments at play within the narrative. Such purposeful utilization of transitions not only enhances thematic coherence but also adds layers of emotional depth and storytelling nuance, making them invaluable tools for filmmakers to communicate and resonate with their audience on a thematic level.

Guiding the Audience Through Time and Place: The Role of Transitions in Cinematic Narrative

Shifts in time or place are frequently signaled in filmmaking through the strategic use of transitions, such as dissolve and wipe, which serve as cinematic signposts guiding the audience through the narrative landscape. Dissolve transitions, for instance, are adept at denoting temporal shifts, seamlessly transporting viewers to flashbacks, or marking changes in the story's timeline by blending one scene into another. On the other hand, wipe transitions can effectively communicate shifts in physical setting or context, smoothly replacing one location with another, allowing the audience to traverse time and place with ease while maintaining narrative cohesion. These transitions, as visual storytelling tools, aid in clarifying temporal and spatial dynamics, contributing to a more immersive and comprehensible cinematic experience by conveying the intricate web of a film's chronology and geography.

Seamless Cinematic Flow: The Art and Impact of Wipe and Dissolve Transitions in Filmmaking

Wipe and dissolve transitions serve as indispensable tools in the filmmaker's arsenal for creating seamless and visually captivating transitions between scenes or shots within a film. These techniques excel at preserving the narrative's flow, allowing for a graceful and fluid progression of the storyline. Wipe transitions, with their dynamic and often thematic shapes, offer an element of visual intrigue, while dissolve transitions provide a gentle and gradual shift between scenes, preventing jarring interruptions. By employing these transitions thoughtfully, filmmakers ensure that the audience remains engrossed and immersed in the storytelling process, as the shifts between different narrative elements become not only aesthetically pleasing but also integral to the overall cinematic experience, enhancing the film's coherence and audience engagement.

Visual Metaphors in Motion: The Art of Shape and Direction in Wipe Transitions

In the area of wipe transitions, filmmakers make meticulous selections regarding the shape and direction of the wipe, a choice that holds profound significance in shaping the emotional tone and thematic resonance of a scene. The chosen shape can be a potent visual metaphor, lending depth and symbolism to the narrative; for instance, a heart-shaped wipe can accentuate romantic themes, while a jagged, irregular shape might signify chaos or conflict. Simultaneously, the direction of the wipe is a crucial element that can imply movement within the story, as it sweeps across the screen. For instance, a wipe moving from top to bottom can suggest a sense of progression or resolution, whereas a wipe from left to right can signify a shift or change in perspective. These nuanced choices in shape and direction not only enhance the visual storytelling but also contribute significantly to the emotional impact and thematic cohesion of the film, allowing filmmakers to convey subtleties that resonate deeply with the audience.

Perfecting Timing: The Artistry of Wipe and Dissolve Transition Placement in Filmmaking

The timing of wipe and dissolve transitions in filmmaking is a delicate and critical task, demanding precision and artistic sensibility. Editors must ensure that these transitions align perfectly with the narrative beats or thematic cues, orchestrating their placement to optimize their impact. The duration of the transition, whether swift or leisurely, plays a pivotal role in shaping the film's pacing, influencing the audience's emotional engagement and comprehension of the storyline. A well-timed transition can emphasize a dramatic revelation or punctuate a pivotal moment, while a poorly executed one can disrupt the flow and coherence of the narrative. Thus, the meticulous control of timing in wipe and dissolve transitions is a testament to the editor's artistry, allowing them to wield these cinematic tools as instruments for enhancing the storytelling experience, deepening audience connection, and ultimately, shaping the film's overall impact and resonance.

Colour and Tone Manipulation in Dissolve Transitions: Crafting Emotional Resonance in Filmmaking

In filmmaking, manipulating color and tone in transition effects like dissolve is an artful technique that enhances emotional resonance and atmosphere in scenes. By adjusting transition colors and tones, filmmakers can align them with the mood and themes of the scene. For instance, warm-toned dissolves create nostalgia and romantic ambiance, while cooler tones or desaturated colors convey detachment or melancholy. This consideration of color and tone enriches visual storytelling, deepens emotional connections with the audience, and harnesses the power of color psychology and symbolism in cinematic storytelling.

Timeless Elegance: The Emotional Power of Dissolve Transitions in 'Kabhi Khushi Kabhie Gham' (K3G)

"Kabhi Khushi Kabhie Gham" (K3G), a cinematic masterpiece celebrated for its opulent storytelling, deftly employs dissolve transitions as a cinematic device to signify shifts in time, particularly when delving into the characters' nostalgic recollections of their childhoods. These dissolve transitions are not just technical tools but integral components of the film's emotional storytelling. By gently fading from one scene to another, K3G manages to transport the audience seamlessly to the past, creating a poignant and sentimental atmosphere. This deliberate use of dissolves serves to heighten the emotional impact of the narrative, forging a deep connection with the audience as they traverse the characters' memories and experiences, adding layers of nostalgia and resonance to the film's grand and emotionally charged storyline.

Heartfelt Romance: The Symbolism of Heart-Shaped Wipe Transitions in 'Dilwale Dulhania Le Jayenge' (DDLJ)

"Dilwale Dulhania Le Jayenge" (DDLJ), a quintessential Bollywood classic, showcases a meticulous use of wipe transitions to amplify the romantic essence of the narrative. Particularly in scenes brimming with heartfelt affection between the two lead characters, DDLJ opts for wipe transitions crafted in the shape of a heart. These heart-shaped wipes serve as potent visual metaphors, accentuating the theme of love at the core of the story. Each heart-shaped wipe not only connects the two characters' emotional journeys but also heightens the film's romantic atmosphere. By strategically employing these wipes, DDLJ infuses the narrative with an extra layer of symbolism and emotion, allowing the audience to become deeply immersed in the love story, making the film an iconic example of how cinematic techniques can enhance and elevate the storytelling experience.

Seamless Historical Saga: The Narrative Function of Wipe Transitions in 'Padmaavat

In "Padmaavat," wipe transitions are skillfully employed as a cinematic tool to depict the passage of time and shifts in location, allowing for seamless transitions between various kingdoms and time periods within the narrative. These wipes serve a crucial function in maintaining the film's pacing and narrative coherence as it navigates through different historical epochs and locales. By using wipe transitions, "Padmaavat" ensures that the audience can effortlessly follow the storyline's intricate web of politics, alliances, and conflicts while also adding an aesthetic dimension to the film's portrayal of history and culture. These transitions, carefully timed and executed, not only contribute to the film's visual appeal but also play a pivotal role in conveying the grandeur and complexity of the historical saga, making "Padmaavat" a visually stunning and immersive cinematic experience.

Elevating Artistry and Narrative Craft: The Multifaceted Role of Wipe and Dissolve Transitions in Indian Cinema

Wipe and dissolve transitions in Indian films are multifaceted tools that play a pivotal role in both artistic and pragmatic aspects of filmmaking. They infuse style and artistry into the visual storytelling, amplifying thematic elements and contributing significantly to the overall cinematic experience. These transitions operate as more than mere visual techniques; they are narrative devices that seamlessly facilitate shifts in time, place, and emotion, enabling filmmakers to engage the audience on multiple sensory levels. Whether conveying the nostalgia of a flashback, the magnitude of a grand love story, or the seamless passage of time, wipe and dissolve transitions in Indian cinema serve as indispensable assets, enriching the storytelling and making it a visually captivating and emotionally resonant experience for the viewers.

P. Colour Correction in Indian Films

Crafting Cinematic Ambiance: The Art of Colour Correction in Filmmaking

Colour correction, a crucial post-production stage in filmmaking, encompasses the meticulous adjustment of colours and the overall visual presentation of footage with the goal of attaining a particular desired look, mood, or aesthetic. It serves as a transformative tool that not only rectifies technical imperfections like inconsistent lighting or white balance but also enhances the storytelling by conveying specific emotions or atmospheres. Colour correction ensures a harmonious and consistent colour quality across all scenes, permitting filmmakers to maintain visual cohesion and fulfill their artistic vision. Whether intensifying the vibrancy of colours for a lively and energetic feel, desaturating hues to evoke a somber or bleak mood, or manipulating colours to reflect a particular time period or genre, this process is integral to a film's storytelling and visual impact, allowing directors and cinematographers to wield colour as a potent storytelling tool.

Purpose of Colour Correction

Colour correction serves several key purposes in Indian films:

Elevating Aesthetics: Crafting Visual Appeal Through Colour Correction in Filmmaking

Aesthetic enhancement through colour correction is a pivotal aspect of filmmaking that elevates the overall visual appeal of a film by achieving a cohesive and pleasing colour palette that aligns precisely with the director's creative vision. This process allows for the fine-tuning of colours to create a distinct and captivating atmosphere that resonates with the film's themes and emotions. It can involve boosting the vibrancy of colours to create a dynamic and energetic mood or subtly adjusting hues to evoke a specific era or setting. By meticulously crafting the colour palette, filmmakers can elicit emotional responses from the audience and immerse them more deeply into the narrative. The aesthetic enhancement aspect of colour correction not only ensures a visually striking and consistent look for the film but also empowers filmmakers to harness colour as a potent storytelling tool, enhancing the overall cinematic experience.

Shaping Emotions and Atmosphere: The Role of Colour Correction in Setting the Cinematic Mood

Colour correction is a dynamic tool in filmmaking that plays a pivotal role in setting the mood and atmosphere of a film. By skillfully manipulating colours, filmmakers can evoke specific emotional responses and establish the desired ambiance within a scene or throughout the entire film. For instance, the infusion of warm, vibrant colours can convey happiness and romance, enveloping the audience in a sense of joy and love. Conversely, the use of desaturated or cooler tones can create a somber, melancholic atmosphere that tugs at the viewer's heartstrings, or they can heighten suspense and tension, immersing the audience in an eerie or mysterious world. Colour correction's ability to shape mood and atmosphere is a powerful storytelling technique that enables directors and cinematographers to connect with their audience on a visceral level, enriching the cinematic experience by leveraging colour as a visual language to communicate and elicit a wide range of emotions and sensations.

Visual Unity and Narrative Flow: The Significance of Consistency in Colour Correction in Filmmaking

Consistency in colour correction is a fundamental aspect of post-production in filmmaking, serving as a critical tool to harmonize the visual elements of a film. It ensures that the colours and overall visual appearance remain uniform and cohesive throughout the movie, even when different shots and scenes have been captured under diverse lighting conditions, settings, or locations. This consistency is essential to prevent jarring disruptions in the viewing experience, as it maintains a seamless visual flow that keeps the audience immersed in the story. By equalizing the colours and tones, colour correction helps bridge any disparities in the raw footage, creating a unified look and feel that aligns with the director's vision, contributing to the film's overall narrative cohesiveness, and preserving a sense of continuity that enhances the audience's engagement with the storytelling.

Technical Precision and Visual Enhancement: The Role of Colour Correction in Addressing Filming Challenges

Colour correction plays a pivotal role in post-production by addressing a wide range of technical issues that may arise during the filming process. One of its primary functions is to rectify exposure problems, ensuring that underexposed or overexposed areas in the footage are corrected to achieve optimal brightness and contrast. Additionally, colour correction can address colour imbalances, where colours may appear skewed due to variations in lighting or camera settings, by aligning them accurately with a reference point. Moreover, it helps mitigate inconsistencies in lighting conditions across different shots or scenes, making sure that the visual quality remains consistent and cohesive throughout the film. In essence, colour correction is a vital tool that not only enhances the film's aesthetic but also resolves technical challenges, allowing filmmakers to deliver a visually polished and technically sound final product to the audience.

Techniques for Colour Correction: Empowering Creativity, The Role of Specialized Software in Colour Correction for Filmmaking

Colour correction is commonly executed with the aid of specialized software applications such as DaVinci Resolve, Adobe Premiere Pro, or Final Cut Pro X. These dedicated tools provide filmmakers and editors with a comprehensive suite of features and controls to meticulously manipulate various colour parameters within the footage. Through these software programs, professionals can fine-tune aspects like brightness, contrast, saturation, and hue, allowing for precise adjustments that cater to the specific needs of the film. Moreover, they offer advanced grading capabilities, including the ability to create custom looks and apply grading presets that help define the film's visual identity. These colour grading software applications have become essential in the post-production process, empowering filmmakers to achieve their desired aesthetic, convey mood and atmosphere, and ensure the overall visual cohesiveness of the film, making them integral components of modern filmmaking workflows.

Shaping Emotion and Continuity: The Art of Colour Temperature Manipulation in Filmmaking

Colour temperature manipulation is a crucial aspect of colour correction and grading, allowing editors and colourists to adjust the warmth or coolness of footage by introducing orange or blue tones, respectively. This technique is a powerful storytelling tool, as it can influence the emotional resonance and atmosphere of a scene. For instance, warming up the colour temperature can evoke feelings of cosiness, nostalgia, or romance, while cooling it down can create a sense of detachment, unease, or suspense. Moreover, colour temperature adjustments play a vital role in ensuring visual consistency by matching different shots within a scene or even across different scenes, mitigating disparities in lighting conditions or camera settings. By skillfully manipulating colour temperature, filmmakers can convey specific moods, enhance visual storytelling, and maintain a harmonious look throughout the film, contributing to a more immersive and emotionally resonant cinematic experience.

Vivid Intensity or Subdued Realism: The Art of Saturation Control in Colour Correction and Grading

Saturation, a crucial component of colour correction and grading, serves as a powerful means to control the vividness and intensity of colours within a film or image. When increased, saturation enhances colours, making them appear more vibrant, vivid, and eye-catching. This heightened saturation is often employed in scenes where the goal is to create a visually striking and attention-grabbing impact, such as in lively celebrations, romantic moments, or fantastical sequences. Conversely, when saturation is decreased, it results in a desaturated or muted look, where colours become less intense and more subdued. This technique is valuable for conveying a sense of realism, nostalgia, or seriousness, effectively toning down the visual intensity for scenes that demand a more restrained or understated aesthetic. Saturation control is an essential tool that allows filmmakers and visual artists to wield colours as a storytelling device, influencing the emotional tone and visual appeal of their work and contributing significantly to the overall narrative and aesthetic experience of the audience.

Shaping Drama and Atmosphere: The Art of Contrast Control in Filmmaking for Visual Impact

Contrast, a key element of colour correction and grading, plays a pivotal role in shaping the visual depth and overall atmosphere of a scene or image. When contrast is increased, it intensifies the differentiation between light and dark areas, creating a more dynamic and striking visual composition. High contrast is often employed in scenes that require a bold and impactful look, such as action sequences or dramatic confrontations, accentuating the dramatic interplay of light and shadow. On the other hand, reducing contrast results in a softer, more subdued effect, which can be used to craft a dreamy or nostalgic ambiance. This lower contrast technique is particularly suitable for conveying a sense of gentleness, romance, or sentimentality. The control of contrast is an essential creative tool that enables filmmakers and visual artists to manipulate the visual mood and narrative impact of their work, contributing significantly to the overall storytelling and aesthetic experience of the audience.

Harmonizing Hues: The Art of Colour Balance in Filmmaking for Natural and Authentic Visuals

Colour balance, a crucial aspect of colour correction and grading in filmmaking, is the process of ensuring that the colours within a film or image appear natural, harmonious, and visually pleasing. This technique involves the correction of colour casts, which may result from varying lighting conditions or the characteristics of the camera equipment used during filming. By addressing these colour casts, colour balance ensures that the colours accurately represent the scene as it would appear to the human eye, eliminating any unwanted shifts or biases in the colour spectrum. Additionally, colour balance plays a significant role in ensuring that whites within the frame appear neutral, free from any warm or cool undertones. By achieving a proper colour balance, filmmakers enhance the visual authenticity of their work, allowing the audience to immerse themselves in the narrative without being distracted by unnatural or skewed colours, thereby contributing to the film's overall aesthetic and storytelling impact.

Collaboration between Editors and Colourists: Editor's Vital Role in Shaping Cinematic Vision, Collaborating on Colour Correction and Grading

The editor's role in the colour correction and grading process is pivotal in translating the director's creative vision into a visually cohesive and emotionally resonant cinematic experience. Editors collaborate closely with colourists to convey the director's intentions for the film's colour palette and mood. They serve as a bridge between the director's narrative objectives and the technical aspects of colour correction, providing essential guidance on which shots or scenes necessitate specific colour adjustments. Editors ensure that the visual storytelling aligns with the narrative, emphasizing key moments, themes, or emotions through colour manipulation. They work in tandem with the colourist to maintain consistency in the visual tone and style throughout the film, ensuring that the final product reflects the director's vision while also meeting technical standards. The editor's role is integral in enhancing the storytelling and aesthetic impact of the film, harmonizing the director's creative vision with the practical execution of colour correction to create a compelling and immersive cinematic narrative.

Mastering Cinematic Visuals: The Role of Colourists in Colour Correction and Grading

Colourists are highly specialized professionals in the field of filmmaking, possessing extensive expertise in the intricate art of colour correction and grading. Their role is to bring the director's creative vision to life by skillfully manipulating colour and visual elements to achieve the desired aesthetic and mood. They have a profound understanding of colour theory, lighting, and the technical aspects of colour grading software, enabling them to make precise adjustments that elevate the overall visual quality of the film. Colourists work collaboratively with the director and editor, using their keen artistic sensibilities and technical prowess to enhance the narrative, evoke specific emotions, and ensure visual consistency across all shots and scenes. Their expertise is invaluable in shaping the film's final look and feel, transforming raw footage into a visually stunning and emotionally resonant cinematic masterpiece that aligns seamlessly with the director's creative vision.

Harmonizing Vision and Technique: Effective Communication in the Collaboration Between Editors and Colourists

Effective communication is a cornerstone of successful collaboration between editors and colourists in the post-production process. Editors play a pivotal role in bridging the gap between the director's creative vision and the technical aspects of colour correction. They articulate the director's intentions, preferences, and narrative objectives, serving as the primary liaison between the creative team and the colourist. In turn, colourists provide valuable feedback and creative suggestions, drawing on their expertise to offer insights into achieving the desired visual style. This collaborative dialogue ensures that the colour correction process aligns closely with the director's vision, while also benefiting from the colourist's technical and artistic proficiency. This dynamic communication allows for the fine-tuning of colour correction to enhance storytelling, evoke specific emotions, and maintain visual consistency, ultimately resulting in a film that seamlessly integrates its creative intent with technical excellence.

Crafting Nostalgia and Emotion: The Role of Colour Correction in 'Barfi!'

In the film "Barfi!", colour correction is a pivotal visual element used to craft a specific and evocative atmosphere. The colourist's expertise is harnessed to create a nostalgic and fairy-tale-like ambiance that envelops the narrative. This is achieved by employing a warm and vibrant colour palette that saturates the scenes with rich, inviting hues. These colours accentuate the film's romantic and emotional elements, infusing them with a sense of vitality and resonance. The meticulous use of colour correction not only enhances the film's visual appeal but also contributes to the audience's immersion in the storytelling, creating a memorable and emotionally resonant cinematic experience that aligns seamlessly with the film's narrative intent.

Weaving History and Memory: The Role of Colour Correction in 'Rang De Basanti

In "Rang De Basanti," colour correction is a storytelling device employed to differentiate between the past and present timelines within the film. The colourist plays a crucial role in this process by applying a distinct colour tone to the sequences set in the past. This deliberate colour grading is designed to evoke a palpable sense of nostalgia and historical context, effectively transporting the audience to a different era and immersing them in the story's rich historical backdrop. By contrasting the colour palettes between past and present scenes, colour correction not only helps distinguish the different timelines but also contributes to the film's emotional depth and thematic resonance, enhancing the audience's connection with the characters and their journey through time, making it an integral part of the film's visual storytelling and narrative impact.

Elegance and Extravagance: Colour Correction in 'Bajirao Mastan

In "Bajirao Mastani," colour correction serves as a pivotal tool for elevating the grandeur and opulence of its historical setting. The colourist's expertise is harnessed to craft a rich and visually striking colour palette that seamlessly aligns with the film's regal and majestic context. This meticulous colour grading enhances the film's visual spectacle, immersing the audience in the grandeur of the era and the opulence of its characters' lives. By intensifying the vibrancy and depth of colours, colour correction not only emphasizes the lavishness of the film's historical backdrop but also elevates the overall cinematic experience. The deliberate use of colour correction in "Bajirao Mastani" contributes significantly to the film's visual storytelling, allowing it to transport viewers to a bygone era of elegance and extravagance, and making it an integral element of the film's narrative impact and aesthetic appeal.

Impact on Indian Film Storytelling: The Art and Significance of Colour Correction in Indian Filmmaking

Colour correction holds a pivotal role in the fabric of Indian filmmaking, serving as a fundamental and multifaceted tool that enriches the storytelling process. This vital post-production technique empowers filmmakers to harness colour as a visual language, effectively conveying emotions, moods, and atmospheres that resonate deeply with the audience. It enhances the audience's engagement by offering a sensory and emotional connection to the narrative. Whether it's the creation of a warm and romantic ambiance or the evocation of a specific historical era, colour correction plays a transformative role in shaping the visual identity and impact of Indian films. Its nuanced application allows for the precise alignment of colour with narrative intent, contributing to the overall emotional depth, aesthetic appeal, and thematic resonance of Indian cinema, making it an indispensable and dynamic element of the filmmaking process.

Q. Visual Effects Integration in Indian Films

Unlocking the Magic of Visual Effects (VFX) in Modern Filmmaking

Visual effects (VFX) constitute a crucial aspect of modern filmmaking, encompassing the creation or manipulation of digital elements to realize scenes and effects that are either logistically challenging or entirely unattainable through practical means. The success of VFX lies in their seamless integration into the film's narrative, ensuring that these digitally crafted elements blend seamlessly with the live-action footage, maintaining visual consistency. When executed effectively, VFX have the power to enhance the storytelling process by expanding the creative possibilities and immersing the audience in fantastical worlds or extraordinary scenarios. Whether it's conjuring mythical creatures, simulating otherworldly environments, or realizing high-octane action sequences, VFX are a versatile and indispensable tool in the filmmaker's arsenal, enabling them to bring their imaginative visions to life on the big screen.

Purpose of VFX integration:

VFX integration in Indian films serves several key purposes:

Bringing Imagination to Life: The Transformative Power of Visual Effects (VFX) in Filmmaking

The utilization of Visual Effects (VFX) in filmmaking is instrumental in enhancing realism by transforming the impossible or imaginary into tangible on-screen experiences. VFX professionals can craft intricate, lifelike digital elements, whether it's creating mythical creatures, simulating otherworldly landscapes, or realizing gravity-defying stunts. These visual effects seamlessly integrate into the live-action footage, blurring the line between reality and fantasy. By doing so, VFX immerse the audience in the film's world, making it more immersive, captivating, and believable. This ability to bring the extraordinary to life not only broadens the creative horizons of filmmakers but also allows viewers to suspend disbelief and fully engage with narratives that venture beyond the boundaries of the physical world, enriching the cinematic experience and expanding the storytelling possibilities in film.

240

Elevating Spectacle: Crafting Awe-Inspiring Moments with Visual Effects (VFX) in Filmmaking

Achieving spectacle through visual effects entails leveraging advanced technology and creative expertise to craft awe-inspiring moments on screen. By seamlessly integrating computer-generated imagery (CGI) with live-action footage, filmmakers can orchestrate breathtaking action sequences where superheroes soar through the skies, massive explosions erupt in vivid detail, and fantastical creatures come to life with astonishing realism. These effects also enable the creation of stunning environments, transporting viewers to otherworldly realms, futuristic cityscapes, or historical periods with meticulous attention to detail. Whether it's the grandeur of a space battle or the intricacies of a microscopic world, visual effects unlock the potential to immerse the audience in larger-than-life visuals that transcend the boundaries of reality, leaving a lasting impact and an indelible mark on the cinematic experience.

Visual Alchemy: Stylistic Explorations through Visual Effects (VFX) in Filmmaking

Stylistic choices in filmmaking encompass the deliberate utilization of visual effects (VFX) to craft distinct and compelling aesthetics that not only complement but also elevate the artistic and thematic dimensions of the film. Through VFX, directors can manipulate colour palettes, lighting, and camera angles, imbuing scenes with a particular mood or atmosphere that reinforces the narrative's emotional resonance. These tools also allow for innovative storytelling techniques, such as surreal dreamscapes, time-bending sequences, or abstract representations of inner thoughts, pushing the boundaries of cinematic expression. Furthermore, VFX can be employed to pay homage to specific artistic movements or eras, invoking a sense of nostalgia or homage, or even to deconstruct conventional visual storytelling norms, offering audiences fresh perspectives and challenging their perceptions. In essence, the judicious use of VFX as stylistic choices empowers filmmakers to infuse their work with a unique visual language that amplifies the film's thematic depth and artistic impact.

Role of Editors in VFX Integration: The Editor's Role in Coordinating VFX with the Director's Vision

Communication is a pivotal role played by editors in the filmmaking process, as they act as a crucial link between the director's creative vision and the VFX team's technical execution. Editors engage in a collaborative dialogue with the director to gain a deep understanding of the intended visual effects, their narrative significance, and emotional impact within the film's overall storytelling. This involves comprehending the director's aesthetic preferences, pacing requirements, and thematic objectives, ensuring that VFX seamlessly integrate into the narrative fabric. By translating the director's conceptual ideas into practical guidelines and by providing essential feedback to the VFX team during post-production, editors help shape and refine the visual effects to align with the director's vision, resulting in a harmonious fusion of storytelling and technical prowess on the cinematic canvas.

Synchronizing the Spectacle: Editors' Role in Sequencing VFX Shots for Narrative Impact

Sequencing is a fundamental responsibility of editors in the filmmaking process, where they meticulously determine the precise placement and timing of VFX shots within the larger context of the film's narrative. Editors play a pivotal role in orchestrating the flow of visual effects to ensure they integrate seamlessly into the storytelling, enhancing the audience's immersion and engagement. By carefully selecting when and where VFX shots are deployed, editors maintain the narrative's pacing, emotional resonance, and overall coherence. They work in tandem with the director's vision to create a dynamic rhythm, using VFX to punctuate key moments, build suspense, or convey essential plot points. In doing so, editors transform a collection of individual shots into a compelling visual story that captivates and resonates with the audience, optimizing the impact and effectiveness of the film's visual effects.

Preserving Visual Harmony: The Editor's Role in Maintaining Consistency Between VFX and Live-Action Sequences

Visual consistency is a paramount concern for editors, who work closely with colourists and VFX artists to ensure that the colour grading, lighting, and visual style of VFX shots harmoniously blend with the surrounding live-action sequences. This meticulous collaboration is essential in maintaining the film's overall aesthetic integrity. Editors are responsible for meticulously reviewing and adjusting the colour balance, contrast, and saturation of VFX shots to match the established look of the film, preserving the continuity of the visual storytelling. They also collaborate with VFX teams to replicate the lighting conditions and atmosphere of the live-action scenes, ensuring that CGI elements seamlessly integrate into the environment. This commitment to visual consistency not only enhances the film's realism but also reinforces its thematic and emotional impact, allowing the audience to immerse themselves fully in the cinematic world and the story being told.

Techniques for VFX Integration: Harmonizing the Palette, Collaborative Colour Grading for Seamless VFX Integration

Colour grading is a critical aspect of post-production, and editors collaborate closely with colourists to meticulously adjust the colour attributes of VFX shots, such as colour temperature, saturation, and contrast, to precisely match the visual characteristics of the live-action footage. This meticulous process is vital for achieving seamless integration of VFX elements into the scenes, as it ensures that CGI elements appear as if they exist within the same environment as the live-action elements. By aligning the colour grading of VFX shots with the surrounding footage, editors not only enhance the visual consistency of the film but also create a cohesive and immersive viewing experience for the audience. This attention to detail allows for a more convincing and captivating storytelling, where VFX elements become indistinguishable from the real-world elements, contributing to the film's overall impact and realism.

Seamless Lighting Integration: Editors' Role in Maintaining VFX Realism

Editors play a crucial role in meticulously scrutinizing the interaction of light and shadows within VFX shots, working diligently to ensure that these elements seamlessly align with the lighting conditions present in the live-action scenes. Achieving consistency in lighting is paramount for maintaining the realism and immersion of the film. Editors work closely with VFX teams to replicate the direction, intensity, and colour temperature of the ambient and key light sources within the live-action shots, ensuring that shadows cast by CGI elements accurately match those cast by real-world objects. This level of attention to lighting detail is indispensable as it prevents discrepancies that could shatter the illusion of a unified cinematic world. By upholding lighting consistency, editors contribute significantly to the overall believability and visual cohesiveness of the film, enabling the audience to fully engage with the narrative without distraction.

Enhancing VFX Realism: The Art of Camera Movement Integration

In visual effects (VFX), the technique of camera movement plays a pivotal role in enhancing the seamless integration of computer-generated imagery (CGI) with live-action footage. Editors employ this approach to infuse a heightened sense of realism and immersion into the final visual product. By introducing subtle camera movements or even controlled shakes, they emulate the dynamic, organic motion typically associated with handheld or live-action cinematography. This artful manipulation of the virtual camera's perspective mimics the natural fluctuations of a real camera operator, forging a convincing connection between the fabricated VFX elements and the genuine surroundings. Consequently, this meticulous attention to camera movement within VFX not only blurs the line between reality and fantasy but also engenders a heightened level of audience engagement and believability, ultimately enriching the overall viewing experience.

The Role of VFX and Editing: "Baahubali: The Beginning" - A Visual Spectacle

"Baahubali: The Beginning" is celebrated for its masterful utilization of visual effects (VFX) to craft awe-inspiring cinematic spectacles. Within this cinematic saga, VFX serves as the transformative element that brings to life epic battle sequences, mythical creatures, and grandiose landscapes. Editors meticulously orchestrated the integration of these VFX shots with live-action footage, achieving a flawless marriage between the two realms. Their careful craftsmanship ensured that the film maintained impeccable visual consistency, where the line between the real and the fantastical became indistinguishable. As a result, "Baahubali: The Beginning" stands as a testament to the unparalleled potential of VFX in storytelling, delivering a cinematic experience that is not only immersive but also a visual extravaganza of unparalleled proportions.

Krrish 3: Blending Superhero Feats with Visual Effects - An Editing Triumph

"Krrish 3," a superhero film, harnessed the power of visual effects (VFX) to vividly portray the titular hero's superhuman capabilities. Editors meticulously orchestrated the incorporation of these VFX sequences, emphasizing the critical need for alignment with the film's overarching visual aesthetics and the real-world backdrop of live-action sequences. Through this deliberate and cohesive approach, "Krrish 3" succeeded in seamlessly merging the extraordinary with the ordinary, rendering the superhero's feats and abilities not only believable but also visually harmonious within the context of the film. The judicious use of VFX thus not only elevated the narrative's impact but also played an integral role in sustaining the film's cohesive visual identity, serving as a vital tool in the creation of an immersive cinematic experience.

2.0: A Visual Effects Extravaganza - Editors as the Architects of Seamless Integration

"2.0," a science fiction masterpiece, showcased a plethora of intricate visual effects (VFX), notably including the creation of a formidable robot army. In this cinematic marvel, editors assumed a pivotal role in the process of flawlessly integrating these elaborate VFX components, ensuring they seamlessly coexisted with the live-action sequences and consistently upheld the film's exceptional visual standards. Their meticulous work was instrumental in preserving the film's high-quality visual effects, allowing the audience to be fully immersed in the awe-inspiring world of sentient robots and cutting-edge technology. By expertly balancing the realms of fantasy and reality, "2.0" not only pushed the boundaries of VFX technology but also reaffirmed the film's position as a groundbreaking achievement in cinematic storytelling, where the fusion of extraordinary visuals and narrative prowess transcended traditional boundaries.

Transforming Indian Cinema: The Art of Seamless VFX Integration and Storytelling Innovation

The effective integration of visual effects (VFX) in Indian films represents a dynamic catalyst for elevating storytelling to unprecedented heights, opening up vast creative horizons, and shattering the traditional confines of cinematic narratives. Collaborative efforts between editors and VFX teams are pivotal in achieving this seamless fusion, enabling filmmakers to transport audiences into immersive and otherworldly realms, craft breathtaking action sequences, and manifest distinctive visual aesthetics that were once only conceivable in dreams. VFX integration serves as an invaluable instrument, empowering Indian filmmakers to weave a tapestry of diverse, visually mesmerizing narratives on the grand canvas of the silver screen, thus redefining the very essence of cinematic expression and captivating the hearts and minds of audiences worldwide.

R. Language and Subtitles

Subtitle Integration in Indian Films

Bridging Language Barriers: The Art of Subtitle Integration in Multilingual Films

The process of subtitle integration in films encompasses the art of introducing translated text or subtitles onto the screen, serving as a vital means of conveying dialogue, narrative nuances, or essential information to viewers who may not comprehend the spoken language used in the film. In the context of multilingual films, subtitles play an indispensable role in transcending language barriers and expanding the accessibility of the film to a broader and more diverse audience. This subtle yet powerful technique enables cinematic storytelling to transcend linguistic boundaries, fostering cross-cultural understanding and enriching the cinematic experience for audiences worldwide by ensuring that the narrative's depth and significance are fully comprehensible and appreciated, irrespective of linguistic differences.

Purpose of Subtitle Integration

Subtitles serve several key purposes in Indian films:

Universal Understanding: The Role of Accessibility Through Subtitles in Global Filmmaking

Accessibility in filmmaking signifies a fundamental commitment to ensuring that the cinematic experience transcends language barriers, granting access to viewers who may not be fluent in the language in which the movie was originally filmed. By incorporating subtitles or translated text, filmmakers extend a welcoming hand to a diverse and global audience, enabling everyone to engage with the story, characters, and emotions on the screen, regardless of linguistic limitations. This act of inclusion and democratization of cinema amplifies cultural exchange, fosters empathy, and cultivates a universal appreciation for the art of filmmaking, affirming that narratives can be universally understood and cherished, reinforcing the notion that cinema is a powerful medium capable of uniting people across the world through the language of storytelling.

Cultural Exchange Beyond Words: Subtitles as a Gateway to Global Diversity in Cinema

Cultural exchange facilitated by subtitles serves as a remarkable gateway to the rich tapestry of global diversity, permitting audiences to not only appreciate but also comprehend the intricacies of various languages, cultural nuances, and references depicted in films. Subtitles effectively bridge the gap between different linguistic worlds, forging connections that transcend borders and enriching the viewer's experience by offering insights into the customs, traditions, and unique aspects of other cultures. In this way, they promote cross-cultural empathy and awareness, fostering a deeper sense of global interconnectedness, and underlining the power of cinema as a conduit for promoting mutual respect, understanding, and celebration of the multifaceted mosaic of human heritage and expression.

Unlocking Global Audiences: The Multilingual Subtitle Strategy in Indian Cinema

The implementation of subtitles in multiple languages within Indian films is a strategic maneuver that significantly amplifies their global reach and broadens their international market appeal. This accessibility initiative transcends linguistic boundaries, making these films comprehensible and relatable to viewers worldwide, irrespective of their native language. Consequently, Indian cinema gains the potential to tap into a vast, diverse, and culturally varied global audience, unlocking new avenues for distribution and commercial success. These subtitles not only facilitate a deeper connection between international viewers and the narrative but also foster cultural exchange and mutual appreciation. Thus, they serve as a pivotal tool in propelling Indian cinema onto the world stage, demonstrating the universality of its themes, and harnessing the magic of storytelling to unite people across continents, showcasing the remarkable potential of film as a medium of global communication and entertainment.

Role of Editors in Subtitle Integration: The Collaborative Art of Communication in Filmmaking

The process of communication within the context of subtitling involves a collaborative effort between editors, translators, subtitlers, and filmmakers, with the primary goal of ensuring a seamless and effective transfer of information to the audience through subtitles. Editors, as intermediaries in this process, play a crucial role by bridging the gap between linguistic experts and filmmakers. They work closely with translators and subtitlers to ascertain precise placement, timing, and content of subtitles, ensuring that the text harmoniously aligns with the film's visuals and audio. Their collaboration extends to frequent consultations with the director to grasp the intended viewing experience, capturing the essence of the narrative, and preserving the director's artistic vision. This meticulous coordination and attention to detail are paramount, as they enable the subtitles to not only convey dialogue accurately but also maintain the film's emotional depth, pacing, and impact, thereby enhancing the overall communication between the film and its diverse audience, regardless of language barriers.

Balancing Act: The Art of Subtitle Integration in Filmmaking

In film communication, editors engage in collaborative efforts with translators, subtitlers, and filmmakers to ensure the flawless integration of subtitles into the visual narrative. Their primary objective is to maintain a seamless and unobtrusive presence of subtitles within the frame, preserving the film's overall flow and aesthetic integrity while effectively conveying dialogue and information to the audience. Editors make strategic choices regarding font selection, text sizes, and positioning on the screen, ensuring that subtitles neither divert attention from the visuals nor disrupt the film's narrative rhythm. By delicately balancing these elements, editors aim to harmonize the textual and visual dimensions of the film, facilitating clear communication without impeding the immersive experience, thereby enabling audiences to fully engage with the story while appreciating the nuances of different languages and cultures represented on screen. This meticulous approach underscores the crucial role of editors in ensuring that subtitles seamlessly become an integral part of the cinematic communication process.

Timing Is Everything: The Precision of Subtitle Synchronization in Filmmaking

Timing within subtitling is a critical responsibility that falls on editors' shoulders, necessitating precise synchronization of subtitles with the spoken dialogue and the overall pacing of the film. Editors meticulously ensure that subtitles appear on screen in perfect harmony with the natural flow of conversation, allowing viewers to read the text comfortably without feeling rushed or delayed. This artful synchronization not only ensures that audiences can fully absorb and comprehend the dialogue but also guarantees that they do not miss any crucial visual or audio elements in the process. The seamless alignment of timing between subtitles and the film's audio-visual components thus contributes significantly to the overall viewing experience, promoting clear communication while upholding the integrity of the narrative and facilitating an uninterrupted connection between the audience and the story being told on screen.

Typography and Styling: Crafting Readable and Harmonious Subtitles in Filmmaking

Font and styling considerations in subtitling involve a meticulous selection process undertaken by editors to enhance readability and visual harmony within the film. Editors make deliberate choices regarding fonts that are not only easy to read but also seamlessly blend with the film's overarching aesthetic and design sensibilities. Additionally, the colour of the subtitles is thoughtfully chosen to ensure high visibility against a variety of background colours and lighting conditions, guaranteeing that the text remains discernible and legible throughout the film. These subtle yet crucial decisions in font, styling, and colour coordination play a pivotal role in making subtitles an unobtrusive and integrated part of the cinematic experience, maintaining clear communication while preserving the film's visual cohesiveness, ultimately contributing to the overall accessibility and enjoyment of the film for a diverse audience.

Strategic Subtitle Placement: Enhancing Readability While Preserving Cinematic Immersion

The art of positioning subtitles within the frame is a meticulous endeavor undertaken by editors to ensure optimal readability and minimal disruption to the viewer's engagement with the film. Editors make deliberate decisions to strategically place subtitles at the bottom of the frame, away from essential visual elements, character faces, or critical action sequences, all in a bid to maintain the subtitles' unobtrusive presence while effectively conveying the dialogue. By adhering to this principle of subtlety and discretion, editors seek to strike a delicate balance between facilitating clear communication for the audience and preserving the immersive quality of the film. This thoughtful positioning of subtitles allows viewers to absorb the textual information seamlessly, fostering an uninterrupted connection with the narrative and enabling them to fully immerse themselves in the cinematic experience without distractions, thereby enhancing both the accessibility and the artistic integrity of the film.

Optimizing Viewer Engagement: Meticulous Line Length and Text Speed in Subtitling

In subtitling, editors pay meticulous attention to line length and text speed, factors crucial for optimizing viewer comprehension and engagement. Editors make deliberate choices to ensure that subtitle lines are of an appropriate length, striking a balance that allows viewers to read them quickly and comfortably without feeling rushed. Moreover, editors synchronize the speed of the subtitles with the natural rhythm and pacing of the dialogue delivery, aligning them seamlessly with the characters' spoken words. This synchronization serves the dual purpose of enabling audiences to keep pace with the conversation while preventing subtitles from either lingering on screen for too long or flashing by too rapidly. These astute adjustments in line length and text speed harmonize the subtitling process with the flow of the film, fostering effective communication and viewer immersion, thus enhancing the overall accessibility and enjoyment of the cinematic experience.

Examples of Subtitle Integration: Bridging Linguistic Divides, The Power of Subtitles in '3 Idiots

"3 Idiots," a multilingual film, leverages the power of subtitles as a transformative tool in bridging linguistic divides, facilitating cultural exchange, and expanding its reach to a global audience. The film utilizes subtitles to seamlessly translate dialogue between Hindi and English, enabling accessibility for both Indian and international viewers. These subtitles are thoughtfully integrated at the bottom of the frame, strategically positioned to avoid essential visual elements or character faces, ensuring that they remain unobtrusive and cohesively integrated with the film's narrative. In doing so, "3 Idiots" not only showcases the universality of its themes and humor but also underscores the pivotal role of subtitles in making cinematic storytelling a truly inclusive and immersive experience, where audiences of diverse backgrounds can revel in the humor, emotion, and depth of the narrative while embracing the rich tapestry of cultures represented on screen.

Breaking Linguistic Barriers: Subtitles in 'Baahubali: The Beginning

"Baahubali: The Beginning," an epic cinematic spectacle, employs subtitles as a vital conduit for breaking linguistic barriers and extending its narrative canvas to a wide-ranging international audience. The film strategically deploys subtitles to translate dialogue from Telugu and Tamil, the original languages, into various languages, including English and Hindi, thus rendering the film accessible to a broader demographic. Careful consideration is given to font selection and positioning, ensuring that the subtitles are clear and legible without obstructing the grandiose visuals that are a hallmark of the film. By skillfully integrating these subtitles, "Baahubali: The Beginning" not only facilitates cross-cultural communication but also preserves the film's immersive quality, permitting audiences to be enraptured by the grandeur of its storytelling while embracing its diverse linguistic dimensions, exemplifying how subtitles can enhance the global appeal of cinematic masterpieces without compromising their artistic integrity.

Seamless Subtitle Integration: 'Parasite' as a Global Cinematic Masterpiece

"Parasite" (Korean Film): While not an Indian film, "Parasite," a Korean cinematic masterpiece, serves as a compelling exemplar of seamless subtitle integration transcending cultural boundaries. The film utilizes subtitles expertly to translate its Korean dialogue into multiple languages, ensuring accessibility to a diverse international audience and contributing significantly to its global acclaim and success. By adopting a careful approach to font selection, positioning, and timing, "Parasite" maintains the immersive quality of its storytelling without undermining the linguistic inclusivity it offers. This cinematic gem underscores the universal appeal of impactful storytelling and demonstrates how well-executed subtitle integration can turn a foreign-language film into a global sensation, emphasizing the pivotal role of subtitles in fostering cross-cultural understanding and appreciation within the area of international cinema.

Bridging Linguistic Diversity: The Role of Subtitles in Indian Cinema

The integration of subtitles in Indian films plays a pivotal role in broadening the accessibility and reach of cinematic works within a linguistically and culturally diverse nation like India. Editors are instrumental in this process, working diligently to seamlessly incorporate subtitles into the film's visual and auditory elements. This skillful integration allows viewers to immerse themselves in the narrative while simultaneously gaining an appreciation for the linguistic and cultural intricacies portrayed on screen. Subtitles serve to enrich the storytelling experience by ensuring that audiences can connect with the narratives, emotions, and artistic expressions presented in these films, regardless of the language in which they are originally produced. This subtitled enrichment contributes to fostering a dynamic cultural exchange within the realm of Indian cinema, serving as a bridge that unites audiences from various linguistic backgrounds and reinforces the idea that cinema is a universal platform for storytelling, capable of transcending boundaries and uniting diverse communities through the shared language of film.

Cinema as a Universal Language: The Inclusive Role of Subtitles in Indian Filmmaking

Moreover, the integration of subtitles in Indian cinema signifies a broader shift in the industry toward a more inclusive and accessible approach to filmmaking. It is an acknowledgment of the diversity of India's linguistic landscape and a commitment to ensuring that films can be enjoyed by a wide array of audiences, irrespective of their native language. By making films more accessible through subtitles, Indian cinema is not only increasing its global appeal but also enhancing its role as a cultural and artistic ambassador. It fosters an environment where audiences from different linguistic and cultural backgrounds can appreciate and connect with the vast array of stories that Indian cinema has to offer. In this sense, subtitles not only serve a practical function but also embody the values of inclusivity, cultural exchange, and the belief that storytelling is a universal language that transcends linguistic barriers.

CHAPTER - 6

6. Gaining Insights Into Diverse Departments

A film director's role necessitates a comprehensive grasp of all aspects of filmmaking, encompassing not only the creative elements but also the technical and logistical facets of the production process. With a clear vision at the helm, the director must be able to communicate this vision coherently to each department, including cinematography, costume design, sound, and editing, among others. This understanding is crucial for ensuring that all team members are aligned with the overarching creative goals and can work collaboratively towards the director's vision. Moreover, it enables the director to make informed decisions, provide effective guidance, and troubleshoot issues that may arise during filming, ultimately facilitating the realization of their cinematic vision on the screen. Here are some of the key departments and areas a film director should be familiar with:

A. The Director's Crucial Connection to Screenwriting

While not primarily responsible for the scriptwriting process, film directors benefit significantly from having a solid grasp of screenwriting principles. This understanding is crucial because it forms the foundation upon which the entire cinematic narrative is built. It allows directors to comprehend the intricacies of storytelling, character arcs, and the essential elements of a script. With this knowledge, directors can collaborate more effectively with screenwriters, providing insightful input, and ensuring that the script aligns with their creative vision. Additionally, a director's understanding of screenwriting facilitates the visualization of scenes and enables them to make informed decisions about shot composition, pacing, and the overall cinematic structure. It empowers directors to contribute creatively to script development and adapt it to the visual medium, thus enhancing their ability to bring their artistic vision to life cohesively and compellingly on the screen. Learning about screenwriting is important for a film director for several crucial reasons:

Mastering Story Structure: A Crucial Skill for Directors in Film and Screenwriting

Understanding story structure through screenwriting knowledge is vital for directors as it equips them with the foundational principles of storytelling, such as the three-act structure, character arcs, and plot development. This proficiency is indispensable in shaping compelling and effectively structured narratives. Directors who comprehend these elements can guide their teams with precision, ensuring that the story's progression is cohesive, characters evolve believably, and plot twists and resolutions are strategically executed, ultimately enhancing the film's overall impact and resonance with the audience.

Fostering Creative Harmony: The Crucial Role of Director-Screenwriter Collaboration in Film Production

Effective collaboration between directors and screenwriters is paramount, particularly during pre-production and production phases. A director's grasp of screenwriting principles facilitates clear and constructive communication with screenwriters, fostering a collaborative environment where ideas can be exchanged, script revisions can be fine-tuned, and the narrative can seamlessly integrate with the director's creative vision. This alignment ensures that the screenplay not only serves as a blueprint for the film but also captures the director's intended tone, style, and storytelling nuances, resulting in a harmonious and cohesive cinematic experience that resonates with the audience.

Elevating Character Depth: The Director's Influence on Character Development in Filmmaking

Character development is a critical aspect of filmmaking, and directors with a solid grasp of screenwriting principles can play an active role in crafting intricate and multifaceted characters. Their understanding enables them to offer valuable insights into character motivations, dynamics, and conflicts, enriching the depth and authenticity of the characters within the film's narrative. This involvement allows directors to guide actors more effectively, ensuring that characters evolve convincingly throughout the story, fostering a deeper emotional connection between the audience and the characters, and ultimately contributing to a more compelling and immersive cinematic experience.

Empowering Visual Storytelling: How Screenwriting Knowledge Elevates Directorial Vision in Filmmaking

Screenwriting encompasses not only dialogue and plot but also vivid descriptions of visual elements, camera angles, and scene transitions. Directors who possess screenwriting knowledge gain a distinct advantage in visual storytelling by being able to more effectively envision and strategize the film's visual components. This proficiency aids in translating the written script into a visually captivating and cohesive cinematic experience. Directors can pre-visualize scenes, consider the most appropriate camera angles and movements to convey emotions or themes, and plan seamless transitions between shots and sequences. As a result, their ability to harness the power of visual storytelling is enhanced, ultimately elevating the film's overall impact and narrative coherence, making it more engaging and memorable for the audience.

Mastering Rhythm and Pacing: How Directors' Screenwriting Knowledge Enhances Film's Narrative Flow

Screenwriting inherently involves crucial decisions regarding pacing and timing within a screenplay, and directors with a solid understanding of these principles can significantly impact the film's overall rhythm and effectiveness. Their insight allows them to actively contribute to the optimization of pacing, ensuring that scenes unfold at a tempo that sustains audience engagement and harmonizes with the film's intended tone. Directors can make informed choices about when to build tension, when to release it, and how to sequence events for maximum impact. This heightened awareness enables them to strike a delicate balance between action, dialogue, and quiet moments, ultimately shaping the film's narrative flow in a way that captivates the viewer and maintains a strong connection with the story, enhancing the overall cinematic experience.

Elevating Character Voices: Directors' Influence on Authentic and Impactful Dialogue in Filmmaking

Mastery of dialogue is a fundamental aspect of effective storytelling, and directors who familiarize themselves with screenwriting principles can offer invaluable insights into this critical element. Their understanding enables them to collaborate closely with screenwriters to craft dialogue that is not only authentic but also serves as a powerful tool for character development and plot advancement. Directors can contribute to the creation of lines that resonate with the characters' personalities, motivations, and arcs, ensuring that every word spoken on screen feels genuine and meaningful. This collaboration between director and screenwriter results in dialogues that not only engage the audience but also play a pivotal role in driving the narrative forward, heightening the emotional impact of the film, and enhancing the overall quality of the storytelling.

Translating Literary Worlds to Screen: How Directors' Screenwriting Expertise Enhances Adaptation Success

Adapting source materials like novels, plays, or other literary works into screenplays is a complex and nuanced process, and directors who possess screenwriting knowledge wield a significant advantage in this endeavor. Their expertise allows them to be active participants in the adaptation process, ensuring that the essence of the original work is preserved while making essential adjustments for the visual medium of film. Directors can collaborate closely with screenwriters to translate intricate narratives, themes, and character developments from the source material into a cinematic format, making decisions on what to include, exclude, or modify to maintain narrative coherence and visual storytelling impact. This collaborative effort ensures that the adapted screenplay not only respects the source material but also thrives as a distinct and compelling cinematic experience that resonates with both fans of the original work and new audiences.

Pitching with Precision: How Screenwriting Knowledge Empowers Directors in Film Development

In the world of filmmaking, pitching and development are critical phases where directors must effectively convey their creative vision to producers, studios, and investors to secure funding and support for their projects. Directors equipped with a solid understanding of screenwriting principles have a distinct advantage in this process. Their knowledge enables them to articulate their film concepts with clarity, coherence, and persuasive power. They can craft compelling narratives and present their ideas in a way that resonates with potential backers, effectively conveying the emotional resonance, thematic depth, and visual potential of their projects. This not only enhances their ability to secure the necessary resources but also fosters trust and confidence in their directorial abilities, laying a strong foundation for the successful development and realization of their films.

Sculpting the Final Narrative: Directors with Screenwriting Insight in Film Editing and Post-Production

Directors with a background in screenwriting bring a unique perspective to the editing and post-production phases of filmmaking. Their knowledge allows them to work in close collaboration with film editors, making informed decisions about how to shape the final narrative. This includes the ability to assess the pacing and timing of scenes, recognize opportunities for restructuring or rearranging sequences to enhance narrative coherence, and ensure that the film aligns closely with the original creative vision. This collaboration streamlines the editing process, as directors can provide precise input on which shots and moments are essential to the story's development, resulting in a more cohesive and impactful final product that resonates with the audience.

Adapting on the Fly: Directors' Screenwriting Knowledge as a Key Asset in Overcoming Script-Related Challenges during Production

Directors equipped with screenwriting knowledge possess a valuable problem-solving skill set that proves instrumental when addressing script-related challenges during production. These challenges can range from logistical constraints to actor improvisation or unexpected weather conditions. In such situations, directors can collaborate effectively with screenwriters, drawing upon their understanding of storytelling principles to devise creative and contextually appropriate solutions. This ability to think on their feet and adapt the script as needed not only maintains the integrity of the narrative but also ensures that the film remains true to the director's vision, fostering a dynamic and flexible production environment that can navigate unexpected hurdles and ultimately deliver a cohesive and engaging cinematic experience.

Cinematic Fusion: Directors' Creative Contributions to Screenwriting

Screenwriting is an inherently creative process, and directors who invest their time in understanding and contributing to it can bring valuable insights to the script's development. This level of involvement enables directors to actively shape the narrative, characters, and thematic elements in a way that aligns seamlessly with their unique artistic vision and storytelling objectives. Directors, with their deep understanding of cinematic language and visual storytelling, can infuse their creative insights into the script. They can suggest imaginative plot twists, character motivations, and visual storytelling elements that not only enhance the story but also contribute to the overall cinematic experience. This collaborative approach creates a synergy between the director's creative instincts and the narrative structure, resulting in a film that not only reflects the director's artistic sensibilities but also resonates with audiences on a profound level. Such films become powerful and memorable works of cinema, as they carry the indelible mark of the director's creative input.

Cinematic Synergy: The Vital Director-Screenwriter Collaboration in Filmmaking

The collaboration between directors and screenwriters is essential in the filmmaking process, as it ensures that the final product is a cohesive and engaging narrative that effectively communicates the director's vision. Directors often have a distinct perspective on how the story should unfold, the visual style it should adopt, and the emotional impact it should convey. When they actively engage with the screenwriting process, they bridge the gap between the written word and its cinematic realization. They bring a holistic understanding of the film's structure, pacing, and visual language, which can lead to more effective storytelling and a deeper connection with the audience. Ultimately, this collaborative effort not only enhances the creative quality of the film but also highlights the importance of the director's role in shaping the narrative and realizing their unique artistic vision on screen.

Empowering Career Growth: How Screenwriting Knowledge Elevates Directors' Opportunities and Prospects in the Film Industry

A comprehensive understanding of screenwriting can significantly bolster a director's career prospects within the film industry. Directors who possess this knowledge are well-positioned to take on a wider array of projects, including those that involve script development, adaptation of source material, or even writing original screenplays. This versatility not only broadens their professional opportunities but also increases their appeal to producers and studios seeking directors who can actively contribute to script refinement and storytelling coherence. Furthermore, directors with a solid grasp of screenwriting may find themselves better equipped to navigate the competitive landscape of filmmaking, as their proficiency allows them to communicate their creative vision more effectively, collaborate seamlessly with writers, and ultimately deliver films that stand out in terms of narrative depth and artistic vision, thereby advancing their career in a highly competitive industry.

B. Director and Director of Photography (DOP)

Collaboration with the director of photography (DOP) is pivotal for a director to attain the envisioned visual style and mood of the film, encompassing aspects such as shot composition, lighting, camera angles, and movement. While a director need not be a cinematography expert, a robust comprehension of cinematographic principles is indispensable for facilitating seamless communication and collaboration with the DOP, thereby actualizing their creative vision. This understanding empowers directors to make informed decisions, amplify storytelling nuances, and craft visually captivating cinematic experiences that resonate with audiences.

Fluent Filmmaking: How Directors' Understanding of Cinematography Enhances Creative Communication and Visual Excellence

Effective communication is a cornerstone of successful filmmaking, and directors benefit immensely from having a fundamental understanding of cinematography. This knowledge equips them with the ability to communicate their creative vision with precision to the cinematographer, facilitating a seamless exchange of ideas. Directors can articulate their concepts more clearly, discussing specific camera angles, shot compositions, lighting preferences, and visual styles. This clarity in communication streamlines the collaboration between the director and the cinematographer, allowing the latter to translate the director's vision into tangible visual elements with greater accuracy. This synergy not only enhances the overall quality of the film's visuals but also ensures that the cinematography aligns closely with the director's artistic intent, contributing to a cohesive and visually stunning cinematic experience for the audience.

Collaborative Mastery: Directors and Cinematographers Uniting through Cinematography Expertise in Filmmaking

Collaboration lies at the heart of filmmaking, and directors who possess a solid understanding of cinematography forge stronger, more effective partnerships with their cinematographers. This shared knowledge fosters a deeper level of collaboration, allowing directors to communicate their creative vision in technical terms, discuss shot compositions, lighting techniques, camera movements, and visual aesthetics with greater precision. This heightened collaboration leads to a harmonious working relationship, where the director and cinematographer can explore creative ideas more fluidly, experiment with visual storytelling techniques, and problem-solve on set in real-time. The result is often a seamless fusion of the director's artistic vision and the cinematographer's technical expertise, resulting in visually stunning and narratively compelling films that resonate deeply with the audience due to the synergy achieved through this collaborative approach.

Crafting Cinematic Artistry: Directors' Mastery of Cinematography for Visual Identity and Impactful Filmmaking

Aesthetic control is a crucial aspect of filmmaking, and directors with a deep comprehension of cinematography wield a powerful tool to shape the visual identity of their films. This knowledge empowers them to exercise meticulous control over every visual element, from framing and composition to lighting and camera movement. Directors can precisely orchestrate the visual mood, tone, and style of the film, ensuring that it aligns seamlessly with their artistic vision and storytelling objectives. This level of control allows for the creation of striking and evocative visuals that not only enhance the narrative but also deeply engage the audience. Directors who understand cinematography can make deliberate and informed choices, resulting in a film that is not only aesthetically captivating but also a true reflection of their creative intent, contributing to a more immersive and impactful cinematic experience.

Elevating Narrative Depth: Directors' Proficiency in Cinematography as a Storytelling Powerhouse in Filmmaking

Cinematography is a potent storytelling tool within the filmmaker's arsenal, and directors with a firm grasp of its principles can harness its capabilities to elevate their storytelling prowess. Through deliberate choices in camera angles, lighting, framing, and camera movement, directors can convey emotions, emphasize character perspectives, and create visual metaphors that enrich the narrative tapestry. These cinematic techniques not only enhance the audience's understanding of the story but also imbue it with depth, subtext, and emotional resonance. Directors can effectively use cinematography to establish mood, build tension, highlight crucial plot points, and guide the viewer's gaze, thereby shaping a more immersive and compelling narrative that resonates on both intellectual and emotional levels, ultimately resulting in a more impactful and memorable cinematic experience.

Cinematography Savvy: How Directors' Expertise Helps Solve Challenges on the Film Set

Problem-solving is a fundamental skill for directors, especially on the ever-changing and often unpredictable terrain of a film set. When directors have a firm understanding of cinematography, they possess a valuable toolkit for addressing unforeseen challenges. They can make real-time decisions about camera placement, framing, and lighting, allowing them to adapt creatively and efficiently to unexpected obstacles, such as changing weather conditions, equipment malfunctions, or scheduling constraints. This agility in problem-solving not only keeps the production on track but also enables directors to maintain the visual consistency and narrative integrity of the film. By leveraging their cinematographic knowledge, directors can navigate these challenges with finesse, ultimately contributing to a smoother production process and a more polished end product.

Budget-Wise Filmmaking: How Directors' Cinematography Expertise Drives Cost Efficiency on Set

Cost efficiency is a paramount concern in filmmaking, and directors with a solid grasp of cinematography can significantly contribute to financial savings throughout the production process. Their understanding enables them to make informed decisions regarding shot selection, camera angles, and lighting setups, optimizing each scene's visual impact while minimizing the likelihood of costly reshoots or extensive post-production adjustments. Directors can efficiently plan and execute shots, ensuring that the desired look and mood are achieved during filming, which can lead to a reduction in the need for costly fixes in post-production. Moreover, this knowledge allows directors to work closely with their cinematographers to maximize the use of available resources, making budget-conscious choices without compromising the overall quality and visual appeal of the film. The result is a more cost-effective production that aligns with the project's financial parameters, ultimately benefiting both the filmmakers and the investors.

Mastering Cinematic Artistry: Directors' Exploration of Visual Style and Self-Expression through Cinematography

Cinematography is undeniably an art form, and directors who recognize its artistic potential can harness it as a powerful means of self-expression. Acquiring knowledge in cinematography empowers directors to delve deeper into the nuances of visual storytelling, enabling them to craft a distinct and signature visual style that distinguishes their work from others. They can experiment with various camera techniques, lighting schemes, framing choices, and camera movements to infuse their films with a personalized aesthetic that resonates with their artistic sensibilities. This creative exploration not only elevates their work to a higher level of artistic expression but also enhances their ability to convey emotions, themes, and narrative concepts through the visual language of cinema, creating a unique cinematic identity that leaves a lasting impact on audiences and the industry at large.

Elevating Visual Precision: Directors' Expertise in Cinematography for Collaborative Excellence with Cinematographers

Having a deep understanding of cinematography equips directors with a critical eye that enables them to evaluate the work of their cinematographer with precision and clarity. They can meticulously assess the visual elements, including framing, lighting, camera angles, and shot composition, against their artistic vision for the film. This critical perspective empowers directors to provide constructive feedback to the cinematographer, guiding the creative process to achieve the desired look, mood, and storytelling impact. This collaborative synergy between director and cinematographer ensures that the visual aesthetics closely align with the director's artistic intent, fostering a harmonious partnership that results in a film that resonates authentically with the director's vision and leaves a lasting impression on the audience.

Strategic Advantages: How Directors' Cinematography Expertise Enhances Career Flexibility and Opportunities in the Film Industry

In the fiercely competitive landscape of the film industry, possessing a diverse skill set is a strategic advantage. Directors who have a deep understanding of cinematography open up a wealth of opportunities and increased career flexibility. This knowledge not only makes them more versatile professionals but also enhances their marketability. Directors with cinematographic expertise can take on a wider range of projects, from small independent films to big-budget productions, and can effectively communicate their creative vision to their teams, producers, and investors. This adaptability and proficiency can lead to more frequent collaborations, as they can contribute meaningfully to various aspects of the filmmaking process, from script development to post-production, increasing their overall appeal to stakeholders. Ultimately, directors who understand cinematography can navigate the competitive film industry more effectively, advance their careers, and leave a lasting mark on the world of cinema.

Fostering Empathy and Collaboration: How Directors' Cinematography Knowledge Enhances Relationships with Film Crew

Cinematography knowledge for directors can cultivate a deeper sense of empathy and mutual understanding between them and their film crew, particularly with cinematographers. By gaining insight into the technical intricacies, challenges, and demands of the cinematographer's role, directors are better equipped to appreciate the complexities of their collaborators' work. This empathy leads to a more positive and collaborative working environment, as directors can effectively anticipate and address the needs and concerns of their crew, ensuring smoother production processes and fostering a strong sense of teamwork. Moreover, this empathetic approach promotes open communication and trust, encouraging creative input from all team members and ultimately resulting in a more harmonious and productive filmmaking experience where everyone's contributions are valued and respected, enhancing the overall quality of the final product.

C. Collaborating with the Production Designer

Collaborating with the production designer is a vital aspect of a film director's job as it allows them to craft the visual aesthetics of the film, encompassing everything from the sets and props to the costumes. Although a director's primary responsibility lies in shaping the narrative and guiding the actors, having an understanding of production design is indispensable. This knowledge enables directors to ensure that the visual elements of the film align with their creative vision, maintaining consistency and thematic depth. By working closely with the production design team, directors can effectively communicate their ideas, fostering a collaborative atmosphere where the physical and visual aspects of the film come together harmoniously. This collaboration is essential in creating a cinematic experience that not only tells a compelling story but also engages the audience through its visual richness, ultimately enhancing the overall impact and effectiveness of the film.

Elevating Narrative through Production Design: Directors' Creative Use of Visual Elements in Cinematic Storytelling

Visual storytelling hinges on the pivotal role of production design, and directors equipped with an understanding of production design principles can harness this creative tool to elevate their narratives, express underlying themes, and fashion a visually immersive and coherent cinematic experience. This comprehension enables directors to collaborate effectively with production designers, art departments, and costume teams to craft sets, props, and wardrobes that seamlessly harmonize with the film's overarching vision. Directors can strategically manipulate colour palettes, aesthetics, and visual motifs to underscore the emotional beats, character developments, and thematic undertones of the story, thereby intensifying the audience's engagement with the narrative. By leveraging the potency of production design, directors can transmute tangible elements into instruments of storytelling, proficiently communicating the subtext, messages, and character arcs, thereby culminating in a more visually captivating, thematically resonant, and artistically unified cinematic masterpiece.

Fostering Creative Harmony: Directors and Production Designers Uniting for Cinematic Excellence

Collaboration is the lifeblood of filmmaking, and directors often form a pivotal partnership with production designers to actualize their creative visions. Directors who delve into the intricacies of production design acquire a valuable skill set that facilitates effective communication and enhances collaboration with the production design team. This understanding enables directors to articulate their ideas more precisely, using visual language to convey their intended mood, tone, and thematic elements. As a result, the production designer and their team can better grasp the director's vision and work in tandem to bring it to life. This collaborative synergy streamlines the creative process, fosters a harmonious working environment, and ultimately ensures that the film's visual aesthetics align seamlessly with the director's artistic intent, thereby contributing to a more cohesive and visually captivating cinematic experience.

Sculpting Visual Aesthetics: Directors' Mastery of Production Design for Cinematic Identity and Impact

Aesthetic control is a pivotal aspect of filmmaking, and directors who possess a deep understanding of production design principles wield a powerful means of shaping the visual identity of their films. This knowledge empowers them to exercise meticulous control over every visual element, including sets, props, costumes, and even colour palettes. Directors can thoughtfully orchestrate the look and feel of the film, ensuring that it harmonizes seamlessly with their artistic vision and storytelling objectives. This level of control allows for the creation of a distinctive and immersive cinematic world that resonates with the director's unique sensibilities. By leveraging their understanding of production design, directors can craft a visual aesthetic that not only enhances the narrative but also establishes a signature style, creating a film that is both visually captivating and a true reflection of their creative intent, ultimately contributing to a more engaging and impactful cinematic experience for the audience.

Elevating Character Depth: How Directors Utilize Production Design for Profound Character Development in Filmmaking

Production design is a dynamic tool for character development within filmmaking. Directors who possess a solid grasp of production design principles recognize that sets, props, and costumes are not mere background elements but essential storytelling devices that can provide profound insights into a character's personality, history, and motivations. They can collaborate effectively with the production designer to create a visual language that enhances character depth and complexity. Through the selection of specific props or the design of a character's living space, directors can convey subtle nuances of the character's identity and experiences. This collaborative effort ensures that every visual element associated with a character aligns seamlessly with their narrative arc, fostering a deeper connection between the audience and the characters. Directors who understand the impact of production design on character development ultimately create more well-rounded and relatable characters, enriching the overall storytelling experience and leaving a lasting impression on the viewer.

Crafting Cinematic Worlds: Directors' Mastery of Production Design for Immersive Storytelling

World-building is a cornerstone of cinematic storytelling, especially in films set in fictional or historical contexts, and production design is the linchpin that brings these worlds to life. Directors who invest in understanding production design principles play a pivotal role in this process, as they can effectively collaborate with production designers to craft immersive and convincing environments that enchant and engage the audience. Through meticulous choices in set design, props, and costumes, directors can meticulously construct the physical and visual elements of these worlds, ensuring that every detail aligns seamlessly with the film's narrative and thematic objectives. This collaborative synergy fosters a sense of authenticity, transporting the audience into these alternate realities, whether they are fantastical realms or historically accurate settings, thus enhancing the film's capacity to captivate, resonate, and leave a lasting impression on viewers through the power of world-building.

Elevating Emotion through Production Design: Directors' Expertise in Crafting Mood and Atmosphere in Cinematic Storytelling

Mood and atmosphere are integral components of cinematic storytelling, and production design stands as a formidable tool for directors to shape these elements to perfection. Directors who possess a profound understanding of production design principles can strategically utilize sets, props, lighting, and even colour schemes to evoke precise emotions and intensify the viewer's cinematic journey. They can collaborate effectively with production designers to craft environments that resonate with the intended mood, whether it's an eerie, suspenseful atmosphere in a thriller or a warm, nostalgic ambiance in a drama. Through meticulous attention to visual details, directors can transport the audience into the heart of the narrative, creating an immersive experience where the settings themselves become vehicles for emotional storytelling. This knowledge enables directors to harness the full potential of production design, forging a profound connection between the film's visuals and its thematic resonance, ultimately resulting in a more impactful and memorable cinematic experience for the audience.

Balancing Creativity and Budget: How Directors' Understanding of Production Design Enhances Cost-Efficient Filmmaking

In filmmaking, cost efficiency is a paramount concern, and directors who possess a comprehensive grasp of production design principles can make judicious decisions that have a direct impact on budget management. This understanding empowers directors to collaborate effectively with production designers, guiding the process of set construction, prop selection, and costume choices in a manner that maximizes resources while minimizing unnecessary expenses. By making informed choices, directors can ensure that every element aligns with the film's artistic vision and narrative requirements, optimizing both the visual and financial aspects of production. This not only contributes to cost-effective filmmaking but also prevents potential overruns and budgetary challenges, allowing for a more streamlined and fiscally responsible production process that benefits both the filmmakers and investors. Ultimately, directors who comprehend production design principles can strike a balance between creative excellence and budgetary constraints, leading to a more efficient and financially sustainable film production.

Creative Solutions: How Directors' Production Design Expertise Enhances Problem-Solving in Filmmaking

Problem-solving is a fundamental skill in filmmaking, and directors with a deep understanding of production design bring a valuable problem-solving perspective to the table. They can effectively collaborate with the production design team to navigate practical challenges such as set construction, location scouting, and prop acquisition. This knowledge enables them to offer creative solutions that not only resolve logistical issues but also enhance the film's visual storytelling. Directors can think innovatively to adapt to changing circumstances on set, ensuring that the film's visual elements seamlessly align with the narrative, tone, and artistic vision. This collaborative problem-solving approach fosters a dynamic and flexible production environment, where challenges are met with creativity and efficiency, ultimately leading to a more cohesive and visually captivating cinematic experience for the audience.

Preserving Visual Continuity: How Directors' Production Design Expertise Enhances Consistency in Filmmaking

Continuity is a paramount concern in filmmaking, and directors with a solid understanding of production design principles play a pivotal role in upholding visual consistency throughout the film. This knowledge empowers directors to work closely with the production design team, ensuring that sets, props, and costumes remain in harmony with the established visual style and artistic vision. They can meticulously oversee details, such as the placement of objects, colours, and lighting choices, to guarantee that the film's visual elements align seamlessly from scene to scene. This meticulous attention to continuity not only enhances the film's overall cohesiveness but also fosters a sense of believability, drawing the audience deeper into the narrative world. Directors who understand production design can thus maintain a tight grip on visual continuity, ensuring that the film's aesthetics remain faithful to their creative intent, thereby contributing to a more immersive and polished cinematic experience.

Elevating Artistic Synergy: Directors and Production Designers Crafting Unique Cinematic Visual Styles

Production design, in its essence, is a form of artistic expression within filmmaking, and directors who recognize this fundamental quality can forge more harmonious and effective collaborations with their production designers. This mutual appreciation allows directors to engage in a creative dialogue with the production design team, enabling them to translate their artistic vision into a visually distinctive and captivating cinematic style. Through this collaboration, directors can explore various artistic elements such as colour palettes, aesthetics, set design, and visual motifs to shape a unique visual language that becomes the hallmark of their work. The resulting synergy between director and production designer elevates the film's aesthetic sensibilities, allowing for the creation of visually arresting and thematically resonant cinematic experiences that leave an indelible mark on both the audience and the art of filmmaking itself.

Fluent Filmmaking: Directors' Enhanced Communication through Understanding of Production Design

Communication forms the bedrock of successful filmmaking, and directors who invest in understanding production design principles bridge a critical gap in this process. By acquiring this knowledge, directors can effectively communicate their artistic vision and creative ideas using the same language as the production design team. This shared understanding fosters a more seamless and productive collaboration, where concepts and visual elements are conveyed with precision, minimizing misunderstandings and streamlining the decision-making process. Directors can articulate their requirements and preferences regarding set design, props, and costumes more clearly, ensuring that every visual element aligns closely with their narrative and thematic intentions. This enhanced communication not only saves valuable time and resources but also results in a more harmonious working environment, ultimately leading to a film where the visual and narrative elements are in perfect sync, resonating more deeply with the audience.

Navigating Career Success: How Directors' Proficiency in Production Design Principles Enhances Opportunities and Versatility in the Film Industry

In the highly competitive landscape of the film industry, directors who possess a profound understanding of production design principles often gain a significant advantage in their careers. This knowledge equips them with a versatile skill set that allows them to take on a broader spectrum of projects, from small-scale independent films to large-scale blockbusters, and from contemporary dramas to period pieces. Directors who appreciate the significance of production design can communicate their creative vision more effectively, collaborate seamlessly with production designers, and make informed decisions about visual aesthetics, all of which enhance their appeal to producers and studios seeking versatile and accomplished directors. This versatility not only opens up a wealth of career opportunities but also provides directors with more avenues for creative expression, allowing them to diversify their portfolio and leave a lasting mark in the film industry through their ability to navigate the complex interplay of narrative and visual elements, ultimately advancing their careers in an industry where expertise and adaptability are highly prized.

D. Directing Aesthetics and Art Department Oversight

The Director's Artistic Vision: Leveraging Art Direction for Visual Storytelling

In the world of filmmaking, where storytelling is paramount, directors who familiarize themselves with art direction principles gain a critical skill set that allows them to meticulously curate the visual elements of their films in alignment with their overarching vision. While a director's primary duty revolves around shaping the narrative and guiding actors, an understanding of art direction empowers them to establish and maintain a consistent and captivating visual identity for the film. By collaborating effectively with the art department, directors can convey their artistic concepts with precision, whether it involves the creation of intricate sets, the selection of props, or the design of costumes and makeup. This collaborative synergy ensures that the visual aesthetics seamlessly harmonize with the narrative and thematic objectives, enhancing the audience's immersive experience. Consequently, directors who appreciate the significance of art direction can weave a more visually engaging and thematically resonant cinematic tapestry that not only complements their storytelling but also elevates the overall quality of the film.

Exploring the Role of Art Direction in Filmmaking: A Director's Perspective

Art direction, as a specialized facet of production design, delves deeply into the visual and artistic aspects of filmmaking. It is the process of meticulously crafting the visual style and look of a film, encompassing everything from sets and props to costumes and colour palettes. Art directors are responsible for ensuring that every visual element aligns with the director's creative vision and the film's thematic intentions. This involves making decisions about the overall artistic tone, style, and mood of the film, as well as the selection of specific design elements to convey those intentions effectively. Art direction is a critical component of cinematic storytelling, as it not only enhances the aesthetic appeal of a film but also plays a fundamental role in conveying emotions, themes, and subtext through the visual language of cinema, ultimately contributing to a more immersive and impactful cinematic experience for the audience. It is essential for a film director to learn about art direction for several important reasons:

Crafting Visual Excellence: Directors' Mastery of Art Direction Principles for Creative Fulfillment in Filmmaking

Aesthetic vision is at the heart of filmmaking, and directors who possess a deep understanding of art direction principles wield a potent tool for realizing their creative aspirations. This knowledge empowers them to collaborate closely and effectively with art directors, allowing them to seamlessly translate their artistic ideas into the film's visual style. Directors can communicate their preferences in terms of colour palettes, set designs, props, and overall aesthetics, enabling the art director and their team to craft environments that harmonize effortlessly with the director's vision. This collaborative synergy ensures that every visual element, from the smallest prop to the grandest set, aligns cohesively with the film's intended mood, tone, and thematic underpinnings. Directors who comprehend art direction principles can thus bring their aesthetic vision to life, transforming the screen into a canvas for their creativity and ensuring that the film resonates as a true manifestation of their artistic intent, resulting in a more visually stunning and emotionally engaging cinematic experience for the audience.

Preserving Visual Harmony: Directors' Role in Maintaining Consistency through Art Direction in Filmmaking

Visual cohesion is a cornerstone of effective filmmaking, and directors with a firm understanding of art direction principles play a pivotal role in upholding this consistency. This knowledge empowers them to collaborate seamlessly with art directors, setting the stage for a unified visual narrative that resonates from start to finish. Directors can oversee the intricate details of sets, props, and costumes, ensuring that every visual element adheres to the established aesthetic, mood, and tone of the film. This meticulous attention to visual continuity guarantees that the audience remains fully immersed in the cinematic world, unburdened by jarring inconsistencies that can disrupt the viewing experience. Directors who comprehend art direction principles thus maintain a tight grip on visual cohesion, preserving the film's integrity as a cohesive and visually captivating work of art, resulting in a more immersive, satisfying, and memorable cinematic journey for the audience.

Fostering Creative Synergy: Directors' Collaboration with Art Direction in Filmmaking

Collaboration is the lifeblood of filmmaking, and directors who invest in understanding art direction principles are better equipped to navigate this critical aspect of the creative process. This knowledge enables directors to communicate their artistic ideas and preferences with clarity and precision, fostering a more productive and harmonious working relationship with the art department. Directors can provide detailed guidance on colour palettes, set designs, props, and other visual elements, ensuring that the entire team is aligned with the film's aesthetic vision. This collaborative synergy results in a more efficient and effective creative process, where the art director and their team can execute the director's ideas with precision and creativity. Directors who comprehend art direction principles can thus orchestrate a dynamic partnership, where their vision is brought to life with artistry and finesse, ultimately contributing to the film's overall success and its ability to captivate and resonate with the audience.

Elevating Emotion Through Art Direction: Directors Crafting Mood and Atmosphere in Cinematic Storytelling

Mood and atmosphere are essential elements of cinematic storytelling, and art direction stands as a crucial tool for directors to craft these aspects to perfection. Directors who possess a deep understanding of art direction principles can strategically utilize sets, props, colour schemes, and visual motifs to evoke precise emotions and intensify the viewer's cinematic experience. They can collaborate effectively with the art director and the team to create environments that resonate with the intended mood, whether it's a haunting, suspenseful ambiance in a thriller or a warm, nostalgic feeling in a drama. Through meticulous attention to visual details, directors can transport the audience into the heart of the narrative, creating an immersive experience where the settings themselves become vehicles for emotional storytelling. This knowledge allows directors to harness the full potential of art direction, forging a profound connection between the film's visuals and its thematic resonance, ultimately resulting in a more impactful and memorable cinematic journey for the audience.

Character Crafting Through Art Direction: Directors Shaping Character Expression in Filmmaking

Character expression is a multi-faceted endeavor in filmmaking, and directors with a comprehensive understanding of art direction principles recognize its pivotal role in character development. This knowledge empowers them to collaborate effectively with the art department, ensuring that costumes, props, and set decoration seamlessly align with the characters' personalities, histories, and narrative arcs. Directors can offer precise guidance on the visual elements associated with each character, delving into the subtleties of colour choices, wardrobe styles, and even the symbolism of props. This collaborative approach results in a cohesive and visually resonant portrayal of characters that enriches their depth and complexity. Directors who grasp the impact of art direction on character expression thus create a more immersive and authentic cinematic experience, where the visual elements serve as powerful tools for conveying the nuances of each character's journey, ultimately enhancing the film's emotional resonance and audience engagement.

Budgetary Mastery Through Art Direction: Directors Navigating Cost Control in Filmmaking

Cost control is a critical aspect of filmmaking, and directors who possess a thorough understanding of art direction principles wield a valuable tool for managing production expenses effectively. This knowledge enables them to collaborate closely with the art department, making informed decisions about where to allocate resources and where to implement cost-saving strategies without sacrificing artistic integrity. Directors can prioritize essential visual elements that are pivotal to the film's narrative and mood, while also identifying areas where budget-friendly alternatives can be employed. This pragmatic approach to cost control ensures that every expenditure aligns with the director's creative vision and storytelling objectives. By striking a balance between fiscal responsibility and artistic excellence, directors who comprehend art direction principles can navigate budget constraints more effectively, ultimately delivering a polished and visually compelling film that resonates with the audience while adhering to financial parameters, benefiting both the filmmakers and investors alike.

Strategic Resource Allocation in Filmmaking: Leveraging Art Direction Principles for Effective Budgeting

Resource allocation is a crucial facet of filmmaking, and directors who invest in understanding art direction principles are better equipped to make informed and strategic decisions regarding budgeting and resource allocation for various components of art direction, including costumes, props, and sets. This knowledge enables directors to prioritize and distribute resources effectively, ensuring that each visual element aligns with the film's artistic vision and narrative requirements. Directors can assess the importance of individual elements, making choices that optimize their impact on storytelling while staying within budgetary constraints. This balanced approach allows for the creation of a cohesive visual world that enhances the film's overall quality and resonance. Directors who comprehend art direction principles can thus make judicious resource allocation decisions, contributing to a more efficient and successful production process that results in a film where every visual element serves a purpose and contributes to the director's creative intent.

Fostering Creativity and Innovation in Art Direction: Collaborative Exploration Between Directors and Art Directors

Creativity and innovation are at the core of art direction, and directors who possess an understanding of this facet of filmmaking can engage in dynamic collaborations with their art directors to cultivate imaginative and inventive artistic concepts. This knowledge empowers directors to think beyond conventional boundaries, explore unconventional visual aesthetics, and experiment with innovative approaches to set design, prop selection, and costume choices. By fostering an environment of creative exploration, directors can challenge the status quo and infuse their films with fresh and distinctive visual styles that captivate and resonate with the audience. This collaborative synergy between director and art director leads to the creation of visually striking and artistically innovative cinematic experiences that push the boundaries of creative expression, setting the film apart as a unique and memorable work of art that reflects the director's commitment to pushing creative boundaries in the art of storytelling.

Art Direction: Creative Problem-Solving in Filmmaking – Director's Expertise

Problem-solving is an integral skill on a film set, and directors who possess a deep understanding of art direction principles bring valuable expertise to address challenges that may arise during production. This knowledge allows them to collaborate effectively with the art department to navigate complex issues, such as sourcing unique or historically accurate props, crafting period-accurate costumes, or achieving specific visual effects. Directors can offer creative solutions, drawing upon their understanding of art direction to devise innovative approaches that align with the film's creative vision and narrative requirements. This collaborative problem-solving approach fosters a dynamic and resourceful production environment, where challenges are met with creativity and efficiency, ultimately resulting in a more polished and visually captivating cinematic experience that remains faithful to the director's artistic intent.

Mastering Visual Storytelling: The Director's Role in Art Direction

Visual storytelling is at the heart of filmmaking, and art direction serves as a powerful tool for directors to masterfully weave visual elements into the narrative fabric of their films. Directors who possess a comprehensive understanding of art direction principles can collaborate effectively with their art directors and teams to craft visually engaging and emotionally resonant cinematic experiences. This knowledge enables directors to strategically utilize sets, props, costumes, and visual motifs to amplify the narrative's emotional beats, underscore thematic elements, and symbolize deeper layers of meaning. Every visual choice becomes a narrative choice, enhancing character development, emphasizing plot points, and immersing the audience in the story world. Directors who comprehend the impact of art direction on visual storytelling create films that are not only visually captivating but also narratively rich, leaving a lasting impression on the audience's hearts and minds through the potent fusion of artistry and storytelling.

Empowerment Through Art Direction: Shaping Cinematic Vision and Creative Control

Empowerment is a pivotal outcome of directors investing in understanding art direction principles. This knowledge equips directors with the confidence and ability to actively shape the visual aesthetics of their films, ensuring that every element aligns with their creative vision. Directors can engage in informed decision-making, collaborating closely with the art department to guide and inspire the creation of sets, props, and costumes that harmonize seamlessly with the narrative, mood, and thematic undertones of the film. This active role in the visual aspect of filmmaking not only enhances creative control but also fosters a sense of ownership and authorship over the project. Directors who appreciate art direction can effectively translate their ideas into reality, forging a more dynamic and collaborative relationship with their art teams. This empowerment allows directors to infuse their films with a unique and personalized visual style, ultimately creating works of cinematic art that reflect their artistic sensibilities and storytelling ambitions, thus leaving an indelible mark on the world of cinema.

Art Direction Mastery: Expanding Horizons and Advancing Careers in the Film Industry

In the fiercely competitive landscape of the film industry, directors who command a comprehensive understanding of art direction principles often enjoy a significant advantage in advancing their careers. This knowledge equips them with a versatile skill set that allows them to tackle a broader spectrum of projects, from intimate independent films to grand-scale blockbusters, and from contemporary narratives to period pieces. Directors who appreciate the significance of art direction can communicate their creative vision with precision, collaborate seamlessly with art directors and their teams, and make informed decisions about visual aesthetics. This versatility not only opens up a wealth of career opportunities but also provides directors with more avenues for creative expression, enabling them to diversify their portfolio and make a lasting impact in the film industry. In an industry where expertise and adaptability are highly valued, directors with knowledge of art direction stand poised for career advancement and a broader spectrum of creative opportunities, ultimately solidifying their position as influential and accomplished filmmakers in the dynamic world of cinema.

E. Collaboration with Actors

Shaping Performances and Character Development Through Collaboration with Actors

Directors play a pivotal role in guiding and collaborating with actors to bring their creative vision to life. Understanding acting principles and techniques is essential because it enables directors to communicate effectively with actors, offering specific direction that aligns with the film's narrative and emotional objectives. Directors can help actors grasp the nuances of their characters, motivating them to deliver authentic and emotionally resonant performances. This collaboration fosters a dynamic and productive working relationship on set, where actors feel supported and empowered to explore their roles more deeply. By working in tandem with actors, directors can ensure that each performance contributes cohesively to the storytelling, creating characters that feel genuine and engaging to the audience. Ultimately, this understanding of acting not only enhances communication but also elevates the overall quality of the film, resulting in a more compelling and artistically satisfying cinematic experience for viewers.

Bridging the Artistic Gap: The Power of Directors' Understanding of Acting Techniques in Effective Communication with Actors

Effective communication is the linchpin of successful filmmaking, and directors who invest in understanding acting techniques and terminology can significantly enhance their ability to convey their creative vision to actors. This knowledge equips directors with a shared vocabulary that bridges the gap between their artistic aspirations and the practical execution of those ideas by the cast. Directors can provide more precise and insightful guidance, helping actors tap into the emotional nuances of their characters and deliver more authentic and compelling performances. By speaking the language of acting, directors foster a collaborative atmosphere where actors feel understood and supported, leading to a more productive and harmonious working relationship. This, in turn, results in performances that align seamlessly with the director's vision, ultimately enriching the narrative and emotional depth of the film and ensuring that the audience is captivated by the characters and their stories.

Elevating Performances through Directorial Mastery of Acting Principles

Performance direction is a cornerstone of effective filmmaking, and directors who possess a comprehensive understanding of acting principles can excel in this crucial aspect of their role. This knowledge equips directors to engage in more nuanced and insightful collaborations with actors, offering specific and constructive feedback that guides performers towards achieving the desired emotional depth, characterization, and subtleties in their roles. Directors can adeptly navigate the intricacies of actor-director communication, using their understanding of acting techniques to elicit authentic and emotionally resonant performances. They can help actors connect with their characters on a profound level, navigate complex emotional arcs, and maintain consistency in their portrayals throughout the film. By providing precise guidance rooted in acting principles, directors ensure that the actors' performances align seamlessly with the film's artistic vision, ultimately elevating the narrative and character-driven aspects of the story and delivering a more engaging and emotionally compelling cinematic experience for the audience.

Fostering Emotional Authenticity: Directorial Mastery of Acting Principles in Cinematic Storytelling

Emotional authenticity lies at the heart of compelling storytelling in film, and directors who possess a firm grasp of acting principles are adept at cultivating this authenticity in their actors. This knowledge enables directors to establish a creative environment where performers feel empowered to explore and express genuine emotions within their characters. Directors can use acting techniques to guide actors in delving deep into their roles, helping them tap into the emotional wellspring of their characters' experiences and motivations. By fostering this emotional connection, directors ensure that the characters resonate with authenticity, enabling the audience to empathize with their struggles, joys, and vulnerabilities. Directors who understand acting principles excel in nurturing performances that transcend the screen, making the characters' emotional journeys palpable and relatable to viewers. This emotional authenticity not only enriches the narrative but also elevates the overall impact of the film, creating a more profound and emotionally resonant cinematic experience that lingers long after the credits roll.

Crafting Compelling Characters: Directorial Proficiency in Acting Principles and Character Development

Character development is pivotal in filmmaking, and directors with a strong grasp of acting principles can excel in this realm. Their knowledge empowers them to collaborate effectively with actors, guiding them to explore characters more deeply. Directors employ acting techniques to unearth nuances in characters' personalities, motivations, and emotions, ensuring consistency and engagement throughout the film. This synergy results in well-rounded characters that evolve organically within the narrative, enhancing storytelling and engaging the audience. Directors who understand acting principles profoundly impact character development, leading to more authentic and resonant films.

Elevating Scene Composition: Directorial Expertise in Acting Principles for Effective Blocking and Movement

Blocking and movement are critical components of effective scene composition in filmmaking, and directors who possess knowledge of acting principles excel in choreographing these elements to serve the narrative. This understanding enables directors to provide precise and insightful guidance to actors, ensuring that their actions, gestures, and interactions within a scene unfold organically and authentically. Directors can use acting techniques to help actors navigate the physicality of their roles, ensuring that blocking enhances the storytelling rather than distracts from it. This collaboration between directors and actors results in fluid and purposeful movement that aligns seamlessly with the film's artistic vision, enhancing the visual and narrative impact of each scene. By applying their understanding of acting to blocking and movement, directors create a more immersive and visually engaging cinematic experience, where every physical action contributes meaningfully to the storytelling and resonates with the audience.

Empathy and Artistry: The Role of Directorial Understanding in Effective Actor Communication

Effective communication with actors is the linchpin of successful filmmaking, and directors who possess an understanding of acting principles are better equipped to navigate the delicate and dynamic actor-director relationship. This knowledge allows directors to engage in nuanced and empathetic dialogues with actors, establishing a foundation of trust and mutual respect. Directors can speak the actors' language, comprehending their process, motivations, and challenges, which in turn facilitates clearer and more insightful guidance.

This empathetic and collaborative approach fosters a positive working environment where actors feel understood, supported, and encouraged to explore the depths of their characters. It results in more authentic and emotionally resonant performances that align seamlessly with the director's vision, enhancing the overall quality of the film. By leveraging their understanding of acting, directors create a harmonious and productive atmosphere that empowers actors to shine and contributes to a more polished and artistically satisfying cinematic production.

Versatility and Artistry: The Director's Adaptability through Understanding Acting Principles

Adaptability is a crucial trait for directors in the dynamic world of filmmaking, and those who possess an understanding of acting principles are inherently more versatile in their directorial approach. This knowledge equips directors to effectively navigate the diversity of actors they encounter, each with unique experiences, skills, and backgrounds. Directors can tailor their communication style, coaching methods, and feedback to suit the specific needs and preferences of each actor, ensuring that every performer reaches their full potential. Whether working with seasoned professionals or newcomers to the industry, directors who understand acting can provide the right guidance and support to foster a collaborative and productive working relationship. This adaptability not only maximizes the actors' abilities but also results in performances that align seamlessly with the film's artistic vision, ultimately enhancing the overall quality and authenticity of the cinematic narrative. Directors who appreciate the value of adaptability through their understanding of acting principles are better equipped to navigate the ever-evolving landscape of filmmaking, ensuring that each actor's unique contributions shine on screen.

Elevating Casting Decisions: The Director's Advantage through Understanding Acting Principles

Casting is a pivotal phase in the filmmaking process, and directors who possess a deep understanding of acting principles wield a significant advantage in making astute casting decisions. This knowledge enables directors to approach the casting process with a discerning eye and a nuanced perspective, ensuring that the actors chosen for each role are not only well-suited to the characters in terms of appearance but also possess the necessary acting skills and emotional range to bring those characters to life authentically. Directors can assess auditions with greater acumen, identifying nuances in performances, chemistry between cast members, and the potential for actors to embody the envisioned roles. By leveraging their understanding of acting, directors can assemble a cast that not only fits the visual aspects of the film but also possesses the acting prowess to deliver the required performances, enhancing the overall quality and authenticity of the cinematic narrative. In essence, directors who appreciate the significance of acting in casting make more informed and discerning choices, ultimately contributing to a more compelling and engaging cinematic experience for the audience.

Harmonious Conflict Resolution: Directorial Proficiency in Managing Actor Conflicts through Understanding Acting Principles

Conflict resolution is an essential skill for directors, and those who possess knowledge of acting principles are better equipped to deftly manage conflicts that may arise between them and actors on set. This understanding allows directors to approach conflicts with empathy and a shared understanding of the creative process, mitigating tensions and fostering an environment of open communication and cooperation. Directors can empathize with the challenges actors face, such as the demands of emotional scenes or the pressure of performance, and use their knowledge to offer constructive solutions and compromises that align with both artistic vision and actor comfort. This collaborative approach not only diffuses conflicts but also transforms them into opportunities for growth and creative problem-solving, ultimately leading to more productive and harmonious working relationships between directors and actors. Directors who appreciate the nuances of acting can navigate conflicts with finesse, preserving the integrity of the production and ensuring that the final performances are authentic and emotionally resonant.

Fostering Artistic Collaboration: The Director's Appreciation of Acting as an Art Form

Artistic collaboration is the lifeblood of filmmaking, and directors who possess an appreciation for acting as an art form in its own right engage in richer and more imaginative collaborations with their actors. This understanding enables directors to approach their working relationships with actors as partnerships in the creative process, fostering an environment where experimentation, exploration, and artistic expression thrive. Directors can tap into their knowledge of acting principles to facilitate dynamic and nuanced character interpretations, encouraging actors to delve into the emotional and psychological depths of their roles. By valuing acting as an art form, directors invite actors to contribute their unique perspectives, instincts, and artistic sensibilities to the characters they portray, resulting in performances that are both authentic and artistically captivating. This collaborative synergy elevates the storytelling, enriches character development, and infuses the film with a distinctive and resonant artistic identity, creating a cinematic work that stands out as a testament to the power of creative collaboration in the world of filmmaking.

Elevating Visual Storytelling: The Director's Proficiency in Shot Selection Rooted in Acting Principles

Storyboarding and shot selection are critical aspects of visual storytelling in filmmaking, and directors who possess a deep understanding of acting principles are better equipped to craft visuals that resonate emotionally with the audience. This knowledge empowers directors to approach scene visualization with a keen focus on performances, ensuring that camera angles, framing, and shot compositions effectively capture the nuances of character interactions and emotions. Directors can anticipate how different shots will convey the subtleties of the actors' performances, enabling them to make informed decisions about camera placement and movement. By leveraging their knowledge of acting, directors create a visual language that harmonizes with the performances, resulting in shots that enhance the storytelling, evoke emotions, and deepen the audience's engagement with the characters and narrative. This synergy between acting and shot selection not only elevates the cinematic experience but also showcases the director's prowess in orchestrating a harmonious marriage of performance and visuals that resonates with viewers on a profound level.

Elevating Filmmaking Versatility: The Role of Acting Principles in Directorial Advancement

Directors who possess a robust understanding of acting principles significantly enhance their prospects for career advancement in the competitive realm of filmmaking. This knowledge equips them with a versatile skill set that extends beyond the confines of specific genres and accommodates a wide range of styles and project requirements. By comprehending acting, directors are better prepared to adapt seamlessly to the unique demands of each film they undertake, nurturing performances that harmonize with the overarching artistic vision. Their ability to communicate effectively with actors, establish collaborative relationships, and navigate the nuances of performance direction is highly esteemed within the industry. Consequently, directors with this expertise often enjoy greater credibility, trust, and recognition, thereby opening doors to a diverse array of projects and collaborations. Their versatility and understanding of acting make them invaluable assets to producers, studios, and fellow filmmakers, ultimately expanding their opportunities for creative expression and career growth. This positions them as highly sought-after directors in the fiercely competitive world of filmmaking.

Enhancing Film Quality: The Impact of Directors with Profound Understanding of Acting Principles

The benefits of directors with a deep understanding of acting principles extend beyond their individual careers; they contribute to the overall quality of the films they work on. Directors who can effectively guide actors often yield performances that are authentic, emotionally resonant, and true to the characters. They can tap into the nuances of human behavior, enabling actors to deliver compelling and multifaceted portrayals. This synergy between directors and actors results in films that engage audiences on a deeper level, bringing characters to life and enhancing the overall cinematic experience. Consequently, directors who comprehend acting principles not only advance their own careers but also elevate the art of filmmaking, enriching the industry and captivating viewers worldwide.

F. Collaborative Decision-Making in Costuming and Makeup

Understanding the nuances of character appearance and wardrobe, in conjunction with the costume and makeup departments, represents a pivotal aspect of a film director's skill set. While the director's primary responsibility revolves around shaping the narrative and eliciting compelling performances from actors, gaining proficiency in costume and makeup coordination is indispensable for ensuring that the visual aspects of characters are in harmony with the director's overarching vision. This knowledge enables directors to make informed and creative choices when it comes to the look and attire of characters, thereby contributing to visual coherence within the film. Moreover, it enhances character development by allowing directors to incorporate visual elements that reflect the character's personality, background, and emotional journey, resulting in more authentic and relatable portrayals. Effective collaboration with costume designers and makeup artists becomes possible when directors possess this expertise, facilitating a shared understanding of the director's creative goals and ensuring that the visual components seamlessly align with the narrative. Ultimately, this comprehensive approach to character appearance enhances the overall quality of the film, making it visually engaging and artistically coherent, while also strengthening the director's ability to bring their creative vision to life on screen. A film director learning about costuming and makeup is important for several key reasons:

Mastering Visual Characterization: The Director's Art in Costume and Makeup

Visual characterization is a fundamental component of filmmaking, and directors who possess an in-depth understanding of costuming and makeup wield these tools adeptly to shape the identity and depth of their characters. This knowledge enables directors to engage in close collaboration with costume designers and makeup artists, facilitating a creative synergy that brings characters to life on screen. Directors can provide precise input on costume choices, guiding the selection of attire that aligns with a character's personality, background, and narrative arc. Likewise, their comprehension of makeup techniques empowers them to convey emotions, age characters convincingly, and enhance physical traits that complement the storytelling. By meticulously overseeing the visual characterization process, directors ensure that characters are not only visually consistent but also resonate authentically with the audience, fostering a deeper emotional connection and enriching the overall cinematic experience.

Crafting Aesthetic Excellence: The Director's Mastery of Costuming and Makeup

Aesthetic control is a pivotal aspect of filmmaking, and directors who possess a comprehensive understanding of costuming and makeup gain a heightened ability to shape the visual aesthetics of their films. This knowledge empowers directors to exercise precision and intentionality in every aspect of a character's appearance, from the choice of clothing to the subtleties of makeup application. They can articulate a cohesive and visually captivating style that aligns seamlessly with their artistic vision, reinforcing the narrative themes and mood of the film. Directors can ensure that characters are not only visually striking but also emblematic of the world they inhabit, evoking a sense of time, place, and cultural context. This level of aesthetic control extends beyond individual characters to encompass the overall visual identity of the film, fostering a cinematic experience that is immersive, evocative, and fully aligned with the director's creative intent.

Weaving Narratives Through Costuming and Makeup: The Director's Art of Visual Storytelling

Storytelling in filmmaking is a multi-layered process, and directors who possess a deep understanding of costuming and makeup harness these elements as powerful tools for narrative enrichment. Through the meticulous selection of costumes and makeup techniques, directors can convey a wealth of information about characters without uttering a word. Attire choices can speak to a character's historical context, social standing, and personal journey, providing the audience with valuable context and cues for interpretation. Makeup can age characters, reveal their emotional states, or emphasize specific traits that align with the storytelling. Directors with this knowledge wield the ability to infuse authenticity and depth into their characters, allowing audiences to connect more profoundly with their struggles, desires, and transformations. By leveraging costuming and makeup as storytelling devices, directors craft narratives that are visually evocative and emotionally resonant, elevating the overall impact and richness of their films.

Time-Traveling Through Costuming and Makeup: Creating Cinematic Authenticity in Historical Settings

Capturing the essence of a particular time period or setting is essential in creating a believable and immersive cinematic experience, and directors who possess a profound understanding of costuming and makeup are well-equipped to achieve this authenticity. Through their knowledge, directors can collaborate effectively with costume designers and makeup artists to ensure that every visual detail aligns with the historical or contextual backdrop of the film. They can make informed decisions about clothing styles, fabrics, accessories, and makeup techniques that resonate with the chosen era, enhancing the overall credibility of the narrative. This attention to detail extends beyond mere accuracy; it allows directors to infuse their films with a sense of time and place that envelops the audience, transporting them to the world of the story. As a result, the film not only reflects historical or contextual accuracy but also reinforces the director's commitment to delivering a rich and believable cinematic reality.

Unlocking Cinematic Synergy: Directors, Costume Designers, and Makeup Artists in Creative Collaboration

Collaboration lies at the heart of successful filmmaking, and directors who possess a comprehensive understanding of costuming and makeup are better equipped to foster productive and creative partnerships with costume designers and makeup artists. Through this shared knowledge, directors can articulate their vision and requirements more precisely, facilitating seamless communication with their creative teams. This clarity of expression leads to a more efficient and harmonious working environment, as each member of the production understands their role and the director's expectations. By fostering open and effective collaboration, directors can ensure that the costumes and makeup align cohesively with the overall visual style of the film, creating a unified and visually compelling cinematic world where every element contributes to the narrative and aesthetic vision.

Strategic Resource Allocation in Filmmaking: Maximizing Visual Impact through Costuming and Makeup Management

Resource allocation is a critical aspect of filmmaking, and directors who possess a comprehensive understanding of costuming and makeup can make judicious decisions when it comes to budgeting and resource management. By leveraging their knowledge, directors can assess the specific requirements of costumes and makeup for each character, scene, or period, allowing them to allocate resources efficiently. This strategic approach ensures that the film maintains its visual integrity while adhering to budget constraints. Directors can prioritize the allocation of resources to scenes or characters that demand more elaborate or historically accurate costumes and makeup, while also identifying opportunities for cost-saving measures where they won't compromise the overall aesthetic or narrative. This astute resource management not only benefits the production's financial health but also guarantees that characters look the part, enhancing the film's credibility and visual impact.

Sustaining Visual Harmony: The Director's Role in Costume and Makeup Continuity

Continuity in costuming and makeup is a fundamental aspect of filmmaking, and directors who possess a deep understanding of these elements play a crucial role in maintaining visual consistency throughout their films. With their knowledge, directors can meticulously oversee every costume and makeup choice, ensuring that characters' appearances seamlessly align from one scene to the next. This consistency extends to wardrobe details, hairstyles, makeup applications, and accessories. Directors can also identify potential pitfalls or challenges related to maintaining continuity, such as weather conditions affecting costumes or the passage of time affecting character appearances. By proactively addressing these issues and working closely with costume and makeup departments, directors can guarantee that the audience remains fully immersed in the narrative, uninterrupted by distracting visual inconsistencies. This meticulous attention to detail enhances the film's overall cohesiveness and elevates the audience's viewing experience.

Metamorphosis in Film: The Director's Art of Character Transformation Through Makeup and Costumes

Character transformation through makeup and costumes is a compelling and transformative element in filmmaking, and directors who possess a thorough understanding of these processes are adept at harnessing their potential. By delving into the intricacies of makeup and costume design, directors can collaborate seamlessly with makeup artists and costume designers to bring about dramatic character changes. They can provide clear directives on the desired transformation, working in tandem to achieve the intended look. This may involve aging characters, creating fantastical creatures, or altering appearances to reflect specific historical or fictional settings. Directors can also contribute valuable insights into the emotional and psychological aspects of character transformation, ensuring that makeup and costumes align with the character's journey and arc within the narrative. This collaborative synergy between directors, makeup artists, and costume designers results in visually striking and emotionally resonant character transformations that enhance the film's storytelling impact.

Casting for Visual Harmony: Directors' Strategic Role in Costume and Makeup-Centric Decision-Making

Casting is a pivotal decision in the filmmaking process, and directors who possess a comprehensive understanding of costuming and makeup can make more informed and strategic choices when selecting actors for their roles. This knowledge allows directors to assess actors not only for their acting prowess but also for their suitability in terms of appearance and the potential for physical transformation. Directors can envision how an actor's natural features may align with the character's look and whether the required makeup or costume alterations are feasible and effective. This insight guides casting decisions, ensuring that actors are not only talented but also well-matched visually to their roles. Directors can also anticipate the collaborative efforts needed between makeup artists, costume designers, and actors to achieve the desired on-screen appearance, leading to smoother production and a more cohesive visual narrative.

Navigating Challenges in Costuming and Makeup: The Director's Role in Creative Problem-Solving

In the dynamic and sometimes unpredictable environment of film production, challenges related to costuming and makeup can indeed emerge, and directors equipped with knowledge in these areas play a crucial role in creative problem-solving. When unexpected issues arise, directors can collaborate closely with the costume and makeup teams to devise innovative solutions that maintain the visual integrity of the film. These challenges could encompass a range of scenarios, from unexpected wardrobe malfunctions to makeup reactions, or even sudden weather-related costume changes. Directors with a solid understanding of costuming and makeup can swiftly assess the situation, suggest adjustments, and facilitate the adaptation of the creative elements to overcome these challenges effectively. This collaborative problem-solving approach ensures that the film stays on track, the characters remain consistent, and the overall production remains fluid, ultimately contributing to the success of the project.

Cultivating Empathy in Filmmaking: Directors' Journey into the World of Costume and Makeup

The process of filmmaking is inherently collaborative, and empathy is a cornerstone of effective teamwork. Directors who invest time in learning about the technical and artistic facets of costuming and makeup demonstrate a deep commitment to understanding the challenges and opportunities faced by the costume and makeup departments. This understanding fosters a sense of empathy, allowing directors to appreciate the intricate processes and decisions involved in these aspects of production. As a result, directors can approach their interactions with costume designers and makeup artists with a greater degree of empathy and respect, recognizing the creativity and problem-solving skills required in their roles. This empathetic approach leads to a more positive and cooperative working environment where ideas are exchanged, challenges are tackled collectively, and the entire team is motivated to contribute their best to the project, ultimately elevating the quality of the film.

Diversifying Directorial Skills: How Costuming and Makeup Proficiency Enhances Career Opportunities in Filmmaking

In the competitive landscape of the film industry, having a well-rounded skill set is often a significant advantage. Directors who possess a strong understanding of costuming and makeup can find themselves in high demand for projects that demand meticulous attention to visual character transformation or historical accuracy. Their expertise allows them to take on a wider array of projects, including those set in specific time periods or genres that require elaborate costumes and makeup. Furthermore, directors who are adept in these areas are seen as valuable assets by producers and studios, as they can contribute to the visual authenticity and storytelling potential of a film. This versatility can lead to more opportunities for career advancement, a diverse portfolio, and the ability to tackle a variety of projects with confidence and finesse, ultimately enhancing their reputation and marketability in the industry.

G. The Director's Role in Location Management

Film directors benefit significantly from understanding location management as it allows them to choose and utilize settings that align with their creative vision. While a director's primary focus revolves around storytelling and guiding performances, a firm grasp of location management ensures visual coherence and enhances collaboration with location professionals. This knowledge enables directors to make informed decisions regarding the choice of locations, ensuring they resonate with the film's narrative and aesthetic requirements. Such mastery empowers directors to create visually engaging films that harmonize with their artistic vision, ultimately contributing to the overall success of the production.

Elevating Filmmaking Through Location Management: Turning Ordinary Places into Extraordinary Storytelling Tools

A director's creative vision is at the heart of every film, and understanding location management is integral to bringing that vision to life. Directors who grasp the intricacies of location management can harness the potential of various settings to align with their storytelling goals. They possess the ability to recognize unique and visually compelling locations that not only serve as backdrops but also become integral elements of the narrative. Whether it's choosing a historic building to convey a sense of time and place, utilizing natural landscapes to symbolize a character's emotional journey, or finding hidden gems that add layers of depth to the story, directors with this understanding can make informed decisions that elevate the visual and thematic aspects of their films. In essence, their grasp of location management empowers them to turn ordinary places into extraordinary storytelling tools, resulting in a more immersive and impactful cinematic experience for the audience.

Crafting Cinematic Aesthetics: The Director's Mastery of Location Management

Achieving aesthetic control is a paramount goal for directors, and a comprehensive understanding of location management is pivotal in this pursuit. Locations serve as the canvas upon which the visual aesthetics of a film are painted. Directors who are well-versed in location management can meticulously select, shape, and customize settings to harmonize with their artistic vision. They can orchestrate the interplay of architecture, natural elements, lighting, and spatial design to evoke specific moods, atmospheres, and visual styles. Whether it's creating a gritty urban backdrop for a crime thriller, capturing the ethereal beauty of a remote wilderness for a drama, or infusing historical authenticity into a period piece, directors with this knowledge wield the power to mold locations into visual masterpieces that seamlessly integrate with their storytelling goals. This heightened control ensures that every frame of the film aligns with the director's artistic vision, resulting in a cohesive and captivating visual experience for the audience.

Location as Narrative Subtext: The Director's Art in Effective Storytelling through Location Management

Location management is an indispensable tool in the director's arsenal for effective storytelling. Directors who possess a deep understanding of location management recognize that locations are not mere backgrounds but active participants in the narrative. They can strategically choose settings that resonate with the story's themes, characters, and emotional arcs, enhancing the storytelling experience. For example, a director may opt for a decaying industrial site to symbolize the decline of a character's life, or they might select a picturesque countryside to underscore the film's themes of renewal and hope. Through their choices, directors can infuse layers of symbolism and subtext into the visual tapestry of the film, allowing locations to serve as visual metaphors that resonate with the audience on a deeper level. This symbiotic relationship between location and storytelling elevates the film's narrative impact, making it a more immersive and emotionally resonant experience for viewers who are attuned to the subtleties of the chosen locations.

Budget-Savvy Filmmaking: The Director's Role in Cost-Effective Location Management

Budget management is a critical aspect of filmmaking, and directors with a firm grasp of location management can play a pivotal role in optimizing the allocation of financial resources. They understand that locations can be a substantial part of a film's budget and can impact the overall cost-effectiveness of the production. These directors can carefully assess location expenses, taking into account factors such as permits, travel, accommodations, and site modifications. With this knowledge, they can make strategic decisions about where to shoot, weighing the visual and narrative benefits against the associated costs. Furthermore, they can employ cost-saving measures, such as selecting nearby locations to minimize travel expenses or negotiating favorable deals with property owners. By balancing the creative potential of locations with budgetary considerations, directors ensure that the chosen settings not only enhance the film's storytelling but also align with the financial constraints of the production, ultimately contributing to a successful and fiscally responsible project.

Smooth Sailing Through Location Management: Directors as Masters of Practical Considerations

Practical considerations are a cornerstone of successful location management, and directors who immerse themselves in this knowledge base can circumvent logistical hurdles with finesse. They recognize that securing permits, arranging access to specific locations, and orchestrating the logistics of a shoot are pivotal aspects of the filmmaking process. Directors versed in location management understand the intricacies of permitting, ensuring that the necessary approvals and paperwork are in place well in advance. They also know how to negotiate access to unique or challenging locations, whether it involves coordinating with property owners, securing permissions, or dealing with local authorities. Furthermore, these directors are well-versed in the practicalities of transporting cast, crew, and equipment to and from remote or challenging locations, minimizing delays and ensuring that the production runs smoothly. Their ability to navigate these practical considerations is akin to the conductor's role in an orchestra, ensuring that every logistical detail harmonizes with the creative vision, ultimately resulting in a seamless and efficient production process.

Strategic Resource Allocation: Directors' Role in Cost-Efficient Location Management

Resource allocation in the context of location management is a critical skill that allows directors to make prudent decisions regarding budgeting and resource allocation for securing and preparing locations. Directors who delve into location management understand that the choice of locations can significantly impact the overall production costs. They can assess the financial implications of scouting and securing specific locations, ensuring that they align with the project's budgetary constraints. Moreover, directors versed in location management know how to allocate resources efficiently to ensure that chosen locations are adequately prepared and meet the creative and logistical requirements of the production. This skill enables directors to strike a balance between achieving their artistic vision and managing costs effectively, ultimately contributing to the success and financial health of the project.

Visual Mastery Through Location Management: Enhancing Filmmaking with Informed Planning

Visual planning is a crucial aspect of filmmaking, and directors who grasp location management principles have a distinct advantage in this regard. Their understanding of location scouting and management allows them to envision how different settings can be maximally utilized within the context of the script. They can plan shots, camera angles, and compositions that not only capture the aesthetics and uniqueness of the chosen locations but also enhance the storytelling. This skill empowers directors to create visually compelling sequences that seamlessly integrate the environment, further immersing the audience in the narrative. It enables them to make informed decisions about framing, lighting, and movement, ultimately ensuring that the visual aspects of the film align with their artistic vision and storytelling goals.

Sustaining Visual Consistency: Directors' Role in Seamless Location Management

Continuity is a vital aspect of filmmaking, and directors with knowledge of location management play a crucial role in maintaining visual consistency throughout the film. They can ensure that the locations chosen for different scenes align with the script's requirements and the established visual style. By understanding location management principles, directors can make informed decisions about how to use and revisit specific locations, taking into account factors like lighting, weather conditions, and the availability of the site. This foresight enables them to plan shooting schedules that prioritize visual continuity, ensuring that scenes shot at different times or on different days seamlessly match in terms of the environment. As a result, the film maintains a cohesive look, enhancing the overall viewing experience and storytelling.

Location-Based Problem Solving: Directors' Resourceful Approach to Overcoming Production Challenges

Problem-solving is an integral skill in filmmaking, and directors who understand location management are better equipped to tackle challenges related to the use of various locations during production. These challenges can range from sudden weather changes that affect outdoor shoots to unexpected noise disturbances or logistical issues. Directors with location management knowledge can collaborate effectively with location managers to brainstorm innovative solutions. For example, if a selected location becomes unavailable at the last minute, they can work together to find suitable alternatives that match the original vision of the scene. This ability to adapt and troubleshoot in real-time not only keeps the production on track but also demonstrates the director's resourcefulness and leadership, contributing to the successful completion of the film.

Streamlining Production Through Efficient Location Management: Directors' Key to Time and Resource Optimization

Efficiency in location management is crucial for optimizing the limited time and resources available during film production. Directors with a solid understanding of location management can play a pivotal role in ensuring that shooting schedules are well-organized and time-efficient. They can work closely with location managers to plan shoot sequences that minimize travel time between locations and capitalize on natural lighting conditions. Additionally, directors can make informed decisions about when and where to shoot based on the availability of locations, ensuring that the production stays on schedule and avoids unnecessary delays. This time-efficient approach not only saves valuable resources but also allows the creative team to focus on capturing the best possible shots and performances, ultimately leading to a smoother and more successful production.

Harmonizing Vision and Logistics: Directors' Collaborative Advantage Through Location Management

Effective collaboration is the cornerstone of successful filmmaking, and directors who understand the intricacies of location management are better equipped to collaborate with location managers and scouts. By learning about location management, directors can communicate their creative vision, logistical needs, and specific requirements with greater clarity and precision. This fosters a productive working relationship where the director's artistic vision aligns seamlessly with the practical aspects of securing and utilizing locations. Directors can work closely with location professionals to explore a wide range of potential settings, ensuring that each location not only fits the narrative but also offers the logistical advantages needed for a smooth production. This collaborative synergy between the director and location experts leads to a more efficient and creative filmmaking process, ultimately enhancing the overall quality of the final product.

Fostering Empathy: Directors' Appreciation of Location Management Challenges

Empathy plays a pivotal role in building productive and harmonious working relationships within the film industry, and directors who invest time in understanding the technical and logistical aspects of location management often develop a deeper sense of empathy for the challenges faced by location teams. By delving into the intricacies involved in securing, preparing, and managing locations, directors can gain a profound appreciation for the meticulous planning, coordination, and problem-solving skills required in this role. This newfound understanding allows directors to approach location professionals with greater empathy, respect, and appreciation for their expertise, creating a positive and collaborative atmosphere on set. When directors acknowledge the efforts and challenges of their location teams, it not only fosters mutual respect but also encourages open communication and teamwork, ultimately contributing to a more efficient and enjoyable filmmaking experience for all involved.

Elevating Filmmaking Quality: The Impact of Director-Empathy in Location Management

The incorporation of empathy into the director-location team dynamic goes beyond the set and influences the final product. Directors who appreciate the complexities of location management are more likely to make informed decisions that positively impact the visual and narrative aspects of their films. They can work in tandem with location managers to find innovative solutions that enhance the storytelling, ensuring that the chosen locations serve the narrative effectively. This collaboration often results in a more seamless and authentic on-screen environment, contributing to the overall quality and authenticity of the film. In essence, directors who invest in understanding the challenges and intricacies of location management not only foster better working relationships but also create an environment conducive to creative problem-solving and a final product that resonates with audiences on a deeper level.

H. The Director's Role in Script Supervision

Script Supervision: Maintaining Narrative Integrity and Continuity on Set

In filmmaking, maintaining continuity and script accuracy during the filming process is paramount to achieving a cohesive and believable narrative. Directors, recognizing the significance of this aspect, often collaborate closely with script supervisors to navigate the intricate nuances of script continuity. By forging a collaborative relationship, directors tap into the expertise of script supervisors, who excel in tracking performance consistency, ensuring storytelling clarity, and organizing scenes effectively. This partnership not only streamlines the production process but also safeguards against discrepancies that could compromise the final product's integrity. Directors and script supervisors become the guardians of the narrative's fidelity, working in tandem to capture the essence of each scene while preserving the flow and authenticity of the story. Their collaboration is akin to a well-choreographed dance, ensuring that every shot and line of dialogue aligns seamlessly with the overarching vision of the film. Collaboration with script supervision is important for a film director for several key reasons:

Script Supervisors: Guardians of Script Accuracy in Filmmaking

Script supervisors are an essential part of a film's production team, and their role in ensuring script accuracy is paramount. Directors who establish a strong working relationship with script supervisors benefit from an extra set of eyes and ears dedicated to the script's details. Script supervisors meticulously document each take, noting dialogue variations, actor movements, and other crucial information. They also help maintain continuity in visual and auditory elements. Directors who collaborate effectively with script supervisors can trust them to catch and rectify any script discrepancies or errors, ensuring that scenes are shot accurately and consistently. This partnership between directors and script supervisors not only upholds the integrity of the script but also allows directors to focus on other creative aspects of filmmaking, knowing that script accuracy is in capable hands. Ultimately, it contributes to a smoother and more cohesive storytelling process, resulting in a more polished final product.

Performance Consistency Mastery: Directors and Script Supervisors in Creative Collaboration

Performance consistency is a fundamental aspect of filmmaking, and script supervisors play a crucial role in achieving it. Directors who collaborate effectively with script supervisors benefit from their expertise in ensuring that actors deliver consistent performances throughout the filming process. Script supervisors meticulously track every aspect of an actor's performance, including dialogue delivery, gestures, and expressions, and cross-reference them with the established character traits and narrative context. This meticulous attention to detail helps directors maintain the integrity of the characters and storyline. By working closely with script supervisors, directors can address any deviations or inconsistencies in real-time, allowing for adjustments that align with the intended character development. This collaboration ensures that the final film presents performances that are not only compelling but also consistent, contributing to a more immersive and believable cinematic experience for the audience.

Shot Planning Prowess: The Collaborative Role of Directors and Script Supervisors

Script supervisors play a vital role in shot planning and execution, collaborating closely with directors to ensure that the visual elements of a film align seamlessly with the script. They work to guarantee that scenes are covered comprehensively, meaning that all essential shots, angles, and details are captured during filming. This meticulous planning helps directors achieve efficient shooting schedules and minimizes the need for costly reshoots. Script supervisors also ensure that transitions between shots and scenes adhere to the narrative flow and continuity specified in the script. Their expertise in shot planning enhances the director's ability to visualize how the script will translate into a cohesive visual story, resulting in a more effective and well-structured film in post-production.

Storytelling Clarity: Directors and Script Supervisors in Synchronized Filmmaking

Script supervisors act as the director's partners in maintaining storytelling clarity throughout the filmmaking process. They meticulously track the script's progression and are vigilant in ensuring that the story unfolds coherently on screen. Directors collaborate closely with script supervisors to monitor the unfolding narrative, helping to identify any potential issues with storytelling, pacing, or continuity. This collaboration allows directors to make real-time adjustments during filming, such as rephrasing dialogue, adjusting actor performances, or refining the sequencing of scenes. By working in tandem with script supervisors, directors can enhance the audience's comprehension of the story, ensuring that the film effectively communicates its intended narrative and emotional beats. This collaborative effort ultimately results in a more engaging and coherent cinematic experience for viewers.

Seamless Collaboration: Directors and Script Supervisors in Effective Communication

Effective communication between directors and script supervisors is a cornerstone of successful filmmaking. Directors who understand the importance of collaborative communication with script supervisors can establish a productive working relationship that significantly contributes to the overall quality of the film. This entails providing clear instructions and guidance regarding the desired performances, scene sequencing, and narrative continuity. Directors can discuss script-related concerns, such as deviations from the script, inconsistencies, or the need for adjustments to enhance storytelling. Open and effective communication ensures that both parties are on the same page, facilitating the seamless execution of the director's vision while maintaining script accuracy and narrative coherence. This collaboration ultimately leads to a smoother production process and a final product that aligns closely with the director's creative intent.

Scene Organization Mastery: Directors and Script Supervisors in Creative Collaboration

Scene organization is a critical aspect of filmmaking, and script supervisors play a pivotal role in maintaining this orderliness. Directors who collaborate effectively with script supervisors benefit from their expertise in structuring scenes and sequences in a logical and efficient manner. Script supervisors help ensure that all required shots are captured, following the script's continuity and the director's vision. This meticulous organization not only streamlines the shooting process but also aids in post-production editing, as it provides editors with a well-structured sequence of shots that can be assembled coherently to tell the story. Directors who understand and work closely with script supervisors can rely on their expertise to maintain scene organization, resulting in a smoother production process and a more cohesive final product.

Efficient Time Management: Directors and Script Supervisors as Partners in Filmmaking

Time management is a critical aspect of filmmaking, and the collaboration between directors and script supervisors is instrumental in achieving efficient use of time during production. Script supervisors play a pivotal role in this regard by meticulously tracking the shooting schedule. They ensure that scenes are completed within the scheduled timeframes and that the production stays within budgetary constraints. Directors who work closely with script supervisors can rely on their expertise to keep the production on track, avoiding costly delays and overages. By maintaining a tight schedule and adhering to time management strategies, directors can optimize their shooting days, make the most of available resources, and ensure a smoother and more cost-effective production process. This collaborative effort between directors and script supervisors is essential for keeping the project on time and within budget while delivering a high-quality final product.

Collaborative Problem-Solving: Directors and Script Supervisors as On-Set Allies in Filmmaking

Problem-solving is an integral part of filmmaking, and directors who collaborate effectively with script supervisors can tap into their expertise when challenges emerge on set. Script supervisors are skilled at identifying and resolving script continuity discrepancies, ensuring that dialogue, actions, and props remain consistent from shot to shot. Additionally, they possess strong logistical skills, helping to manage the practical aspects of shooting, such as tracking continuity, documenting shot takes, and ensuring that actors maintain consistent performances. When unforeseen issues arise, directors can turn to script supervisors for innovative solutions, whether it's adapting a scene due to unexpected weather conditions or addressing script adjustments on the fly. This collaborative problem-solving dynamic between directors and script supervisors ensures that production hurdles are met with creative and effective solutions, ultimately contributing to the successful realization of the director's vision.

Strategic Resource Allocation: Directors and Script Supervisors as Partners in Efficient Filmmaking

Resource allocation is a critical aspect of film production, and the collaboration between directors and script supervisors plays a pivotal role in this regard. Script supervisors provide valuable insights into the script's demands, including the complexity of scenes, the number of shots required, and any specific logistical considerations. Directors can draw upon their expertise to strategically allocate resources, such as shooting days, equipment, and crew members, to ensure that the most critical and challenging scenes receive the necessary attention and resources. This collaboration helps directors optimize their production schedules, making efficient use of limited resources and adhering to budget constraints while still delivering the best possible results in line with the script's requirements. It ensures that the director's creative vision is realized within the practical constraints of the production process.

Visual and Narrative Consistency: The Collaborative Role of Directors and Script Supervisors in Filmmaking

Visual and narrative consistency are fundamental aspects of filmmaking, and the collaboration between directors and script supervisors plays a pivotal role in achieving this consistency. Script supervisors meticulously track every detail of the script during filming, including dialogue, character actions, props, and costume continuity. This attention to detail helps directors maintain a cohesive visual and narrative flow throughout the film. Directors can rely on script supervisors to catch any discrepancies or errors that might disrupt the film's consistency and work with them to rectify these issues promptly. By maintaining this consistency, directors ensure that the audience's immersion in the story remains intact, enhancing the overall viewing experience and allowing the narrative to unfold seamlessly on screen.

Fostering Empathy: Strengthening the Director-Script Supervisor Relationship in Filmmaking

Empathy is a fundamental element in any collaborative creative process, and when it comes to filmmaking, fostering empathy between directors and script supervisors is of utmost importance. Directors who invest time in understanding the intricate responsibilities and challenges faced by script supervisors gain a deeper appreciation for the indispensable role they play in maintaining script continuity and overall production consistency. This understanding not only elevates their respect for the script supervisor's expertise but also encourages directors to communicate more effectively, provide clear instructions, and address script-related concerns with empathy and respect.

Fostering Empathy: A Blueprint for a Successful Director-Script Supervisor Partnership in Filmmaking

The establishment of empathy in the director-script supervisor relationship creates a positive and collaborative working environment where both parties can work together seamlessly. Script supervisors are often tasked with tracking details related to continuity, ensuring that each scene adheres to the script, and taking detailed notes that assist in editing and post-production processes. Directors who acknowledge the challenges and intricacies of the script supervision role are better equipped to provide the necessary support and guidance. This collaboration ultimately leads to a more successful and harmonious filmmaking process, as the director-script supervisor team can focus on creative aspects, knowing that the script's integrity is being upheld diligently. In essence, fostering empathy in this relationship not only improves the overall efficiency of the production but also enhances the final product's quality, ensuring that it meets the highest standards of storytelling and continuity.

I. Director's Artistic Vision and Art of Production

Mastering the Art of Production: Navigating Logistics, Schedules, and Resources

In the intricate world of filmmaking, the director's artistic vision and storytelling prowess often take center stage. However, behind the scenes, an equally crucial role is played by production management, a multifaceted discipline encompassing scheduling, budgeting, and resource allocation. For directors, delving into production management is akin to mastering the conductor's baton in an orchestra. It empowers them to orchestrate the symphony of creativity while adhering to the practical constraints of time and money. By immersing themselves in production management principles, directors can navigate the labyrinth of logistics, make informed decisions about resource allocation, and meticulously plan each phase of the production process. This comprehensive understanding allows them to bring their creative vision to life efficiently, ensuring that every aspect of the film, from pre-production to post-production, aligns seamlessly with the established budget and schedule. In essence, directors who grasp production management strike a harmonious balance between artistry and pragmatism, ultimately contributing to the successful realization of their cinematic visions. Learning about production management is important for a film director for several key reasons:

Optimizing Resource Allocation: Directors and Production Managers in Synchronized Filmmaking

Efficient resource allocation is a cornerstone of successful filmmaking, and directors who comprehend the principles of production management can engage in fruitful collaborations with production managers. These managers play a pivotal role in overseeing and allocating various resources, from budgeting for specific needs to scheduling shoots and coordinating personnel. Directors who possess knowledge in production management can effectively communicate their creative vision and requirements to production managers, facilitating a smooth workflow that optimizes resource allocation. This collaboration ensures that resources are used judiciously, preventing overspending or wastage while aligning every aspect of the production with the director's artistic intent.

Strategic Budget Control: The Collaborative Role of Directors and Production Managers

Budget control is a crucial aspect of filmmaking, and directors who understand production management can collaborate effectively with production managers to maintain financial discipline throughout the project. Production managers play a pivotal role in budgeting, allocating funds to various departments, and monitoring expenditures. Directors with knowledge in production management can provide valuable input during the budgeting process, ensuring that creative needs are considered while avoiding unnecessary expenses. Throughout production, this collaboration allows directors to make informed decisions, prioritize spending, and prevent budget overruns, all while ensuring that the film aligns with their artistic vision without compromising financial stability. This efficient budget control is essential for the successful completion of a film within its financial constraints.

Efficient Time Management: The Synergy Between Directors and Production Managers

Time management is a critical aspect of filmmaking, and directors who understand production management principles can collaborate effectively with production managers to optimize the efficient use of time during a film's production. Production managers are responsible for developing and maintaining shooting schedules that outline when and where each scene will be filmed. Directors with knowledge in production management can work closely with production managers to ensure that the shooting timeline aligns with the creative vision of the film. This collaboration allows directors to make informed decisions about scene order, set preparation, and other logistical considerations, ensuring that scenes are shot efficiently and within the allotted time frame. Effective time management is essential for staying on schedule and within budget while still achieving the artistic goals of the film.

Optimizing Logistics: How Directors and Production Managers Collaborate for a Smooth Film Production

Logistics play a pivotal role in the successful execution of a film production, and directors who have a grasp of production management can collaborate effectively with production managers to streamline logistical planning. Production managers are responsible for coordinating various logistics, including securing necessary equipment, arranging transportation for the cast and crew, and managing location logistics. Directors who are knowledgeable about production management can provide valuable input on these logistical aspects, helping to ensure that the production runs smoothly. This collaboration allows directors to contribute to decisions regarding equipment selection, transportation options, and location choices, all of which impact the efficiency and effectiveness of the filmmaking process. By working closely with production managers on logistics, directors can help create an environment in which the creative vision can be realized efficiently and without unnecessary disruptions.

Strategic Resource Planning: How Directors and Production Managers Collaborate for Efficient Resource Allocation in Film Production

Resource planning is a critical aspect of film production, and directors who understand production management can make well-informed decisions about how to allocate limited resources effectively. This involves determining which crew members are essential for specific scenes or sequences, selecting the appropriate equipment for achieving desired shots, and making strategic choices regarding location usage. Directors who have knowledge in production management can assess the creative needs of the project and prioritize resource allocation accordingly. For example, they can allocate more crew members and equipment to complex action sequences, while being more resource-efficient for smaller, dialogue-driven scenes. This resource optimization not only helps control costs but also ensures that the creative vision is realized without compromising quality or efficiency, ultimately contributing to a successful film production.

Creative Problem-Solving: How Directors Utilize Production Management Knowledge to Overcome Challenges in Film Production

During the production of a film, various challenges and unexpected issues can crop up, ranging from unfavorable weather conditions to scheduling conflicts or equipment malfunctions. Directors who possess knowledge in production management are better equipped to tackle these challenges effectively. They can work closely with the production team, including producers, production managers, and department heads, to find creative and practical solutions. For instance, if a key location suddenly becomes unavailable, a director well-versed in production management can quickly adapt by identifying alternative locations that fit the creative vision and scheduling requirements. This problem-solving ability not only helps keep the production on track but also demonstrates the director's leadership and adaptability, contributing to a smoother and more successful filmmaking process.

Enhancing Filmmaking Through Effective Communication: Collaboration Between Directors and Production Managers

Effective communication between directors and production managers is a cornerstone of successful filmmaking. Directors who take the time to learn about production management develop a common language with the production team, fostering clear and efficient communication. This shared understanding enables directors to convey their creative vision, priorities, and logistical requirements effectively to the production managers. In return, production managers can provide valuable insights on the feasibility of various creative choices and offer solutions to challenges based on their logistical expertise. This collaborative and well-informed communication not only streamlines decision-making but also creates a harmonious working environment, where everyone is aligned toward achieving the project's goals efficiently and with a shared sense of purpose.

Proactive Risk Mitigation: Collaboration Between Directors and Production Managers in Filmmaking

Collaborating with production managers is crucial for effective risk mitigation in filmmaking. Directors who understand the principles of production management can actively contribute to identifying potential risks and challenges during pre-production, production, and post-production phases. By working closely with production managers, directors can develop proactive strategies to mitigate these risks, whether they are related to budget overruns, scheduling conflicts, logistical issues, or unforeseen obstacles on set. This collaboration allows directors to make informed decisions that minimize the impact of potential setbacks, ensuring that the project stays on track and within budget while maintaining the creative integrity of the film.

Facilitating Effective Crew Coordination: The Role of Directors in Production Management

Effective crew coordination is vital for a successful film production, and directors who grasp the principles of production management can facilitate seamless collaboration with key crew members. This understanding enables directors to communicate their creative vision, goals, and expectations clearly to the cinematographer, production designer, costume designer, and other essential team members. Directors can work closely with each department, ensuring that the visual aesthetics, set designs, and costumes align with the overall artistic vision of the film. Additionally, directors can coordinate schedules, allocate resources, and address any logistical or production-related challenges efficiently, fostering a productive and cohesive working environment that contributes to the film's overall quality and success.

From Vision to Reality: How Directors and Production Managers Collaborate to Execute the Filmmaker's Creative Vision

Collaborating with production managers is instrumental in translating a director's artistic vision into a tangible and well-executed film. Directors often have a clear creative vision for how they want the story to unfold, the visual style they wish to convey, and the emotions they want to evoke in the audience. Production managers play a crucial role in bridging the gap between this artistic vision and the practicalities of film production. They handle the logistics, resource allocation, budgeting, and scheduling, ensuring that the director's vision can be realized within the available resources and constraints. This collaboration allows directors to concentrate their energy on storytelling, working with actors, and crafting the overall aesthetic, knowing that the production manager is managing the operational aspects to bring their artistic vision to life effectively.

Creating a Secure Film Set: Collaborative Safety Planning Between Directors and Production Managers

Safety is a paramount concern on any film set, and it is the director's responsibility to prioritize and maintain a safe working environment for the entire cast and crew. Production managers, as part of their role, are involved in safety planning and execution, which includes assessing potential risks, implementing safety protocols, and coordinating emergency procedures. Directors who have a solid understanding of production management can collaborate effectively with production managers to address safety concerns. This collaboration involves identifying potential hazards related to stunts, special effects, or location-specific challenges and ensuring that safety measures are in place to mitigate these risks. By working closely with production managers, directors can create a culture of safety on set, instilling confidence in the team and allowing everyone to focus on their roles with peace of mind, ultimately contributing to a successful and secure production.

Career Advancement and Versatility: How Production Management Knowledge Elevates a Director's Opportunities in the Film Industry

Having a strong grasp of production management principles can significantly enhance a director's career prospects in the film industry. Directors who possess this knowledge are well-equipped to handle a diverse array of projects, from small-scale independent films to large-budget productions, and they can navigate the complexities of each with confidence. This adaptability allows them to work effectively within various budget constraints, timelines, and logistical challenges, making them valuable assets to production companies and studios. Furthermore, their ability to maintain efficient resource allocation, control costs, and manage risks positions them as reliable and skilled leaders in the industry, opening doors to a broader range of creative opportunities and career advancement. Whether working on blockbuster films or indie projects, directors with a strong understanding of production management can demonstrate their versatility and competence, ultimately propelling their careers to new heights.

J. Role of Directors in Action Sequences and Stunt Work

Collaborating with Stunt Coordinators and Performers in Action Sequences

Directors who engage in the art of crafting action scenes and collaborate effectively with stunt coordinators and performers bring a valuable layer of expertise to their filmmaking toolkit. By gaining insight into the intricacies of stunts and action sequences, directors can contribute significantly to the visual storytelling and overall impact of their films. This knowledge allows them to envision action sequences that are not only thrilling but also serve the narrative, character arcs, and emotional beats of the story. Directors can work closely with stunt coordinators, conveying their creative vision while respecting safety measures and choreography intricacies. This collaborative effort ensures that action sequences are executed safely, efficiently, and with artistic finesse, ultimately enhancing the audience's cinematic experience. Whether it's a high-octane chase scene, a meticulously choreographed fight, or a gravity-defying stunt, directors versed in the language of action sequences can translate their visions into compelling, adrenaline-pumping moments on screen while prioritizing the well-being of the performers and crew.

Prioritizing Safety on Film Sets: The Crucial Role of Directors in Action Sequences and Stunt Work

Safety on a film set, particularly during action sequences involving stunts, is a paramount concern for directors. Those who possess a comprehensive understanding of stunts are well-equipped to prioritize and maintain a safe working environment for the entire cast and crew. This involves collaborating closely with experienced stunt coordinators to ensure that meticulous safety precautions, such as harnesses, crash mats, and protective gear, are in place and rigorously adhered to during stunt rehearsals and filming. Directors must also have a keen eye for detail, ensuring that the choreography of action sequences minimizes risks and potential hazards. By fostering a culture of safety and clear communication on set, directors can inspire confidence in their team and lead by example, promoting a secure working environment that enables creative, yet risk-free, execution of thrilling stunts essential to the storytelling process.

Crafting Authentic Action Sequences: The Director's Role in Achieving Realism Through Stunts

Creating a sense of realism in action sequences is a fundamental goal for directors, and understanding the intricacies of stunts is crucial in achieving this objective. Directors who delve into the world of stunts can collaborate effectively with experienced stunt coordinators to design action scenes that not only look authentic but also resonate with the audience. This collaboration involves meticulous choreography, precision in timing, and attention to detail in both the physical movements of the actors and the technical aspects, such as camera angles and editing. Directors can work closely with the stunt team to ensure that every punch, jump, or fall aligns seamlessly with the narrative and character motivations, enhancing the overall impact and believability of the action sequences. Ultimately, this pursuit of realism contributes to a heightened cinematic experience that immerses the audience in the story and leaves a lasting impression.

Elevating Visual Storytelling: How Stunts Enhance Narrative Impact in Filmmaking

Visual storytelling is at the heart of effective filmmaking, and understanding stunt techniques allows directors to harness their potential as compelling narrative devices. Action sequences, often involving stunts, serve as dynamic storytelling tools that can convey essential elements of character development, plot progression, and emotional depth. Directors who delve into the intricacies of stunts can collaborate closely with stunt coordinators to craft action scenes that are not just visually engaging but also rich in narrative significance. Through careful choreography and creative planning, they can orchestrate stunts that reveal character traits, showcase the evolution of relationships, or mark pivotal moments in the story. Whether it's a breathtaking chase sequence, a climactic battle, or a daring escape, these action scenes, when executed with a deep understanding of stunt techniques, become integral to the film's narrative fabric, enhancing the audience's emotional investment and overall cinematic experience.

Balancing Safety and Performance: The Director's Role in Coordinating Action Sequences and Stunts

Performance coordination in action sequences is a delicate balance between ensuring the safety and believability of stunts while extracting the best performances from actors. Directors who possess an understanding of stunt work can play a pivotal role in this process by guiding actors effectively during physically demanding scenes. They can communicate with actors in a language that bridges the gap between the storytelling needs and the technical intricacies of stunts. This not only helps actors feel more comfortable and confident while performing challenging actions but also enables directors to elicit nuanced and emotionally resonant performances. By having a grasp of stunt techniques, directors can choreograph action sequences that align with the characters' motivations and story arcs, ensuring that the physicality of the scene seamlessly integrates with the broader narrative, resulting in both visually stunning and emotionally impactful performances.

Crafting Dynamic Stunt Sequences: The Director's Art of Effective Shot Planning

Effective shot planning is essential in capturing the intricacies and excitement of stunt sequences on film. Directors who understand stunt work can collaborate seamlessly with stunt coordinators to plan and execute shots that not only ensure the safety of the performers but also maximize the visual impact of the action. By comprehending the technical aspects of stunts, directors can envision dynamic camera angles, shot compositions, and movements that accentuate the choreographed sequences, making them more engaging and cinematic. This collaboration enables directors to create a visual narrative within the action sequences, conveying critical story points, character development, and emotional intensity through the carefully planned shots. As a result, the audience is not only immersed in the excitement of the stunt but also connected to the broader storytelling, elevating the overall cinematic experience.

Enhancing Visual Aesthetics: The Director's Collaboration with Cinematographers in Action Sequences

The visual aesthetics of action sequences are crucial in creating an engaging and memorable cinematic experience. Directors who have a solid understanding of stunts can collaborate effectively with cinematographers to ensure that the action is captured in a visually compelling manner. This collaboration involves careful consideration of camera angles, framing, and movement to highlight the agility, power, and intensity of the stunts. Directors can work with cinematographers to choose the right lenses, camera positions, and lighting setups that enhance the visual impact of the action, making it not only exciting but also aesthetically pleasing. By aligning the technical aspects of stunts with the cinematographic vision, directors can create action sequences that not only thrill audiences with their daring feats but also captivate them with their striking visual beauty, adding depth and artistry to the overall film.

Maintaining Continuity in Action Sequences: How Directors with Stunt Knowledge Keep the Flow Intact

Continuity is a critical aspect of filmmaking, and it becomes especially challenging to maintain during action sequences where characters are engaged in complex movements and stunts. Directors who understand stunt work are better equipped to ensure continuity in action scenes. They can work closely with stunt coordinators and choreographers to plan and execute sequences that flow seamlessly from one shot to another. This involves meticulous attention to the placement and timing of actors and stunt performers, as well as the consistency of their actions and expressions. Directors can also use techniques like shot-listing and storyboarding to visualize the sequence and identify potential continuity issues in advance. By coordinating the various elements of the action sequence effectively, directors can ensure that the final result is a visually coherent and immersive experience for the audience, where the excitement and impact of the action are not compromised by inconsistencies.

Elevating Characters through Stunt Techniques: A Director's Art of Performance Enhancement

Performance enhancement through stunt techniques is a powerful tool in a director's arsenal for character development and storytelling. Directors who understand stunts can collaborate closely with stunt coordinators and performers to choreograph action sequences that amplify the physicality of characters, making them more dynamic and compelling. Through well-executed stunts, directors can depict characters as skilled fighters, daring adventurers, or even vulnerable individuals pushed to their limits. These sequences not only serve as thrilling spectacle but also provide opportunities for character growth and emotional depth. Directors can use stunts to convey character traits, showcase personal transformations, or emphasize a character's determination, courage, or vulnerability. This creative use of stunt techniques enhances the overall narrative and leaves a lasting impact on the audience, contributing significantly to character-driven storytelling in the world of cinema.

Unleashing Creativity: How Directors Embrace Stunt Innovation for Extraordinary Action Sequences

Stunt work in filmmaking is a realm of boundless creativity, and directors who understand its potential can use it to craft exceptional action sequences. Their grasp of stunts allows them to collaborate with stunt coordinators and create imaginative, visually stunning choreography. Directors can push the boundaries of what's possible on screen, designing sequences that captivate audiences and define their films with signature style. From gravity-defying acrobatics to thrilling vehicle chases, this creative use of stunt techniques enhances the movie's visual appeal and sets it apart in the competitive world of filmmaking.

Navigating Challenges in Action Sequences: How Directors with Stunt Knowledge Find Innovative Solutions

The world of stunts and action sequences in filmmaking often presents a myriad of challenges and unexpected hurdles. Directors who have a firm understanding of this domain can effectively collaborate with stunt teams to navigate and solve these complex issues. Whether it's devising alternative methods for a particularly daring stunt, adjusting choreography to accommodate an actor's limitations, or mitigating unforeseen safety concerns on set, directors with insight into stunt work can tap into their problem-solving skills to find innovative solutions. This collaborative problem-solving not only ensures the safety of the cast and crew but also ensures that the vision for the action sequence is realized, ultimately contributing to the success and impact of the film. Directors who appreciate the creative problem-solving aspects of stunt work can transform potential setbacks into opportunities for enhancing the overall quality of their movie.

Strategic Budget Management in Stunt Production: How Directors with Stunt Knowledge Optimize Resources

Budget management is a critical aspect of filmmaking, and directors who possess an understanding of stunt production can make more informed and strategic decisions when it comes to allocating resources. Stunt work often involves expenses related to safety equipment, specialized training, and potentially increased insurance costs due to the inherent risks. Directors with this knowledge can collaborate effectively with their production teams to prioritize where to invest their resources to achieve impactful action sequences while also adhering to budget constraints. They can make choices that maximize the visual and narrative impact of stunts without overspending, ensuring that the film's financial resources are utilized efficiently and effectively to bring their creative vision to life on screen. This ability to strike a balance between creative ambition and fiscal responsibility is essential for successful filmmaking, as it enables directors to deliver thrilling action without breaking the bank.

Elevating Your Filmmaking Career: How Stunt Knowledge Opens Doors to Versatility and Opportunities

Career advancement in the film industry often hinges on a director's ability to take on a wide range of projects and demonstrate versatility in storytelling. Directors who possess a solid understanding of stunts and action sequences have a competitive edge, as they can confidently tackle projects that demand intricate choreography and dynamic physical performances. This expertise allows them to collaborate seamlessly with stunt coordinators and performers, resulting in more authentic and thrilling action scenes that captivate audiences. As a result, directors with this skill set can expand their portfolio to include action-oriented genres, such as action-adventure, thriller, or superhero films, broadening their career prospects and attracting diverse opportunities. Their ability to craft high-impact action sequences, while ensuring the safety and professionalism of the stunt team, enhances their reputation in the industry and positions them as sought-after directors for action-packed projects, ultimately contributing to their career advancement and long-term success.

K. The Director's Role in Post-Production Storytelling

Collaborating with Post-Production Teams for Film Perfection

Collaborating with post-production teams involves working closely with professionals responsible for various aspects of post-production, such as colour correction and sound mixing, to fine-tune the film's visual and auditory elements. Directors who engage in this phase of filmmaking can communicate their creative preferences and make critical decisions that influence the final product. For instance, during colour correction, they can ensure that the film's colour palette matches the intended mood and atmosphere, enhancing the storytelling. In sound mixing, directors can refine the audio elements, including dialogue, music, and sound effects, to achieve a balanced and immersive auditory experience. By actively participating in post-production, directors maintain creative control over the project, refine the film's narrative coherence, and ensure that the end result aligns closely with their artistic vision. This collaboration is essential for bringing the film to its full potential, as it allows directors to address any discrepancies or issues that may have arisen during filming, ultimately contributing to the film's overall quality and impact.

Empowering Creative Control: The Impact of Directorial Knowledge in Post-Production Processes

Directors who possess a deep understanding of post-production processes wield a powerful tool for maintaining creative control over their films. This knowledge empowers them to communicate effectively with editors, colourists, and sound engineers, guiding these professionals to bring their artistic vision to life. Directors can make informed decisions about pacing, shot selection, and narrative flow during the editing process, ensuring that the final product aligns with their creative intent. Additionally, their grasp of colour correction techniques allows them to influence the film's visual aesthetics, enhancing or altering colours to evoke specific moods or atmospheres. In the sound mixing stage, directors can work closely with sound designers and engineers to achieve the desired auditory experience, from subtle nuances to impactful soundscapes. Ultimately, this comprehensive understanding of post-production enables directors to shape the film's final form, maintaining artistic integrity and realizing their creative vision on the screen.

Preserving Narrative Continuity: The Director's Role in Post-Production Storytelling

Directors who engage deeply in the post-production phase of filmmaking play a crucial role in preserving storytelling continuity. During editing, they work closely with editors to ensure that the narrative structure maintains its coherence and emotional impact. Directors can make decisions about the arrangement of scenes, the pacing of the story, and the transitions between shots, ensuring that the film effectively conveys its intended message and engages the audience emotionally. Moreover, their involvement in sound mixing allows them to fine-tune the auditory elements to complement the storytelling, ensuring that dialogue, music, and sound effects enhance the narrative's emotional resonance. By actively participating in post-production, directors can safeguard the consistency of the storytelling, resulting in a more compelling and emotionally resonant cinematic experience for the audience.

Mastering Visual Aesthetics: The Director's Role in Colour Correction and Grading in Post-Production

In post-production, directors who possess a comprehension of colour correction and grading wield a critical influence over a film's visual aesthetics. This understanding allows them to work closely with colourists to achieve the exact mood, atmosphere, and visual style that align with their creative vision. During colour correction, directors can fine-tune the colours in each shot, ensuring that they convey the intended emotions and enhance the overall storytelling. Moreover, in the grading process, directors can make decisions about the film's overall colour palette, allowing them to evoke specific feelings and visual motifs throughout the narrative. With this knowledge, directors can maintain full control over the film's visual identity, resulting in a coherent and visually captivating cinematic experience that resonates with their artistic vision and the audience's emotions.

Crafting Cinematic Soundscapes: The Director's Role in Sound Mixing and Design

Sound design is an integral part of filmmaking that profoundly influences the audience's emotional engagement with the story. Directors who actively participate in sound mixing and design discussions play a pivotal role in shaping the auditory landscape of their films. They collaborate closely with sound professionals, such as sound designers and mixers, to ensure that the film's audio elements harmonize seamlessly with the visuals and narrative. This involvement allows directors to make decisions about the placement of sound effects, music, and dialogue, enhancing the storytelling by creating mood, tension, and immersion. They can fine-tune the balance between dialogue and background sounds, ensuring clarity and emotional resonance in the characters' voices. Additionally, directors can work on the selection and integration of music, using it as a powerful tool to evoke specific emotions and reinforce the film's themes. Ultimately, directors who understand sound design can elevate their films by crafting an auditory experience that captivates the audience, deepens their emotional connection to the story, and contributes significantly to the overall impact of the film.

Elevating Performances in Post-Production: The Director's Role in Editing and Sound Mixing

Directors play a crucial role in enhancing the performances of actors through active involvement in the editing and sound mixing processes during post-production. By collaborating closely with editors and sound designers, directors can make precise adjustments that elevate the quality and impact of the performances. In the editing room, directors can fine-tune the timing of individual shots and sequences, ensuring that the actors' expressions, gestures, and emotions are conveyed effectively. They can trim or extend scenes to optimize the pacing, allowing moments of tension, humor, or drama to resonate with the audience. Moreover, directors can work with sound designers to craft aural nuances that complement the actors' performances, adding depth and emotional resonance. This may include adjusting the volume and placement of dialogue, enhancing the use of ambient sounds, or incorporating music cues that heighten the emotional intensity of a scene. Overall, directors who engage in performance enhancement during post-production can refine the actors' work, resulting in more compelling, resonant performances that contribute significantly to the overall impact of the film.

Facilitating Creative Harmony: Directors' Effective Communication in Post-Production Collaboration

Directors' effective collaboration with post-production teams relies on clear communication and feedback. When directors have a comprehensive understanding of post-production terminology and processes, they can engage in more specific and constructive discussions with editors, colourists, sound designers, and other professionals. This level of communication ensures that the director's creative vision and expectations are effectively conveyed, reducing the likelihood of misunderstandings or misinterpretations during the editing, colour correction, and sound mixing stages. Directors can articulate their preferences regarding pacing, visual aesthetics, soundscapes, and narrative flow with greater precision, enabling the post-production team to execute changes and enhancements efficiently. This streamlined workflow not only saves time and resources but also results in a final product that aligns closely with the director's original vision, fostering a collaborative and productive post-production environment.

Mastering the Art of Visual Effects Integration: Directors and their Role in Post-Production VFX

Directors who possess a strong understanding of post-production can play a pivotal role in the successful integration of visual effects (VFX) into their films. They can collaborate closely with VFX artists and supervisors to ensure that digital elements blend seamlessly with live-action footage, achieving a cohesive visual style. Directors can provide specific guidance on the intended look and feel of the VFX, offering insights into how these elements should interact with the narrative and enhance the storytelling. Their understanding of post-production processes enables them to anticipate the technical challenges and creative opportunities that VFX bring, leading to more effective planning and execution. This collaboration results in VFX that not only meet the director's creative vision but also align with the overall aesthetics and narrative continuity of the film, enhancing the audience's immersive experience.

Guardians of Excellence: The Director's Role in Post-Production Quality Control Top of Form

Quality control is a vital aspect of a director's role during post-production. Directors are responsible for meticulously reviewing drafts, edits, and sound mixes to ensure that the final product aligns with their creative vision and maintains the desired level of excellence. They scrutinize every aspect of the film, from the pacing of scenes to the colour grading and sound design, seeking to identify any inconsistencies or discrepancies. Directors use their deep understanding of the film's narrative, character development, and visual aesthetics to assess whether each element contributes effectively to the overall storytelling and emotional impact. This attention to detail and commitment to quality control ensures that the final product meets the director's artistic standards and resonates with the audience as intended, ultimately delivering a compelling and immersive cinematic experience.

Navigating Post-Production Challenges: How Directors with Post-Production Knowledge Find Solutions

Directors often face various challenges and unexpected issues during the post-production phase of filmmaking. These can range from technical glitches in the editing software to the discovery of missing or damaged footage. Directors who possess a deep understanding of post-production processes are well-equipped to tackle these challenges and find creative solutions. They can collaborate closely with editors, sound designers, and other post-production professionals to troubleshoot technical issues, rework scenes that may not be achieving the desired impact, or even explore alternative narrative approaches when necessary. This problem-solving ability not only helps maintain the project's timeline but also ensures that the final product meets the director's artistic vision and storytelling goals, even in the face of unexpected setbacks.

Strategic Budget Management in Post-Production: How Directors with Post-Production Knowledge Optimize Resources

Post-production is a crucial phase of filmmaking that often commands a substantial portion of the budget. Directors who possess a strong understanding of post-production processes are better equipped to manage budgetary considerations effectively. They can make informed decisions about how to allocate resources to various aspects of post-production, such as editing, visual effects, sound design, and colour correction. This knowledge allows directors to prioritize the elements that are essential to achieving their creative vision while also ensuring that the budget is used efficiently and that resources are not squandered. By making strategic budgetary choices during post-production, directors can strike a balance between realizing their artistic goals and maintaining fiscal responsibility, which is vital for the overall success of the film.

Directors' Role in Film Marketing: Leveraging Understanding of Post-Production for Promotion

During post-production, directors often play a role in shaping promotional materials and trailers for their films. Having an understanding of marketing and distribution principles is valuable in this phase, as it enables directors to actively contribute to marketing efforts. They can ensure that promotional materials effectively represent the film's content, style, and themes, aligning with the final vision. Directors can collaborate with marketing teams to craft compelling trailers and promotional campaigns that resonate with the target audience. This involvement not only enhances the film's marketing strategy but also ensures that the promotional materials accurately convey the film's unique selling points, ultimately contributing to its success in the competitive landscape of the film industry.

Exercising Creative Control: The Director's Role in Post-Production Editing

Post-production is the pivotal phase in the filmmaking process where directors hold the authority to shape the final edit of the film. A deep understanding of post-production processes is paramount for directors to wield this authority effectively. It allows them to collaborate closely with editors, making precise adjustments to the pacing, timing, and sequencing of scenes. Directors can ensure that the narrative maintains its coherence, emotional impact, and alignment with their initial creative vision. Furthermore, their comprehension of post-production extends to collaborating with sound designers and colorists to refine the film's visual and auditory aesthetics. This knowledge empowers directors to exercise full control over the editing process, enabling them to mold the final product to best convey their storytelling intentions and artistic vision to the audience. It is in the post-production phase that the director's vision is finely honed and polished, ensuring the film's impact and resonance with viewers.

Career Advancement Through Post-Production Expertise: A Competitive Edge for Directors

Directors with a comprehensive understanding of post-production processes gain a significant edge in their careers, as this knowledge enhances their capacity to collaborate seamlessly with post-production teams. Such collaboration fosters efficient workflows and productive working relationships, resulting in a smoother and more streamlined production process. As a result, directors are better equipped to take on a wide array of projects, spanning diverse genres and styles, from independent films to large-scale productions. Their ability to navigate the intricacies of post-production, including editing, sound design, and visual effects, also enhances their reputation in the industry, making them highly sought-after collaborators for producers, studios, and fellow filmmakers. In the ever-evolving landscape of filmmaking, directors with a strong grasp of post-production can effectively adapt to changing technological trends and market demands, ultimately opening up more opportunities for career advancement and creative expression. This expertise not only broadens their creative horizons but also solidifies their position as accomplished and adaptable filmmakers in the dynamic world of cinema.

L. Collaborating with Film Editors in Post-Production

Understanding the intricacies of the post-production process and establishing a collaborative relationship with the film editor is an essential aspect of a director's toolkit. While directors need not become editing experts, their grasp of the editing process plays a pivotal role in realizing their creative vision and enhancing overall efficiency during production. This understanding empowers directors to wield greater influence over their films, enabling them to craft more resonant and engaging narratives. With insights into pacing, shot selection, and continuity, directors can make informed decisions from the outset, which not only streamlines production but also results in a more cohesive and powerful final product. This synergy between directors and editors fosters open communication, allowing for a deeper exploration of storytelling possibilities, and ultimately, it elevates the quality and impact of the films they create.

Unlocking Creative Control: The Role of Editing Mastery in Filmmaking

Creative control is a fundamental aspiration for directors in the filmmaking process, and a deep comprehension of the editing process is a critical means by which they can realize this ambition. Directors who possess a comprehensive understanding of editing principles wield a powerful tool to shape the visual and narrative aspects of their films. This knowledge enables them to visualize how individual scenes will ultimately come together during post-production, allowing them to make informed decisions during filming that are conducive to smoother and more effective editing. By foreseeing how various elements like shot composition, pacing, and continuity will impact the final product, directors can exercise precise control over the film's overall tone, rhythm, and storytelling impact. This not only streamlines the editing process but also empowers directors to craft a more cohesive, emotionally resonant, and artistically satisfying cinematic experience, ultimately ensuring that their creative vision is realized to its fullest extent on the screen.

The Art of Editing Mastery: Shaping the Film's Narrative Journey"

Editing is commonly referred to as the "final rewrite" of a film, and directors who possess a profound understanding of editing principles wield a pivotal tool for refining the storytelling process. This knowledge empowers them to make critical decisions during filming that directly impact the film's narrative flow, pacing, and overall coherence. Directors can anticipate how various shots and scenes will come together in the editing room, allowing them to prioritize shot selection, framing, and timing to ensure that each element serves the narrative's thematic and emotional objectives. This foresight enables directors to craft a more engaging and impactful storytelling experience, where the audience is guided through the narrative with precision and emotional resonance. By comprehending the transformative power of editing, directors can effectively contribute to the shaping of the film's final narrative, ultimately resulting in a more compelling, cohesive, and artistically satisfying cinematic journey for viewers.

Efficiency Through Editing Mastery: Optimizing Film Production

Efficient production is a paramount goal in filmmaking, and directors who possess a keen understanding of the editing process are better equipped to optimize the efficiency of their shoots. This knowledge allows directors to plan meticulously, making informed decisions about shot composition, coverage, and sequencing during filming. By visualizing how scenes will come together in post-production, directors can avoid unnecessary takes, superfluous coverage, and time-consuming retakes, which can lead to significant time and cost savings on set. This streamlined approach not only conserves valuable resources but also contributes to a more focused and productive shooting environment. Directors who comprehend the intricacies of the editing process can thus work more efficiently, ensuring that every moment spent on set serves the narrative and artistic vision while minimizing wastage of time and resources, ultimately leading to a more cost-effective and successful production.

Mastering Visual Language: The Art of Editing in Cinematic Storytelling

Visual language is a cornerstone of cinematic storytelling, and editing stands as a vital component of this language. Directors who possess a deep understanding of editing principles wield a powerful tool to communicate emotions, build tension, and convey meaning in their films with precision and impact. This knowledge empowers directors to make deliberate choices in terms of shot selection, pacing, and sequencing, allowing them to orchestrate the visual narrative in a manner that resonates with the audience on an emotional and intellectual level. They can use editing techniques such as cuts, transitions, and juxtaposition to manipulate time, space, and perspective, thus imbuing scenes with depth, subtext, and layers of meaning. Directors who grasp the intricacies of the visual language of editing can craft films that not only engage the senses but also provoke thought and evoke profound emotional responses, ensuring that their storytelling is as visually compelling as it is narratively resonant, resulting in a more impactful and memorable cinematic experience for the audience.

Enhancing Filmmaking Through Director-Editor Collaboration: The Power of Understanding Editing Principles

Collaboration is an essential aspect of filmmaking, and directors who possess a solid understanding of editing principles can foster more effective partnerships with their editors. This knowledge enables directors to articulate their creative vision with precision, ensuring that the editor fully comprehends their intended narrative and emotional objectives. Directors can provide clearer guidance on pacing, shot selection, and the desired thematic or tonal nuances, streamlining the editing process and minimizing the need for extensive revisions. This collaborative synergy not only enhances communication but also encourages a more harmonious and productive working relationship between director and editor. Directors who grasp the intricacies of editing can thus work hand in hand with their editors, aligning their creative goals and vision to achieve a more polished and artistically satisfying final product, ultimately benefiting both the filmmaking process and the audience's cinematic experience.

Mastering Problem-Solving in Post-Production: Leveraging Editing Expertise for Creative Solutions

Problem-solving is an indispensable skill in post-production, and directors who possess a comprehensive understanding of editing principles bring valuable expertise to address unexpected challenges that may emerge during this phase. This knowledge allows directors to collaborate effectively with their editors, offering creative solutions to a wide range of issues, from narrative restructuring to salvaging footage that may not have initially met their expectations. Directors can tap into their understanding of pacing, shot selection, and narrative flow to devise innovative approaches that align with the film's creative vision and storytelling objectives. This collaborative problem-solving dynamic fosters a flexible and resourceful post-production environment, where unforeseen hurdles are met with creativity and efficiency. Directors who comprehend the intricacies of editing can thus work hand in hand with their editors to navigate the complex landscape of post-production, ensuring that the final film is a cohesive, visually engaging, and narratively satisfying work that remains faithful to the director's artistic intent.

Unlocking Cost Efficiency in Filmmaking: The Role of Directorial Understanding in Editing

Cost efficiency is a paramount concern in filmmaking, and directors who possess a comprehensive understanding of how editing functions are better equipped to make judicious decisions during filming that can result in substantial savings. This knowledge empowers directors to plan meticulously, anticipate the requirements of the editing process, and ensure that they capture the necessary coverage and shots during production. By avoiding the need for costly reshoots or additional days on set, directors can optimize the allocation of resources, making every moment spent on set a cost-effective investment in the final product. This approach not only conserves budget but also promotes a disciplined and efficient production environment. Directors who comprehend the intricacies of editing can thus contribute significantly to cost efficiency, ensuring that the film remains on budget while adhering to the artistic vision and storytelling objectives, ultimately benefiting both the filmmakers and investors by maximizing the return on their investment.

Sustaining Consistency in Filmmaking: The Role of Directorial Understanding in Editing and Narrative Cohesion

Consistency is a fundamental goal in filmmaking, and directors who possess a strong understanding of editing principles are well-equipped to maintain this consistency in their storytelling and visual style throughout the film. This knowledge empowers directors to envision how individual scenes will connect and flow in post-production, allowing them to make informed decisions during filming that contribute to narrative coherence and visual uniformity. Directors can ensure that elements such as shot composition, pacing, and continuity align with the established tone and style of the film, creating a seamless and harmonious viewing experience. By maintaining this consistency, directors not only enhance the audience's immersion in the narrative but also reinforce the film's thematic and emotional resonance. Directors who comprehend the nuances of editing can thus orchestrate a cohesive and artistically satisfying cinematic journey, where every scene and shot contributes to the overall storytelling and visual integrity, ultimately resulting in a more compelling and memorable cinematic work.

Elevating Artistic Expression in Filmmaking: The Artistry of Editing and Collaborative Creative Vision

Artistic expression is at the heart of filmmaking, and editing stands as a distinct and powerful art form within the cinematic process. Directors who possess a deep appreciation for the artistry of editing recognize it as a potent means of creative expression. This knowledge empowers directors to engage in dynamic collaborations with their editors, fostering an environment of artistic exploration and innovation. Directors can work closely with editors to shape the film's emotional tone, rhythm, and mood, making deliberate choices in areas such as pacing, shot selection, and sequencing to align with their artistic vision. By harnessing the transformative potential of editing, directors can infuse their films with a unique and personalized cinematic style, one that communicates their creative sensibilities and storytelling ambitions to the audience. This partnership between director and editor results in films that not only engage the senses but also provoke thought and evoke profound emotional responses, ultimately showcasing the director's ability to wield the art of editing as a medium for artistic expression and storytelling, leaving an indelible mark in the world of cinema.

Expanding Filmmaking Horizons: The Career Advantages of Directors with Editing Proficiency

Career advancement in the filmmaking industry often depends on a director's versatility and proficiency across various aspects of the craft, and possessing knowledge of editing can significantly expand a director's career horizons. Directors with editing expertise are well-equipped to take on a wider range of projects, including those with limited budgets where resourcefulness and the ability to wear multiple hats, including that of an editor, are invaluable. This versatility not only increases their employability but also offers greater creative control over their work. Directors who understand editing principles can effectively communicate their artistic vision to editors, collaborate seamlessly, and, if needed, step into the editing role themselves. This adaptability allows directors to thrive in a variety of production scenarios, from independent films to low-budget passion projects, enhancing their career prospects and establishing them as accomplished filmmakers capable of bringing their creative visions to life across diverse budget constraints, ultimately advancing their careers and broadening their influence in the dynamic world of cinema.

Fostering Empathy in Filmmaking: Directors and Editors Building Collaborative Bonds through Understanding

Empathy is a vital ingredient in the collaborative process of filmmaking, and directors who invest in understanding the intricacies of the editing process can cultivate deeper empathy for their editors. This knowledge allows directors to appreciate the challenges and creative potential that editors grapple with during post-production. Directors who comprehend the art of editing are more likely to engage in empathetic, constructive, and mutually beneficial relationships with their editing teams. They can offer better support and guidance to editors, effectively communicate their creative vision, and respect the craft of editing. This empathetic approach fosters a harmonious and productive post-production environment, where creative insights and ideas can flow freely, ultimately leading to a more polished and artistically satisfying final product. Directors who appreciate the challenges and opportunities in editing are better equipped to forge strong bonds with their editing teams, facilitating collaboration that elevates the film and enriches the cinematic storytelling experience for the audience.

M. Collaborating with the Sound Department

Collaborating with the Sound Department for Cinematic Audio Excellence

Collaborating with the sound department during filmmaking involves several aspects. Firstly, it entails ensuring that high-quality audio is captured on set, which is vital for a seamless and professional end product. This includes managing elements like mic placement, background noise control, and on-set dialogue recording. Furthermore, directors play a pivotal role in sound design, where they make creative decisions about how sound is used to enhance the narrative and atmosphere of the film. This involves selecting and manipulating various audio elements, such as sound effects and ambient noise, to evoke specific emotions or emphasize key moments in the story. Additionally, directors have a say in the choice and integration of music into the film, deciding on its placement and impact within the storytelling. Finally, effective communication with the sound team is essential, as directors need to convey their creative vision and expectations clearly. While directors don't need to be sound experts themselves, having a foundational understanding of sound principles and techniques is crucial for maintaining artistic control, ensuring storytelling consistency, and delivering a cinematic experience that deeply engages the audience on both visual and auditory levels, ultimately elevating the impact and immersion of the final product.

Crafting Cinematic Stories through Sound: The Transformative Role of Directors in Sound Design

Storytelling in filmmaking is a multi-sensory experience, and sound plays a pivotal role in this narrative tapestry. Directors who possess a profound understanding of sound principles recognize its transformative potential as a storytelling tool. This knowledge empowers directors to make deliberate choices in sound design, encompassing elements such as music, dialogue, ambient noise, and sound effects, to amplify the narrative's emotional impact, build atmosphere, and convey characters' emotions more poignantly. They can orchestrate soundscapes that immerse the audience in the story world, manipulating sound dynamics to evoke tension, excitement, or tranquility as needed. By harnessing the evocative power of sound, directors can shape the audience's emotional journey and enhance the film's thematic resonance, ultimately creating a more immersive, emotionally resonant, and artistically satisfying cinematic experience. Directors who grasp the nuances of sound design are thus adept at using sound as a storytelling ally, ensuring that their films communicate on a sensory and emotional level that transcends the visual, enriching the narrative tapestry and leaving a lasting impact on the audience.

Elevating Emotional Impact: The Art of Sound in Filmmaking and its Directorial Mastery

The emotional impact of sound in filmmaking is profound, and directors who possess a comprehensive understanding of sound principles can wield this tool to tremendous effect. Sound encompasses not only music and sound effects but also the nuances of dialogue delivery and ambient noise, all of which play a pivotal role in shaping the audience's emotional response. Directors can strategically deploy music to underscore the mood of a scene, heightening tension or eliciting empathy as needed. They can use sound effects to immerse the audience in the film's world, making action sequences more exhilarating or horror scenes more chilling. Moreover, directors who appreciate the subtleties of dialogue delivery can guide actors to convey emotions more authentically, further intensifying the audience's emotional engagement. By orchestrating sound with precision, directors create a more immersive viewing experience, where the audience is not just witnessing the narrative but also feeling it on a visceral level. This mastery of sound allows directors to manipulate emotions, foster empathy, and ultimately craft films that resonate deeply with viewers, leaving a lasting emotional impact long after the credits roll.

Sculpting Aesthetic Soundscapes: Directorial Mastery of Sound Principles in Filmmaking

Aesthetic control is a fundamental aspiration for directors in the filmmaking process, and sound represents a critical component of a film's overall aesthetic. Directors who possess a deep understanding of sound principles can actively shape the auditory atmosphere and tonal nuances of their films in collaboration with sound designers and composers. This knowledge empowers directors to communicate their creative vision with precision, guiding the sonic elements to align with the film's thematic undertones and emotional resonance. They can strategically employ music, sound effects, and dialogue to create a soundscape that is not only harmonious with the visual aesthetics but also enhances the film's narrative impact. By engaging in a collaborative partnership with sound experts, directors ensure that every auditory choice contributes to the desired mood, atmosphere, and emotional texture of the film, resulting in a more cohesive and artistically satisfying cinematic experience that resonates with the audience on a sensory and aesthetic level.

Bridging the Gap: The Power of Sound Understanding in Director-Sound Department Communication

Effective communication is at the heart of successful filmmaking, and directors who invest in understanding sound terminology and techniques can bridge the gap between their creative vision and the expertise of the sound department. This knowledge equips directors to articulate their ideas with clarity, enabling them to communicate their desired auditory atmosphere, tone, and emotional nuances effectively. Directors can speak the same creative language as sound professionals, facilitating a more productive and collaborative working relationship. By understanding sound principles, directors can provide precise guidance on music choices, sound effects, and dialogue delivery, ensuring that each element aligns with the film's artistic vision. This streamlined communication process not only fosters mutual understanding but also empowers directors to harness the full creative potential of sound in their films, ultimately enhancing the narrative impact and sensory experience for the audience. Directors who grasp the intricacies of sound communication can thus collaborate more seamlessly with their sound departments, resulting in a more polished and artistically satisfying final product.

Sculpting Cinematic Rhythm: The Director's Mastery of Sound for Pacing and Flow

Pacing and rhythm are pivotal elements in cinematic storytelling, and directors who comprehend the influence of sound on these aspects are better equipped to orchestrate the tempo and flow of their films with precision. This knowledge empowers directors to make insightful choices during both filming and editing, ensuring that the auditory components, including music, sound effects, and dialogue, align seamlessly with the film's intended pacing and rhythm. Directors can use sound to control the audience's emotional journey, modulating the speed and intensity of scenes to evoke tension, excitement, or reflection as required by the narrative. By strategically utilizing sound, directors can sculpt the film's rhythm to enhance dramatic impact, maintain audience engagement, and deliver a satisfying cinematic experience. Whether it's through the rhythmic beat of a musical score or the deliberate use of silence, directors who understand sound's influence on pacing can guide their films to unfold at the precise tempo that best serves the story, resulting in a more engaging, emotionally resonant, and artistically satisfying cinematic journey for viewers.

Mastering Visual-Audio Synchronization: The Director's Proficiency in Sound Principles

Visual-audio synchronization is a fundamental requirement in filmmaking, and directors who possess a thorough understanding of sound principles are well-equipped to orchestrate this synchronization with precision. This knowledge allows directors to coordinate actions, dialogues, and visual elements in a manner that aligns seamlessly with the audio track. They can ensure that every footstep, word of dialogue, or visual effect syncs harmoniously with the accompanying sound, creating a cohesive and immersive viewing experience. Directors who appreciate the intricacies of sound timing can make informed decisions during both filming and editing, fostering a sense of visual-audio unity that enhances the film's narrative impact. By achieving flawless synchronization, directors not only elevate the overall production quality but also contribute to a more polished and artistically satisfying cinematic presentation, where the audience is fully immersed in a world where sight and sound work in perfect harmony to convey the story and emotions effectively.

Elevating Audio Excellence: Directorial Proficiency in Sound Recording and Mixing Technicalities

Technical considerations in sound recording and mixing are crucial aspects that directors should be aware of to ensure the highest audio quality in their films. A comprehensive understanding of concepts like microphone placement, sound levels, and acoustics equips directors with the knowledge needed to prevent common sound-related issues during production. Directors can make informed decisions regarding microphone selection and placement to capture clean and clear audio, taking into account factors such as the shooting location's acoustics and ambient noise. They can also monitor sound levels to prevent distortion or unwanted noise, ensuring that dialogue and other audio elements are recorded at optimal quality. By being well-versed in these technical aspects, directors can proactively address potential challenges and work more effectively with their sound teams, resulting in a smoother and more successful sound recording process and ultimately contributing to a film with exceptional sound quality.

Harmonizing Creativity: Director-Sound Team Collaboration and the Art of Sound Principles

Collaboration is a cornerstone of successful filmmaking, and directors who possess a solid understanding of sound principles can engage in more effective partnerships with their sound teams. This knowledge enables directors to communicate their creative vision with precision, ensuring that sound professionals fully grasp the desired auditory atmosphere, tone, and emotional nuances. Directors can provide clearer guidance on music choices, sound effects, and dialogue delivery, facilitating a more seamless and productive working relationship with sound designers, composers, and engineers. This collaborative synergy not only enhances communication but also encourages a more harmonious and creative environment, where ideas can flow freely, and sound experts can contribute their expertise to enrich the film's auditory experience. Directors who comprehend the intricacies of sound collaboration can thus work hand in hand with their sound teams to achieve a more polished and artistically satisfying final product, one where sound is a powerful storytelling ally that resonates deeply with the audience and enhances the cinematic narrative.

Optimizing Budgets through Sound Proficiency: The Director's Role in Cost-Efficient Filmmaking

Cost efficiency is a paramount concern in filmmaking, and directors who possess a comprehensive understanding of sound principles can significantly contribute to this goal. This knowledge empowers directors to make judicious decisions during production, ensuring that sound recording receives appropriate attention in scenes where it is pivotal to the narrative or emotional impact. By prioritizing sound recording on set, directors can avoid the need for costly post-production fixes or extensive ADR (Automated Dialogue Replacement) sessions. This proactive approach not only conserves budget but also streamlines the production process, saving both time and resources. Directors who comprehend the nuances of sound can thus make cost-effective choices that align with their artistic vision, ultimately benefiting both the filmmaking team and investors by maximizing the return on investment while delivering a high-quality auditory experience to the audience.

Elevating Artistry through Sound: Directors as Masters of Cinematic Auditory Expression

Sound is a nuanced and expressive art form within filmmaking, and directors who recognize its artistic potential can harness it as a potent creative tool to enrich their cinematic vision. This knowledge empowers directors to engage in imaginative collaborations with sound professionals, composers, and sound designers, enabling them to sculpt unique and emotionally resonant auditory landscapes that complement their storytelling objectives. Directors can use sound to evoke specific emotions, underscore themes, and deepen the audience's connection with characters and narrative arcs. Whether through the selection of a distinctive musical score, the careful placement of sound effects, or the manipulation of ambient noise, directors who appreciate the artistic dimension of sound can infuse their films with a singular and evocative auditory identity. This heightened level of artistic expression not only enhances the sensory experience for the audience but also distinguishes the director's work as a singular and compelling contribution to the cinematic landscape, leaving a lasting impact and enriching the storytelling tapestry of their films.

Safeguarding Sonic Excellence: The Director's Role in Quality Control through Sound Principles

Quality control is a paramount consideration in filmmaking, and directors who possess a solid understanding of sound principles are better equipped to exercise precise oversight throughout the production process. This knowledge empowers directors to critically evaluate the quality of sound recording and mixing, allowing them to assess whether the auditory elements align with their artistic vision and storytelling goals. Directors can identify issues such as background noise, distortion, or inconsistencies in dialogue delivery more effectively, addressing them promptly to maintain audio quality. By actively monitoring sound quality, directors ensure that the final product meets their standards and maintains a high level of sonic excellence, enhancing the overall cinematic experience for the audience. This quality control not only upholds the director's artistic integrity but also contributes to a polished and artistically satisfying final product, where sound is a powerful and seamless element that resonates deeply with viewers.

The Auditory Conductor: Sound Expertise in the Competitive Filmmaking Landscape

In the fiercely competitive landscape of filmmaking, a director's career is a relentless pursuit, one in which success hinges on their versatility and proficiency across various facets of the craft. A director is not merely a visual storyteller but also an auditory conductor. Those who possess a comprehensive understanding of sound principles hold a distinct advantage in this multifaceted industry. They have the power to elevate the sensory experience of the audience by expertly manipulating sound to enhance the narrative. This proficiency grants them a unique and invaluable skill set that they can offer to prospective film projects.

Sound Expertise: Enhancing Directorial Versatility and Employability in the Film Industry

The advantage of sound knowledge extends beyond the purely creative sphere. It enhances a director's employability, making them more appealing to producers and studios seeking individuals who can bring a holistic approach to filmmaking. Directors with sound expertise can take on a broader range of projects, from intimate independent films to grand high-budget productions. Their ability to effectively shape and integrate sound into the narrative is a sought-after asset in an industry where audience engagement and immersion are paramount. This versatility not only broadens their creative horizons but also affords them greater creative control over their projects, allowing them to deliver more polished and artistically satisfying films. In essence, directors who understand sound can navigate the competitive and ever-evolving film industry more adeptly, opening doors to a broader range of opportunities and solidifying their position as accomplished and adaptable filmmakers in the dynamic world of cinema. Sound, in their hands, becomes a powerful tool for emotional resonance, adding a new dimension to their storytelling capabilities and cementing their reputation as multifaceted visionaries in the realm of filmmaking.

N. Director's Role in Special and Visual Effects Collaboration

In the contemporary filmmaking landscape, with special and visual effects playing pivotal roles in numerous productions, it is imperative that directors possess a fundamental understanding of these processes and maintain close collaboration with the specialized departments responsible for executing them. By doing so, directors not only ensure seamless integration of these effects into their films but also harness a competitive advantage that allows them to craft visually stunning and captivating cinematic experiences that closely align with their creative visions. In an industry where technological advancements continuously redefine the boundaries of visual storytelling, directors who invest in learning about SFX and VFX empower themselves to navigate this evolving terrain effectively, thus enhancing their ability to deliver films that captivate audiences and stand out in the highly competitive world of filmmaking.

Enhancing Creative Vision: The Art of Seamlessly Incorporating Special Effects (SFX) and Visual Effects (VFX) in Filmmaking

Creative vision in filmmaking is greatly enhanced when directors possess a comprehensive understanding of special effects (SFX) and visual effects (VFX). This knowledge equips directors with the ability to envision and plan for the seamless integration of these elements into their films, ensuring that they align harmoniously with the overarching artistic vision. Directors can pre-visualize how SFX and VFX will augment the storytelling, enrich visual aesthetics, and contribute to the overall narrative impact. Their understanding enables them to communicate their creative ideas more effectively to SFX and VFX teams, fostering a collaborative environment where innovative concepts are explored and refined. By leveraging their expertise, directors can harness the transformative potential of SFX and VFX to bring their imaginative worlds, fantastical creatures, or awe-inspiring environments to life with precision and authenticity. This holistic approach to creative vision not only elevates the quality of the film but also empowers directors to achieve their artistic aspirations with finesse and precision, resulting in a cinematic experience that captivates and resonates with audiences on both visual and emotional levels.

Elevating Filmmaking with Special Effects (SFX) and Visual Effects (VFX): The Director's Art of Storytelling

In filmmaking, storytelling is greatly enhanced when directors possess a comprehensive understanding of special effects (SFX) and visual effects (VFX). These effects serve as potent storytelling tools that allow directors to transcend the boundaries of the physical world and convey intricate ideas, otherworldly realms, and extraordinary events with unparalleled depth and impact. Directors who are well-versed in SFX and VFX can strategically employ these techniques to breathe life into their narratives, immersing audiences in fantastical and immersive worlds that captivate the imagination. These effects enable directors to visualize and manifest complex plot elements, dynamic action sequences, and visually stunning environments that might otherwise be challenging to depict convincingly. By leveraging their knowledge, directors infuse their storytelling with a rich tapestry of visual and emotional dimensions, creating a cinematic experience that resonates deeply with audiences and leaves a lasting impression long after the credits roll.

The Power of Precision: Directors' Enhanced Communication with SFX and VFX Teams

Effective communication is the bedrock of successful filmmaking, and directors with a deep understanding of special effects (SFX) and visual effects (VFX) have a distinct advantage. This knowledge empowers directors to communicate clearly and precisely with SFX and VFX teams, ensuring that their creative concepts are understood and executed accurately. They can convey technical specifications, visual aesthetics, and narrative nuances with precision, facilitating a smoother collaborative process. This enhanced communication minimizes misunderstandings, expedites decision-making, and encourages innovative problem-solving. The end result is a more faithful realization of the director's artistic vision, where SFX and VFX seamlessly integrate with the narrative, enhancing the overall cinematic experience and elevating the film artistically.

Strategic Budget Management in SFX and VFX: How Directors Optimize Resources

Effective budget management is paramount in filmmaking, and directors who possess a solid understanding of special effects (SFX) and visual effects (VFX) can navigate the financial aspects of their projects with greater finesse. This knowledge allows directors to make informed and strategic decisions regarding the allocation of resources for SFX and VFX, ensuring that these effects are employed judiciously to maximize their impact within the confines of the budget. Directors can identify key moments in the narrative where SFX and VFX will have the most significant storytelling and visual impact, and prioritize investments accordingly. Moreover, they can collaborate with production and post-production teams to identify cost-effective solutions, streamline processes, and avoid unnecessary expenditures. By leveraging their understanding of the cost implications, directors strike a balance between creative vision and fiscal responsibility, ensuring that SFX and VFX are used strategically to enhance the cinematic experience without exceeding budgetary constraints, ultimately leading to a more efficient and financially sustainable filmmaking endeavor.

Ensuring Safety in Practical Special Effects (SFX): The Director's Role in Protecting the Film Crew

Safety on a film set is paramount, especially with practical special effects (SFX) like stunts and explosions. Directors well-versed in safety considerations play a crucial role in protecting the entire cast and crew. They collaborate closely with the SFX team to establish and enforce stringent safety protocols, ensuring necessary precautions. Directors oversee safety measures, conduct risk assessments, and make informed decisions regarding SFX sequences to maintain everyone's safety. Prioritizing safety fosters a creative environment within responsible filmmaking, safeguarding the well-being of the cast and crew for a successful and secure production.

Mastering the Technical Art of Filmmaking: How Directorial Knowledge in SFX and VFX Enhances Precision and Efficacy

Technical knowledge is a potent tool in the director's arsenal, and those who invest in learning about special effects (SFX) and visual effects (VFX) acquire a valuable understanding that enhances their ability to plan and execute scenes with precision and efficacy. This expertise empowers directors to navigate the intricate technical aspects of filmmaking, ensuring that practical and digital effects are seamlessly integrated with live-action footage. Directors can envision how SFX and VFX elements will interact with the actors and the environment, allowing for more informed decisions during the shooting process. They can coordinate camera angles, lighting, and choreography to harmonize with the planned effects, fostering a cohesive visual narrative. By leveraging their technical knowledge, directors create a cohesive cinematic experience where SFX and VFX augment the storytelling seamlessly, making for a film that captivates audiences with its flawless integration of practical and digital elements.

Crafting Cinematic Shots with SFX and VFX: The Director's Advantage in Visual Planning

Visual planning is a foundational element of filmmaking, and directors who possess knowledge of special effects (SFX) and visual effects (VFX) have a distinct advantage in crafting shots and camera movements that harmonize with these effects. This understanding allows directors to pre-visualize how a scene will evolve, taking into account the interplay between practical and digital elements. Directors can anticipate how SFX and VFX will influence the composition, lighting, and dynamics of a shot, enabling them to plan camera angles, movement, and framing that seamlessly integrate with the effects. This meticulous planning ensures that the final shot not only serves the narrative but also aligns cohesively with the film's visual aesthetics, resulting in a visual language that communicates the director's creative vision with precision and impact. Directors who leverage their knowledge of SFX and VFX in visual planning create a cinematic experience where every shot is purposeful, evocative, and in perfect alignment with the overarching artistic vision of the film.

Harmonizing Creativity and Technology: Directors' Collaboration with SFX and VFX Teams

Directors with a deep understanding of special effects (SFX) and visual effects (VFX) play a crucial role in fostering effective collaboration with these essential teams in filmmaking. Their knowledge serves as a bridge between their creative vision and the technical expertise of SFX and VFX professionals, leading to smoother communication and more productive dialogues. This collaboration cultivates an environment where innovative ideas are explored, refined, and seamlessly integrated into the filmmaking process. Directors can provide precise guidance and informed decisions, aligning their creative concepts with the technical capabilities of the SFX and VFX teams. The outcome is a more cohesive and impactful cinematic experience, with practical and digital effects enhancing the storytelling, visual aesthetics, and overall quality of the film.

Transforming Challenges into Creative Opportunities: How Directors with SFX and VFX Knowledge Excel in Problem-Solving

In the dynamic environment of filmmaking, unforeseen challenges and technical issues related to special effects (SFX) and visual effects (VFX) can surface during production. Directors who possess a deep understanding of these effects play a pivotal role in creative problem-solving. Their knowledge empowers them to collaborate closely with SFX and VFX teams, offering valuable insights and alternative approaches to tackle issues efficiently. Directors can navigate technical complexities, troubleshoot unforeseen complications, and adapt their creative vision to address constraints without sacrificing artistic integrity. This collaborative problem-solving fosters an environment where innovative solutions emerge, enabling directors to transform challenges into opportunities for creativity and ingenuity. Ultimately, directors with SFX and VFX knowledge lead productions that are agile and resilient, capable of surmounting obstacles and delivering a final product that reflects their artistic vision with finesse and creativity.

Sustaining Visual Continuity with Special Effects (SFX) and Visual Effects (VFX): The Director's Expertise

Directors who possess a solid understanding of special effects (SFX) and visual effects (VFX) play a vital role in achieving visual consistency and continuity in filmmaking. Their knowledge empowers them to seamlessly integrate SFX and VFX in alignment with the film's narrative and visual language. Directors can meticulously plan the deployment of these effects, ensuring they adhere to established rules and aesthetics across various scenes. This attention to detail extends to factors like lighting, color grading, and post-production techniques, where SFX and VFX must harmonize with live-action footage. By maintaining this continuity, directors create a unified cinematic experience that enhances audience immersion in the narrative and reinforces the director's artistic vision throughout the entire film.

Crafting Cinematic Art: The Artistic Potential of SFX and VFX in Filmmaking

Artistic expression lies at the heart of filmmaking, and directors who grasp the creative potential of special effects (SFX) and visual effects (VFX) are equipped with potent tools to shape their artistic vision. These directors recognize that SFX and VFX are not merely technical elements but mediums for storytelling. By understanding and appreciating the artistic possibilities of these effects, directors open doors to a world of creative exploration. This understanding allows them to engage in close collaboration with effects artists, forging a creative synergy that transcends the ordinary.

Pushing Boundaries: The Artistic Journey of Directors with SFX and VFX

In this collaborative process, directors can embark on journeys of innovation, experimentation, and visionary storytelling. They have the capacity to bring to life sequences that are not only visually stunning but also narratively impactful. By pushing the boundaries of traditional storytelling, directors can create moments that leave an indelible mark on the audience's memory. It is through this artistic collaboration that directors can fully realize their unique cinematic style, infusing their films with a distinctive visual identity that sets them apart from the rest and elevates their work to the realm of true artistic expression. SFX and VFX become more than technical tools; they are the paintbrushes directors use to craft visual masterpieces that resonate with viewers on a profound artistic and emotional level, making their mark in the annals of cinema.

Elevating Career Prospects with SFX and VFX Expertise: Directors' Competitive Edge

In the competitive landscape of the film industry, career advancement is often facilitated by a diverse skill set, and directors who possess a robust understanding of special effects (SFX) and visual effects (VFX) enjoy a distinct advantage. Their knowledge equips them to tackle a wide range of projects, from those demanding intricate and cutting-edge visual effects to those exploring the latest technological trends. This adaptability enhances their marketability in an industry that continually evolves, as they can readily embrace emerging technologies and leverage their expertise to craft visually stunning and technically sophisticated films. Directors with SFX and VFX proficiency are sought after for their ability to navigate the complexities of modern filmmaking, and their capacity to deliver visually striking narratives opens doors to a broader spectrum of opportunities, contributing significantly to their career growth and standing in the industry.

O. Directors' Role in Marketability and Distribution

Beyond the Director's Chair: Navigating the Film's Marketability and Distribution Potential

Understanding the target audience and the marketability of a film's vision is pivotal for a director's success, as it equips them with the knowledge needed to make strategic decisions throughout the filmmaking process. By delving into marketing and distribution principles, directors can tailor their creative choices to better resonate with their intended viewers, increasing the film's appeal and potential for success. This understanding enables directors to participate actively in decisions related to promotional materials, distribution strategies, and audience engagement. They can collaborate more effectively with marketing teams to craft trailers and campaigns that accurately represent the film, aligning with its unique selling points and appealing to the right demographic. In doing so, directors not only enhance the film's marketability but also ensure that their creative vision reaches the widest possible audience, contributing to both the film's commercial viability and its artistic impact.

Audience-Centric Filmmaking: Leveraging Marketing Knowledge for Directorial Success

Audience understanding is a vital aspect of filmmaking, and directors who possess knowledge about marketing can effectively connect with and engage their target audience. This understanding goes beyond demographics and delves into the psychology and preferences of the viewers. Directors can use this insight to make informed creative and narrative decisions that resonate with the intended audience, from crafting relatable characters to developing storylines that address specific themes or concerns. Additionally, marketing-savvy directors can strategize how to position and promote their films, identifying the most suitable distribution channels, release dates, and marketing campaigns to maximize reach and impact. Ultimately, this audience-centric approach enhances the film's chances of success, as it is more likely to captivate and resonate with viewers, leading to positive reviews, word-of-mouth recommendations, and box office success, all of which contribute to the director's career advancement in the competitive film industry.

Navigating the Market: The Role of Marketing and Distribution Knowledge in Filmmaking Success

Commercial viability is a crucial consideration for filmmakers, and directors with a solid understanding of marketing and distribution are well-equipped to assess and enhance the chances of their projects succeeding in the market. By delving into market research, they can gauge the demand for specific genres, styles, or subject matters and tailor their creative choices accordingly. This includes making decisions on script development, casting, and production values that align with the preferences of the target audience. Furthermore, directors with marketing knowledge can strategize the release timing and distribution plan, selecting the right platforms or theaters to maximize exposure and profitability. This awareness of the commercial landscape not only increases the likelihood of financial success but also opens doors to future projects and career advancement in the competitive film industry.

The Financial Blueprint: Integrating Marketing and Distribution Costs into Film Budgeting

Budgeting and resource allocation are integral aspects of film production, and directors who have a grasp of marketing and distribution understand the importance of factoring in the costs related to promoting and distributing their films. By incorporating marketing and distribution expenses into the budgeting process, directors can make more informed decisions about how to allocate resources efficiently. They can earmark funds for advertising, public relations, film festival submissions, and other promotional efforts that are crucial for building anticipation and buzz around their movie. Simultaneously, directors can strategize on distribution methods, whether through traditional theatrical releases, streaming platforms, or international markets, while considering the associated costs. This holistic approach to budgeting ensures that financial resources are managed judiciously, preventing unexpected overruns and contributing to the overall success of the project.

Creative Collaboration: Directors' Role in Crafting Effective Film Promotional Materials

Understanding marketing principles empowers directors to actively participate in the creation of promotional materials for their films. Directors who are knowledgeable about marketing can provide valuable input and creative direction to marketing teams, graphic designers, and editors working on trailers, posters, and social media content. They can ensure that these materials align with the film's tone, themes, and target audience, effectively conveying the essence of the movie. By infusing their creative vision into promotional materials, directors can play a pivotal role in generating excitement and anticipation among potential viewers, ultimately contributing to the film's success at the box office or on streaming platforms. This collaborative approach between directors and marketing teams results in promotional materials that resonate with audiences and enhance the film's visibility in a competitive market.

Strategic Film Festival Submissions: How Directors with Marketing Insight Make a Difference

Directors who possess knowledge of marketing can work closely with film distributors to formulate a strategic plan for film festival submissions. This festival strategy involves selecting the most suitable festivals based on the film's genre, style, and target audience. Directors can leverage their marketing understanding to assess which festivals align with the film's commercial and artistic goals. Additionally, they can assist in crafting compelling festival submissions, including engaging synopses, eye-catching posters, and captivating trailers, all designed to pique the interest of festival programmers. By actively participating in the festival strategy, directors can increase the film's chances of acceptance into prestigious festivals, where it can garner critical acclaim and industry attention, ultimately boosting its prospects for wider distribution and commercial success.

Navigating the Changing Tides: How Directors Stay Informed About Marketing and Distribution Trends in the Film Industry

Staying informed about marketing trends and emerging distribution platforms is crucial for directors in today's dynamic film industry. By keeping a finger on the pulse of market trends, directors can adapt their strategies to align with changing audience preferences and consumption habits. For instance, understanding the rise of streaming platforms and the growth of online content consumption allows directors to explore digital distribution options and create content tailored for online audiences. Moreover, staying attuned to marketing trends enables directors to employ innovative promotional techniques, such as influencer partnerships or interactive social media campaigns, to engage with their target audience effectively. By embracing these trends, directors can ensure that their films remain relevant, accessible, and competitive in a rapidly evolving landscape, ultimately increasing their chances of commercial success.

Strategic Decision-Making: Understanding Distribution Options in Filmmaking

Understanding distribution options is paramount for directors as it empowers them to make informed decisions that align with their film's goals and intended audience. Traditional theatrical releases offer the grandeur of the big screen and can build buzz and prestige, but they often require substantial marketing budgets and face competition for screen time. Streaming platforms provide broader accessibility and the potential for global reach, catering to the convenience of modern audiences, but they may involve negotiations with platforms and face challenges in standing out in a crowded digital landscape. Hybrid distribution models allow directors to combine the best of both worlds, tailoring their release strategy to leverage the strengths of different distribution channels. By comprehending these choices, directors can strategically plan how to maximize their film's exposure, profitability, and impact while considering budget constraints and audience demographics.

Proactive Marketing and Engagement: Directors' Role in Building Buzz During Production

Directors can play a crucial role in the marketing and distribution process by engaging in promotional activities during the production phase. This proactive approach involves creating and sharing behind-the-scenes content, such as interviews with cast and crew, production diaries, and teaser materials, to generate excitement and anticipation among potential audiences. Leveraging social media platforms and online communities, directors can interact directly with fans and followers, providing updates, sneak peeks, and exclusive content related to the film. This not only builds a dedicated fan base but also creates a sense of community and engagement around the project. By incorporating marketing efforts into the production process, directors can lay a strong foundation for successful distribution and ensure that their film gains visibility and traction in an increasingly competitive media landscape.

Building Personal Brand and Industry Reputation: The Impact of Directors' Active Engagement in Marketing

Directors who actively engage in marketing efforts can significantly contribute to building their personal brand and reputation as filmmakers. By maintaining a strong online presence and regularly interacting with fans and followers, directors can establish themselves as accessible and relatable figures in the industry. This engagement not only fosters a dedicated fan base but also creates a loyal community of supporters who are more likely to follow a director's future projects. Additionally, by consistently delivering quality content and sharing insights into their filmmaking journey, directors can enhance their credibility and position themselves as experts in their field. This, in turn, can lead to increased recognition, better career opportunities, and a lasting impact on the film industry.

Maximizing Exposure and Impact: The Art of Cross-Promotion in Filmmaking

Directors who actively engage in marketing efforts can leverage cross-promotion as a powerful strategy to enhance the visibility and appeal of their films. Collaborating with marketing teams, directors can identify synergies with other films, brands, or media outlets that share a similar target audience or thematic resonance. This collaboration allows for mutually beneficial promotional activities, such as joint advertising campaigns, special screenings, or cross-branded merchandise, which can expand the film's reach and generate buzz. Cross-promotion not only amplifies the film's marketing impact but also creates valuable partnerships that can lead to broader opportunities for exposure and success in the competitive film industry.

Strategic Release Planning: Timing Film Launches for Optimal Impact

Directors who possess a deep understanding of marketing principles can strategically plan the timing of their film releases to maximize their chances of success. This involves considering various factors such as the competitive landscape, the availability of similar films, and potential blockbuster releases during the same period. Directors can also take advantage of holidays, cultural events, or seasonal trends that align with their film's theme or genre, as this can significantly impact audience interest and box office performance. By carefully analyzing these variables and making informed decisions, directors can ensure that their films are launched at the right moment, increasing their visibility and the likelihood of resonating with their target audience.

Building Fan Loyalty: Directors as Engaging Digital Storytellers

Directors who actively engage with their audience through social media and other digital platforms can cultivate a dedicated fan base that is enthusiastic about their work. This engagement goes beyond traditional marketing and allows directors to connect directly with viewers, sharing insights, updates, and behind-the-scenes content related to their projects. By fostering a sense of community and interaction, directors can generate anticipation and excitement among their followers, which can translate into strong word-of-mouth marketing. This, in turn, can contribute to a robust opening for their film, as fans are more likely to spread the word, attend screenings, and support the director's creative endeavors, ultimately enhancing the film's visibility and success.

The Strategic Advantage: How Marketing and Distribution Understanding Elevates Directors in the Film Industry

Directors who possess a solid understanding of marketing and distribution can significantly advance their careers in the film industry. Their ability to actively contribute to the promotion and distribution strategies of their projects sets them apart as proactive and informed filmmakers. This knowledge equips them to make strategic decisions about their films' release, audience targeting, and promotional efforts, ultimately increasing the chances of their work reaching a wider audience and achieving commercial success. Additionally, such directors are more attractive to producers and studios, as they bring a well-rounded skill set that extends beyond the creative aspects of filmmaking. They can collaborate more effectively with marketing and distribution teams, making them valuable assets in the competitive world of cinema, opening doors to a broader range of projects and opportunities.

P. Director's Awareness of Rights and Contracts

Director's Awareness of Rights and Contracts in Filmmaking

Being aware of legal and contractual aspects related to filmmaking is crucial for film directors, as it equips them with the knowledge and tools necessary to safeguard their creative rights, negotiate contracts with actors, crew, and studios effectively, ensure legal compliance throughout the production, and adeptly navigate the intricate legal landscape of filmmaking. This understanding empowers directors to make informed decisions that align with their artistic vision, protect their financial and creative interests, and ultimately minimize potential legal risks that can arise during film production, ensuring a smoother and more successful filmmaking process.

Empowering Filmmakers: The Crucial Role of Legal Knowledge in Safeguarding Creative Rights

Directors who have a solid grasp of legal concepts and the intricacies of entertainment law can effectively safeguard their creative rights throughout the filmmaking process. This understanding empowers them to negotiate contracts and agreements that protect their artistic vision, ensuring that their input and decisions are respected and maintained during production, post-production, and distribution. Additionally, legal knowledge enables directors to navigate potential conflicts or disputes, such as disagreements with producers or distributors, in a manner that upholds their creative integrity. By having a firm legal foundation, directors can confidently assert their rights, including issues related to copyright, intellectual property, and contractual obligations, ultimately preserving their artistic vision and the integrity of their work in the often complex and highly regulated world of filmmaking.

Contracts and Filmmaking: Empowering Directors to Navigate Negotiations and Protect Creative Interests

Directors who possess a strong understanding of contract law are better equipped to navigate the complex web of negotiations that are integral to filmmaking. They can actively participate in contract negotiations with a wide range of stakeholders, including actors, crew members, producers, and distributors. This legal knowledge empowers directors to advocate for their creative vision and interests effectively. They can ensure that contractual agreements align with their expectations, from securing the right talent and crew to protecting their artistic control and ensuring fair compensation. Additionally, directors can leverage their legal acumen to address potential issues that may arise during production or distribution, mitigating disputes and ensuring that contracts serve as a solid foundation for successful collaboration and the realization of their artistic vision.

Intellectual Property Empowerment: How Directors Can Safeguard and Maximize Their Creative Works

Directors with a grasp of intellectual property rights have the ability to safeguard their creative works and make informed decisions about how their films are used and distributed. Copyright law knowledge, in particular, allows directors to protect their films from unauthorized copying or distribution. They can negotiate licensing agreements with distributors or streaming platforms, ensuring that their intellectual property is used in a manner consistent with their intentions. Additionally, an understanding of trademarks can be valuable in branding and marketing efforts, allowing directors to protect their film titles, logos, or associated merchandise. Overall, this legal expertise empowers directors to have greater control over their intellectual property, both during the filmmaking process and in the subsequent exploitation and promotion of their work.

Legal Compliance Mastery: Navigating the Filmmaking Landscape with Knowledge and Integrity

Directors who are well-versed in legal compliance are better equipped to navigate the complex web of legal regulations that govern the filmmaking industry. This knowledge extends to areas such as labor laws, which dictate fair working conditions and compensation for the cast and crew, ensuring a harmonious and legally sound production environment. Understanding tax codes is crucial for managing the financial aspects of filmmaking, as it allows directors to optimize tax incentives and credits, ultimately contributing to cost-effective production. Furthermore, copyright laws play a pivotal role in protecting the intellectual property of the film, including its script, music, and visual elements. Directors who comprehend these laws can ensure that their projects adhere to copyright regulations, mitigating the risk of legal disputes that could delay or jeopardize the film's release. Legal compliance knowledge is essential for directors to operate within the boundaries of the law, maintain ethical production practices, and safeguard their projects from potential legal entanglements.

Financial Responsibility in Filmmaking: Empowering Directors to Secure Fair Compensation and Protect Creative Rights

Directors who possess a strong grasp of financial responsibility are well-prepared to navigate the financial aspects of filmmaking effectively. This includes understanding the intricacies of contract terms, which are vital in ensuring that the director's role, compensation, and creative rights are clearly defined and protected. Additionally, knowledge of royalties and profit participation agreements allows directors to negotiate fair and equitable compensation structures, ensuring that they receive a share of the film's financial success in line with their contributions. This financial acumen not only safeguards the director's financial interests but also fosters transparency and trust among all stakeholders involved in the project. Ultimately, directors who are financially literate can make informed decisions that contribute to the financial success of the film and protect their financial well-being in the industry.

Clearance and Licensing Mastery: Directors as Guardians of Legal Integrity in Filmmaking

Directors who comprehend the intricacies of clearance and licensing play a pivotal role in ensuring the legal integrity of their films. This knowledge involves understanding the legal obligations associated with using copyrighted materials, such as music, artwork, or even branded products, within their productions. It also extends to obtaining the necessary permissions and releases from individuals, including actors, crew members, and even extras, whose likenesses and performances may be featured in the film. Furthermore, directors need to secure location releases when filming in private or public spaces to prevent legal complications. This legal literacy not only mitigates the risk of copyright infringement and legal disputes but also demonstrates a commitment to ethical and responsible filmmaking practices. Directors who prioritize clearance and licensing contribute to the film's overall compliance with legal standards and the protection of intellectual property rights.

Unlocking Success: The Director's Guide to Navigating Distribution Agreements in Filmmaking

Understanding distribution agreements is essential for directors as they navigate the complex process of bringing their films to audiences. This knowledge involves comprehending the contractual terms and conditions set forth by distribution companies, including aspects such as territories, release platforms, revenue-sharing arrangements, marketing commitments, and the duration of the distribution license. Directors need to be well-versed in their distribution rights to protect their creative vision and ensure that their films receive the best possible exposure and revenue potential. Negotiating favorable terms in these agreements can be crucial in maximizing a film's success and financial returns. Moreover, directors who understand distribution contracts are better equipped to collaborate with distribution partners, fostering a productive working relationship that benefits both parties and ultimately brings the film to a wider and more appreciative audience.

Safety First: Legal Liability and Risk Management for Directors in Filmmaking

Directors must have a grasp of legal liability and risk management to ensure the safety of their cast and crew and safeguard themselves from potential legal consequences. This understanding involves identifying potential risks associated with various aspects of production, from stunts and special effects to location shooting and equipment use. Directors should implement safety protocols and procedures, secure the necessary permits and insurance coverage, and ensure that the set adheres to safety standards and regulations. By doing so, they can minimize the likelihood of accidents and injuries on set, reducing both physical and legal risks. Additionally, directors should be aware of their contractual and legal obligations to mitigate liability, such as including indemnification clauses in contracts and obtaining the required permissions and clearances for copyrighted materials and locations. Overall, a strong understanding of legal liability and risk management is crucial for responsible filmmaking and the protection of all involved parties.

Harmonizing Filmmaking: The Director's Guide to Effective Dispute Resolution

Directors need to be well-versed in dispute resolution mechanisms to manage conflicts that may arise during the filmmaking process. Whether it's contractual disputes with cast and crew, disagreements with producers or financiers, or creative differences with fellow collaborators, understanding dispute resolution options is essential. Mediation, for instance, allows for a neutral third party to facilitate discussions and negotiations to reach a mutually acceptable resolution. Arbitration provides a more formal process where an arbitrator makes a binding decision based on presented evidence. Directors who comprehend these options can choose the most suitable method for addressing conflicts, potentially saving time, costs, and preserving professional relationships. It also ensures that disputes are handled efficiently, allowing the filmmaking process to continue without significant disruptions.

Insurance Mastery: How Directors Secure a Safe and Smooth Filmmaking Production

Directors must have a grasp of insurance requirements and policies to safeguard the production and manage potential liabilities effectively. They play a crucial role in ensuring that the production has the appropriate insurance coverage. This includes coverage for various aspects such as equipment, liability, cast and crew, and even adverse weather conditions that might disrupt filming. Directors need to work closely with production managers and insurance professionals to assess the specific needs of the production, identify potential risks, and tailor insurance policies accordingly. In doing so, they can mitigate financial risks, protect the well-being of the cast and crew, and provide a safety net in case unexpected issues or accidents occur during the filmmaking process. This understanding of insurance is fundamental in maintaining a secure and smooth production.

Global Filmmaking: Navigating International Legal Complexities for Directors

Directors must be well-versed in international legal considerations to successfully navigate the complexities of filmmaking that involve international collaborations, co-productions, and multi-country distribution. These considerations encompass a broad range of issues, including intellectual property rights in different jurisdictions, tax incentives and treaties, visa and work permit requirements for international cast and crew, import and export regulations for equipment, and compliance with local censorship and content regulations. Directors need to work closely with legal experts who specialize in international entertainment law to ensure that their projects are legally sound across borders. Understanding these international legal intricacies is paramount for filmmakers looking to expand their reach to global audiences while avoiding legal pitfalls that could hinder their projects or lead to costly disputes.

Elevating Your Filmmaking Career: The Impact of Legal Knowledge and Contract Expertise for Directors

Directors who possess a strong understanding of legal matters and contract negotiation can advance their careers in the film industry significantly. This expertise not only allows them to protect their creative and financial interests in projects but also positions them as reliable and knowledgeable collaborators. Directors with legal acumen are better equipped to negotiate favorable terms in contracts, safeguard their intellectual property rights, and ensure proper compensation. Moreover, their ability to navigate complex legal issues and mitigate risks enhances their reputation in the industry, making them more attractive candidates for a variety of projects and collaborations. In a highly competitive field like filmmaking, this comprehensive skill set can open doors to diverse opportunities and provide a solid foundation for long-term career growth.

Q. Director's Insight into Film Marketing and Promotion

While promoting and marketing a film is not traditionally within a director's primary scope of duties, having a strong understanding of these aspects can be invaluable for ensuring the success of their work. Acquiring knowledge about marketing and promotion equips directors with the tools to establish a direct connection with their target audience, enabling them to shape their creative decisions to resonate with current market trends and audience preferences. This understanding empowers directors to actively participate in the promotion process, building their personal brand and engaging with fans, which can significantly contribute to both the commercial and artistic triumph of their films. Essentially, directors who grasp the fundamentals of marketing and promotion can leverage this knowledge to not only enhance their work's visibility but also to craft a more rewarding and impactful career in the highly competitive area of filmmaking.

Mastering Audience Engagement: How Directors Enhance Film Visibility and Build Lasting Connections

Directors who possess a deep understanding of marketing and promotion strategies have a distinct advantage when it comes to engaging with their film's audience. They can actively participate in the development of promotional materials, leveraging their creative insights to craft compelling trailers, posters, and social media content that resonate with viewers. By connecting with their audience through various online platforms, directors can build a loyal fan base and generate buzz surrounding their project long before its release. This engagement fosters a sense of community and anticipation among the audience, increasing the likelihood of a strong opening and positive word-of-mouth marketing. Directors who excel in audience engagement not only enhance the visibility of their films but also forge a lasting connection with viewers, creating a dedicated following that can extend beyond a single project and benefit their future endeavors in the industry.

Strategic Filmmaking: How Directors Align Creative Choices with Target Audience Preferences for Success

Directors who possess a comprehensive understanding of marketing principles can strategically align their creative choices with the preferences and expectations of their target audience. By analyzing market research and demographic data, they can tailor the film's storytelling, style, and thematic elements to resonate with the intended viewers. This alignment not only enhances the film's overall appeal but also increases the likelihood of a positive reception by the target audience. Directors can make informed decisions about the film's tone, genre, and narrative approach, ensuring that it effectively captures the attention and emotions of those they aim to reach. As a result, the film becomes more relatable and engaging for its target demographic, ultimately leading to a stronger connection between the audience and the director's creative vision, which is essential for a film's success in today's competitive cinematic landscape.

Crafting Artful Promotion: How Directors Elevate the Creative Direction of Marketing Campaigns

Directors, armed with their deep understanding of the film's artistic vision, can play a pivotal role in shaping the creative direction of marketing campaigns and promotional materials. By actively participating in the marketing process, they can ensure that these materials effectively convey the film's unique style, themes, and overall essence to the audience. Directors can collaborate closely with marketing teams, providing insights and ideas that align with the narrative's emotional core and visual aesthetics. This collaborative approach allows them to maintain consistency between the promotional materials and the film itself, creating a cohesive and compelling marketing campaign that resonates with potential viewers. By infusing their creative input into the marketing process, directors not only enhance the film's appeal but also bridge the gap between the artistic intent and audience expectations, ultimately increasing the film's chances of success in a highly competitive industry.

Strategic Branding: How Active Marketing Involvement Elevates a Director's Career and Reputation

Participating actively in marketing and promotion is a strategic move that can significantly enhance a director's personal brand and reputation within the film industry. By engaging with audiences through social media, interviews, and public appearances related to the film, directors can establish a unique and recognizable presence. This not only fosters a loyal fan base but also positions the director as a prominent figure in the industry. A strong online presence, combined with a consistent and appealing public image, can open doors to new opportunities, such as attracting investors and collaborators for future projects. Moreover, it can generate industry recognition and credibility, making the director a sought-after talent in a competitive field. In essence, brand building through active marketing involvement can be a catalyst for a director's career advancement and long-term success in the film world.

Amplifying Filmmaking: The Power of Social Media Engagement for Directors

Social media engagement has become a vital tool for directors to connect directly with their audience and amplify the visibility of their films. Directors can leverage platforms like Twitter, Instagram, Facebook, and even TikTok to provide fans with exclusive behind-the-scenes content, such as photos, videos, and insights into the filmmaking process. This engagement not only creates excitement and anticipation among fans but also fosters a sense of connection and loyalty. Directors can also use social media to share updates, respond to fan inquiries, and participate in conversations related to their work. By actively engaging with fans, directors can build a dedicated online community that serves as a powerful promotional force when the film is released. Additionally, social media provides a direct channel for feedback, allowing directors to gauge audience reactions and adjust their marketing strategies accordingly. Overall, social media engagement has become an indispensable tool for directors in the modern filmmaking landscape, enabling them to extend their reach and enhance the visibility of their films.

Unlocking Festival Success: The Director's Guide to Crafting Effective Film Festival Strategies

Film festival strategies are a crucial aspect of a director's role in marketing and promoting their film. Directors can work closely with their distributors to develop a well-planned festival strategy that aligns with the film's goals and target audience. This strategy involves selecting the right film festivals based on factors such as the festival's prestige, genre focus, and geographical location. Directors can also help craft compelling festival submissions, including strong press kits, trailers, and promotional materials, to make their film stand out in a competitive festival environment. Attending key festivals and engaging with audiences, critics, and industry professionals can further enhance a film's reputation and visibility. Winning awards or receiving critical acclaim at festivals can generate buzz around the film and attract the attention of distributors and potential buyers. A well-executed festival strategy not only increases the film's chances of success on the festival circuit but also paves the way for successful distribution, reaching a wider audience and maximizing the film's commercial potential.

Market Savvy Filmmaking: How Directors Harness Market Insights for Commercial Success

Understanding the market is a fundamental aspect of a director's role in ensuring a film's commercial success. Directors who take the time to study market trends and analyze audience preferences gain valuable insights into what types of films are currently in demand. This knowledge allows them to tailor their creative choices, such as selecting genres, themes, or storytelling approaches that align with prevailing market trends.

Directors can also make strategic decisions about the film's target audience, determining which demographic groups are likely to be most interested in their project. Additionally, understanding the market helps directors plan their release strategy effectively, considering factors such as the competitive landscape, release timing, and distribution platforms that are currently popular among audiences. By aligning their creative vision with market realities, directors increase the likelihood of their film resonating with audiences, achieving commercial success, and making a positive impact in the industry.

Strategic Budget Allocation: How Directors Optimize Resources for Effective Film Promotion

Budget allocation is a critical aspect of filmmaking, and directors who possess knowledge of marketing principles can make strategic decisions to optimize their budget for promotional efforts. Understanding the costs associated with marketing campaigns, advertising, and promotional materials allows directors to allocate resources in a way that maximizes the film's visibility and impact. They can identify key areas where investments are needed, such as creating compelling trailers, designing eye-catching posters, or running effective social media advertising campaigns. Additionally, directors can prioritize marketing strategies based on the target audience and market trends, ensuring that their budget is spent efficiently on reaching the right viewers. This informed approach to budget allocation not only helps the film gain better exposure but also prevents unnecessary overspending, ultimately contributing to the film's overall success within the constraints of the budget.

Crafting Impactful Promotion: How Directors Shape Marketing Materials to Enhance Film Visibility

Directors' involvement in the creation of promotional materials is a crucial component of a film's marketing campaign. By understanding marketing principles and having an intimate knowledge of their film's themes, characters, and artistic vision, directors can actively shape and contribute to the development of these materials. For instance, they can collaborate closely with editors and marketing teams to craft engaging and impactful trailers that effectively convey the essence of the film's narrative and style, ensuring they resonate with the target audience. Directors can also work with graphic designers to design visually compelling posters that capture the film's unique identity and appeal to potential viewers. Additionally, their insights into the film's creative elements enable directors to provide valuable input for social media content, ensuring that it aligns with the film's overall marketing strategy. This hands-on involvement not only ensures that promotional materials authentically represent the film but also enhances its marketability by effectively communicating its distinctive qualities, ultimately contributing to the film's success in the competitive market.

Directorial Presence: How Directors Elevate Film Premieres and Promotional Events for Success

Directors' presence at film premieres and promotional events is a pivotal component of a movie's marketing strategy. Directors who comprehend the promotional aspect can maximize the impact of these occasions by strategically engaging with the media, fans, and industry professionals. They can articulate their creative vision, share insights into the filmmaking process, and provide context for the film, enriching the audience's understanding and connection to the project. Moreover, directors can use these events as platforms to build their personal brand, fostering a deeper connection with fans and enhancing their reputation as filmmakers. By actively participating in red carpet interviews, press conferences, and fan interactions, directors contribute significantly to generating buzz and excitement around the film, ultimately increasing its visibility and commercial success.

Listening to the Audience: How Director-Viewer Interaction Shapes Future Filmmaking Success

Directors who actively engage with marketing efforts have the opportunity to collect invaluable feedback from the audience, which can profoundly influence their future projects and creative choices. By monitoring social media conversations, attending screenings, and participating in Q&A sessions, directors gain insights into how viewers perceive and respond to their films. This feedback can encompass a wide range of elements, from narrative preferences and character likability to visual aesthetics and emotional impact. Directors can use this feedback as a powerful tool for refining their storytelling techniques, enhancing their understanding of their target audience, and tailoring their future projects to better align with audience expectations and desires. Additionally, this direct engagement with the audience fosters a sense of connection and community, strengthening the bond between directors and their fan base, which can be instrumental in building a lasting and successful filmmaking career.

Strategic Collaborations: Directors Expanding Film Visibility Through Cross-Promotion

Directors can strategically collaborate with distributors and various stakeholders to identify opportunities for cross-promotion, which can significantly enhance a film's visibility and appeal. Cross-promotion involves partnering with other films, brands, or products that share a similar target audience or thematic resonance. By leveraging these partnerships, directors can tap into existing fan bases and customer networks, reaching a broader and more engaged audience. For example, a director of a suspenseful thriller may collaborate with a popular streaming platform to promote their film alongside other suspenseful content. This can involve joint marketing campaigns, special screenings, or even co-branded merchandise. Cross-promotion not only extends a film's reach but also allows it to benefit from the established credibility and recognition of its partners, ultimately increasing its chances of success in a competitive market.

Global Outreach: How Directors Harness an International Fan Base Through Online Presence

An active online presence is a powerful tool for directors to connect with a global audience and cultivate an international fan base, which is increasingly valuable for successful film distribution in diverse markets. Directors can use various digital platforms, including social media, official websites, and streaming platforms, to engage with fans, share behind-the-scenes content, and promote their work. By consistently interacting with followers and responding to their feedback, directors can create a sense of community and loyalty among their online fan base. This not only generates anticipation for their current project but also builds brand recognition and trust. With an international fan base, directors can leverage their reach to secure distribution deals in multiple countries, tapping into the enthusiasm and support of their followers to bolster their film's success on a global scale. Additionally, an online presence enables directors to stay informed about emerging market trends and audience preferences, helping them tailor their future projects to meet the demands of various international markets.

The Power of Word-of-Mouth: How Effective Marketing Drives Film Audiences

Effective marketing strategies have the capacity to generate positive word-of-mouth, a potent force in driving audiences to see a film. When a film is promoted skillfully, capturing the interest and curiosity of potential viewers, it sparks conversations and discussions among friends, family, and social circles. These conversations, often fueled by excitement or intrigue, serve as endorsements that can significantly influence people's decisions to watch a film. Positive word-of-mouth creates a ripple effect, expanding the film's reach beyond its initial target audience as those who have seen it recommend it to others. In today's interconnected digital age, word-of-mouth extends to social media platforms, online reviews, and discussions, amplifying its impact even further. Directors who understand the value of word-of-mouth as a byproduct of effective marketing can harness this organic promotion to boost their film's viewership, ultimately contributing to its success at the box office and beyond.

Directorial Advancement: How Marketing and Promotion Expertise Elevates Careers in Filmmaking

Directors who possess a solid understanding of marketing and promotion often enjoy a significant advantage in their careers within the film industry. This advantage stems from their ability to actively engage in the promotion of their projects, which not only demonstrates their commitment but also enhances their value to studios and production companies. By collaborating effectively with marketing professionals, these directors can align their creative vision with promotional strategies, ensuring that the marketing materials accurately represent the film's essence. This collaboration can lead to a more harmonious working relationship between the creative and marketing teams, resulting in more effective promotional campaigns. Additionally, directors who actively contribute to marketing efforts can help their projects stand out in an increasingly competitive landscape, leading to increased opportunities for their films to succeed commercially. Ultimately, a director's ability to understand and participate in marketing and promotion can be a key factor in their career advancement within the industry.

The Director's Art of Communication: Bringing Creative Vision to Life in Filmmaking

Directors serve as the creative visionaries of a film, and while they don't need to possess expertise in every technical department, having a well-defined creative vision and effective communication skills are paramount. Directors rely on their ability to translate their artistic concepts into actionable instructions that their department heads and crew can understand and execute. Effective communication is the linchpin of successful filmmaking, as directors work closely with heads of departments such as cinematography, production design, costume and makeup, sound, and editing, among others. They must articulate their vision, provide guidance, and foster collaboration to ensure that every element of the film aligns with the intended narrative and aesthetic. By nurturing a collaborative and communicative environment, directors can harness the collective talents of their team, turning their vision into a cohesive and compelling cinematic experience.

CHAPTER - 7

7. Script Development and Screenwriting

A. Crafting the Narrative: The importance of strong scripts

Crafting Cinematic Magic: The Power of Narrative Substance, Robust Scripts, and Character Development

Narrative substance is the cornerstone of a film's ability to captivate audiences, with a robust script serving as its foundation. A strong script intricately weaves together characters, conflicts, and themes, driving the narrative forward with depth and intrigue. Well-developed characters, each with their unique motivations, flaws, and growth arcs, infuse the story with relatability and emotional resonance. Their interactions and transformations contribute to the plot's momentum, inviting audiences to invest emotionally in their journeys. A compelling narrative, guided by a skilled director, envelops viewers in a world that offers both escapism and reflection, weaving together themes and conflicts that evoke thought and empathy. This synergy between script, character development, and directorial finesse brings about an immersive cinematic experience that lingers long after the credits roll.

The Heartfelt Alchemy: Script, Character, and Emotion in Cinema

The potency of emotional resonance in cinema lies within the pages of a compelling script, which serves as a conduit for audiences to forge profound connections with characters and their journeys. A powerful script possesses the ability to evoke a wide spectrum of emotions, from joy to sorrow, empathy to catharsis. When relatable characters navigate situations that mirror universal human experiences, viewers find themselves drawn into a shared emotional space, forming a genuine bond with the narrative. These characters become vessels through which audiences can explore their own emotions, perspectives, and reflections. Directors who recognize the script's potential to kindle emotional engagement infuse scenes with authenticity, guiding actors to deliver performances that heighten the impact of these emotions. In these moments, the convergence of skilled direction, heartfelt performances, and a resonant script creates a profound connection between the film and its viewers, reminding us of cinema's unique power to elicit deep and lasting feelings.

Pioneering Originality: Directors and the Cinematic Quest for Uniqueness

Amidst the bustling landscape of the film industry, originality and uniqueness shine as beacons of distinction, capturing the attention of audiences and industry insiders alike. Original scripts carve a niche by offering narratives that break away from conventional norms, presenting fresh perspectives and innovative storytelling. Directors who champion such scripts are catalysts for pushing the boundaries of cinematic creativity, guiding the manifestation of thought-provoking concepts and unexplored themes onto the screen. These films stand as a testament to the power of original ideas to captivate, inspire, and challenge preconceived notions. By defying predictability, directors infuse their projects with a sense of curiosity, inciting curiosity and fascination in viewers who seek narratives that stand apart from the familiar, demonstrating the enduring allure of cinematic ingenuity.

Illuminating Society: Cinema's Role in Addressing Pertinent Social Issues

Scripts that delve into pertinent social issues not only entertain but also serve as catalysts for meaningful conversations and societal reflection. These films possess the power to illuminate neglected corners of society, shining a spotlight on topics often relegated to the shadows. Directors who tackle these scripts navigate the delicate balance between artistic expression and social responsibility, crafting narratives that resonate deeply with audiences' personal experiences and collective consciousness. By bringing these issues to the forefront, these films inspire viewers to engage in dialogue, fostering awareness, empathy, and advocacy. Through the director's lens, societal narratives gain a potent tool for catalyzing change, proving that cinema is more than mere entertainment – it's a dynamic force that shapes perceptions, challenges norms, and paves the way for a more enlightened and compassionate world.

Mastering the Cinematic Symphony: Pacing and Structure in Film

Pacing and structure in a script are the orchestrators of a film's rhythm, ensuring a seamless journey that captivates audiences from start to finish. A well-structured script, meticulously guided by the director's vision, skillfully balances exposition, rising action, and resolution. This careful orchestration ensures that the narrative unfolds in a way that sustains tension, anticipation, and emotional investment. Directors adeptly maneuver the script's pacing, allowing it to ebb and flow in harmony with the story's natural cadence. By judiciously managing the tempo of revelations, confrontations, and resolutions, directors create a dynamic viewing experience that holds the audience's attention, leading them through the narrative's peaks and valleys while maintaining a sense of intrigue and emotional resonance. In this delicate interplay between script and direction, filmmakers craft a symphony of storytelling that envelops audiences, leaving them both satisfied and yearning for more.

Sculpting Character and Story: The Art of Dialogue in Cinema

Dialogues serve as windows into characters' souls, revealing their innermost thoughts, desires, and conflicts, while also propelling the narrative forward. Directors, in collaboration with screenwriters and actors, shape these dialogues to encapsulate the essence of characters, reflecting their unique personalities and motivations. The director's insight guides the delivery, pacing, and emotional nuances of dialogues, ensuring they align with the characters' journeys. Memorable lines etched into the script resonate with audiences, becoming cultural touchpoints and lending the film a sense of timelessness. Directors who harness the power of well-crafted dialogues infuse their films with a dynamic dimension, enriching characters and relationships, and bestowing quotability that reverberates far beyond the cinema screen. Through careful direction, these lines become indelible markers in the audience's memory, underscoring the director's role in shaping a film's linguistic tapestry and its enduring impact.

Visual Alchemy: The Director's Craft in Cinematic Storytelling

Visual storytelling stands as the complementary partner to the written script, translating narrative nuances and emotional depth into a language understood universally by audiences. A strong script serves as the foundation upon which the director builds a visual tapestry, dictating shot composition, camera movements, lighting, and overall aesthetics. Directors employ visual elements to not only enhance the narrative's impact but also to convey subtle subtexts and thematic undercurrents. The director's expertise in visual storytelling comes to the fore as they interpret the script's emotional beats, pacing, and mood, and then translate these elements into cinematic language. Whether through vivid colours, stark contrasts, sweeping vistas, or intimate close-ups, directors wield visual cues to deepen the audience's engagement and emotional connection. In this dynamic interplay between script and direction, the director's vision brings the narrative to life, enveloping audiences in a multi-sensory experience that lingers long after the credits roll.

Unlocking Hidden Dimensions: The Art of Subtext and Layered Storytelling in Cinema

Subtext and layered storytelling enrich a film's narrative by infusing it with hidden meanings, nuances, and complexities that extend beyond the surface plot. Directors skillfully incorporate subtext through visual cues, dialogue, and character interactions, allowing astute viewers to uncover deeper layers of meaning. This approach creates a multi-dimensional experience, where the audience not only engages with the immediate storyline but also delves into the underlying themes, emotions, and social commentary. The director's adept handling of subtext fosters a sense of discovery for the audience, prompting varied interpretations and inviting discussions that transcend the screen. Through these nuanced layers, directors encourage viewers to engage actively, forming connections that extend beyond the confines of the film, thus underscoring the director's mastery in crafting narratives that resonate on both immediate and profound levels.

Genre Mastery: Balancing Expectations and Creative Innovation in Film Direction

The seamless alignment between a script's genre and audience expectations plays a pivotal role in determining a film's resonance and success. Directors carefully consider the genre's conventions, tropes, and storytelling patterns to cater to the preferences and anticipations of their target audience. Staying within these boundaries can evoke familiarity and comfort, drawing audiences into a world they understand and enjoy. However, directors also have the creative latitude to innovate and subvert genre norms, injecting fresh perspectives and unexpected twists that elevate the viewing experience. Skillful deviations from genre conventions can captivate audiences by defying predictability, adding depth to characters, and encouraging deeper engagement. Nonetheless, directors must tread carefully to maintain a balance between genre suitability and audience expectations, as straying too far from established norms might risk alienating viewers. Ultimately, the director's mastery lies in orchestrating a delicate dance between genre conventions and creative freedom, ensuring that the film resonates while offering a refreshing perspective that satisfies both traditional expectations and the desire for novel storytelling.

Adapting Source Material: The Director's Balancing Act in Cinematic Storytelling

Adapting novels, plays, or real-life events into film scripts is a delicate process that involves preserving the source material's essence while effectively translating it to the visual and narrative medium. Directors must condense the original content, making creative choices like altering timelines, merging characters, and adjusting plot structures, all while retaining the core message and spirit. Their role is to capture the narrative's essence and utilize cinematic tools to enhance its impact, evoking emotions and engaging the audience. This adaptation process requires a deep understanding of the strengths and limitations of both literature or historical events and cinema. Successful directors maintain the original's integrity while crafting a cinematic experience that resonates with audiences.

Collaborative Script Development: Crafting a Compelling Narrative Through Creative Exchange

The process of script development is inherently collaborative, involving a dynamic interplay of creative minds such as writers, directors, and producers. Through a series of drafts and revisions, the script evolves as each collaborator contributes their insights and expertise. Writers infuse the initial concept with characters, dialogue, and narrative structure, while directors bring their vision for visual storytelling and pacing. Producers provide feedback based on market trends, feasibility, and budget considerations. This iterative process of refinement ensures that the script's nuances are enriched and its coherence solidified. The back-and-forth exchange of ideas, viewpoints, and expertise contributes to a robust and well-rounded final script that encompasses the best of all perspectives. This collaborative spirit underscores the importance of teamwork in crafting a compelling story that resonates with audiences while meeting commercial and artistic objectives.

Eternal Scripts: The Timeless Power of Cinematic Storytelling

Films endowed with strong scripts have the remarkable ability to transcend their immediate era and continue to captivate audiences across generations. A well-crafted script, rich in storytelling depth, relatable characters, and meaningful themes, resonates with universal human experiences, making it timeless and enduring. These films are not merely confined to their original release; they become cultural touchstones that continue to be celebrated, analyzed, and referenced, shaping the evolution of cinematic storytelling. Their impact goes beyond individual viewing experiences to influence storytelling trends and inspire filmmakers to strive for narrative excellence. Such scripts set a benchmark for aspiring writers and directors, showcasing the power of storytelling that withstands the test of time, leaving an indelible mark on the cinematic landscape and contributing to the enduring legacy of the medium.

A strong script is the backbone of successful Indian films, influencing emotional impact, character dynamics, and thematic depth. It guides the entire production and resonates with a diverse audience, encapsulating Indian culture and societal nuances. The script's dialogue, storytelling, and underlying messages evoke emotions, drive social conversations, and reflect the evolving Indian ethos. In Indian cinema, the script is the critical cornerstone, responsible for crafting compelling narratives that deeply engage viewers.

B. Collaborating with screenwriters to adapt stories for audiences

Cinematic Localization: Crafting Narratives for the Indian Audience

Recognizing the significance of cultural context and localization, filmmakers embark on a transformative journey to tailor narratives to resonate deeply with the Indian audience. This process involves more than mere translation; it entails a nuanced understanding of the cultural nuances, societal values, and norms that shape the local experience. Collaboration between directors and screenwriters becomes paramount, as it ensures that the storytelling remains authentic and relatable to the intended audience. By infusing Indian elements, traditions, and perspectives into the narrative fabric, filmmakers create a narrative landscape that feels familiar yet distinct, allowing viewers to connect emotionally and intellectually with the story's characters and situations. This intricate balance between global storytelling and localized authenticity is a testament to the directors' dedication to crafting narratives that find a meaningful place within the hearts and minds of their target audience.

Mastering Source Material Understanding: The Key to Effective Screenwriting Adaptation

Source Material Understanding is a critical facet of screenwriting, encompassing the profound exploration of a variety of source materials, such as books, plays, or real-life events, by screenwriters. In this intricate process, screenwriters delve beyond the superficial narrative to grasp the core essence, themes, emotions, and intricacies embedded within the source material. By meticulously dissecting and comprehending these underlying elements, screenwriters equip themselves with a comprehensive framework that guides the adaptation process. This understanding acts as a compass, steering the decisions in scriptwriting, character development, dialogue construction, and scene selection, ensuring that the adapted screenplay remains faithful to the essence of the source material while effectively accommodating the nuances of the visual medium. Thus, source material understanding emerges as the cornerstone of successful adaptation, enabling screenwriters to intricately weave the soul of the original work into the fabric of the cinematic narrative, fostering a compelling and resonant storytelling experience for the audience.

Preserving Core Themes: The Art of Adapting Narrative Essence in Screenwriting

Maintaining Core Themes involves a collaborative endeavour aimed at preserving the fundamental essence of a narrative's themes, emotions, and messages, ensuring their seamless transition from the source material to the adapted screenplay. In this intricate process, screenwriters collaborate closely with directors, producers, and fellow creative professionals to identify and extract the central elements that define the original story's depth and resonance. Through meticulous analysis, they distil these core themes and emotions, comprehending their significance within the narrative's context. This understanding guides the screenwriters in making informed decisions during the adaptation, from character arcs and dialogue to plot structure and visual representation. By harnessing their craft and leveraging the cinematic medium's unique tools, screenwriters adeptly transpose these pivotal themes into a new form, seamlessly interweaving them with the visual and auditory aspects of storytelling. This dedication to upholding the heart of the original narrative while respecting the demands of the cinematic medium ultimately leads to a powerful and resonant adaptation that honours the source material's intrinsic essence, effectively engaging audiences and conveying the story's enduring messages.

Harmonizing Narrative Adjustments and Pacing: Crafting the Indian Cinematic Experience

In Indian cinema, Narrative Adjustments and Pacing constitute a multifaceted process through which screenwriters adeptly reconfigure narratives to align with the distinct pacing and structural dynamics inherent in this cinematic tradition. Skilfully navigating the intricate interplay between cultural norms, audience expectations, and the constraints of film duration, screenwriters embark on a thoughtful journey of revaluation and adaptation. With an astute understanding of their target audience's preferences for immersive storytelling, screenwriters meticulously assess the original source material, identifying narrative threads that can be condensed or expanded without compromising the core essence. This process involves an intricate dance between retaining pivotal plot points, character developments, and thematic richness while seamlessly integrating song-and-dance sequences, dramatic dialogues, and emotional crescendos that are quintessential to Indian cinema. Through these nuanced narrative adjustments, screenwriters cater to the sensory and emotional sensibilities of the audience, crafting a rhythm that ebbs and flows harmoniously. This results in a captivating cinematic experience where the storyline remains coherent, emotionally resonant, and attuned to the expectations of Indian cinema enthusiasts, ultimately contributing to the distinctive tapestry of storytelling that characterizes the industry.

Character Transformation in Indian Cinema: Balancing Authenticity and Cultural Connection

In Indian cinema, character transformation is a complex process led by screenwriters who balance cultural sensitivity and creative finesse. They navigate the delicate task of adapting characters to connect with India's diverse audience, considering societal norms, history, and contemporary values. Motivations are adjusted to align with cultural values, making characters more relatable. Dialogues are crafted with linguistic nuances that capture regional tones and idioms, adding realism and depth. Character arcs are molded to incorporate personal growth within the context of Indian cinematic grandeur, including musical elements and dramatic climaxes. Screenwriters strive for a delicate balance between character evolution and cultural cohesion, creating personas that resonate globally while retaining their unique Indian identity, resulting in a cinematic experience that deeply connects with Indian society.

The Linguistic Tapestry: Navigating Language and Dialogues in Indian Cinema

Language and Dialogues constitute a multifaceted terrain where screenwriters navigate the intricate art of translation and cultural resonance, reflecting the unique challenges and opportunities of Indian cinema. Within this domain, screenwriters grapple with the intricate task of transposing dialogues and wordplay from their source material, while meticulously upholding cultural relevance and linguistic nuances. This endeavor involves transcending linguistic boundaries, capturing the essence of humor, emotion, and context in dialogues that seamlessly traverse from one language to another. The complexity lies in preserving the wit, idiomatic expressions, and regional flavor that imbue the original dialogues while ensuring that the adapted lines resonate with the diverse linguistic tapestry of India. This demands a profound understanding of regional dialects, socio-linguistic norms, and historical linguistic evolution. By adroitly harnessing the kaleidoscope of Indian languages, screenwriters embrace the intricate symphony of accents, vocabularies, and linguistic subtleties, enriching the characters' authenticity and the narrative's texture. Thus, the artistry of language and dialogues in Indian cinema resides in the screenwriters' ability to transcend linguistic barriers, interweaving eloquence and cultural resonance, and ultimately crafting a cinematic discourse that transcends linguistic diversity to strike a chord with audiences across the nation.

Visual Adaptation: Bridging the Gap Between Literature and Cinema

Visual Adaptation constitutes a dynamic partnership between screenwriters and directors, an intricate orchestration of creative vision that bridges the literature or other source materials with the cinematic canvas. In this collaborative endeavor, screenwriters work harmoniously with directors to meticulously transpose the vivid visual elements intrinsic to the source material into a visual language that resonates with the audience. This involves a delicate fusion of narrative fidelity and cinematic sensibilities, where screenwriters provide essential descriptive cues that enable directors to translate the ambience, settings, and atmospheres of the original work onto the screen. Challenges arise in the translation of elaborate descriptions and subtleties, requiring an artful balance between remaining faithful to the source material and allowing the visual medium to breathe life into the story. By distilling the essence of these descriptions and collaborating closely with directors, screenwriters contribute to the creation of visual worlds that amplify the narrative's emotional depth. This dynamic collaboration ultimately results in a harmonious convergence of literary imagination and cinematic ingenuity, enhancing the audience's engagement and providing a compelling visual rendition of the source material's essence.

Balancing Global and Local Appeal: Crafting Stories for Diverse Audiences in Indian Cinema

Balancing Global Appeal requires screenwriters to navigate the intricate interplay between preserving the story's universal resonance and tailoring it to resonate with the nuanced sensibilities of the Indian audience. In this delicate endeavor, screenwriters operate as cultural translators, deftly calibrating narrative elements to transcend geographical confines while staying true to the authenticity of the source material. They engage in a meticulous process of sifting through the narrative's thematic core and characters' emotional arcs, identifying elements that possess a universal human quality. By honing in on these aspects, screenwriters create a narrative framework that resonates across cultures, rendering the story's emotional landscape relatable to audiences worldwide. Simultaneously, screenwriters grapple with the task of integrating Indian cultural nuances, societal dynamics, and contextual elements that enrich the story's texture for local audiences. This process often involves infusing regional traditions, idiomatic expressions, and sociopolitical currents that resonate with Indian viewers without alienating international spectators. The challenge lies in striking a harmonious equilibrium that neither dilutes the global universality nor overwhelms with culturally specific references. Through this intricate navigation, screenwriters craft narratives that manage to be both internationally accessible and deeply resonant within the Indian context, fostering a storytelling tapestry that bridges cultures and fosters a shared narrative experience.

Creative Interpretation: Infusing Indian Culture into Screenwriting

Creative interpretation in screenwriting for Indian cinema involves skillfully adapting source material to resonate with Indian audiences by infusing it with a unique cultural essence. This process requires identifying narrative elements that can be transformed to align with local cultural norms, traditions, and societal contexts. Screenwriters incorporate culturally relevant nuances into characters' motivations, dialogues, and interactions. This creative infusion extends to settings, celebrations, and interpersonal dynamics, enriching the narrative's texture. By leveraging cultural touchpoints, screenwriters create an intimate connection between the story and the audience, offering a cinematic experience that is both globally resonant and distinctly Indian.

Collaborating with Authors: Translating Vision from Page to Screen

Engaging the Author's Vision encapsulates the collaborative dynamics between screenwriters and original authors, a symbiotic relationship that occasionally extends beyond the written page to the cinematic world. In cases where the authors are involved, screenwriters embark on a dialogue that honors the intrinsic essence of the source material while navigating the unique demands of the visual medium. This collaborative process can span from consultations on character motivations, thematic depth, and narrative intricacies to even more active roles such as co-writing or consulting on the adaptation. Authors bring invaluable insights into the subtext, emotional undercurrents, and thematic subtleties of their work, enabling screenwriters to seamlessly translate these elements into the cinematic language. Their input often results in a harmonious interplay between the core narrative and the film's visual execution, leading to a layered and resonant adaptation that retains the author's signature vision while embracing the transformative power of the cinematic experience.

Refining the Adapted Script: The Collaborative Journey of Feedback and Iteration

Feedback and Iteration epitomize the collaborative synergy among directors, producers, and screenwriters, culminating in a refined and polished adapted script. In this intricate dance, the screenwriter's initial draft serves as a blueprint that undergoes a dynamic evolution through the discerning lenses of the creative team. Directors contribute their visual acumen, envisioning how the narrative will unfold on screen, while producers offer perspectives grounded in market trends and audience preferences. As the adapted script is reviewed, a robust feedback loop emerges, facilitating a discourse that nurtures the narrative's growth. Revisions are informed by a synthesis of creative visions, aiming to harmonize thematic depth, pacing, character arcs, and cinematic feasibility. This iterative process of fine-tuning involves meticulous reshaping of dialogues, scenes, and structures, guided by a collective desire to sculpt a compelling cinematic experience. While at times this exchange may entail constructive debates, the amalgamation of perspectives enriches the storytelling tapestry. Through this collaborative alchemy, the adapted script evolves into a refined masterpiece, a testament to the collaborative spirit that propels it from the initial screenwriter's vision to a collective realization of cinematic excellence.

Innovative Twists and Enhancements: Elevating Adaptations with Creative Ingenuity

Innovative Twists and Enhancements exemplify screenwriters' artful ingenuity as they introduce novel elements to amplify the impact of an adaptation, infusing it with a distinct flair that resonates both with the source material and the cinematic medium. In select instances, screenwriters adeptly intertwine imaginative additions—be they new characters, subplots, or reinterpretations of existing elements—aligning seamlessly with the original narrative's essence while elevating its visual and emotional impact. These creative interventions often leverage the cinematic canvas to heighten drama, suspense, or emotional depth, providing unexpected surprises that captivate audiences anew. Such enhancements, when skillfully executed, create a layered storytelling experience that surprises, intrigues, and engages viewers on multiple levels. The screenwriter's ability to harmonize the familiar with the fresh, in service of the story's core, underlines their role as narrative architects who craft adaptations that not only honor the source material but also carve a unique niche within the cinematic landscape.

The collaboration between screenwriters, directors, and creative teams in adapting stories for Indian audiences is a nuanced process. It involves preserving the core essence of the source material while reimagining it within the context of Indian culture. This dynamic interplay transforms narratives into a form that resonates with the diverse and dynamic Indian audience, transcending linguistic and cultural barriers. Through this intricate dance of adaptation, storytelling becomes a bridge between different cultures, enriching the cinematic experience and forging a profound connection with the Indian audience.

Addressing Cultural Nuances and Societal Themes Through Scriptwriting

Cultural Authenticity in Scriptwriting: Forging Connections with Audiences

Cultural authenticity holds paramount significance in scriptwriting as it encompasses the meticulous depiction of cultural nuances, ensuring genuine representation and fostering a profound connection between narratives and audiences. By adeptly capturing the subtleties of a culture's language, traditions, social dynamics, and values, scripts not only avoid perpetuating stereotypes and misrepresentations but also elevate storytelling to a level where it becomes a mirror for the audience's own cultural identity. In this symbiotic relationship, audiences are not only entertained but also validated, as well-crafted narratives mirror their experiences and allow them to see their worldviews, struggles, and aspirations accurately reflected on screen. This resonance cultivates a powerful emotional engagement, enabling individuals to forge a stronger bond with the story and its characters, ultimately leading to a more profound and enduring impact.

Scripting Social Change: Films as Catalysts for Conversations on Pressing Issues

Scripts play a pivotal role in addressing and dissecting pressing societal challenges, functioning as potent catalysts that ignite conversations and bolster awareness. By skillfully interweaving narratives with pertinent social issues, scripts possess the capability to spotlight the intricacies of subjects like gender equality and caste dynamics, offering audiences a nuanced lens through which to view and comprehend these complexities. Films that delve into these themes not only shed light on the often-neglected aspects of these issues but also challenge prevailing norms, biases, and injustices, thus prompting viewers to question and reevaluate their own perspectives. Through authentic character portrayals, gripping plotlines, and thought-provoking dialogues, such scripts can cultivate empathy, empathy, and introspection, driving viewers to engage in vital dialogues that propel societal transformation.

Character Contextualization: Weaving Cultural Authenticity into Script Narratives

The contextualization of characters within scripts involves a profound analysis of how their backgrounds and interactions intricately mirror the tapestry of cultural norms and values. By meticulously crafting characters that resonate with their cultural milieu, scripts unveil a vivid portrayal of how familial relationships, traditions, and interactions are inextricably interwoven within their specific cultural contexts. This portrayal not only captures the nuances of interpersonal dynamics but also provides a lens through which audiences can glimpse the intricate web of values and beliefs that shape characters' decisions and behaviors. As characters navigate their lives within the framework of their cultural backdrop, the script masterfully showcases how external influences and internal convictions intersect, highlighting the delicate balance between individual aspirations and societal expectations. This contextual authenticity not only enriches the narrative's depth but also invites audiences to immerse themselves in a world that resonates with their own experiences and cultural identities, fostering a powerful connection between the characters and the viewers.

Linguistic Tapestry: Enriching Scripts with Regional Authenticity and Nuances

The strategic employment of language and dialects within scripts serves as a gateway to capturing regional authenticity, enriching the narrative with a tapestry of linguistic nuances. By deftly incorporating local languages and dialects, scripts infuse the story with an authentic flavor that resonates deeply with the cultural and geographical context, facilitating a more immersive experience for the audience. These linguistic choices go beyond mere dialogue, encapsulating the essence of regional idioms, colloquialisms, and expressions that not only reflect the characters' backgrounds but also enhance their relatability and relatability and relatability and relatability and relatability and relatability and relatability to the audience. Moreover, the interplay of languages can contribute to the overarching ambiance of the narrative, setting the tone, and even symbolizing power dynamics, social hierarchies, or cultural clashes. In this intricate dance of words, the script leverages language as a powerful tool to evoke emotions, bridge cultural gaps, and foster a deeper connection between the narrative and its viewers, culminating in a storytelling experience that transcends linguistic boundaries.

Scripting the Past and Mythology: Layering Depth into Narrative Context

The incorporation of historical events or mythological references within scripts lends a profound layer of depth to narratives by weaving them into the fabric of the story. By seamlessly integrating these elements, scripts bridge the gap between the past and present, offering audiences a multidimensional perspective on societal narratives. Films that skillfully intertwine historical contexts or draw parallels with mythological themes not only transport viewers to different eras but also highlight the timeless essence of human experiences, struggles, and triumphs. These references can serve as poignant metaphors, shedding light on contemporary challenges by juxtaposing them against lessons from the past. In doing so, the script not only educates but also ignites critical discourse by encouraging audiences to ponder the relevance of history and mythology in shaping our collective identity. This interplay between history, mythology, and the present narrative creates a rich tapestry that not only entertains but also invites reflection, fostering a more profound engagement with the story's underlying messages and themes.

Celebrating Culture: Festivals as Heartfelt Narrative Elements

Films intricately capture the essence of cultural celebrations and festivals, infusing narratives with the vibrancy and emotion that accompany these cherished communal events. By meticulously recreating the sights, sounds, and rituals of these festivities, films transport audiences into the heart of cultural traditions, creating an immersive experience that resonates with viewers' cultural identities. These elements are more than mere set pieces; they serve as powerful tools that contribute to the film's atmosphere and storytelling. Festivals become pivotal backdrops that mirror characters' journeys, infusing pivotal moments with heightened emotion or catalyzing pivotal changes. The sights of jubilant crowds, the sounds of traditional music, and the depiction of age-old customs not only envelop the audience in a palpable ambiance but also deepen their connection to the characters and their arcs. Through these celebrations, films subtly communicate themes of unity, heritage, and shared values, inviting viewers to reflect on their own cultural legacies and prompting an emotional investment in the narrative's resolution.

Subtext and Symbolism: Unveiling Hidden Cultural Narratives in Film Scripts

The artful incorporation of subtext and symbolism within scripts offers a multi-layered approach to conveying profound cultural meanings, enriching narratives with hidden depths that engage astute audiences. Through the deft manipulation of subtext, scripts communicate underlying themes, cultural critiques, or societal commentary that may not be explicitly stated in the dialogue. Employing visual metaphors and allegorical storytelling, films transcend the surface plot, allowing for a more nuanced exploration of cultural nuances, beliefs, and values. These symbols can serve as a bridge between the conscious and subconscious, invoking visceral reactions and inviting introspection. By intertwining subtext and symbolism, scripts encourage viewers to embark on an intellectual and emotional journey, decoding hidden meanings and connecting them to their own cultural experiences. This narrative layering not only deepens the story's impact but also opens avenues for dialogue and interpretation, fostering a richer appreciation for the intricate tapestry of cultural narratives.

Amplifying Diversity and Voices in Film Scripts: Crafting Authentic and Inclusive Narratives

Incorporating diverse perspectives and voices within scripts is paramount as it enriches storytelling by mirroring the intricacies of the real world and promoting empathy among audiences. By weaving in a tapestry of viewpoints stemming from various cultural, social, and personal backgrounds, narratives become more authentic, relatable, and reflective of the multifaceted human experience. This inclusivity not only breaks down stereotypes and fosters understanding but also amplifies voices that have historically been sidelined. Films that give voice to marginalized communities serve as powerful mediums for shedding light on their struggles, achievements, and resilience. Works like "Moonlight," directed by Barry Jenkins, delve into the complexities of Black identity and sexuality, while "Parasite," directed by Bong Joon-ho, confronts class disparities. These films not only offer a platform for underrepresented stories but also contribute to a more comprehensive cinematic landscape that celebrates the full spectrum of human narratives.

Cultural Clashes and Synthesis in Film: Navigating Identities in a Globalized World

Narratives delving into cultural clashes and synthesis encapsulate the dynamic interplay between diverse societies, capturing the intricate dance of traditions, values, and ideologies in an increasingly interconnected world. Such stories, like "The Namesake" by Jhumpa Lahiri, illuminate the clash between generations rooted in their native culture and their offspring navigating the complexities of a new land. They expose the tensions arising from the juxtaposition of traditions, leading to both estrangement and growth, and yet, within these tensions lie opportunities for profound understanding and adaptation. Through works like "Bend It Like Beckham," directed by Gurinder Chadha, and "Crazy Rich Asians," directed by Jon M. Chu, the narratives unveil the potential for synthesis, where cultures blend and evolve, often resulting in unexpected harmonies. These stories mirror contemporary realities, showcasing the challenges of identity negotiation and the possibilities of harmonious coexistence, serving as mirrors reflecting the complexities of a globalized world while advocating for cross-cultural empathy and dialogue.

Evolution of Traditions in Film: Navigating Change While Preserving Cultural Heritage

Scripts that delve into the evolution of traditions intricately navigate the delicate balance between the preservation of cultural heritage and the inevitable shifts brought about by the winds of modernity. These narratives, often like "Fiddler on the Roof" by Joseph Stein, follow characters grappling with the changing times as long-standing customs intersect with contemporary realities. Through the lenses of these stories, the tension between the sanctity of tradition and the demands of progress become palpable, encapsulating the poignant struggles faced by communities seeking to uphold their roots while navigating the challenges of an ever-transforming world. Whether in "Coco," directed by Lee Unkrich, which illuminates the intersection of family bonds and ancestral reverence, or in "The Joy Luck Club," directed by Wayne Wang, which showcases the intricate connections between generations, these scripts magnify the intricacies of adaptation and resilience. These narratives not only depict the shifts in traditions but also highlight the enduring essence that can persist even as practices transform, offering insights into the ways in which societies grapple with change while staying anchored to their core values.

Unraveling the Struggle of Identity and Society: Narratives of Personal Desires and Societal Expectations in Literature and Film

Scripts that delve into the interplay between personal desires and societal expectations unravel the intricate tapestry of characters' journeys, often becoming mirrors to the universal struggle between individual identity and collective norms. These narratives, such as "Pride and Prejudice" by Jane Austen, delve into characters' battles to align their inner aspirations with the external pressures imposed by their cultures and communities. Through their narratives, the inherent tension between individual dreams and the weight of familial, cultural, or societal obligations is palpably showcased, often leading to internal conflict and external drama. Whether it's the clash between romance and duty as seen in "Romeo and Juliet" by William Shakespeare or the negotiation of career choices in the face of familial expectations as portrayed in "Bend It Like Beckham," directed by Gurinder Chadha, these scripts lay bare the emotional struggle and the complex decisions individuals face when striving to define their unique paths amidst established norms. Such stories not only shed light on the profound dilemmas characters confront but also offer a platform for audiences to contemplate their own experiences of identity, autonomy, and the intricate dance between personal fulfillment and collective responsibilities.

Timeless Mirrors: Scripts as Reflections of Evolving Societal Norms and Universal Human Struggles

Furthermore, these scripts often serve as mirrors reflecting the evolving societal norms and expectations of their respective eras. They capture the spirit of their times and, in doing so, provide a historical and cultural context that allows contemporary audiences to connect with the struggles and dilemmas of characters from different time periods. The narratives provide insights into the constraints, conventions, and prejudices that individuals grapple with and the ways in which they navigate these challenges. In essence, these scripts transcend their immediate narratives to become timeless tales of the human experience, resonating across generations. They invite audiences to question the extent to which societal expectations should influence personal choices, and to consider the complexity of the journey to self-discovery and the pursuit of individual dreams within the intricate fabric of the collective consciousness. In this way, they not only entertain but also offer profound opportunities for introspection, making them enduring and cherished pieces of storytelling.

Films as Catalysts for Societal Change: Shaping Discourse, Fostering Empathy, and Mobilizing Action

Films that tackle cultural and societal themes wield the transformative power to catalyze tangible real-world impact and societal change. These narratives, serving as both mirrors and catalysts, possess the potential to ignite conversations, foster empathy, and mobilize collective action. Works like "12 Years a Slave," directed by Steve McQueen, or "Schindler's List," directed by Steven Spielberg, transcend their cinematic boundaries to reshape public discourse, amplifying awareness about historical injustices and human rights. Furthermore, films like "An Inconvenient Truth," directed by Davis Guggenheim, have been instrumental in shifting the environmental dialogue and policy-making. By authentically portraying marginalized voices and inciting empathy, these films have triggered social movements, policy revisions, and a heightened global consciousness. In doing so, they underscore the unique role that storytelling and visual artistry play in shaping society, motivating individuals to confront uncomfortable truths, challenge established norms, and strive collectively for a more equitable and just world.

The art of scriptwriting holds a profound power to address cultural nuances and societal themes, serving as a driving force in shaping public perceptions and fostering vital dialogue. Through the creation of authentic characters, thought-provoking narratives, and resonant storytelling, scripts become potent vehicles for the exploration of cultural richness and the illumination of complex societal issues. They offer a window into diverse worlds, providing audiences with a deeper understanding of the multifaceted tapestry of human experiences, traditions, and challenges. Moreover, scripts have the potential to bridge gaps of understanding, create empathy, and provoke conversations about important topics, thereby acting as catalysts for positive change and social growth. In essence, scriptwriting becomes a dynamic art form that not only entertains but also enlightens, providing a platform for cultural appreciation and the discussion of critical social matters.

CHAPTER - 8

8. The Art of Casting And Character Development

The art of casting and character development in Indian films is a complex and essential process that contributes significantly to compelling cinematic narratives. Casting directors seek performers who not only match the physical attributes but also embody the depth and versatility required for their roles. Given India's diverse cultural landscape, casting involves a nuanced understanding of regional sensibilities and cultural diversity.

Character development is intertwined with casting, as writers and directors craft intricate backstories and motivations, shaping the characters' personalities and arcs. This process extends to supporting and ensemble characters, enriching the storytelling's authenticity.

Authentic and well-developed characters are vital in Indian cinema, driving emotional engagement and resonance with the audience. Exploring human emotions, relationships, and societal dynamics within the Indian context is at the core of character development, reflecting the evolving cultural and social landscape of the country. The successful marriage of casting and character development defines the cinematic experience in India.

A. The Art of Casting and Selecting Actors

The Significance of Character Alignment in Indian Cinema: Elevating Authenticity and Impact

The significance of character alignment is strikingly evident in Indian cinema as well. In films like "Deewar," Amitabh Bachchan's portrayal of Vijay Verma perfectly aligns with the character's righteous anger and determination, leaving an indelible mark. Rajkummar Rao's role in "Shahid" showcases his exceptional alignment with the real-life character, adding authenticity to the story. Ranveer Singh's performance in "Bajirao Mastani" captures the essence of the historical figure, while Vidya Balan's role in "Kahaani" is both convincing and emotionally resonant. Aamir Khan's dedication to his character in "Lagaan" transforms the film into a memorable sports drama. These examples illustrate how well-matched actors in Indian cinema can elevate the authenticity and impact of a story, making it relatable and emotionally resonant for audiences.

Physical Transformations in Indian Cinema: Dedication, Authenticity, and the Art of Character Portrayal

In Indian cinema, actors have also displayed an unwavering commitment to their craft by undergoing remarkable physical transformations to authentically portray characters. A notable example is Aamir Khan's stunning metamorphosis for his role in "Dangal," where he transformed his physique to convincingly portray an aging wrestler. Khan gained a significant amount of weight to embody the character's later years and then shed it to depict the wrestler in his prime, showcasing the dedication required to authentically convey the character's journey. Another striking instance is Randeep Hooda's portrayal of Sarabjit Singh in the biographical drama "Sarbjit." Hooda underwent a drastic weight loss to accurately depict the physical toll of imprisonment on the character. Priyanka Chopra's commitment to her role as the legendary boxer Mary Kom involved intensive training to emulate the physical strength and agility of the champion. Furthermore, Ranbir Kapoor's striking physical resemblance to Sanjay Dutt in "Sanju" contributed significantly to the film's immersive experience, enhancing the believability of the character's life journey. These examples from Indian cinema underscore how actors harness their physical attributes to enrich their performances, adding depth and authenticity to the characters they portray, while exemplifying their unwavering dedication to faithfully interpreting the essence of the roles they inhabit.

Emotional Depth in Indian Cinema: Forging Lasting Connections Through Authentic Performances

In Indian cinema, too, actors have showcased their exceptional ability to infuse characters with emotional depth, forging a profound connection with audiences. A standout example is Irrfan Khan in "The Lunchbox," where he portrays a lonely office worker with subtlety and grace, eliciting empathy for his character's quiet yearning and solitude. Deepika Padukone's portrayal of a woman dealing with depression in "Chhapaak" is another poignant instance, as she channels the character's pain and resilience with authenticity, shedding light on an important social issue. Additionally, Rajkummar Rao's versatile performances in films like "Trapped" and "Shahid" showcase his ability to embody a wide range of emotions, drawing viewers into the intricate emotional journeys of his characters. These Indian actors, like their international counterparts, demonstrate the profound impact of authentic emotional expression, forging a deep and lasting connection between the audience and the narratives they bring to life on screen.

Cultural Alignment in Indian Cinema: Enriching Narratives Through Authentic Casting

In Indian cinema, casting actors with cultural alignment has been a significant practice that enriches storytelling with authenticity. Films like "Lagaan," directed by Ashutosh Gowariker, stand as prime examples where the cast's cultural background plays a pivotal role in enhancing the narrative. In this epic sports drama set during the British Raj, the actors' deep understanding of rural Indian life, language, and customs is palpable, bringing an unparalleled depth to their portrayals. Similarly, in "Dilwale Dulhania Le Jayenge," directed by Aditya Chopra, the lead actors Shah Rukh Khan and Kajol, both of whom have strong roots in Indian culture, infuse their characters with an innate understanding of the diaspora experience, resonating with millions of Indians living abroad. These instances illustrate how cultural alignment between actors and their characters not only lends authenticity but also allows for a more profound exploration of cultural nuances, ultimately fostering a stronger connection between the audience and the narratives that reflect their own cultural heritage.

Language Mastery in Indian Cinema: Elevating Character Authenticity Through Dialects and Languages

In Indian cinema, the mastery of dialects and languages specific to characters is a hallmark of exceptional performances, enriching the storytelling experience. A prime example can be found in the film "Pakeezah," directed by Kamal Amrohi, where the legendary actress Meena Kumari impeccably portrayed the character Sahibjaan, a courtesan with a refined Urdu-speaking background. Meena Kumari's command over the Urdu language and her ability to convey the character's emotions and struggles through her diction and dialogue delivery added a layer of authenticity that resonated deeply with the audience. Similarly, in "Gangs of Wasseypur," directed by Anurag Kashyap, the ensemble cast adeptly navigated the Bihari dialect, immersing themselves in the linguistic nuances of the region and creating characters that felt rooted in the cultural fabric of Bihar. These instances highlight how linguistic mastery in Indian cinema serves as a bridge connecting characters to their cultural and linguistic backgrounds, allowing audiences to engage more deeply with the narrative and its emotional resonance.

Method Acting in Indian Cinema: Crafting Authentic Characters Through Research and Dedication

Method acting, enriched by thorough research, is a testament to the commitment of actors to bring their characters to life with unparalleled authenticity, transcending the boundaries of the script. Indian cinema, too, has witnessed remarkable instances of method acting and diligent research. A striking example is Aamir Khan's portrayal of Mahavir Singh Phogat in "Dangal," directed by Nitesh Tiwari. Khan underwent a rigorous physical transformation, gaining weight to portray the character accurately. He also delved deep into the sport of wrestling, training extensively to authentically depict the struggles, dedication, and aspirations of a wrestler. His meticulous approach, coupled with the physical and emotional dedication he poured into the role, resonated profoundly with the audience and contributed to the film's massive success. Similarly, in "Bhaag Milkha Bhaag," directed by Rakeysh Omprakash Mehra, Farhan Akhtar underwent intensive physical training and immersed himself in the life of the legendary athlete Milkha Singh. These Indian examples mirror the transformative potential of method acting, where actors, through their meticulous preparation and commitment, breathe life into characters, forging a connection with the audience that goes beyond mere performance.

Believable Chemistry: Iconic Actor Pairings in Indian Cinema

The establishment of believable chemistry and interactions between well-cast actors is indeed a pivotal element of a narrative's emotional resonance, and Indian cinema has witnessed several remarkable instances of such on-screen chemistry. One notable example is the pairing of Shah Rukh Khan and Kajol in films like "Dilwale Dulhania Le Jayenge" and "Kabhi Khushi Kabhie Gham." Their effortless camaraderie and palpable chemistry have made them one of Indian cinema's most iconic on-screen couples, evoking both romance and relatability. Similarly, the father-son relationship depicted by Amitabh Bachchan and Hrishikesh Mukherjee in "Anand" showcased a heartwarming bond that left a lasting impact on audiences. These Indian film examples illustrate how well-matched actors can bring characters' relationships to life, making them not just a part of the story but a reflection of the genuine human connections that resonate deeply with viewers, ultimately contributing to the enduring appeal of these films.

Period Authenticity: Casting in Historical Roles in Indian Cinema

Casting actors in historical or period roles presents a multifaceted challenge, requiring a delicate balance between embodying characters' essence and adhering to historical accuracy. Navigating the complexities of time, culture, and societal norms demands actors who can not only bring characters to life but also authentically transport audiences to a bygone era. Attention to historical accuracy is crucial, as it extends beyond physical appearance and encompasses behaviors, dialects, and social contexts specific to the period. Films like "Lagaan," directed by Ashutosh Gowariker, exemplify this commitment, with Aamir Khan and the ensemble cast capturing not only the physicality but also the mannerisms, language, and cultural nuances of characters set in colonial India. Such meticulous casting not only enhances the film's veracity but also allows viewers to engage more deeply with the narrative, immersing themselves in an intricately reconstructed world that enriches their understanding of history, culture, and the timeless human experience.

The Art of Subtle Expressions: Crafting Authentic Performances in Indian Cinema

Actors infuse their performances with a profound layer of authenticity through the mastery of subtle expressions and nuanced gestures, which mirror authentic emotions and reactions. These microcosmic details, often imperceptible yet deeply resonant, serve as windows into characters' inner worlds, forging a genuine connection between the portrayed emotions and the audience's own experiences. Such finesse in acting is exemplified by performances like Amitabh Bachchan's portrayal of Anthony Gonsalves in "Amar Akbar Anthony," where the subtleties in his expressions convey a wide range of emotions, or Irrfan Khan's nuanced acting in "The Lunchbox," which captures the complexity of human connections through subtle glances and gestures. These delicate expressions can reveal unspoken intentions, suppressed fears, or the nuances of relationships, enhancing the portrayal's depth and emotional resonance. By incorporating these minute yet powerful elements, actors unveil the multidimensionality of their characters, underscoring the intricate artistry that transforms acting into a reflection of the human psyche, creating performances that linger in the memory and echo the profound intricacies of life itself.

Breaking the Mold: When Indian Actors Defy Expectations and Redefine Versatility

Casting against type, a strategic departure from an actor's familiar roles, often yields captivating performances that defy expectations and showcase their versatility. Instances of actors breaking their mold to embrace characters outside their comfort zones can result in transformative portrayals that expand their artistic horizons. This approach not only challenges actors to step into unfamiliar territories but also offers audiences a fresh perspective, breaking down preconceived notions. Examples like Aamir Khan's exceptional transformation for his role in "Dangal," where he played a wrestler and underwent a significant physical change, or Vidya Balan's shift from glamorous roles to portraying strong, unconventional characters in films like "Kahaani" and "Tumhari Sulu," emphasize the extraordinary depth of talent these actors possess. These departures enable them to channel uncharted emotional nuances, embody different personas, and shed light on unexplored dimensions of their skills, culminating in performances that linger in cinematic memory and redefine their careers, illustrating how venturing beyond established typecasts can lead to extraordinary revelations in the world of acting.

Chameleons of the Silver Screen: India's Versatile Actors Redefining the Art of Transformation

The remarkable ability of actors to adapt their personas across diverse genres and character types serves as a testament to their artistic prowess, enabling them to seamlessly transform into the heart of various narratives. Versatile actors, chameleonic in nature, possess an innate capacity to shed their own identities and fully embody the essence of characters, whether comedic, dramatic, heroic, or villainous. This fluidity allows them to transcend limitations, reshaping their physicality, mannerisms, and emotional dynamics to seamlessly blend with the demands of each role. Performers such as Irrfan Khan, who effortlessly transitions from intense dramatic roles in films like "The Lunchbox" to comedic roles in movies like "Piku," or Tabu, who excels in diverse roles ranging from a conflicted mother in "Haider" to a mysterious spy in "Andhadhun," contribute immeasurably to the authenticity of various narratives. Their malleability injects layers of believability, enabling audiences to suspend disbelief and immerse themselves in stories that span the gamut of human experiences, showcasing the transformative power of acting at its finest.

Unveiling the Art of Casting Directors: Shaping Characters and Narratives in Filmmaking

Casting directors are the unsung heroes of the filmmaking process, playing a pivotal role in bringing a director's vision to life by meticulously identifying actors who seamlessly align with the characters envisioned in the script. Their expertise transcends the superficial aspects of appearance; instead, they delve deep into the art of recognizing talents that can authentically breathe life into the characters, navigating the complex intricacies of emotions, dynamics, and intentions. Their discerning eye and creative insight are honed through years of experience, and it is their responsibility to sift through a vast and diverse pool of performers to handpick individuals whose potential to inhabit roles with depth and resonance is readily apparent.

The Artistic Alchemy of Casting Directors: Crafting Cohesive Narratives and Authentic Performances

The work of casting directors goes beyond mere selection; they are the architects of a harmonious convergence between the written characters and the actors who will bring them to life. Their artistry lies in understanding the director's interpretation of the narrative and identifying actors who can not only individually excel but also interact seamlessly, coalescing into a cohesive and captivating narrative mosaic. In essence, casting directors sculpt the very foundation upon which authentic, compelling, and emotionally resonant performances are built. They contribute to the chemistry within the ensemble cast, ensuring that the interactions between characters feel genuine and immersive. Through their tireless dedication and the finesse with which they match actors to their roles, casting directors wield a profound influence over the very heart of cinematic storytelling, contributing to the magic that unfolds on the silver screen.

The art of casting goes beyond the mere selection of popular or well-known actors; it encompasses the intricate task of identifying individuals who possess the ability to infuse authenticity, emotional depth, and cultural resonance into the characters they portray. When actors seamlessly merge their skills, craft, and personal experiences with the essence of their roles, they elevate the film's authenticity and create narratives that resonate profoundly with audiences. This harmonious alignment between actors and their characters is a cornerstone of impactful storytelling, as it allows viewers to not only witness but also emotionally connect with the unfolding narrative. The result is a more immersive cinematic experience, where characters feel like real people with relatable struggles, aspirations, and dilemmas, making the storytelling more powerful and enduring.

B. Creating memorable characters that resonate with audiences

Relatable Characters and Universal Emotions: Bridging Lives Through Indian Cinema

The interplay between relatable traits and universal emotions within characters renders them accessible touchpoints for a diverse audience, engendering a profound sense of connection and empathy. Characters whose experiences mirror those of viewers establish a unique bridge between the on-screen narrative and the personal lives of the audience. Instances like the coming-of-age struggles depicted in "Wake Up Sid" or the exploration of love and identity in "Dil Chahta Hai" resonate deeply because they evoke emotions and scenarios familiar to many. These characters act as conduits for audiences to explore their own feelings and experiences, allowing them to witness their own lives through the lens of another. This relatability endows characters with authenticity, blurring the line between fiction and reality, and engendering a profound resonance that transforms storytelling into a shared human experience, illustrating the remarkable ability of cinema to bridge diverse lives and unite them under the umbrella of universal emotions and experiences within the context of Indian cinema.

Cultural Specificity in Character Creation: Crafting Authentic Narratives in Indian Cinema

Cultural specificity in character creation is essential in Indian cinema to establish familiarity and authenticity. By incorporating language, attire, festivals, and social norms into characters, storytellers create relatable figures that resonate deeply with the audience. This immersion in cultural nuances strengthens the audience's connection to the characters, making them see their own lives reflected in the narrative. Characters like Piku from "Piku" and Murad from "Gully Boy" exemplify this authenticity, bridging the gap between the cinematic world and the viewers' realities. Cultural specificity fosters emotional engagement, turning characters into symbolic representations of the audience's cultural identity.

Exploring Flaws and Vulnerabilities: Crafting Multifaceted Characters in Indian Cinema

Endowing characters with flaws and vulnerabilities is essential in sculpting multidimensional personas that reflect the complexity of the human experience. These imperfections serve as windows into characters' inner struggles, insecurities, and growth arcs, making them remarkably relatable and evoking profound empathy from audiences. Characters like Aman Mathur in "Kal Ho Naa Ho" or Kabir Khan in "Chak De! India" illustrate this depth, as their personal challenges, insecurities, and evolving perspectives highlight their humanity, rendering them three-dimensional and compelling. By portraying characters with flaws, Indian cinema writers and creators cultivate a space for transformation, allowing them to journey from their weaknesses towards self-discovery and redemption. This journey resonates with viewers who identify with the universal experience of navigating imperfection and adversity, forging an unbreakable connection that transcends fiction and solidifies the bond between the audience and the characters, thus underscoring how embracing flaws leads to storytelling that mirrors the intricate tapestry of real life within the context of Indian cinema.

Diverse Characters: The Vibrant Tapestry of Human Experience in Indian Cinema

Bestowing characters with distinct personalities and traits is the cornerstone of crafting a vibrant narrative tapestry that reflects the diversity and complexity of the human spectrum in the context of Indian cinema. By infusing each character with unique mannerisms, beliefs, quirks, and motivations, Indian filmmakers create an intricate web of relationships that mirrors the multifaceted nature of Indian society. These diverse personalities not only enhance the narrative's authenticity but also facilitate a dynamic interplay of dynamics, forging connections that drive the plot and infuse depth into interactions. Characters as varied as the introspective Rani in "Queen" or the relentless Kabir Khan in "Chak De! India" exemplify this diversity, as their individuality propels the storyline and provides viewers with a broad spectrum of perspectives to engage with. Thus, the significance of distinct personalities is immeasurable, as it crafts a rich tapestry of human experiences that resonates with Indian audiences, transcending the bounds of fiction to reflect the kaleidoscope of life itself within the context of Indian cinema.

Motivations and Goals: Driving Indian Cinema's Narrative Tapestry

Characters' motivations and goals are the engine propelling the plot in the context of Indian cinema, acting as catalysts that ignite the narrative's forward momentum. These driving forces, whether they stem from desires for love, justice, redemption, or social change, not only serve as the focal point of characters' arcs but also imbue the storyline with depth and complexity. By delving into characters' aspirations, dreams, and inner conflicts, Indian filmmakers craft multidimensional personas whose actions resonate with their core motivations, making their journeys compelling and relatable for Indian audiences. Characters like Rani in "Queen" or Murad in "Gully Boy" exemplify how these motives propel narratives, leading to internal transformations and external conflicts that grip viewers. The interplay between motivations and goals provides the canvas upon which characters evolve, as their pursuit of these objectives unveils their resilience, vulnerabilities, and growth, thereby shaping a tapestry of storytelling that mirrors the intricate pathways of human ambition and emotion in the context of Indian cinema.

Memorable Dialogues: Crafting Character Identities in Indian Cinema

Memorable dialogues and catchphrases serve as defining threads that intricately weave the fabric of character identity in Indian cinema, embedding distinct personality traits, emotions, and intentions into the very words they utter. These lines possess the power to encapsulate the essence of a character's beliefs, humor, or worldview, acting as verbal signatures that resonate long after the screen fades. Instances like Amitabh Bachchan's iconic "Don ko pakadna mushkil hi nahin, namumkin hai" from "Don" or Shah Rukh Khan's "Bade bade deshon mein aisi chhoti chhoti baatein hoti rehti hai, Senorita" from "Dilwale Dulhania Le Jayenge" exemplify how these lines transcend the script, becoming cultural touchstones that are universally recognized and evoke immediate associations with the characters who delivered them. The impact of such dialogues transcends the boundaries of fiction, imprinting themselves onto popular culture, becoming part of everyday discourse, and exemplifying how characters' voices can transcend the cinematic realm to become ingrained in the collective consciousness of Indian society at large.

Character Transformations: The Heartbeats of Journeys in Indian Cinema

Characters' growth arcs and transformations within Indian cinema often serve as the heartbeats that breathe life into their journeys, showcasing the profound impact of experiences on their personalities and perspectives. The evolution of characters not only propels the storyline but also adds layers of authenticity and relatability to their personas. As they navigate challenges, make choices, and confront their flaws, characters like Munna in "Munna Bhai M.B.B.S." or Geet in "Jab We Met" undergo metamorphoses that mirror the complexities of real life. These developmental trajectories unveil dimensions of characters that go beyond initial impressions, revealing their vulnerabilities, strengths, and ultimately their humanity. Through their transformations, characters become living embodiments of the themes and messages of the narrative, underscoring the dynamic nature of human experiences and crafting stories that resonate deeply with audiences who witness not just plots unfolding, but souls evolving.

The Power of Symbolic Characters: Unveiling Deeper Meanings in Literature

Symbolism involves the use of characters, objects, or elements within a literary work to represent deeper, abstract concepts or themes. When characters are analyzed as symbolic representations of larger themes or archetypes, it means that they embody universal, recurring patterns of human behavior and experiences. These archetypes, rooted in the collective unconscious, serve as recognizable prototypes that audiences can easily identify with and understand. For instance, a hero's journey can symbolize the path of self-discovery and growth. The choice of an innocent character may symbolize purity or vulnerability. These representations resonate with cultural and societal contexts as they tap into shared beliefs, values, and narratives prevalent in a particular time and place. The hero's journey might mirror a society's quest for progress, while the innocent character could embody society's yearning for a return to a simpler, more virtuous state. These symbolic characterizations thus offer a layered reading experience, inviting readers to explore both the individual character's narrative and its broader significance within the intricate web of cultural and societal interpretations.

Beyond Stereotypes: Crafting Multidimensional Characters in Literature

Navigating the terrain of character creation involves the delicate task of steering clear of stereotypes, which oversimplify and pigeonhole individuals based on preconceived notions. This challenge demands a nuanced approach wherein characters are crafted with depth and authenticity, transcending one-dimensional portrayals. Multidimensional characters that defy expectations are vital because they mirror the complexities of real people and offer a richer, more engaging narrative. By shattering stereotypes, authors not only avoid perpetuating harmful biases but also cultivate a broader understanding of diverse perspectives. These multifaceted characters possess internal conflicts, evolving motivations, and diverse traits that mirror the intricacies of human nature. Through them, readers can grapple with a more truthful reflection of the world, prompting empathy, dismantling misconceptions, and fostering a greater appreciation for the vast spectrum of identities and experiences.

Interpersonal Dynamics: The Heart of Narrative Connection

Interpersonal dynamics within a narrative weave a crucial tapestry, anchoring the story in relatable human experiences. Characters' relationships and interactions serve as a driving force, propelling plot developments, revealing hidden facets, and igniting emotional resonance. These dynamics not only mirror the intricate web of connections in reality but also amplify the narrative's impact by infusing it with authenticity and depth. Through conflicts, alliances, romances, and rivalries, readers witness the characters' vulnerabilities, desires, and growth. Memorable moments are born from the clash and convergence of these intricate bonds, enriching the narrative with tension, catharsis, and revelation. The emotional connections formed between characters and readers stem from shared empathetic responses to love, loss, camaraderie, and discord, fostering a profound investment in the unfolding story. As these interpersonal dynamics unfold, readers find a mirror to their own relationships and a gateway to understanding the complexities of human connections, making the narrative both a mirror and a lens through which they explore their own emotional landscapes.

Diverse Characters: Reshaping Perceptions and Fostering Inclusion in Narratives

The presence of characters from diverse backgrounds within a narrative landscape holds the power to reshape societal norms and perceptions through enhanced social representation. When characters authentically embody a range of identities, experiences, and cultures, they challenge stereotypes, broaden perspectives, and foster a more inclusive understanding of the world. By presenting characters from marginalized or underrepresented groups, narratives become mirrors that reflect the multifaceted realities of society, validating the existence and narratives of individuals who have historically been sidelined. This kind of representation holds a profound positive influence as it offers individuals, especially those belonging to these groups, the opportunity to see themselves authentically portrayed on screen. This validation and visibility not only provide a sense of belonging and empowerment but also counter feelings of isolation and erasure, enabling audiences to form meaningful connections with characters and narratives. In turn, this can encourage empathy, promote understanding, and spark meaningful dialogues that contribute to broader social change, fostering a more equitable and compassionate society.

Empowering Characters: Inspiring Resilience, Courage, and Determination in Audiences

Characters imbued with qualities like resilience, courage, and determination serve as powerful conduits of audience engagement and empowerment. When characters overcome adversities and navigate complex situations, they not only resonate deeply with viewers but also evoke a sense of relatability and inspiration. These characters become beacons of hope and sources of encouragement, demonstrating that challenges can be confronted and conquered through tenacity and inner strength. Their journeys often parallel real-life struggles, offering audiences a sense of validation and the belief that they, too, can surmount obstacles. As viewers witness characters surmounting seemingly insurmountable odds, they vicariously experience the emotional transformation of triumph over adversity, fostering a personal connection that transcends fiction. These characters serve as role models, igniting a spark within the audience to confront their own challenges with renewed resolve. By fostering empathy and reminding audiences of their own capacity for growth, these characters inspire real-world change and encourage viewers to embrace their own agency in shaping their destinies.

Creating memorable characters involves a blend of relatability, depth, uniqueness, and cultural authenticity. When characters resonate with Indian audiences, they become more than just figures on screen; they become conduits through which viewers experience emotions, connect with themes, and explore the human experience in a way that is both personal and universal.

C. Balancing star power with character-driven storytelling

Character-Centric Storytelling: The Heart of Indian Cinema

Character-centric storytelling stands at the heart of Indian cinema, emphasizing the profound impact of well-crafted characters and their transformative journeys. Indian filmmakers recognize that strong characters are the emotional anchors of their narratives, capable of resonating deeply with audiences. These characters are not mere protagonists but vessels through which the complexities of human existence are explored. Their well-developed arcs serve as emotional compasses, guiding viewers through the vicissitudes of joy, sorrow, triumph, and adversity. Audiences become emotionally invested in these characters, witnessing their growth, transformation, and inner conflicts. This emotional engagement transcends cultural boundaries, forming a universal bridge between the screen and the spectator. Whether it's the hero's quest for justice, the heroine's resilience against societal norms, or the antagonist's journey towards redemption, Indian cinema thrives on character-driven storytelling that fosters empathy, introspection, and a profound connection between the storytellers and their audience.

The Impact of Star Power: Elevating Characters in Indian Cinema

The infusion of star power into character-driven Indian films is a strategic masterstroke, elevating not just the appeal but also the authenticity and relatability of the characters on screen. Well-known actors bring their charisma, acting prowess, and established personas to their roles, instantly drawing audiences into the narrative. Their mere presence can transform characters into iconic figures, making them more engaging and memorable. The audience's familiarity with the actor's previous work and public persona often adds depth and nuance to their portrayal, making the characters more relatable and convincing. In many cases, star power enhances the authenticity of the characters, as the actors bring a wealth of experience and a deep understanding of their craft to their roles. This synergy between well-known actors and character-driven narratives creates a compelling cinematic experience, where the characters come alive with a blend of the actor's unique charisma and the writer's vision, forging a powerful connection between the audience and the characters they are watching unfold on screen.

Balancing Stardom and Character Depth: The Art of Filmmaking in Indian Cinema

Balancing character depth with the presence of a popular star in Indian cinema can be a delicate tightrope walk. The challenge lies in ensuring that the star's larger-than-life persona does not overshadow the intricacies and nuances of the character they are portraying. Directors must strike a delicate equilibrium between the actor's established image and the character's depth and complexity. They often achieve this by tailoring roles to align with the star's strengths and persona, but also by delving into the character's psyche, crafting layers that the actor can explore. In doing so, directors aim to harness the star's charisma to enhance the character's relatability while maintaining the character's integrity and emotional resonance. This delicate balance results in character-driven narratives where the star's presence elevates rather than detracts from the storyline, ultimately delivering a compelling cinematic experience where character depth and stardom coexist harmoniously.

Transformative Portrayals: Stars Redefining Themselves Through Character-Driven Indian Cinema

The involvement of stars in character-driven Indian cinema often leads to transformative portrayals that challenge both the actor's established on-screen image and the audience's perceptions. Renowned actors frequently embrace roles that push the boundaries of their comfort zones, embarking on a journey of character transformation. This willingness to shed their established personas and inhabit diverse, multifaceted characters demonstrates their commitment to their craft and their willingness to explore uncharted territories. Such transformations can be physical, emotional, or psychological, as actors undergo rigorous preparations, including changes in appearance, dialect, and behavior, to fully embody their characters. These immersive portrayals not only showcase the actors' versatility but also offer audiences a glimpse into their dedication to the art of storytelling. This mutual exploration between actors and their roles results in character-driven narratives that resonate deeply, challenging preconceived notions and leaving a lasting impact on both the actor's career and the audience's cinematic experience.

The Dynamic Interplay: Star Power and Character Depth in Indian Cinema

Star power plays a pivotal role in engaging audiences, particularly in character-driven narratives within Indian cinema. The allure of well-known actors draws viewers to the theaters, creating an initial connection between the audience and the characters they portray. Once this connection is established, the art lies in keeping viewers deeply invested in the characters' emotional journeys. Directors and writers employ various techniques, such as crafting compelling character arcs, introducing relatable conflicts, and orchestrating moments of emotional intensity. The characters' growth and transformation resonate with the audience, fostering empathy and emotional involvement. Viewers become active participants in the characters' struggles and triumphs, forming a profound connection that transcends the screen. This sustained engagement is a testament to the power of character-driven storytelling, where star power serves as the initial spark, and the emotional depth of the characters keeps the audience captivated until the closing credits roll.

Icons Beyond Stars: Unforgettable Characters in Indian Cinema

In character-driven Indian cinema, certain characters possess the remarkable ability to leave indelible impressions, regardless of the actor's star status. These characters are meticulously crafted, with layers of depth, relatability, and authenticity that transcend the actor portraying them. Such roles become emblematic not only of the film itself but also of the cultural and societal narratives they represent. Their impact extends beyond the screen, sparking discussions, influencing fashion trends, and even becoming touchstones of popular culture. Whether it's the resilient village woman fighting against social injustice, the charismatic rebel challenging the status quo, or the introspective artist navigating the complexities of life, these characters resonate deeply with audiences, forging emotional connections that endure long after the film has concluded. Their lasting impact underscores the importance of well-crafted roles that contribute significantly to a film's resonance and its enduring place in the annals of Indian cinema.

Harmonizing Artistry: The Director-Star Collaboration in Enriching Character-Driven Narratives in Indian Cinema

The collaboration between directors and stars in Indian cinema is a dynamic interplay of creativity that enriches character depth and narrative substance. Directors leverage their artistic vision and storytelling acumen to craft characters that resonate with the audience, while stars bring their unique charisma, acting prowess, and insights to breathe life into these roles. This partnership often involves open dialogues and creative exchanges, where directors encourage actors to contribute their perspectives and ideas, fostering a sense of ownership and authenticity in the portrayal. The blending of star power and creative insights infuses characters with complexity, making them more relatable and engaging. This collaborative synergy enhances character depth by delving into the nuances of their personalities, motivations, and emotional journeys. The result is character-driven narratives that not only captivate audiences but also reflect the harmonious blend of artistic vision and the transformative power of stellar performances.

Starry Encounters: Exploring Character Dynamics in Star-Studded Ensembles in Indian Cinema

Character dynamics play a pivotal role in driving the plot forward in Indian cinema, and when these dynamics involve star-studded ensembles, they can create intriguing and captivating narratives. The interactions and relationships between characters, often shaped by their individual backgrounds, motivations, and conflicts, provide the emotional core of character-driven storytelling. Star-studded ensembles bring a wealth of talent and charisma to these dynamics, intensifying the chemistry between characters and adding layers of complexity to their relationships. These interactions can range from the camaraderie of friends to the tensions within a family, from the clashes of ideologies to the blossoming of love. The presence of well-known actors in these ensembles elevates the dramatic stakes, making character-driven narratives all the more compelling. As these characters navigate their journeys and relationships, audiences become engrossed in the emotional intricacies of their interactions, ultimately becoming active participants in the unfolding drama.

Harmonious Ensemble: Balancing Character Spotlight in Indian Cinema's Character-Driven Narratives

Character-driven storytelling in Indian cinema excels in its ability to balance the spotlight among various characters, allowing each to shine within the narrative's framework. While stars often bring their substantial presence to the screen, collaboration takes precedence over overshadowing. Ensemble casts frequently consist of accomplished actors who understand the importance of serving the narrative and its thematic depth. This collaborative spirit ensures that characters are not only well-defined but also contribute meaningfully to the overarching story. Directors adeptly distribute moments of focus and character development, allowing each actor to explore their role's nuances and emotional depths. As a result, viewers are treated to a symphony of performances, each character leaving a unique imprint on the audience's cinematic experience. This harmonious balance between star power and narrative serves as a testament to the artistry and professionalism of Indian cinema, where the story takes precedence over individual stardom.

Navigating Expectations: The Art of Leveraging Star Power in Character-Driven Indian Cinema

Audiences often come to star-driven films with specific expectations, anticipating the charisma and star power of their favorite actors. Directors in character-driven Indian cinema understand this familiarity and use it to their advantage. They leverage the audience's preconceived notions of their stars' personas and qualities to create characters that resonate on a deeper level. By subtly subverting or enriching these expectations, directors craft characters that surprise, engage, and challenge viewers. This approach allows for a symbiotic relationship between the actor's established image and the character's complexity. Audiences are drawn in by the familiar star presence but are then pleasantly taken aback by the character's depth and emotional journey. This interplay between expectations and narrative innovation elevates the character-driven storytelling experience, making it a compelling blend of audience anticipation and creative exploration.

The Perfect Alignment: When Stars and Characters Merge in Character-Driven Indian Cinema

In character-driven Indian cinema, there are instances where stars align perfectly with the characters they portray, creating a seamless synergy that enhances the narrative. When casting choices align with the essence of the character, it can result in performances that transcend the screen. Actors who naturally embody the traits, emotions, and nuances of their characters bring an unparalleled authenticity to their roles. This synergy between actor and character resonates with audiences on a profound level, allowing viewers to immerse themselves fully in the character's journey. Whether it's the intense dedication of an actor to a physically demanding role, the innate charm of a star aligning with a charismatic character, or the emotional depth they bring to a complex role, these instances of perfect alignment elevate character-driven narratives to a realm of cinematic excellence, leaving a lasting impact on the audience's collective memory.

The Timeless Allure: How Character-Driven Indian Cinema Transcends Trends and Endures Through Generations

Character-driven films in Indian cinema often possess a remarkable endurance, standing the test of time and remaining relevant despite changing industry trends. The enduring quality of such films lies in the strength of the characters themselves. Well-developed characters with relatable emotions, flaws, and aspirations resonate with audiences across generations. Their universal themes and timeless narratives continue to captivate viewers, making these films enduring classics. The emotional connection that audiences forge with these characters transcends the superficial trends of the industry, ensuring that these films retain their appeal over the years. Moreover, the memorable performances by actors who have brought these characters to life leave an indelible mark on cinematic history. As a result, character-driven films maintain their relevance and continue to be celebrated, serving as a testament to the enduring power of well-crafted characters in Indian cinema.

Balancing star power with character-driven storytelling is an intricate dance that demands a delicate touch from directors in the realm of filmmaking. It involves the art of harnessing the charisma and popularity of well-known actors, often referred to as "stars," while concurrently upholding the integrity of well-crafted, multi-dimensional characters within the narrative. This delicate equilibrium is crucial in ensuring that the allure of star actors does not overshadow the essence of the story or compromise the authenticity of the characters. When successfully executed, this harmonious convergence of star power and character-driven storytelling gives rise to films that resonate deeply with audiences. It draws viewers into emotionally charged, relatable, and immersive cinematic experiences, where they not only appreciate the performances of their favorite actors but also connect with the struggles, emotions, and dilemmas of the characters they portray. In this way, the dynamic interplay between star power and storytelling enriches the cinematic landscape, creating narratives that are not only commercially successful but also artistically meaningful and emotionally resonant.

CHAPTER - 9

9. Essential Pre-Production Steps

A. The Intricacies of Pre-Production Planning

Essential Pre-Production Elements: Crafting a Film's Foundation

The process of script development and selection in Indian cinema is a critical and intricate one, where numerous factors must align to create a compelling narrative. It often begins with the director's vision, a creative concept, or a story idea that resonates with them. From there, writers collaborate closely with the director, taking into account market trends, audience expectations, and the film's intended genre and tone. The script is meticulously crafted, with attention to character development, plot intricacies, and thematic depth. This collaborative effort also involves input from producers, who play a pivotal role in ensuring the script is not only artistically sound but also financially viable. Together, the creative team works to strike a balance between artistic integrity and commercial appeal, with the goal of producing a script that captivates audiences while meeting the demands of the industry. This process of script development and selection sets the foundation for the entire filmmaking journey, emphasizing the importance of a well-crafted narrative in Indian cinema.

Behind the Scenes: Navigating the Intricate Process of Budgeting and Financing in Indian Film Production

The budgeting and financing of an Indian film production is a meticulous and multi-faceted process. It begins with the estimation of the budget required for the entire production, taking into account various elements such as pre-production, location costs, actor salaries, crew expenses, visual effects, marketing, and distribution. Once the budget is determined, filmmakers embark on securing funding from a variety of sources. Producers often play a central role in providing financial backing, investing their resources into the project.

Studios and production houses may also get involved, especially in larger-scale productions. Additionally, filmmakers seek investments from individual investors or financiers who believe in the project's potential for success. In some cases, distributors may advance funds for distribution rights, helping to offset production costs. The combination of these financial sources, along with careful budgeting and financial planning, ensures that the film has the necessary resources to bring the director's vision to life while also meeting the economic realities of the industry. This intricate process of budgeting and financing is crucial to the successful execution of Indian cinema projects.

The Art of Casting: Selecting the Right Talents to Bring Characters to Life in Indian Cinema

The casting and talent acquisition process in Indian cinema is a meticulous and crucial aspect of filmmaking, driven by the need to find actors who can embody the characters authentically and bring the director's vision to life. Casting directors play a pivotal role in this process, collaborating closely with the director to identify suitable talents. They meticulously review portfolios, conduct auditions, and assess actors' suitability for specific roles based on their acting skills, physical appearance, and emotional depth. In the context of character-driven storytelling, casting becomes even more critical, as the success of the film often hinges on the audience's emotional connection with the characters. This process involves not only selecting lead actors but also supporting cast members, ensuring that each role contributes to the overall narrative cohesively. The collaboration between casting directors, directors, and producers is instrumental in assembling a talented ensemble that can breathe life into the characters and make them relatable to the audience. It's a process where the choice of actors can profoundly impact the film's success, making casting and talent acquisition an art form in itself within the Indian film industry.

Creating Cinematic Worlds: The Art of Location Scouting and Set Design in Indian Cinema

The process of location scouting and set design in Indian cinema is a meticulous and creative endeavor that contributes significantly to the visual and thematic aspects of a film. Location managers, in collaboration with the director and production team, embark on a thorough search for appropriate filming locations that align with the script's requirements. This involves traveling to various regions, both urban and rural, to find settings that resonate with the narrative. Once suitable locations are identified, art directors and production designers come into play, working closely with the director to transform these spaces into authentic, cinematic settings. They pay meticulous attention to detail, ensuring that the sets not only reflect the visual aesthetics of the script but also convey the cultural and emotional nuances of the story. The collaboration between location managers, art directors, and production designers is instrumental in creating the immersive world in which the characters and story come to life. This intricate process showcases the importance of both real-world locations and meticulously crafted sets in Indian cinema, as they serve as the canvas on which the director's vision is realized.

Crafting the Visual Language: The Significance of Storyboarding and Shot Planning in Indian Cinema

Storyboarding and shot planning are essential steps in the filmmaking process that help translate the director's vision into a cohesive visual narrative. The creation of storyboards involves illustrating each scene with detailed drawings or digital renderings, providing a visual blueprint for how the director intends to frame and capture the action. This meticulous planning allows for a precise visualization of camera angles, compositions, and movements, ensuring that the visual storytelling aligns with the intended emotional impact of the scene. Shot planning, in conjunction with storyboarding, influences the overall visual aesthetics and narrative flow of the film. It helps determine whether a scene should be shot in a single take for a continuous and immersive experience or broken down into multiple shots for emphasis and dramatic effect. This collaborative process, involving the director, cinematographer, and other key members of the crew, ensures that every frame serves a purpose in advancing the story and engaging the audience visually. Storyboarding and shot planning, therefore, play a crucial role in shaping the cinematic language of Indian films, contributing to their artistic and narrative excellence.

Dressing the Part: The Art of Costume Design in Indian Cinema

Costume design and wardrobe selection in Indian cinema are integral components of the filmmaking process that contribute significantly to character development, authenticity, and visual storytelling. The meticulous process involves selecting costumes that not only align with the character's personality, role, and journey but also adhere to the film's time period and setting. Costume designers collaborate closely with the director to create a wardrobe that enhances character identity and complements the narrative. They consider factors such as colour symbolism, cultural nuances, and the emotional arc of the characters to make informed choices. Whether it's the opulent attire of historical epics or the contemporary fashion of modern dramas, costume designers play a pivotal role in ensuring that the characters' visual aesthetics resonate with the audience and contribute to their believability. This attention to detail in costume design adds depth to the characters and elevates the overall visual impact of Indian films, making it an essential aspect of the cinematic storytelling process.

Behind the Scenes: Crafting Cinematic Excellence through Crew Selection and Coordination in Indian Cinema

The process of assembling a skilled and efficient crew is a crucial aspect of filmmaking in India, involving meticulous selection of professionals across various departments. This includes cinematographers, sound engineers, editors, production designers, and many others, each contributing their expertise to bring the director's vision to life. The coordination among these individuals is vital to ensure the smooth logistics of production, from scheduling shoots at diverse locations to managing complex equipment setups. Additionally, collaboration between the director and department heads is essential to maintain a unified creative vision throughout the filmmaking process. This well-coordinated effort enables the seamless execution of the film's technical aspects, ensuring that the visual and auditory elements align with the narrative's emotional and storytelling requirements. In the Indian film industry, where diversity and complexity are inherent, effective crew selection and logistical planning play a pivotal role in delivering cinematic excellence to audiences.

Crafting Cinematic Excellence: The Art of Technical and Equipment Planning in Indian Filmmaking

The process of technical and equipment planning in Indian filmmaking involves meticulous consideration of various elements crucial for capturing the director's vision. This includes the selection and arrangement of technical equipment such as cameras, lighting setups, sound recording gear, and more. Cinematographers work closely with the director to determine the visual style that best suits the film, whether it's the grandeur of epic historical dramas or the intimate aesthetic of character-driven narratives. Lighting plays a pivotal role in setting the mood and atmosphere of scenes, and careful choices are made to ensure that it complements the emotional resonance of the story. Sound engineers, on the other hand, focus on capturing clear and immersive audio that enhances the audience's engagement with the characters and the plot. The seamless integration of these technical elements is essential for creating a cohesive cinematic experience that aligns with the storytelling needs, making it a critical component of Indian film production.

Legal and Contractual Formalities in Indian Filmmaking: Navigating the Path to a Trouble-Free Production

In Indian filmmaking, the process of legal and contractual formalities is a crucial aspect of ensuring a smooth and trouble-free production. Filmmakers must meticulously navigate the legal landscape, which includes securing rights for scripts, music, and any other copyrighted material. Contracts with actors, crew members, and other stakeholders must be drafted and finalized, outlining their roles, responsibilities, and compensation. Additionally, obtaining the necessary permits and clearances from relevant authorities is essential to avoid legal complications during production. This can encompass location permits, permissions for shooting in public spaces, and compliance with labor laws. Any oversight in these legal matters can lead to delays, disputes, or even legal actions that may disrupt the filmmaking process. Therefore, attention to legal and contractual formalities is paramount to the successful execution of Indian film projects.

Scheduling and Timeline Management in Indian Filmmaking: The Art of Efficient Production Planning

The process of scheduling and timeline management in Indian filmmaking is a meticulous and essential aspect of production planning. Filmmakers carefully map out the production schedule, considering various factors such as shooting sequences, locations, and the availability of cast and crew. Each day on set is meticulously planned to optimize productivity and minimize downtime. Adhering to the established timeline is critical for managing production costs and ensuring that the project stays on track. Delays can lead to increased expenses, which can have a cascading effect on the overall budget. Moreover, timely completion is crucial for meeting release deadlines and avoiding scheduling conflicts that can disrupt the availability of talent and post-production resources. Therefore, effective scheduling and adherence to timelines are paramount in the successful execution of Indian film projects, helping ensure both financial efficiency and artistic integrity.

The Art of Stunts and Special Effects in Indian Filmmaking: Crafting Spectacular Action Sequences

The planning and execution of stunts and special effects in Indian filmmaking are complex and crucial aspects of pre-production. Filmmakers engage in meticulous choreography and planning to ensure the safety of actors and stunt performers during action sequences. This includes assessing the physical requirements of each stunt, identifying potential risks, and implementing safety measures. Moreover, the coordination between stunt directors, performers, and the rest of the crew is essential for seamless execution. In parallel, the planning for special effects sequences, including visual and practical effects, is carried out to align with the script's requirements. This involves determining the technical equipment needed, such as pyrotechnics or CGI, and ensuring that these effects integrate seamlessly into the narrative. Proper planning and safety protocols are paramount, not only to protect the well-being of the cast and crew but also to achieve the desired visual impact and cinematic spectacle that Indian films are known for.

Pre-Production Harmony: The Key to a Seamless Filmmaking Process in Indian Cinema

Clear communication and collaboration are the linchpins of a successful pre-production phase in Indian filmmaking. It's essential that every department, from scriptwriters to costume designers, art directors, and technical crews, is on the same page regarding the director's vision and the film's overall objectives. Effective coordination among these departments ensures that all elements, whether it's the script, sets, costumes, or technical aspects like lighting and sound, align cohesively with the intended narrative and visual aesthetics. This synergy not only streamlines the transition from pre-production to production but also saves valuable time and resources by minimizing miscommunication and redundancy. In the collaborative and intricate world of Indian cinema, where films often involve large crews and extensive logistical planning, a well-orchestrated pre-production phase is pivotal for the successful execution of the final product on screen.

Pre-production planning is a meticulous and complex phase that lays the groundwork for the entire filmmaking process. The collaborative efforts of various departments, meticulous attention to detail, and adherence to schedules contribute to the successful execution of a film's creative vision.

B. Location scouting, production design and costume selection

Location Scouting:

The Crucial Role of Script Analysis in Filmmaking's Pre-Production Phase

Script analysis is a fundamental step in the pre-production process of filmmaking as it serves as the foundation upon which all other elements are built. It involves a comprehensive examination of the script to understand the specific settings and environments required for each scene. This analysis goes beyond just identifying locations; it delves into the emotional and thematic nuances of the script, determining how settings can contribute to the storytelling. It involves considering factors such as time periods, cultural contexts, and character interactions to ensure that the chosen locations and sets align with the director's vision and the overall narrative. Script analysis not only guides the location scouting and set design teams but also informs decisions related to costume design, lighting, and cinematography, ensuring that every aspect of the production works in harmony to bring the script to life on screen.

Transforming Creative Concepts into Cinematic Settings: The Vital Role of Location Scouts in Filmmaking

In the intricate process of filmmaking, location scouts play a pivotal role in bringing the director's vision to life. They work closely with the director to translate the script's narrative and emotional requirements into tangible locations. This collaborative effort involves understanding the director's visual aesthetic, mood, and cinematic style, ensuring that the chosen locations align seamlessly with the storytelling objectives. Location scouts are adept at recognizing the unique qualities of potential sites, whether it's capturing the essence of a historical period, evoking a particular atmosphere, or conveying a specific emotion. Their keen eye for detail helps them identify the perfect settings that not only serve as backdrops but become integral to the narrative, enhancing the overall cinematic experience. Through effective communication and a deep understanding of the director's vision, location scouts play a crucial role in turning creative concepts into real-world locations that enrich the film's visual storytelling.

The Cinematic Role of Locations: Enhancing Authenticity and Immersion in Filmmaking

Locations in filmmaking are not mere settings; they are integral elements that contribute significantly to the authenticity and atmosphere of a film. The choice of locations plays a crucial role in transporting the audience into the world of the narrative. Whether it's a bustling metropolitan city, a serene countryside, a historical monument, or a fictional realm, locations set the stage for the characters' journeys and interactions. Authentic locations resonate with the audience, making the storytelling more immersive and believable. The atmosphere and ambiance of these settings can evoke emotions, convey cultural nuances, and establish the film's mood. A well-selected location becomes a character in itself, influencing the narrative's dynamics. The attention to detail in choosing locations, from architectural elements to natural landscapes, ensures that the film's visual language aligns harmoniously with the director's vision, enriching the overall cinematic experience for the audience.

Logistical Considerations in Film Location Selection: Balancing Creativity with Practicality

Logistical considerations are paramount when selecting film locations. Accessibility, permits, and their implications on production schedules are crucial factors that determine the feasibility of a location. Ensuring that the chosen locations are easily accessible to the cast, crew, and equipment is essential to maintain the efficiency of the production process. Additionally, acquiring the necessary permits and legal clearances is vital to avoid disruptions during filming and potential legal complications later on. Balancing the creative vision with the practicalities of shooting on location is a delicate task for filmmakers. It requires meticulous planning and coordination to address the logistical challenges that can arise, such as transportation of equipment, accommodation for the crew, and adherence to local regulations. These logistical considerations play a pivotal role in the successful execution of a film's production phase, ensuring that the director's vision can be realized within the constraints of real-world logistics.

Cultural Significance of Film Locations: Enhancing Narrative Authenticity and Immersion.

The cultural relevance of chosen locations in filmmaking cannot be overstated. Locations serve as more than just backdrops; they become integral components of the storytelling process. By selecting locations that authentically reflect the cultural context of the film, directors and production designers add depth and authenticity to the narrative. These locations become visual cues that enhance the audience's understanding of the story, its characters, and the world they inhabit. For instance, a historical epic set in ancient India gains cultural richness when shot amidst the architectural marvels of a historic city like Jaipur or Varanasi. Similarly, a contemporary urban drama set in Mumbai's bustling streets captures the essence of modern Indian culture. By immersing the audience in these culturally relevant environments, filmmakers can evoke a stronger emotional connection and provide a more immersive cinematic experience, making the cultural relevance of locations a crucial aspect of pre-production planning and storytelling.

Scouting for Cinematic Perfection: The Meticulous Process of Location Selection in Filmmaking

The scouting process in filmmaking is a meticulous and essential phase of pre-production. It involves the director, location manager, and sometimes the production designer visiting potential locations to assess their suitability for various scenes in the script. During these visits, they take photographs and detailed notes, capturing not only the visual elements but also the logistical aspects of each location. This process allows the team to evaluate whether a location aligns with the director's vision, the script's requirements, and the overall mood and atmosphere desired for the film. Factors such as lighting conditions, accessibility, proximity to the base of operations, and permits required are all carefully considered. The scouting process often requires multiple visits to different locations to ensure that the chosen settings complement each other and create a cohesive visual narrative. It's a critical step that lays the foundation for the visual storytelling and ensures that the selected locations enhance the overall cinematic experience.

Diverse Location Scouting: Enriching the Cinematic Palette for Authentic Storytelling

Scouting diverse locations is of paramount importance in the filmmaking process, as it ensures that the film can authentically depict a wide range of scenes and settings. Filmmakers often seek out locations that can serve as backdrops for various elements of the story, such as urban environments, rural landscapes, historic sites, or contemporary interiors. This variety adds depth to the narrative, allowing the film to transport the audience to different worlds within the same story. It also showcases the versatility of the filmmaking team and their ability to adapt locations to match the script's requirements. Whether it's a bustling city street, a serene countryside, or a grand historical monument, diverse locations enrich the visual palette of the film, making it more engaging and immersive for the audience.

Digital Tools Revolutionizing Location Scouting in Modern Filmmaking

In the modern filmmaking landscape, digital tools have become invaluable for virtual location scouting. Filmmakers and location scouts use advanced digital mapping tools and software to explore potential locations without physically visiting them. These tools provide detailed satellite imagery, 3D models, and virtual tours of various places, allowing the production team to assess their suitability for filming. This not only saves time and resources but also opens up opportunities to scout locations from anywhere in the world, which can be especially useful for international productions. Digital tools enhance the efficiency of location scouting, enabling filmmakers to make informed decisions about the best settings to bring their creative vision to life.

Production Design:

Crafting the Visual World of a Film: The Role of Production Design

Creating the visual world of a film is a collaborative and artistic endeavor where production designers play a crucial role in bringing the director's vision to life. This collaboration begins with extensive discussions between the director and production designer to understand the film's thematic elements, time period, cultural context, and emotional tone. The director conveys their artistic aspirations, and the production designer translates these concepts into tangible visual elements. Extensive research follows, involving the study of historical references, art, architecture, and cultural nuances relevant to the film's setting. Mood boards, concept sketches, and storyboards are created to visualize the sets, costumes, and overall aesthetic. The production designer works closely with the art department, costume designers, and the director of photography to ensure a seamless integration of visual elements. Sets are constructed or locations are scouted to match the envisioned world, and every detail, from colour palettes to lighting schemes, is meticulously considered. The production designer's role extends into overseeing the creation of props, set dressing, and ensuring visual consistency throughout the production. The result is a captivating and immersive visual world that enhances the storytelling, making it a vital aspect of cinematic artistry.

From Script to Set: The Art of Set Design and Construction in Filmmaking

Set design and construction are essential aspects of filmmaking that involve translating the script's locations and environments into tangible sets. The process begins with a detailed analysis of the script and discussions with the director to understand the creative vision and practical requirements. Once the concept is finalized, production designers and their teams create intricate blueprints and design plans, considering factors such as spatial layout, architectural style, and period accuracy. Skilled carpenters, painters, and craftsmen then bring these designs to life, constructing the physical sets with meticulous attention to detail. Set decorators and prop masters work on furnishing and accessorizing the sets, ensuring that every item aligns with the story's context. Lighting designers collaborate to create appropriate atmospheres, while the director of photography fine-tunes camera angles to capture the sets effectively. Throughout the process, set designers and builders must balance creativity with practicality, ensuring that sets are functional for filming and adaptable to various scenes. The result is a visually compelling and immersive backdrop that enhances the storytelling, making the audience feel transported into the world of the film.

The Art of Immersion: How Attention to Detail in Set Design Elevates Cinematic Realism

Attention to detail in set design is paramount to creating a believable and immersive cinematic experience. Production designers and their teams meticulously craft every element within a set, from the placement of furniture and decor to the choice of props and even the subtlest textures on walls and floors. These details serve as visual cues that contribute to the authenticity of the film's world, reflecting the time period, cultural context, and the characters' personalities. For example, in a period piece, historical accuracy in set details can transport the audience to a different era. In a contemporary setting, carefully chosen details can provide insights into a character's background or state of mind. The cumulative effect of these details ensures that the audience not only watches the film but also feels a part of it, heightening their emotional engagement and overall cinematic experience.

The Art of Cinematic Aesthetics: How Colour Palettes and Design Elements Enhance Storytelling

Colour palettes and aesthetics are powerful tools in the hands of production designers, allowing them to visually convey emotions, themes, and atmospheres within a film. By carefully selecting colours and design elements for sets and props, they can evoke particular moods and enhance the storytelling. For example, warm and vibrant colours might be used in romantic comedies to create a cheerful and inviting ambiance, while cooler, muted tones could be employed in a thriller to instill tension and unease. The colour choices can also reflect cultural or historical contexts, with period pieces often featuring palettes that align with the time they depict. Additionally, the juxtaposition of colours can be used to symbolize character relationships or transitions in a character's journey. The aesthetics extend beyond colour to encompass architectural styles, furniture, and decor, all of which contribute to the visual language of the film and its ability to immerse the audience in the narrative.

From Research to Fantasy: The Role of Production Design in Crafting Historical Accuracy and Genre-Specific Worlds

Recreating historical periods or capturing the essence of specific film genres through production design is a demanding yet essential aspect of filmmaking. When dealing with historical accuracy, production designers must conduct meticulous research to ensure that every detail, from costumes to props to set pieces, aligns with the chosen time frame. This commitment to accuracy helps transport the audience to a different era, immersing them in the world of the film. Likewise, in genre-specific films such as science fiction or fantasy, the production design plays a pivotal role in crafting a distinct visual language. Creating futuristic worlds or magical realms requires innovative design choices and a keen understanding of the genre's conventions. Balancing historical accuracy or genre adherence with the film's overall aesthetic and storytelling objectives is a challenge that skilled production designers take on, as it directly impacts the film's ability to transport viewers into unique and captivating worlds.

Fostering Visual Synergy: How Production Design Collaborates Across Departments to Enrich Cinematic Experiences

Collaboration with other departments is integral to achieving a cohesive visual experience in filmmaking, and the production design department plays a central role in orchestrating this synergy. Production designers work closely with cinematographers to ensure that the sets they create are conducive to the desired camera angles, movements, and lighting schemes. This collaboration ensures that the visual storytelling aligns with the narrative's emotional beats, enhancing the audience's engagement. Additionally, production designers collaborate with the lighting department to optimize the interplay of natural and artificial light within the designed spaces, creating atmosphere and mood. Furthermore, coordination with the costume department is crucial to maintain visual consistency, as costumes and set designs must harmonize in terms of colour palettes, textures, and overall aesthetics. This multidisciplinary collaboration ensures that every visual element on screen complements and enhances the overall cinematic experience, immersing the audience in the world of the film while serving the storytelling.

Crafting Cinematic Worlds on a Budget: The Art of Balancing Creative Vision with Financial Constraints in Production Design

Production designers face the challenging task of balancing their creative vision with budgetary constraints, a crucial aspect of filmmaking. While they strive to create visually stunning and immersive worlds that align with the director's vision, they must also work within the financial limits set for the production. This often requires making strategic decisions regarding which aspects of the set or design should receive more significant investments and which can be achieved with cost-effective solutions. Creativity and resourcefulness play a pivotal role in finding innovative ways to achieve the desired look and feel of the film while adhering to the budget. Negotiations with suppliers, the efficient use of available resources, and a keen eye for cost-effective alternatives become essential skills in ensuring that the production design remains visually captivating while staying within financial boundaries. Ultimately, this delicate balance between creative ambition and fiscal responsibility is what allows production designers to bring captivating visual worlds to the screen.

Costume Selection:

Unveiling the Characters: The Crucial Role of Character Analysis in Pre-Production

Character analysis is a fundamental step in the pre-production process, where filmmakers delve into the intricacies of each character to bring them to life on screen. This involves a comprehensive examination of the character's personality traits, motivations, histories, and psychological profiles. Filmmakers aim to understand the characters' emotional landscapes, their past experiences that shape their behaviors, and the dynamics they share with other characters. This analysis not only helps actors embody their roles more authentically but also guides other departments, such as costume and makeup, in creating a visual representation that aligns with the character's essence. Directors and writers often collaborate closely during this stage to ensure that character development aligns with the film's overall narrative arc and themes. In essence, character analysis serves as the foundation upon which the entire storytelling process is built, enabling characters to resonate with audiences on a profound level.

Dressing the Part: The Art and Significance of Costume Design in Filmmaking

Costume design in filmmaking is a meticulous art that goes far beyond simply clothing the characters. It involves a deep understanding of the film's time period, culture, and socio-economic context, as costumes play a pivotal role in establishing the setting and enhancing the storytelling. The costume designer's task is to transport the audience into the world of the film by meticulously crafting attire that is not only historically accurate but also visually compelling. They research the fashions, fabrics, and styles of the era, paying careful attention to the societal norms and class distinctions of the time. Each costume choice is a deliberate visual cue, conveying information about the characters' backgrounds, personalities, and arcs. Furthermore, costumes must facilitate the actors' performances, allowing them to embody their characters fully. This intersection of historical accuracy, cultural context, and character psychology makes costume design a crucial element in the creation of a believable and immersive cinematic experience.

Fashioning the Cinematic World: Collaborative Synergy Between Costume and Production Design

Collaboration between costume designers and production designers is a vital aspect of filmmaking, as it ensures that costumes seamlessly integrate with the film's overall visual design. Costume designers and production designers work closely to create a harmonious and visually coherent cinematic world. This involves discussions about colour palettes, aesthetics, and the mood of the film to ensure that costumes not only complement the sets and locations but also contribute to the storytelling. For example, if a production designer creates a lush and opulent set, the costume designer may choose costumes that reflect the same grandeur, creating a unified visual experience. Conversely, in a minimalist setting, costumes might convey character traits or plot elements more vividly. This synergy between costume and production design plays a pivotal role in conveying the director's vision and enriching the cinematic narrative.

Costume Transitions: The Visual Language of Character Development in Film

Costumes play a significant role in character transformation within the context of a film's narrative. They are not just a visual aspect but a storytelling tool that aids in character development. Through costume changes, audiences can visually grasp a character's evolution, emotional journey, or shifts in circumstances. For instance, a character may start in humble attire and, as they progress or change, transition to more sophisticated or powerful clothing, symbolizing their growth or change in status. Conversely, a character in a position of power might undergo a transformation where they shed their formal attire for something more casual or disheveled to reflect a shift in their life. These changes in costumes provide a visual cue for the audience, reinforcing character arcs and aiding in the storytelling process, making the character's journey more relatable and emotionally resonant.

Material Matters: The Role of Fabrics and Textures in Costume Design for Film

The selection of materials and fabrics for costumes in filmmaking is a meticulous process that significantly contributes to the authenticity of a character's portrayal. Costume designers carefully consider the character's background, profession, social status, and the film's historical or contemporary setting. For example, a character from a historical period piece may require costumes made from authentic materials of that era to transport the audience to that time. Additionally, the choice of materials helps convey specific character traits; rich, luxurious fabrics might be chosen for a character in a high-society role, while more practical and rugged materials could be selected for a character with a working-class background. Texture and material choices also impact how costumes interact with lighting and camera work, further enhancing the character's visual presence on screen. Ultimately, the attention to materials ensures that costumes not only look accurate but also feel authentic, contributing to a deeper immersion into the film's world and the characters' lives.

Dressing the Part: The Significance of Costume Fittings in Filmmaking

Costume fittings are a crucial aspect of the costume design process in filmmaking, serving multiple purposes. They provide an opportunity for costume designers to ensure that the costumes fit the actors properly and are comfortable to wear during long shooting days. This is essential for the actors' ease of movement and overall performance. Fittings also allow actors to get a feel for their costumes, which can help them inhabit their characters more convincingly. Moreover, trial fittings provide a platform for testing how costumes look under various lighting conditions, ensuring that they appear as intended on screen. Costume designers can make any necessary adjustments based on how the costumes behave during fittings, ensuring that they meet both aesthetic and practical requirements. Ultimately, costume fittings play a vital role in achieving the desired look, comfort, and authenticity of the characters' attire, enhancing the overall quality of the film.

Colour Psychology: Elevating Character Depth through Costume Design in Filmmaking

Colour psychology is a fundamental aspect of costume design in filmmaking, as it wields a powerful influence on how characters are perceived and how their emotional states are conveyed to the audience. Costume designers carefully select colours to align with the personalities and traits of the characters. For instance, warm colours like reds and yellows often symbolize passion, energy, and power, while cooler tones like blues and greens may represent calmness or melancholy. The use of vibrant and contrasting colours can accentuate a character's vivacity, whereas muted or monochromatic palettes may suggest subtlety or conformity. Moreover, colour choices can signal transitions or character arcs, with shifts in colour reflecting changes in a character's emotional journey. Overall, the skillful application of colour psychology in costume design enhances storytelling by adding depth to characters and evoking emotional responses from the audience.

Continuity and Practicality: Balancing Costume Design in Filmmaking

Costume designers face the challenge of ensuring both continuity and practicality when creating outfits for film characters. Continuity is vital to maintain a seamless visual narrative, where a character's appearance remains consistent from one scene to the next. This involves meticulous attention to detail, including the placement of accessories, hairstyle, and even the creases on clothing. Additionally, costumes must be practical for actors to perform in comfortably, allowing them to move freely and convey emotions convincingly. This balance is particularly crucial in action sequences or emotionally charged moments. Practical considerations such as the weight of costumes, the ease of quick changes, and the choice of materials all play a role in facilitating the actor's performance. Ultimately, costume designers must excel in both maintaining continuity for the film's visual coherence and ensuring that actors can embody their characters authentically and comfortably.

The collaboration between location scouts, production designers, and costume designers is essential for creating a visually immersive and authentic cinematic experience. Their combined efforts contribute to the visual storytelling, character depth, and overall impact of the film.

C. Building a collaborative and efficient pre-production team

Project Management Essentials: Vision and Communication

Clear vision and communication are vital aspects of successful project management. Firstly, defining the project's vision, tone, and objectives is crucial as it sets the foundation for the entire endeavor. This involves clarifying what the project aims to achieve, its scope, and the desired outcomes. When everyone involved in the project, from team members to stakeholders, is aligned with this vision, it minimizes confusion and ensures that efforts are collectively directed towards a common goal. Equally important is establishing open lines of communication. Effective project management relies on transparent and ongoing exchanges of information and ideas among team members. This can involve regular team meetings, progress reports, and feedback sessions. Open communication not only fosters collaboration but also allows for the early identification and resolution of issues or roadblocks. It creates an environment where team members feel comfortable sharing their insights and concerns, ultimately leading to more informed decision-making and a higher likelihood of project success.

Seasoned Leadership in Pre-Production: A Recipe for Success

Appointing an experienced producer or production manager to lead the pre-production process is a pivotal step in ensuring the project's success. Seasoned leadership brings a wealth of industry knowledge and expertise to the table, which is invaluable during the complex and multifaceted pre-production phase. These leaders can effectively guide the team through various aspects of pre-production, including script development, budgeting, scheduling, and resource allocation. They often have established networks within the industry, allowing them to secure the necessary talent, locations, and equipment efficiently. Additionally, experienced leaders are adept at identifying and mitigating potential challenges, making strategic decisions, and ensuring that the project stays on track both creatively and logistically. Their ability to navigate the intricacies of pre-production enhances the project's overall efficiency, quality, and likelihood of achieving its goals.

Building a Pre-Production Dream Team: From Casting to Set Design

The effectiveness of the pre-production phase hinges on the composition of a team with a diverse array of skills and expertise, collectively spanning all aspects of the filmmaking process prior to shooting. This multifaceted team is essential for orchestrating a seamless and well-prepared production. It begins with casting directors, who play a pivotal role in selecting the right talent to bring the script's characters to life. Location scouts are crucial for identifying and securing suitable filming locations that align with the director's vision. Art directors and production designers collaborate to conceptualize and create the visual world of the film, ensuring that every detail, from set design to props, complements the narrative. Costume designers meticulously craft attire that not only suits the characters but also adds authenticity and depth to the storytelling. Additionally, the team may encompass experts in cinematography, lighting, sound, and special effects, among others, to address various technical and creative aspects. The amalgamation of these specialized roles allows for a well-rounded and comprehensive approach to pre-production, ensuring that the film's vision is thoroughly realized, and every logistical and artistic detail is accounted for. Collaborative synergy among these diverse talents is paramount in laying a strong foundation for a successful filmmaking endeavor.

Fostering Collaboration in Pre-Production: A Key to Filmmaking Success

Fostering a collaborative mindset within the pre-production team is pivotal for the success of any film project. It starts with carefully selecting team members who not only excel in their respective roles but also possess the willingness to collaborate and share ideas. Emphasizing the value of constructive feedback is essential, as it allows for the refinement and improvement of various aspects of the project, from the script to casting choices and visual design. Creative collaboration, where team members from diverse backgrounds and skill sets come together to brainstorm and innovate, can often lead to breakthrough ideas and enhance the overall quality of the film. Encouraging open communication, mutual respect, and a shared commitment to the project's vision are fundamental components of building a cohesive and effective pre-production team.

Leadership in Pre-Production: The Role of Department Heads in Crafting Cinematic Excellence

Appointing capable department heads is pivotal in orchestrating a successful pre-production phase in filmmaking. Each department head assumes a leadership role in their respective domain, fostering collaboration and cohesion among their teams to collectively work toward achieving the film's overarching vision. The production designer, for instance, is tasked with crafting the visual world of the film in tandem with the director, while the costume designer meticulously tailors the attire of characters to align with the narrative and period. The location scouting head identifies suitable filming locations that harmonize with the script's demands, and the casting director handpicks actors whose talents and personas seamlessly blend with the characters they portray. Additionally, art directors oversee the artistic aspects, ensuring the film's visual consistency, while technical heads manage the intricate technical facets, maintaining industry standards for quality. The synergy among these department heads is fundamental in translating creative concepts into a unified and compelling cinematic experience.

The Power of Pre-Production Meetings: Collaborative Planning for Cinematic Success

Pre-production meetings are the cornerstone of effective project planning in filmmaking. These meetings provide a structured platform for the team to convene, share insights, and make collective decisions. Regularly scheduled meetings serve as touchpoints to gauge progress, identify challenges, and strategize solutions. They facilitate open and transparent communication among department heads, ensuring that everyone is aligned with the project's vision, objectives, and timeline. Key decisions, whether related to casting, location scouting, budget allocation, or creative choices, are deliberated upon collectively, benefiting from the wealth of expertise within the team. These meetings not only enhance teamwork but also foster a sense of shared ownership, vital for the successful execution of a film project.

Clarity in Pre-Production Roles: Streamlining Filmmaking Efficiency

Establishing clear roles and responsibilities within a film's pre-production team is fundamental for efficient project management. Each team member's duties and areas of expertise should be explicitly defined to prevent overlaps or gaps in responsibilities, which could lead to confusion and inefficiencies. By assigning specific tasks and roles, from casting directors to location scouts, costume designers, and art directors, the team can function seamlessly. This clarity streamlines the workflow, allowing each member to focus on their designated tasks and make significant contributions to the project. Clear role definitions also promote accountability and help keep the project on track, ensuring that everyone understands their contributions to the film's success.

Meticulous Planning: The Role of Attention to Detail in Pre-Production

Attention to detail is a critical trait for team members involved in the pre-production phase of filmmaking. Pre-production is a stage where meticulous planning and organization are paramount, as it involves mapping out every aspect of the film, from casting choices to location selections, script revisions, and budget allocations. Team members who possess a keen eye for detail are instrumental in preventing oversights that could disrupt the smooth execution of the project during filming. They meticulously review contracts, schedules, permits, and budgets, ensuring that all elements align with the project's vision and objectives. This attention to detail not only maintains the project's integrity but also saves valuable time and resources by addressing potential issues proactively. Whether it's scrutinizing the script for continuity or double-checking the logistics of a complex scene, detail-oriented team members play a crucial role in the success of pre-production efforts.

Efficiency Under Pressure: The Role of Problem-Solving in Pre-Production

The ability to think critically and solve problems efficiently is a valuable trait when assembling a pre-production team for a film. In the dynamic environment of filmmaking, unforeseen challenges can arise at any moment, from last-minute location changes to budget constraints or weather-related issues. Team members who possess strong problem-solving skills can analyze situations, identify viable solutions, and make decisions under pressure. They are instrumental in adapting to changing circumstances and ensuring that the production stays on track. Whether it's finding creative workarounds to budget constraints or adjusting shooting schedules due to weather conditions, these individuals play a crucial role in maintaining the project's momentum and ensuring its successful execution. Their ability to navigate unexpected obstacles contributes significantly to the efficiency and effectiveness of the pre-production phase.

Thriving Amid Uncertainty: The Role of Adaptability in Film Pre-Production

Adaptability is a fundamental quality to seek in pre-production team members for film projects. In the dynamic world of filmmaking, plans are rarely set in stone, and unexpected changes can occur at any stage of production. Whether it's a sudden change in the script, adjustments to shooting schedules due to weather conditions, or modifications to the budget, individuals who can quickly pivot and adapt to these changes are invaluable. Their ability to remain composed, think on their feet, and find effective solutions is critical for keeping the production on track and ensuring that the project's vision is realized, even in the face of unforeseen challenges. Adaptability fosters a collaborative and resilient environment, enabling the team to navigate complexities and deliver a successful film.

Seamless Collaboration: The Crucial Role of Communication in Film Pre-Production

Strong communication skills are paramount in the pre-production phase of filmmaking, where collaboration and coordination among diverse team members are essential. Team members who can articulate their ideas, listen actively to others, and convey information clearly foster a productive working environment. Effective communication extends beyond the immediate team; it involves liaising with actors, directors, producers, and other key stakeholders. Clear communication helps ensure that everyone understands the project's objectives, timelines, and creative vision. It also aids in troubleshooting issues that may arise during pre-production, such as scheduling conflicts or budget considerations. Ultimately, strong communication is the linchpin that holds the various elements of pre-production together, facilitating a smooth workflow and contributing to the overall success of the film project.

Fostering a Positive Work Environment: Key to Pre-Production Success

Creating a positive work environment is essential for the success of any pre-production team. When team members feel valued, respected, and supported, they are more likely to be motivated and engaged in their work. This positive atmosphere encourages creativity and open communication, as team members feel comfortable sharing their ideas and opinions without fear of criticism. Collaboration thrives in such an environment, as individuals are more willing to work together to solve problems and achieve common goals. Morale remains high when team members feel appreciated for their contributions, leading to increased productivity and a smoother pre-production process. Ultimately, a positive work environment not only benefits the team but also has a direct impact on the quality of the final film product.

Team-Building Activities: Strengthening Unity and Collaboration in Pre-Production Teams

Team-building activities play a crucial role in fostering a sense of unity and collaboration among pre-production teams. These activities, whether they involve icebreakers, workshops, or outdoor adventures, help team members get to know each other on a personal level, creating stronger interpersonal connections. As a result, team members are more likely to communicate openly, trust each other's judgments, and work together seamlessly when tackling the various challenges that arise during pre-production. Team-building activities not only improve morale but also enhance problem-solving skills, as team members learn to adapt to different personalities and work styles. In the fast-paced and often high-pressure world of filmmaking, these bonds forged through team-building activities can make a significant difference in the overall success of a project.

Team-Building Activities: Strengthening Unity and Collaboration in Pre-Production Teams

Continuous learning is a vital element in the success of any pre-production team in the film industry. Encouraging team members to engage in ongoing skill development and stay abreast of industry trends is essential for maintaining a competitive edge. The world of filmmaking is dynamic, with technologies, techniques, and storytelling methods evolving constantly. Pre-production team members, whether they are involved in casting, location scouting, art direction, or any other role, benefit from continuous learning by staying updated on the latest tools, software, and methodologies. This commitment to learning not only enhances their individual capabilities but also bolsters the collective knowledge of the team. It fosters an environment where creative problem-solving and innovation thrive, allowing the team to adapt to changing project needs and industry standards. Moreover, as filmmaking often involves interdisciplinary collaboration, team members who continually expand their skill sets can contribute more effectively to the project, facilitating a smoother and more efficient pre-production process.

Creating a cohesive and effective pre-production team requires a careful selection of individuals who not only excel in their designated roles but also function harmoniously as a unit. A successful pre-production team possesses a diverse yet complementary skill set, where each member's expertise contributes to the overall project's success. Effective leadership within the team guides the creative vision and ensures that everyone's efforts align with the project's goals. Strong communication is paramount, fostering clarity and a shared understanding of the project's requirements and objectives. Beyond their individual abilities, team members should share a common commitment to the film's success, working together seamlessly to address challenges and drive the production forward. In essence, a well-balanced pre-production team serves as the cornerstone of a successful film production, combining talent, leadership, effective communication, and a shared dedication to bring the creative vision to life.

CHAPTER - 10

10. The Filmmaking Process

An In-Depth Look at the Various Stages of Filmmaking, from Shooting to Editing

The filmmaking process for Indian cinema, much like the global filmmaking industry, involves several intricately connected stages that collectively contribute to the creation of compelling narratives on the silver screen. It commences with pre-production, where the groundwork is laid, encompassing tasks such as script development, casting, location scouting, and logistical planning, all of which are often deeply intertwined with India's rich cultural diversity and geographical heterogeneity. The subsequent phase is production, where the script is brought to life through the collaborative efforts of the director, cast, and crew, often incorporating the vibrancy of India's varied cultural and geographical settings. Post-production is the final critical stage, involving editing, sound design, visual effects, and music composition, with a focus on creating a seamless and immersive cinematic experience that resonates with India's diverse audiences. Throughout these stages, Indian filmmaking also emphasizes the fusion of music, dance, and cultural elements, adding a distinct flair that distinguishes it from other film industries. The process is a dynamic amalgamation of creative storytelling and technical finesse, with each stage contributing to the film's narrative, visual style, and emotional resonance, allowing Indian cinema to engage and captivate audiences on both a national and global scale.

A. Shooting

Principal Photography: Capturing the Cinematic Essence in the 'Shooting' Phase of Filmmaking

Principal photography, often referred to as the "shooting" phase of filmmaking, is a crucial stage where the meticulously planned pre-production work comes to life. During this phase, scenes are filmed with actors, and the primary focus is on capturing their performances, dialogues, and actions as scripted. The director, as the creative visionary behind the project, plays a central role in guiding the actors to bring characters to life and ensuring that the scenes align with the film's overall vision. The cinematographer, in collaboration with the camera crew, is responsible for translating the director's vision into compelling visuals by choosing camera angles, framing shots, and managing lighting to achieve the desired mood and tone. Principal photography is a complex and dynamic process that demands precision, creativity, and effective communication among the entire crew to capture the essence of the story while adhering to the shooting schedule and budget. It's a phase where the magic of filmmaking truly unfolds, and the synergy between the director, actors, and the technical team is paramount in achieving the desired cinematic results.

Cinematography: Crafting Visual Narratives and Emotions in Filmmaking

Cinematography is a fundamental aspect of filmmaking where skilled cinematographers employ a symphony of visual elements to convey emotions and elevate storytelling. Through the deft manipulation of lighting, they craft moods and atmospheres that intensify the audience's emotional connection to the narrative. The choice of camera angles, whether it's a low-angle shot to accentuate dominance or a high-angle shot to evoke vulnerability, serves as a powerful tool for character and plot development. Movements of the camera, such as tracking shots that smoothly follow the action, or handheld shots that create a sense of immediacy and chaos, bring dynamism to scenes. Additionally, cinematographers employ techniques like close-ups to magnify subtle facial expressions, thereby delving into the depth of characters' emotions, or wide shots to establish a sense of scale and geography within the story's world. This intricate dance of visual storytelling, where every frame and composition is meticulously crafted, ensures that cinematography plays an integral role in shaping the cinematic experience and allows audiences to truly immerse themselves in the story being told.

Set Management and Direction: Orchestrating Creative and Technical Elements in Filmmaking

Set management and direction in filmmaking involve a meticulous orchestration of creative and technical elements, where the director serves as the linchpin in ensuring the realization of their vision. The director collaborates closely with numerous departments, including production design, costume, and cinematography, to ensure that every element within a scene aligns with the overarching narrative and visual style. Effective direction is pivotal in guiding actors to deliver performances that resonate with the intended character depth and emotional tone of the story. This involves not only conveying character motivations and relationships but also fostering an environment where actors can explore their roles authentically. Furthermore, the director plays a crucial role in capturing the desired mood and atmosphere by working closely with the cinematographer to establish visual aesthetics and with the production design team to create a cohesive and immersive world. Ultimately, the seamless coordination between the director and these various departments is essential in bringing a cinematic vision to life, ensuring that scenes are executed as planned, and compelling storytelling is achieved on screen.

Shooting on Location: Balancing Authenticity and Practicality in Filmmaking

Shooting on location in filmmaking is a complex endeavor, balancing authenticity with practicality. It involves overcoming logistical challenges, such as transporting equipment and crew to remote or unconventional sites. Unpredictable weather can disrupt schedules, adding uncertainty. Securing permits for filming in various locations is a bureaucratic process. Despite these hurdles, the decision to shoot on location is driven by the desire to capture a genuine atmosphere, adding realism to the narrative. Filmmakers must balance these challenges creatively, often requiring on-the-spot problem-solving. Unexpected events can lead to serendipitous moments, enriching the storytelling. Ultimately, shooting on location, while challenging, can result in a more immersive cinematic experience that resonates with the audience.

Executing Action Scenes, Stunts, and Visual Effects: Crafting Thrills Safely and Realistically in Filmmaking

The execution of action scenes, stunts, and visual effects in filmmaking is a complex and intricate process that demands the utmost attention to safety and realism. Stunt coordinators, often unsung heroes of the industry, work meticulously to choreograph and oversee high-risk sequences, ensuring the well-being of the performers. Their expertise lies in designing stunts that not only appear thrilling but can be performed safely through rigorous training and rehearsal. Special effects teams are instrumental in crafting awe-inspiring visuals, from explosive pyrotechnics to computer-generated imagery (CGI), seamlessly integrating them into the narrative. The collaboration between these teams and the director is paramount, as the director's vision guides the creative direction of action scenes, while the technical expertise of the coordinators and effects teams transforms that vision into a tangible reality. The result is a cinematic spectacle where the line between reality and illusion blurs, captivating audiences with the adrenaline-pumping excitement of stunts and the dazzling spectacle of special effects while maintaining the safety and well-being of all involved.

B. Post-Production

The Art of Film Editing: Crafting the Invisible Narrative

Editing is the invisible art of filmmaking that wields a profound influence on the narrative, pacing, and emotional resonance of a film. Editors are storytellers in their own right, responsible for selecting the most compelling shots, arranging them in a coherent sequence, and crafting a seamless narrative flow. They determine the rhythm of the film, manipulating time and space to evoke desired emotions and maintain audience engagement. Through the juxtaposition of images, the editor shapes character development, builds tension, and orchestrates dramatic climaxes. The art of editing lies in the ability to distill hours of footage into a cohesive and impactful story, making choices about what to include, what to omit, and when to transition between scenes. These decisions have a profound impact on the audience's experience, guiding their emotional journey and leaving a lasting impression. In essence, the editor is the guardian of a film's soul, responsible for transforming raw footage into a polished masterpiece that resonates deeply with viewers.

Sculpting Emotion: The Power of Sound Design and Music in Filmmaking

Sound design and music in filmmaking are essential elements that intricately shape the film's atmosphere and emotional depth. Sound designers meticulously craft aural landscapes by incorporating elements such as sound effects and ambient noise, seamlessly integrating them into the visual narrative to immerse the audience in the film's world. These sonic details breathe life into scenes, from the rustling of leaves in a serene forest to the thunderous roar of a spaceship's engines. Composers, on the other hand, compose original scores or select pre-existing music to evoke emotions, underscore character arcs, and underscore pivotal moments. The collaboration between sound designers, composers, and editors is paramount, as they work in harmony to ensure that every sound complements the visual storytelling, reinforcing mood and narrative beats. The result is a symphony of sound that enhances the audience's emotional connection to the film, making it an integral part of the cinematic experience that lingers long after the credits roll.

Pushing Boundaries: The Magic of Visual Effects (VFX) and CGI in Modern Filmmaking

Visual Effects (VFX) and CGI play a transformative role in modern filmmaking, enabling the creation of stunning visuals, fantastical worlds, and extraordinary creatures that enhance scenes and immerse the audience in alternate realities. These techniques involve the integration of computer-generated imagery (CGI) into live-action footage, where skilled artists and technicians meticulously blend the real and virtual worlds. The process typically begins during pre-production with detailed planning and storyboarding to determine where VFX will be applied. During filming, markers, green screens, and motion-capture technology are often used to provide reference points for later digital integration. In post-production, VFX artists and animators work tirelessly to create, refine, and seamlessly insert CGI elements into the live-action shots. This involves precise rendering, texturing, and lighting to ensure the virtual objects or characters appear as if they exist in the same physical space as the actors. The result is a seamless fusion of practical and digital effects, where the boundaries of imagination are pushed, and filmmakers can transport audiences to worlds previously unattainable through traditional filmmaking methods.

Crafting Cinematic Ambiance: The Art of Colour Correction and Grading in Post-Production

Colour correction and grading are vital post-production processes in filmmaking involving the expert manipulation of color tones and hues for specific visual aesthetics and narrative goals. Colourists ensure color consistency and coherence throughout the film, correcting deviations due to factors like lighting during filming. Beyond the technical aspect, color grading is where the creative magic happens. It's the process of enhancing the film's mood and storytelling through color. By adjusting the color palette, saturation, contrast, and brightness, colorists can evoke emotions, set atmospheres, and convey character development. This subtle yet powerful art deepens the audience's visceral engagement with the story.

C. Finalization

Harmonizing Cinematic Soundscapes: The Art of the Final Sound Mix in Post-Production

The final sound mix in filmmaking is the critical stage where the various sonic elements, including dialogues, sound effects, and music, are meticulously combined to create a cohesive and immersive soundtrack. Sound mixers and engineers carefully balance these elements to ensure that the audience can clearly hear and understand the dialogue while experiencing the full impact of sound effects and music. Achieving this balance is essential for storytelling, as it allows the audience to engage with the narrative without distraction. The process involves adjusting volumes, equalization, and spatial placement to give each sound its proper space in the audio landscape. Furthermore, the final mix aims to create a dynamic range that enhances emotional depth and impact, using subtle nuances in sound to accentuate the mood and intensity of a scene. A well-executed final sound mix not only elevates the film's overall audio quality but also plays a crucial role in immersing the audience in the cinematic world, ensuring that every sound contributes to the storytelling experience.

Elevating the Cinematic Experience: The Vital Role of Visual and Sound Quality Control in Filmmaking

Visual and sound quality control is an indispensable phase in the filmmaking process, involving a rigorous and meticulous review of the film's visuals and sound to identify and rectify any technical issues. This critical step ensures that the final product meets the highest quality standards and delivers an optimal viewing and listening experience for the audience. Visual quality control scrutinizes aspects such as image resolution, colour consistency, and visual continuity, addressing issues like colour grading discrepancies or visual artifacts. Sound quality control, on the other hand, focuses on audio clarity, ensuring that dialogues are intelligible, sound effects are well-balanced, and the music enhances the narrative without overpowering the other elements. This process may involve extensive testing on various screens and audio systems to guarantee that the film will look and sound its best in diverse viewing environments. The commitment to visual and sound quality control is fundamental in delivering a polished, professional, and captivating cinematic experience, where technical excellence underpins the storytelling artistry.

From Production to Public: Navigating the Distribution and Release Phase of Filmmaking

The distribution and release phase of filmmaking involves a carefully orchestrated series of steps to prepare the film for its intended audience across various platforms. Firstly, decisions are made regarding the formats in which the film will be distributed, whether it's for traditional theatrical release, streaming platforms, DVDs, or a combination of these. For theaters, the film must be converted to specific formats, often adhering to industry standards for audio and visual quality. For streaming services, digital encoding and file preparation are necessary to ensure smooth online delivery. Once the technical aspects are in place, marketing strategies and promotions come into play. This includes creating trailers, posters, and other promotional materials to generate buzz and anticipation. Release schedules are meticulously planned to maximize the film's exposure and potential box office earnings. This might involve premiering at film festivals, regional or international releases, and coordination with streaming platforms to reach a global audience. Ultimately, the distribution and release phase is a critical juncture where the film transitions from production to becoming a marketable product, requiring a well-coordinated effort to ensure that it reaches its intended viewers in the most effective and engaging manner possible.

D. Feedback and Refinement

Refining the Art: The Significance of Test Screenings in Filmmaking

Test screenings are a valuable practice in filmmaking, involving the presentation of a film to a select audience before its wide release to gather feedback and assess audience reactions. This process serves multiple crucial purposes. Firstly, it allows filmmakers to gauge how their work resonates with a real audience, gaining insights into which aspects engage viewers and which might need improvement. It provides an opportunity to identify pacing issues, plot holes, or unclear storytelling elements that might have gone unnoticed during the editing process. The audience's emotional responses, such as laughter, tears, or tension, are invaluable indicators of the film's impact. Subsequently, based on this feedback, filmmakers can make final adjustments, including re-editing sequences, reshooting scenes, or refining the sound and visual effects. These changes aim to enhance the overall quality and viewer experience, ensuring the film's resonance with its intended audience. Ultimately, test screenings play a pivotal role in fine-tuning the film's storytelling and emotional impact, contributing to its success upon wider release.

Director's Cuts and Alternate Versions: Exploring the Evolution of Filmmaking

The concept of a "director's cut" and the release of alternate versions of a film offer an intriguing dimension of filmmaking, allowing filmmakers to revisit and recontextualize their work. A director's cut typically represents the director's original artistic vision, with re-edits and alterations made to align the film more closely with their creative intent. These versions may include added scenes, pacing changes, or shifts in narrative focus, providing viewers with a deeper understanding of the director's vision. In contrast, alternate versions are often tailored to specific audiences or markets, featuring localized dialogues or cultural adjustments. These versions can sometimes differ significantly from the original, offering unique perspectives and storytelling experiences. The release of these versions highlights the dynamic nature of filmmaking, where a single narrative can be presented in various ways, inviting audiences to engage with the film on different levels and appreciate the nuances of the creative process.

The filmmaking process is a collaborative journey with distinct stages that collectively shape the final cinematic experience. Pre-production initiates the process, involving tasks like script development, casting, location scouting, and logistical planning. Production follows, where the script is realized through the collaborative efforts of the director, cast, and crew. Post-production comes next, encompassing editing, sound design, visual effects, and music composition to create a seamless cinematic experience. This intricate balance of creativity, technical expertise, and storytelling mastery results in films that captivate audiences worldwide, combining visual and auditory elements with narrative prowess to evoke emotions, provoke thoughts, and offer unforgettable storytelling on the silver screen.

E. Managing production challenges, maintaining creative integrity

Comprehensive Pre-Production Planning: The Foundation for Filmmaking Success

Comprehensive planning in pre-production is the cornerstone of a successful filmmaking endeavor, as it lays the groundwork for anticipating and mitigating potential challenges that may arise during filming. It involves meticulous attention to detail, from script breakdowns to location scouting, budgeting, and scheduling, with the goal of identifying and addressing any logistical, technical, or creative issues in advance. Experienced production managers play a pivotal role in this process, drawing upon their expertise to foresee potential obstacles and develop contingency plans. These plans encompass solutions for scenarios ranging from adverse weather conditions to actor unavailability, equipment malfunctions, or unexpected changes in the script. By having contingency plans in place, the production team can respond swiftly and effectively when challenges inevitably emerge, minimizing disruptions and ensuring that the project stays on track. Thorough pre-production planning not only enhances the efficiency and cost-effectiveness of the filmmaking process but also provides a solid foundation for creative exploration and innovation, ultimately contributing to the realization of the director's vision with fewer surprises and setbacks.

Embracing Flexibility and Adaptability: Thriving in the Unpredictable World of Filmmaking

Flexibility and adaptability are indispensable qualities in the world of filmmaking, where unpredictability often becomes the norm. Filming on location means contending with ever-changing weather conditions, unforeseen technical glitches, or even unexpected changes in the script or actor availability. In such scenarios, a flexible mindset becomes a filmmaker's greatest asset, enabling quick thinking and creative problem-solving on the spot. It's about finding alternative solutions, whether it's rewriting a scene to accommodate unexpected rain, improvising with available resources, or reworking the shooting schedule to accommodate last-minute changes. Moreover, embracing flexibility can lead to serendipitous moments of inspiration and innovation, where spontaneous decisions result in memorable scenes or sequences. Filmmaking is an organic and collaborative process, and those who embrace flexibility are better equipped to navigate its twists and turns, ultimately yielding a more dynamic and resilient creative outcome.

Striking a Balance: Managing Budget Constraints in Filmmaking

Navigating budget constraints is a perpetual challenge in filmmaking, as the cost of production can skyrocket quickly. It necessitates a delicate balance between optimizing resources while upholding the creative vision. This often involves meticulous pre-production planning to identify cost-effective solutions, such as choosing practical locations over elaborate set builds or maximizing the utility of existing props and costumes. Filmmakers also employ strategies like script revisions to reduce expensive sequences or exploring alternative shooting methods to save on time and expenses. Collaborations with local organizations or negotiating deals with suppliers can further stretch the budget. However, it's essential to recognize that budget constraints can be a double-edged sword, as they can foster creativity by necessitating innovative problem-solving. They encourage filmmakers to think outside the box, which often leads to inventive, resourceful solutions that enrich the storytelling. In essence, managing budget constraints is a delicate dance that requires a combination of fiscal discipline, creative ingenuity, and effective collaboration to ensure that the final product both aligns with the director's vision and remains financially viable.

Time Management in Filmmaking: Striking a Balance Between Efficiency and Creativity

Time management is a critical aspect of filmmaking, with time constraints exerting a pervasive influence on every stage of the production process. Tight shooting schedules demand meticulous planning and efficient execution to capture all necessary footage within the allocated time, often leading to long and demanding workdays. Editing timelines are similarly subject to time pressures, as editors must sift through hours of footage and craft a coherent narrative within strict deadlines. In post-production, visual effects, sound design, and colour grading must be synchronized to ensure timely delivery. To streamline processes without compromising quality, filmmakers rely on strategies such as pre-visualization, storyboarding, and meticulous script breakdowns during pre-production. Efficient on-set workflows, clear communication, and judicious time allocation help optimize shooting schedules. In post-production, collaborative digital tools and effective project management software are employed to expedite tasks. However, it's essential to maintain a balance between efficiency and creativity, as rushing through critical processes can potentially undermine the quality of the final product. Thus, time management in filmmaking requires a delicate equilibrium, where careful planning and strategic optimization ensure that deadlines are met while artistic integrity is upheld.

Crew Coordination in Filmmaking: The Art of Effective Communication and Collaboration

Crew coordination in filmmaking is the backbone of a successful production, emphasizing the profound significance of effective communication and collaboration among various departments. Filmmaking is inherently collaborative, with each department playing a crucial role in bringing the director's vision to life. Clear and open channels of communication are essential to address challenges collectively, from coordinating complex camera movements to troubleshooting technical issues on set. Effective leadership is pivotal in fostering a cohesive and harmonious working environment, where the director, producers, and department heads provide direction, motivation, and support to their teams. This leadership ensures that everyone is aligned with the project's objectives, facilitating creative problem-solving and preventing conflicts that can derail production. Crew coordination, underpinned by strong communication and leadership, not only results in a smoother workflow but also nurtures a sense of camaraderie and shared purpose, ultimately contributing to the success of the film.

Overcoming Logistical Hurdles in Filmmaking: A Symphony of Coordination and Resourcefulness

Logistical hurdles in filmmaking encompass a multitude of challenges, from coordinating location logistics to transporting equipment and securing the necessary permits. Location logistics can be particularly demanding, involving scouting, securing permissions, and ensuring the accessibility of remote or challenging filming sites. Equipment transport entails not only the safe shipping of cameras, lights, and sound gear but also their efficient setup and maintenance on location. Additionally, obtaining permits for filming in public or private spaces can be a bureaucratic labyrinth, necessitating meticulous planning and negotiation. Successful navigation of these logistical challenges hinges on collaborative efforts among various departments, including location managers, production coordinators, and transportation teams. Effective communication and teamwork are paramount to ensure that everything runs smoothly on set, from managing the movement of cast and crew to coordinating catering and ensuring the timely arrival of equipment. The ability to tackle logistical hurdles seamlessly is a testament to the resourcefulness and adaptability of the filmmaking team, ultimately ensuring that the production stays on track and that the creative vision is realized despite the myriad of practical obstacles.

Navigating Unpredictable Elements in Filmmaking: Agility, Innovation, and the Art of Adaptation

Unpredictable elements are a constant challenge in filmmaking, encompassing factors like ever-changing weather conditions, last-minute actor unavailability, or unforeseen technical glitches that can disrupt even the most well-planned productions. Filmmakers must be agile and adaptable to tackle these challenges effectively. Strategies to minimize disruptions include having contingency plans in place for weather-related issues, such as scheduling alternative indoor scenes or investing in weather-resistant equipment. For actor availability, flexible shooting schedules or standby replacements can be considered, while technical glitches often require experienced crew members and backup equipment to swiftly troubleshoot and resume filming. Embracing spontaneity in the face of unexpected situations can also lead to serendipitous moments that enhance the film's creativity and authenticity. Ultimately, successful filmmakers learn to accept the unpredictability of the process and approach each challenge as an opportunity for innovation, demonstrating their resilience and ability to adapt in the ever-evolving world of cinema.

Preserving the Director's Vision: Guiding the Filmmaking Process from Conception to Completion

Maintaining the director's creative vision is paramount throughout every stage of production, serving as the North Star that guides decision-making and shapes the entire filmmaking process. This vision encompasses the director's unique interpretation of the script, visual aesthetics, narrative tone, and character development. It not only informs the artistic choices, such as cinematography, production design, and costume, but also guides decisions related to casting, performance direction, and editing. Amidst the myriad of challenges and practical considerations inherent to filmmaking, keeping the director's vision at the forefront ensures a cohesive and unified storytelling experience. Clear communication and collaboration among the crew are essential in aligning everyone with this vision, allowing for creative exploration within established parameters. Additionally, the director's vision provides a touchstone for decision-making when unexpected issues arise, offering a basis for choosing solutions that harmonize with the overarching artistic goals. Ultimately, prioritizing the director's creative vision is a testament to the collaborative nature of filmmaking, where a shared commitment to bringing a singular vision to life leads to a resonant and compelling cinematic work.

Fostering Collaborative Problem-Solving: Leveraging the Collective Expertise of the Film Production Team

Involving the entire production team in finding solutions to challenges is not only important but also essential for the success of a film project. Filmmaking is inherently collaborative, with each department bringing a unique set of skills, knowledge, and perspectives to the table. When faced with obstacles or unexpected problems, tapping into this diversity of viewpoints fosters innovative problem-solving. For example, a lighting technician might offer insights on how to achieve a particular mood or effect more efficiently, a costume designer may suggest alterations that improve actor comfort and performance, and an editor might propose creative editing techniques to overcome continuity issues. Moreover, the collective brainpower of the team encourages creative thinking and fosters a sense of ownership and commitment to the project's success. Collaborative solutions not only lead to practical answers but also enhance the overall quality and creativity of the film, demonstrating that filmmaking is not the product of a single visionary, but the collective effort and ingenuity of the entire production team.

Harmonizing Creative Vision and Financial Considerations: The Role of Effective Communication with Stakeholders in Filmmaking

Effective communication with producers, financiers, and other stakeholders is a linchpin in the filmmaking process, as it ensures alignment between creative aspirations and financial considerations. Transparent and clear communication is crucial to convey the director's creative vision, providing stakeholders with a comprehensive understanding of the project's artistic goals and intended impact. It also facilitates a constructive dialogue where concerns, constraints, and expectations can be openly addressed. This alignment is vital to avoid misunderstandings that can arise when creative ambitions clash with budgetary or scheduling realities. Collaboration between creative teams and stakeholders allows for informed decision-making, enabling adjustments that respect the creative integrity of the project while maintaining fiscal responsibility. Moreover, it engenders trust and a sense of shared purpose, fostering an environment where all parties are motivated to work together toward a common goal—the successful realization of the film. Ultimately, effective communication with stakeholders is a cornerstone of a harmonious and productive filmmaking process, where creative vision and financial feasibility are brought into harmonious equilibrium.

Preserving Storytelling Intent in Filmmaking: Balancing Adaptation and Narrative Integrity Amid Challenges

Protecting storytelling intention in filmmaking requires a delicate balancing act between adapting to challenges and preserving the essence of the narrative. While unforeseen obstacles often demand creative problem-solving and flexibility, the core elements of the story—the character arcs, thematic depth, and emotional resonance—must remain intact. Filmmakers employ various strategies to address challenges without compromising the story's integrity. This might involve reworking scenes, adjusting the shooting schedule, or embracing the spontaneity of unexpected situations to infuse authenticity into the narrative. It also entails prioritizing storytelling over superficial perfection, as sometimes imperfections can enhance the film's realism and emotional impact. Maintaining a strong collaboration between the director, screenwriter, and production team is crucial, as it ensures that creative decisions align with the narrative's original intent. Ultimately, the goal is to navigate challenges in a way that enriches the storytelling rather than dilutes it, honoring the film's unique vision while embracing the ever-evolving nature of the filmmaking process.

Crafting Cinematic Vision: The Pivotal Role of Directors in Filmmaking

The role of the director in filmmaking is undeniably pivotal, serving as the creative mastermind and guiding force that shapes the entire project. Directors not only conceive the artistic vision but also communicate and execute it, making them the linchpin of the production. Their strong directorial presence is crucial in maintaining the project's creative integrity and inspiring confidence within the production crew. By providing a clear and unifying vision, directors keep the team aligned and motivated, even when faced with unexpected challenges. They make crucial decisions on set, from guiding actors' performances to selecting shots and controlling pacing, always with an unwavering focus on storytelling and character development.

The Director's Commitment: Forging Cohesion and Authenticity in Filmmaking

The unwavering commitment of directors to realizing the project's creative vision instills confidence in the crew, encouraging them to invest their best efforts in the production. Effective communication, strong leadership, and the ability to adapt to unforeseen circumstances are the hallmarks of a great director. Through these qualities, directors guide the team towards a cohesive and harmonious collaboration, resulting in a compelling and authentic cinematic experience. The director's role transcends mere decision-making; it encompasses the orchestration of a multitude of creative and technical elements to craft a narrative that resonates with audiences, making them the driving force behind the magic that unfolds on the silver screen.

Managing production challenges while preserving creative integrity necessitates a delicate balancing act that encompasses logistical expertise, adaptability, and an unwavering artistic vision. This intricate process involves the cultivation of a collaborative environment where all stakeholders, from the director and cast to the production crew and financiers, work in unison to confront the myriad challenges that often arise during filmmaking. At the heart of this endeavor lies the commitment to prioritize the essence of the story, ensuring that the narrative's emotional and thematic core remains intact despite the hurdles encountered. By fostering this collaborative spirit, aligning the collective vision, and remaining steadfast in their dedication to storytelling, filmmakers can not only surmount production challenges but also craft films that resonate authentically with audiences, resulting in cinematic experiences that leave a lasting impact.

F. Incorporating song-and-dance sequences in Indian films

Exploring the Rich Cultural Heritage: The Evolution of Song-and-Dance Sequences in Indian Cinema

Song-and-dance sequences in Indian cinema have a rich and intricate history deeply rooted in the country's cultural traditions. These sequences trace their origins to classical Indian performing arts, where music, dance, and storytelling have been intertwined for centuries. The Indian subcontinent's diverse cultural tapestry, with its multitude of regional languages, folklore, and traditions, has greatly influenced the cinematic representation of song and dance. The elaborate choreography and vibrant costumes seen in these sequences often draw inspiration from classical dance forms like Bharatanatyam, Kathak, and Odissi, with their intricate footwork, expressive gestures, and storytelling elements. Additionally, the influence of traditional musical theater forms, such as the folk dances of various regions and the grandeur of Bollywood-style productions, has contributed to the evolution of song-and-dance sequences in Indian cinema. These sequences serve as a reflection of India's cultural diversity, acting as a bridge between the ancient traditions of the past and the contemporary storytelling of the present, while captivating audiences worldwide with their vibrancy and emotional resonance.

The Multifaceted Role of Song-and-Dance Sequences in Indian Cinema: Emotions, Plot Advancement, and Subtext

Song-and-dance sequences in Indian cinema are versatile narrative tools that go beyond mere entertainment, functioning as expressive mediums that convey a myriad of emotions, advance the plot, and subtly communicate subtext. These sequences serve as emotional outlets, allowing characters to express their innermost feelings and desires, whether it's love, joy, sorrow, or even conflict. They possess the unique ability to encapsulate complex emotions that might be challenging to convey through dialogue alone. Moreover, song-and-dance sequences often act as pivotal plot progressors, propelling the narrative forward by introducing new developments, conflicts, or resolutions. They can also serve as symbolic representations of a character's inner journey, revealing their growth, transformation, or internal conflicts. Furthermore, these sequences carry an inherent subtext that can add layers of meaning to the story. Through symbolism, metaphor, and visual storytelling, they can subtly convey themes, social commentary, or cultural values. In essence, song-and-dance sequences in Indian cinema are not mere embellishments but essential narrative devices that enrich the storytelling tapestry, engaging audiences on emotional, thematic, and plot-driven levels.

The Emotional Resonance of Music and Dance in Indian Cinema: Elevating Cinematic Moments with Joy, Sorrow, and Love

Music and dance in Indian cinema serve as powerful conduits for emotional resonance, infusing scenes with a depth of feeling that lingers in the hearts and minds of audiences long after the credits roll. These elements elevate emotional impact by synchronizing with the characters' experiences, intensifying their expressions of joy, sorrow, love, or even conflict. The rhythm and melodies of the music create a visceral connection with the audience, as the beats and tunes mirror the ebb and flow of human emotions. Dance, with its expressive movements and gestures, becomes a visual representation of the characters' inner feelings, transcending linguistic and cultural barriers to convey universal sentiments. The synergy between music and dance not only enhances the audience's connection to the characters but also invites them to participate in the emotional journey, amplifying the impact of pivotal moments in the storyline. Whether it's a celebratory dance at a wedding, a poignant melody during a farewell, or an energetic performance in a moment of triumph, the emotional resonance of song-and-dance sequences in Indian cinema is a testament to their enduring appeal and their unique ability to make cinematic moments unforgettable.

Extravagance and Artistry: The Spectacular Visual Elements of Song-and-Dance Sequences in Indian Cinema

Song-and-dance sequences in Indian cinema are the crown jewels of cinematic spectacle, transforming films into visually stunning feasts for the eyes. These sequences are marked by their elaborate costumes, intricate choreography, and opulent set designs that transport audiences to a world of heightened reality. The resplendent attire, often adorned with intricate embroidery, sequins, and vibrant colours, adds a touch of grandeur to the visual landscape, making each character a visual masterpiece in their own right. Choreography, inspired by classical dance forms and contemporary dance styles, infuses the sequences with elegance, precision, and emotional depth. The coordination of multiple dancers, intricate formations, and graceful movements create a symphony of visual poetry. Set designs transport viewers to enchanting locales, from historic palaces to picturesque landscapes, providing a sense of escapism and wonder. These cinematic spectacles, with their captivating blend of music, dance, costume, and scenery, transcend the ordinary and elevate the cinematic experience to a realm of heightened beauty and artistic expression, leaving an indelible mark on the audience's imagination.

Song-and-Dance Sequences in Indian Cinema: Celebrating India's Cultural Diversity

Song-and-dance sequences in Indian cinema serve as vibrant showcases of the nation's rich tapestry of cultural diversity, acting as windows into the myriad traditions, languages, and artistic expressions that define India's unique identity. They are a testament to the inclusivity of Indian cinema, often featuring a harmonious blend of regional dance forms, attire, and music. Whether it's the graceful Kathak of North India, the exuberant Bhangra of Punjab, the sensual Odissi of the East, or the energetic Garba of Gujarat, these sequences celebrate the country's unity in diversity. Through elaborate costumes, choreography, and music that are specific to each region, these sequences not only preserve and showcase traditional art forms but also introduce audiences to the cultural heritage of India's various states and communities. They emphasize the beauty of India's multiculturalism, acting as a bridge between different linguistic, regional, and religious groups. In doing so, song-and-dance sequences encapsulate the essence of a culturally vibrant and diverse nation, offering a glimpse into the kaleidoscope of traditions that make India a tapestry of colours, rhythms, and stories.

Dancing into the Hearts and Minds: Character Development through Song-and-Dance Sequences in Indian Cinema

Song-and-dance sequences in Indian cinema are exquisite windows into the inner worlds of characters, allowing them to reveal facets of their personalities, dreams, and conflicts in a manner that transcends verbal expression. These sequences serve as dynamic character development tools, offering a visual and emotional journey into the psyche of the protagonists. Through dance movements, facial expressions, and body language, characters convey their emotions and desires, whether it's the exuberance of newfound love, the melancholy of unfulfilled dreams, or the determination to overcome adversity. The choice of dance style, costume, and choreography is tailored to each character's traits and narrative arc, reflecting their individuality. For example, a reserved character may gradually evolve from hesitant movements to confident dance steps, signifying their personal growth. Conversely, a character in turmoil may express their inner conflicts through frenetic, chaotic dance sequences. These moments of artistic expression become mirrors into the characters' hearts, making them relatable, multidimensional, and deeply human, and allowing audiences to connect with their joys, struggles, and aspirations on a profound level.

Harmonizing Traditions and Modernity: The Fusion of Traditional and Contemporary Music in Indian Cinema

The fusion of traditional Indian music with contemporary genres in Indian cinema is a sonic tapestry that reflects the ever-evolving tastes and cultural dynamics of the nation. These cinematic soundscapes are a testament to India's ability to seamlessly blend its rich musical heritage with modern influences, creating a unique and eclectic musical identity. While traditional instruments like the sitar, tabla, and flute continue to hold sway in the background, contemporary music elements such as electronic beats, Western harmonies, and global rhythms have been integrated to cater to a diverse and modern audience. This fusion allows Indian cinema to transcend geographic and generational boundaries, resonating with viewers worldwide. It captures the essence of India's cultural fluidity, where the old and new coexist harmoniously, and tradition embraces innovation. Whether it's a classical raag fused with a pulsating hip-hop rhythm or a soulful melody enhanced by electronic synthesizers, this musical fusion not only underscores the diversity of Indian cinema but also showcases its ability to adapt and remain relevant in an ever-changing world of entertainment.

Transforming Viewers into Participants: The Interactive Magic of Song-and-Dance Sequences in Indian Cinema

Song-and-dance sequences in Indian cinema are extraordinary instruments of audience engagement, offering sublime moments of entertainment that forge an intimate connection between the screen and the viewers. These sequences are meticulously designed to be interactive experiences, inviting the audience to become active participants in the cinematic journey. As the music swells and the dancers take the stage, viewers often find themselves singing along with the catchy tunes and mimicking the dance moves. It's a phenomenon where the cinema hall transforms into a theater of collective joy, where audiences join in the celebration of life, love, and emotion. This interactive nature not only elevates the entertainment value but also strengthens the emotional bond between the narrative and the viewer. The songs and dances become a shared experience, fostering a sense of togetherness and community within the audience. Whether it's the exuberance of a peppy dance number or the nostalgia of a soulful melody, these sequences transcend the screen, becoming moments of joy, celebration, and cultural connection that linger long after the film ends. In essence, song-and-dance sequences in Indian cinema are the bridge that transforms passive spectators into active participants, making the cinematic experience not just a visual and auditory delight but a cherished memory to be sung and danced to for generations.

Iconic Song-and-Dance Sequences: Cinematic Landmarks in Indian Cinema's Collective Consciousness

Iconic song-and-dance sequences in Indian cinema are timeless cultural touchstones and cinematic landmarks that transcend their respective films, etching themselves into the collective consciousness of a nation and beyond. These moments are the stuff of legend, often indelibly associated with specific actors, filmmakers, and eras. For example, the rain-soaked dance of Raj and Simran in "Dilwale Dulhania Le Jayenge" or the exuberant train-top dance in "Chaiyya Chaiyya" from "Dil Se" have become emblematic of romance and vitality in Bollywood. Such sequences are celebrated not just for their stunning choreography and melodious tunes but for the emotions they evoke and the cultural impact they've had. They transcend the filmic realm to become ingrained in popular culture, influencing fashion trends, inspiring parodies, and serving as reference points in conversations and celebrations. These moments are more than just entertainment; they are shared experiences that connect generations, bridging the past with the present and carrying the promise of a vibrant cinematic future. In essence, iconic song-and-dance sequences are the heartbeats of Indian cinema, pulsating with the energy of creativity and the enduring spirit of storytelling that continues to captivate and unite audiences worldwide.

The Global Allure of Song-and-Dance Sequences: Indian Cinema's Cultural Ambassadors

Song-and-dance sequences play a pivotal role in the commercial success and global appeal of Indian cinema. They are not just artistic expressions but potent marketing tools that serve as cultural ambassadors, introducing audiences worldwide to the charm, vibrancy, and emotional depth of Indian storytelling. These sequences, often accompanied by catchy music and stunning visuals, create a unique cinematic identity that sets Indian films apart on the global stage. They cater to a diverse range of tastes, combining elements of drama, romance, comedy, and action, ensuring that Indian films resonate with a broad spectrum of viewers. Furthermore, the universal language of music and dance transcends linguistic barriers, allowing Indian cinema to communicate its narratives to international audiences effectively. These sequences often serve as the first impression of Indian cinema for many viewers, leaving a lasting impact and piquing interest in exploring more of this rich cinematic tradition. As a result, song-and-dance sequences act as powerful magnets, drawing global audiences into the world of Indian cinema and contributing significantly to its ever-expanding global footprint.

The Art of Choreography in Indian Song-and-Dance Sequences: Translating Narrative into Movement

Choreography in song-and-dance sequences is an art form in itself, and it plays a crucial role in translating a film's themes, emotions, and narrative into captivating visual storytelling. Choreographers are the unsung heroes behind the intricate dance routines that become the highlight of many Indian films. They work closely with the director to understand the characters, the storyline, and the emotional context of the sequence, ensuring that every dance step aligns with the narrative's intentions. Choreographers must balance creativity with cultural authenticity, often drawing inspiration from traditional Indian dance forms while infusing modern elements to keep the choreography fresh and relevant. Moreover, they adapt to changing dance trends and styles, incorporating contemporary moves like hip-hop or salsa to appeal to a wide audience. The result is a seamless fusion of tradition and innovation, where choreography becomes a powerful tool for storytelling, character development, and entertainment. It's a testament to the choreographer's ability to transform dance into a language that transcends words, allowing characters to express their deepest emotions and desires through every graceful or energetic movement. In essence, choreography in song-and-dance sequences is the marriage of artistic creativity and narrative precision, ensuring that these moments become not just dance performances but vital components of cinematic storytelling.

Seamless Integration of Song-and-Dance Sequences: Elevating Indian Film Narratives with Artistic Finesse

Integrating song-and-dance sequences in Indian films requires meticulous craftsmanship. These sequences should seamlessly blend with the story, enhancing it by advancing the plot, revealing character dynamics, or deepening emotions. Continuity in character behavior and tone is crucial, and transitions in and out of these sequences must be smooth to maintain the film's flow. Successful integration relies on artistic cohesion, where choreography, music, and visuals harmonize with storytelling, creating an immersive experience. When done masterfully, these sequences become narrative gems that enrich the cinematic experience.

In Indian cinema, song-and-dance sequences are more than just musical interludes; they are a vital part of the cinematic experience, blending cultural heritage, storytelling, and entertainment. These sequences add emotional depth, visual splendor, and a distinct flavor to Indian movies. They serve as a unique tool to convey emotions, highlight key moments, and showcase Indian culture. Often transcending realism, they create a heightened reality for expressing deep emotions and exploring themes like love, celebration, and cultural identity. Beyond entertainment, these sequences represent the fusion of artistic expression and cultural representation in Indian cinema, making them an enduring and beloved aspect that resonates with global audiences.

CHAPTER - 11

11. Cultural Sensitivity and Diversity

Navigating Cultural Sensitivities While Telling Stories from Diverse Indian Backgrounds

Cultural Authenticity in Filmmaking: The Crucial Role of Thorough Research

Thorough research is the bedrock upon which authentic and respectful portrayal of diverse cultural backgrounds in cinema is built. Filmmakers must commit to in-depth research to gain a deep understanding of the intricacies, nuances, and sensibilities of the cultures they aim to represent. This research extends to every facet of filmmaking, from character dynamics and their beliefs to the settings, traditions, and societal norms that shape their lives. It involves engaging with cultural experts, consulting with community representatives, and immersing oneself in the language, history, and customs of the culture in question. By doing so, filmmakers ensure that their work does not perpetuate stereotypes or misrepresent the people and traditions they are portraying. Instead, research allows for a nuanced and empathetic portrayal that respects the integrity of the culture while contributing to a more diverse and inclusive cinematic landscape. Ultimately, thorough research is an ethical imperative in filmmaking, fostering cross-cultural understanding and celebrating the richness of the world's diverse tapestry of stories and experiences.

Cultural Expert Consultation: Fostering Authentic and Respectful Film Portrayals

Consulting with experts from the cultures being portrayed in a film is an invaluable step in the quest for authenticity and respectful representation. Cultural consultants offer a profound understanding of the nuances, traditions, and sensibilities that might elude filmmakers from outside those cultures. They serve as bridges between the creative team and the community they aim to depict, providing invaluable insights that extend beyond mere research. These experts can elucidate subtle intricacies, from language nuances and non-verbal communication to the intricacies of daily life and societal norms. They help filmmakers navigate potential pitfalls and ensure that the portrayal is accurate, respectful, and devoid of stereotypes or misinterpretations. Consulting with experts is not just a matter of authenticity but also a commitment to ethical storytelling and cultural sensitivity. It is a collaborative process that enriches the filmmaking journey, fostering cross-cultural understanding and celebrating the diverse tapestry of human experiences on the cinematic canvas.

Respectful Cultural Portrayals: The Role of Well-Rounded Characters in Cinema

The imperative of respectful portrayals of cultures in cinema underscores the responsibility of filmmakers to approach their subject matter with sensitivity and depth. It necessitates a departure from stereotypes, caricatures, or one-dimensional representations that perpetuate misconceptions and biases. Instead, well-rounded characters are essential in achieving a nuanced and respectful depiction. These characters possess complexity, individuality, and authenticity that reflect the diversity and depth of real people within a given culture. They exhibit a range of emotions, beliefs, and motivations that challenge preconceived notions and offer a more profound understanding of their world. By focusing on well-rounded characters, filmmakers humanize their subjects, portraying them as multifaceted individuals with their own aspirations, struggles, and growth arcs. This approach not only promotes cultural authenticity but also fosters empathy and cross-cultural understanding among audiences. It encourages viewers to see the common humanity that transcends cultural differences, promoting respectful and inclusive storytelling that contributes to a richer and more compassionate cinematic landscape.

Enriching Cinematic Authenticity: The Significance of Cultural Nuances and Traditions

Attention to cultural nuances and traditions is the cornerstone of imbuing characters and settings with depth and authenticity in filmmaking. It involves a meticulous examination of the rituals, ceremonies, and social interactions that are integral to a specific culture. Accurately depicting these elements enriches the narrative by providing a deeper understanding of the characters' lives and the world they inhabit. For instance, the celebration of festivals, the observance of rites of passage, or the dynamics of familial relationships are not merely superficial details but windows into the characters' values, beliefs, and emotional landscapes. By respecting and accurately portraying these cultural aspects, filmmakers create a more immersive and relatable experience for audiences. It not only lends credibility to the storytelling but also demonstrates a profound respect for the culture being depicted. In essence, the commitment to cultural nuances and traditions elevates the cinematic narrative, turning it into a respectful and enlightening exploration of the complexities of human existence within a specific cultural context.

Balancing Act: Navigating Sensitive and Controversial Topics in Cultural Contexts in Filmmaking

Addressing sensitive and controversial topics within different cultural contexts in filmmaking presents a complex and delicate challenge. Filmmakers must navigate a fine line between sparking meaningful dialogue and potentially causing offense or harm. It involves a profound understanding of the cultural, historical, and social nuances that surround these topics. The key lies in approaching such subjects with sensitivity, empathy, and a commitment to responsible storytelling. This can be achieved by portraying diverse perspectives, engaging with experts and community representatives, and involving affected communities in the creative process. Moreover, narratives should strive for nuance, avoiding oversimplification or sensationalization. Filmmakers should be open to criticism and feedback, recognizing that respectful and constructive discourse can arise from the portrayal of controversial topics. Ultimately, the goal is to create films that encourage introspection, empathy, and cross-cultural understanding while respecting the boundaries and sensitivities of different cultural contexts. In essence, addressing controversial topics in cinema is an art of storytelling that, when executed with care and respect, can contribute to meaningful dialogue and societal growth.

Harmonizing Creativity and Authenticity: Striking the Balance in Filmmaking

Balancing creative freedom and cultural authenticity in filmmaking is a nuanced task that requires a delicate touch. Creative storytelling often involves imaginative interpretations and artistic liberties, which, if taken too far, can risk misrepresenting or disrespecting the cultures being depicted. However, it's essential to recognize that storytelling thrives on creativity and innovation. To maintain this balance, filmmakers should begin with a foundation of thorough research and consultation with cultural experts or community representatives. This ensures a deep understanding of the culture's nuances and values, allowing for respectful adaptation within the creative process. Filmmakers can then weave cultural authenticity into their narratives, infusing stories with the spirit and essence of the culture while retaining room for artistic interpretation. It's crucial to approach creative liberties with sensitivity, ensuring that any departures from strict cultural accuracy serve the narrative's purpose without causing harm or perpetuating stereotypes. Ultimately, the goal is to strike a harmonious balance where creative storytelling enriches the cinematic experience while respecting and celebrating the diversity and authenticity of cultures depicted on screen.

Avoiding Tokenism: Crafting Authentic and Complex Characters in Filmmaking

Avoiding tokenism in filmmaking is a critical step towards promoting diversity and cultural authenticity. Token characters, often included to represent a specific culture, risk reducing complex identities to mere stereotypes or shallow caricatures. To steer clear of this pitfall, characters should be crafted with depth and complexity that extends beyond their cultural identity. They should possess their own motivations, arcs, and individuality, just like any other character. It's vital to view cultural identity as one facet of a character's personality rather than their defining trait. By doing so, filmmakers can create authentic, relatable, and well-rounded characters that resonate with audiences on a human level, transcending cultural boundaries. This approach not only enriches storytelling but also contributes to more inclusive and respectful portrayals of diverse cultures, fostering a cinematic landscape where every character, regardless of their cultural background, is portrayed with authenticity, dignity, and depth.

Cultural Diversification in Filmmaking: Enriching Narratives and Fostering Inclusivity

The cultural diversification of filmmakers is pivotal in ensuring authentic and inclusive storytelling. When filmmakers from diverse backgrounds are involved in the creative process, it brings a wealth of perspectives, experiences, and insights to the narratives they craft. This diversity enriches storytelling by providing a more comprehensive understanding of cultural nuances, traditions, and sensibilities, leading to more accurate and respectful portrayals of diverse communities. It allows for a broadening of narrative horizons, enabling stories that may have been marginalized or overlooked to come to the forefront. Moreover, it fosters a more inclusive industry, where voices that have historically been underrepresented gain a platform to tell their stories authentically. In this way, cultural diversification of filmmakers not only enhances the authenticity of cinema but also contributes to a more vibrant, empathetic, and interconnected cinematic landscape that reflects the tapestry of human experiences.

Incorporating Cultural Insiders' Feedback and Collaboration: Nurturing Authentic and Respectful Filmmaking

Feedback and collaboration with individuals from the cultures being portrayed in filmmaking are invaluable for creating nuanced and authentic narratives. When filmmakers actively involve cultural insiders, they gain access to firsthand experiences, perspectives, and cultural insights that may otherwise be overlooked. These collaborations foster a respectful and open dialogue, allowing for a more accurate and nuanced portrayal of cultural elements, traditions, and societal norms. By listening to feedback and engaging in collaborative processes, filmmakers can avoid missteps, stereotypes, or misunderstandings, ensuring that the final product is culturally sensitive and representative. It's an approach that not only elevates storytelling but also promotes mutual understanding and respect, fostering a more inclusive and empathetic cinematic landscape where diverse voices are heard and celebrated.

Cinema's Universal Language: Fostering Empathy for Cross-Cultural Storytelling

Empathy plays a pivotal role in the creation of narratives that transcend cultural boundaries. Filmmakers who approach their subjects with empathy can craft stories that resonate on a universal level, tapping into shared human experiences and emotions that connect us all. While cultures may differ in their customs, languages, and traditions, the fundamental aspects of the human condition remain remarkably consistent. Love, loss, hope, fear, joy, and sorrow are emotions that know no cultural boundaries, and when depicted with authenticity, they become the threads that bind diverse audiences to a story. By focusing on these universal themes, filmmakers can bridge cultural gaps, enabling viewers from different backgrounds to relate to and empathize with the characters and their journeys. This empathetic approach fosters cross-cultural understanding and appreciation, turning cinema into a powerful medium for not only celebrating diversity but also highlighting our shared humanity.

Fostering Empathy and Cultural Understanding: The Power of Intercultural Relationships in Cinema

Narratives that explore intercultural relationships and conflicts provide a unique opportunity to promote understanding and acceptance in cinema. By delving into the complexities of relationships between individuals from diverse cultural backgrounds, filmmakers can shed light on the challenges, joys, and nuances that arise in such dynamics. These stories often portray the initial misunderstandings and cultural clashes, but they also have the power to showcase the growth, empathy, and ultimately, the bridge-building that can occur when people from different cultures come together. By addressing these themes in a sensitive and nuanced manner, filmmakers can inspire audiences to reflect on their own prejudices and biases, encouraging them to embrace diversity and engage in more open and empathetic dialogue. Intercultural narratives thus serve as a catalyst for meaningful discussions about acceptance, tolerance, and the richness that arises from embracing the mosaic of cultural diversity in our interconnected world.

Shaping Societal Change: The Impact of Films that Navigate Cultural Sensitivities

Stories that navigate cultural sensitivities in cinema have the potential to create a profound impact and catalyze positive societal changes. By addressing cultural nuances and challenging stereotypes, these narratives raise awareness about the importance of cultural inclusivity and understanding. They have the capacity to spark conversations on a global scale, encouraging audiences to critically examine their preconceived notions and biases. Instances abound where films have served as catalysts for such discussions, leading to increased awareness and advocacy for cultural diversity, tolerance, and inclusivity. These films not only shed light on the challenges faced by marginalized communities but also inspire viewers to take action, whether through education, advocacy, or simply fostering a more empathetic and accepting worldview. In this way, cinema becomes a powerful tool for social change, as it engages audiences in dialogue, promotes empathy, and contributes to a more inclusive and equitable society.

Navigating cultural sensitivities is essential to crafting stories that honor the diverse fabric of Indian society. By conducting thorough research, respecting traditions, and collaborating with experts, filmmakers can create narratives that not only entertain but also foster cross-cultural understanding and appreciation.

Addressing issues of representation and inclusion in Indian cinema

Diverse Storytelling in Indian Cinema: Beyond Mainstream Narratives

The importance of diverse storytelling in Indian cinema cannot be overstated. It goes beyond merely reflecting the cultural mosaic of the country; it is a testament to the richness and complexity of Indian society. Indian films have traditionally been known for their mainstream narratives, which often center on common themes and characters. However, there is a growing recognition of the need to explore stories from marginalized perspectives, representing a wide range of experiences, cultures, and identities. This inclusivity not only fosters empathy and understanding but also celebrates the diversity within the country. By telling stories from different backgrounds, whether it's regional, linguistic, ethnic, or socioeconomic, Indian cinema has the potential to break stereotypes, challenge prejudices, and inspire audiences to appreciate the multifaceted nature of their society. It also provides a platform for voices that have historically been underrepresented, allowing for more authentic and resonant storytelling that truly reflects the kaleidoscope of India's cultural heritage and contemporary realities.

Inclusive Casting: Authentic Representation and Diversity on Screen

Inclusive casting holds immense significance in the film industry as it goes beyond mere performance and plays a crucial role in authentic representation on screen. When filmmakers cast actors from various backgrounds, ethnicities, and communities to portray characters, they not only ensure a more accurate depiction of the diverse world we live in but also send a powerful message about inclusivity and representation. Inclusive casting allows stories to reflect the reality that people from different backgrounds exist within the same society, breaking away from the limitations of homogenous casting that perpetuates stereotypes and biases. It empowers actors from marginalized communities to share their voices, stories, and experiences, enriching the narrative landscape and fostering greater empathy among audiences. Inclusive casting is a catalyst for change, as it not only broadens opportunities for actors but also paves the way for more authentic, relatable, and resonant storytelling that reflects the multifaceted nature of human existence and the tapestry of diverse identities that make up our world.

Breaking Stereotypes: Subverting Conventions in Indian Cinema for a More Inclusive Future

Breaking stereotypes in Indian cinema is a complex but essential endeavor. For decades, Indian films have perpetuated certain stereotypes related to gender, caste, religion, and regional identity. These stereotypes have not only reinforced biases but also limited the creative potential of storytelling. The challenge lies in subverting these expectations and presenting characters that defy traditional norms. This involves creating narratives that showcase the diversity and complexity of individuals beyond the confines of their stereotypes. For instance, portraying strong, independent female characters who challenge gender roles or showcasing inter-caste or inter-religious relationships that defy societal norms can be powerful ways to challenge entrenched stereotypes. When films embrace these opportunities for creative subversion, they not only contribute to a more inclusive and equitable cinematic landscape but also have the potential to influence societal attitudes and perceptions, paving the way for positive social change.

Championing Underrepresented Voices: The Transformative Power of Inclusive Cinema

Championing underrepresented voices in cinema is a vital step towards fostering a more inclusive and equitable society. It's crucial to recognize that films have the power to shape public opinion, influence attitudes, and spark important conversations about marginalized communities. By giving voice to groups such as the LGBTQ+ community, differently-abled individuals, and others who have historically been marginalized, cinema plays a transformative role in challenging societal biases and prejudices. These narratives empower these voices, providing a platform for their stories to be heard, understood, and empathized with by a wider audience. They serve as a mirror to society, prompting introspection and dialogue about issues that have long been ignored or stigmatized. By championing underrepresented voices, filmmakers not only contribute to a more inclusive cinematic landscape but also inspire real-world change, fostering greater acceptance, empathy, and respect for all members of society, regardless of their background or identity.

Empowerment Through Storytelling: Inspiring Resilience, Advocating for Change, and Celebrating Diverse Voices in Cinema

Empowerment through storytelling is a profound aspect of cinema's impact on society. Narratives that depict characters facing adversity, battling against odds, and ultimately triumphing are not only compelling but also deeply inspirational. These stories resonate with audiences on a visceral level, reminding them of the indomitable human spirit and the capacity for resilience in the face of challenges. Cinema has a unique power to shine a spotlight on underrepresented communities and individuals, shedding light on their struggles and triumphs. When marginalized voices are authentically represented on screen, it fosters empathy and understanding among viewers. Moreover, these narratives can serve as a catalyst for social change by highlighting injustices, sparking conversations, and inspiring action. By portraying stories of empowerment, cinema becomes a potent tool for advocating for positive societal transformation and ensuring that everyone's voice and experiences are recognized, valued, and celebrated.

Authentic Portrayals in Cinema: Fostering Empathy, Breaking Stereotypes, and Promoting Inclusivity

Authenticity in the portrayal of underrepresented communities in cinema holds immense significance. When filmmakers take the time to conduct thorough research, consult with cultural insiders, and represent these communities in a genuine and respectful manner, it not only honors the diversity of human experiences but also has a profound impact on fostering empathy and understanding among audiences. Authentic portrayals help dispel stereotypes and biases, providing a more accurate and nuanced view of these communities' struggles, triumphs, and everyday lives. Such representation humanizes individuals who have often been marginalized or misunderstood, bridging gaps in perception and creating a space for empathy to flourish. It allows viewers to connect on a deeper level with characters and their stories, forging a sense of common humanity that transcends cultural, social, or linguistic differences. In this way, authentic portrayals in cinema serve as a powerful instrument for promoting tolerance, respect, and a more inclusive society that values the richness of diversity in all its forms.

Beyond Clichés: Expanding Cinematic Horizons with Diverse Narratives

The exploration of storylines beyond clichés and formulaic plots is crucial in expanding the horizons of cinema and creating a more inclusive cinematic landscape. Diverse narratives that break away from stereotypes and tired tropes offer a breath of fresh air to the industry. By delving into uncharted territory, filmmakers can uncover hidden gems of storytelling, showcasing the complexity of human experiences and the myriad ways in which stories can be told. These fresh narratives not only engage and captivate audiences but also challenge the status quo, pushing the boundaries of creativity and representation. They reflect the richness of the real world, where life unfolds in unexpected and multifaceted ways. By embracing diverse storylines, cinema celebrates the myriad perspectives, voices, and cultures that make up our global society, ultimately contributing to a more dynamic, empathetic, and vibrant cinematic landscape that reflects the rich tapestry of human existence.

Fostering Authentic Narratives: The Impact of Collaborating with Underrepresented Voices in Filmmaking

Collaborating with writers, directors, and crew members from underrepresented backgrounds is not only valuable but essential in enriching the storytelling process. It brings fresh, diverse perspectives to the creative table, infusing narratives with authenticity and depth. When individuals from underrepresented communities are actively involved in the filmmaking process, their unique experiences and insights help shape narratives that resonate more profoundly with audiences. This collaboration not only contributes to more accurate and respectful portrayals but also fosters a more inclusive and equitable industry.

By giving underrepresented talent the opportunity to share their voices, stories, and expertise, filmmakers can create narratives that reflect the multifaceted nature of our world, challenging stereotypes, and broadening the horizons of cinematic storytelling. Ultimately, this collaborative approach strengthens the industry as a whole, making it more reflective of the diverse society it seeks to represent and entertain.

Embracing Intersectionality: Crafting Authentic Narratives in a Diverse World

Intersectionality, the recognition of individuals' multiple and intersecting identities and experiences, presents both challenges and opportunities in storytelling. Addressing intersectionality in narratives is complex because it requires a nuanced understanding of how various aspects of a person's identity, such as race, gender, sexuality, class, and ability, intersect and influence their experiences. The challenge lies in authentically representing these multifaceted identities without reducing characters to stereotypes or tokenism. However, by navigating this complexity skillfully, filmmakers have the opportunity to create narratives that resonate deeply with diverse audiences. These narratives can shed light on the unique challenges faced by individuals at the intersections of multiple identities, fostering greater empathy and understanding. They also have the potential to inspire discussions about privilege, discrimination, and social justice. In embracing intersectionality, storytelling becomes a powerful tool for promoting inclusivity and acknowledging the rich tapestry of human experiences, encouraging audiences to see and celebrate the multifaceted nature of individuals and their stories.

Fostering a More Inclusive Society: The Filmmaker's Responsibility for Authentic Representation

The responsibility of filmmakers to approach representation with sensitivity and authenticity cannot be overstated. When creators fail to depict underrepresented communities with care and respect, the consequences can be detrimental. Misrepresentations can perpetuate harm, reinforce stereotypes, and deepen societal biases. Filmmakers must recognize that their work has a profound impact on how audiences perceive and understand these communities. Authenticity in representation is not just a matter of storytelling integrity; it's a moral and ethical imperative. By taking the time to engage in thorough research, consult with cultural insiders, and prioritize accurate and respectful portrayals, filmmakers can ensure that their work contributes to positive social change rather than perpetuating harm. Sensitivity to the nuances of different identities and experiences is paramount, and creators should be committed to fostering a more inclusive and empathetic society through their storytelling.

Empowering Audiences Through Positive Role Models: The Impact of Diverse Representation in Cinema

The impact of presenting positive role models from various backgrounds in cinema is profound, as these characters have the potential to inspire and empower audiences. Positive role models challenge societal norms and stereotypes, offering viewers alternative narratives and representations. They encourage individuals to envision themselves as agents of change, transcending barriers and limitations imposed by their circumstances. When films feature characters who defy expectations and overcome adversity, they not only resonate with viewers but also serve as beacons of hope and motivation. These characters become sources of inspiration, reminding audiences that resilience, determination, and integrity can lead to personal growth and positive social change. Ultimately, cinema's ability to depict positive role models from diverse backgrounds contributes to a more inclusive and equitable world by demonstrating that strength, courage, and compassion know no boundaries and are qualities found in every corner of society.

The Era of Inclusive Storytelling: How Audience Demand Shapes the Entertainment Industry

Audience awareness and demand for diverse and inclusive stories have become pivotal factors shaping the entertainment industry. In recent years, there has been a growing recognition that audiences are hungry for narratives that reflect the complexity of our diverse world. This demand has prompted a shift in the industry, with filmmakers, studios, and streaming platforms increasingly prioritizing inclusive storytelling. The box office success and critical acclaim of films that authentically represent underrepresented communities have served as compelling evidence that diversity not only enriches narratives but also drives commercial success. This trend has encouraged more inclusive filmmaking practices, as creators recognize that stories with broad appeal can resonate with a wide range of viewers. As a result, the industry is moving toward greater diversity both in front of and behind the camera, ultimately reshaping the landscape of cinema to better reflect the diverse experiences and perspectives of its global audience.

Addressing representation and inclusion issues in Indian cinema necessitates a comprehensive and deliberate approach that goes beyond mere surface-level diversity. To make meaningful strides, filmmakers must champion marginalized voices, break free from stereotypes, and prioritize the telling of authentic stories that resonate with a broader spectrum of Indian society. This entails giving underrepresented communities, whether defined by gender, caste, religion, or regional background, the opportunity to share their narratives and experiences, resulting in a more inclusive cinematic landscape. By doing so, Indian cinema not only fosters social awareness and empathy but also enriches its storytelling by tapping into the wealth of diverse perspectives, ultimately reflecting the true richness and complexity of Indian society and its multifaceted narratives.

Case studies of films that have successfully balanced cultural authenticity with global appeal

"Slumdog Millionaire" (2008):

"Slumdog Millionaire" (2008) is a cinematic masterpiece that brilliantly captured the essence of Mumbai's slums while resonating with international audiences. Director Danny Boyle skillfully blended Indian cultural elements with a universal narrative of hope and determination to create a film that transcends borders.

Firstly, the film's success in capturing the essence of Mumbai's slums can be attributed to its meticulous attention to detail. The gritty, realistic portrayal of the slum's environment, coupled with authentic locations and settings, provided an immersive experience for viewers. The film's cinematography, with its vibrant and chaotic depiction of the city, offered a window into the daily life of the slum dwellers. This authenticity not only lent credibility to the narrative but also showcased the resilience and spirit of the people living in such challenging conditions.

Moreover, "Slumdog Millionaire" masterfully blended Indian cultural elements, such as music and dance, with a universal narrative. The film's soundtrack, composed by A.R. Rahman, featured a fusion of traditional Indian instruments and modern beats, creating a musical backdrop that was both culturally rich and accessible to a global audience. The use of Bollywood-style dance sequences, like the iconic "Jai Ho" performance, added an element of spectacle and entertainment while reinforcing the film's underlying themes of love and aspiration.

At its core, "Slumdog Millionaire" tells a universal story of hope, determination, and the relentless pursuit of dreams. The narrative of Jamal Malik, a young boy from the slums who defies the odds to participate in a quiz show, struck a chord with audiences worldwide. It resonated because it tapped into the universal themes of love, destiny, and the idea that anyone, regardless of their background, can achieve greatness.

"Slumdog Millionaire" succeeded in capturing the essence of Mumbai's slums by meticulously portraying their environment while appealing to international audiences through a blend of Indian cultural elements and a universal narrative of hope and determination. The film's ability to bridge cultural divides and connect with viewers on a profound emotional level is a testament to its exceptional storytelling and filmmaking.

"Lagaan" (2001):

"Lagaan" (2001) stands as a cinematic marvel for its ability to seamlessly blend traditional Indian settings and cricket with a universally relatable underdog story. The film, directed by Ashutosh Gowariker, transcended cultural boundaries by weaving together elements that resonated with both Indian and international audiences.

Firstly, "Lagaan" is set in the backdrop of rural India during the British colonial era, a historical context that immediately immerses viewers in the rich tapestry of Indian culture and heritage. The film's depiction of rural life, complete with vibrant costumes, folk music, and traditional rituals, authentically captured the essence of rural India. The cricket matches, which are central to the plot, were ingeniously integrated into this setting, making them an integral part of the narrative.

Cricket, a sport deeply cherished in India, served as a unifying element, allowing audiences to connect with the story on a personal level. The underdog theme, where a group of villagers takes on the oppressive British rulers in a high-stakes cricket match, is a universally relatable and timeless narrative. The idea of a marginalized community defying odds and challenging a powerful oppressor strikes a chord with people from diverse backgrounds, as it taps into the human desire for justice, freedom, and triumph against adversity.

"Lagaan" delves into themes of unity, resistance, and cultural pride, which resonate with viewers globally. The film portrays the villagers coming together, transcending differences of caste and creed, to fight for a common cause. This theme of unity in the face of adversity is a universal one, touching the hearts of audiences regardless of their cultural background.

The concept of resistance against injustice is another theme that holds cross-cultural appeal. The villagers' struggle against the unjust tax imposed by the British is a story of resilience and the indomitable human spirit. It sends a message that resonates with anyone who values the principles of fairness and equality.

"Lagaan" masterfully combined traditional Indian settings and cricket with a universally relatable underdog story. Its historical context, themes of unity and resistance, and the portrayal of the human spirit's triumph against adversity made it a film that appealed to diverse audiences around the world. The film's ability to transcend cultural boundaries while celebrating India's rich heritage and values is a testament to its storytelling prowess and its lasting impact on the global cinematic landscape.

"My Name is Khan" (2010):

"My Name is Khan" (2010), directed by Karan Johar, is a powerful film that delicately addresses cultural and religious sensitivities while conveying a resounding message of inclusivity. It achieves this by exploring the global resonance of its themes related to discrimination, love, and personal growth.

The film centers on Rizwan Khan, played by Shah Rukh Khan, an autistic man of Muslim descent living in the United States. His journey unfolds against the backdrop of post-9/11 America, a time marked by heightened cultural and religious tensions. Rizwan's character is portrayed with sensitivity, offering a nuanced representation of autism and challenging stereotypes surrounding it.

One of the film's remarkable achievements is its exploration of cultural and religious sensitivities. It presents the struggles faced by Rizwan and his wife, Mandira, played by Kajol, as they encounter prejudice and discrimination in the aftermath of 9/11. The film addresses the Islamophobia and xenophobia prevalent during that time, shedding light on the challenges faced by Muslim communities, not just in the U.S. but globally. By doing so, "My Name is Khan" prompts a reflection on the importance of understanding and embracing diversity, regardless of one's cultural or religious background.

Moreover, the film's central message of inclusivity is deeply resonant on a global scale. It highlights the universality of human emotions and the capacity for love and compassion to transcend differences. Rizwan's journey to meet the President of the United States to convey his message, "My name is Khan, and I am not a terrorist," symbolizes the power of an individual's actions to make a difference and challenge societal prejudices.

The film also emphasizes the transformative power of personal growth and understanding. Rizwan's journey is not just about confronting discrimination but also about his own self-discovery and growth as an individual. His determination to spread a message of love and acceptance underscores the idea that change begins with one person and can have a ripple effect on society.

"My Name is Khan" gained international recognition for its nuanced portrayal of cultural and religious sensitivities, and its themes of discrimination, love, and personal growth resonate with audiences worldwide. It serves as a reminder that cinema has the capacity to bridge divides, foster empathy, and promote inclusivity, making it a powerful medium for addressing complex and sensitive issues on a global stage.

"Bend It Like Beckham" (2002):

"Bend It Like Beckham" (2002), directed by Gurinder Chadha, is a delightful film that adeptly navigates cultural expectations, family dynamics, and women's empowerment. It achieves this by presenting a relatable coming-of-age narrative that transcends cultural boundaries.

The film revolves around the story of Jess Bhamra, a British-Indian teenager played by Parminder Nagra, who aspires to become a professional soccer player, inspired by her idol David Beckham. However, her dreams clash with the traditional values and expectations of her Sikh family, who expect her to conform to cultural norms and focus on marriage and domestic life.

One of the film's strengths is its exploration of cultural expectations and the tension between generations. It portrays the struggle many first-generation immigrants face in balancing their heritage with the desire to embrace the opportunities of their adopted country. The clash between Jess's passion for soccer and her family's expectations creates a narrative that resonates with individuals from diverse cultural backgrounds who have grappled with similar dilemmas.

The family dynamics in "Bend It Like Beckham" are portrayed with depth and nuance. The film showcases the love and warmth within Jess's family while also addressing the generational divide and the challenges of intercultural communication. The characters, especially Jess's parents, are depicted as complex individuals with their own hopes, fears, and dreams. This portrayal humanizes them and fosters empathy, allowing audiences to understand their concerns even as they root for Jess to pursue her dreams.

Women's empowerment is a central theme in the film. Jess and her friend Jules, portrayed by Keira Knightley, are determined to challenge stereotypes and break gender barriers in soccer. Their journey represents the broader struggle for gender equality and empowerment. Jess's resilience and determination serve as an inspiration to women and girls, irrespective of their cultural backgrounds, encouraging them to pursue their passions and defy societal limitations.

"Bend It Like Beckham" is a coming-of-age story that resonates universally. Jess's journey of self-discovery, her friendships, and her pursuit of her dreams are relatable to young people worldwide who navigate the complexities of adolescence and the desire to assert their individuality. The film's humor, heart, and authenticity make it accessible and enjoyable for a global audience.

"Bend It Like Beckham" skillfully navigates cultural expectations, family dynamics, and women's empowerment through a relatable coming-of-age narrative. Its ability to explore these themes while maintaining a universal appeal has made it a beloved film that transcends cultural boundaries. It serves as a celebration of diversity and a testament to the power of storytelling to bridge cultural divides and inspire audiences around the world.

"Life of Pi" (2012):

"Life of Pi" (2012), directed by Ang Lee, is a visually captivating film that masterfully merges Indian spirituality and storytelling with a universal tale of survival. It achieves this by using symbolism and rich cultural imagery that resonated with global audiences.

The film is based on Yann Martel's novel and follows the journey of Pi Patel, a young Indian man played by Suraj Sharma, who survives a shipwreck and finds himself stranded on a lifeboat in the Pacific Ocean with a Bengal tiger named Richard Parker. The narrative unfolds as Pi navigates the challenges of survival and forms an unlikely bond with the tiger.

One of the film's remarkable features is its exploration of spirituality and faith. Pi is a devout follower of Hinduism, Christianity, and Islam, a unique aspect of his character that reflects India's religious diversity. The film beautifully portrays his faith as a source of strength and solace during his ordeal. This aspect of the story not only adds depth to the character but also underscores the theme of the coexistence of different beliefs and the power of spirituality in the face of adversity.

"Life of Pi" utilizes symbolism in a profound way, drawing from Indian cultural and spiritual imagery. The presence of the tiger, Richard Parker, is symbolic of Pi's inner strength, survival instincts, and his ability to confront the wild and untamed aspects of his own nature. The film's use of metaphorical storytelling, combined with stunning visual effects, creates a rich tapestry of symbolism that resonates on both a spiritual and emotional level.

The film's rich cultural imagery extends beyond symbolism. The visual aesthetics of the movie are heavily influenced by Indian art and spirituality. The vibrant colours, intricate patterns, and the use of water as a metaphor for life and transformation all draw from Indian artistic traditions. These elements create a visually stunning and immersive cinematic experience that captures the essence of India's cultural and spiritual richness.

"Life of Pi" resonated with global audiences because it told a universal story of survival, self-discovery, and the resilience of the human spirit. The film's themes of faith, belief, and the interconnectedness of all living beings transcend cultural boundaries, making it relatable to viewers from diverse backgrounds. It also serves as a testament to the power of storytelling to bridge cultural divides and ignite a sense of wonder and introspection.

I"Life of Pi" successfully merges Indian spirituality and storytelling with a universal survival narrative. Through its use of symbolism, rich cultural imagery, and exploration of faith, it resonates with global audiences and leaves a lasting impact. The film is a testament to the power of cinema to convey profound and universal themes while celebrating the beauty of cultural diversity.

"The Lunchbox" (2013):

"The Lunchbox" (2013), directed by Ritesh Batra, is a beautifully crafted film that delicately explores urban loneliness and human connections against the backdrop of Mumbai's lunchbox delivery system, the dabbawala network. What makes this film particularly remarkable is its ability to convey emotional depth and relatable themes that transcend cultural specificities.

The film's narrative revolves around two central characters: Saajan Fernandes, played by Irrfan Khan, a middle-aged office worker on the verge of retirement, and Ila, portrayed by Nimrat Kaur, a lonely housewife seeking to rekindle her husband's affection. Their lives become unexpectedly entwined when a lunchbox, prepared by Ila, is mistakenly delivered to Saajan instead of her husband.

The lunchbox delivery system, an integral part of Mumbai's culture, serves as the backdrop for the film. It's not merely a logistical concept but a metaphor for the intricate connections that exist in a bustling city where millions coexist but often remain isolated. The film uses this system to symbolize the idea that meaningful connections can emerge from the most mundane and routine aspects of life.

At its core, "The Lunchbox" is a story about loneliness and the yearning for human connection. Saajan and Ila, both trapped in their respective lives, find solace and companionship through handwritten notes exchanged via the lunchbox. These notes become a lifeline, allowing them to share their thoughts, dreams, and emotions. The film beautifully portrays the emotional intimacy that develops between the characters, even though they have never met in person.

What makes "The Lunchbox" universally relatable is its exploration of fundamental human emotions—loneliness, longing, and the search for meaning. The characters' experiences resonate with viewers from all walks of life who have, at some point, felt disconnected or yearned for a deeper connection. While the film is rooted in the specific setting of Mumbai, its themes are universal and strike a chord with audiences worldwide.

The film's emotional depth is further enhanced by outstanding performances from Irrfan Khan and Nimrat Kaur. Their subtle and nuanced acting brings the characters to life, making their journey of self-discovery and connection profoundly moving. The chemistry between the two actors is palpable, despite their limited on-screen interaction, highlighting the power of human connection.

"The Lunchbox" is a testament to the ability of cinema to explore complex themes of urban loneliness and human connection while transcending cultural specificities. It captures the essence of Mumbai's bustling life while telling a universally relatable story of love, longing, and the transformative power of human connection. The film's emotional depth and universal appeal make it a standout piece of cinema that continues to resonate with audiences around the world.

"Queen" (2014):

"Queen" (2014), directed by Vikas Bahl, is a groundbreaking Indian film that empowers its protagonist, Rani, to embark on a transformative journey of self-discovery after her wedding is abruptly canceled. What sets this film apart is its themes of independence and self-empowerment, which resonated not only with Indian audiences but also with viewers worldwide.

The film begins with Rani, played by Kangana Ranaut, in a state of shock and despair after her fiancé calls off their wedding. Initially devastated, she makes a bold decision to go on her honeymoon trip to Europe alone, a destination originally planned for her honeymoon. This decision marks the beginning of Rani's journey towards self-rediscovery.

"Queen" is a coming-of-age story that explores Rani's personal growth and her realization of her own worth and potential. As she travels through Europe, she encounters various characters and experiences that challenge her preconceptions and encourage her to step out of her comfort zone. Her journey of self-discovery is not only about geographical exploration but also about finding her inner strength and independence.

One of the film's most striking aspects is its depiction of Rani's transformation. She evolves from a timid, sheltered woman bound by societal expectations into a confident and self-assured individual who embraces life's challenges. The film's message is clear: a woman doesn't need a man to complete her; she can find fulfillment and happiness within herself.

"Queen" addresses universal themes of independence and self-empowerment that resonate with audiences worldwide. Rani's journey is a testament to the idea that anyone can break free from societal constraints and discover their true potential. Her story is one of empowerment, and it serves as an inspiration to individuals who may feel trapped by societal expectations or personal insecurities.

Kangana Ranaut's portrayal of Rani earned her widespread acclaim, and her character became an iconic symbol of female empowerment. Rani's relatability and her journey towards self-discovery transcended cultural boundaries, making her a beloved character not just in India but also among international audiences.

"Queen" is a remarkable film that empowers its protagonist to embark on a transformative journey of self-discovery. Its themes of independence and self-empowerment struck a chord with viewers beyond India, making it a universally relatable and inspirational story. The film's message—that one can find strength and happiness within oneself—is a powerful and enduring one that continues to resonate with audiences around the world.

"Dangal" (2016):

"Dangal" (2016), directed by Nitesh Tiwari, is a critically acclaimed Indian film that celebrated female athletes and challenged gender stereotypes within the context of India's wrestling culture. This sports biopic also explored universal themes of ambition, perseverance, and parent-child relationships, making it a resonant and inspirational story for audiences worldwide.

The film is based on the real-life story of Mahavir Singh Phogat, played by Aamir Khan, a former wrestler who had to give up his dreams of winning a gold medal for India due to family and financial constraints. Determined to fulfill his dream through his children, Phogat defies societal norms by training his daughters, Geeta and Babita, in the male-dominated sport of wrestling.

"Dangal" stands out for its portrayal of strong and determined female athletes who break barriers and prove themselves in a sport traditionally dominated by men. Geeta Phogat, played by Fatima Sana Shaikh, and Babita Kumari, portrayed by Sanya Malhotra, undergo rigorous training, face societal opposition, and eventually become successful wrestlers, with Geeta winning a gold medal at the Commonwealth Games. The film not only celebrates their achievements but also challenges the notion that women are less capable than men in any field.

The film also delves into the complexities of parent-child relationships, particularly the father-daughter bond. Mahavir Singh Phogat's unwavering belief in his daughters' potential and his relentless training methods, which include breaking gender norms, are met with resistance initially. However, the story beautifully portrays the evolving relationship between the father and his daughters as they begin to understand his vision and dedication. This emotional depth adds a universal appeal to the film, as it explores themes of ambition, sacrifice, and the pursuit of excellence.

"Dangal" transcends cultural boundaries with its universal themes of ambition, perseverance, and the power of family bonds. The film's message—that gender should not limit one's aspirations and capabilities—is a message that resonates not only in India but also with audiences worldwide. The inspiring journey of Geeta and Babita Phogat serves as a testament to the human spirit's ability to overcome obstacles and achieve greatness.

Aamir Khan's exceptional performance as Mahavir Singh Phogat earned him critical acclaim, and his dedication to the role, including undergoing a remarkable physical transformation, added authenticity to the character. The performances of the young actors who portrayed Geeta and Babita were also widely praised for their portrayal of determined and resilient athletes.

"Dangal" is a powerful film that celebrates female athletes, challenges gender stereotypes, and explores universal themes of ambition and parent-child relationships. Its inspirational story of the Phogat sisters' journey to success resonates with audiences around the world, making it a culturally significant and emotionally compelling cinematic experience.

"The Namesake" (2006):

"The Namesake" (2006), directed by Mira Nair and based on Jhumpa Lahiri's novel of the same name, is a poignant exploration of the immigrant experience, capturing the struggles of first-generation immigrants in the United States while remaining deeply rooted in Indian cultural experiences. The film portrays the complexities of generational and cultural identity conflicts, making it a compelling narrative that resonates with a diverse audience.

The film's central character, Gogol Ganguli, played by Kal Penn, is born to Bengali immigrant parents, Ashoke and Ashima Ganguli, portrayed by Irrfan Khan and Tabu, in the United States. Gogol's name itself becomes a symbol of his cultural duality, as he is named after the famous Russian author, Nikolai Gogol, which reflects his parents' aspirations for assimilation into American society. However, Gogol grapples with his unusual name and the tension between his Indian heritage and American upbringing throughout the film.

One of the film's strengths lies in its portrayal of the immigrant experience, from the challenges of adapting to a new culture to the sense of displacement and longing for one's homeland. The Ganguli family's struggle to balance their Indian traditions and values with the cultural influences of their new home is a theme that resonates deeply with immigrants from various backgrounds. The film captures the essence of the Indian-American diaspora, highlighting the importance of preserving one's cultural heritage while embracing the opportunities of a new world.

"The Namesake" also explores generational conflicts within immigrant families. Gogol's parents, who cling to their Indian customs and traditions, often clash with their American-born children, who are more assimilated into Western culture. This intergenerational tension is a universal theme that transcends cultural boundaries, as it reflects the challenges faced by immigrant families worldwide when navigating the delicate balance between preserving their cultural roots and adapting to a new environment.

The film's narrative is woven with emotional depth, touching on themes of identity, belonging, and the search for one's place in the world. Gogol's journey of self-discovery and acceptance of his heritage is a relatable narrative that resonates with audiences of diverse backgrounds. It emphasizes the importance of understanding and embracing one's cultural identity as an integral part of who they are.

Mira Nair's direction infuses the film with a rich visual and emotional tapestry, capturing the vibrancy of Indian culture and the quiet moments of introspection experienced by the characters. The performances, particularly by Irrfan Khan and Tabu, are exceptional and add authenticity to the portrayal of the Ganguli family's experiences.

"The Namesake" is a heartfelt exploration of the immigrant experience, delving into the struggles of first-generation immigrants in the United States while remaining deeply rooted in Indian cultural experiences. Its portrayal of generational and cultural identity conflicts makes it a universally resonant film that speaks to the complexities of the human experience, making it a significant and emotionally engaging cinematic work.

"Pad Man" (2018):

"Pad Man" (2018), directed by R. Balki and inspired by the life of Arunachalam Muruganantham, is a groundbreaking Indian film that fearlessly addresses the taboo topic of menstrual hygiene in India while promoting empowerment, advocacy for social change, and resonating with global conversations around women's rights.

The film revolves around the life of Lakshmi Chauhan, played by Akshay Kumar, a small-town mechanic who becomes obsessed with the issue of menstrual hygiene after realizing the dire consequences of using unsanitary rags during menstruation. Fueled by a desire to help his wife and other women in his community, he embarks on a mission to create affordable and accessible sanitary napkins. Lakshmi's journey from being an outsider to a menstrual hygiene innovator is at the heart of the film's narrative.

One of the film's notable strengths is its bold approach to addressing a topic that has been shrouded in silence and stigma in India for centuries. Menstrual hygiene, often considered a deeply private and taboo subject, is brought to the forefront of public discourse through the film's compelling storytelling. "Pad Man" takes an unflinching look at the challenges women face due to the lack of access to safe menstrual hygiene products and challenges societal norms that have perpetuated this silence.

The film promotes empowerment by showcasing the determination and resourcefulness of its protagonist, Lakshmi, who defies societal norms and confronts entrenched patriarchal attitudes to pursue his mission. Lakshmi's character embodies the spirit of empowerment, as he not only invents a low-cost sanitary pad-making machine but also encourages women to use them and break free from the shackles of menstrual stigma. His unwavering commitment to change the status quo serves as an inspirational story of an individual's capacity to bring about transformative social change.

"Pad Man" advocates for social change by shedding light on the economic, health, and social consequences of inadequate menstrual hygiene practices. It challenges the silence and ignorance surrounding menstruation and calls for open discussions and awareness campaigns. The film's impact extends beyond the screen, as it has been credited with sparking conversations and initiatives related to menstrual hygiene, not only in India but also on the global stage.

The film's resonation with global conversations around women's rights is significant. "Pad Man" aligns with the broader movement advocating for women's empowerment, gender equality, and access to healthcare. Its message transcends borders, making it relatable to audiences worldwide who are engaged in discussions about breaking taboos, promoting women's health, and challenging societal norms.

R. Balki's direction combines elements of drama, humor, and social commentary, making the film both entertaining and thought-provoking. Akshay Kumar's portrayal of Lakshmi is both endearing and inspiring, and the supporting cast delivers strong performances.

"Pad Man" is a powerful film that fearlessly tackles the taboo subject of menstrual hygiene in India while promoting empowerment, advocating for social change, and resonating with global conversations around women's rights. Its bold approach, inspirational storytelling, and impactful message have made it a significant contribution to the discourse on a crucial and long-overlooked issue, sparking meaningful change and awareness.

"Dilwale Dulhania Le Jayenge" (1995):

"Dilwale Dulhania Le Jayenge" (DDLJ), released in 1995 and directed by Aditya Chopra, stands as an iconic Bollywood film that masterfully balanced Indian family values and traditions with a universal love story, achieving enduring popularity across cultures and generations.

At its core, DDLJ is a classic romantic tale of two young individuals, Raj and Simran, played by Shah Rukh Khan and Kajol, who meet while traveling in Europe. The film's initial setting in London and Switzerland adds a refreshing international flavor to the narrative, setting it apart from the traditional Bollywood love stories of the time. However, it's the film's ability to seamlessly weave in Indian family values and traditions that makes it a timeless classic.

The film begins with the introduction of Raj and Simran, who come from contrasting backgrounds. Simran belongs to a conservative Punjabi family settled in London, while Raj is an NRI (Non-Resident Indian) who grew up in London but retains a strong connection to his Indian roots. As the story unfolds, DDLJ explores the complexities of love and cultural identity.

One of the film's defining characteristics is its portrayal of traditional Indian family values, particularly the close-knit and emotionally charged relationships within an Indian family. Simran's relationship with her father, played by Amrish Puri, is central to the film. Her father's strict adherence to tradition and his initial reluctance to accept Raj as a suitor forms the crux of the conflict in the story. This conflict resonated deeply with Indian audiences, as it mirrored the generational clashes that often occur within traditional families when it comes to matters of love and marriage.

Despite these cultural conflicts, DDLJ managed to appeal to a global audience due to its universal themes of love, determination, and the importance of family. The film beautifully portrays the idea that love can transcend cultural boundaries and differences. Raj's relentless pursuit of Simran, his unwavering commitment to winning her father's approval, and the iconic train station climax scene became iconic moments that resonated with viewers worldwide.

The music of DDLJ, composed by Jatin-Lalit with lyrics by Anand Bakshi, played a pivotal role in its popularity. The songs, including "Tujhe Dekha Toh," "Mere Khwabon Mein," and "Tum Hi Ho Bandhu," are timeless classics that continue to be cherished by audiences of all ages. The music added an emotional depth to the narrative, enhancing the film's universal appeal.

What sets DDLJ apart is its ability to strike a balance between traditional values and contemporary aspirations. It acknowledges the importance of respecting cultural traditions while also encouraging individuals to follow their hearts. This message of cultural acceptance and love prevailing over cultural differences has made DDLJ a beloved film not only in India but also among the Indian diaspora and global audiences.

The film's enduring popularity can be attributed to its ability to connect with different generations. It has become a cultural touchstone, with families often passing down their love for DDLJ to younger generations. The characters of Raj and Simran have become iconic, and the film's dialogues and scenes are widely quoted and imitated.

"Dilwale Dulhania Le Jayenge" is a classic romantic film that successfully balanced Indian family values and traditions with a universal love story. Its enduring popularity across cultures and generations is a testament to its timeless appeal and the universal themes it explores, making it one of the most beloved and iconic films in the history of Indian cinema.

These case studies illustrate how certain films managed to strike a balance between their cultural authenticity and global appeal. By weaving culturally specific elements into universally resonant narratives, these films engaged audiences around the world while also celebrating the uniqueness of Indian culture and perspectives.

CHAPTER - 12

12. Distribution and Marketing

The Evolving Landscape of Film Distribution and Marketing in India

Evolution of Theatrical Distribution: From Single-Screen Theaters to Multiplex Cinemas

The traditional theatrical release has historically been the dominant distribution channel for films, serving as the primary platform for showcasing cinematic creations to audiences. This model has been a cornerstone of the film industry for decades, with single-screen theaters being the primary exhibition venues. These single-screen theaters, often grand and opulent, were the go-to destinations for moviegoers, offering a communal and immersive experience. However, as the film industry evolved, the transition to multiplexes became evident. Multiplex cinemas introduced the concept of multiple screens under one roof, offering audiences a wider choice of films and showtimes, as well as enhanced amenities like comfortable seating, better sound systems, and improved concessions. This shift aimed to provide a more diverse and enjoyable cinematic experience, catering to a broader range of tastes and preferences. While traditional theatrical releases have faced challenges in recent years, including competition from digital platforms, they continue to play a vital role in the film industry, providing a communal and immersive setting for audiences to enjoy the magic of cinema.

The Digital Disruption: How Streaming Platforms Have Transformed Film Distribution

The emergence of digital platforms and streaming services has brought about a significant disruption in the landscape of film distribution. Over-the-top (OTT) platforms such as Netflix, Amazon Prime Video, Disney+ Hotstar, and many others have revolutionized the way films are consumed. These platforms offer a wide array of content that is accessible anytime, anywhere, and on multiple devices, providing unprecedented convenience to viewers. This shift has not only expanded the reach of films to a global audience but has also challenged the traditional theatrical release model. Filmmakers and studios now have additional avenues to release their work, leading to greater diversity in content and the ability to cater to niche audiences. Furthermore, the convenience of streaming services has been particularly advantageous during periods of restricted theatrical access, as seen during the COVID-19 pandemic. However, this digital disruption has also raised questions about the future of movie theaters and the economics of filmmaking, as the balance between theatrical releases and digital distribution continues to evolve.

The Rise of Direct-to-OTT Releases: Transforming Film Distribution in the Digital Age

Direct-to-OTT (Over-The-Top) releases have emerged as a prominent distribution strategy, allowing films to bypass traditional theatrical releases and debut directly on digital platforms. This approach offers several advantages, including the ability to reach a global audience instantaneously, eliminating geographical limitations. Filmmakers can leverage the extensive subscriber bases of platforms like Netflix, Amazon Prime Video, and Disney+ Hotstar to ensure widespread visibility for their work. However, it also presents challenges, particularly in terms of revenue sharing. The traditional box office model, where theaters share a portion of ticket sales with studios, has been disrupted, prompting discussions about fair compensation in the digital landscape. Additionally, while direct-to-OTT releases offer accessibility, they can sometimes lack the communal and immersive experience of theaters. Nonetheless, this distribution model has become increasingly relevant, especially during periods of restricted theatrical access, and has forever altered the film industry's distribution dynamics.

The Hybrid Release Model: Navigating the Convergence of Theatrical and OTT Distribution in Film

Hybrid release models, where films are simultaneously released in theaters and on Over-The-Top (OTT) platforms, have gained prominence as a response to changing audience preferences and industry dynamics. This approach offers several benefits, most notably the flexibility to cater to diverse audience preferences. While some viewers may prefer the traditional cinematic experience of theaters, others seek the convenience and accessibility of streaming platforms. Hybrid releases strike a balance by allowing filmmakers to tap into both markets simultaneously, maximizing their reach and revenue potential. This model has been particularly effective during the COVID-19 pandemic when theaters faced restrictions, demonstrating the adaptability and resilience of the film industry in meeting evolving audience demands. It also opens up new avenues for collaboration between studios, distributors, and streaming platforms, shaping the future of film distribution.

The Resurgence of Regional Cinema: A Paradigm Shift in Indian Film Distribution

The resurgence of regional cinema is a testament to the evolving landscape of Indian film distribution. Regional films, produced in languages other than Hindi, have gained immense popularity and expanded their reach beyond their traditional markets, largely due to the digital revolution and the presence of these films on Over-The-Top (OTT) platforms. This phenomenon is driven by several factors, including the unique storytelling, cultural authenticity, and relatability of regional narratives. Audiences are increasingly seeking diverse and culturally rich content, which regional cinema readily provides. Additionally, streaming platforms have made these films accessible to a global audience, breaking language barriers and enabling subtitles and dubbing options. As a result, regional films are not only finding new audiences within India but are also gaining international recognition. This trend showcases the rich tapestry of Indian cinema and reinforces the idea that storytelling transcends language, making regional cinema a vital and integral part of the industry's growth and diversification.

The Digital Revolution: Transforming Film Marketing Through Social Media Platforms

The film industry has witnessed a significant shift towards online marketing, primarily driven by the pervasive influence of social media platforms. Filmmakers and studios now recognize the immense potential of platforms like Facebook, Twitter, Instagram, and YouTube in creating pre-release buzz and engaging audiences directly. Trailers, posters, and teaser content are strategically shared across these platforms, generating excitement and anticipation among fans and followers. Interactive marketing campaigns, such as hashtag challenges, live Q&A sessions with cast and crew, and behind-the-scenes glimpses, provide a more immersive experience, forging a deeper connection between the film and its audience. This approach not only reaches a wider demographic but also allows for real-time feedback and instant engagement, fostering a sense of community around the film. The democratization of marketing through social media has empowered smaller productions to compete on a level playing field with larger studios, making online marketing an indispensable tool in the modern film industry's promotional arsenal.

The Data-Driven Revolution: Optimizing Film Marketing and Distribution in the Digital Age

In the contemporary film industry, data-driven strategies have become instrumental in optimizing marketing campaigns and distribution decisions. Through sophisticated data analytics, filmmakers and studios can gain valuable insights into their target demographics, enabling them to craft highly personalized marketing efforts. By analyzing factors like audience behavior, preferences, and viewing habits, they can create content that resonates more effectively with potential viewers. Additionally, data analytics extends its influence to distribution decisions, helping filmmakers determine the most suitable release platforms and geographic regions. This data-driven approach not only enhances the efficiency of marketing expenditure but also increases the likelihood of a film's success by aligning it with the preferences of the intended audience. It exemplifies how the integration of technology and data science has revolutionized the film industry, offering a more precise and strategic approach to both marketing and distribution.

Innovative Film Promotion: Beyond Advertising - Engaging Audiences with Celebrity Endorsements, Interactive Events, and Viral Challenges

In the dynamic landscape of film promotion, innovative campaigns have emerged as powerful tools for creating engagement and anticipation among audiences. These strategies often go beyond traditional advertising and tap into the realms of social media and interactive events. Celebrity endorsements, where popular figures from the film industry or other domains lend their support, lend credibility and star power to a project. Interactive events, such as virtual premieres or live Q&A sessions with the cast and crew, provide fans with direct access to the film's creators, fostering a sense of community and excitement. Viral challenges, where fans are encouraged to participate in creative challenges related to the film, not only generate buzz but also turn audiences into active participants in the promotional process. These innovative approaches not only capture the attention of potential viewers but also leverage their active involvement in shaping the film's narrative, resulting in heightened anticipation and a more interactive and immersive experience leading up to the film's release.

Enhancing Global Accessibility: The Role of Subtitles and Dubbing in International Distribution of Indian Films

The international distribution of Indian films through OTT (Over-The-Top) platforms has opened up new frontiers for the Indian film industry, allowing it to reach a global audience. However, to make these films truly accessible and enjoyable to viewers around the world, localization efforts play a pivotal role. Subtitles and dubbing are two key elements in this process. Subtitles provide translations of dialogue and on-screen text, allowing non-Indian audiences to follow the story while still hearing the original language. On the other hand, dubbing involves replacing the original language soundtrack with a voiceover in the viewer's preferred language, ensuring a more immersive experience. These localization efforts not only break down language barriers but also enable Indian cinema to connect with a diverse global audience, enhancing its international appeal and fostering cross-cultural understanding. In essence, they transform Indian films into a global commodity, making them more accessible and enjoyable for viewers across the world.

Expanding Horizons: The Transformative Impact of Regional and Global Collaborations in Indian Cinema

The rise of regional and global collaborations in the Indian film industry has significantly diversified both content and distribution opportunities. Indian filmmakers are increasingly partnering with international production and distribution companies, leading to a fusion of creative ideas and storytelling styles. These collaborations bring together the expertise of Indian cinema, known for its rich narratives and vibrant cultural elements, with the global reach and resources of international partners. This not only results in the creation of films with broader international appeal but also facilitates the distribution of Indian cinema to a wider audience around the world. Moreover, these collaborations often bring in international talent, fostering a cross-pollination of skills and ideas that enrich the creative landscape of Indian cinema. Overall, such partnerships reflect the evolving nature of the industry and its readiness to embrace diverse influences and audiences, making Indian films more globally relevant than ever before.

Embracing the Virtual: The Phenomenon of Digital Film Premieres and Online Launch Events

The trend of virtual film premieres and online launch events has gained significant traction in recent times, primarily driven by the need to adapt to changing circumstances, including the COVID-19 pandemic. These digital premieres and events have proven highly effective in reaching wider and more diverse audiences globally. By leveraging the power of online platforms and social media, filmmakers can create buzz and anticipation for their films, engaging with fans and critics alike in real-time. This approach allows for broader accessibility, enabling viewers from different regions to participate and celebrate the film's release simultaneously. Moreover, the interactive nature of virtual events, such as live Q&A sessions with the cast and crew, provides a unique opportunity for fans to connect with their favorite filmmakers and gain insights into the creative process. As a result, digital premieres and virtual launch events have become a valuable addition to the film marketing and distribution landscape, offering both convenience and an enhanced sense of community for movie enthusiasts.

Reimagining Revenue: The Transition from Box Office to Subscription-Based Models in the Film Industry

The shift from traditional box office revenue to subscription-based models on OTT (Over-The-Top) platforms represents a significant transformation in the film industry's revenue landscape. While box office earnings have long been the primary source of income for filmmakers, the advent of OTT platforms has introduced a new era of monetization. Subscription-based models offer a steady and predictable stream of revenue, as viewers pay a monthly fee for access to a vast library of content. This shift has opened up opportunities for filmmakers to create diverse and niche content that might not have thrived solely on theatrical releases. However, it also poses challenges, such as increased competition for audience attention and the need for platforms to continuously generate fresh, compelling content to retain subscribers. Additionally, the traditional film distribution ecosystem, including theaters and distributors, is undergoing significant changes, and stakeholders must adapt to this evolving landscape. Ultimately, this shift reflects a broader transformation in the media and entertainment industry, where digital platforms are redefining how content is produced, distributed, and monetized.

The landscape of film distribution sond marketing in India has transformed significantly with the rise of digital platforms and changing audience behaviors. The traditional theatrical model coexists with online streaming, offering filmmakers diverse avenues to reach their target audiences. The blending of technology, data-driven strategies, and innovative marketing campaigns is shaping a dynamic and multifaceted distribution ecosystem.

Strategies for reaching diverse audiences across different regions and languages

Cultural Sensitivity in Storytelling: Bridging Global Audiences through Authentic Representation

Cultural sensitivity is a fundamental aspect of successful storytelling, particularly when it comes to creating content that resonates with diverse global audiences. It involves a deep understanding of the cultural nuances, customs, and values of different regions and communities. Filmmakers and content creators who prioritize cultural sensitivity not only avoid perpetuating harmful stereotypes but also demonstrate respect for local traditions and beliefs. This approach not only fosters a more authentic representation of the cultures depicted but also enhances the audience's connection to the narrative. When audiences see their cultures and experiences portrayed with authenticity and respect on screen, it can lead to a stronger emotional engagement, a sense of inclusion, and a greater appreciation for the story being told. In an era of global connectivity, cultural sensitivity has become an essential element in bridging cultural gaps and fostering a deeper appreciation of the diverse world we live in through the medium of film.

Localized Marketing: Crafting Connection with Regional Audiences in a Global Film Landscape

Localized marketing plays a pivotal role in the success of a film's distribution strategy, especially in a diverse and culturally rich global landscape. It involves the meticulous customization of marketing campaigns to align with the unique preferences, sensibilities, and expectations of specific regional audiences. This can encompass a range of elements, from adapting promotional materials, such as posters and trailers, to featuring regional celebrities in endorsements and advertisements. The goal is to create a connection between the film and the audience by speaking directly to their cultural and emotional sensibilities. This approach not only enhances the relatability of the film but also demonstrates a genuine effort to engage with local communities. Ultimately, localized marketing is a testament to the importance of cultural awareness in the film industry, recognizing that successful storytelling goes beyond the screen and into the hearts and minds of audiences around the world.

Regional Partnerships in Film Distribution: Navigating Diverse Markets for Local Success

Regional partnerships in film distribution are instrumental in navigating the complexities of diverse markets and ensuring a film's success on a local level. These collaborations involve forging alliances with local distributors, production houses, and influential figures within the regional entertainment industry. Such partnerships are pivotal in understanding the nuances of each market, from cultural sensitivities to distribution logistics. Local distributors possess valuable insights into the tastes and preferences of their audience, enabling filmmakers to tailor their release strategies effectively. Moreover, collaborating with regional production houses can provide access to local talent, resources, and expertise, further enhancing the film's authenticity and resonance. Engaging with influencers who have a strong presence and following in specific regions can also significantly boost a film's visibility and engagement with the local audience. These partnerships, built on mutual trust and shared objectives, not only expand the film's reach but also strengthen the ties between the global film industry and local communities, fostering a more inclusive and culturally sensitive approach to storytelling.

Multi-Language Releases: Bridging Audiences and Celebrating Linguistic Diversity in Cinema

Multi-language releases have become a common and effective strategy in the film industry, especially in diverse and multilingual countries like India. This approach involves launching a film in multiple languages simultaneously, allowing it to reach a wider and more diverse audience. It broadens the film's appeal by breaking down language barriers, ensuring that viewers from different regions can access and enjoy the same content. This strategy not only maximizes the film's box office potential but also fosters inclusivity by acknowledging the linguistic diversity within the country. Moreover, it capitalizes on the star power of actors and the popularity of directors, transcending regional boundaries and creating a unified cinematic experience. Multi-language releases have proven to be a successful formula, driving box office revenues and expanding a film's cultural impact. They exemplify the film industry's adaptability in catering to diverse audiences while celebrating the rich tapestry of languages and cultures within a country.

Language Accessibility in Cinema: The Role of Subtitling and Dubbing in Global Film Engagement

Dubbing and subtitles play a pivotal role in ensuring that films can reach and engage audiences who are not proficient in the film's original language. Subtitling, the practice of adding translated text at the bottom of the screen, allows viewers to hear the original dialogue while reading a translation. This maintains the authenticity of the actors' voices and emotional nuances, making it a preferred choice for cinephiles who wish to experience the film as closely as possible to the director's intent. On the other hand, dubbing involves re-recording the dialogue in the target language, with voice actors replacing the original performers. When executed skillfully, dubbing can be seamless and provide a natural viewing experience. However, it requires meticulous casting and syncing to ensure that the new voices match the characters' expressions and emotions accurately. Both subtitling and dubbing are crucial tools in making cinema accessible to a global audience, allowing films to transcend language barriers and resonate with viewers from diverse linguistic backgrounds while preserving the integrity of the original content.

Cultural Sensitivity and Global Engagement: The Significance of Content Localization

The localization of content involves tailoring films, television shows, or digital content to reflect the culture, language, and customs of a specific region or audience. This approach offers several advantages in terms of audience engagement and resonance. Firstly, localized content establishes a stronger emotional connection with viewers, as it speaks directly to their cultural and linguistic identity. When characters, settings, and narratives align with local norms and values, audiences can more easily relate to and invest in the storytelling. Secondly, localization enhances accessibility. By presenting content in the viewer's native language, it removes language barriers, making it easier for a broader range of individuals to enjoy the content. Moreover, it can foster a sense of pride and ownership among local audiences, as they see their culture and language represented in the media they consume. Overall, localization is a powerful strategy for content creators seeking to expand their reach and create a meaningful connection with diverse audiences worldwide.

Engaging Local Audiences: The Impact of Regional Premieres and Promotional Events

Regional premieres and promotional events play a crucial role in connecting with local audiences and generating excitement around a film or television show. These events provide a platform for filmmakers, actors, and production teams to interact directly with viewers in specific regions, fostering a sense of community and shared enthusiasm. By tailoring premieres and promotions to local tastes and preferences, content creators can establish a deeper connection with the audience, making them feel valued and understood. Moreover, regional events often attract local media attention, increasing visibility and word-of-mouth promotion within the target market. This localized approach not only boosts initial viewership but can also lead to sustained support and loyalty from regional audiences, contributing to the long-term success of the content. Overall, regional premieres and promotions are powerful tools for content creators to engage with diverse audiences on a more personal and meaningful level, ultimately enhancing the overall impact and reception of their work.

Fostering Deeper Connections: The Power of Social Media Engagement in Regional Languages

Social media engagement in regional languages has become a pivotal strategy for content creators and businesses alike, enabling them to connect with audiences on a personal and culturally resonant level. By crafting content in regional languages, brands and creators demonstrate their commitment to understanding and valuing the linguistic diversity of their audience. This not only fosters a sense of community but also deepens the engagement as it aligns with the audience's preferred mode of communication. Moreover, content in regional languages can be more relatable, addressing local concerns, interests, and cultural nuances. This approach enhances the likelihood of content being shared within regional communities, contributing to organic growth and expanding the reach of the message or product. Overall, social media engagement in regional languages not only builds stronger connections with audiences but also reinforces the idea that brands and creators are attuned to the cultural fabric of their diverse fan base.

Nurturing Stronger Bonds: The Significance of Community Outreach Initiatives

Community outreach initiatives play a vital role in building meaningful connections between creators, brands, or organizations and local communities. These efforts often involve a range of activities such as workshops, screenings, and interactive sessions that aim to engage with communities on a deeper level. Workshops, for instance, provide opportunities for skill development, education, and collaboration, fostering a sense of empowerment and self-improvement. Screenings of relevant content can spark discussions and raise awareness about important issues, while interactive sessions create spaces for open dialogue and feedback. These initiatives not only demonstrate a commitment to local engagement but also contribute to a sense of trust and mutual understanding. By investing time and resources in community outreach, creators and organizations not only establish a strong local presence but also gain valuable insights that can inform their content, products, or services, making them more resonant and impactful within those communities.

Local Box Office Wisdom: Adapting Distribution Strategies to Regional Film Trends

Understanding local film trends and preferences is paramount in devising effective distribution strategies. Regional variations in cinematic tastes and trends can greatly influence a film's reception and success. By closely monitoring local box office hits and content trends, distributors and filmmakers gain valuable insights into what resonates with specific audiences. This knowledge allows them to tailor their distribution strategies, from release timing to marketing campaigns, to align with local preferences. It also helps in making informed decisions about localization efforts, such as dubbing or subtitling, to ensure that the film is accessible and relatable to the target audience. Staying attuned to local trends not only enhances the chances of a film's success but also demonstrates a commitment to respecting and connecting with regional audiences on a deeper level, fostering a sense of authenticity and cultural sensitivity in the distribution process.

Adapting Film Themes for Global Audiences: Balancing Cultural Sensitivity and Narrative Integrity

Adapting film themes to suit different regions is a nuanced and essential aspect of global distribution. While some universal themes may resonate across cultures, others may require careful consideration and adjustment. Recognizing that certain narrative elements, cultural values, and sensitivities can vary significantly, distributors and filmmakers must be willing to adapt to these differences. This adaptation may involve modifying dialogues, scenes, or character motivations to align with local sensibilities without compromising the core essence of the story. This approach not only ensures that the film remains respectful and relatable to the target audience but also demonstrates a commitment to cultural sensitivity, ultimately enhancing the film's reception and impact in diverse regions. By striking the right balance between maintaining the film's integrity and accommodating regional nuances, filmmakers can create a bridge that allows their stories to resonate authentically with audiences worldwide.

Feedback and Iteration: Enhancing Film Distribution Strategies through Audience Insights and Adaptations

Feedback and iteration play a pivotal role in refining distribution strategies for global markets. Collecting feedback from local audiences following film releases is a valuable practice that offers insights into the effectiveness of distribution approaches and the reception of the content. This feedback loop allows distributors and filmmakers to identify areas that require improvement and make necessary adjustments for future outreach efforts. It encompasses various aspects, including marketing campaigns, cultural adaptation, and distribution channels. By actively listening to the audience's response, distributors can fine-tune their strategies, ensuring that subsequent releases align more closely with local preferences and expectations. This iterative process not only strengthens the connection between the film and its audience but also demonstrates a commitment to ongoing improvement, fostering a more successful and culturally resonant film distribution ecosystem in diverse regions around the world.

To reach diverse audiences across various regions and languages, filmmakers need to adopt a multifaceted approach that combines cultural sensitivity, targeted marketing, and adaptability. Embracing a localized approach entails a deep understanding of the unique cultural nuances, preferences, and sensibilities of each region or linguistic group. By tailoring their marketing strategies and storytelling to resonate with these specific communities, filmmakers can effectively bridge language and cultural barriers, making their films more relatable and accessible. This approach not only fosters broader audience engagement but also promotes a sense of cultural authenticity, enhancing the film's reception and appreciation among diverse viewers. In doing so, filmmakers create a dynamic and inclusive cinematic landscape that celebrates the rich diversity of languages and cultures found within a country, while still maintaining a global appeal.

Leveraging digital platforms and social media for promotional purposes

Digital Platforms and Social Media: Revolutionizing Global Audience Reach in Film Distribution

The advent of digital platforms and social media has revolutionized audience reach in the world of film distribution. These online avenues offer an unprecedented global reach, allowing filmmakers and distributors to connect with audiences across the world. What sets them apart is their capacity to target specific demographics with pinpoint accuracy. Through data analytics and user profiling, these platforms can identify audiences based on their interests, behaviors, and preferences. This targeted approach enables customized marketing campaigns and content recommendations, ensuring that films reach the most receptive viewers. Whether it's promoting niche independent films or blockbuster releases, digital platforms and social media have become powerful tools for reaching diverse audiences on a global scale, reshaping the landscape of film distribution in the process.

Crafting Engaging Content: The Art of Film Marketing in the Digital Age

In the ever-evolving landscape of film marketing, creating engaging content has become a cornerstone strategy for capturing users' attention and generating excitement. The traditional film trailer has evolved into a meticulously crafted art form, offering tantalizing glimpses of the story, characters, and visual spectacles. Additionally, behind-the-scenes footage and teasers have become valuable tools for building anticipation and fostering a sense of connection between audiences and filmmakers. These snippets of the filmmaking process, often shared on social media platforms and official websites, provide viewers with a sneak peek into the creative journey, offering a more immersive and interactive experience. By strategically utilizing visually appealing and interactive content, film marketers not only pique curiosity but also cultivate a dedicated and engaged fan base that eagerly awaits each new release.

Fostering Connection through Real-Time Interaction: A Dynamic Approach to Film Marketing

In film marketing, real-time interaction with the audience has emerged as a powerful and invaluable strategy. This approach involves engaging directly with viewers through comments on social media platforms, live streaming events, and interactive Q&A sessions. By doing so, filmmakers and actors can create a more intimate and personal connection with their fan base, bridging the gap between the screen and the audience. Real-time

437

interaction humanizes promotional efforts, allowing fans to see the personalities behind the films and fostering a sense of community. This engagement not only builds anticipation for upcoming releases but also provides a platform for fans to express their thoughts, ask questions, and feel actively involved in the filmmaking journey. Ultimately, this two-way communication enhances the overall film experience and strengthens the bond between creators and their audience, leading to a more loyal and enthusiastic fan base.

Amplifying Film Marketing: Leveraging the Power of Influencer Collaborations

In film marketing, collaborating with influencers who have a substantial and relevant following has become a highly effective strategy. This approach involves partnering with social media personalities, YouTubers, bloggers, or individuals with a strong online presence and a keen interest in the film's genre or subject matter. Influencers act as intermediaries who can connect filmmakers with their dedicated followers, and their endorsements are often seen as credible and trustworthy. By leveraging influencers, filmmakers can tap into established online communities, gain access to niche audiences, and generate buzz around their projects. These collaborations can take various forms, such as sponsored content, live-streamed discussions, or exclusive sneak peeks, and they allow for creative and engaging ways to promote films. Ultimately, influencer collaborations not only amplify the reach of marketing efforts but also enhance the film's credibility and appeal to a broader and more diverse audience.

Elevating Film Marketing: Harnessing the Potential of Hashtag Campaigns

Utilizing hashtag campaigns as a marketing strategy has proven to be a powerful tool in building anticipation and engagement around a film. By strategically choosing or creating relevant and catchy hashtags, filmmakers can tap into existing online conversations and trends, effectively becoming part of a broader cultural dialogue. This approach encourages audiences to participate by using the designated hashtags in their own posts, generating user-generated content that serves as organic promotion. As a result, discussions about the film extend beyond the immediate fan base, reaching a wider and more diverse audience. The real-time nature of social media amplifies the impact of these campaigns, creating a sense of excitement and community among potential viewers. Whether it's encouraging fans to share their favorite moments, speculate about plot twists, or participate in challenges related to the film, hashtag campaigns provide an interactive and inclusive marketing strategy that capitalizes on the viral nature of online content.

The Art of Anticipation: Crafting Effective Teaser Campaigns in Film Marketing

Teaser campaigns have become a vital component of film marketing, effectively whetting the audience's appetite and generating anticipation before the release of a full-length trailer. These short, tantalizing clips offer a sneak peek into the film's visuals, characters, or a particularly compelling scene, often leaving viewers with intriguing questions and a desire for more. Teasers play a crucial role in setting the tone, style, and mood of the film, creating a buzz that extends well beyond their brief duration. They serve as conversation starters, prompting discussions, speculations, and fan theories across social media platforms. Additionally, the carefully timed release of teasers keeps the audience engaged throughout the pre-release phase, helping maintain interest and excitement until the film's premiere. In the age of digital media, where attention spans are short and competition for viewers' time and interest is fierce, teaser campaigns offer filmmakers a dynamic and effective tool for building a loyal and enthusiastic fan base.

Engaging the Audience: Interactive Challenges and Contests in Film Promotion

Interactive challenges and contests have emerged as innovative ways to engage the audience in the promotion of films. By creating viral challenges, often tied to a film's themes or iconic scenes, filmmakers tap into the participatory nature of social media. These challenges encourage users to become active participants, whether by recreating memorable moments, sharing their interpretations, or showcasing their creativity. The beauty of these campaigns lies in their ability to foster a sense of community among fans and participants, who connect over their shared enthusiasm for the film. As users take on these challenges, they generate user-generated content, from videos to artwork, which becomes a powerful form of word-of-mouth promotion. This organic spread of content not only extends the film's reach but also amplifies the buzz and excitement surrounding its release. In an era when audiences value their role as content creators and influencers, interactive challenges empower them to become brand advocates and integral contributors to a film's marketing campaign.

Unlocking the Magic: Behind-the-Scenes Insights in Film Marketing

Sharing behind-the-scenes insights has become a compelling marketing strategy in the film industry, offering audiences a captivating peek into the intricate process of bringing a cinematic masterpiece to life. These glimpses not only demystify the glamour associated with the world of cinema but also humanize the cast and crew, transforming them from distant celebrities into relatable individuals with passions and challenges. Audiences are drawn to the authenticity of behind-the-scenes content, as it reveals the dedication, hard work, and creativity that go into every frame of a film. This transparency builds a profound connection between filmmakers and viewers, fostering a sense of involvement and investment in the project. Fans eagerly follow the journey from script to screen, from the camaraderie on set to the technical wizardry in post-production, and their curiosity and emotional attachment translate into increased engagement and anticipation for the film's release. As the boundary between creators and consumers blurs in the digital age, behind-the-scenes insights play a vital role in building lasting relationships between filmmakers and their global audience.

The Power of Time: Countdowns and Countdown Posts in Film Marketing

Countdowns and countdown posts have proven to be potent tools in the modern film marketing arsenal, strategically harnessing the element of time to heighten anticipation and engagement. By announcing a release date and initiating a countdown, filmmakers create a sense of urgency, effectively marking the days until the film's debut. This anticipation cultivates excitement among fans and followers, turning the waiting period into a communal experience. Countdown posts, shared on social media platforms and other digital channels, serve as daily reminders and teasers, each post unveiling a new piece of information or exclusive content. These posts keep the audience engaged throughout the countdown, offering a constant stream of updates, posters, trailers, or behind-the-scenes snippets. As the clock ticks down, the excitement intensifies, and the audience becomes emotionally invested in the film's release. In essence, countdowns and their accompanying posts not only serve as marketing tactics but also as a storytelling technique that enhances the overall narrative of the film's journey to the big screen.

The Ephemeral Art: Leveraging Stories and Reels in Film Marketing on Social Media

Utilizing stories and reels on social media platforms, particularly Instagram, has become a dynamic strategy in film marketing, harnessing the ephemeral nature of these features to captivate audiences effectively. Stories and reels offer a unique advantage in their temporary, time-bound format, making them ideal for sharing bite-sized, visually engaging content. Filmmakers can leverage this brevity to tease trailers, share exclusive behind-the-scenes glimpses, and even run short-lived contests or interactive polls. The impermanence of these features creates a sense of urgency among viewers, compelling them to regularly check for updates to avoid missing out. Additionally, the creative potential of stories and reels enables filmmakers to experiment with various formats, filters, and interactive elements, enhancing user engagement. As a result, these short-lived posts not only keep audiences informed and entertained but also foster a sense of real-time connection between the film and its followers, making them integral components of a modern film marketing toolkit.

Digital Advertising: Targeted Strategies and Real-Time Insights in Film Marketing

Paid advertising on digital platforms has revolutionized film marketing by offering an efficient way to reach diverse and expansive audiences. The key advantage lies in the precision of targeting options that allow filmmakers to tailor their ad campaigns based on demographics, interests, behaviors, and more. This ensures that promotional content reaches the most relevant viewers, maximizing the impact of the campaign. Additionally, paid advertising offers flexibility in terms of budget allocation and campaign duration, enabling filmmakers to optimize their strategies according to the film's release schedule and audience engagement patterns. Various ad formats, such as display ads, video ads, and social media promotions, cater to different consumer behaviors and preferences. The ability to track and analyze the performance of ad campaigns in real-time provides valuable insights that help refine targeting and content for better results. In a digital age, paid advertising remains a powerful tool for filmmakers to enhance the visibility of their films, connect with wider audiences, and generate buzz around their projects.

Data Analytics: Driving Effective Film Marketing Campaigns in the Digital Age

Data analytics has become an indispensable tool in evaluating the effectiveness of film promotional efforts in the digital age. It plays a crucial role in assessing various aspects of a campaign, from audience engagement to click-through rates and conversion metrics. By leveraging data analytics, filmmakers and marketing teams can gain in-depth insights into how audiences are responding to their promotional content. This information allows for data-driven decision-making, enabling adjustments to be made in real-time to optimize the campaign's performance. For instance, if certain ads or content formats are proving more engaging than others, resources can be reallocated to capitalize on what works best. Moreover, data analytics provides the ability to measure the return on investment (ROI) of marketing campaigns, ensuring that resources are allocated effectively to generate the desired results. Ultimately, data analytics empowers filmmakers to fine-tune their promotional strategies, enhancing their ability to connect with audiences and drive interest and anticipation for their films.

Leveraging digital platforms and social media for promotional purposes provides filmmakers with a powerful and interactive means to connect with their audience. Through these platforms, filmmakers can create and share engaging content that offers behind-the-scenes glimpses, interactive Q&A sessions, and teaser trailers, building a sense of anticipation and excitement among their followers. Moreover, these digital spaces allow filmmakers to cultivate a sense of community and direct engagement, where fans can share their thoughts, feedback, and excitement for upcoming projects. Utilizing various features such as live streaming, interactive polls, and hashtag campaigns further amplifies their reach, generating buzz and interest in their work. By harnessing the potential of digital platforms and social media, filmmakers can establish a direct and enduring connection with their audience, creating a lasting impact and fostering a sense of involvement and loyalty among their fans.

CHAPTER - 13

13. The Future of Indian Filmmaking

Digital-First Releases:

The Digital-First Film Release Revolution: Navigating the Shift from Theatrical Debuts to Streaming Platforms

The trend of digital-first film releases represents a significant paradigm shift in the film industry, marking a departure from the traditional theatrical debuts. This transformation has been accelerated by the ascent of streaming platforms like Netflix, Amazon Prime Video, and Disney+. One of the key advantages of this approach is the heightened accessibility and convenience it provides to audiences. By releasing films directly on digital platforms, viewers have the flexibility to watch them from the comfort of their own homes, circumventing the need for physical visits to movie theaters. This convenience aligns seamlessly with evolving viewer habits, where on-demand access to content is increasingly prevalent. It also capitalizes on the global reach of digital platforms, ensuring that films can swiftly connect with diverse audiences worldwide, transcending geographical boundaries and time zones. Furthermore, digital-first releases introduce a level of agility in terms of release schedules, allowing filmmakers to engage with their audiences more promptly and responsively. This means that films can be released in a more timely manner in response to current events, cultural shifts, or audience demand. Such agility reduces the delays and complexities associated with traditional distribution methods, where films must navigate intricate release schedules and vie for limited screen time in theaters.

Digital-First Film Releases: Challenges and Opportunities in the Evolution of Cinema Distribution

However, while digital-first releases come with a host of advantages, they have also ignited substantial discussions within the film industry. These discussions revolve around the evolving dynamics between traditional cinema exhibition and digital streaming platforms. The traditional theatrical experience, which has been a cornerstone of the film industry for decades, now contends with new challenges as digital-first releases offer a direct path to audiences. This has raised concerns about the financial sustainability of traditional theaters, as they may face declines in box office revenues due to this shift. Additionally, the trend has raised important questions about the viability of existing revenue models in the film industry. While digital-first releases democratize access to films, they can potentially disrupt the established financial structure of the film industry, leading to further exploration of innovative revenue strategies. Consequently, digital-first releases are reshaping the film industry, and the ongoing interplay between traditional cinema exhibition and digital distribution will likely shape its future trajectory. This transformative trend has blurred the lines between cinematic formats and spurred an industry-wide reevaluation of how films are produced, distributed, and consumed.

Unlocking Accessibility and Convenience: How Digital-First Releases Have Revolutionized Film Viewing

The digital-first release approach has significantly expanded accessibility and convenience for audiences in several key ways. Firstly, it eliminates geographical barriers, allowing viewers from different regions and countries to access the film simultaneously, promoting a sense of global connectivity. Secondly, it offers flexibility in terms of viewing time, as audiences can watch the film at their convenience, pausing, rewinding, or resuming as needed. This convenience is particularly appealing to individuals with busy schedules who may not have the time to visit a physical theater. Furthermore, digital-first releases often come with various viewing options, including different languages and subtitles, catering to a diverse audience. Additionally, viewers can access these films on various devices, from smartphones and tablets to smart TVs, enhancing flexibility in where and how they consume content. Overall, digital-first releases have transformed the film-watching experience, making it more inclusive and adaptable to the lifestyles of modern audiences.

A. Emerging trends and innovations in Indian cinema

The Shift Towards Digital-First Film Releases: Transforming Accessibility and Convenience

The trend of digital-first film releases signifies a transformative shift in the film industry's distribution landscape, propelled largely by the dominance of streaming platforms. This shift comes with a range of compelling advantages, chiefly marked by heightened accessibility and convenience for audiences. Digital-first releases allow viewers to enjoy films from the comfort of their homes, obviating the need for physical visits to movie theaters. This convenience resonates with evolving viewer preferences and the extensive global outreach of digital platforms. It means that films can promptly and effortlessly connect with diverse audiences across the world, transcending geographical boundaries and accommodating different time zones. Furthermore, digital-first releases bring about a significant degree of flexibility in release schedules, enabling filmmakers to engage with their audiences more responsively. This flexibility allows films to be launched in response to current events, cultural trends, or audience demands, reducing the complexities and delays associated with traditional distribution methods.

Digital-First Film Releases: Transforming Industry Dynamics and Revenue Models

Nonetheless, the rise of digital-first releases has prompted extensive discourse within the film industry. These discussions are primarily centered around the evolving dynamics between traditional cinema exhibition and digital streaming platforms. Traditional theaters, which have long been the bedrock of film distribution, are grappling with new challenges as digital-first releases offer a direct pathway to audiences. These challenges have provoked concerns about the economic viability of traditional theaters, particularly the potential decline in box office revenues resulting from this shift. In addition, this trend has instigated vital discussions about the sustainability of existing revenue models in the film industry. While digital-first releases democratize film access, they have the potential to disrupt the established financial structure of the film industry, sparking further exploration of innovative revenue strategies. Consequently, digital-first releases are reshaping the film industry, and the ongoing interplay between traditional cinema exhibition and digital distribution will likely define the industry's future trajectory. This transformative trend has blurred the lines between cinematic formats and spurred an industry-wide reevaluation of how films are produced, distributed, and consumed.

Enhancing Accessibility and Convenience: The Impact of Digital-First Film Releases on Audiences

The digital-first release approach has significantly expanded accessibility and convenience for audiences in several key ways. Firstly, it eliminates geographical barriers, allowing viewers from different regions and countries to access the film simultaneously, promoting a sense of global connectivity. Secondly, it offers flexibility in terms of viewing time, as audiences can watch the film at their convenience, pausing, rewinding, or resuming as needed. This convenience is particularly appealing to individuals with busy schedules who may not have the time to visit a physical theater. Furthermore, digital-first releases often come with various viewing options, including different languages and subtitles, catering to a diverse audience. Additionally, viewers can access these films on various devices, from smartphones and tablets to smart TVs, enhancing flexibility in where and how they consume content. Overall, digital-first releases have transformed the film-watching experience, making it more inclusive and adaptable to the lifestyles of modern audiences.

B. Web Series and Streaming Content:

Highlight the rise of high-quality web series on OTT platforms.

The Web Series Revolution: Transforming Television and Film with Over-the-Top (OTT) Platforms

The rise of high-quality web series on Over-the-Top (OTT) platforms represents a significant transformation in the entertainment industry. These platforms have become hubs for original, diverse, and often boundary-pushing content that caters to a wide range of tastes and preferences. Unlike traditional television, web series are not bound by time constraints, allowing for more intricate storytelling, character development, and exploration of complex themes. This freedom has attracted not only emerging talents but also established actors, directors, and writers who see web series as a platform to experiment and create content that might not fit the conventional television mold. With easy accessibility through digital streaming, viewers can binge-watch entire seasons at their convenience, making it a popular choice for modern audiences seeking immersive, long-form storytelling. The success of web series has also led to increased competition among streaming platforms, driving the production of higher quality content, innovative narratives, and international collaborations, ultimately reshaping the way we consume and engage with television and film.

Unlocking Creative Freedom: The Impact of Web Series on Diverse Storytelling and Character Development

Web series have revolutionized the world of entertainment by offering an unprecedented degree of creative freedom, diverse storytelling, and extended character development. These digital platforms provide creators with the space to explore unconventional narratives, complex characters, and a wide range of genres that may not find a place within the constraints of traditional television or film. With no fixed episode durations, web series allow for flexible storytelling, letting the plot unfold at its own pace, delving deeper into character motivations, and even experimenting with non-linear narratives. Moreover, web series have become a haven for representation, featuring a more diverse array of characters from various backgrounds and experiences, thus reflecting a broader and more inclusive range of stories. This freedom and diversity have not only attracted emerging talents but also renowned actors, directors, and writers, drawn to the opportunity to engage in unconventional and innovative projects. As viewers increasingly turn to streaming platforms for their entertainment, web series have cemented their place as a dynamic and influential medium capable of pushing creative boundaries and engaging audiences in fresh and exciting ways.

Beyond Convention: The Impact of Unconventional Genres on Modern Filmmaking

The exploration of unconventional genres beyond mainstream cinema marks a dynamic shift in the world of filmmaking. While mainstream cinema traditionally adheres to well-established genres like romance, drama, and action, the emergence of unconventional genres such as horror, science fiction, and fantasy has broadened the horizons of storytelling. These genres offer filmmakers the creative freedom to delve into uncharted territory, often pushing the boundaries of imagination and thematic depth. Horror explores the darkest corners of human fears and psychology, while science fiction allows for speculative narratives about the future, technology, and the human condition. Fantasy transports audiences to magical realms filled with mythical creatures and epic adventures. The allure of these genres lies in their ability to captivate audiences with unique and often thought-provoking narratives, challenging the notion that unconventional genres are limited to niche audiences. As these genres continue to gain popularity and critical acclaim, they are reshaping the cinematic landscape, enriching storytelling possibilities, and captivating audiences with narratives that defy convention.

Exploring the Unconventional: The Rise of Horror, Science Fiction, and Fantasy Genres in Indian Cinema

The emergence of horror, science fiction, and fantasy genres in Indian cinema represents a notable departure from the traditional dominance of Bollywood's romantic and dramatic narratives. These unconventional genres have been steadily gaining popularity among Indian audiences. For instance, the film "Tumbbad" (2018) successfully blends horror and fantasy elements, immersing viewers in a dark and mythical world, and it received critical acclaim for its innovative storytelling. Additionally, "Stree" (2018) introduced a unique blend of horror and comedy, offering a refreshing take on the genre. In science fiction, "Koi... Mil Gaya" (2003) and its sequels explored extraterrestrial encounters, while "PK" (2014) delved into thought-provoking themes within a sci-fi framework. These films not only entertained but also opened the door to fresh and imaginative storytelling, expanding the horizons of Indian cinema and reflecting the growing appetite for diverse genres among audiences.

Breaking Boundaries: Narrative Experimentation in Indian Cinema

Narrative experimentation has witnessed a significant surge in Indian cinema, with filmmakers pushing the boundaries of traditional storytelling by embracing nonlinear narratives, multiple timelines, and intricate techniques. A notable example is the Indian film "Kahaani" (2012), directed by Sujoy Ghosh, which combines a thrilling detective story with a non-linear narrative structure. The film keeps audiences guessing as the protagonist's journey unravels through multiple timelines and unexpected twists. Another remarkable Indian film, "Rang De Basanti" (2006), directed by Rakeysh Omprakash Mehra, blends historical and contemporary narratives through its unique storytelling approach. Internationally, Indian-American director M. Night Shyamalan has also contributed to this trend with films like "The Sixth Sense" (1999), known for its unexpected twists and non-linear storytelling. These examples highlight how narrative experimentation is enriching Indian cinema, engaging viewers with intellectually stimulating narratives that challenge traditional conventions.

Engaging Uncertainty: The Impact of Narrative Experimentation on Audiences in Indian Cinema

Narrative experimentation challenges audiences by disrupting conventional storytelling structures, thus offering unique and thought-provoking viewing experiences. These approaches demand active engagement from viewers as they navigate non-linear timelines, decipher complex narratives, and uncover hidden connections within the story. The element of surprise and the need for attentive observation create a more immersive cinematic journey, making audiences feel like active participants rather than passive spectators. Such films often provoke discussions and interpretations, fostering a deeper connection between the film and its viewers. By pushing the boundaries of storytelling, narrative experimentation invites audiences to embrace the thrill of uncertainty and complexity, expanding the horizons of cinematic narratives.

Empowering Women on Screen: The Rise of Female-Centric Narratives in Indian Cinema

In Indian cinema, there has been a notable surge in the prominence of female-centric narratives, signaling a significant shift in storytelling paradigms. These films have placed strong and complex female characters at their forefront, moving beyond conventional gender roles and offering fresh perspectives on women's lives. Traditionally, Indian cinema has been criticized for its portrayal of women as mere love interests or stereotypes. However, this new wave of female-centric narratives has sought to challenge these norms and showcase women as multi-dimensional individuals with their own aspirations, ambitions, and agency.

Breaking Stereotypes: Female-Centric Narratives in Indian Cinema Addressing Gender Equality

These films explore a wide range of themes, including women's empowerment, resilience, self-discovery, and the pursuit of dreams. They often navigate complex societal issues such as gender discrimination, patriarchy, and societal expectations, shedding light on the challenges women face while advocating for gender equality. One notable example is "Kahaani," where Vidya Balan's character takes on the role of a determined, resourceful woman searching for her missing husband in the bustling streets of Kolkata. Such narratives not only resonate with female audiences but also encourage a broader conversation about gender dynamics in Indian society. They challenge long-held stereotypes and offer a more inclusive and progressive vision of women in cinema, inspiring not just Indian audiences but also contributing to the global discourse on gender representation and equality in film.

Realism and Social Relevance: A New Wave of Indian Cinema

In recent years, Indian cinema has undergone a notable transformation with a growing trend towards realistic portrayals of characters and narratives. Filmmakers have recognized the importance of crafting stories that resonate with contemporary audiences and tackle pressing social issues. This shift towards realism has enabled Indian cinema to confront topics that were previously considered taboo or ignored altogether. From addressing social issues like poverty, discrimination, and corruption to delving into the nuances of mental health and complex human emotions, Indian films are now taking on a broader spectrum of subject matter.

Societal Issues and Realism: Indian Cinema's Evolution in Storytelling

This evolution in storytelling reflects a more mature and socially aware approach within the industry. Films such as "Article 15" and "Tumhari Sulu" have delved into the complexities of caste discrimination and the challenges faced by working-class women, respectively. Additionally, movies like "Dear Zindagi" have explored the theme of mental health, breaking down stigmas and fostering discussions on these important topics. By grounding their narratives in reality and depicting relatable characters, Indian filmmakers are not only engaging audiences on a deeper level but also contributing to important societal dialogues. This trend showcases the industry's willingness to evolve and adapt to the changing needs and sensibilities of its viewers while championing socially relevant storytelling.

Regional Cinema in India: Achieving Global Recognition and Critical Acclaim

Regional cinema in India has made significant strides in achieving international recognition, transcending linguistic and cultural boundaries. These films have been increasingly featured in prestigious film festivals worldwide, where they have garnered critical acclaim and accolades. For example, Malayalam cinema has gained attention for its exceptional storytelling and cinematic craftsmanship, with films like "Jallikattu" even being India's official entry to the Oscars. Similarly, Marathi films like "Court" have won awards at prominent festivals, showcasing the diversity and richness of India's regional cinema..

Global Reach: How Streaming Platforms are Taking Indian Regional Cinema Worldwide

The availability of regional films on global digital platforms has also played a pivotal role in expanding their reach and impact. Streaming services like Netflix and Amazon Prime have provided a global audience access to a wide array of Indian regional films, complete with subtitles and dubbing options, making them more accessible and comprehensible to viewers worldwide. This not only promotes cross-cultural understanding but also encourages international audiences to explore India's diverse linguistic and cultural tapestry through the lens of its regional cinema. As a result, regional cinema has not only gained global recognition but has also enriched the global cinematic landscape with its unique stories, cultural nuances, and artistic expressions.

Exploring New Realities: The Impact of Virtual Reality and Augmented Reality on Indian Cinema

Virtual Reality (VR) and Augmented Reality (AR) are emerging technologies that have begun to make their mark in Indian cinema, transforming storytelling and audience engagement. VR immerses viewers in a completely virtual world, while AR overlays digital elements onto the real world. Indian filmmakers are increasingly exploring these technologies to create unique and interactive cinematic experiences. Incorporating VR and AR in storytelling has the potential to transport audiences to diverse and captivating settings. Filmmakers can use VR to place viewers directly into the heart of a narrative, allowing them to explore the film's environment from a first-person perspective. For instance, a historical drama set in ancient India can use VR to recreate historical landmarks and immerse viewers in the rich cultural tapestry of that era. AR, on the other hand, can enhance real-world environments by adding digital elements. This can be used to provide additional context or information to audiences, such as displaying subtitles or translating dialogues in real-time during foreign-language films.

Additionally, these technologies offer a high level of interactivity, allowing viewers to actively engage with the narrative. For example, VR headset users can make choices that impact the storyline, becoming participants in the narrative. This interactivity enhances audience engagement and opens up new storytelling possibilities. Indian cinema has begun experimenting with interactive narratives, especially in genres like suspense and horror, where viewers' choices influence the plot's direction, adding unpredictability and excitement.

VR and AR in Indian Cinema: Transforming Education and Storytelling

Another aspect of VR and AR in Indian cinema is their potential for educational and historical storytelling. VR can be used to recreate historical events, providing an immersive learning experience for students and history enthusiasts. Similarly, AR can overlay informative content onto documentaries, making them more engaging and informative. However, it's worth noting that the adoption of VR and AR in Indian cinema is still in its early stages, and there are challenges to overcome, such as the cost of production and accessibility of VR headsets and AR devices. Nevertheless, these technologies hold tremendous potential to revolutionize storytelling in Indian cinema, offering audiences more immersive, interactive, and educational cinematic experiences. As technology continues to advance and become more accessible, we can expect to see a growing integration of VR and AR in Indian filmmaking, pushing the boundaries of narrative and audience engagement.

Global Collaborations in Indian Cinema: A New Era of Cross-Cultural Filmmaking

The trend of Indian filmmakers collaborating with international talents represents a transformative phase in the Indian cinema landscape, opening up exciting possibilities for cross-cultural storytelling and groundbreaking filmmaking. This trend has been catalyzed by the globalization of the entertainment industry, allowing Indian filmmakers to tap into a global audience while enriching their narratives with fresh perspectives and diverse skills.

Universal Themes and Global Narratives: The Impact of Cross-Cultural Collaborations in Indian Cinema

These cross-cultural collaborations often lead to the creation of films that transcend geographical and cultural boundaries. Indian filmmakers partnering with international talents bring forth narratives that appeal to a wide, international audience by tapping into shared human experiences and universal themes. These films often explore themes such as love, identity, and social issues from a more global perspective, offering viewers a chance to connect with characters and stories that reflect the collective human condition. The result is a richer and more inclusive cinematic landscape that fosters cultural exchange and greater understanding among audiences worldwide.

These collaborations usher in innovative approaches to filmmaking. When Indian and international talents join forces, they combine their unique artistic sensibilities, technical prowess, and creative visions. This fusion often leads to films that push artistic boundaries, experiment with visual aesthetics, and explore novel storytelling techniques. For example, collaborations with foreign cinematographers may introduce distinctive visual styles, while partnerships with international composers can result in groundbreaking soundtracks that meld diverse musical traditions. The outcome is a fresh and dynamic cinematic experience that elevates Indian cinema's global profile and positions it as a vibrant contributor to the evolving world of storytelling.

Beyond Entertainment: The Role of Social Impact Cinema in Addressing Societal Challenges in India

Social impact cinema has emerged as a powerful tool for raising awareness about pressing social issues and advocating for positive change. In recent years, Indian filmmakers have been increasingly drawn to storytelling that transcends mere entertainment and delves into the heart of societal challenges. Films such as "Article 15" (2019), "Toilet: Ek Prem Katha" (2017), and "Mardaani" (2014) are notable examples that have tackled issues like caste-based discrimination, sanitation, and human trafficking, respectively. These films employ compelling narratives and compelling characters to shed light on deeply rooted problems and stimulate conversations around them.

Indian Cinema as a Catalyst for Social Change: Amplifying Voices and Driving Positive Transformation

Indian cinema's ability to reach wide and diverse audiences makes it a potent platform for social advocacy. These films not only bring marginalized issues to the forefront but also encourage viewers to reflect on their own attitudes and actions, sparking conversations that can lead to social change. Furthermore, filmmakers often collaborate with non-governmental organizations (NGOs) and activists to ensure that their stories are rooted in reality and aligned with the objectives of social justice. In this way, Indian cinema is not only entertaining but also a catalyst for societal transformation, using the art of storytelling to drive positive change and amplify the voices of those who need to be heard. As this trend continues to grow, Indian cinema is poised to become an even more influential agent of social impact and advocacy.

Revolutionizing Film Marketing in Indian Cinema: Interactive Campaigns and Audience Engagement

The landscape of marketing in Indian cinema has undergone a significant transformation, characterized by experimentation and innovation. Filmmakers and studios are increasingly exploring interactive and audience-centric approaches to create buzz around their films. One noteworthy trend is the use of interactive social media campaigns. Films like "Andhadhun" (2018) and "Stree" (2018) leveraged social media platforms like Twitter, Instagram, and TikTok to engage audiences through challenges, contests, and viral marketing campaigns. For instance, the "Stree" team launched the #MardKoDardHoga challenge, inviting fans to share their quirky take on the film's catchphrase, which not only generated excitement but also amplified the film's visibility.

Digital Premieres and Online Launch Events: Transforming Film Marketing in Indian Cinema

Another emerging trend is virtual premieres and online launch events. The COVID-19 pandemic accelerated the adoption of digital premieres, allowing filmmakers to connect directly with their audience. For instance, "Ludo" (2020) had a virtual premiere event attended by the cast and crew, which was streamed live on YouTube. This approach not only adhered to social distancing measures but also allowed fans to participate in real-time, creating a sense of shared excitement and intimacy. These innovations in marketing are not only engaging but also cost-effective, making them an integral part of contemporary Indian cinema's promotional strategy. As technology continues to evolve, one can expect further experimentation and boundary-pushing marketing campaigns that cater to the ever-evolving tastes and preferences of the audience.

Sustainable Filmmaking in Indian Cinema: Nurturing the Environment While Creating Art

Sustainable filmmaking has emerged as a significant trend in Indian cinema, reflecting a growing awareness of environmental issues and the need to adopt eco-friendly production practices. Filmmakers and production crews are increasingly recognizing their responsibility to minimize the environmental impact of their projects. This includes reducing waste, conserving resources, and adopting sustainable technologies. For instance, "Paani" (2022), a film directed by Shekhar Kapur, prioritized water conservation during production by using advanced filtration systems and reusing water on set. Such practices not only reduce the film industry's water footprint but also set a commendable example for other sectors.

Sustainable Storytelling: Indian Cinema's Role in Environmental Advocacy

Sustainable filmmaking goes beyond production practices and extends to storytelling itself. Films like "Kadvi Hawa" (2017) and "Water" (2005) have addressed climate change and water scarcity as central themes, aiming to raise awareness and inspire action. By incorporating environmental narratives, Indian cinema can play a pivotal role in advocacy and education, fostering a sense of responsibility among audiences. As the global consciousness regarding environmental issues continues to grow, sustainable filmmaking in Indian cinema not only reduces its carbon footprint but also contributes to a broader dialogue on environmental conservation and climate change mitigation. This trend is likely to gain even more prominence as both filmmakers and audiences become increasingly environmentally conscious.

The Indian cinema landscape is evolving rapidly, embracing new genres, storytelling techniques, and technological advancements. As filmmakers explore uncharted territories and engage with diverse narratives, Indian cinema continues to captivate audiences both domestically and on a global stage.

C. The Globalization and Digital Revolution

The Impact of Globalization and Digital Platforms on Storytelling and Production

Breaking Boundaries: How Digital Platforms are Redefining the Global Reach of Entertainment Content

Digital platforms have shattered geographical barriers, ushering in an era where content can effortlessly reach a global audience. Unlike traditional distribution models that were often limited by regional releases and the logistics of physical media, digital platforms provide a borderless platform for content creators. This newfound global reach has profound implications for the film and entertainment industry, allowing movies, series, and other forms of content to transcend cultural and linguistic boundaries. For example, a film produced in India can now be streamed and enjoyed by audiences in the United States, the United Kingdom, Australia, and countless other countries simultaneously. This phenomenon has not only expanded the potential audience for content but has also accelerated the exchange of cultural influences on a global scale.

Enriching Storytelling Through Globalization: How Diverse Cultural Perspectives Shape Modern Content Creation

Globalization, facilitated by digital platforms, has enriched storytelling by exposing creators to a diverse array of cultural perspectives and ideas. Filmmakers now have access to a global audience that brings its own unique sensibilities and preferences, leading to the creation of content that caters to a broader spectrum of tastes and interests. This cross-cultural pollination can be observed in the content itself, as narratives increasingly incorporate elements from different regions and cultures. For instance, a series set in Asia might feature characters from various nationalities, allowing for multifaceted storytelling that appeals to a worldwide audience. This global audience reach has not only democratized content distribution but has also fostered a more interconnected and culturally rich entertainment landscape, where audiences from different parts of the world can appreciate and engage with each other's stories.

Cultural Exchange and Fusion: Redefining Narratives in Contemporary Indian Cinema

Cultural exchange and fusion have become prevalent themes in contemporary Indian cinema, reflecting the interconnectedness of the global world. Filmmakers are increasingly recognizing the value of incorporating diverse cultural elements into their narratives to create more layered and relatable stories. This trend goes beyond mere globalization and embraces the idea of cross-cultural storytelling, where different cultures enrich and complement each other. For example, films like "The Lunchbox" (2013) seamlessly blend Indian and Western elements in their narratives, highlighting the universality of human emotions while celebrating cultural diversity.

Harmonizing Cultures Through Music: The Fusion of Traditions in Contemporary Indian Cinema

One significant aspect of this trend is the fusion of music and themes. Indian cinema has a long history of integrating music and dance into its storytelling, and in recent years, filmmakers have skillfully blended traditional Indian melodies with contemporary genres to cater to modern tastes. This fusion creates a unique musical identity in Indian cinema and resonates with a diverse and global audience. The embrace of cultural exchange and fusion not only broadens the horizons of Indian cinema but also promotes understanding and appreciation of different cultures, fostering a sense of unity in diversity on the global cinematic stage.

Cinematic Perspectives Enriched by Global Exposure: A Shift Towards Inclusive Storytelling in Indian Films

The exposure to global content has undeniably had a transformative impact on Indian filmmakers' perspectives, pushing them to embrace more inclusive and diverse storytelling. With the easy accessibility of international films and series through digital platforms, Indian directors and writers have been exposed to a wide range of narratives that extend beyond their local and cultural boundaries. This exposure has broadened their horizons, making them more aware of the multiplicity of human experiences and perspectives. As a result, many Indian filmmakers are now weaving stories that reflect the complex tapestry of society, including narratives centered around underrepresented communities, marginalized voices, and unconventional themes.

Diverse and Authentic Narratives: The Impact of Global Exposure on Indian Cinema

This shift towards more inclusive storytelling is not just about diversity for diversity's sake; it's a reflection of a changing world where audiences demand authenticity and a broader representation of human experiences. Filmmakers are responding to this demand by creating narratives that challenge norms, break stereotypes, and celebrate the richness of diversity. This change is not limited to Bollywood but is also evident in regional cinema, where filmmakers are increasingly exploring narratives that reflect the cultural and social diversity of their respective regions. In essence, exposure to global content has opened the doors to a more inclusive and varied cinematic landscape in India, enriching the storytelling tapestry and ensuring that a wider range of voices and perspectives find their way to the silver screen.

Unlocking Global Potential: The Rise of Cross-Border Collaborations in Cinema

The trend of cross-border collaborations and co-productions in the world of cinema has been on the rise, and it's not limited to Indian cinema alone. Filmmakers are increasingly recognizing the benefits of such partnerships, which bring together talent and resources from different countries to create compelling and globally appealing stories. These collaborations enable the pooling of creative minds, technical expertise, and financial resources, ultimately resulting in films that have a broader international appeal.

Cultural Fusion and Creative Synergy: The Impact of Cross-Border Collaborations in Cinema

One of the significant advantages of cross-border collaborations is the diversity of perspectives they bring to the table. When filmmakers from different cultural backgrounds come together, they bring unique storytelling traditions, visual aesthetics, and thematic elements into the mix. This fusion of cultural influences often leads to the creation of narratives that resonate with a global audience while offering fresh and innovative perspectives. Additionally, co-productions help mitigate financial risks by sharing production costs, making it possible to create high-quality films that might have been challenging to produce independently. Overall, cross-border collaborations and co-productions have become a driving force behind the globalization of cinema, enriching the industry with a diverse array of narratives and fostering greater cultural exchange on the silver screen.

Digital Platforms: Revolutionizing Film Production with Advanced Technology and Equipment

The advent of digital platforms has revolutionized the filmmaking industry, offering filmmakers access to cutting-edge technology that significantly elevates the quality and capabilities of film production and post-production processes. In terms of production, digital platforms provide a wide array of tools and equipment that can capture high-resolution, cinematic-quality images and videos. This access to advanced cameras, lenses, and other filmmaking equipment enables filmmakers to achieve stunning visuals and capture intricate details, enriching the overall visual storytelling.

Digital Platforms: Transforming Filmmaking with Advanced VFX, Post-Production, and Sound Design Tools

Furthermore, digital platforms have democratized the field of visual effects (VFX) and post-production. Filmmakers can now harness powerful software and hardware solutions for VFX, compositing, and colour grading, among others. These technologies empower filmmakers to create seamless and immersive visual effects, from jaw-dropping action sequences to fantastical worlds. Additionally, advancements in sound design and mixing tools allow for precise control over audio elements, resulting in immersive and impactful soundscapes that enhance the viewer's emotional engagement with the film. In essence, the integration of advanced technology through digital platforms has not only improved the technical aspects of filmmaking but has also expanded creative possibilities, enabling filmmakers to tell their stories with unprecedented visual and auditory richness.

Unleashing Creative Freedom: How Digital Platforms Empower Filmmakers to Explore Niche and Unconventional Narratives

Digital platforms have ushered in an era of unparalleled creative freedom for filmmakers, liberating them from the constraints of traditional box office pressures and mainstream conventions. Unlike the traditional film industry, where box office success often dictates the kinds of stories that get greenlit, digital platforms have provided a space where experimental and unconventional storytelling can flourish. Filmmakers are no longer bound by the need to appeal to the broadest possible audience to ensure profitability. Instead, they can delve into niche or thought-provoking narratives that may not have mass market appeal but can deeply resonate with specific audiences.

Embracing Diversity: How Digital Platforms Fuel a New Wave of Filmmaking and Storytelling Innovation

This newfound creative freedom has led to the emergence of a diverse range of films that challenge norms and push the boundaries of storytelling. Filmmakers can experiment with narrative structures, character development, and themes without fear of commercial failure. This has resulted in a vibrant landscape of films that tackle complex and sometimes controversial topics, fostering a greater diversity of voices and perspectives in the cinematic world. In essence, digital platforms have democratized creativity, allowing filmmakers to follow their artistic instincts and produce works that may not have found a place in the traditional film industry, ultimately enriching the cinematic landscape with fresh and innovative narratives.

Real-Time Feedback Loops: Harnessing Audience Insights in the Digital Filmmaking Era

Digital platforms offer filmmakers a unique advantage in the form of instantaneous feedback from audiences. Unlike traditional theatrical releases where filmmakers have limited access to real-time audience reactions, digital platforms allow for immediate responses through comments, likes, shares, and user reviews. This direct interaction between creators and viewers creates a dynamic feedback loop that can significantly impact content creation. Filmmakers can gauge audience preferences, opinions, and criticisms almost instantly, helping them understand what works and what doesn't.

Fostering a Symbiotic Relationship: How Real-Time Audience Feedback Shapes Future Filmmaking

This feedback loop extends beyond individual films and can influence future productions. Filmmakers can use audience responses to fine-tune their storytelling, character development, and thematic choices. It provides an opportunity for continuous improvement and refinement of their craft. Additionally, this real-time engagement can foster a sense of community and collaboration between creators and viewers, as audiences feel heard and valued when their feedback is acknowledged and incorporated into the creative process. In this way, digital platforms not only democratize filmmaking but also create a more symbiotic relationship between filmmakers and their audience, ultimately leading to more audience-centric content.

Unlocking the Power of Episodic Storytelling: How Digital Platforms Redefine Narrative Formats

Digital platforms have revolutionized storytelling, with a focus on short-form content and episodic series. Unlike traditional cinema, which often relies on feature-length films, digital platforms embrace shorter, bite-sized narratives. This has given rise to web series, where stories are divided into compact episodes, allowing for in-depth character development and complex plots. Episodic series cater to diverse audience preferences, offering quick, engaging stories for short breaks and more immersive, long-form narratives that span multiple seasons.

Short-Form Content and Episodic Series: A Playground for Diverse Storytelling

Short-form content and episodic series on digital platforms offer storytelling flexibility. Filmmakers can experiment with various genres, tones, and formats to suit their narratives. This results in a diverse range of content, from drama and comedy to science fiction and horror, all in digestible formats. Additionally, these series often tap into binge-watching culture, where viewers watch multiple episodes at once, creating a unique sense of anticipation and engagement. This trend has not only changed the way stories are told but also expanded creative and narrative possibilities for filmmakers and storytellers, transcending the constraints of traditional cinema.

Revolutionizing Audience Engagement: Real-Time Interaction on Digital Platforms

Digital platforms have revolutionized audience engagement by providing interactive tools that facilitate direct communication between viewers and content creators. Unlike traditional cinema, where audience reactions are often limited to post-screening discussions, digital platforms enable real-time interactions. Viewers can leave comments, ratings, and engage in discussions about the content they're consuming. This immediate feedback loop has a profound impact on storytelling approaches, as filmmakers can gauge audience reactions, preferences, and sentiments almost instantaneously. They can adjust their storytelling strategies based on the feedback, leading to a more responsive and dynamic approach to content creation.

Empathetic Storytelling: Tailoring Character Development through Direct Audience Engagement

Furthermore, this direct audience engagement extends to character development and plot progression. Creators can monitor the audience's emotional responses and attachment to specific characters. They can then tailor character arcs and narrative trajectories to align with audience expectations and preferences, resulting in more relatable and compelling stories. Additionally, the ability to engage with viewers on a personal level fosters a sense of community and connection, making audiences more invested in the characters and their journeys. This feedback-driven approach has become a powerful tool in the digital age, allowing content creators to build stronger relationships with their audiences and create content that resonates on a deeper level.

Data-Driven Storytelling: Leveraging Analytics for Informed Creative Decisions

Data analytics has emerged as a fundamental driver of decision-making in the digital era of content creation. Digital platforms provide content creators with an extensive array of data related to viewership patterns, audience demographics, engagement metrics, and more. This wealth of information offers invaluable insights into what works and what doesn't in the world of storytelling. Filmmakers and content producers can analyze these data points to make informed decisions about content creation, distribution, and marketing. For example, by examining which scenes or episodes of a series garnered the most attention, creators can understand audience preferences and adapt their narratives accordingly.

Data-Driven Content Creation: Crafting Narratives and Strategies Aligned with Audience Preferences

One of the most significant impacts of data-driven decision-making is its ability to guide narrative choices and production strategies. Filmmakers can use data analytics to identify popular genres, themes, or character archetypes within their target audience, allowing them to craft narratives that align with these preferences. Additionally, viewership data can reveal the effectiveness of storytelling techniques, helping creators refine their storytelling craft. For instance, if data indicates that viewers tend to drop off during certain plot developments, creators can adjust the pacing or narrative structure to maintain engagement. Ultimately, data-driven content creation not only ensures that content resonates with the audience but also optimizes the allocation of resources, making it a vital aspect of modern digital content production.

The Digital Platform Revolution: Empowering Niche Content and Subcultures Worldwide

The rise of digital platforms has ushered in an era where niche content and subcultures find their rightful place in the spotlight. Unlike traditional media, digital platforms can afford to produce and distribute content that caters to specific, often underserved, audiences. This shift has allowed for a flourishing of diverse content that addresses unique interests, hobbies, and subcultures. For instance, platforms like YouTube and Vimeo have become homes for a wide range of niche communities, from tabletop gamers and comic book enthusiasts to knitting aficionados and urban explorers. Content creators within these niches can produce videos, documentaries, tutorials, and more, connecting with like-minded individuals worldwide who share their passions.

Fostering Understanding and Empowerment: The Role of Digital Platforms in Exploring Diverse Subcultures and Hobbies

The diversification of content on digital platforms not only provides an outlet for enthusiasts but also encourages cultural and subcultural exploration. Audiences can delve into worlds and perspectives they might have never encountered in mainstream media. This expansion of content has the power to bridge gaps, foster understanding, and empower communities. For example, documentaries exploring subcultures or obscure hobbies shed light on the dedication and creativity of individuals within these communities, challenging stereotypes and creating a sense of belonging for those who might have felt marginalized. In essence, digital platforms have democratized content creation, enabling even the most niche interests to thrive and connect globally.

The Digital Revolution: How Accessibility and Convenience Are Reshaping Audience Engagement

The advent of digital platforms has revolutionized the way content is consumed, primarily by making it incredibly accessible and convenient for audiences worldwide. Unlike traditional modes of content distribution, which often required viewers to adhere to set schedules and physical locations, digital platforms offer the flexibility to access content at any time and from virtually anywhere with an internet connection. This accessibility has profoundly impacted audience engagement, as individuals are no longer constrained by the limitations of broadcast or theater showtimes. They can watch movies, series, documentaries, or any form of content at their own pace, whether it's during their daily commute, a lunch break, or late at night.

The Streaming Revolution: Redefining Audience Engagement Through Convenience and Personalization

The convenience offered by digital platforms has become a significant driver of audience engagement and content consumption. Streaming services, for instance, allow users to create their personalized viewing schedules, pause, rewind, or fast-forward content, and seamlessly switch between devices. This level of control not only enhances the viewing experience but also encourages binge-watching and repeat viewing, as viewers can revisit their favorite shows or movies without any hassle. Additionally, the convenience factor extends to the breadth of content available, as audiences can explore a vast library of options catering to their specific interests, resulting in more engaged and satisfied viewers.

In essence, digital platforms have redefined the way audiences interact with content, making it more accessible and convenient than ever before.

D. Virtual production in context of Indian film

This innovative approach is revolutionizing Indian cinema in several ways. Firstly, it offers a cost-effective solution, as it eliminates the need for extensive location shoots and costly practical effects. By creating virtual environments and scenarios, filmmakers can reduce production costs while still delivering high-quality visual storytelling. Additionally, virtual production allows for greater creative control and flexibility, enabling directors and cinematographers to experiment with different visual styles and settings. As Indian filmmakers continue to explore and refine these techniques, we can expect even more visually breathtaking and ambitious films in the years to come. This marks a significant shift in the industry, with virtual production becoming an integral part of the creative process and contributing to the creation of visually immersive and captivating stories that resonate with audiences. Here's a detailed discussion of virtual production in the context of Indian cinema:

Immersive Storytelling:

Immersive storytelling through virtual production has undoubtedly transformed the landscape of Indian cinema, offering filmmakers an unprecedented toolbox to craft visually spectacular and emotionally engaging narratives. One of the most iconic examples of this transformation is the "Baahubali" film series, directed by S.S. Rajamouli. These films stand as a testament to how virtual production has elevated Indian cinema to international standards of grandeur and imagination.

Firstly, virtual production has facilitated the seamless integration of real-world elements with digital environments, breaking the boundaries of what was once thought possible in Indian filmmaking. "Baahubali: The Beginning" and "Baahubali: The Conclusion" capitalized on this technology to transport audiences to the fictional kingdom of Mahishmati, replete with awe-inspiring waterfalls, towering palaces, and epic battles. The extensive use of virtual production not only enabled the creation of these breathtaking visuals but also lent a sense of authenticity and scale to the narrative. Viewers were not merely spectators but participants in the mythical world, emotionally invested in the characters' journeys.

Moreover, these films redefined the scale and ambition of Indian cinema. They showcased the immense potential of virtual production to bring epic stories and historical or mythological narratives to life with unparalleled grandeur. The success of "Baahubali" opened doors for other filmmakers to explore immersive storytelling, challenging traditional limits. By pushing the boundaries of creativity and technology, virtual production has reinvigorated Indian cinema, offering audiences a visual and emotional experience like never before. In essence, it has revolutionized the way stories are told and perceived on the Indian silver screen, leaving an indelible mark on the industry's future.

Cost Efficiency:

Cost efficiency has emerged as a significant advantage of virtual production in Indian cinema. It has revolutionized the way filmmakers approach ambitious projects with extensive visual effects requirements. A prime example is "2.0," the highly anticipated sequel to "Robot" (also known as "Enthiran"). This film harnessed the power of virtual production to deliver jaw-dropping visual effects sequences while maintaining budgetary constraints. Traditionally, creating such sequences involved significant expenditures on physical sets, on-location shoots, and post-production expenses. However, with virtual production, filmmakers can achieve comparable or even superior results at a fraction of the cost. The technology allows for the creation of digital environments and effects that look astonishingly real, making it an attractive option for Indian productions seeking to compete on a global scale without exhausting their financial resources.

Virtual production offers cost efficiency beyond visual effects by streamlining the filmmaking process. It reduces expenses related to location scouting, set construction, and travel, enabling Indian filmmakers to experiment with genres, push creative boundaries, and maintain tight budgets. This cost-effective approach has democratized access to advanced filmmaking tools, leading to innovative storytelling, imaginative narratives, and visually stunning productions in Indian cinema. In essence, virtual production has ushered in a new era of creative exploration and competitiveness within the Indian film industry.

Realistic Visual Effects:

Virtual production has played a pivotal role in elevating the realism of visual effects in Indian cinema, catering to genres that demand immersive and convincing digital elements. Genres like science fiction, fantasy, and historical dramas, which were once considered challenging due to their reliance on visual effects, are now being wholeheartedly embraced by Indian filmmakers. A prime example of this transformation is evident in "Krrish 3," a superhero film that used virtual production techniques to depict the superhero's extraordinary powers and the fantastical world of mutants with remarkable authenticity. Virtual production enabled the film to achieve a level of visual fidelity that was previously elusive, immersing audiences in a believable and visually stunning superhero narrative.

In the context of Indian cinema, where storytelling often encompasses mythology, folklore, and larger-than-life tales, the ability to create realistic visual effects is a game-changer.

Filmmakers can now bring ancient legends and epic stories to life with unprecedented visual richness and precision, enhancing the cinematic experience for audiences. Whether it's recreating historical eras, simulating intergalactic battles, or conjuring mythical creatures, virtual production empowers Indian filmmakers to realize their creative visions with a level of realism that resonates deeply with viewers. This shift towards realistic visual effects not only expands the creative horizons of Indian cinema but also positions it on a global stage, where audiences increasingly seek high-quality visual storytelling across a spectrum of genres.

Efficient Pre-Visualization:

Efficient pre-visualization is a significant advantage offered by virtual production in Indian filmmaking. It empowers directors and cinematographers to plan and execute intricate shots and sequences with precision. This meticulous planning not only saves time but also optimizes the utilization of resources during the production phase. "Tumbbad," an acclaimed Indian film known for its unique and otherworldly environments, effectively utilized virtual production to pre-visualize the intricate sets and settings crucial to the film's narrative. By doing so, the filmmakers were able to translate their creative vision into reality efficiently. This approach not only resulted in visually stunning sequences but also contributed to the film's overall success.

In the context of Indian cinema, where budgets and resources are often constraints, efficient pre-visualization through virtual production becomes a valuable tool. It allows filmmakers to make the most of their available resources, ensuring that every aspect of the production aligns with the artistic vision. By seamlessly integrating digital elements into the pre-production process, Indian filmmakers can create visually captivating and narratively engaging films while staying within budgetary limitations. This streamlined approach not only benefits individual projects but also enhances the overall productivity and competitiveness of the Indian film industry.

Collaborative Filmmaking:

Collaborative filmmaking is a cornerstone of the success of virtual production in Indian cinema. By bringing together various departments, such as cinematography, visual effects, and art direction, filmmakers can work in synergy to achieve a visually cohesive and captivating final product. The process involves close coordination between these departments to ensure that real-world elements seamlessly merge with digital environments, resulting in a more immersive and visually satisfying cinematic experience. For instance, in the Bollywood film "Zero," virtual production played a pivotal role in achieving a seamless integration of real-world and virtual environments. The collaborative efforts of the different departments ensured that the film's unique visual effects and storytelling elements came together harmoniously.

In the Indian film industry, where storytelling often relies heavily on visuals and aesthetics, the collaborative potential of virtual production is a game-changer. It allows filmmakers to push creative boundaries and craft visually stunning narratives that captivate audiences. Moreover, the collaborative approach fosters a sense of innovation and experimentation, which is essential for pushing the envelope in terms of storytelling and visual storytelling in Indian cinema. As filmmakers continue to explore the possibilities offered by virtual production, collaborative filmmaking will remain a driving force behind the industry's evolution and its ability to deliver visually impressive and emotionally resonant films.

Skill Development and Technological Growth:

Skill development and technological growth are integral aspects of the impact of virtual production in Indian cinema. As virtual production technology continues to advance, Indian filmmakers and technicians are embracing these tools and enhancing their proficiency. This not only fosters a pool of skilled professionals but also contributes significantly to the overall growth of the Indian film industry's technical capabilities. The expertise gained in virtual production techniques empowers filmmakers to create more visually immersive and technically sophisticated films, whether they belong to the blockbuster genre or independent cinema.

Furthermore, the democratization of virtual production technology is making it more accessible to a wider range of Indian filmmakers. It is no longer restricted to big-budget productions alone. Smaller-scale films and independent filmmakers are also beginning to explore and utilize virtual production techniques. This democratization signifies that the technology is becoming more inclusive and adaptable to various budget constraints. As a result, it not only enhances the storytelling potential but also opens up avenues for creative expression and innovation across different segments of the Indian film industry, contributing to its overall growth and diversity.

Future Potential

The future potential of virtual production in the Indian film industry is undeniably promising. While it is currently in its nascent stages, the technology is poised to play a pivotal role in the evolution of Indian cinema. As virtual production tools become more refined, user-friendly, and cost-effective, we can anticipate a wider adoption across the industry.

One of the most exciting aspects of virtual production is its ability to enhance storytelling across a diverse array of genres. From grand mythological epics that require epic landscapes and otherworldly environments to contemporary dramas seeking realistic and immersive settings, virtual production offers a versatile canvas for Indian filmmakers to bring their visions to life. This means that the future of Indian cinema will likely see a broader spectrum of stories, ranging from historical epics to cutting-edge science fiction, benefiting from the capabilities of virtual production. As filmmakers become increasingly adept at using these tools, we can look forward to more visually captivating and narratively innovative films that challenge conventions and elevate the cinematic experience for Indian audiences and beyond.

E. 3D and 360-degree Filmmaking future in India

The future of 3D and 360-degree filmmaking in India holds tremendous potential, offering new dimensions to storytelling and audience engagement. Here's a discussion of these two emerging cinematic technologies and their prospects in the Indian film industry:

3D Filmmaking:

3D filmmaking has indeed made noteworthy progress in India, marked by the release of several Bollywood and regional films in 3D formats. This technology has opened up exciting possibilities for filmmakers to craft immersive visual experiences by introducing depth and dimension to their storytelling. Here's an in-depth exploration of 3D filmmaking in India:

3D filmmaking offers a unique way to engage the audience by creating a heightened sense of immersion. By using stereoscopic technology, filmmakers can present images with depth, making objects appear closer or farther away. This technique goes beyond traditional 2D filmmaking, allowing viewers to feel like they are inside the film's world rather than just spectators. This immersive quality is particularly well-suited for genres like action, adventure, fantasy, and animation, where visual spectacle plays a crucial role in storytelling.

India experienced an initial wave of enthusiasm for 3D cinema, partly driven by global trends and Hollywood blockbusters that embraced the technology. Bollywood and regional film industries also sought to capitalize on this excitement by releasing 3D films. However, this initial enthusiasm encountered challenges. Some 3D films were criticized for prioritizing visual effects over storytelling, leading to a perception that 3D was more of a gimmick than a storytelling tool. Additionally, the need for specialized equipment and higher production costs posed challenges, limiting the number of 3D releases.

Despite these challenges and the tapering of initial fervor, there's still a promising future for 3D filmmaking in India. Filmmakers are becoming more discerning in their use of 3D, understanding that it should complement and enhance storytelling rather than overshadow it. As technology continues to evolve, it's likely that more cost-effective and user-friendly 3D solutions will become available. These developments could make 3D a more viable option for a broader range of Indian filmmakers, including independent and emerging talents.

The future of 3D in India lies in its ability to serve the narrative. Filmmakers will likely explore how 3D can be employed to deepen emotional connections with characters and create more immersive storytelling. For instance, 3D can be used to enhance the viewer's perception of scale, emphasizing the grandeur of historical epics or the intimacy of character-driven dramas. As filmmakers become more adept at integrating 3D seamlessly into their narratives, it has the potential to become a valuable storytelling tool rather than just a visual spectacle.

In the coming years, there is a growing expectation that Indian filmmakers will increasingly view 3D as a potent storytelling tool rather than a mere gimmick. This shift indicates a more mature and refined approach to utilizing 3D technology to enhance the narrative, immerse the audience in the cinematic world, and create emotionally resonant experiences. Here's a detailed exploration of what this evolving landscape might look like:

The future of 3D filmmaking in India revolves around its capacity to serve the narrative. Filmmakers are likely to focus on how 3D can be employed to deepen the audience's engagement with the story and characters. Instead of relying solely on visual spectacle, 3D will be used strategically to emphasize key elements of the narrative. For instance, in a historical epic, 3D might be employed to convey the scale and majesty of ancient landscapes and battles, creating a more immersive experience. In character-driven dramas, 3D could be harnessed to heighten emotional connections by allowing viewers to feel more intimately involved in the characters' journeys.

One of the strengths of 3D is its ability to transport audiences into the heart of the cinematic world. Indian filmmakers will likely focus on maximizing this aspect to create environments that feel tangible and immersive. Whether it's the bustling streets of a vibrant city, the vastness of a natural landscape, or the intricate details of a fantasy realm, 3D can make these settings come alive. This immersive quality can engage viewers on a deeper level, making them feel like active participants in the story rather than passive observers.

As 3D technology continues to advance, it is poised to become more accessible to a wider audience. Innovations like glasses-free 3D displays are on the horizon, potentially eliminating the need for specialized eyewear. This could be a game-changer, as it addresses one of the barriers to 3D adoption—the discomfort or inconvenience of wearing glasses. With more accessible technology, 3D films may become a more inclusive cinematic experience, appealing to a broader demographic.

One of the key challenges in utilizing 3D effectively lies in striking a balance between the visual spectacle and storytelling. Filmmakers will need to ensure that 3D enhances the narrative rather than distracting from it. This means judiciously using 3D effects to draw the audience's attention to narrative elements, heightening emotional moments, and creating a sense of presence, all while avoiding the temptation to overuse the technology for the sake of spectacle alone.

The future of 3D filmmaking in India holds exciting prospects, with filmmakers increasingly recognizing its potential as a storytelling tool. By focusing on narrative enhancement, immersive experiences, accessibility, and maintaining a balance between spectacle and storytelling, 3D cinema in India has the potential to offer audiences richer and more emotionally resonant cinematic journeys.

360-Degree Filmmaking:

360-degree filmmaking, often associated with virtual reality (VR) and immersive experiences, is also gaining traction in India. While VR content is not yet as mainstream as traditional cinema, it has found a niche audience, particularly in the gaming and entertainment sectors. In the future, we can anticipate several developments:

VR (Virtual Reality)-enhanced storytelling represents an exciting frontier in filmmaking, and its future in India is poised for exploration and innovation. Here's an in-depth look at what this emerging trend entails and how it might evolve:

VR technology offers the unique capability to place the audience directly inside the story, providing an unparalleled level of immersion. Filmmakers in India will increasingly experiment with VR to create narratives where viewers are not just spectators but active participants. This shift fundamentally alters the traditional role of the audience, enabling them to interact with the story's environment and characters in a deeply engaging way. For example, in a crime thriller, viewers could become detectives, exploring crime scenes and piecing together clues, or in a historical drama, they might step back in time to witness historic events unfold around them.

The adoption of VR in storytelling will demand innovative approaches to narrative structure. Indian filmmakers will need to adapt their craft to fully harness the potential of this medium. Instead of linear storytelling, VR narratives may branch out, allowing viewers to make choices that affect the progression of the story. This nonlinear approach has the potential to create unique and personalized experiences for each viewer. Filmmakers may experiment with multiple storylines and perspectives, blurring the lines between traditional genres and inviting viewers to explore stories from various angles.

VR-enhanced storytelling hinges on interactivity. It's not just about passively watching a film; it's about actively engaging with it. This level of interactivity can lead to deeper emotional connections with characters and a heightened sense of presence within the story's world. In Indian cinema, this could mean viewers participating in Bollywood dance sequences, solving mysteries in a detective thriller, or experiencing the vibrancy of an Indian market firsthand. The potential for emotional impact and audience engagement is immense.

While the possibilities of VR-enhanced storytelling are exciting, they also come with technical and creative challenges. Filmmakers will need to adapt to new technologies, such as 360-degree cameras and VR headsets, and understand how to craft narratives that work seamlessly in a VR environment. Moreover, storytelling in VR requires a different set of skills than traditional filmmaking, including a deep understanding of spatial storytelling, sound design, and user interaction. Indian storytellers will need to undergo a learning curve to make the most of this medium.

VR-enhanced storytelling holds the promise of revolutionizing the way narratives are experienced in Indian cinema. It offers immersive, interactive, and personalized experiences that can transport audiences to new realms of storytelling. As filmmakers adapt to this evolving medium, we can anticipate a wave of innovative narratives and immersive experiences that push the boundaries of traditional cinema in India.

360-Degree Videos:

The utilization of 360-degree videos, a subset of immersive technology, presents significant opportunities for Indian filmmakers beyond traditional entertainment. Here's an in-depth exploration of this trend and its potential applications:

360-degree videos are relatively more accessible than full-fledged VR experiences as they can be viewed on regular screens, such as computers and mobile devices, without the need for specialized headsets. This accessibility opens up a world of possibilities for Indian filmmakers to reach wider audiences, including those who may not have VR headsets. Furthermore, 360-degree videos are versatile and can cater to a variety of sectors and industries, making them a valuable storytelling tool.

360-degree videos find applications across diverse industries beyond entertainment. For instance, in tourism, Indian filmmakers can create immersive virtual tours of historical monuments, scenic landscapes, and cultural experiences, allowing viewers to explore India's rich heritage and natural beauty from the comfort of their homes. Similarly, in education, 360-degree videos can be used to transport students to historical events, scientific expeditions, or even virtual classrooms, enhancing learning experiences. Real estate can benefit from 360-degree videos by offering virtual property tours, helping potential buyers explore homes and spaces remotely.

One of the key advantages of 360-degree videos is their ability to provide an engaging and interactive experience. Filmmakers can place viewers in the center of the action, allowing them to control their perspective and explore the surroundings. In the context of Indian cinema, this could mean immersive sequences like being part of a Bollywood dance performance, experiencing the chaos of a bustling Indian market, or even being a spectator at a cricket match. This heightened engagement can foster a deeper emotional connection between viewers and the content, regardless of the industry or sector.

Creating high-quality 360-degree videos requires specialized equipment, such as 360-degree cameras, and expertise in spatial storytelling. Filmmakers need to consider factors like stitching together footage from multiple cameras, spatial audio design, and user interaction. While the technology and techniques can be complex, they are becoming more accessible, and Indian filmmakers can collaborate with experts or undergo training to master the art of 360-degree video production.

360-degree videos offer Indian filmmakers a versatile and accessible medium for storytelling that extends far beyond traditional entertainment. The ability to engage audiences across various industries, from tourism to education and real estate, presents a broad spectrum of creative and commercial opportunities. As technology continues to evolve, we can expect Indian filmmakers to explore and expand the horizons of 360-degree video storytelling, creating immersive and engaging experiences for audiences both in India and around the world.

F. VR Filmmaking :

The increasing accessibility and affordability of virtual reality (VR) filmmaking tools are poised to have a significant impact on Indian cinema, particularly for independent and emerging filmmakers. Here's a detailed exploration of this trend:

As VR equipment and software become more user-friendly and cost-effective, they lower the entry barrier for independent and emerging Indian filmmakers. Unlike traditional filmmaking, VR doesn't always require massive budgets for sets, location shoots, or intricate post-production work. This accessibility empowers storytellers with limited resources to explore and experiment with immersive narratives.

VR offers an entirely new canvas for storytelling. Filmmakers can place viewers inside the story, allowing them to interact with the environment and characters. This level of immersion opens up possibilities for innovative narrative structures and experiences that are uniquely tailored to the medium. Independent filmmakers, unburdened by the constraints of mainstream cinema, may be more inclined to take creative risks and explore unconventional storytelling techniques.

VR is not just an extension of traditional cinema; it's an entirely different medium. This means that Indian filmmakers can tackle subjects and genres that may not be well-suited to conventional filmmaking. For example, documentaries can offer deeply immersive experiences by transporting viewers to remote locations or historical events. Horror films can create an unparalleled sense of dread, and educational content can provide hands-on learning experiences. Independent filmmakers, driven by their passion and creative vision, may find VR an ideal medium to tell niche or unconventional stories.

The rise of VR content in India may lead to the emergence of VR festivals and events dedicated to showcasing immersive storytelling experiences. These platforms could provide much-needed exposure for independent filmmakers who are pushing the boundaries of VR filmmaking. Such festivals can help foster a community of VR enthusiasts, technologists, and creators, encouraging collaboration and innovation in the medium.

While the democratization of VR filmmaking is exciting, it's essential to acknowledge that VR presents a unique set of challenges and requires a learning curve. Filmmakers need to master new techniques for spatial storytelling, 360-degree camera operation, spatial audio design, and user interaction. However, with resources like online tutorials, workshops, and a growing community of VR creators, the learning curve is becoming more manageable for independent talents.

The growing accessibility and affordability of VR filmmaking tools in India present significant opportunities for independent and emerging filmmakers, encouraging creativity, experimentation, and innovative storytelling. As the VR ecosystem evolves, we can expect the rise of VR festivals and platforms in India that promote and celebrate VR content, providing creators with exposure and the chance to engage with audiences seeking immersive storytelling experiences.

3D and 360-degree filmmaking hold promise for the future of Indian cinema. While 3D may find renewed relevance when used thoughtfully to enhance storytelling, 360-degree and VR filmmaking are poised to revolutionize the way stories are told, offering immersive and interactive experiences to audiences across India and the world. The key to success will be a careful balance between technological innovation and compelling storytelling.

G. Impact of Artificial Intelligence (AI)

How Artificial Intelligence (AI) Enhances Creativity and Efficiency

Artificial Intelligence (AI) holds immense promise in transforming the Indian filmmaking process by offering a dual advantage of heightened creativity and improved efficiency. AI-powered tools and algorithms can analyze vast datasets of scripts, identifying patterns in storytelling, character development, and pacing, providing invaluable insights to screenwriters and directors. This analytical prowess aids in script refinement and creative enhancement. Additionally, AI can generate entirely new script ideas based on specific genres or themes, stimulating fresh creativity. In production, AI streamlines tasks like location scouting, scheduling, and even visual effects and animation, reducing time and costs while enhancing the overall quality of the film. AI can also bolster marketing and distribution strategies by analyzing audience data and predicting box office performance.

Ultimately, AI's role in Indian cinema is a transformative force, fostering innovation and efficiency while preserving the rich artistic tradition of storytelling that defines Indian cinema. Here are some ways in which AI can be integrated into Indian filmmaking:

AI-Powered Script Development: Transforming Storytelling in the Digital Age

Artificial Intelligence (AI) has ushered in a new era in storytelling and script development. AI tools can analyze existing scripts, dissecting them to provide valuable insights into elements such as story structure, character development, and pacing. This analytical prowess aids screenwriters in honing their scripts, identifying weaknesses, and enhancing their overall quality. Additionally, AI's creative capabilities are expanding, as it can generate entirely new scripts tailored to specific genres, styles, or themes. This not only offers screenwriters fresh ideas and inspiration but also showcases the potential for AI to become a collaborator in the creative process, suggesting narrative directions and plot twists that human writers might not have considered. Thus, AI's impact on storytelling and script development is multifaceted, bridging the realms of analysis and creativity to reshape how stories are crafted in the digital age.

AI-Enhanced Casting: Revolutionizing Actor Selection in Entertainment

Artificial Intelligence (AI) plays a pivotal role in streamlining casting decisions in the entertainment industry. By analyzing actors' past performances, audience preferences, and the suitability of actors for specific roles based on factors such as age, gender, and acting style, AI can provide valuable insights to casting directors and filmmakers. Moreover, AI's facial recognition technology enables the matching of actors to historical or fictional characters, ensuring a better fit in terms of physical appearance and potential resonance with the audience. This technology not only expedites the casting process but also enhances the likelihood of creating a more immersive and believable cinematic experience by aligning the actors closely with the envisioned characters. In essence, AI revolutionizes the casting landscape by leveraging data-driven analysis and cutting-edge technology to make casting decisions more informed, efficient, and aligned with creative visions.

AI-Enhanced Location Scouting: Revolutionizing Filmmaking Efficiency and Precision

Artificial Intelligence (AI) proves invaluable in the process of scouting filming locations, significantly enhancing efficiency and precision. By analyzing vast datasets of images and videos, AI can swiftly identify potential locations that align with the director's creative vision. This includes matching the aesthetic, ambiance, and overall look desired for the film. Furthermore, AI can provide comprehensive information about weather conditions, including historical data and forecasts, helping filmmakers plan shoots to coincide with optimal weather. Additionally, it can offer insights into permits and logistical considerations specific to chosen locations, such as legal requirements, accessibility, and infrastructure. In essence, AI streamlines the scouting process by harnessing data-driven analysis, empowering filmmakers with the information needed to make informed decisions and select the ideal settings for their cinematic endeavors.

AI-Optimized Production Scheduling: Enhancing Efficiency and Resilience in Filmmaking

Artificial Intelligence (AI) plays a pivotal role in optimizing production schedules in the film and television industry. By analyzing a multitude of factors such as actor availability, location availability, and equipment requirements, AI can create highly efficient and realistic shooting schedules. This ensures that the project runs smoothly and minimizes downtime. Moreover, AI's predictive capabilities allow it to anticipate potential delays, whether due to weather, logistical challenges, or other unforeseen circumstances. When such delays are anticipated, AI can recommend solutions to mitigate their impact and keep the project on track, such as rescheduling shoots, reallocating resources, or adjusting the overall timeline. In essence, AI revolutionizes the production planning process, offering invaluable insights and adaptability to meet the demands of the dynamic and often unpredictable world of filmmaking, ultimately leading to more efficient and cost-effective productions.

AI-Driven Visual Effects and Animation: Revolutionizing Quality and Efficiency in Filmmaking

AI-powered tools have significantly expedited the creation of visual effects and animation, bringing both cost-efficiency and efficiency to the forefront of the entertainment industry. Deep learning algorithms, a subset of AI, excel in generating incredibly realistic computer-generated imagery (CGI) characters and environments with remarkable precision. This technology minimizes the need for labor-intensive manual work traditionally required in animation and VFX production, thereby reducing both time and costs. AI-driven solutions can swiftly generate intricate details, from lifelike facial expressions to complex background scenery, streamlining the production process and enabling artists and animators to focus their efforts on refining and perfecting the creative elements of the visuals. This synergy of human creativity and AI-driven automation not only accelerates project timelines but also significantly enhances the overall quality of visual effects and animation, contributing to a new era of cinematic storytelling.

AI-Enhanced Video Editing: Transforming Post-Production in the Film Industry

Artificial Intelligence (AI) has emerged as a powerful ally in the domain of video editing, offering a range of capabilities that streamline the post-production process. AI algorithms can swiftly analyze video footage to automatically identify the best takes, reducing the time and effort required for editors to sift through extensive footage manually. Additionally, AI can enhance the overall visual quality by automatically correcting colour grading, ensuring consistency and a polished look throughout the film. AI's creative potential extends to suggesting suitable music tracks and sound effects that align with the film's mood and narrative, further expediting the editing process and enhancing the overall audio-visual experience. Moreover, AI's language processing abilities are leveraged for subtitling and dubbing, enabling faster and more accurate translations, making Indian films accessible to a broader global audience by breaking down language barriers. In essence, AI revolutionizes video editing by offering a combination of automation and creative support, significantly boosting the efficiency and quality of post-production in the film industry.

AI-Powered Film Marketing and Distribution: Leveraging Data for Success in Cinema

Artificial Intelligence (AI) has transformed the landscape of film marketing and distribution by harnessing the power of data analysis and predictive capabilities. AI algorithms can meticulously analyze audience data and feedback gleaned from social media, online platforms, and other sources to gain valuable insights into viewer preferences, trends, and sentiments. Armed with this knowledge, filmmakers and studios can tailor their marketing strategies to engage specific demographics effectively, ensuring that promotional efforts resonate with the intended audience. Moreover, AI's predictive models can forecast a film's box office performance based on historical data, market trends, and other relevant factors, aiding in strategic release planning. This enables filmmakers to choose the optimal release date, select target markets, and allocate resources wisely, ultimately maximizing a film's commercial success and cultural impact. AI empowers the film industry with data-driven precision, allowing for more effective marketing strategies and informed decision-making in the competitive world of cinema.

AI-Driven Film Distribution: Maximizing Revenue and Safeguarding Content

Artificial Intelligence (AI) plays a pivotal role in optimizing film distribution strategies by leveraging data analysis and predictive capabilities. AI algorithms can meticulously examine audience preferences, historical data, and market trends to identify the most profitable distribution channels for a given film. This enables filmmakers and distributors to make informed decisions about how and where to release their content to maximize revenue and viewership. Furthermore, AI is a powerful tool in combating piracy, a significant threat to the film industry. It can monitor online platforms and detect unauthorized copies of films, taking proactive measures to prevent piracy and protect the revenue generated from the film. By combining distribution optimization and anti-piracy efforts, AI contributes to the sustainability and profitability of the film industry, ensuring that creators and stakeholders reap the full benefits of their cinematic endeavors.

AI-Enhanced User Experience: Personalized Streaming Recommendations in India

Streaming platforms in India are harnessing the power of Artificial Intelligence (AI) to revolutionize the user experience. AI algorithms analyze the viewing history and preferences of users, creating personalized recommendations that cater to individual tastes.

By understanding user behavior and content preferences, these platforms can curate a tailored selection of films and shows, ensuring that users discover content they are likely to enjoy. This not only enhances user engagement but also extends the reach of lesser-known films, contributing to a diverse and dynamic viewing landscape. AI-powered recommendations have become a cornerstone of the streaming industry, creating a win-win scenario where users discover content they love, and platforms increase user satisfaction and retention, ultimately reshaping how Indian audiences consume and interact with cinematic content.

AI-Enhanced Global Accessibility: Breaking Language Barriers for Indian Films

For Indian films seeking global recognition and audiences, Artificial Intelligence (AI) plays a pivotal role in breaking down language barriers and expanding accessibility. AI-driven language processing tools excel in translating subtitles and facilitating dubbing into multiple languages efficiently and accurately. This not only ensures that the film's dialogues and narratives are comprehensible to international viewers but also enhances the overall viewing experience by maintaining linguistic and cultural nuances. As a result, Indian films can transcend linguistic boundaries, reach a broader and more diverse global audience, and gain a foothold in the international market. AI's contribution in this realm not only increases the global visibility of Indian cinema but also fosters cross-cultural exchange, enriching the cinematic landscape and promoting cultural diversity in the global entertainment industry.

Harmonizing AI and Human Creativity: The Evolving Role of Technology in Indian Filmmaking

The potential of AI in Indian filmmaking is undeniable, but it must be embraced as a tool to augment rather than supplant human creativity and expertise. Filmmaking is fundamentally a collaborative and artistic endeavor that thrives on human innovation, intuition, and emotion. AI's role should be to enhance and streamline various aspects of the process, from script analysis to visual effects, without overshadowing the vision and artistry of filmmakers. It's crucial to approach AI integration in filmmaking with a consciousness of ethical considerations, data privacy, and potential biases in AI algorithms. Protecting sensitive data, ensuring fair representation, and maintaining creative integrity are paramount. By striking a balance between the capabilities of AI and the human touch, Indian filmmakers can harness the full potential of this technology while preserving the soul and authenticity of their craft, paving the way for a harmonious coexistence of AI and human creativity in the world of cinema.

H. Predictions for the Evolution of Indian Filmmaking

The Digital Evolution: A Catalyst for Inclusive Storytelling in the Entertainment Industry

The digital revolution in the entertainment industry is poised to usher in a new era of storytelling that prioritizes diverse and inclusive narratives. As digital platforms continue to break down traditional barriers, content creators are increasingly recognizing the importance of representing a broader spectrum of voices and experiences in their storytelling. This shift towards inclusivity not only promotes social justice and representation but also enriches the narratives themselves. Audiences are craving stories that reflect the complexity of the real world, and digital platforms provide a space for these stories to flourish. This change in the narrative landscape goes beyond tokenism; it's about giving underrepresented communities and marginalized voices the platform they deserve to share their stories authentically.

Empowering Through Representation: The Social Impact of Underrepresented Stories in the Digital Age

As underrepresented stories gain prominence in digital media, they have the potential to drive significant social change. These narratives can challenge stereotypes, dismantle biases, and foster empathy among audiences, ultimately contributing to a more equitable and inclusive society. When stories that have historically been marginalized or overlooked take center stage, they empower individuals from these communities and inspire a sense of belonging and pride. The impact extends beyond the screen, as it encourages real-world conversations, policy changes, and greater acceptance of diversity. In essence, the digital revolution is propelling narratives towards a future where every voice is heard, and the power of storytelling as a catalyst for social transformation is fully realized.

Hybrid Distribution: The Convergence of Theatrical Releases and Digital Premieres in the Future of Content Delivery

The future of content delivery is likely to be a hybrid model that combines both traditional theatrical releases and digital premieres. While the digital revolution has opened up new avenues for content distribution and consumption, the appeal of the cinematic experience in theaters remains strong. Filmmakers and studios will continue to recognize the value of a theatrical release, especially for big-budget productions and films that offer a visually immersive experience. The grandeur of the big screen, state-of-the-art sound systems, and communal viewing in theaters provide a unique cinematic experience that can't be replicated at home. Therefore, the hybrid approach will allow filmmakers to cater to both audiences who prefer the spectacle of the cinema and those who seek the convenience of digital platforms.

Flexible Distribution Strategies: Adapting to the Needs of Traditional and Digital Audiences

Filmmakers will increasingly tailor their distribution strategies to cater to both traditional and digital audiences. They will carefully assess the content and target demographics of their films to determine the most suitable release format. Smaller indie films and niche content may find success through digital premieres, reaching a global audience without the need for extensive theatrical releases. On the other hand, blockbuster movies and visually stunning films will still benefit from a traditional theatrical release to maximize their impact. The key will be flexibility, allowing filmmakers to adapt their distribution models based on the specific needs and expectations of their target audience, thereby ensuring that both the traditional and digital realms of entertainment continue to thrive in harmony.

Global Rise of Regional Cinema: How Digital Platforms Are Changing the Landscape

The expansion of regional cinema's global influence within the Indian film industry is a promising trend that is expected to gain significant momentum in the coming years. Digital platforms and streaming services have played a pivotal role in enabling regional films to transcend geographical boundaries. These platforms have made it easier for audiences worldwide to access and appreciate the rich diversity of Indian cinema beyond the traditionally dominant Bollywood productions. As a result, regional films, whether in Tamil, Telugu, Bengali, Malayalam, or other languages, are gaining recognition and a dedicated global viewership.

Regional Cinema's Global Ascent: A New Era of Indian Film Diversity

Film festivals and international streaming platforms are essential catalysts in this process, offering regional films a global stage to shine. When these films receive critical acclaim and accolades at prestigious festivals, they often secure international distribution deals, further expanding their reach. For example, films like "Baahubali" (Telugu) and "KGF" (Kannada) achieved immense success not only in India but also among international audiences. The appeal of regional cinema lies in its unique storytelling, cultural authenticity, and fresh narratives that resonate with audiences worldwide. As filmmakers from various regions continue to produce innovative and compelling content, regional cinema's influence on the global stage is poised to grow, contributing to a more diverse and inclusive Indian film industry that caters to both local and international audiences.

Redefining Indian Cinema with Immersive Technologies: VR, AR, and CGI Integration

The integration of advanced technologies like virtual reality (VR), augmented reality (AR), and cutting-edge CGI is set to revolutionize the Indian cinema landscape, offering filmmakers innovative tools to create immersive and visually stunning experiences. VR and AR technologies, in particular, have the potential to transport viewers into the heart of the narrative, allowing them to interact with the film's world in unprecedented ways. For instance, VR can enable audiences to step into a character's shoes and experience the storyline from their perspective, creating a deeper emotional connection. AR can blend digital elements seamlessly with the real world, enhancing the storytelling experience both in cinemas and through mobile applications. These technologies are not only engaging but also offer opportunities for marketing, merchandise, and extended universe storytelling.

Pushing Boundaries: The Future of Indian Cinema with Advanced CGI and Visual Effects

Furthermore, the advancement of CGI and visual effects (VFX) is expected to push the boundaries of creativity in Indian cinema. Filmmakers will increasingly use CGI to create breathtaking landscapes, otherworldly creatures, and larger-than-life action sequences. With the growing demand for high-quality VFX, Indian studios are investing in talent and technology, leading to a higher standard of visual storytelling. As these technologies become more accessible and cost-effective, we can anticipate a surge in innovative narratives that leverage these tools to captivate audiences, making Indian cinema more competitive on a global scale. The future of Indian cinema promises not only more visually spectacular films but also a deeper level of engagement and immersion for viewers, setting new benchmarks in storytelling and cinematic experiences.

Beyond Passive Viewing: The Rise of Interactive and Participatory Content in Indian Cinema

The future of Indian cinema is poised for a transformative shift towards interactive and participatory content, offering a departure from passive viewing and fostering active engagement. This paradigm change is driven by the convergence of cutting-edge technology and the profound impact of digital platforms, enabling filmmakers to explore novel ways of involving audiences in the co-creation of narratives. This evolution is likely to manifest in a variety of forms, most notably through interactive movies, where viewers are empowered to make critical decisions that directly influence the plot's direction and outcomes. In this immersive narrative experience, audiences take on roles akin to video game players, actively shaping the storyline, and thus, leading to multiple branching narrative possibilities and highly personalized cinematic journeys. This transformation not only offers a fresh dimension to storytelling but also augments audience agency and emotional investment in the cinematic process, reflecting the dynamic evolution of Indian cinema in the digital age.

Empowering the Audience: The Advent of Real-Time Participation in Indian Cinema

Additionally, participatory content could include real-time voting during live events or interactive screenings, where viewers collectively influence the story's progression or character choices. This shift towards audience agency not only enhances engagement but also creates a sense of ownership over the narrative, fostering deeper connections with the content. Furthermore, as digital platforms enable seamless interactivity and feedback mechanisms, Indian cinema is likely to experiment with these innovative approaches, offering viewers more dynamic and personalized storytelling experiences. This transformation aligns with the evolving expectations of modern audiences who seek more than just passive entertainment, and it has the potential to revolutionize the way Indian films are created and consumed.

Global Filmmaking Synergy: The Future of Cross-Border Collaborations in Indian Cinema

The future of Indian cinema is poised for an increase in cross-border collaborations and co-productions, reflecting a globalized entertainment landscape. With digital platforms erasing geographical boundaries, filmmakers from India are likely to seek international partnerships to create content that resonates with a broader global audience. These collaborations hold the promise of blending diverse talents, cultures, and storytelling sensibilities, resulting in unique narratives with universal appeal.

Transcending Borders: The Promise of Global Stories in Indian Cinema Through Cross-Border Collaborations

These international partnerships are expected to produce films that transcend cultural boundaries and offer fresh perspectives. Indian cinema has a rich and diverse storytelling tradition, and when combined with the global influence of filmmakers from other countries, it can create narratives that are both culturally rooted and globally relevant. Such collaborations can also bring together talent from different parts of the world, leading to innovative storytelling techniques, advanced production values, and diverse casts. As Indian cinema continues to gain prominence on the global stage, these cross-border collaborations will play a pivotal role in shaping the future of the industry, fostering creative exchanges and giving rise to cinematic experiences that capture the essence of a globalized world.

Eco-Friendly Filmmaking: Sustainable Practices in the Future of Indian Cinema

The future of Indian cinema is likely to witness a significant shift towards sustainability initiatives, with filmmakers and production houses increasingly prioritizing environmentally conscious practices. As the world grapples with pressing environmental issues, the entertainment industry, including Indian cinema, is expected to acknowledge its carbon footprint and work towards minimizing its impact on the environment. This shift can encompass various aspects of filmmaking, including production processes, set design, waste management, and transportation.

Eco-Conscious Production: Redefining Sustainability in the Future of Indian Cinema

Filmmakers are likely to explore sustainable alternatives for various aspects of production, such as opting for renewable energy sources on sets, reducing single-use plastics, and implementing eco-friendly transportation solutions. Set design could also see a shift towards more sustainable materials and practices, minimizing the environmental impact of constructing and dismantling elaborate sets. Additionally, waste management practices on film sets are expected to improve, with a focus on recycling and responsible disposal. By embracing these sustainable practices, Indian cinema can set a responsible example for the industry and contribute to global efforts to combat climate change and promote environmental stewardship.

The Rise of Independent Filmmaking: A New Frontier in Indian Cinema's Future

The future of Indian cinema is likely to witness a significant rise in independent filmmaking, largely propelled by increased access to digital platforms and the democratization of content creation. Independent filmmakers have already made their mark in recent years, delivering thought-provoking and unconventional narratives that challenge the traditional norms of mainstream cinema. With digital platforms providing a more accessible and cost-effective distribution channel, aspiring filmmakers are expected to have a broader avenue to showcase their creativity.

The Future of Indian Cinema: Independent Filmmaking and Narrative Diversity

This surge in independent filmmaking will encourage experimentation and innovation in storytelling. Independent filmmakers often have more creative freedom and are not bound by the commercial constraints that often dictate mainstream cinema. As a result, audiences can anticipate a wider range of narratives, from unique and niche stories to thought-provoking social commentaries. This diversity of voices and storytelling styles will enrich

Indian cinema, fostering a more inclusive and dynamic cinematic landscape that caters to a broad spectrum of tastes and preferences. Additionally, the rise of independent filmmaking may also serve as a source of fresh talent, bringing new actors, directors, and writers to the forefront of the industry, ultimately contributing to the continued growth and evolution of Indian cinema.

AI and Machine Learning in Indian Cinema: Transforming Content Recommendations and Audience Insights

The integration of AI and machine learning in Indian cinema represents a promising avenue for the industry's future. AI-powered technologies are poised to play a pivotal role in various aspects of filmmaking, from content creation to marketing. One significant application is in the area of content recommendations. AI algorithms can analyze vast datasets of viewer preferences and behaviors to offer personalized movie recommendations. This not only enhances the user experience on streaming platforms but also helps filmmakers and studios understand audience preferences better, aiding in the development of content that aligns more closely with what viewers want.

Leveraging AI and Machine Learning in Indian Cinema: From Creative Enhancement to Targeted Marketing and Beyond

Moreover, AI and machine learning can be utilized in the creative process itself. These technologies can analyze scripts, dialogues, and historical data to predict the potential success of a film concept. They can help filmmakers optimize elements like pacing, story structure, and character development, thereby increasing the chances of producing content that resonates with audiences. Additionally, AI-driven visual effects and CGI tools can enhance post-production, making it more efficient and cost-effective. In marketing, AI can automate the process of targeting specific audience segments with tailored promotional materials and even predict a film's potential box office performance. By harnessing AI's capabilities, Indian cinema can not only streamline various production and marketing processes but also deliver content that caters more precisely to the tastes and preferences of a diverse audience, ultimately driving the industry's growth and competitiveness in the digital age.

Virtual Production in Indian Cinema: A Technological Revolution for Visual Storytelling

The adoption of virtual production techniques in Indian cinema is poised to be a transformative trend, revolutionizing the way films are created. As technology continues to advance, virtual production allows filmmakers to create immersive and visually stunning worlds within a controlled studio environment, reducing the need for extensive on-location shoots. This not only makes the production process more cost-effective but also provides greater creative control over every aspect of the film.

Revolutionizing Pre-Production: Virtual Production's Impact on Indian Filmmaking

One of the most significant advantages of virtual production is its ability to streamline the pre-production process. Filmmakers can now use virtual sets and environments to plan and visualize scenes well before shooting begins. This level of pre-visualization enhances the storytelling process, allowing directors to experiment with different visual styles and camera angles in real-time. Moreover, virtual production enables Indian filmmakers to tackle ambitious projects that might have been logistically challenging or financially prohibitive in the past. By leveraging virtual production techniques, the Indian film industry can produce visually captivating and ambitious projects, ultimately offering audiences a more immersive and captivating cinematic experience.

Elevating the Art of Storytelling: A Renaissance in Indian Cinema

The resurgence of storytelling craftsmanship is a promising trend in Indian cinema, where narratives are expected to take center stage once again. In a landscape where technological advancements and visual spectacle often dominate discussions, this shift places the essence of storytelling and character development at the forefront. Indian filmmakers are increasingly recognizing that an engaging and well-crafted narrative is the backbone of any successful film.

The Resurgence of Storytelling: Meeting the Demands of Discerning Audiences in Indian Cinema

Audiences are becoming more discerning, seeking out films that offer meaningful and emotionally resonant stories. Filmmakers are responding to this demand by investing in strong screenplays, character development, and nuanced storytelling techniques. As a result, audiences can expect more relatable and immersive cinematic experiences, where the art of storytelling is celebrated and prioritized. This trend aligns with the global appreciation for well-crafted narratives and reinforces the enduring power of storytelling in connecting with viewers on a deeper level.

Elevating Indian Cinema Through Universal Storytelling: Crafting Narratives with Global Appeal

In this evolving landscape, storytelling craftsmanship will not only elevate the quality of Indian cinema but also contribute to a broader recognition of Indian films on the international stage. Films that resonate with universal themes and emotions, driven by compelling storytelling, have the potential to cross cultural boundaries and find audiences worldwide. This renewed emphasis on storytelling craft is a testament to the enduring impact of narratives that move, inspire, and provoke thought, making it a positive development for the Indian film industry and its global audience.

Reimagining the Cinematic Experience: The Future of Theaters in Indian Cinema

The exhibition landscape in Indian cinema is on the cusp of transformation, driven by the need to adapt to changing audience preferences. As digital platforms offer convenient and on-demand access to a plethora of content, traditional theaters are reevaluating their role in the entertainment ecosystem. One significant adaptation could be the creation of unique cinematic experiences within theaters. To compete with the convenience of streaming at home, cinemas may focus on providing immersive experiences that go beyond the mere act of screening a film. This could include enhanced sound systems, high-quality projection technology, and even augmented or virtual reality elements integrated into certain screenings, making the theater visit a multisensory event.

Revitalizing Cinemas: Fostering Immersive and Interactive Theatrical Experiences in Indian Cinema

Moreover, the theatrical experience may evolve to cater to diverse audience needs. Alongside traditional screenings, theaters might diversify their offerings by hosting live events, Q&A sessions with filmmakers and actors, and interactive experiences that engage the audience on a deeper level. The goal will be to create a sense of community and anticipation that can't be replicated in a living room. In essence, the changing exhibition landscape in Indian cinema will likely focus on making the act of going to the movies an event in itself, offering unique and memorable experiences that extend beyond the boundaries of traditional film viewing.

A New Dawn for Traditional Cinemas: Evolving to Thrive in the Digital Age

However, this transformation doesn't necessarily signal the end of traditional cinema but rather its adaptation to contemporary demands. While digital platforms offer convenience and flexibility, theaters can still carve out a niche by offering exceptional experiences that celebrate the magic of cinema on the big screen. This shift aligns with the global trend of reimagining theaters as cultural hubs, where film is just one component of a broader entertainment ecosystem, ensuring that the appeal of theatrical viewing endures in the face of digital competition. The evolution of Indian filmmaking in the coming years will be marked by diversity, innovation, and adaptability. Filmmakers will explore new technologies, embrace global perspectives, and craft narratives that resonate with audiences on a profound level. As the industry continues to evolve, Indian cinema will remain a vibrant force in the global cinematic landscape.

CHAPTER - 14

14. Conclusion

"Directing Indian Cinema" is a valuable resource that illuminates the multifaceted role of directors in the world of Indian cinema. This book caters to a diverse audience, including budding filmmakers seeking to enter the industry, experienced directors looking to hone their craft, and cinephiles eager to gain a deeper understanding of the intricate workings of Indian cinema.

One of the core strengths of this book lies in its comprehensive approach. It delves into the director's pivotal role in shaping the narrative, aesthetics, and overall impact of a film. By offering a blend of analysis, case studies, and practical insights, it provides readers with a holistic view of the directorial process. This multifaceted approach allows readers to explore the theoretical and practical aspects of filmmaking, from script development and pre-production to on-set direction and post-production.

The inclusion of case studies is particularly enlightening. These real-world examples dissect notable films, dissecting the director's decisions and their impact on the final product. By dissecting the works of both renowned and emerging directors, the book offers a diverse range of perspectives and approaches to storytelling. These case studies provide invaluable lessons and inspirations for aspiring directors, offering a deeper understanding of how directors can harness their creative vision to craft compelling narratives.

Furthermore, "Directing Indian Cinema" acknowledges the unique cultural and artistic elements that define Indian cinema. It doesn't merely provide a generic overview of filmmaking but underscores the distinct characteristics of Indian storytelling, aesthetics, and societal influences. This contextual understanding is crucial for anyone aiming to engage with Indian cinema, whether as a creator or an audience member.

"Directing Indian Cinema" serves as a guiding light by offering a comprehensive and insightful exploration of the director's role in Indian filmmaking. Its blend of theory, practical guidance, and case studies makes it an invaluable resource for those passionate about Indian cinema, offering a deeper appreciation of the artistry and craftsmanship that go into creating the captivating narratives that define this vibrant cinematic landscape.